BENCHMARK SERIES

MICROSOFT® EXCEL® 2013

LEVELS 1 & 2

NITA RUTKOSKY
Pierce College at Puyallup
Puyallup, Washington

DENISE SEGUIN
Fanshawe College
London, Ontario

JAN DAVIDSON
Lambton College
Sarnia, Ontario

AUDREY ROGGENKAMP
Pierce College at Puyallup
Puyallup, Washington

IAN RUTKOSKY
Pierce College at Puyallup
Puyallup, Washington

PARADIGM
EDUCATION SOLUTIONS
St. Paul

Director of Editorial: Christine Hurney
Director of Production: Timothy W. Larson
Production Editor: Lori Michelle Ryan
Assistant Production Editor: Katherine Lee
Cover Designers: Leslie Anderson and Valerie King
Design & Production Specialist: Valerie King

ISBN 978-0-76385-453-9 (Text + Disc)
ISBN 978-0-76385-382-2 (Text)

875 Montreal Way
St. Paul, MN 55102
Email: educate@emcp.com
Website: www.emcp.com

Printed in the United States of America

22 21 20 19 18 17 16 15 14 2 3 4 5 6 7 8 9 10

Contents

PLANNING *Guidelines for Choosing Outcomes, Instructional Approach, Resources, and Assessments*

Note: Lesson Blueprints providing detailed lesson plans for a 16-week course are provided on the Instructor disc and on the Internet Resource Center.

ASSESSMENT *Resources for Evaluating Student Achievement*

Note: Project Model Answers are provided in the student textbook at the beginning of each chapter.

Planning the Course

Most educators would agree that the key to teaching a successful course is careful, thorough planning. And, as noted in *Exceptional Teaching: Ideas in Action*, published by Paradigm Publishing, "Instructors assess, plan, implement, and evaluate . . . repeatedly. They do this based on many of the factors that make teaching learner-centered and on several other variables. Before students even think about entering or logging into the classroom, instructors make decisions about the course. These begin with identifying the heart of the course. That is, what, exactly, are the most important outcomes that students should achieve? And what plan of action can the instructor devise that will help ensure those outcomes?" Thinking through a course action plan typically includes four phases:

1. Developing course outcomes
2. Determining the course delivery mode and structure (dividing the course into parts, each with outcomes)
3. Selecting the instructional approach, resources, and activities of the course
4. Developing an assessment strategy

Developing Course Outcomes

In developing course outcomes, some of the key issues to consider are the following:

- When this course is complete, in what ways will the learner be permanently changed? Should instruction result in
    - building knowledge?
    - developing higher-order thinking?
    - developing independent learning skills?
    - developing technical literacy?
- What problems are encountered that are related to course content?
    - What must be communicated?
    - How will the learner find out whether the work is satisfactory?
    - How will the learner receive feedback?

Considering these questions, a set of end-of-course outcomes for a one-semester course on Microsoft Excel 2013 could include the following items, stated as performance objectives.

At course conclusion, the student will be able to:

- Create and edit spreadsheets of varying complexity
- Format cells, columns, and rows as well as entire workbooks in a uniform, attractive style
- Analyze numerical data and project outcomes to make informed decisions
- Plan, research, create, revise and publish worksheets and workbooks to meet specific communication needs
- Given a workplace scenario requiring a numbers-based solution, assess the information requirements and then prepare the materials that achieve the goal efficiently and effectively

Determining the Course Delivery Mode and Structure

Frequently, the course structure has been determined in advance by your department. However, if you are in a position to develop a plan or modify an existing structure, consider these questions:

- What topics in each subject area are essential for demonstrating the course outcomes?
- Is this the only course that will address this subject and skill set?
- What do students already know about each subject? What can they learn on their own without your direct instruction?
- Where in each subject will the instruction begin and end?

Your answers to these questions will help you divide the course content into parts and identify the associated learning outcomes (also called performance objectives). Note that course outcomes are marked by higher and more challenging skill sets and typically require the integration of many skills, while unit or part outcomes are more narrowly defined and focused.

Course Delivery: Traditional Classroom, Online (Distance Learning), or Hybrid?

While the core considerations are the same whether you are planning a traditional on-campus course, an online course (also called a distance learning course), or a hybrid of the two, the instructional delivery differences create distinct needs you must address in the planning stage.

A critical challenge in teaching online courses is the issue of interacting with students. How will you communicate with them? How will they submit assignments and tests? How will you deliver feedback? How will you get to know your students? Here are some additional questions to consider when planning an online or hybrid course:

- What course management system will you use: Blackboard or some other platform?
- Will students work independently offline? How will they use the course management system to review course outcomes, the syllabus, and assignment due dates? How will they communicate with you, take online quizzes, transmit completed work, and participate in chat sessions?
- Will you be able to offer an on-campus orientation meeting for students at the beginning of the course? If so, how will you prepare to answer the questions students will likely have?
- Will students come to the campus or school to take exams? If not, will students be directed to offsite locations where exams can be administered to verify that the person taking the exam is indeed the person getting credit for the course?
- What hardware configuration and/or software requirements must a student have to participate in your course?

Both the student and instructor resources offered with *Benchmark Series Microsoft Excel 2013, Levels 1 & 2* can be adapted for use in an online learning environment or a hybrid of traditional and online learning contexts. The SNAP Training and Assessment product, in particular, is well suited for these course delivery modes, and these online files are also designed for distance-learning situations.

The Syllabus

A comprehensive syllabus will help you and your students prepare for each part of the course. A well-planned syllabus is useful for traditional, on-campus courses as well as for courses that are delivered online. A syllabus normally includes:

1. Course-identifying data
2. Prerequisites
3. Instructor contact information
4. Course outcomes
5. Required course resources
6. Major assignments
7. Grade composition
8. Class structure
9. Course schedule
10. College/school requirements

Figure 1 shows a traditional, on-campus course syllabus for a 16-week course that meets three times a week and uses *Benchmark Excel 2013, Levels 1 & 2* as the core courseware. Lesson plans are referenced in the sample syllabus and are available on the Instructor Resources disc as well as on the password-protected part of the Internet Resource Center (IRC) for *Benchmark Excel 2013* at www.paradigmcollege.net/BenchmarkExcel13.

FIGURE 1 Traditional 16-Week Semester Syllabus Example Using Benchmark Office 2013

Course Description

This course prepares students to work with Microsoft Office 2013 applications in a career setting or for personal use. Using courseware that incorporates a step-by-step, project-based approach, students develop a introductory-level competency in Word, Excel, Access, and PowerPoint 2013 and explore the essential features of Windows 8 and Internet Explorer 10. Students also develop an understanding of fundamental computer hardware and software concepts.

Prerequisites: None

Instructor Contact Information

Name:	**Office Location:**
Office Phone:	**Office Hours:**
Office Email:	

Required Course Resources

Benchmark Series Microsoft Excel 2013, Levels 1 & 2
by Rutkosky, Seguin, Davidson, Roggenkamp, and Rutkosky © Paradigm Publishing, Inc.
Student Resources CD (provided with textbook)
Internet Resource Center, www.paradigmcollege.net/BenchmarkExcel13
SNAP Training and Assessment account, snap2013.emcp.com
USB flash drive or other storage medium

Computer Time

Approximately six to eight hours per week of computer time outside of class is recommended for successful completion of course requirements.

Grading

Final grades will be calculated as an average of all of the following assignments:

- Concepts Check 5%
- Skills Check (SNAP Grade It) 10%
- Visual Benchmark 15%
- Case Study 15%
- Unit Performance Assessment 15%
- SNAP Performance Evaluations 20%
- Exams 20%

College and Course Policy Information

- This college conforms to the provisions of the Americans with Disabilities Act. You are invited to report any special needs to your instructor.
- Your attendance is expected at all class sessions.
- We subscribe to the college policy on academic honesty found in the school catalog.

Course Schedule—Benchmark Excel 2013

16-week semester, three 1-hour classes per week

Week	Class	Chapter	Lesson Plan File	Description
1	Class 1	Getting Started/ Windows 8	BM-Excel2013-L1-Session01	Intro to course, Getting Started, Using Windows 8
	Class 2	Windows 8/ Internet Explorer	BM-Excel2013-L1-Session02	Finish Windows 8, Internet Explorer, Working with Data Files
	Class 3	Level 1, Ch 1	BM-Excel2013-L1-Session03	Preparing an Excel Worksheet
2	Class 4	Level 1, Ch 1	BM-Excel2013-L1-Session04	Preparing an Excel Worksheet
	Class 5	Level 1, Ch 2	BM-Excel2013-L1-Session05	Inserting Formulas in a Worksheet
	Class 6	Level 1, Ch 2	BM-Excel2013-L1-Session06	Inserting Formulas in a Worksheet
3	Class 7	Level 1, Ch 2	BM-Excel2013-L1-Session07	Inserting Formulas in a Worksheet
	Class 8	Level 1, Ch 3	BM-Excel2013-L1-Session08	Formatting an Excel Worksheet
	Class 9	Level 1, Ch 3	BM-Excel2013-L1-Session09	Formatting an Excel Worksheet
4	Class 10	Level 1, Ch 4	BM-Excel2013-L1-Session10	Enhancing a Worksheet
	Class 11	Level 1, Ch 4	BM-Excel2013-L1-Session11	Enhancing a Worksheet
	Class 12	**Level 1, U1**	BM-Excel2013-L1-Session12	**Level 1, U1 Performance Assessments**
5	Class 13	Level 1, Ch 5	BM-Excel2013-L1-Session13	Moving Data Within and Between Workbooks
	Class 14	Level 1, Ch 5	BM-Excel2013-L1-Session14	Moving Data Within and Between Workbooks
	Class 15	Level 1, Ch 6	BM-Excel2013-L1-Session15	Maintaining Workbooks
6	Class 16	Level 1, Ch 6	BM-Excel2013-L1-Session16	Maintaining Workbooks
	Class 17	Level 1, Ch 7	BM-Excel2013-L1-Session17	Creating a Chart in Excel
	Class 18	Level 1, Ch 7	BM-Excel2013-L1-Session18	Creating a Chart in Excel

Week	Class	Chapter	Lesson Plan File	Description
7	Class 19	Level 1, Ch 8	BM-Excel2013-L1-Session19	Adding Visual Interest to Workbooks
	Class 20	Level 1, Ch 8	BM-Excel2013-L1-Session20	Adding Visual Interest to Workbooks
	Class 21	Level 1, Ch 8	BM-Excel2013-L1-Session21	Adding Visual Interest to Workbooks
8	Class 22	**Level 1, U2**	BM-Excel2013-L1-Session22	**Level 1, U2 Performance Assessments**
	Class 23	**TEST**	BM-Excel2013-L1-Session23	**Excel Level 1 Test**
	Class 24	Level 2, Ch 1	BM-Excel2013-L2-Session24	Advanced Formatting Techniques
9	Class 25	Level 2, Ch 1	BM-Excel2013-L2-Session25	Advanced Formatting Techniques
	Class 26	Level 2, Ch 1	BM-Excel2013-L2-Session26	Advanced Formatting Techniques
	Class 27	Level 2, Ch 2	BM-Excel2013-L2-Session27	Advanced Functions and Formulas
10	Class 28	Level 2, Ch 2	BM-Excel2013-L2-Session28	Advanced Functions and Formulas
	Class 29	Level 2, Ch 3	BM-Excel2013-L2-Session29	Working with Tables and Data Features
	Class 30	Level 2, Ch 3	BM-Excel2013-L2-Session30	Working with Tables and Data Features
11	Class 31	Level 2, Ch 4	BM-Excel2013-L2-Session31	Summarizing and Consolidating Data
	Class 32	Level 2, Ch 4	BM-Excel2013-L2-Session32	Summarizing and Consolidating Data
	Class 33	Level 2, Ch 4	BM-Excel2013-L2-Session33	Summarizing and Consolidating Data
12	Class 34	**Level 2, U1**	BM-Excel2013-L2-Session34	**Level 2, U1 Performance Assessments**
	Class 35	Level 2, Ch 5	BM-Excel2013-L2-Session35	Using Data Analysis Features
	Class 36	Level 2, Ch 5	BM-Excel2013-L2-Session36	Using Data Analysis Features
13	Class 37	Level 2, Ch 5	BM-Excel2013-L2-Session37	Using Data Analysis Features
	Class 38	Level 2, Ch 6	BM-Excel2013-L2-Session38	Protecting and Sharing Workbooks
	Class 39	Level 2, Ch 6	BM-Excel2013-L2-Session39	Protecting and Sharing Workbooks
14	Class 40	Level 2, Ch 7	BM-Excel2013-L2-Session40	Automating Repetitive Tasks and Customizing Excel
	Class 41	Level 2, Ch 7	BM-Excel2013-L2-Session41	Automating Repetitive Tasks and Customizing Excel
	Class 42	Level 2, Ch 8	BM-Excel2013-L2-Session42	Importing, Exporting and Distributing Data
15	Class 43	Level 2, Ch 8	BM-Excel2013-L2-Session43	Importing, Exporting and Distributing Data
	Class 44	Level 2, Ch 8	BM-Excel2013-L2-Session44	Importing, Exporting and Distributing Data
	Class 45	**Level 2, U2**	BM-Excel2013-L2-Session45	**Level 2, U2 Performance Assessments**
16	Class 46	**TEST**	BM-Excel2013-L2-Session46	**Excel Level 2 Test**

Selecting the Instructional Approach, Resources, and Activities

After the course outcomes and structure are determined, it is important to plan the main content of the course. This includes selecting courseware, identifying resources for English language learners, considering instructional support materials, and reviewing other resources.

Student Courseware

Selecting high-quality student courseware is an important step in the planning process. Learning materials should be engaging and accessible. The Benchmark Series offers several valuable learning tools to support course performance objectives.

- *Benchmark Excel 2013, Levels 1 & 2 textbook* with Student Resources CD
- eBook
- Student Internet Resource Center at www.paradigmcollege.net/BenchmarkExcel13
- SNAP Training and Assessment software
- SNAP Tutorials CD
- Blackboard cartridge

Textbook Structure and Features

Benchmark Excel 2013 prepares students to work with Microsoft Excel 2013 in business and academic settings, and also for personal use. Incorporating a project-based approach that organizes instruction and guided exercises around related program features, this text builds student competency in the 2013 version of Excel and the essential features of Windows 8 and Internet Explorer 10.

The *Excel 2013 Levels 1 & 2* text is just one book in the Benchmark Series. The Benchmark Series contains the following eleven textbooks:

- *Benchmark Series Microsoft Office 2013*
    - Getting Started (essential computer hardware and software concepts)
    - Windows 8
    - Internet Explorer 10
    - Word 2013 (8 chapters)
    - Excel 2013 (8 chapters)
    - Access 2013 (8 chapters)
    - PowerPoint 2013 (8 chapters)
    - Integrating Office 2013 Programs
- *Benchmark Series Microsoft Word 2013 Levels 1 and 2*
    - Getting Started
    - Windows 8
    - Internet Explorer 10
    - Word 2013 Level 1 (8 chapters)
    - Word 2013 Level 2 (8 chapters)
- *Benchmark Series Microsoft Word 2013 Level 1*
    - Getting Started
    - Windows 8
    - Internet Explorer 10
    - Word 2013 Level 1 (8 chapters)
- *Benchmark Series Microsoft Word 2013 Level 2*
    - Word 2013 Level 2 (8 chapters)
- *Benchmark Series Microsoft Excel 2013 Levels 1 and 2*
    - Getting Started
    - Windows 8
    - Internet Explorer 10

    - Excel 2013 Level 1 (8 chapters)
    - Excel 2013 Level 2 (8 chapters)
- *Benchmark Series Microsoft Excel 2013 Level 1*
    - Getting Started
    - Windows 8
    - Internet Explorer 10
    - Excel 2013 Level 1 (8 chapters)
- *Benchmark Series Microsoft Excel 2013 Level 2*
    - Excel 2013 Level 2 (8 chapters)
- *Benchmark Series Microsoft Access 2013 Levels 1 and 2*
    - Getting Started
    - Windows 8
    - Internet Explorer 10
    - Access 2013 Level 1 (8 chapters)
    - Access 2013 Level 2 (8 chapters)
- *Benchmark Series Microsoft Access 2013 Level 1*
    - Getting Started
    - Windows 8
    - Internet Explorer 10
    - Access 2013 Level 1 (8 chapters)
- *Benchmark Series Microsoft Access 2013 Level 2*
    - Access 2013 Level 2 (8 chapters)
- *Benchmark Series Microsoft PowerPoint 2013*
    - Getting Started
    - Windows 8
    - Internet Explorer 10
    - PowerPoint 2013 (8 chapters)

The main Microsoft application sections of each book in the Benchmark Series contain eight chapters, split into two units. The opening page of a unit lists the four chapter titles included in the unit. Each chapter opener presents the chapter's Performance Objectives, an overview of the skills taught in the chapter, a listing of the SNAP tutorials that support the chapter content, and a CD icon and text identifying a folder of data files to be copied to the student's storage medium. These files are used to complete chapter projects and end-of-chapter activities. Following the opening page, the chapter begins with model answers of the chapter projects that students can reference to confirm they have completed the chapter projects correctly.

Skills instruction in the text is organized around projects that require using a group of related features to complete a document or build a file. A project overview, which lists the project number and title, identifies tasks to accomplish and the features to use in completing the work. The project overview also identifies the number of parts that make up the project. Following each project part (identified with the project number and letter), the text presents instruction on the features and skills necessary to accomplish the next section of the project. Typically, a file remains open throughout all parts of the project. Students save their work incrementally and usually print only at the end of the entire project. Instructors have access to the live project model answer files for the completed project as well as the project parts on the Instructor Resources disc and on the password-protected Instructor section of www.paradigmcollege.net/BenchmarkExcel13.

Page margins include the following elements:

- Quick Steps—brief feature summaries for reference and review
- Hint boxes—trouble-shooting ideas and additional useful information
- Button graphics

Each chapter ends with the following review elements and exercises:

- Chapter Summary—A bulleted list captures the purpose and execution of key features.
- Commands Review—Commands taught in the chapter are listed with button, ribbon tab, and keyboard actions.
- Concepts Check—Short-answer questions allow students to test their comprehension and recall of program features, terminology, and functions. Printouts of the Concepts Check answer keys are provided in the print *Instructor's Guide* and electronic files are available on the Instructor Resources disc and on the password-protected Instructor section of www.paradigmcollege.net/BenchmarkExcel13.
- Skills Check—Semi-guided exercises ask students to demonstrate their mastery of the major features and program skills taught in the chapter. The *Instructor's Guide* includes printed versions of the Skills Check model answers along with rubrics to assess student work. In addition, rubric Word documents, PDF files of the model answers, and live application model answers are available for instructors on the Instructor Resources disc and on the password-protected Instructor section of www.paradigmcollege.net/BenchmarkExcel13. Items marked with a SNAP Grade It icon have corresponding SNAP activities available online.
- Visual Benchmark—With limited guidance, students are challenged to use their problem-solving skills and mastery of program features to build a file that matches a shown sample file. Grading rubrics, PDF files, and live application model answers are available to instructors to support these activities.
- Case Study—Framed in a workplace project perspective, these less-guided assessments evaluate students' abilities to apply chapter skills and concepts in solving realistic problems. Case Study activities require demonstrating program skills as well as decision-making skills and include Help and Internet-based activities. Grading rubrics, PDF files, and live application model answers are available to instructors to support these activities.

Unit Performance Assessments follow each set of four chapters and offer opportunities for cross-disciplinary, comprehensive evaluation. There are four types of Unit Performance Assessments. Assessing Proficiency is a group of gently guided exercises. Writing Activities involve applying program skills in a communication context. An Internet Research project reinforces research, writing, and program skills. A Job Study activity in the Unit 2 Performance Assessment presents a capstone assessment requiring critical thinking and problem solving. Annotated printouts of the model answers and rubrics for evaluating student work are included in the *Instructor's Guide*. The Instructor Resources disc and the password-protected Instructor section of www.paradigmcollege.net/BenchmarkExcel13 include live file model answers and rubric Word document files for these assessments.

Student Resources CD

Files that serve as a starting point for completing many of the project and end-of-chapter exercises are included on the CD that accompanies the student text. Typically, students are directed to open one of these files, save the file with a new name, and then edit and print the file. Some chapter work requires the students to start an activity from a blank file. As students begin a chapter, they should copy the folder of files for the chapter exercises to the storage medium of their choice. This folder name is displayed next to a CD icon on the first page of the chapter.

eBook

For student who prefer studying with an eBook, the texts in the Benchmark Series are available in an electronic form. The web-based, password-protected eBooks feature dynamic navigation tools, including bookmarking, a linked table of contents, and the ability to jump to a specific page. The eBook format also supports helpful study tools, such as highlighting and note taking.

Benchmark Excel 2013 Internet Resource Center

The Benchmark Excel 2013 Resource Center at www.paradigmcollege.net/BenchmarkExcel13 offers valuable information for both instructors and students. For students, the Internet Resource Center includes quick access to the student data files, informational Web links, study aids such as online quizzes, and more. All instructor resources posted on the website are password protected and are not accessible by students.

SNAP Training and Assessment

SNAP is a web-based training and assessment program designed to optimize skill-based learning for Word, Excel, Access, and PowerPoint along with Windows and Internet Explorer. SNAP creates a virtual classroom on the Web, allowing instructors to employ an electronic grade book and schedule tutorials, skill and concept exams, Grade It end-of-chapter Skills Check activities, and comprehensive performance evaluations.

SNAP contains:

- a bank of 154 interactive, gradable, multimedia tutorials, aligned to textbook chapters, that can be used for direct instruction or remediation (See Table 1 for a listing of the SNAP tutorials for that are available for Benchmark Excel 2013.)
- a bank of 306 performance skill items in which students perform tasks in Microsoft Excel 2013 that are reported in the learning management system; instructors can assign pre-defined skills exams or create their own
- a bank of 58 Grade It Skills Check assessment activities, which correspond to end-of-chapter activities
- comprehensive Performance Evaluation activities, one per chapter and one per unit, for comprehensive evaluation of skills mastery
- a bank of 875 concept items that can be used to monitor student understanding of computer literacy and technical knowledge; instructors can assign pre-defined concepts exams or create their own

TABLE 1 Benchmark SNAP Tutorials Correlation

Benchmark Windows 8 SNAP Tutorials

Tutorial	Tutorial Title
1	Exploring the Windows 8 Start Screen
2	Exploring the Windows 8 Desktop
3	Opening and Using Windows
4	Exploring the Taskbar and the Charm Bar
5	Browsing Devices and Files
6	Selecting, Copying, and Moving Folders and Files
7	Changing Folder and View Options
8	Creating a Folder and Renaming a Folder or File
9	Using the Recycle Bin
10	Customizing the Desktop
11	Exploring the Control Panel
12	Getting Help in Windows 8
13	Using Windows Search Tools

Benchmark Internet Explorer SNAP Tutorials

Tutorial	Tutorial Title
1	Navigating the Internet Using Web Addresses
2	Finding Information Using Search Tools
3	Researching Information Using Advanced Search Tools
4	Downloading Content from a Web Page

Benchmark Excel Level 1 SNAP Tutorials

Chapter	Tutorial	Tutorial Title
1	1.1	Opening, Saving, and Closing an Excel Workbook
1	1.2	Entering Data in Cells and Saving a Workbook with a New Name
1	1.3	Editing Cells and Using Proofing Tools
1	1.4	Printing a Worksheet
1	1.5	Applying Formatting; Using Undo and Redo; Changing Alignment
1	1.6	Navigating and Scrolling in a Worksheet
1	1.7	Applying Basic Formatting
1	1.8	Applying Number Formatting
1	1.9	Getting Help at the Excel Help Window
2	2.1	Performing Calculations Using Formulas
2	2.2	Copying and Testing Formulas
2	2.3	Using Statistical Functions
2	2.4	Writing Formulas with Date Functions and Dates
2	2.5	Displaying Formulas in a Worksheet
2	2.6	Creating Formulas and Absolute Addressing
3	3.1	Adjusting Column Width and Row Height
3	3.2	Inserting and Deleting Columns and Rows
3	3.3	Applying Font Formatting
3	3.4	Applying Alignment Formatting
3	3.5	Applying Cell Styles and Themes
3	3.6	Formatting Numbers
3	3.7	Adding Borders and Shading to Cells
3	3.8	Using Format Painter
3	3.9	Hiding and Unhiding Columns and/or Rows

Benchmark Excel Level 1 SNAP Tutorials

Chapter	Tutorial	Tutorial Title
4	4.1	Changing Page Layout Options
4	4.2	Formatting a Worksheet Page for Printing
4	4.3	Using Page Break Preview
4	4.4	Inserting Headers and Footers
4	4.5	Formatting and Printing Multiple Worksheets
4	4.6	Completing a Spelling Check
4	4.7	Using Undo and Redo
4	4.8	Using Find and Replace
4	4.9	Finding and Replacing Text and Formatting
4	4.10	Sorting Data
4	4.11	Filtering Data Using a Custom AutoFilter
5	5.1	Moving and Copying Cells
5	5.2	Inserting, Moving, Renaming, and Deleting a Worksheet
5	5.3	Formatting Multiple Worksheets
5	5.4	Using Paste Options
5	5.5	Printing a Workbook Containing Multiple Worksheets
5	5.6	Freezing Panes and Changing the Zoom
5	5.7	Splitting a Worksheet into Windows
5	5.8	Naming and Using a Range
5	5.9	Working with Windows
5	5.10	Linking Data between Worksheets
5	5.11	Copying and Pasting Data between Programs
6	6.2	Managing Folders
6	6.3	Managing the Recent Workbooks List
6	6.4	Managing Worksheets
6	6.5	Formatting with Cell Styles
6	6.6	Inserting Hyperlinks
6	6.7	Using Excel Templates
7	7.1	Creating Charts in Excel
7	7.2	Editing Chart Data
7	7.3	Formatting with Chart Buttons
7	7.4	Printing Charts
7	7.5	Changing Chart Design
7	7.6	Changing Chart Formatting
7	7.7	Inserting and Formatting a Shape
7	7.8	Moving, Sizing, and Deleting a Chart
7	7.9	Using Financial Functions
7	7.10	Using the Logical IF Function
8	8.1	Inserting Symbols and Special Characters
8	8.2	Inserting and Modifying Images
8	8.3	Inserting and Modifying Clip Art Images
8	8.4	Creating and Inserting Screenshots
8	8.5	Inserting and Copying Shapes
8	8.6	Drawing and Formatting Text Boxes

Benchmark Excel Level 1 SNAP Tutorials

Chapter	Tutorial	Tutorial Title
8	8.7	Inserting a Picture as a Watermark
8	8.8	Inserting and Formatting a SmartArt Graphic
8	8.9	Creating WordArt

Benchmark Excel Level 2 SNAP Tutorials

Chapter	Tutorial	Tutorial Title
1	1.1	Applying Conditional Formatting
1	1.2	Applying Conditional Formatting Using Icon Sets
1	1.3	Applying Conditional Formatting Using Data Bars and Color Scales
1	1.4	Applying Conditional Formatting Using a Formula
1	1.5	Using Fraction, Scientific, and Special Number Formatting
1	1.6	Creating a Custom Number Format
1	1.7	Wrapping and Shrinking Text to Fit within a Cell
1	1.8	Filtering and Sorting Data Using Conditional Formatting and Cell Attributes
1	1.9	Using Text Functions
1	1.10	Filtering a Worksheet Using a Custom AutoFilter
2	2.1	Creating and Managing Range Names
2	2.2	Using Statistical Functions: COUNT, COUNTA, COUNTIF, and COUNTIFS Functions
2	2.3	Using Statistical Functions: AVERAGEIF and AVERAGEIFS
2	2.4	Using Math and Trigonometry Functions: SUMIF and SUMIFS
2	2.5	Using Lookup Functions
2	2.6	Using the PPMT Function
2	2.7	Using Logical Functions
3	3.1	Creating and Modifying Tables
3	3.2	Adding Rows to a Table
3	3.3	Formatting Data as a Table
3	3.4	Using the Sort Feature in Tables
3	3.5	Filtering a Table
3	3.6	Using Data Tools
3	3.7	Removing Duplicate Records
3	3.8	Validating and Restricting Data Entry
3	3.9	Converting a Table to a Normal Range; Subtotalling Related Data
3	3.10	Grouping and Ungrouping Data
4	4.1	Summarizing Data in Multiple Worksheets Using Range Names and 3-D References
4	4.2	Summarizing Data by Linking Ranges in Other Worksheets or Workbooks
4	4.3	Summarizing Data Using the Consolidate Feature
4	4.4	Creating a PivotTable Report
4	4.5	Filtering a PivotTable Using Slicers
4	4.6	Filtering a PivotTable Using a Timeline
4	4.7	Creating a PivotChart
4	4.8	Summarizing Data with Sparklines
5	5.1	Pasting Data Using Paste Special Options
5	5.2	Using Goal Seek to Populate a Cell
5	5.3	Using Scenario Manager

Benchmark Excel Level 2 SNAP Tutorials

Chapter	Tutorial	Tutorial Title
5	5.4	Performing What-If Analysis Using Data Tables
5	5.5	Using Auditing Tools
5	5.6	Circling Invalid Data and Watching Formulas
6	6.1	Inserting and Editing Comments
6	6.2	Adding Workbook Properties
6	6.3	Printing and Editing Comments
6	6.4	Sharing a Workbook
6	6.5	Resolving Conflicts in a Shared Workbook
6	6.6	Saving a Workbook to Windows SkyDrive, Inviting People to Share a Workbook, and Sending a Workbook via Email
6	6.7	Protecting and Unprotecting Worksheets
6	6.8	Protecting and Unprotecting the Structure of a Workbook
6	6.9	Adding Password Protection to a Workbook
6	6.10	Tracking Changes
7	7.1	Using Macros
7	7.2	Editing a Macro
7	7.3	Managing Macros
7	7.4	Pinning Workbooks to the Recent Workbooks List
7	7.5	Customizing the Work Area
7	7.6	Customizing the Ribbon
7	7.7	Customizing the Quick Access Toolbar
7	7.8	Using Custom Templates
8	8.1	Importing Data from Access, a Text File, or a Website
8	8.2	Exporting Data from Excel
8	8.3	Copying and Pasting Worksheet Data between Programs
8	8.4	Copying and Pasting Worksheet Data to a Word Document
8	8.5	Exporting Data as a Text File
8	8.6	Preparing a Worksheet for Distribution
8	8.7	Saving a Workbook in a Different File Format
8	8.8	Viewing Trust Center Settings
8	8.9	Creating a PDF/XPS Copy of a Workbook
8	8.10	Publishing a Worksheet as a Web Page

SNAP Tutorials CD

A CD of tutorials teaching the basics of Office, Windows, and Internet Explorer is also available if instructors wish to assign SNAP tutorial work without using the web-based SNAP program.

Blackboard Cartridge

This set of files allows instructors to create a personalized website for their course and provides course content, tests, and the mechanisms for establishing communication via e-discussions and online group conferences. Available content includes a syllabus, test banks, PowerPoint presentations with lecture notes, and supplementary course materials. Upon request, the files can be available within 24–48 hours. Hosting the site is the responsibility of the educational institution.

Resources for English Language Learners[1]

One of the fastest growing groups of students in higher education is comprised of students whose first language is not English and whose English is not yet equivalent to that of native English speakers in lexicon and syntax. The wide differences in fluency among limited English speakers makes planning for meeting their needs somewhat more complex—and very important.

Many instructors find that they must meet the needs of students who are learning English and who need additional help. Because your goal is to help *all* the students in your course meet the intended outcomes, plan how you're going to assist students with limited English skills.

Begin by assessing the language abilities of your students:

1. One method is a "one-minute preview." Provide sheets of paper and ask students two questions. Give them one minute or so to write their answers. The questions could be about their language skills, but it might be better to ask about something else. That way you get a short writing sample plus information about something, such as why they are taking the course, what they would like to learn, the types of activities they enjoy, or what they are most worried about in the course. You will be able to see which students will need additional help.
2. If your class is small, conduct a discussion early in the course. Make sure you hear each student answer a question or ask one.
3. If you are conducting a pretest for the course, include some questions that ask students if they need to improve their English or writing skills.
4. Tell students to email you if they think they will need language help or extra exam time for reading assignments or tests.

In addition to the suggestions above, consider preparing a list of terms for each session that might be difficult for English language learners. You can suggest that students arrange for tutors to assist them with completing the unguided assessments. You may also want to dedicate a session (or part of one) to instruction on how to prepare the work you expect.

Instructor Resources

Along with the *Instructor's Guide*, instructional materials available with *Benchmark Excel 2013, Levels 1 & 2* include:

- Instructor Resources disc with electronic files for all resources included in the *Instructor's Guide*. The disc also offers the model answer files for end-of-chapter work in live program format and annotated PDF format, PowerPoint presentations with lecture notes, and detailed lesson plans, which include lecture/demonstration notes, discussion topics, tips for students, and possible work for advanced students.
- Instructor resources available at the Internet Resource Center at www.paradigmcollege.net/BenchmarkExcel13, which includes all of the materials in the print *Instructor's Guide* and on the Instructor Resources disc.

[1] Excerpted from *Exceptional Teaching: Ideas in Action,* published by Paradigm Publishing, Inc.

- ExamView® Assessment Suite and test banks with approximately 875 multiple-choice items to create customized web-based or print tests.

Information about Microsoft Office 2013

Microsoft Office 2013 operates on the Windows 8 operating system, as well as on Windows 7.

Video on the What's New in Office 2013

Microsoft Corporation offers its own downloadable video presentation on the new features in Office 2013 at this address: http://office.microsoft.com/en-us/support/video-whats-new-in-office-2013-VA103147615.aspx?CTT=1http

Quick Start Guides

Microsoft provides a series of Quick Start Guides for the applications in Office 2013 at http://office.microsoft.com/en-us/support/office-2013-quick-start-guides-HA103673669.aspx?CTT=1

Certification: Microsoft Office Specialist

With the release of Office 2013, Microsoft has developed a new set of certification objectives, which are available at http://www.microsoft.com/learning/en/us/mos-certification.aspx. The following books in the Benchmark Series have been validated and approved by ProCert Labs (www.procert.com) as courseware covering the Core-level objectives in the Microsoft Office Specialist Certification exam.

- *Benchmark Series Microsoft Word 2013 Levels 1 & 2*
- *Benchmark Series Microsoft Excel 2013 Levels 1 & 2*
- *Benchmark Series Microsoft Access 2013 Levels 1 & 2*
- *Benchmark Series Microsoft PowerPoint 2013*

Table 2 correlates the Benchmark Excel 2013 Levels 1 & 2 text with the certification exam objectives.

TABLE 2 Benchmark Excel Levels 1 & 2 and Microsoft Office Specialist Certification Exam Correlation

Certification Exam Objective	Text Reference
1.0 Create and Manage Worksheets and Workbooks	
1.1 Create Worksheets and Workbooks	
1.1.1 create new blank workbooks	L1C1, pgs. 5-9
1.1.2 create new workbooks use templates	L1C6, pgs. 217-219
1.1.3 import files	L2C8, pgs. 270-277
1.1.4 open non-native files directly in Excel	L2C8, pgs. 276-277
1.1.5 add worksheets to existing workbooks	L1C5, pgs. 153-154
1.1.6 copy and move worksheets	L1C6, pgs. 200-203
1.2 Navigate through Worksheets and Workbooks	
1.2.1 search for data within a workbook	L1C4, pgs. 120-124
1.2.2 insert hyperlinks	L1C6, pgs. 212-217
1.2.3 change worksheet order	L1C5, pgs. 160-161

Certification Exam Objective	Text Reference
1.2.4 demonstrate how to use Go To	L1C1, pgs. 7, 10-11; L1C3, pg. 86
1.2.5 demonstrate how to use Name Box	L1C5, pgs. 167-168, L2C2, pg. 42, L2C4, pgs. 107-108
1.3 Format Worksheets and Workbooks	
1.3.1 change worksheet tab color	L1C5, pgs. 160-161
1.3.2 modify page setup	L1C4, pgs. 101-107
1.3.3 insert and delete columns and rows	L1C3, pgs. 66-69
1.3.4 change workbook themes	L1C3, pgs. 73-74
1.3.5 adjust row height and column width	L1C3, pgs. 63-66
1.3.6 insert watermarks	L1C8, pgs. 286-287
1.3.7 insert headers and footers	L1C4, pgs. 112-117
1.3.8 set data validation	L2C3, pgs. 84-89
1.4 Customize Options and Views for Worksheets and Workbooks	
1.4.1 hide worksheets	L1C5, pgs. 162-163
1.4.2 hide columns and rows	L1C3, pgs. 86-87
1.4.3 customize the Quick Access toolbar	L2C7, pgs. 240, 245-247
1.4.4 customize the Ribbon	L2C7, pgs. 240-245
1.4.5 manage macro security	L2C7, pgs. 231-233, L2C8, pgs. 296-297
1.4.6 change workbook views	L1C4, pgs. 104-107; 112-114, L2C7 pgs. 237-238, 248-250
1.4.7 record simple macros	L2C7, pgs. 227-229, 231-233
1.4.8 add values to workbook properties	L2C6, pgs. 187-189
1.4.9 demonstrate how to use zoom	L1C5, pgs. 164-166
1.4.10 display formulas	L1C2, pg. 49, L2C5, pgs. 170-171
1.4.11 freeze panes	L1C5, pgs. 165-166
1.4.12 assign shortcut keys	L2C7, pgs. 227, 231-233
1.4.13 split the window	L1C5, pgs. 165-166
1.5 Configure Worksheets and Workbooks to Print or Save	
1.5.1 set a print area	L1C4, pgs. 110-111
1.5.2 save workbooks in alternate file formats	L2C8, pgs. 298-301
1.5.3 print individual worksheets	L1C4, pgs. 117-118; L1C5, ps. 163-164
1.5.4 set print scaling	L1C4, pgs. 108-109
1.5.5 repeat headers and footers	L1C4, pgs. 112-117
1.5.6 maintain backward compatibility	L2C8, pgs. 294-295
1.5.7 configure workbooks to print	L1C4, pgs. 107-111; 117-118
1.5.8 save files to remote locations	L1C1, pgs. 8-9; L2C6, pgs. 199-202
2.0 Create Cells and Ranges	
2.1 Insert Data in Cells and Ranges	
2.1.1 append data to worksheets	L1C5, pgs. 154-160, L2C8, pgs. 271-272
2.1.2 find and replace data	L1C4, pgs. 120-124
2.1.3 copy and paste data	L1C5, pgs. 154-160
2.1.4 demonstrate how to use AutoFill tool	L1C1, pgs. 13, 15-17

Certification Exam Objective	Text Reference
2.1.5 expand data across columns	L1C1, pgs. 21-22
2.1.6 insert and delete cells	L1C3, pgs. 66-69
2.2 Format Cells and Ranges	
2.2.1 merge cells	L1C3, pgs. 70-72
2.2.2 modify cell alignment and indentation	L1C3, pgs. 70-72; 78-80
2.2.3 change font and font styles	L1C3, pgs. 69-72; 78-81
2.2.4 use Format Painter	L1C3, pg. 86
2.2.5 wrap text within cells	L1C3, pgs. 71, 78, L2C1 pg. 22
2.2.6 apply Number formats	L1C3, pgs. 74-78, L2C1, pgs. 16-22
2.2.7 apply highlighting	L1C3, pgs. 70, 72, 75, 84-85 (fill color)
2.2.8 apply cell styles	L1C6, pgs. 204-211
2.2.9 change text to WordArt	L1C8, pgs. 293-294
2.3 Order and Group Cells and Ranges	
2.3.1 apply conditional formatting	L2C1, pgs. 6-16
2.3.2 insert sparklines	L2C4, pgs. 130-132
2.3.3 transpose columns and rows	L2C5, pgs. 156-158
2.3.4 create named ranges	L1C5, pgs. 167-168, L2C2, pgs. 41-42
2.3.5 create outlines	L2C3, pgs. 89-94
2.3.6 collapse groups of data in outlines	L2C3, pgs. 89-94
2.3.7 insert subtotals	L2C3, pgs. 89-93
3.0 Create Tables	
3.1 Create a Table	
3.1.1 move between tables and ranges	L2C3, pgs. 74-75, 89-92
3.1.2 add and remove cells within tables	L2C3, pgs. 75-76, 82-84, 86-89
3.1.3 define titles	L2C3, pgs. 76-78
3.2 Modify a Table	
3.2.1 apply styles to tables	L2C3, pgs. 76-78
3.2.2 band rows and columns	L2C3, pgs. 76-78
3.2.3 insert total rows	L2C3, pgs. 76-78
3.2.4 remove styles from tables	L2C3, pgs. 77-78, 89-92
3.3 Filter and Sort a Table	
3.3.1 filter records	L1C4, pgs. 127-129, L2C3, pgs. 78-79
3.3.2 sort data on multiple columns	L1C4, pgs. 125, 127, L2C3, pgs. 78-79, 90-92
3.3.3 change sort order	L1C4, pgs. 125-127, L2C3 pgs. 80-81
3.3.4 remove duplicates	L2C3, pgs. 82-84
4.0 Apply Formulas and Functions	
4.1 Apply Cell Ranges and References in Formulas and Functions	
4.1.1 demonstrate how to use references (relative, mixed, absolute)	L1C2, pgs. 50-53
4.1.2 define order of operations	L1C2, pgs. 40-42
4.1.3 reference cell ranges in formulas	L1C2, pgs. 40, 42, 44, 46-48,

Certification Exam Objective	Text Reference
4.2 Summarize Data with Functions	
4.2.1 demonstrate how to apply the SUM function	L1C1, pgs. 18-19
4.2.2 demonstrate how to apply the MIN and MAX functions	L1C2, pgs. 46-48
4.2.3 demonstrate how to apply the COUNT function	L1C2, pgs. 45, 48
4.2.4 demonstrate how to apply the AVERAGE function	L1C1, pgs. 19; L1C2, pgs. 45-46
4.3 Apply Conditional Logic in Functions	
4.3.1 demonstrate how to apply the SUMIF function	L2C2, pgs. 49-50
4.3.2 demonstrate how to apply the AVERAGEIF function	L2C2, pgs. 46-47
4.3.3 demonstrate how to apply the COUNTIF function	L2C2, pgs. 43-44
4.4 Format and Modify Text with Functions	
4.4.1 demonstrate how to use the RIGHT, LEFT and MID functions	L2C1, pgs. 23-24, 26
4.4.2 demonstrate how to use the TRIM function	L2C1, pgs. 23-24, 26
4.4.3 demonstrate how to use the UPPER and LOWER functions	L2C1, pgs. 23-25,
4.4.4 demonstrate how to use the CONCATENATE function	L2C3, pgs. 81-83
5.0 Create Charts and Objects	
5.1 Create a Chart	
5.1.1 create charts and graphs	L1C7, pgs. 232-251
5.1.2 add additional data series	L1C7, pgs. 233, 235-236
5.1.3 switch between rows and columns in source data	L1C7, pgs. 240-241
5.1.4 demonstrate how to use Quick Analysis	L2C1, pgs. 6-7, 11, L2C3, pgs. 74
5.2 Format a Chart	
5.2.1 add legends	L1C7, pgs. 236-237, 242-243, 246
5.2.2 resize charts and graphs	L1C7, pgs. 233-235
5.2.3 modify chart and graph parameters	L1C7, pgs. 236-238 (filter)
5.2.4 apply chart layouts and styles	L1C7, pgs. 239-241, 243
5.2.5 position charts and graphs	L1C7, pgs. 233, 235, 242-244
5.3 Insert and Format an Object	
5.3.1 insert text boxes	L1C8, pgs. 284-286
5.3.2 insert SmartArt	L1C8, pgs. 288-292
5.3.3 insert images	L1C8, pgs. 275-279
5.3.4 add borders to objects	L1C8, pgs. 276, 279
5.3.5 add styles and effects to objects	L1C8, pgs. 276-277, 279, 281-283
5.3.6 change object colors	L1C8, pgs. 276-277; 283, 290
5.3.7 modify object properties	L1C8, pgs. 278-279
5.3.8 position objects	L1C8, pgs. 276-277, 283, 289, 294

Microsoft Office 2013 Product Editions

Microsoft Office 2013 is available in the following editions:

- Microsoft Office Starter
- Office Home and Student
- Office Home and Business
- Office Professional
- Microsoft Office Professional Plus
- Microsoft Office Standard
- Microsoft Office Professional Academic

The programs included in each edition at http://office.microsoft.com/en-us/products/FX101635841033.aspx.

Microsoft Office 2013 System Requirements

This interactive text is designed for the student to complete chapter work on a computer running a standard installation of Microsoft Office 2013, Office Professional Edition, and the Microsoft Windows 8 operating system. To effectively run the Microsoft Office 2013 suite and operating system, your computer should be outfitted with the following:

- 1 gigahertz (GHz) processor or higher; 1 gigabyte (GB) of RAM
- 3 GB of available hard-disk space
- .NET version 3.5, 4.0, or 4.5
- DirectX 10 graphics card
- Minimum 1024 × 576 monitor resolution (or 1366 × 768 to use the Windows Snap feature)
- Computer mouse, multi-touch device, or compatible pointing device

Office 2013 will also operate on computers running the Windows XP Service Pack 3 or the Windows Vista operating system.

Screen captures for the books in the Benchmark Series were created using a screen resolution display setting of 1600 × 900. Refer to the *Customizing Settings* section of *Getting Started in Office 2013,* which follows the textbook's preface for instructions on changing a monitor's resolution. Figure G.10 on page 10 of the textbook illustrates the Microsoft Office Word ribbon at three resolutions for comparison purposes. Choose the resolution that best matches your computer; however, be aware that using a resolution other than 1600 × 900 means that your screens may not match the illustrations in this book.

Developing an Assessment Strategy

The final major phase of planning a course is to develop an assessment strategy based on the purpose of evaluation and on your philosophy of what constitutes high-quality assessments. The obvious purpose of assessing students' learning is to determine whether students have achieved the goals of the course and, if they have, to what degree, resulting in a grade for credits earned. Other functions of evaluation include motivating students, determining the overall effectiveness of your teaching, and meeting accreditation requirements.

In developing your philosophy of assessment, consider these suggestions from Paradigm Publishing's *Exceptional Teaching.*

Assessments should:

- contribute to students' learning by asking them to apply their skills in out-of-school or workplace situations.
- be planned as an integral part of the course design in terms of timing, content, and form.
- have a clear purpose.
- be appropriate for the purpose in terms of content and format.
- be scored as consistently and objectively as possible.
- provide students with feedback on their learning.
- emphasize intellectual traits of value—analytical reading, thinking, decision making, and research skills along with individual creativity and intelligence.
- be conducted at specific, planned checkpoints.
- be conducted in a positive learning environment, with every effort made to lower students' test anxieties.
- allow students to demonstrate their accomplishment of outcomes in various ways, including ways that fit their individual learning styles.

Determining the Number, Level, and Type of Assessments

Formulate your evaluation and grading strategy by answering these course-level questions. Consider if you should include:

- a course pre-assessment?
- a course comprehensive assessment that will determine students' mastery of the major intended outcomes for the entire course?
- pre-assessments for each section?
- comprehensive assessments for each section that assess students' mastery of the major intended outcomes for that section?
- interim or checkpoint assessments that assess students' mastery of intended outcomes of learning within units? How many? How often?

Also ask yourself: once my system is in place, will my students know that I value *how* and *how well* they think?

These questions will help you establish approximately how many assessments you wish to include and their place in the course.

The next decisions concern which types of assessment to use: traditional cognitive (objective) tests and/or performance-based assessments. Each of these two major categories of tests has its merits. Traditional cognitive tests such as multiple-choice exams usually work best for testing information recall, comprehension, and analysis. They also are reliable and efficient, and relatively easy to score. On the down side, objective-type tests are criticized for not representing how students will use their new skills in an unfamiliar setting or in the real world of work. On the other hand, performance-based testing requires students to demonstrate what they have learned and to apply it in a realistic context that closely approximates an on-the-job situation. These tests measure how well students can do what the course intended to teach them. As emphasized in

Exceptional Teaching, "Authentic, performance-based assessments ask students to integrate what they have learned and apply it to resolve an issue, solve a problem, create something new, work collaboratively, or use their written and oral communication skills. Authentic assessments stress the process of learning as well as the outcomes of learning."

Creating a Grading Plan

By choosing the types of assessments that will measure students' achievement of course and program outcomes, you will already have established a schema of the major grading components. The next step is to weight the scores before entering them into a grade calculation system, such as, an Excel spreadsheet.

Will you include other factors such as effort and attendance in students' grades? If so, consider how to measure those elements. While it is simple to track attendance, it is not as easy to objectively evaluate effort and attitude. Some experts recommend that teachers provide regular verbal and written feedback on these factors, but confine grades to academic achievement.

The following grading plan, which is part of the sample syllabus presented earlier in this section, offers a starting point as you develop your comprehensive grading strategy:

- Concepts Check assignments 5%
- Skills Check (SNAP Grade It) assignments 10%
- Visual Benchmark assignments 15%
- Case Study assignments 15%
- SNAP Performance Evaluations 20%
- Unit Performance Assessments 15%
- Exams 20%

For More Information

Much of the content of this "Planning the Course" article is based on information found in *Exceptional Teaching: Ideas in Action*. To order a copy of this resource, please visit www.ParadigmCollege.com or contact Customer Care at 800-535-6865, or educate@emcp.com.

Overview
Using Windows 8

Performance Objectives

- Use the Start screen to launch programs
- Use desktop icons and the Taskbar to launch programs and open files or folders
- Organize and manage data, including copying moving, creating, and deleting files and folders; and create a shortcut
- Explore the Control Panel and personalize the desktop
- Use the Windows Help and Support features
- Use search tools
- Customize monitor settings

Projects

Project 1	Opening Programs, Switching between Programs, and Manipulating Windows
Project 2	Changing Taskbar Properties
Project 3	Copying a File and Folder and Deleting a File
Project 4	Copying and Deleting Files
Project 5	Creating a New Folder
Project 6	Deleting Files to and Restoring Files from the Recycle Bin
Project 7	Emptying the Recycle Bin
Project 8	Creating a Shortcut
Project 9	Changing the Desktop Theme
Project 10	Customizing the Mouse
Project 11	Customizing with a Shortcut Command
Project12	Getting Help
Project 13	Searching for Programs and Files

Overview
Browsing the Internet Using Internet Explorer 10

Performance Objectives

- Navigate the Internet using URLs and hyperlinks
- Use search engines to locate information
- Download web pages and images

Projects

Project 1	Browsing the Internet Using URLs
Project 2	Navigating Using Hyperlinks
Project 3	Searching for Information by Topic
Project 4	Searching with a Metasearch Search Engine
Project 5	Narrowing a Search
Project 6	Downloading Images and Web Pages
Project 7	Opening the Saved Web Page and Image in a Word Document

Overview
Excel 2013 Level 1, Chapter 1
Preparing an Excel Workbook

Performance Objectives
- Identify the various elements of an Excel workbook
- Create, save, and print a workbook
- Enter data in a workbook
- Edit data in a workbook
- Insert a formula using the AutoSum button
- Apply basic formatting to cells in a workbook
- Use the Help feature

Projects
Project 1	Prepare a Worksheet with Employee Information
1a	Creating and Saving a Document
1b	Editing Data in a Cell
1c	Inserting Data in Cells with AutoComplete
Project 2	Open and Format a Workbook and Insert Formulas
2a	Inserting Data in Cells with the Fill Handle
2b	Adding Values with the AutoSum Button
2c	Inserting the AVERAGE Function and Copying a Formula Relatively
Project 3	Format a Worksheet
3a	Changing Column Width and Merging and Centering Cells
3b	Formatting Numbers
Project 4	Use the Help Feature
4a	Using the Help Feature
4b	Getting Help in a Dialog Box and Backstage Area

Overview
Excel 2013 Level 1, Chapter 2
Inserting Formulas in a Worksheet

Performance Objectives

- Write formulas with mathematical operators
- Type a formula in the Formula bar
- Copy a formula
- Use the Insert Function feature to insert a formula in a cell
- Write formulas with the AVERAGE, MAX, MIN, COUNT, NOW, and TODAY functions
- Create absolute and mixed cell references

Projects

Project 1	Insert Formulas in a Worksheet
1a	Finding Differences by Inserting and Copying a Formula
1b	Calculating Salary by Inserting and Copying a Formula with the Fill Handle
1c	Writing a Formula by Pointing that Calculates Percentage of Actual Budget
1d	Writing a Formula by Pointing That Calculates Percentage of Down Time
Project 2	Insert Formulas with Statistical Functions
2a	Averaging Test Scores in a Worksheet
2b	Finding Maximum and Minimum Values in a Worksheet
2c	Counting the Number of Students Taking Tests
2d	Using a NOW Function and Displaying Formulas
Project 3	Insert Formulas Using Absolute and Mixed Cell References
3a	Inserting and Copying a Formula with an Absolute Cell Reference
3b	Inserting and Copying a Formula with Multiple Absolute Cell References
3c	Determining Payroll Using Formulas with Absolute and Mixed Cell References
3d	Determining Simple Interest Using a Formula with Mixed Cell References

Overview
Excel 2013 Level 1, Chapter 3
Formatting an Excel Worksheet

Performance Objectives

- Change column widths
- Change row heights
- Insert rows and columns in a worksheet
- Delete cells, rows, and columns in a worksheet
- Clear data in cells
- Apply formatting to data in cells
- Apply formatting to selected data using the Mini toolbar
- Apply a theme and customize the theme font and color
- Format numbers
- Repeat the last action
- Automate formatting with Format Painter
- Hide and unhide rows and columns

Projects

Project 1	Format a Product Pricing Worksheet
1a	Changing Column Width Using a Column Boundary
1b	Changing Column Width at the Column Width Dialog Box
1c	Changing Row Height
1d	Inserting Rows
1e	Inserting a Column
1f	Deleting and Clearing Rows in a Worksheet
1g	Applying Font and Alignment Formatting
Project 2	Apply a Theme to a Payroll Worksheet
2	Applying a Theme
Project 3	Format an Invoices Worksheet
3a	Formatting Numbers with Buttons in the Number Group
3b	Formatting Numbers at the Format Cells Dialog Box
Project 4	Format a Company Budget Worksheet
4a	Aligning and Rotating Data in Cells
4b	Applying Font Formatting at the Format Cells Dialog Box
4c	Adding Borders to Cells
4d	Adding Fill Color and Shading to Cells
4e	Formatting with Format Painter
4f	Hiding and Unhiding Columns and Rows

Overview
Excel 2013 Level 1, Chapter 4
Enhancing a Worksheet

Performance Objectives

- Change worksheet margins
- Center a worksheet horizontally and vertically on the page
- Insert a page break in a worksheet
- Print gridlines and row and column headings
- Set and clear a print area
- Insert headers and footers
- Customize print jobs
- Complete a spelling check on a worksheet
- Find and replace data and cell formatting in a worksheet
- Sort data in cells in ascending and descending order
- Filter a list using AutoFilter

Projects

Project 1	Format a Yearly Budget Worksheet
1a	Changing Margins and Horizontally and Vertically Centering a Worksheet
1b	Changing Page Orientation and Size
1c	Inserting a Page Break in a Worksheet
1d	Printing Column Titles on Each Page of a Worksheet
1e	Scaling Data to Fit on One Page and Printing Row Titles on Each Page
1f	Inserting a Background Picture
1g	Printing Gridlines and Row and Column Headings
1h	Printing Specific Areas
1i	Inserting a Header in a Worksheet
1j	Inserting a Footer and Modifying a Header in a Worksheet
1k	Creating Different Odd and Even Page Headers and Footers and a Different First Page Header and Footer
1l	Printing Specific Pages of a Worksheet
Project 2	Format a May Sales and Commissions Worksheet
2a	Spell Checking and Formatting a Worksheet
2b	Finding and Replacing Data
2c	Finding and Replacing Cell Formatting
Project 3	Format a Billing Worksheet
3a	Sorting Data
3b	Sorting Data Using the Sort Dialog Box
3c	Sorting Data in Two Columns
3d	Filtering Data

Overview
Excel 2013 Level 1, Chapter 5
Moving Data within and between Workbooks

Performance Objectives

- Create a workbook with multiple worksheets
- Move, copy, and paste cells within and between worksheets
- Split a worksheet into windows and freeze panes
- Name a range of cells and use a range in a formula
- Open multiple workbooks
- Arrange, size, and move workbooks
- Copy and paste data between workbooks
- Link data between worksheets

Projects

Project 1	Manage Data in a Multiple-Worksheet Account Workbook
1a	Inserting, Deleting, Selecting, Copying, Pasting, and Formatting Worksheets
1b	Copying and Moving Cells and Pasting Cells Using Paste Options
1c	Copying and Pasting Cells Using the Clipboard Task Pane
1d	Copying and Pasting Values
1e	Selecting, Moving, Renaming, and Changing the Color of Worksheet Tabs
1f	Hiding a Worksheet and Formatting Multiple Worksheets
1g	Printing All Worksheets in a Workbook
Project 2	Write Formulas Using Ranges in an Equipment Usage Workbook
2a	Using Zoom, Splitting Windows, and Editing Cells
2b	Naming a Range and Using a Range in a Formula
Project 3	Arrange, Size, and Copy Data between Workbooks
3a	Opening, Arranging, and Hiding/Unhiding Workbooks
3b	Minimizing, Maximizing, and Restoring Workbooks
3c	Copying Selected Cells from One Open Worksheet to Another
Project 4	Linking and Copying Data within and between Worksheets and Word
4a	Linking Cells between Worksheets
4b	Copying and Pasting Excel Data into a Word Document

Overview
Excel 2013 Level 1, Chapter 6
Maintaining Workbooks

Performance Objectives

- Create and rename a folder
- Delete workbooks and folders
- Copy and move workbooks within and between folders
- Copy and move worksheets between workbooks
- Maintain consistent formatting with styles
- Insert, modify, and remove hyperlinks
- Create financial forms using templates

Projects

Project 1	Manage Workbooks
1a	Creating a Folder
1b	Renaming a Folder
1c	Selecting and Deleting Workbooks
1d	Saving a Copy of an Open Workbook to Another Folder
1e	Copying a Workbook at the Open Dialog Box
1f	Cutting and Pasting a Workbook
1g	Renaming a Workbook
1h	Deleting a Folder and Its Contents
Project 2	Copy and Move Worksheets into an Equipment Rental Workbook
2a	Managing Workbooks at the Open Backstage Area
2b	Copying a Worksheet to Another Workbook
2c	Moving a Worksheet to Another Workbook
Project 3	Create and Apply Styles to a Payroll Workbook
3a	Formatting with Cell Styles
3b	Defining and Applying a Style
3c	Defining a Style without First Applying Formatting
3d	Modifying Styles
3e	Copying Styles
Project 4	Insert, Modify, and Remove Hyperlinks
4a	Linking to a Website and Another Workbook
4b	Linking to a Place in a Workbook, to Another Workbook, and Using a Graphic
4c	Modifying, Editing, and Removing a Hyperlink
Project 5	Create a Billing Statement Workbook Using a Template
5	Preparing a Billing Statement Using a Template

Overview
Excel 2013 Level 1, Chapter 7
Creating Charts and Inserting Formulas

Performance Objectives

- Create a chart with data in an Excel worksheet
- Size, move, edit, format. and delete charts
- Print a selected chart and print a worksheet containing a chart
- Change chart location
- Insert, move, size, and delete chart elements and shapes
- Write formulas with the PMT and FV financial functions
- Write formulas with the IF logical function

Projects

Project 1	Create a Quarterly Sales Column Chart
1a	Creating a Chart
1b	Formatting with Chart Buttons
1c	Printing a Chart
Project 2	Create a Technology Purchases Bar Chart and Column Chart
2a	Creating a Chart and Changing the Design
2b	Changing Chart Layout and Location and Adding Chart Elements
Project 3	Create a Population Comparison Line Chart
3a	Creating and Formatting a Line Chart
3b	Inserting and Customizing a Shape
Project 4	Create a Costs Percentage Pie Chart
4	Deleting a Chart and Creating and Formatting a Pie Chart
Project 5	Calculate Payments and the Future Value of an Investment
5a	Calculating Payments
5b	Finding the Future Value of an Investment
Project 6	Insert Formulas with the IF Logical Function
6a	Writing a Formula with an IF Function
6b	Writing a Formula with an IF Function Using the Function Arguments Palette
6c	Writing IF Statements Containing Text

Overview
Excel 2013 Level 1, Chapter 8
Adding Visual Interest to Workbooks

Performance Objectives

- Insert symbols and special characters
- Insert, size, move, and format images
- Insert a screenshot
- Draw, format, and copy shapes
- Insert, format, and type text in a text box
- Insert a picture image as a watermark
- Insert and format SmartArt graphics
- Insert and format WordArt

Projects

Project 1	Insert a Clip Art Image and Shapes in a Financial Analysis Workbook
1a	Inserting Symbols and Special Characters
1b	Formatting an Image
1c	Inserting and Formatting a Clip Art Image
1d	Inserting and Formatting a Screenshot
1e	Drawing Arrow Shapes
Project 2	Insert a Picture and Text Box in a Division Sales Workbook
2	Inserting and Customizing a Picture and Text Box
Project 3	Insert a Watermark in an Equipment Usage Workbook
3	Inserting a Picture as a Watermark
Project 4	Insert and Format SmartArt Graphics in a Company Sales Workbook
4a	Inserting, Moving, and Sizing a SmartArt Graphic in a Worksheet
4b	Changing the SmartArt Graphic Design
4c	Changing the SmartArt Graphic Formatting
4d	Inserting and Formatting WordArt

Overview
Excel 2013 Level 2, Chapter 1
Advanced Formatting Techniques

Performance Objectives

- Apply conditional formatting by entering parameters for a rule
- Apply conditional formatting using a predefined rule
- Create and apply a new rule for conditional formatting
- Edit, delete, and clear conditional formatting rules
- Apply conditional formatting using an icon set, data bars, and color scale
- Apply conditional formatting using a formula
- Apply fraction and scientific formatting
- Apply a special format for a number
- Create a custom number format
- Apply wrap text and shrink to fit text control options
- Modify text using the text functions PROPER, UPPER, LOWER, SUBSTITUTE, RIGHT, MID, and TRIM
- Filter a worksheet using a custom AutoFilter
- Filter and sort a worksheet using conditional formatting or cell attributes

Projects

Project 1	Format Cells Based on Values
1a	Using Quick Analysis to Format Cells Based on a Value Comparison
1b	Formatting Cells Based on Top/Bottom Rules
Project 2	Apply Conditional Formatting to Insurance Policy Data
2a	Creating and Applying New Formatting Rules
2b	Creating, Editing, and Deleting a Formatting Rule
2c	Applying Conditional Formatting Using an Icon Set
2d	Applying Conditional Formatting Using a Formula
Project 3	Using Fraction and Scientific Formatting Options
3	Applying Fraction and Scientific Formatting
Project 4	Apply Advanced Formatting Options
4a	Applying Special Formatting
4b	Creating a Custom Number Format
4c	Applying Wrap Text and Shrink to Fit Text Control Options
Project 5	Convert Text Using Text Functions
5a	Converting Text Using SUBSTITUTE, LOWER, and UPPER Text Functions
5b	Extracting Text Using RIGHT, LEFT, MID, and TRIM Functions
Project 6	Filter and Sort Data Based on Values, Icon Set, and Font Color
6a	Filtering Policy Information
6b	Filtering by Icon Set
6c	Filtering by Font Color
6d	Sorting by Cell Color

Overview
Excel 2013 Level 2, Chapter 2
Advanced Functions and Formulas

Performance Objectives

- Create and use named ranges in formulas
- Use the functions COUNTA, COUNTIF, and COUNTIFS
- Use the functions AVERAGEIF and AVERAGEIFS
- Use the functions SUMIF and SUMIFS
- Edit a named range
- Rename and delete a named range
- Look up date using the lookup functions VLOOKUP and HLOOKUP
- Analyze loan payments using PPMT
- Use the conditional logic functions IF, AND, and OR

Projects

Project 1	Calculate Statistics and Sums Using Conditional Formulas
1a	Creating Range Names
1b	Creating COUNTIF Functions
1c	Creating COUNTIFS Functions
1d	Creating AVERAGEIF Functions
1e	Creating AVERAGEIFS Functions
1f	Creating SUMIF Functions
1g	Editing and Deleting a Range Name
Project 2	Populate Cells by Looking up Data
2	Creating a VLOOKUP Function
Project 3	Analyze an Expansion Project Loan
3	Calculating Principal Portions of Loan Payments
Project 4	Calculate Benefit Costs Using Conditional Logic
4a	Calculating Pension Costs Using Nested IF and AND Functions
4b	Calculating Health and Dental Costs Using Nested IF and OR Functions

Overview
Excel 2013 Level 2, Chapter 3
Working with Tables and Data Features

Performance Objectives

- Create a table in a worksheet
- Expand a table to include new rows and columns
- Add a calculated column in a table
- Format a table by applying table styles and table style options
- Add a *Total* row to a table and formulas to total cells
- Sort and filter a table
- Split contents of a cell into separate columns
- Use Flash Fill
- Remove duplicate records
- Restrict data entry by creating validation criteria
- Convert a table to a normal range
- Create subtotals in groups of related data
- Group and ungroup data

Projects

Project 1	Create and Modify a Table
1a	Converting a Range to a Table
1b	Adding a Row and Calculated Column to a Table
1c	Formatting a Table and Adding a *Total* Row
1d	Sorting and Filtering a Table
Project 2	Use Data Tools to Split Data and Ensure Data Integrity
2a	Separating Client Names into Two Columns
2b	Combining Client and File Numbers to Create Case Codes
2c	Removing Duplicate Rows
2d	Restricting Data Entry to Dates Within a Range
2e	Restricting Data Entry to Values Within a List
2f	Ensuring Data Entered Is a Specified Text Length
Project 3	Group and Subtotal Related Records
3a	Converting a Table to a Range and Creating Subtotals
3b	Modifying Subtotals
3c	Grouping and Ungrouping Data

Overview
Excel 2013 Level 2, Chapter 4
Summarizing and Consolidating Data

Performance Objectives

- Summarize data by creating formulas with range names that reference other worksheets
- Modify the range assigned to a range name
- Summarize data by creating 3.D references
- Create formulas that link to cells in other worksheets or workbooks
- Edit a link to a source workbook
- Break a link to an external reference
- Use the Consolidate feature to summarize data in multiple worksheets
- Create, edit, and format a PivotTable
- Filter a PivotTable using Slicers
- Filter a PivotTable using Timelines
- Create and format a PivotChart
- Create and format Sparklines

Projects

Project 1	Calculate Park Attendance Totals
1a	Modifying a Named Range and Summarizing Data in Multiple Worksheets
1b	Summarizing Data in Multiple Worksheets Using a 3-D Reference Formula
1c	Summarizing Data by Linking to Another Workbook
1d	Editing Source Data and Updating an External Link
1e	Removing a Linked External Reference
Project 2	Calculate Total Fees Billed by Three Dentists
2	Summarizing Data Using the Consolidate Feature
Project 3	Analyze Fitness Equipment Sales Data in a PivotTable and PivotChart
3a	Creating a PivotTable Using Recommended PivotTables
3b	Building a PivotTable
3c	Formatting and Filtering a PivotTable
3d	Using a Slicer to Filter a PivotTable
3e	Using a Timeline to Filter a PivotTable
3f	Changing the Values Function in a PivotTable
3g	Creating a PivotChart
3h	Crating a PivotChart from Scratch
Project 4	Add Sparklines in a Worksheet to Show Trends
4a	Creating Sparklines
4b	Customizing Sparklines

Overview
Excel 2013 Level 2, Chapter 5
Using Data Analysis Features

Performance Objectives

- Switch data arranged in columns to rows and vice versa
- Perform a mathematical operation during a paste routine
- Populate a cell using Goal Seek
- Save and display various worksheet models using Scenario Manager
- Create a scenario summary report
- Create a one-variable data table to analyze various outcomes
- Create a two-variable data table to analyze various outcomes
- View relationships between cells in formulas
- Identify Excel error codes and troubleshoot a formula using formula auditing tools
- Circle invalid data
- Use the Watch Window to track a value

Projects

Project 1	Analyze Data Using Paste Special Options
1a	Converting Data from Rows to Columns
1b	Multiplying the Source Cells by the Destination Cells
Project 2	Calculate a Target Test Score
2	Using Goal Seek to Return a Target Value
Project 3	Forecast a Budget Based on Various Inflation Rates
3a	Adding Scenarios to a Worksheet Model
3b	Applying a Scenario's Values to a Worksheet
3c	Generating a Scenario Summary Report
Project 4	Compare the Impacts of Various Inputs Related to Cost and Sales Pricing
4a	Creating a One-Variable Data Table
4b	Crating a Two-Variable Data Table
Project 5	Audit a Worksheet to View and Troubleshoot Formulas
5a	Viewing Relationships between Cells and Formulas
5b	Troubleshooting Formulas
5c	Circling Invalid Data and Watching a Formula Cell

Overview
Excel 2013 Level 2, Chapter 6
Using Access Tools and Managing Objects

Performance Objectives

- Create a new database using a template
- Add a group of objects to a database using an Application Parts template
- Save a database as a template
- Create a new form using an Application Parts Blank Form
- Create a form to be used as a template in a database
- Create a table by copying the structure of another table
- Evaluate a table using the Table Analyzer Wizard
- Evaluate a database using the Performance Analyzer
- Split a database
- Print documentation about a database using the Database Documenter
- Rename and delete objects

Projects

Project 1	Create a New Database Using a Template
1a	Creating a New Contacts Database Using a Template
1b	Entering and Viewing Data in the Contacts Database
1c	Saving a Database as a Template
Project 2	Create Objects Using a Template
2a	Creating a Contacts Table, a Query, Forms, and Reports Using a Template
2b	Creating a New Form Using an Application Parts Blank Form
2c	Creating and Using a User-Defined Form Template
Project 3	Copy Table Structure
3	Copying a Table Structure to Create a New Table
Project 4	Use Access Tools to Optimize and Document a Database
4a	Splitting a Table Using the Table Analyzer Wizard
4b	Analyzing a Database to Improve Performance
4c	Splitting a Database
4d	Generating a Table Definition Documentation Report
4e	Renaming and Deleting Database Objects
Project 5	Create a Database Using Templates, Application Parts, Quick Start and Wizards

Overview
Excel 2013 Level 2, Chapter 7
Automating Repetitive Tasks and Customizing Excel

Performance Objectives

- Record, run, and edit a macro
- Save a workbook containing macros as a macro-enabled workbook
- Create a macro that is run using a shortcut key combination
- Pin and unpin a frequently used file to the Recent Workbooks list
- Customize the display options for Excel
- Hide the ribbon to increase space in the work area
- Customize the ribbon by creating a custom tab and adding buttons
- Add and remove buttons for frequently used commands to the Quick Access toolbar
- Create and apply custom views
- Create and use a template
- Customize save options for AutoRecover files

Projects

Project 1	Create Macros
1a	Creating a Macro and Saving a Workbook as a Macro-Enabled Workbook
1b	Running a Macro
1c	Creating and Running a Macro Using a Shortcut Key
1d	Editing a Macro
Project 2	Customize the Excel Work Environment
2a	Pinning a Frequently Used Workbook to the Recent Workbooks List
2b	Customizing Display Options and Minimizing the Ribbon
2c	Restoring Default Display Options
2d	Exporting Customizations
2e	Customizing the Ribbon
2f	Adding Commands to the Quick Access Toolbar
2g	Importing Ribbon and Quick Access Toolbar Customizations
2h	Creating and Applying Custom Views
Project 3	Save a Workbook as a Template
3a	Saving a Workbook as a Template
3b	Using a Custom Template
Project 4	Managing Excel's Save Options
4a	Customizing Save Options
4b	Recovering a Workbook

Overview
Excel 2013 Level 2, Chapter 8
Importing, Exporting, and Distributing Data

Performance Objectives

- Import data from an Access table, website, and text file
- Append data from an Excel worksheet to an Access table
- Embed and link data in an Excel worksheet to a Word document
- Copy and paste data in an Excel worksheet to a PowerPoint presentation
- Export data as a text file
- Scan and remove private or confidential information from a workbook
- Mark a workbook as final
- Check a workbook for features incompatible with earlier versions of Excel
- View Trust Center settings
- Save an Excel workbook as a PDF or XPS file
- Save an Excel worksheet as a web page

Projects

Project 1	Import Data from External Sources to Excel
1a	Importing Data from an Access Database
1b	Importing a Table from a Web Page
1c	Importing Data from a Comma Separated Text File
Project 2	Export Data in Excel
2a	Copying and Pasting Excel Data to an Access Datasheet
2b	Embedding Excel Data in a Word Document
2c	Linking Excel Data in a Word Document
2d	Breaking a Link
2e	Embedding Excel Data in a PowerPoint Presentation
2f	Exporting a Worksheet as a Text File
Project 3	Prepare a Workbook for Distribution
3a	Removing Private and Confidential Data from a Workbook
3b	Marking a Workbook as Final
3c	Checking a Workbook for Compatibility with Earlier Versions of Excel
3d	Exploring Trust Center Settings
Project 4	Distributing Workbooks
4a	Publishing a Workbook as a PDF Document
4b	Publishing a Workbook as an XPS Document
4c	Publishing a Worksheet as a Web Page

Overview of Assessment Venues

The grading sheet on the following pages can be used as a resource to create your grading plan. An electronic copy of this table is provided on the Instructor Resources disc, and you can alter this file to meet your specific course needs. Several venues of different types are available for assessing student achievement in your course.

Comprehension-Based Assessments

- Concepts Check questions appear at the end of each chapter. These short-answer questions test student comprehension and recall of program features, terminology, and functions. Answer keys are included in the *Instructor's Guide*, on the Instructor Resources disc, and on the password-protected Instructor section of the Internet Resource Center. Matching activities based on the Concepts Check questions are available in SNAP.
- ExamView® test generating software and test banks includes multiple-choice items for each chapter of the text. Use ExamView to create web-based or print tests.
- SNAP web-based assessments include multiple-choice items for each chapter of the text (prepared from the ExamView test banks). Instructors can assign pre-designed concepts exams or create their own.
- Quizzes of multiple-choice items for each chapter of the text (different from the items in the ExamView test banks) are available on the Internet Resource Center. Students can take quizzes in either practice mode with immediate feedback or in scores-reported mode with results emailed to the instructor.

Performance-Based Assessments

- End-of-chapter assessments are provided to assess student understanding of major features and program skills taught in the chapter. Instructor support for these assessments is included in the *Instructor's Guide*, on the Instructor Resources disc and, on the password-protected Instructor section of the Internet Resource Center.
    - Skills Check assessments provide additional hands-on computer exercises to reinforce learning. These exercises include some guidance, but less than the chapter projects. Items marked with a SNAP Grade It icon have a corresponding activity available in SNAP, which will automatically score student work. Grading rubrics, annotated PDF files, and live application files are available to instructors to support these activities.
    - Visual Benchmark activities provide limited guidance and challenge students to use their problem-solving skills and mastery of program features to build a file that matches a file displayed with the exercise. Grading rubrics, PDF files, and live application files are available to instructors to support these activities.
    - Case Studies offer realistic scenarios that require taking initiative and determining solutions using skills developed throughout the chapter. Students search the Internet or the program's Help feature to find the additional information they need to create final documents and files. Student work will vary, but grading rubrics, PDF files, and live application files are available to instructors to support these activities.

- Unit Performance Assessments are separate sections at the end of each group of four chapters that include a range of activities to evaluate student achievement. Grading rubrics are provided to instructors to support these activities.
  - Assessing Proficiency exercises involve using program features to create a variety of documents, all with little or no assistance. Annotated PDF files and live application files are available to instructors to support these activities.
  - Writing Activities stress the vital cross-disciplinary skill of writing clearly during the course of preparing specific documents.
  - Internet Research is a scenario-based activity requiring Internet navigation and searching plus information analysis and presentation.
  - Job Study is a culminating case study exercise that simulates workplace tasks and challenges. This Performance Assessment type is found in Unit 2 Performance Assessments.
- SNAP is a web-based training and assessment program designed to optimize skill-based learning. SNAP includes a learning management system that creates a virtual classroom on the Web, allowing the instructor to schedule tutorials, exams, and textbook assignments and to employ an electronic grade book. SNAP support for the *Benchmark Series* includes the following:
  - A bank of 154 interactive, gradable, multimedia tutorials, aligned to support activities found in textbook sections, that can be used for direct instruction or remediation.
  - A bank of 306 performance skill items in which students perform tasks in Microsoft Excel 2013 that are evaluated and reported in the learning management system. Instructors can assign pre-defined skill exams or create their own exams from the item bank.
  - A bank of 58 Grade It Skills Check assessment activities, with immediate, automatic scoring with individualized feedback of student work, align with select Skills Check activities in the textbook.
  - Comprehensive Performance Evaluation activities, one per chapter and one per unit, for comprehensive evaluation of skills mastery.
  - Over 875 concept items that can be used to monitor student understanding computer literacy and technical knowledge as well as a concept item generator that will allow instructors to create up to ten kinds of new concept items
- Supplemental activities are provided for use in evaluating student comprehension of program skills. Resources for these assessments are included in the *Instructor's Guide*, on the Instructor Resources disc, and on the Instructor section of the Internet Resource Center.
  - Supplemental Assessments are similar in format to the end-of-chapter Skills Check or Visual Benchmark assessments, and are supported with data files, model answer files, and rubrics. There is one Supplemental Assessment for each unit, or two for each level.
  - Supplemental Case Studies are similar in format to the end-of-chapter Case Studies, and are supported with, data files, model answer files, and rubrics. There is one Supplemental Case Study for each application level.

Using the Microsoft Office 2013 Compare Features

Microsoft Office 2013 offers features you can use to compare students' completed files against the live model answer files provided to instructors to support evaluation of student work for textbooks in the *Benchmark Series*. The compare features are available in Word, Excel, and PowerPoint, and they work a little differently in each of those applications. A compare feature is not available in Access.

In Excel

Compare Files is a new feature for Excel 2013. It does not come preloaded in Excel but is one of the tools in the Inquire add-in, which can be installed in some versions of the application, including Microsoft Office Professional Plus 2013. Once you have installed the add-in, you will see the INQUIRE tab on your Excel ribbon, and you can use the Excel Compare Files button on that tab to compare students' files against the model answer files.

Instructions for Installing the Inquire Add-in

1. Close all open Excel files.
2. Open a new, blank Excel workbook.
3. Click the FILE tab.
4. Click *Options* and then click *Add-ins*.
5. Click the *Manage* option box arrow, click the *COM Add-ins* option in the drop-down list, and then click the Go button.
6. In the COM Add-ins dialog box, make sure the *Inquire* check box contains a check mark. ***Note: If you do not see an entry for the Inquire add-in, either your version of Office or Excel does not include it, or your organization's system administrator has made it unavailable. Microsoft Office Professional Plus 2013 includes the Inquire add-in for Excel.***
7. Click OK. You should now see the INQUIRE tab on the ribbon in your Excel file.

Instructions for Using Excel's Compare Files Feature

1. Make sure you have installed the Inquire add-in as instructed above.
2. Close all open Excel files.
3. Open the model answer file.
4. Open the student's file.
5. With the student's file the active file, click the INQUIRE tab.
6. Click the Compare Files button in the Compare group to open the Select Files To Compare dialog box. By default, Excel fills in the name of the model answer file in the *Compare* option box and the name of the student's file in the *To* option box. Verify that those names are correct. ***Note: If you have not closed all other open Excel files, you may see the name of another file in one or both of these option boxes. Click the option box arrow to display a list of all open Excel documents, and select the correct file from the list.***

7. Click the Compare button. Excel opens a new Spreadsheet Compare window showing any differences between the files.
8. Click the Export Results button in the Export group on the Home tab, and save the exported workbook. You may want to name this file with the student's last name, the model answer file name, and *-compare* at the end.
9. Close the Spreadsheet Compare window and open the exported compare file. Notice that the Compare file has two sheets—Differences and Setup. In the Differences sheet, the *Old Value* column lists entries from the model answer file, the *New Value* column lists entries from the student's file, and the *Description* column explains what is different between the two entries.
10. You can provide the student with the compare file as an Excel workbook, a hard-copy printout, or a PDF. ***Note: When you print the compare file as a hard copy or export it to a PDF, you need to print or export each tab separately. Review the information on the Setup tab and determine whether it will be useful for the student.***

Using the Microsoft Excel 2013 Compare Feature

Compare Files is a new feature for Excel 2013. It does not come preloaded in Excel but is one of the tools in the Inquire add-in, which can be installed in some versions of the application, including Microsoft Office Professional Plus 2013. Once you have installed the add-in, you will see the INQUIRE tab on your Excel ribbon, and you can use the Excel Compare Files button on that tab to compare students' files against the model answer files.

Instructions for Installing the Inquire Add-in

1. Close all open Excel files.
2. Open a new, blank Excel workbook.
3. Click the FILE tab.
4. Click *Options* and then click *Add-ins*.
5. Click the *Manage* option box arrow, click the *COM Add-ins* option in the drop-down list, and then click the Go button.
6. In the COM Add-ins dialog box, make sure the *Inquire* check box contains a check mark. ***Note: If you do not see an entry for the Inquire add-in, either your version of Office or Excel does not include it, or your organization's system administrator has made it unavailable. Microsoft Office Professional Plus 2013 includes the Inquire add-in for Excel.***
7. Click OK. You should now see the INQUIRE tab on the ribbon in your Excel file.

Instructions for Using Excel's Compare Files Feature

1. Make sure you have installed the Inquire add-in as instructed above.
2. Close all open Excel files.
3. Open the model answer file.
4. Open the student's file.
5. With the student's file the active file, click the INQUIRE tab.

6. Click the Compare Files button in the Compare group to open the Select Files To Compare dialog box. By default, Excel fills in the name of the model answer file in the *Compare* option box and the name of the student's file in the *To* option box. Verify that those names are correct. ***Note: If you have not closed all other open Excel files, you may see the name of another file in one or both of these option boxes. Click the option box arrow to display a list of all open Excel documents, and select the correct file from the list.***
7. Click the Compare button. Excel opens a new Spreadsheet Compare window showing any differences between the files.
8. Click the Export Results button in the Export group on the Home tab, and save the exported workbook. You may want to name this file with the student's last name, the model answer file name, and *-compare* at the end.
9. Close the Spreadsheet Compare window and open the exported compare file. Notice that the Compare file has two sheets—Differences and Setup. In the Differences sheet, the *Old Value* column lists entries from the model answer file, the *New Value* column lists entries from the student's file, and the *Description* column explains what is different between the two entries.
10. You can provide the student with the compare file as an Excel workbook, a hard-copy printout, or a PDF. ***Note: When you print the compare file as a hard copy or export it to a PDF, you need to print or export each tab separately. Review the information on the Setup tab and determine whether it will be useful for the student.***

Grading Sheet

Benchmark Series Microsoft Excel 2013 Level 1

Assignment	Title	Start from Scratch	SNAP Grade It	Date Due	Grade
Unit 1: Preparing and Formatting Worksheets					
Chapter 1 Preparing an Excel Workbook					
Concepts Check			✓		
Skills Check Assessment 1	Create a Worksheet Using AutoComplete	✓	✓		
Skills Check Assessment 2	Create and Format a Worksheet	✓	✓		
Skills Check Assessment 3	Create a Worksheet Using the Fill Handle	✓	✓		
Skills Check Assessment 4	Insert Formulas in a Worksheet		✓		
Visual Benchmark	Create, Format, and Insert Formulas in a Worksheet	✓			
Case Study Part 1	Deering Industries: Calendar				
Case Study Part 2	Deering Industries: Quarterly Purchases				
Case Study Part 3	Deering Industries: Expenditures Memo				
Case Study Part 4	Deering Industries: Copy Machines (Internet)	✓			
SNAP Tutorial 1.1	Opening, Saving, and Closing an Excel Workbook				
SNAP Tutorial 1.2	Entering Data in Cells and Saving a Workbook with a New Name				
SNAP Tutorial 1.3	Editing Cells and Using Proofing Tools				
SNAP Tutorial 1.4	Printing a Worksheet				
SNAP Tutorial 1.5	Applying Formatting; Using Undo and Redo; Changing Alignment				
SNAP Tutorial 1.6	Navigating and Scrolling in a Worksheet				
SNAP Tutorial 1.7	Applying Basic Formatting				
SNAP Tutorial 1.8	Applying Number Formatting				

Assignment	Title	Start from Scratch	SNAP Grade It	Date Due	Grade
SNAP Tutorial 1.9	Getting Help at the Excel Help Window				
IRC Quiz	Study Quiz				
SNAP Concepts	Quiz				
SNAP Skill Items	Quiz				
SNAP PE	Comprehensive Performance Evaluation				
Chapter 2 Inserting Formulas in a Worksheet					
Concepts Check			✓		
Skills Check Assessment 1	Insert AVERAGE, MAX, and MIN Functions		✓		
Skills Check Assessment 2	Insert the SUM Function and Enter Formulas with Mathematical Operators		✓		
Skills Check Assessment 3	Write Formulas with Absolute Cell References		✓		
Skills Check Assessment 4	Write Formulas with Mixed Cell References		✓		
Skills Check Assessment 5	Use Help to Learn About Excel Options	✓			
Visual Benchmark	Create a Worksheet and Insert Formulas	✓			
Case Study Part 1	Allenmore Auto Sales: Monthly Sales Worksheet				
Case Study Part 2	Allenmore Auto Sales: Formulas				
Case Study Part 3	Allenmore Auto Sales: Wholesaled data				
Case Study Part 4	Allenmore Auto Sales: Estimates (Help, Internet)				
SNAP Tutorial 2.1	Performing Calculations Using Formulas				
SNAP Tutorial 2.2	Copying and Testing Formulas				
SNAP Tutorial 2.3	Using Statistical Functions				
SNAP Tutorial 2.4	Writing Formulas with Date Functions and Dates				
SNAP Tutorial 2.5	Displaying Formulas in a Worksheet				
SNAP Tutorial 2.6	Creating Formulas and Absolute Addressing				
IRC Quiz	Study Quiz				
SNAP Concepts	Quiz				
SNAP Skill Items	Quiz				

Assignment	Title	Start from Scratch	SNAP Grade It	Date Due	Grade
SNAP PE	Comprehensive Performance Evaluation				
Chapter 3 Formatting an Excel Worksheet					
Concepts Check			✓		
Skills Check Assessment 1	Format a Sales and Bonuses Worksheet		✓		
Skills Check Assessment 2	Format an Overdue Accounts Worksheet		✓		
Skills Check Assessment 3	Format a Supplies and Equipment Worksheet		✓		
Skills Check Assessment 4	Format a Financial Analysis Worksheet		✓		
Visual Benchmark	Create a Worksheet and Insert Formulas	✓			
Case Study Part 1	HealthWise Fitness Center: Dues				
Case Study Part 2	HealthWise Fitness Center: Payroll Sheet	✓			
Case Study Part 3	HealthWise Fitness Center: New Equipment (Internet)	✓			
Case Study Part 4	HealthWise Fitness Center: Prospective Clients	✓			
SNAP Tutorial 3.1	Adjusting Column Width and Row Height				
SNAP Tutorial 3.2	Inserting and Deleting Columns and Rows				
SNAP Tutorial 3.3	Applying Font Formatting				
SNAP Tutorial 3.4	Applying Alignment Formatting				
SNAP Tutorial 3.5	Applying Cell Styles and Themes				
SNAP Tutorial 3.6	Formatting Numbers				
SNAP Tutorial 3.7	Adding Borders and Shading to Cells				
SNAP Tutorial 3.8	Using Format Painter				
SNAP Tutorial 3.9	Hiding and Unhiding Columns and/or Rows				
IRC Quiz	Study Quiz				
SNAP Concepts	Quiz				
SNAP Skill Items	Quiz				
SNAP PE	Comprehensive Performance Evaluation				
Chapter 4 Enhancing a Worksheet					
Concepts Check			✓		

Assignment	Title	Start from Scratch	SNAP Grade It	Date Due	Grade
Skills Check Assessment 1	Format a Data Analysis Worksheet		✓		
Skills Check Assessment 2	Format a Test Results Worksheet		✓		
Skills Check Assessment 3	Format an Equipment Rental Worksheet		✓		
Skills Check Assessment 4	Format an Invoices Worksheet		✓		
Skills Check Assessment 5	Create a Worksheet Containing Keyboard Shortcuts (Help)	✓			
Visual Benchmark	Create and Format an Expense Worksheet	✓			
Case Study Part 1	Macadam Realty: Sample Mortgages				
Case Study Part 2	Macadam Realty: Sales and Commissions				
Case Study Part 3	Macadam Realty: Conversion Worksheet (Internet)	✓			
SNAP Tutorial 4.1	Changing Page Layout Options				
SNAP Tutorial 4.2	Formatting a Worksheet Page for Printing				
SNAP Tutorial 4.3	Using Page Break Preview				
SNAP Tutorial 4.4	Inserting Headers and Footers				
SNAP Tutorial 4.5	Formatting and Printing Multiple Worksheets				
SNAP Tutorial 4.6	Completing a Spelling Check				
SNAP Tutorial 4.7	Using Undo and Redo				
SNAP Tutorial 4.8	Using Find and Replace				
SNAP Tutorial 4.9	Finding and Replacing Text and Formatting				
SNAP Tutorial 4.10	Sorting Data				
SNAP Tutorial 4.11	Filtering Data Using a Custom AutoFilter				
IRC Quiz	Study Quiz				
SNAP Concepts	Quiz				
SNAP Skill Items	Quiz				
SNAP PE	Comprehensive Performance Evaluation				
Unit 1 Performance Assessments					
Assessment 1	Calculate Total, Maximum, Minimum, and Average Yearly Sales				

Assignment	Title	Start from Scratch	SNAP Grade It	Date Due	Grade
Assessment 2	Create Worksheet with AutoFill and Calculate Hours and Gross Pay	✓			
Assessment 3	Sales Bonuses Workbook	✓			
Assessment 4	Format First-Quarter Sales Workbook				
Assessment 5	Format Weekly Payroll Workbook				
Assessment 6	Format Customer Sales Analysis Workbook				
Assessment 7	Format Invoices Workbook				
Writing Activity 1	Plan and Prepare Orders Summary Workbook	✓			
Writing Activity 2	Prepare Depreciation Workbook	✓			
Writing Activity 3	Insert Straight-Line Depreciation Formula				
Internet Research	Create a Travel Planning Worksheet	✓			
Supplemental Assessment 1	Doctor Visits	✓			
Supplemental Assessment 2	Doctor Visits	✓			
SNAP PE	Comprehensive Performance Evaluation				
Unit 2: Enhancing the Display of Workbooks					
Chapter 5 Moving Data within and between Workbooks					
Concepts Check			✓		
Skills Check Assessment 1	Copy and Paste Data Between Worksheets in a Sales Workbook		✓		
Skills Check Assessment 2	Copy, Paste, and Format Worksheets in an Income Statement Workbook		✓		
Skills Check Assessment 3	Freeze and Unfreeze Window Panes in a Test Scores Workbook		✓		
Skills Check Assessment 4	Create, Copy, Paste, and Format Cells in an Equipment Usage Workbook	✓			
Skills Check Assessment 5	Copying and Linking Data in a Word Document				
Visual Benchmark	Create and Format a Sales Worksheet Using Formulas	✓			
Case Study Part 1	Gateway Global: Supplies and Equipment Purchases	✓			
Case Study Part 2	Gateway Global: Softball Statistics (Help)	✓			
Case Study Part 3	Gateway Global: Length, Weight, and Volume Conversions (Internet)	✓			

Assignment	Title	Start from Scratch	SNAP Grade It	Date Due	Grade
Case Study Part 4	Gateway Global: Placing an Excel Image in a Letter	✓			
SNAP Tutorial 5.1	Moving and Copying Cells				
SNAP Tutorial 5.2	Inserting, Moving, Renaming, and Deleting a Worksheet				
SNAP Tutorial 5.3	Formatting Multiple Worksheets				
SNAP Tutorial 5.4	Using Paste Options				
SNAP Tutorial 5.5	Printing a Workbook Containing Multiple Worksheets				
SNAP Tutorial 5.6	Freezing Panes and Changing the Zoom				
SNAP Tutorial 5.7	Splitting a Worksheet into Windows				
SNAP Tutorial 5.8	Naming and Using a Range				
SNAP Tutorial 5.9	Working with Windows				
SNAP Tutorial 5.10	Linking Data between Worksheets				
SNAP Tutorial 5.11	Copying and Pasting Data between Programs				
IRC Quiz	Study Quiz				
SNAP Concepts	Quiz				
SNAP Skill Items	Quiz				
SNAP PE	Comprehensive Performance Evaluation				
Chapter 6 Maintaining Workbooks					
Concepts Check			✓		
Skills Check Assessment 1	Manage Workbooks	✓			
Skills Check Assessment 2	Move and Copy Worksheets Between Sales Analysis Workbooks		✓		
Skills Check Assessment 3	Define and Apply Styles to a Projected Earnings Workbook	✓	✓		
Skills Check Assessment 4	Insert Hyperlinks in a Bookstore Workbook		✓		
Skills Check Assessment 5	Apply Conditional Formatting to a Sales Workbook (Help)	✓			
Visual Benchmark	Fill in an Expense Report Form	✓			
Case Study Part 1	Leeward Marine: Expenses Summary				
Case Study Part 2	Leeward Marine: Estimated Expenses				
Case Study Part 3	Leeward Marine: Format Worksheet	✓			
Case Study Part 4	Leeward Marine: Product List	✓			
SNAP Tutorial 6.1	Maintaining Workbooks				

Assignment	Title	Start from Scratch	SNAP Grade It	Date Due	Grade
SNAP Tutorial 6.2	Managing Folders				
SNAP Tutorial 6.3	Managing the Recent Workbooks List				
SNAP Tutorial 6.4	Managing Worksheets				
SNAP Tutorial 6.5	Formatting with Cell Styles				
SNAP Tutorial 6.6	Inserting Hyperlinks				
SNAP Tutorial 6.7	Using Excel Templates				
IRC Quiz	Study Quiz				
SNAP Concepts	Quiz				
SNAP Skill Items	Quiz				
SNAP PE	Comprehensive Performance Evaluation				
Chapter 7 Creating Charts and Inserting Formulas					
Concepts Check			✓		
Skills Check Assessment 1	Create a Net Profit Chart		✓		
Skills Check Assessment 2	Create a Company Sales Column Chart		✓		
Skills Check Assessment 3	Create Quarterly Cosmetic and Foreign Sales Bar Chart		✓		
Skills Check Assessment 4	Create a Fund Allocations Pie Chart		✓		
Skills Check Assessment 5	Write a Formula with the PMT Function		✓		
Skills Check Assessment 6	Write a Formula with the FV Function		✓		
Skills Check Assessment 7	Write a Formula with the IF Function		✓		
Skills Check Assessment 8	Create a Stacked Cylinder Chart				
Skills Check Assessment 9	Learn about Excel Options	✓			
Visual Benchmark	Create and Format a Pie Chart	✓			
Case Study Part 1	Dollar Wise Financial Services: Loan Amounts	✓			
Case Study Part 2	Dollar Wise Financial Services: Budget	✓			
Case Study Part 3	Dollar Wise Financial Services: Interest Rates				
Case Study Part 4	Dollar Wise Financial Services: IF Statement				
Case Study Part 5	Dollar Wise Financial Services: Mortgage Rates (Internet)	✓			

Assignment	Title	Start from Scratch	SNAP Grade It	Date Due	Grade
SNAP Tutorial 7.1	Creating Charts in Excel				
SNAP Tutorial 7.2	Editing Chart Data				
SNAP Tutorial 7.3	Formatting with Chart Buttons				
SNAP Tutorial 7.4	Printing Charts				
SNAP Tutorial 7.5	Changing Chart Design				
SNAP Tutorial 7.6	Changing Chart Formatting				
SNAP Tutorial 7.7	Inserting and Formatting a Shape				
SNAP Tutorial 7.8	Moving, Sizing, and Deleting a Chart				
SNAP Tutorial 7.9	Using Financial Functions				
SNAP Tutorial 7.10	Using the Logical IF Function				
IRC Quiz	Study Quiz				
SNAP Concepts	Quiz				
SNAP Skill Items	Quiz				
SNAP PE	Comprehensive Performance Evaluation				
Chapter 8 Adding Visual Interest to Workbooks					
Concepts Check			✓		
Skills Check Assessment 1	Insert a Clip Art Image and WordArt in an Equipment Sales Workbook		✓		
Skills Check Assessment 2	Insert Formulas and Format a Travel Company Workbook		✓		
Skills Check Assessment 3	Insert and Format Shapes in a Company Sales Workbook		✓		
Skills Check Assessment 4	Insert and Format a SmartArt Graphic in a Sales Workbook				
Skills Check Assessment 5	Create and Insert a Screenshot				
Visual Benchmark	Insert Formulas, WordArt, and Clip Art in a Worksheet				
Case Study Part 1	Ocean Truck Sales: Truck and SUV Inventory				
Case Study Part 2	Ocean Truck Sales: Truck and SUV Inventory				
Case Study Part 3	Ocean Truck Sales: Posting to a Web Page				
Case Study Part 4	Ocean Truck Sales: Incentive Diagram in PowerPoint				
SNAP Tutorial 8.1	Inserting Symbols and Special Characters				
SNAP Tutorial 8.2	Inserting and Modifying Images				

Assignment	Title	Start from Scratch	SNAP Grade It	Date Due	Grade
SNAP Tutorial 8.3	Inserting and Modifying Clip Art Images				
SNAP Tutorial 8.4	Creating and Inserting Screenshots				
SNAP Tutorial 8.5	Inserting and Formatting a Shape				
SNAP Tutorial 8.6	Drawing and Formatting Text Boxes				
SNAP Tutorial 8.7	Inserting a Picture as a Watermark				
SNAP Tutorial 8.8	Inserting and Formatting a SmartArt Graphic				
SNAP Tutorial 8.9	Creating WordArt				
IRC Quiz	Study Quiz				
SNAP Concepts	Quiz				
SNAP Skill Items	Quiz				
SNAP PE	Comprehensive Performance Evaluation				
Unit 2 Performance Assessments					
Assessment 1	Copy and Paste Data and Insert WordArt in a Training Scores Workbook				
Assessment 2	Manage Multiple Worksheets in a Projected Earnings Workbook				
Assessment 3	Create Charts in Worksheets in a Sales Totals Workbook				
Assessment 4	Create and Format a Line Chart				
Assessment 5	Create and Format a Pie Chart				
Assessment 6	Use the PMT Function and Apply Formatting to a Workbook				
Assessment 7	Use the IF Function and Apply Formatting to a Workbook				
Assessment 8	Insert a Text Box and Hyperlinks in a Travel Workbook				
Assessment 9	Insert an Image and a SmartArt Graphic in a Workbook				
Assessment 10	Insert Symbol, Clip Art, and WordArt in a Sales Workbook				
Assessment 11	Insert and Format a Shape in a Budget Workbook				
Writing Activity 1	Prepare a Projected Budget	✓			
Writing Activity 2	Create a Travel Tours Bar Chart	✓			
Writing Activity 3	Prepare a Ski Vacation Worksheet	✓			
Internet Research	Find Information on Excel Books and Present the Data in a Worksheet	✓			

Assignment	Title	Start from Scratch	SNAP Grade It	Date Due	Grade
Job Study	Create a Customized Time Card for a Landscaping Company				
Supplemental Assessment 1	Stock Portfolio	✓			
Supplemental Assessment 2	Roller Coaster Statistics	✓			
Final Case Study	Body Mechanics & Rehabilitation				
SNAP PE	Comprehensive Performance Evaluation				

Grading Sheet

Benchmark Series Office Microsoft Excel 2013 Level 2

Assignment	Title	Start from Scratch	SNAP Grade It	Date Due	Grade
Unit 1: Advanced Formatting, Formulas, and Data Management					
Chapter 1 Advanced Formatting Techniques					
Concepts Check		✓	✓		
Skills Check Assessment 1	Use Conditional and Fraction Formatting		✓		
Skills Check Assessment 2	Apply Custom Number Formatting		✓		
Skills Check Assessment 3	Use Custom AutoFilter; Filter and Sort by Color		✓		
Skills Check Assessment 4	Create, Edit, and Delete Formatting Rules		✓		
Visual Benchmark	Format a Billing Summary				
Case Study Part 1	NuTrends Market Research: Income Statistics				
Case Study Part 2	NuTrends Market Research: Income Statistics				
Case Study Part 3	NuTrends Market Research: Income Statistics				
Case Study Part 4	NuTrends Market Research: Income Statistics (Internet)	✓			
SNAP Tutorial 1.1	Applying Conditional Formatting				
SNAP Tutorial 1.2	Applying Conditional Formatting Using Icon Sets				
SNAP Tutorial 1.3	Applying Conditional Formatting Using Data Bars and Color Scales				
SNAP Tutorial 1.4	Applying Conditional Formatting Using a Formula				
SNAP Tutorial 1.5	Using Fraction, Scientific, and Special Number Format				
SNAP Tutorial 1.6	Creating a Custom Number Format				
SNAP Tutorial 1.7	Wrapping and Shrinking Text to Fit within a Cell				
SNAP Tutorial 1.8	Filtering and Sorting Data Using Conditional Formatting and Cell Attributes				
SNAP Tutorial 1.9	Using Text Functions				

Assignment	Title	Start from Scratch	SNAP Grade It	Date Due	Grade
SNAP Tutorial 1.10	Filtering a Worksheet Using a Custom AutoFilter				
IRC Quiz	Study Quiz				
SNAP Concepts	Quiz				
SNAP Skill Items	Quiz				
SNAP PE	Comprehensive Performance Evaluation				
Chapter 2 Advanced Functions and Formulas					
Concepts Check		✓	✓		
Skills Check Assessment 1	Create Range Names and use the Lookup Function		✓		
Skills Check Assessment 2	Use Conditional Statistical and Math Functions		✓		
Skills Check Assessment 3	Use Financial Functions and PMT and PPMT		✓		
Skills Check Assessment 4	Use Logical Functions		✓		
Skills Check Assessment 5	Use the HLOOKUP Function		✓		
Visual Benchmark 1	Use Lookup, Statistical, and Math Functions in a Billing Summary				
Visual Benchmark 2	Use Lookup and Logical Functions to Calculate Cardiology Costs				
Case Study Part 1	NuTrends Market Research: Pizza by Mario Sales				
Case Study Part 2	NuTrends Market Research: Pizza by Mario Sales				
Case Study Part 3	NuTrends Market Research: Pizza by Mario Sales (Help)				
Case Study Part 4	NuTrends Market Research: Pizza by Mario Sales (Internet)				
SNAP Tutorial 2.1	Creating and Managing Range Names				
SNAP Tutorial 2.2	Using Statistical Functions: COUNT, COUNTA, COUNTIF, and COUNTIFS				
SNAP Tutorial 2.3	Using Statistical Functions: AVERAGEIF and AVERAGEIFS				
SNAP Tutorial 2.4	Using Math and Trigonometry Functions: SUMIF AND SUMIFS				
SNAP Tutorial 2.5	Using Lookup Functions				
SNAP Tutorial 2.6	Using the PPMT Function				
SNAP Tutorial 2.7	Using Logical Functions				
IRC Quiz	Study Quiz				

Assignment	Title	Start from Scratch	SNAP Grade It	Date Due	Grade
SNAP Concepts	Quiz				
SNAP Skill Items	Quiz				
SNAP PE	Comprehensive Performance Evaluation				
Chapter 3 Working with Tables and Data Features					
Concepts Check		✓	✓		
Skills Check Assessment 1	Create and Format a Table		✓		
Skills Check Assessment 2	Use Data Tools		✓		
Skills Check Assessment 3	Subtotal Records		✓		
Visual Benchmark 1	Using Table and Data Tools in a Call List				
Visual Benchmark 2	Using Subtotals in a Call List				
Case Study Part 1	NuTrends Market Research: Marketing Plans				
Case Study Part 2	NuTrends Market Research: Marketing Plans				
Case Study Part 3	NuTrends Market Research: Marketing Plans (Help)				
Case Study Part 4	NuTrends Market Research: Marketing Plans (Internet)	✓			
SNAP Tutorial 3.1	Creating and Modifying Tables				
SNAP Tutorial 3.2	Adding Rows to a Table				
SNAP Tutorial 3.3	Formatting Data as a Table				
SNAP Tutorial 3.4	Using the Sort Feature in Tables				
SNAP Tutorial 3.5	Filtering a Table				
SNAP Tutorial 3.6	Using Data Tools				
SNAP Tutorial 3.7	Removing Duplicate Records				
SNAP Tutorial 3.8	Validating and Restricting Data Entry				
SNAP Tutorial 3.9	Converting a Table to a Normal Range; Subtotaling Related Data				
SNAP Tutorial 3.10	Grouping and Ungrouping Data				
IRC Quiz	Study Quiz				
SNAP Concepts	Quiz				
SNAP Skill Items	Quiz				
SNAP PE	Comprehensive Performance Evaluation				

Assignment	Title	Start from Scratch	SNAP Grade It	Date Due	Grade
Chapter 4 Summarizing and Consolidating Data					
Concepts Check		✓	✓		
Skills Check Assessment 1	Summarize Data in Multiple Worksheets using Range Names		✓		
Skills Check Assessment 2	Summarize Data Using Linked External References				
Skills Check Assessment 3	Break Linked References		✓		
Skills Check Assessment 4	Summarize Data Using 3-D References		✓		
Skills Check Assessment 5	Filtering a PivotTable using a Slicer and Timeline		✓		
Skills Check Assessment 6	Creating and Customizing Sparklines		✓		
Visual Benchmark	Summarizing Real Estate Sales and Commission Data				
Case Study Part 1	NutTrends Market Research: Pizza by Mario				
Case Study Part 2	NutTrends Market Research: Pizza by Mario	✓			
Case Study Part 3	NutTrends Market Research: Pizza by Mario (Help)				
Case Study Part 4	NutTrends Market Research: Franchise Comparison (Interent)	✓			
SNAP Tutorial 4.1	Summarizing Data in Multiple Worksheets Using Range Names and 3-D References				
SNAP Tutorial 4.2	Summarizing Data by Linking Ranges in Other Worksheets or Workbooks				
SNAP Tutorial 4.3	Summarizing Data Using the Consolidate Feature				
SNAP Tutorial 4.4	Creating a PivotTable				
SNAP Tutorial 4.5	Filtering a PivotTable Using Slicers				
SNAP Tutorial 4.6	Filtering a PivotTable Using a Timeline				
SNAP Tutorial 4.7	Creating a PivotChart				
SNAP Tutorial 4.8	Summarizing Data with Sparklines				
IRC Quiz	Study Quiz				
SNAP Concepts	Quiz				
SNAP Skill Items	Quiz				
SNAP PE	Comprehensive Performance Evaluation				

Assignment	Title	Start from Scratch	SNAP Grade It	Date Due	Grade
Unit 1 Performance Assessments					
Assessment 1	Conditionally Format and Filter a Help Desk Worksheet				
Assessment 2	Use Conditional Logic Formulas in a Help Desk Worksheet				
Assessment 3	Use Table and Data Management Features in a Help Desk Worksheet				
Assessment 4	Add Subtotals and Outline a Help Desk Worksheet				
Assessment 5	Use Financial and Text Functions to Analyze Data for a Project				
Assessment 6	Analyze Sales Using a PivotTable, PivotChart, and Sparklines				
Assessment 7	Link to an External Data Source and Calculate Distributor Payments				
Writing Activity 1	Create a Worksheet to Track Movie Rental Memberships	✓			
Writing Activity 2	Create a Worksheet to Log Hours Walked in a Company Fitness Contents	✓			
Internet Research	Create a Worksheet to Compare Online Auction Listing Fees	✓			
Supplemental Assessment 1	Gradebook	✓			
Supplemental Assessment 2	Lab Revenue				
SNAP PE	Comprehensive Performance Evaluation				
Unit 2: Managing and Integrating Data and the Excel Environment					
Chapter 5 Using Data Analysis Features					
Concepts Check		✓	✓		
Skills Check Assessment 1	Convert Columns to Rows; Add Source Cells to Destination Cells; Filter		✓		
Skills Check Assessment 2	Use Goal Seek		✓		
Skills Check Assessment 3	Use Scenario Manager		✓		
Skills Check Assessment 4	Create a Two-Variable Data Table		✓		
Skills Check Assessment 5	Find and Correct Formula Errors		✓		

Assignment	Title	Start from Scratch	SNAP Grade It	Date Due	Grade
Visual Benchmark 1	Find the Base Hourly Rate for Drum Lessons				
Visual Benchmark 2	Create Scenarios for Drum Lesson Revenue				
Case Study Part 1	NuTrends Market Research: Pizza by Mario Startup				
Case Study Part 2	NuTrends Market Research: Pizza by Mario Startup				
Case Study Part 3	NuTrends Market Research: Pizza by Mario Startup (Help)				
Case Study Part 4	NuTrends Market Research: Pizza by Mario Startup (Internet)				
SNAP Tutorial 5.1	Pasting Data Using Paste Special Options				
SNAP Tutorial 5.2	Using Goal Seek to Populate a Cell				
SNAP Tutorial 5.3	Using Scenario Manager				
SNAP Tutorial 5.4	Performing What-If Analysis Using Data Tables				
SNAP Tutorial 5.5	Using Auditing Tools				
SNAP Tutorial 5.6	Circling Invalid Data and Watching Formulas				
IRC Quiz	Study Quiz				
SNAP Concepts	Quiz				
SNAP Skill Items	Quiz				
SNAP PE	Comprehensive Performance Evaluation				
Chapter 6 Protecting and Sharing Workbooks					
Concepts Check		✓	✓		
Skills Check Assessment 1	Enter and Display Workbook Properties and Insert Comments		✓		
Skills Check Assessment 2	Share a Worksheet, Edit a Shared Workbook, and Print a History Sheet				
Skills Check Assessment 3	Remove Shared Access		✓		
Skills Check Assessment 4	Protect an Entire Worksheet and Add a Password to a Workbook		✓		
Skills Check Assessment 5	Unlock Cells and Protect a Worksheet and Protect Workbook Structure		✓		
Skills Check Assessment 6	Track Changes, Accept/Reject Changes, and Print a History Sheet				
Visual Benchmark	Track Changes; Insert Comments				

Assignment	Title	Start from Scratch	SNAP Grade It	Date Due	Grade
Case Study Part 1	NuTrends Market Research: Pizza by Mario New Franchises				
Case Study Part 2	NuTrends Market Research: Pizza by Mario New Franchises				
Case Study Part 3	NuTrends Market Research: Pizza by Mario New Franchises				
Case Study Part 4	NuTrends Market Research: Pizza by Mario New Franchises (Internet)	✓			
SNAP Tutorial 6.1	Inserting and Editing Comments				
SNAP Tutorial 6.2	Adding Workbook Properties				
SNAP Tutorial 6.3	Printing and Editing Comments				
SNAP Tutorial 6.4	Sharing a Workbook				
SNAP Tutorial 6.5	Resolving Conflicts in a Shared Workbook				
SNAP Tutorial 6.6	Saving a Workbook to Windows SkyDrive, Inviting People to Share a Workbook, and Sending a Workbook via Email				
SNAP Tutorial 6.7	Protecting and Unprotecting Worksheets				
SNAP Tutorial 6.8	Protecting and Unprotecting the Structure of a Workbook				
SNAP Tutorial 6.9	Adding Password Protection to a Workbook				
SNAP Tutorial 6.10	Tracking Changes				
IRC Quiz	Study Quiz				
SNAP Concepts	Quiz				
SNAP Skill Items	Quiz				
SNAP PE	Comprehensive Performance Evaluation				
Chapter 7 Automating Repetitive Tasks and Customizing Excel					
Concepts Check		✓	✓		
Skills Check Assessment 1	Create Macros	✓	✓		
Skills Check Assessment 2	Run Macros		✓		
Skills Check Assessment 3	Create Macros; Save as a Macro-Enabled Workbook		✓		
Skills Check Assessment 4	Print Macros		✓		
Skills Check Assessment 5	Customize the Excel Environment		✓		

Assignment	Title	Start from Scratch	SNAP Grade It	Date Due	Grade
Skills Check Assessment 6	Create Custom Views		✓		
Skills Check Assessment 7	Create and Use a Template				
Visual Benchmark 1	Customize the Ribbon	✓			
Visual Benchmark 2	Create a Custom Template	✓			
Case Study Part 1	NuTrends Market Research: Macros				
Case Study Part 2	NuTrends Market Research: Pizza by Mario Macros				
Case Study Part 3	NuTrends Market Research: Quick Access Toolbar (Help)	✓			
Case Study Part 4	NuTrends Market Research: Document Recovery	✓			
SNAP Tutorial 7.1	Using Macros				
SNAP Tutorial 7.2	Editing a Macro				
SNAP Tutorial 7.3	Managing Macros				
SNAP Tutorial 7.4	Pinning Workbooks to the Recent Workbooks List				
SNAP Tutorial 7.5	Customizing the Work Area				
SNAP Tutorial 7.6	Customizing the Ribbon				
SNAP Tutorial 7.7	Customizing the Quick Access Toolbar				
SNAP Tutorial 7.8	Using Custom Templates				
IRC Quiz	Study Quiz				
SNAP Concepts	Quiz				
SNAP Skill Items	Quiz				
SNAP PE	Comprehensive Performance Evaluation				
Chapter 8 Importing, Exporting, and Distributing Data					
Concepts Check		✓	✓		
Skills Check Assessment 1	Import Data from Access and a Text File		✓		
Skills Check Assessment 2	Link Data to a Word Document				
Skills Check Assessment 3	Embed Data in a PowerPoint Presentation				
Skills Check Assessment 4	Export Data as a Text File				
Skills Check Assessment 5	Prepare a Workbook for Distribution				

Assignment	Title	Start from Scratch	SNAP Grade It	Date Due	Grade
Skills Check Assessment 6	Prepare and Distribute a Workbook				
Visual Benchmark	Import, Analyze, and Export Population Data				
Case Study Part 1	NuTrends Market Research: Pizza by Mario Research Data				
Case Study Part 2	NuTrends Market Research: Pizza by Mario Expansion Research				
Case Study Part 3	NuTrends Market Research: Research Data (Help)				
Case Study Part 4	NuTrends Market Research: Internet Fax Memo (Internet)	✓			
SNAP Tutorial 8.1	Importing Data from Access, a Text File, or a Website				
SNAP Tutorial 8.2	Exporting Data from Excel				
SNAP Tutorial 8.3	Copying and Pasting Worksheet Data between Programs				
SNAP Tutorial 8.4	Copying and Pasting Worksheet Data to a Word Document				
SNAP Tutorial 8.5	Exporting Data as a Text File				
SNAP Tutorial 8.6	Preparing a Worksheet for Distribution				
SNAP Tutorial 8.7	Saving a Workbook in a Different File Format				
SNAP Tutorial 8.8	Viewing Trust Center Settings				
SNAP Tutorial 8.9	Publishing a Worksheet as a Web Page				
IRC Quiz	Study Quiz				
SNAP Concepts	Quiz				
SNAP Skill Items	Quiz				
SNAP PE	Comprehensive Performance Evaluation				
Unit 2 Performance Assessments					
Assessment 1	Use Goal Seek and Scenario Manager to Calculate Investment Proposals				
Assessment 2	Calculate Investment Outcomes for a Portfolio Using a Two-Variable Data Table				
Assessment 3	Solve an Error and Check for Accuracy in Investment Commission Formulas				

Assignment	Title	Start from Scratch	SNAP Grade It	Date Due	Grade
Assessment 4	Document and Share a Workbook and Manage Changes in an Investment Portfolio Worksheet				
Assessment 5	Insert Comments and Protect a Confidential Investment Portfolio Workbook				
Assessment 6	Automate and Customize an Investment Portfolio Workbook				
Assessment 7	Create and Use an Investment Planner Template				
Assessment 8	Export a Chart and Prepare and Distribute an Investment Portfolio Worksheet				
Writing Activity	Create a Computer Maintenance Template	✓			
Internet Research 1	Apply What-If Analysis to a Planned Move	✓			
Internet Research 2	Research and Compare Smartphones	✓			
Job Study	Prepare a Wages Budget and Link the Budget to a Word Document	✓			
Supplemental Assessment 1	Calculate Monthly House Payments	✓			
Supplemental Assessment 2	Travel Routes Mileage Spreadsheet and Memo				
Final Case Study	Worldwide Enterprises Human Resources				
SNAP PE	Comprehensive Performance Evaluation				

Concepts Check Answer Key

Benchmark Excel 2013, Level 1, Chapter 1

1.	The horizontal and vertical lines that define the cells in a worksheet area are referred to as this.	gridlines	page 7
2.	Columns in a worksheet are labeled with these.	letters	page 7
3.	Rows in a worksheet are labeled with these.	numbers	page 7
4.	Press this key on the keyboard to move the insertion point to the next cell.	Tab	page 7 (Table 1.2)
5.	Press these keys on the keyboard to move the insertion point to the previous cell.	Shift + Tab	page 7 (Table 1.2)
6.	Data being typed in a cell displays in the cell as well as here.	Formula bar	page 7
7.	If a number entered in a cell is too long to fit inside the cell, the number is changed to this.	number symbols (###)	page 8
8.	This feature automatically inserts words, numbers, or formulas in a series.	AutoFill	page 13
9.	This is the name of the small black square that displays in the bottom right corner of the active cell.	AutoFill fill handle **OR** fill handle	page 15
10.	Use this button in the Editing group on the HOME tab to insert a formula in a cell.	AutoSum	page 18
11.	With this function, a range of cells are added together and then divided by the number of cell entries.	AVERAGE	page 19
12.	To select nonadjacent columns using the mouse, hold down this key on the keyboard while clicking the column headers.	Ctrl	page 20 (Table 1.4)
13.	Click this button to merge selected cells and center data within the merged cells.	Merge & Center	page 21
14.	The Accounting Number Format button is located in this group on the HOME tab.	Number	page 23
15.	Press this function key to display the Excel Help window.	F1	page 25

Concepts Check Answer Key

Benchmark Excel 2013, Level 1, Chapter 2

1.	When typing a formula, begin the formula with this sign.	= (equals sign)	page 37
2.	This is the operator for division that is used when writing a formula.	/ (forward slash)	page 38 (Table 2.1)
3.	This is the operator for multiplication that is used when writing a formula.	* (asterisk)	page 38 (Table 2.1)
4.	As an alternative to the fill handle, use this button to copy a formula relatively in a worksheet.	Fill	page 38
5.	To display cell references for a formula, perform this action on a cell containing a formula.	double-click the cell	page 39
6.	A formula's order of operations can be modified with these.	parentheses	page 40
7.	Excel inserts this symbol in a cell that may contain a possible error.	dark green triangle	page 41
8.	A function operates on this, which may consist of a constant, a cell reference, or another function.	argument	page 43
9.	This function returns the largest value in a set of values.	MAX	page 45
10.	This is the keyboard shortcut to display formulas in a worksheet.	Ctrl + ` (grave accent)	page 49
11.	This function returns the current date and time.	NOW	page 49
12.	To identify an absolute cell reference, type this symbol before the column and row.	$ (dollar sign)	page 50

Concepts Check Answer Key

Benchmark Excel 2013, Level 1, Chapter 3

1.	By default, a column is inserted on this side of the column containing the active cell.	left	page 67
2.	To delete a row, select the row and then click the Delete button in this group on the HOME tab.	Cells	page 68
3.	Use the options at this button's drop-down list to clear the contents of the cell or selected cells.	Clear	page 69
4.	Use this button to insert color in the active cell or selected cells.	Fill Color	page 70
5.	Select data in a cell and this displays above the selected text.	Mini toolbar	page 70
6.	By default, numbers are aligned at this side of a cell.	right	page 74
7.	Click this button in the Alignment group on the HOME tab to rotate data in a cell.	Orientation	page 71
8.	The Themes button is located on this tab.	PAGE LAYOUT	page 73
9.	If you type a number with a dollar sign, such as *$50.25*, Excel automatically applies this formatting to the number.	currency	page 74
10.	If you type a number with a percent sign, such as *25%*, Excel automatically applies this formatting to the number.	percent	page 74
11.	Align and indent data in cells using buttons in the Alignment group on the HOME tab or with options at this dialog box with the Alignment tab selected.	Format Cells	page 78
12.	You can repeat the last action performed by pressing Ctrl + Y or this function key.	F4	page 84
13.	The Format Painter button is located in this group on the HOME tab.	Clipboard	page 86
14.	To hide a column, select the column, click this button in the Cells group on the HOME tab, point to *Hide & Unhide*, and then click *Hide Columns*.	Format	page 86

Concepts Check Answer Key

Benchmark Excel 2013, Level 1, Chapter 4

1.	This is the default left and right margin measurement.	0.7 inch	page 101
2.	This is the default top and bottom margin measurement.	0.75 inch	page 101
3.	The Margins button is located on this tab.	PAGE LAYOUT	page 101
4.	By default, a worksheet prints in this orientation on a page.	portrait	page 104
5.	Click the Print Titles button in the Page Setup group on the PAGE LAYOUT tab and the Page Setup dialog box displays with this tab selected.	Sheet	page 107
6.	Use options in this group on the PAGE LAYOUT tab to adjust the printed output by a percentage to fit the number of pages specified.	Scale to Fit	page 108
7.	Use this button in the Page Setup group on the PAGE LAYOUT tab to select and print specific areas in a worksheet.	Print Area	page 110
8.	Click the Header & Footer button in the Text group on the INSERT tab and the worksheet displays in this view.	Page Layout	page 112
9.	This tab contains options for formatting and customizing a header and/or footer.	HEADER & FOOTER TOOLS DESIGN	page 112
10.	Click this tab to display the Spelling button.	REVIEW	page 118
11.	The Undo and Redo buttons are located on this toolbar.	Quick Access	page 118
12.	Click this button in the Find and Replace dialog box to expand the dialog box.	Options	page 121
13.	Use these buttons at the expanded Find and Replace dialog box to search for specific cell formatting and replace it with other formatting.	Format	page 123
14.	Use this button in the Editing group on the HOME tab to sort data in a worksheet.	Sort & Filter	page 125
15.	Use this feature to temporarily isolate specific data in a worksheet.	filter	page 127

Concepts Check Answer Key

Benchmark Excel 2013, Level 1, Chapter 5

1.	By default, a workbook contains this number of worksheets.	one	page 153
2.	Click this button to insert a new worksheet in a workbook.	New sheet	page 153
3.	To select nonadjacent worksheet tabs, click the first tab, hold down this key, and then click any other tabs you want selected.	Ctrl	page 153
4.	To select adjacent worksheet tabs, click the first tab, hold down this key, and then click the last tab.	Shift	page 153
5.	The Cut, Copy, and Paste buttons are located in this group on the HOME tab.	Clipboard	page 154
6.	This button displays in the lower right corner of pasted cells.	Paste Options	page 155
7.	Use this task pane to copy and paste multiple items.	Clipboard	page 157
8.	Click this option at the worksheet tab shortcut menu to apply a color to a worksheet tab.	*Tab Color*	page 160
9.	To print all of the worksheets in a workbook, display the Print backstage area, click the first gallery in the *Settings* category, and then click this option at the drop-down list.	*Print Entire Workbook*	page 163
10.	The Split button is located on this tab.	VIEW	page 164
11.	Display the Arrange Windows dialog box by clicking this button in the Window group on the VIEW tab.	Arrange All	page 169
12.	Click this button to make the active workbook expand to fill the screen.	Maximize	page 172
13.	Click this button to reduce the active workbook to a layer behind the Excel button on the Taskbar.	Minimize	page 172
14.	When linking data between worksheets, the worksheet containing the original data is called this.	source	page 174

Concepts Check Answer Key

Benchmark Excel 2013, Level 1, Chapter 6

1.	Perform file management tasks, such as copying, moving, and deleting workbooks, with options at the Open dialog box or this dialog box.	Save As	page 190
2.	At the Open dialog box, a list of folders and files displays in this pane.	Content	page 191
3.	Rename a folder or file at the Open dialog box using a shortcut menu or this button.	Organize	page 192
4.	At the Open dialog box, hold down this key while selecting nonadjacent workbooks.	Ctrl	page 192
5.	Workbooks deleted from the hard drive are automatically sent to this location.	Windows Recycle Bin	page 193
6.	The most recently opened workbook names display in this list, which displays when the *Recent Workbooks* option is selected at the Open backstage area.	Recent Workbooks	page 197
7.	Do this to a workbook name you want to remain at the top of the *Recent Workbooks* list at the Open backstage area.	pin it	page 198
8.	If you close a workbook without saving it, you can recover it with this option at the Open backstage area.	*Recover Unsaved Workbooks*	page 198
9.	The Cell Styles button is located in this group on the HOME tab.	Styles	page 204
10.	Click the *New Cell Style* option at the Cell Styles button drop-down gallery and this dialog box displays.	Style	page 205
11.	A style you create displays in this section of the Cell Styles button drop-down gallery.	*Custom*	page 205
12.	Copy styles from one workbook to another with options at this dialog box.	Merge Styles	page 210
13.	To link a workbook to another workbook, click this button in the *Link to* section of the Insert Hyperlink dialog box.	Existing File or Web Page	page 213
14.	Templates display at this backstage area.	New	page 217

Concepts Check Answer Key

Benchmark Excel 2013, Level 1, Chapter 7

1.	Let Excel determine a chart type for selected data in a worksheet by clicking this button in the Charts group on the INSERT tab.	Recommended Charts	page 232
2.	This type of chart shows proportions and relationships of the parts to the whole.	pie	page 233 (Table 7.1)
3.	When you create a chart, the chart is inserted in this location by default.	worksheet containing data or same worksheet as selected cells	page 233
4.	Size a chart by dragging one of these on the selected chart border.	sizing handle	page 233
5.	When a chart is selected, three buttons display at the right side of the chart border: the Chart Elements button, the Chart Styles button, and this button.	Chart Filters	page 236
6.	Select a chart in a worksheet, display the Print backstage area, and the first gallery in the *Settings* category is automatically changed to this option.	*Print Selected Chart*	page 238
7.	The Switch Row/Column button is location in this group on the CHART TOOLS DESIGN tab.	Data	page 240
8.	Click this option at the Move Chart dialog box to move the chart to a separate sheet.	*New sheet*	page 242
9.	Insert a shape in a chart and this tab is active.	DRAWING TOOLS FORMAT tab	page 246
10.	Select a chart (not a chart element), click the Format Selection button in the Current Selection group on the CHART TOOLS FORMAT tab, and this task pane displays at the right side of the screen.	Format Chart Area	page 248
11.	This function finds the payment for a loan based on constant payments and a constant interest rate.	PMT	page 252
12.	Suppose cell B2 contains the total sales amount. Write a formula that inserts the word *BONUS* in cell C2 if the sales amount is greater than $49,999 and inserts the words *NO BONUS* if the sales amount is not greater than $49,999.	=IF(B2>49999, "BONUS", "NO BONUS")	page 256

Concepts Check Answer Key

Benchmark Excel 2013, Level 1, Chapter 8

1.	The Symbol button is located on this tab.	INSERT	page 273
2.	The *Font* option is available at the Symbol dialog box with this tab selected.	Symbols	page 273
3.	Insert a picture, clip art image, screenshot, shape, or SmartArt graphic with buttons in this group on the INSERT tab.	Illustrations	page 275
4.	Display the Insert Pictures window by clicking this button on the INSERT tab.	Pictures	page 275
5.	When you insert an image, such as a picture or clip art, in a worksheet, this tab is active.	PICTURE TOOLS FORMAT	page 275
6.	Maintain the proportions of an image by holding down this key while dragging a sizing handle.	Shift	page 276
7.	To move an image, position the mouse pointer on the image border until the mouse pointer displays with this attached and then drag the image to the desired location.	four-headed arrow	page 276
8.	To capture a portion of a screen, click the Screenshot button and then click this option at the drop-down list.	*Screen Clipping*	page 280
9.	To copy a shape, hold down this key while dragging the shape.	Ctrl	page 281
10.	When you draw a text box in a worksheet and then release the mouse button, this tab is active.	DRAWING TOOLS FORMAT	page 284
11.	This term refers to a lightened image that displays behind data in a file.	watermark	page 286
12.	Click the SmartArt button in the Illustrations group on the INSERT tab and this dialog box displays.	Choose a SmartArt Graphic	page 288

Concepts Check Answer Key

Benchmark Excel 2013, Level 2, Chapter 1

1.	Point to this option at the Conditional Formatting button drop-down list to format cells based on a comparison operator such as greater than.	Highlight Cells Rules	page 7 (Figure 1.2)
2.	To conditionally format a range using the Above Average condition, click this option at the Conditional Formatting button drop-down list.	Top/Bottom Rules	page 7 (Figure 1.2)
3.	Open this dialog box to create, edit, or delete a conditional formatting rule.	Conditional Formatting Rules Manager	page 10
4.	Excel uses threshold values to classify data into three to five categories when applying conditional formatting using this option.	Icon Sets	page 12
5.	Click this option in the Select a Rule Type section of the New Formatting Rule dialog box to create a rule that conditionally formats cells based on the value(s) in another cell.	Use a formula to determine which cells to format	page 15
6.	Open this dialog box with this tab active to format a selected range as fractions and select the type of fraction to display.	Format Cells dialog box with Number tab active	page 16
7.	Scientific formatting is used by scientists and others who need to write very large numbers using this notation.	exponential	page 16
8.	The special number format options displayed in the Type list box are dependent on the setting in this option box.	Locale	page 18
9.	If you type 156.3568 in a cell with the custom number format code ###.## applied, this result will display.	156.36	page 20 (Table 1.1)
10.	Use either of these two text control options to format a long label within the existing column width.	Wrap text or Shrink to fit	page 22
11.	Use this text function to change existing text in the source cell to new text in the formula cell.	SUBSTITUTE	page 23 (Table 1.2)
12.	Open this dialog box to filter by more than one criterion using a comparison operator.	Custom AutoFilter	page 27
13.	A worksheet can be filtered by a cell color that has been applied manually or by this feature.	conditional formatting	page 29
14.	Open this dialog box to organize cells in a worksheet by more than one color.	Sort	page 30

Concepts Check Answer Key

Benchmark Excel 2013, Level 2, Chapter 2

1.	Assign a name to a selected range by typing the desired name in this box.	Name	page 41
2.	A range name can be a combination of letters, numbers, underscore characters, and this punctuation character.	period	page 41
3.	Use this function to count cells that contain text or a combination of text and numbers.	COUNTA	page 42
4.	Write the COUNTIF function that will count the number of cells in a range named Sales in which the values are greater than $50,000.	=COUNTIF(sales,">50000")	page 43
5.	Use this statistical function to find the mean of a range based on two criteria.	AVERAGEIFS	page 46
6.	SUMIF is found in this category of functions.	Math & Trig	page 49
7.	Open this dialog box to delete a range name.	Name Manager	page 51
8.	Use this lookup function to locate a value in a reference table in which the comparison data is arranged in rows.	HLOOKUP	page 55
9.	This financial function returns the principal portion of a specified loan payment.	PPMT	page 56
10.	Access the IF function from this button in the Function Library group on the FORMULAS tab.	Logical	page 58
11.	This term refers to a formula in which one function is created inside another function.	nested function	page 58
12.	Excel's AND and OR functions use this type of logic to construct conditional tests.	Boolean	page 59

Concepts Check Answer Key

Benchmark Excel 2013, Level 2, Chapter 3

1.	The first row of a table that contains the column headings is called the field names row or this row.	header row	page 74
2.	Typing a formula in the first record of a column in a table causes Excel to define the field as this type of column.	calculated	page 75
3.	Change the visual appearance of a table using this gallery in the TABLE TOOLS DESIGN tab.	Table Styles	page 76
4.	This term describes the formatting feature in a table in which even-numbered rows are formatted differently from odd-numbered rows.	banding	page 76
5.	Clicking this button causes the Convert Text to Columns Wizard to appear.	Text to Columns	page 80
6.	Open this dialog box to instruct Excel to compare the entries in the columns you specify and automatically delete rows that contain repeated data.	Remove Duplicates	page 82
7.	Open this dialog box to restrict entries in a cell to those that you set up in a drop-down list.	Data Validation	page 84
8.	This option in the Allow option box is used to require that data entered into a cell be a specific number of characters.	Text length	page 85 (Figure 3.6)
9.	This is the default error alert style that prevents invalid data from being entered into a cell.	Stop	page 85 (Table 3.1)
10.	The Convert to Range button is found on this tab.	TABLE TOOLS DESIGN	page 89
11.	Prior to creating subtotals using the Subtotal button in the Outline group of the DATA tab, arrange the data in this order.	By the fields in which the records should be grouped	page 89
12.	In a worksheet with subtotal rows only displayed, click this button next to a subtotal row to view the grouped rows.	Show Detail	page 89–90 (Figure 3.7)
13.	Click this button in an outlined worksheet to collapse the rows for a group.	Hide Detail	page 89–90 (Figure 3.7)
14.	In an outlined worksheet, use this button to collapse all records and display only the row with the grand total.	level 1	page 92
15.	Clicking this button in an outlined worksheet will cause the Hide Detail button for the selected rows to be removed.	Ungroup	page 93

Concepts Check Answer Key

Benchmark Excel 2013, Level 2, Chapter 4

1.	This symbol separates a worksheet reference from a cell reference.	exclamation point	page 106
2.	This term describes a formula that references the same cell in a range that spans two or more worksheets.	3-D reference	page 106
3.	Assume that a workbook contains the following defined range names that reference cells in four worksheets: Qtr1, Qtr2, Qtr3, and Qtr4. Provide the formula to add the data in the four ranges.	=Qtr1+Qtr2+Qtr3+Qtr4 or =Sum(Qtr1,Qtr2,Qtr3,Qtr4)	page 106
4.	Create this formula entry for QtrlySales.xlsx to link to an external reference cell C12 in a worksheet named Summary.	=[QtrlySales.xlsx]Summary!C12	page 110
5.	Open this dialog box to change the source of a linked external reference after moving the source workbook to another folder.	Edit Links	page 111
6.	Click this button to permanently remove a linked external reference and convert the linked cells to their existing values.	Break Link	page 111
7.	This default function is active when you open the Consolidate dialog box.	Sum	page 115
8.	Use this button to preview different PivotTable scenarios.	Recommended PivotTables	page 117
9.	Add fields to a PivotTable by clicking the field check box in this task pane.	PivotTable Fields	page 118
10.	The PivotTable Styles gallery is accessible from this tab.	PIVOTTABLE TOOLS DESIGN	page 121
11..	Insert this type of pane to filter a PivotTable with one mouse click.	Slicer	page 122
12.	Insert this type of pane to filter a PivotTable by dates.	Timeline	page 124
13.	Choose a function other than Sum for a PivotTable numeric field by clicking this button in the Active Field group on the PivotTable Tools Analyze tab.	Field Settings	page 126
14.	The buttons to filter a PivotChart are found here.	the legend or the axis field buttons located on the PivotChart	page 127
15.	This is the first step in adding Sparklines to a worksheet.	Select the empty cell range in which to insert Sparklines.	page 130
16.	Click this tab to customize Sparklines.	SPARKLINE TOOLS DESIGN	page 132

Concepts Check Answer Key

Benchmark Excel 2013, Level 2, Chapter 5

1.	This option from the Paste drop-down gallery converts columns to rows and rows to columns.	Transpose	page 156
2.	Open this dialog box to perform a mathematical operation while pasting the copied range to the destination cells.	Paste Special	page 158
3.	Use this feature if you know the result you want to obtain but are not sure what input value you need to achieve that result.	Goal Seek	page 159
4.	This feature allows you to store various sets of data for specified cells under a name.	Scenario Manager	page 161
5.	This report compares various saved data sets side by side so you can view all of the results on one page.	Scenario Summary	page 165
6.	In a one-variable data table, the source formula is entered at this location within the data table range.	one cell above and one column right of input values	page 166
7.	The Data Table feature is accessed from this button.	What-If Analysis	page 166
8.	In a two-variable data table, the source formula is entered at this location within the data table range.	top left cell	page 168
9.	Click this button to draw arrows to cells that feed data into the active cell.	Trace Precedents	page 170
10.	Click this button to draw arrows to cells that use the data in the active cell.	Trace Dependents	page 170
11.	This type of error occurs when the formula has correct syntax but is not correct for the data or situation.	logic	page 171
12.	This type of formula is entered outside the main worksheet area and used to check key figures within the worksheet.	proof formula	page 171
13.	Use this button in the Formula Auditing group to assist with locating the source cell that is causing an error code.	Error Checking	page 172
14.	This error code indicates that a value needed by the formula to calculate the result is not available.	#N/A	page 172 (Table 5.1)
15.	Use this feature to test existing data in a worksheet that has had a new data validation rule created.	Circle Invalid Data	page 174

Concepts Check Answer Key

Benchmark Excel 2013, Level 2, Chapter 6

1.	Open this view to add descriptive information about a workbook, such as a title or subject heading.	Info backstage area	page 187
2.	This panel displays the workbook's properties between the ribbon and worksheet.	document information panel	page 188
3.	A small, red, diagonal triangle in the upper right corner of a cell indicates that this box will pop up when the mouse pointer rests on the cell.	comment	page 189
4.	Open this dialog box to turn on the feature that allows changes to be made by more than one user at the same time.	Share Workbook	page 192
5.	Change the user name for the computer that you are using by opening this dialog box.	Excel Options	page 194
6.	When two users have the same workbook open at the same time and both make changes to the same cell, this dialog box appears when the second person saves the workbook.	Resolve Conflicts	page 196
7.	Open this dialog box to create a history sheet , which includes a record of all of the changes made to a shared workbook.	Highlight Changes	page 198
8.	Select a cell that you want to allow changes to and then click this button and menu option to unlock the cell before protecting the worksheet.	Format, Lock Cell	page 204
9.	At this dialog box, you can add a password that is required to unprotect a worksheet.	Protect Sheet	page 204
10.	Prevent users from inserting or deleting worksheets in a workbook by opening this dialog box.	Protect Structure and Windows	page 207
11.	Click this option from the Protect Workbook drop-down list at the Info backstage area view to assign a password to open a workbook.	Encrypt with Password	page 208
12.	Turn on this feature and Excel automatically changes the workbook to a shared workbook, if it is not already shared.	Track Changes	page 211
13.	Excel applies this formatting to cells in a shared workbook that have been modified to make the revised cells stand out.	Colored border, with each user's changes in a different color	page 211 (Figure 6.14)
14.	Use this feature to navigate to each changed cell in a shared workbook and decide whether to keep the change or restore the cell back to its previous value.	Accept/Reject Changes	page 212
15.	This feature is not available to restore cells to their previous values after you have finished reviewing tracked changes.	Undo	page 212

Concepts Check Answer Key

Benchmark Excel 2013, Level 2, Chapter 7

1.	A macro name must begin with a letter and can contain a combination of letters, numbers, and this character.	underscore character	page 227
2.	Click this button to indicate that you have finished the tasks or keystrokes you want saved in the macro.	Stop Recording	page 228
3.	A workbook containing a macro is saved in this file format.	Excel Macro-Enabled Workbook (*.xlsm)	page 228
4.	A macro can be assigned to a shortcut key that is a combination of a lowercase or uppercase letter and this key.	Ctrl	page 231
5.	Macro instructions are stored in this program code.	Visual Basic for Applications (VBA)	page 233
6.	A workbook that you use frequently can be permanently added to the Recent Workbooks list by clicking this icon next to the workbook name.	pin icon	page 236
7.	Display options are shown in the Excel Options dialog box with this option selected in the left pane.	Advanced	page 236
8.	Click this button to minimize the ribbon and provide more space in the work area.	Ribbon Display Options	page 238
9.	Click this option in the left pane at the Excel Options dialog box to create a custom ribbon tab.	Customize Ribbon	page 240
10.	Click this option at the Customize Quick Access Toolbar drop-down list to locate a feature to add to the toolbar from the commands list box.	More Commands	page 245
11.	Click this button at the Custom Views dialog box to create a new custom view that will save the current display settings for the active worksheet.	Add	page 248
12.	Change Save as type to this option at the Save As dialog box to save the current workbook as a standard workbook that can be opened from the New dialog box.	Excel Template (*.xltx)	page 250
13.	This task pane opens when Excel is restarted after the previous session ended abnormally.	Document Recovery	page 253

Concepts Check Answer Key

Benchmark Excel 2013, Level 2, Chapter 8

1.	This group on the DATA tab contains buttons for importing data into Access.	Get External Data	page 270
2.	If the source database used to import data contains more than one table, this dialog box appears after you select the data source to allow you to choose the desired table.	Select Table	page 271
3.	To import tables from a web page, open this dialog box to browse to the website and click arrows next to tables on the page that you want to import.	New Web Query	page 272
4.	These are the two commonly used delimiter characters in delimited text file formats.	tab, comma	page 275
5.	To add to the bottom of the active Access datasheet cells that have been copied to the Clipboard, click this option at the Paste button drop-down list.	Paste Append	page 278-279
6.	Choosing Microsoft Excel Worksheet Object at the Paste Special dialog box in a Word document and then clicking OK inserts the copied cells as this type of object.	embedded	page 280
7.	If the Excel data you are pasting into a Word document will likely be updated in the future and you will want the Word document to reflect the updated values, paste the data as this type of object.	linked	page 280
8.	A chart copied from Excel and pasted to a slide in a PowerPoint presentation is pasted as this type of object by default.	embedded	page 284
9.	Click this option in the Other File Types section of the Export backstage area to select the CSV file format to export the active worksheet as a text file.	Change File Type	page 286
10.	This feature scans the open workbook for personal and hidden information and provides you with the opportunity to review and remove the items.	Document Inspector	page 289
11.	A workbook that has been marked as final is changed to this type of workbook to prevent additions, deletions, and modifications to cells.	read-only	page 292
12.	Use this feature to check the current workbook for formatting or features that are not available with versions of Excel prior to Excel 2007 and that could cause loss of functionality if saved in the earlier file format.	Compatibility Checker	page 294
13.	Save a worksheet in either of these fixed-layout formats, which preserve Excel's formatting and layout features while allowing distribution of the file to others who may not have Excel installed on their computers.	PDF or XPS	page 298
14.	Click this button in the Save As dialog box once the Save as type option has been changed to a web page file format to type a page title.	Change Title	page 302

Excel Level 1, Chapter 1 Model Answers

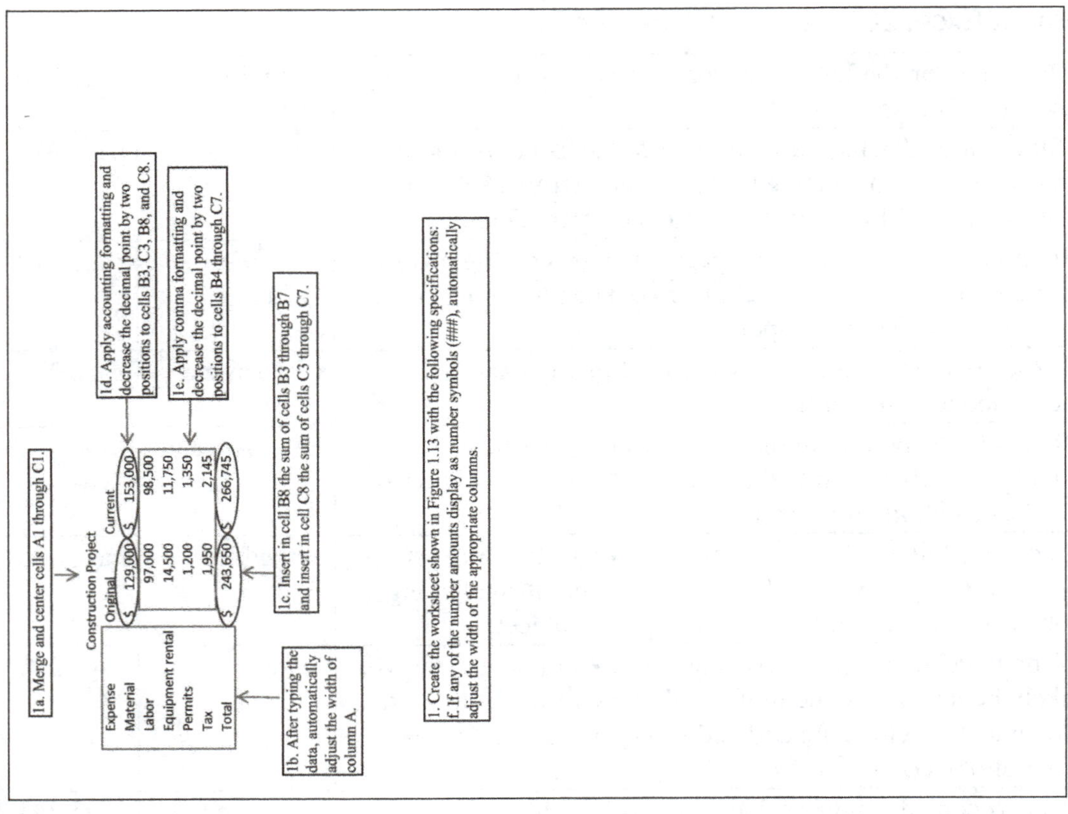

EL1-C1-A2-Exp(A2).xlsx

EL1-C1-A1-Plan(A1).xlsx

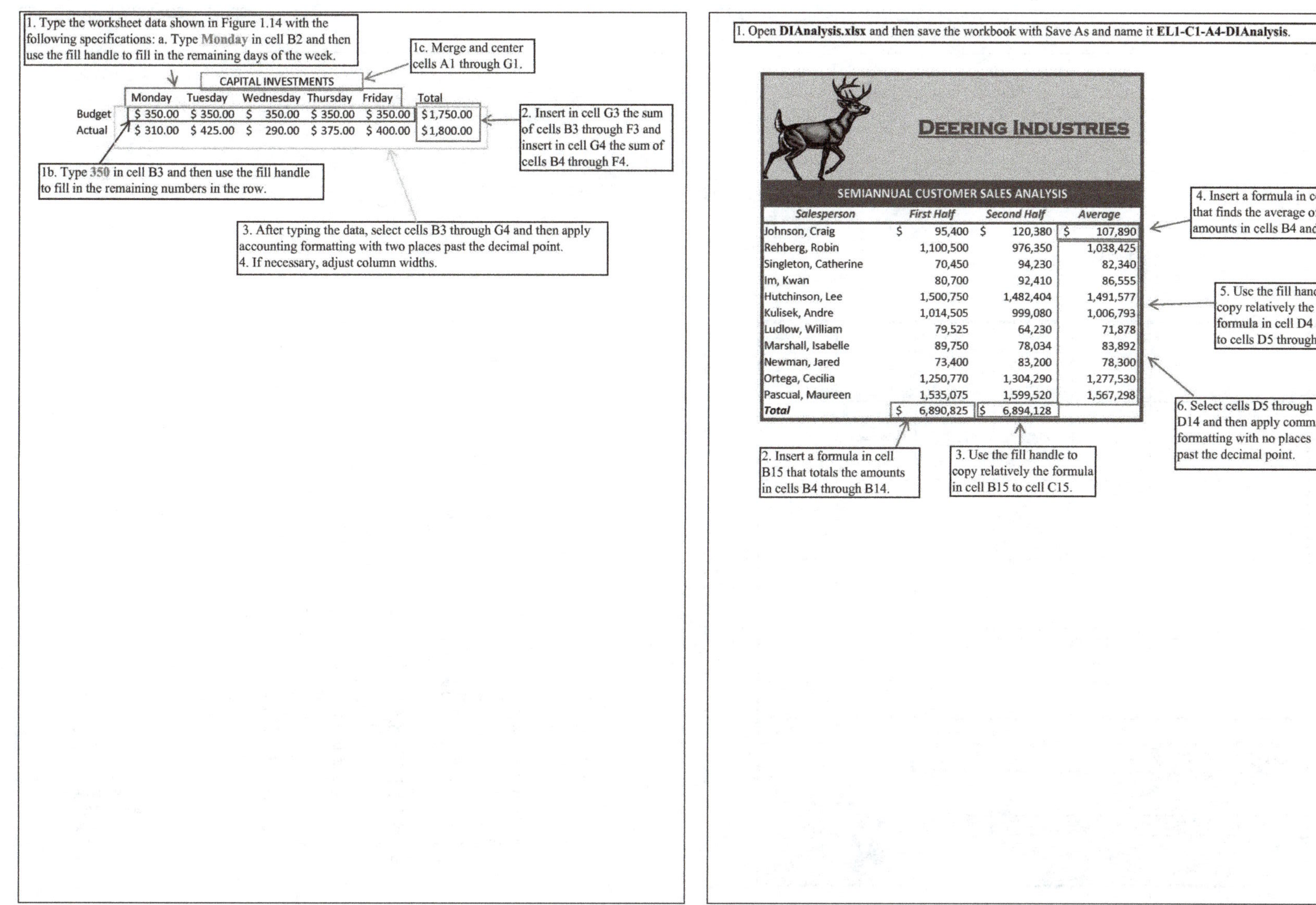

CAPITAL INVESTMENTS						
	Monday	Tuesday	Wednesday	Thursday	Friday	Total
Budget	$ 350.00	$ 350.00	$ 350.00	$ 350.00	$ 350.00	$1,750.00
Actual	$ 310.00	$ 425.00	$ 290.00	$ 375.00	$ 400.00	$1,800.00

EL1-C1-A3-Invest(A3).xlsx

SEMIANNUAL CUSTOMER SALES ANALYSIS			
Salesperson	First Half	Second Half	Average
Johnson, Craig	$ 95,400	$ 120,380	$ 107,890
Rehberg, Robin	1,100,500	976,350	1,038,425
Singleton, Catherine	70,450	94,230	82,340
Im, Kwan	80,700	92,410	86,555
Hutchinson, Lee	1,500,750	1,482,404	1,491,577
Kulisek, Andre	1,014,505	999,080	1,006,793
Ludlow, William	79,525	64,230	71,878
Marshall, Isabelle	89,750	78,034	83,892
Newman, Jared	73,400	83,200	78,300
Ortega, Cecilia	1,250,770	1,304,290	1,277,530
Pascual, Maureen	1,535,075	1,599,520	1,567,298
Total	$ 6,890,825	$ 6,894,128	

EL1-C1-A4-DIAnalysis(A4).xlsx

Personal Expenses - July through December

Expense	July	August	September	October	November	December	Average
Rent	$ 850	$ 850	$ 850	$ 850	$ 850	$ 850	$ 850
Rental insurance	55	55	55	55	55	55	55
Health insurance	120	120	120	120	120	120	120
Electricity	129	135	110	151	168	173	144
Utilities	53	62	49	32	55	61	52
Telephone	73	81	67	80	82	75	76
Groceries	143	137	126	150	147	173	146
Gasoline	89	101	86	99	76	116	95
Total	$ 1,512	$ 1,541	$ 1,463	$ 1,537	$ 1,553	$ 1,623	$ 1,538

EL1-C1-VB-PersExps(VB).xlsx

DEERING INDUSTRIES

NOVEMBER, 2015

SUNDAY	MONDAY	TUESDAY	WEDNESDAY	THURSDAY	FRIDAY	SATURDAY
1	2	3	4	5 Excel Training 9-11 a.m.	6 Time Card Due	7
8	9 Staff Meeting 9-10 a.m.	10	11	12	13	14
15	16	17	18	19	20 Time Card Due	21
22	23 Staff Meeting 9-10 a.m.	24 Production Team Meeting 1-3 p.m.	25	26	27	28
29	30					

EL1-C1-CS-DICalendar(CS1).xlsx

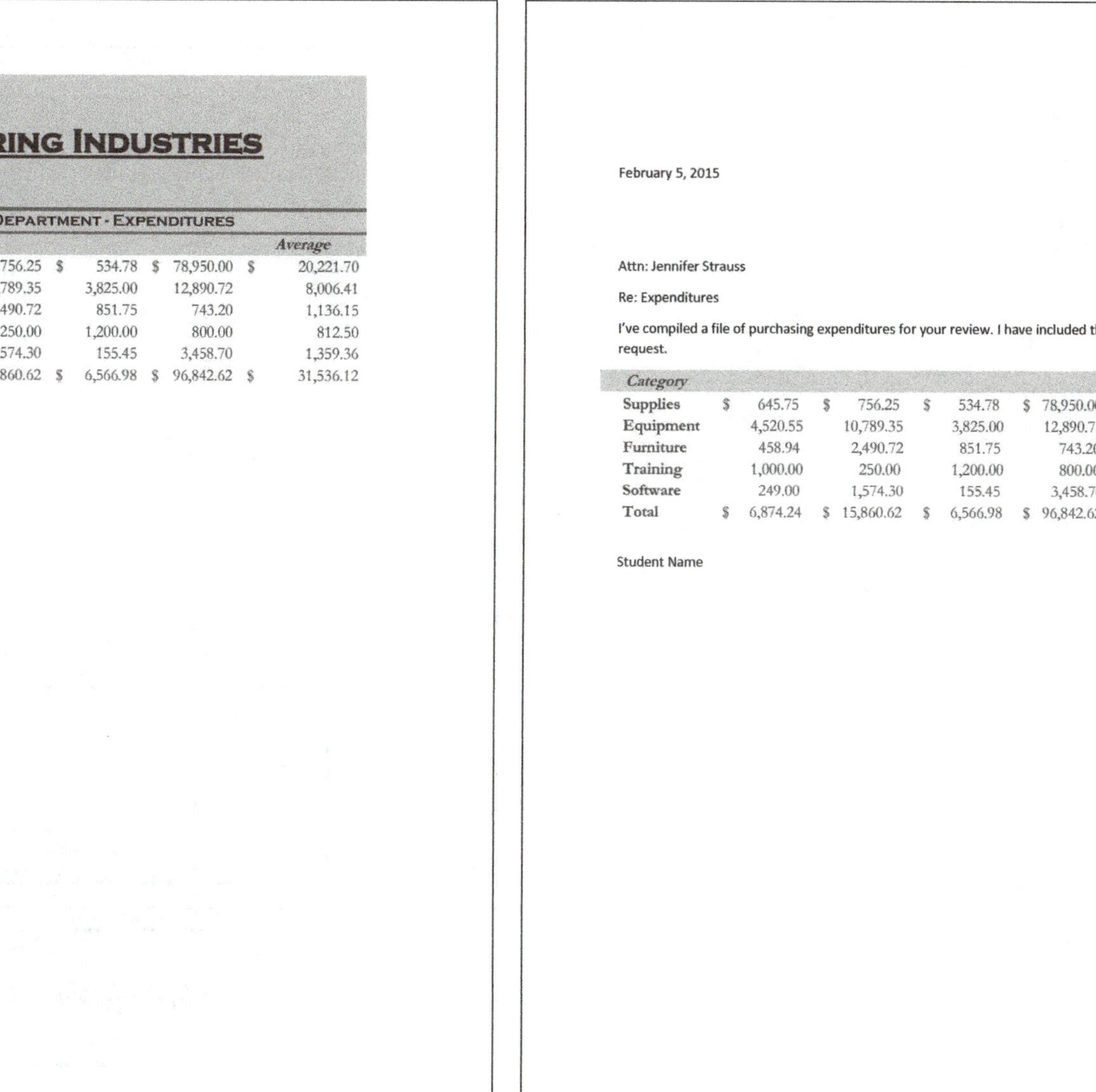

DEERING INDUSTRIES

PURCHASING DEPARTMENT - EXPENDITURES

Category					Average
Supplies	$ 645.75	$ 756.25	$ 534.78	$ 78,950.00	$ 20,221.70
Equipment	4,520.55	10,789.35	3,825.00	12,890.72	8,006.41
Furniture	458.94	2,490.72	851.75	743.20	1,136.15
Training	1,000.00	250.00	1,200.00	800.00	812.50
Software	249.00	1,574.30	155.45	3,458.70	1,359.36
Total	$ 6,874.24	$ 15,860.62	$ 6,566.98	$ 96,842.62	$ 31,536.12

EL1-C1-CS-DIExpenditures(CS2).xlsx

February 5, 2015

Attn: Jennifer Strauss

Re: Expenditures

I've compiled a file of purchasing expenditures for your review. I have included the information per your request.

Category					Average
Supplies	$ 645.75	$ 756.25	$ 534.78	$ 78,950.00	$ 20,221.70
Equipment	4,520.55	10,789.35	3,825.00	12,890.72	8,006.41
Furniture	458.94	2,490.72	851.75	743.20	1,136.15
Training	1,000.00	250.00	1,200.00	800.00	812.50
Software	249.00	1,574.30	155.45	3,458.70	1,359.36
Total	$ 6,874.24	$ 15,860.62	$ 6,566.98	$ 96,842.62	$ 31,536.12

Student Name

EL1-C1-CS-DINotetoJS(CS3).xlsx

DEERING INDUSTRIES		
PURCHASING DEPARTMENT - COPIERS		
Company	Model	Price
Canon	ImageCLASS D1120	$ 330.00
Xerox	WorkCenter 4250XF	$ 2,390.00
Sharp	AL-1631 Digtal Laser	$ 589.00

EL1-C1-CS-DICopiers(CS4).xlsx

Excel Level 1, Chapter 2 Model Answers

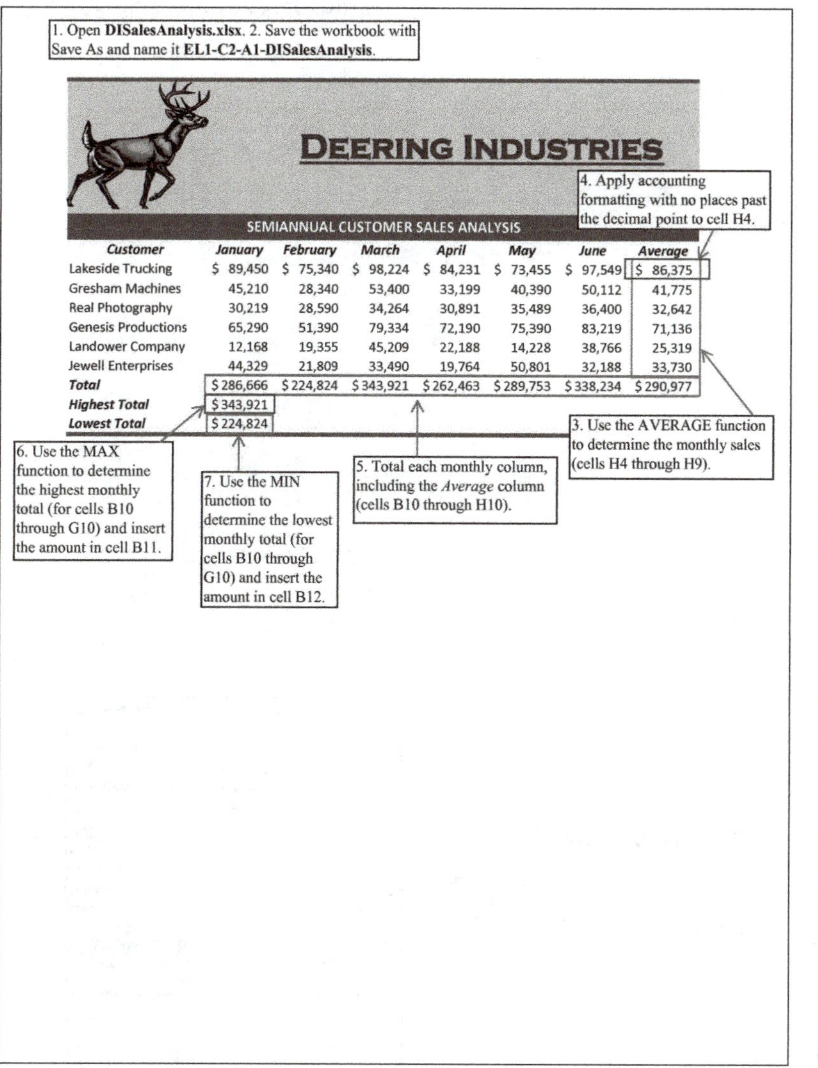

Customer	January	February	March	April	May	June	Average
Lakeside Trucking	$ 89,450	$ 75,340	$ 98,224	$ 84,231	$ 73,455	$ 97,549	$ 86,375
Gresham Machines	45,210	28,340	53,400	33,199	40,390	50,112	41,775
Real Photography	30,219	28,590	34,264	30,891	35,489	36,400	32,642
Genesis Productions	65,290	51,390	79,334	72,190	75,390	83,219	71,136
Landower Company	12,168	19,355	45,209	22,188	14,228	38,766	25,319
Jewell Enterprises	44,329	21,809	33,490	19,764	50,801	32,188	33,730
Total	$ 286,666	$ 224,824	$ 343,921	$ 262,463	$ 289,753	$ 338,234	$ 290,977
Highest Total	$ 343,921						
Lowest Total	$ 224,824						

EL1-C2-A1-DISalesAnalysis(A1).xlsx

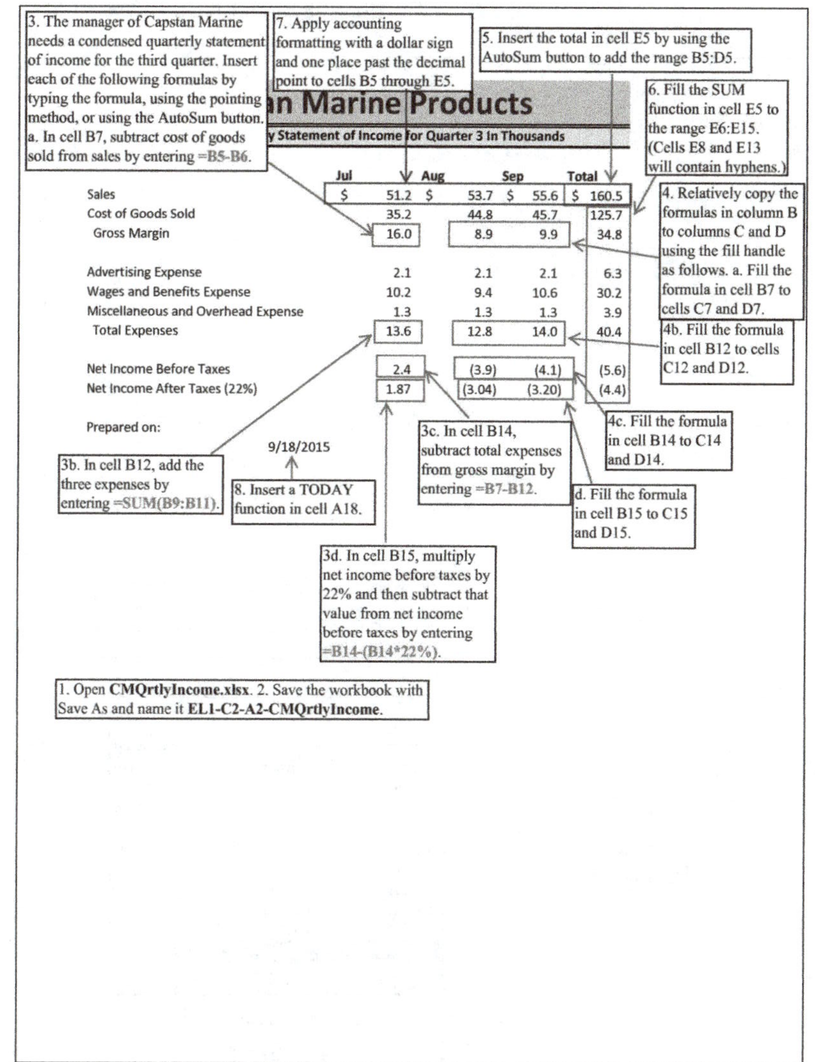

	Jul	Aug	Sep	Total
Sales	$ 51.2	$ 53.7	$ 55.6	$ 160.5
Cost of Goods Sold	35.2	44.8	45.7	125.7
Gross Margin	16.0	8.9	9.9	34.8
Advertising Expense	2.1	2.1	2.1	6.3
Wages and Benefits Expense	10.2	9.4	10.6	30.2
Miscellaneous and Overhead Expense	1.3	1.3	1.3	3.9
Total Expenses	13.6	12.8	14.0	40.4
Net Income Before Taxes	2.4	(3.9)	(4.1)	(5.6)
Net Income After Taxes (22%)	1.87	(3.04)	(3.20)	(4.4)
Prepared on:	9/18/2015			

EL1-C2-A2-CMQrtlyIncome(A2).xlsx

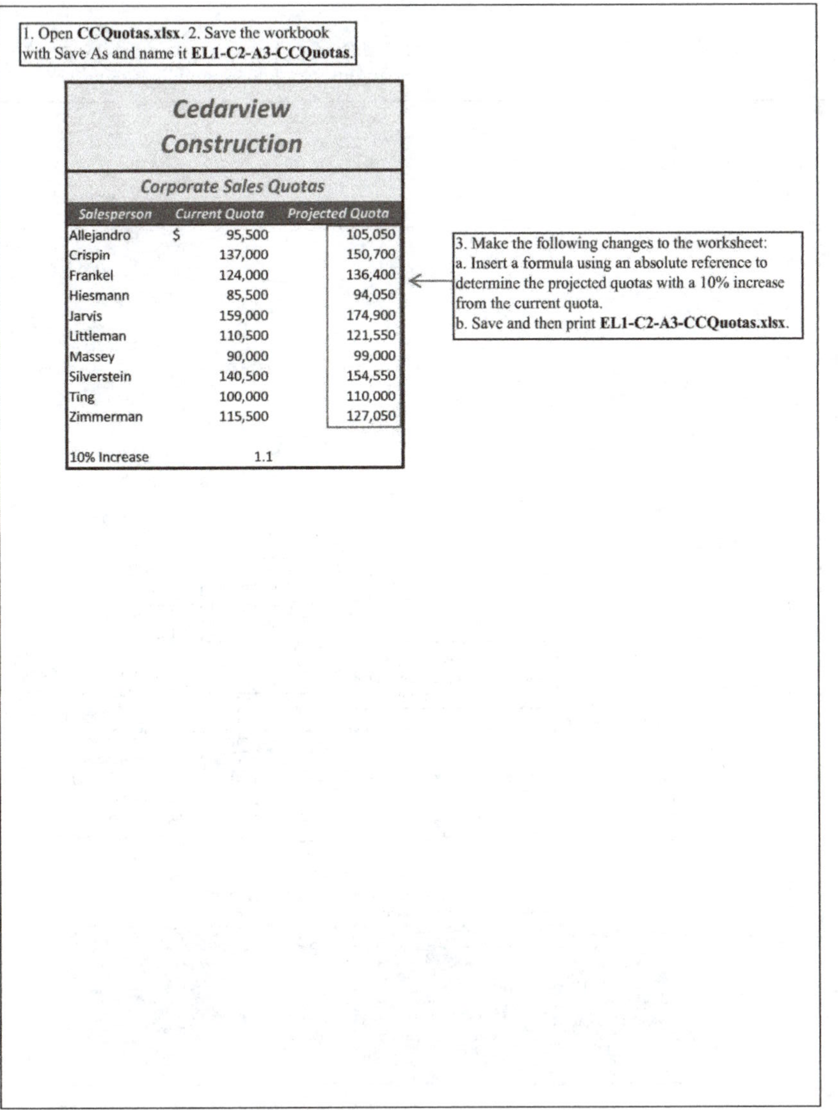

1. Open **CCQuotas.xlsx**. 2. Save the workbook with Save As and name it **EL1-C2-A3-CCQuotas**.

Cedarview Construction		
Corporate Sales Quotas		
Salesperson	*Current Quota*	*Projected Quota*
Allejandro	$ 95,500	105,050
Crispin	137,000	150,700
Frankel	124,000	136,400
Hiesmann	85,500	94,050
Jarvis	159,000	174,900
Littleman	110,500	121,550
Massey	90,000	99,000
Silverstein	140,500	154,550
Ting	100,000	110,000
Zimmerman	115,500	127,050
10% Increase	1.1	

3. Make the following changes to the worksheet:
a. Insert a formula using an absolute reference to determine the projected quotas with a 10% increase from the current quota.
b. Save and then print **EL1-C2-A3-CCQuotas.xlsx**.

EL1-C2-A3-CCQuotes(A2,Step3b).xlsx

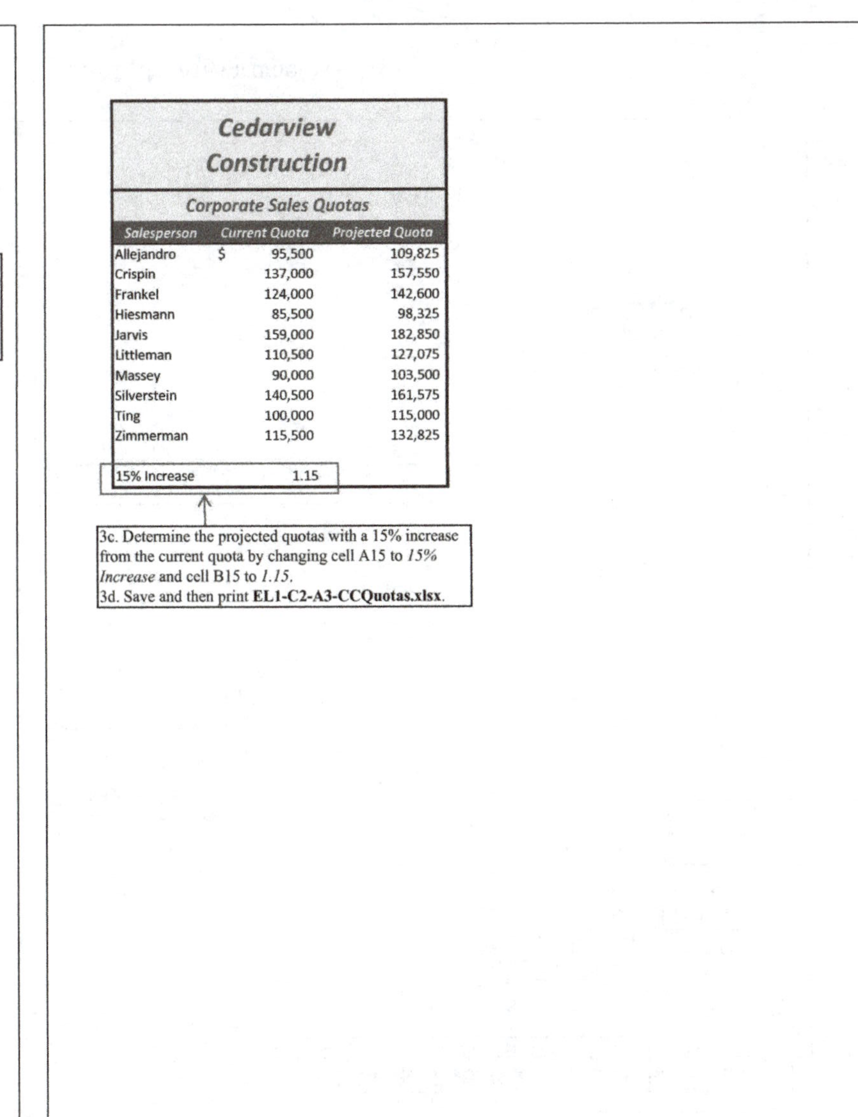

Cedarview Construction		
Corporate Sales Quotas		
Salesperson	*Current Quota*	*Projected Quota*
Allejandro	$ 95,500	109,825
Crispin	137,000	157,550
Frankel	124,000	142,600
Hiesmann	85,500	98,325
Jarvis	159,000	182,850
Littleman	110,500	127,075
Massey	90,000	103,500
Silverstein	140,500	161,575
Ting	100,000	115,000
Zimmerman	115,500	132,825
15% Increase	1.15	

3c. Determine the projected quotas with a 15% increase from the current quota by changing cell A15 to *15% Increase* and cell B15 to *1.15*.
3d. Save and then print **EL1-C2-A3-CCQuotas.xlsx**.

EL1-C2-A3-CCQuotas(A3,Step3d).xlsx

Cedarview Construction

Corporate Sales Quotas

Salesperson	Current Quota	Projected Quota
Allejandro	$ 95,500	$ 114,600
Crispin	137,000	164,400
Frankel	124,000	148,800
Hiesmann	85,500	102,600
Jarvis	159,000	190,800
Littleman	110,500	132,600
Massey	90,000	108,000
Silverstein	140,500	168,600
Ting	100,000	120,000
Zimmerman	115,500	138,600
20% Increase	1.2	

4. Apply accounting formatting with no places after the decimal point to cell C4.

3e. Determine the projected quotas with a 20% increase from the current quota.

EL1-C2-A3-CCQuotas(A3,Step5).xlsx

1. Open **AASMileageChart.xlsx**. 2. Save the workbook with Save As and name it **EL1-C2-A4-AASMileageChart**.

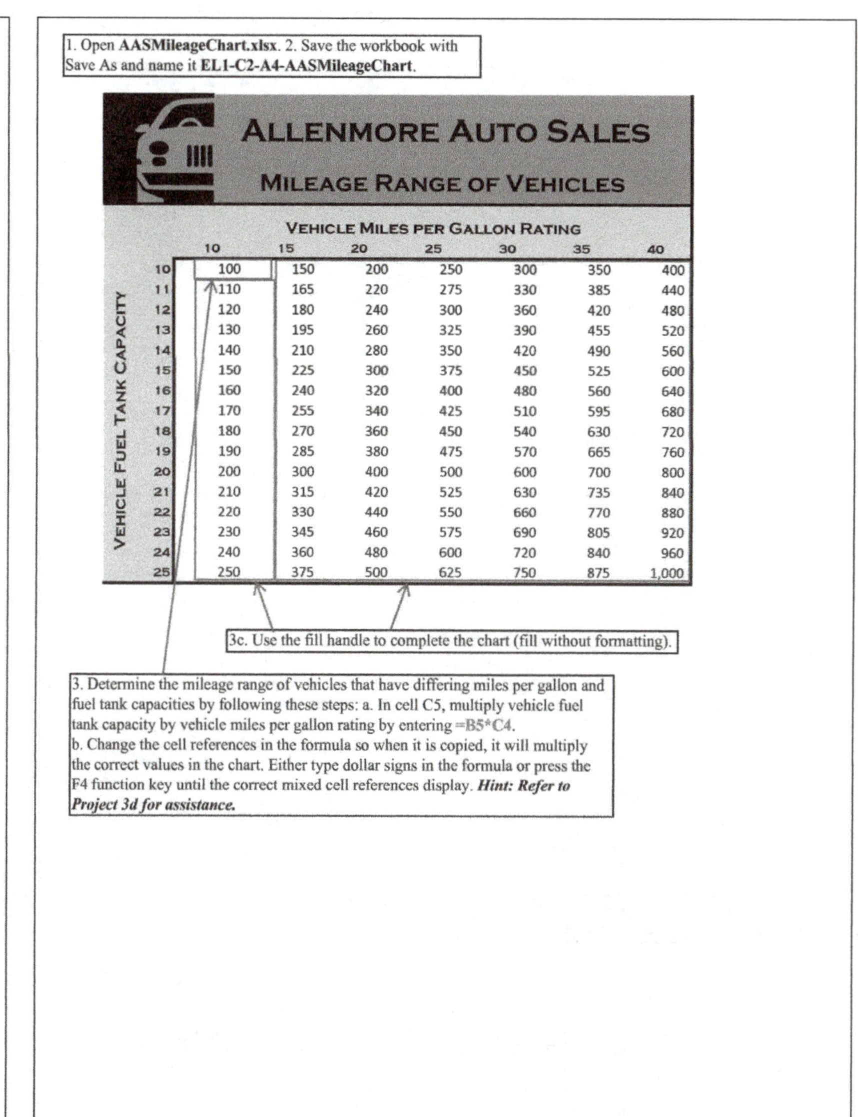

Allenmore Auto Sales

Mileage Range of Vehicles

Vehicle Miles per Gallon Rating (columns) / Vehicle Fuel Tank Capacity (rows)

	10	15	20	25	30	35	40
10	100	150	200	250	300	350	400
11	110	165	220	275	330	385	440
12	120	180	240	300	360	420	480
13	130	195	260	325	390	455	520
14	140	210	280	350	420	490	560
15	150	225	300	375	450	525	600
16	160	240	320	400	480	560	640
17	170	255	340	425	510	595	680
18	180	270	360	450	540	630	720
19	190	285	380	475	570	665	760
20	200	300	400	500	600	700	800
21	210	315	420	525	630	735	840
22	220	330	440	550	660	770	880
23	230	345	460	575	690	805	920
24	240	360	480	600	720	840	960
25	250	375	500	625	750	875	1,000

3c. Use the fill handle to complete the chart (fill without formatting).

3. Determine the mileage range of vehicles that have differing miles per gallon and fuel tank capacities by following these steps: a. In cell C5, multiply vehicle fuel tank capacity by vehicle miles per gallon rating by entering =B5*C4.
b. Change the cell references in the formula so when it is copied, it will multiply the correct values in the chart. Either type dollar signs in the formula or press the F4 function key until the correct mixed cell references display. ***Hint: Refer to Project 3d for assistance.***

EL1-C2-A4-AASMileageChart(A4).xlsx

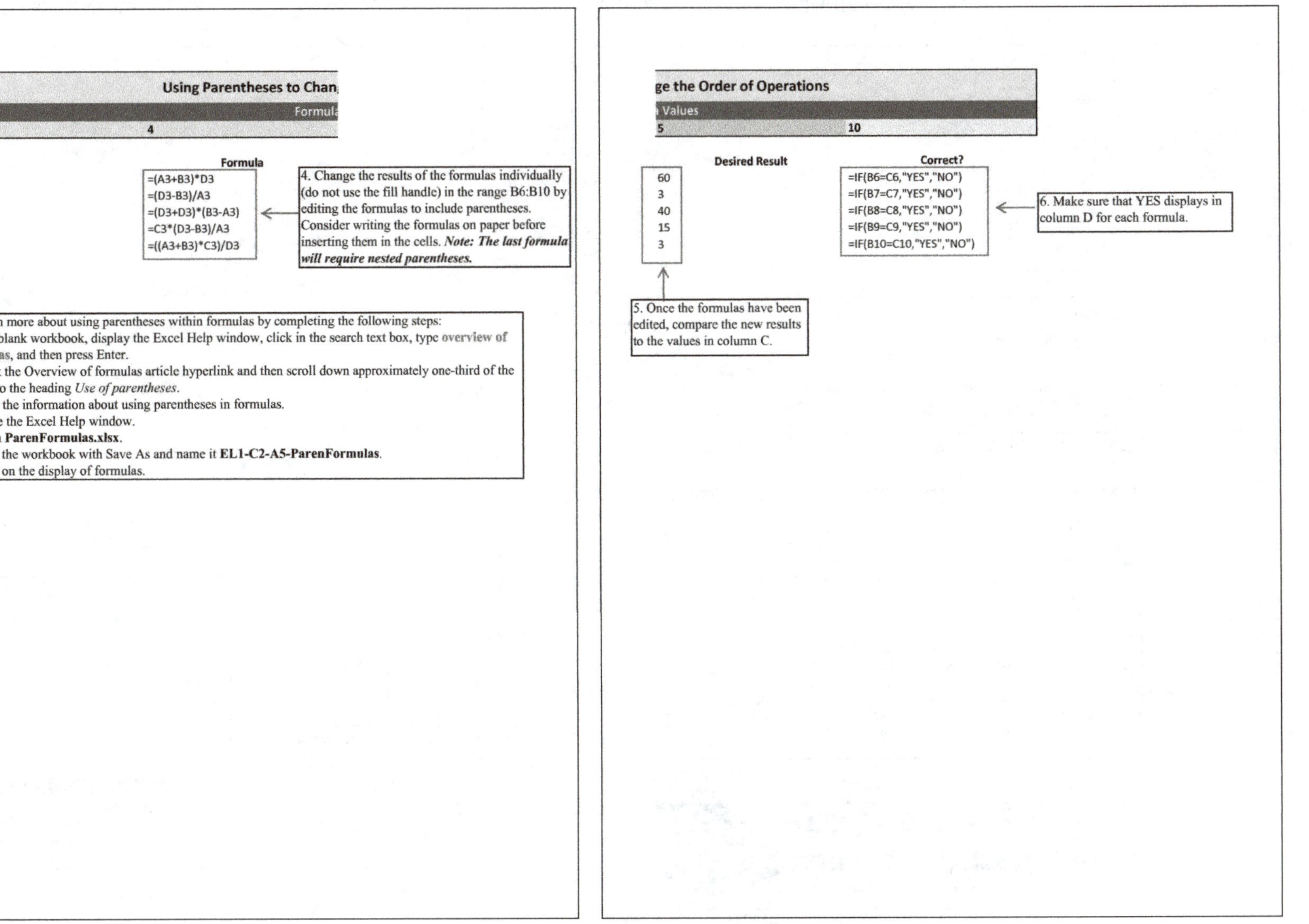

Using Parentheses to Chan

Formul

2	4

	Formula
1	=(A3+B3)*D3
2	=(D3-B3)/A3
3	=(D3+D3)*(B3-A3)
4	=C3*(D3-B3)/A3
5	=((A3+B3)*C3)/D3

4. Change the results of the formulas individually (do not use the fill handle) in the range B6:B10 by editing the formulas to include parentheses. Consider writing the formulas on paper before inserting them in the cells. ***Note: The last formula will require nested parentheses.***

1. Learn more about using parentheses within formulas by completing the following steps:
a. At a blank workbook, display the Excel Help window, click in the search text box, type **overview of formulas**, and then press Enter.
b. Click the Overview of formulas article hyperlink and then scroll down approximately one-third of the article to the heading *Use of parentheses*.
c. Read the information about using parentheses in formulas.
d. Close the Excel Help window.
2. Open **ParenFormulas.xlsx**.
3. Save the workbook with Save As and name it **EL1-C2-A5-ParenFormulas**.
7. Turn on the display of formulas.

EL1-C2-A5-ParenFormulas(A5,Step8).xlsx (1 of 2)

ge the Order of Operations

Values

5	10

Desired Result	Correct?
60	=IF(B6=C6,"YES","NO")
3	=IF(B7=C7,"YES","NO")
40	=IF(B8=C8,"YES","NO")
15	=IF(B9=C9,"YES","NO")
3	=IF(B10=C10,"YES","NO")

5. Once the formulas have been edited, compare the new results to the values in column C.

6. Make sure that YES displays in column D for each formula.

EL1-C2-A5-ParenFormulas(A5,Step8).xlsx (2 of 2)

Weekly Payroll

Employee	Hours	Rate	Salary
Alvarez, Rita	40	$ 22.50	$ 900.00
Campbell, Owen	15	22.50	337.50
Heitmann, Luanne	25	19.00	475.00
Malina, Susan	40	18.75	750.00
Parker, Kenneth	40	18.75	750.00
Reitz, Collette	20	15.00	300.00
Shepard, Gregory	15	12.00	180.00

Construction Projects

Project	Projected	Actual	Difference
South Cascade	$145,000	$ 141,597	$ (3,403)
Rogue River Park	120,000	124,670	4,670
Meridian	120,500	99,450	(21,050)
Lowell Ridge	95,250	98,455	3,205
Walker Canyon	70,000	68,420	(1,580)
Nettleson Creek	52,000	49,517	(2,483)

Test Scores

Employee	Test No. 1	Test No. 2	Test No. 3	Wgt. Avg.
Coffey, Annette	62%	64%	76%	70%
Halverson, Ted	88%	96%	90%	91%
Kohler, Jeremy	80%	76%	82%	80%
McKnight, Carol	68%	72%	78%	74%
Parkhurst, Jody	98%	96%	98%	98%
Test Averages	79%	81%	85%	
Test Weights	25%	25%	50%	

EL1-C2-VB-Formulas(VB,Step4).xlsx

Weekly Payroll

Employee	Hours	Rate
Alvarez, Rita	40	22.5
Campbell, Owen	15	22.5
Heitmann, Luanne	25	19
Malina, Susan	40	18.75
Parker, Kenneth	40	18.75
Reitz, Collette	20	15
Shepard, Gregory	15	12

Construction Projects

Project	Projected	Actual
South Cascade	145000	141597
Rogue River Park	120000	124670
Meridian	120500	99450
Lowell Ridge	95250	98455
Walker Canyon	70000	68420
Nettleson Creek	52000	49517

Test Scores

Employee	Test No. 1	Test No. 2
Coffey, Annette	0.62	0.64
Halverson, Ted	0.88	0.96
Kohler, Jeremy	0.8	0.76
McKnight, Carol	0.68	0.72
Parkhurst, Jody	0.98	0.96
Test Averages	=AVERAGE(B24:B28)	=AVERAGE(C24:C28)
Test Weights	0.25	0.25

EL1-C2-VB-Formulas(VB,Step5).xlsx (1 of 2)

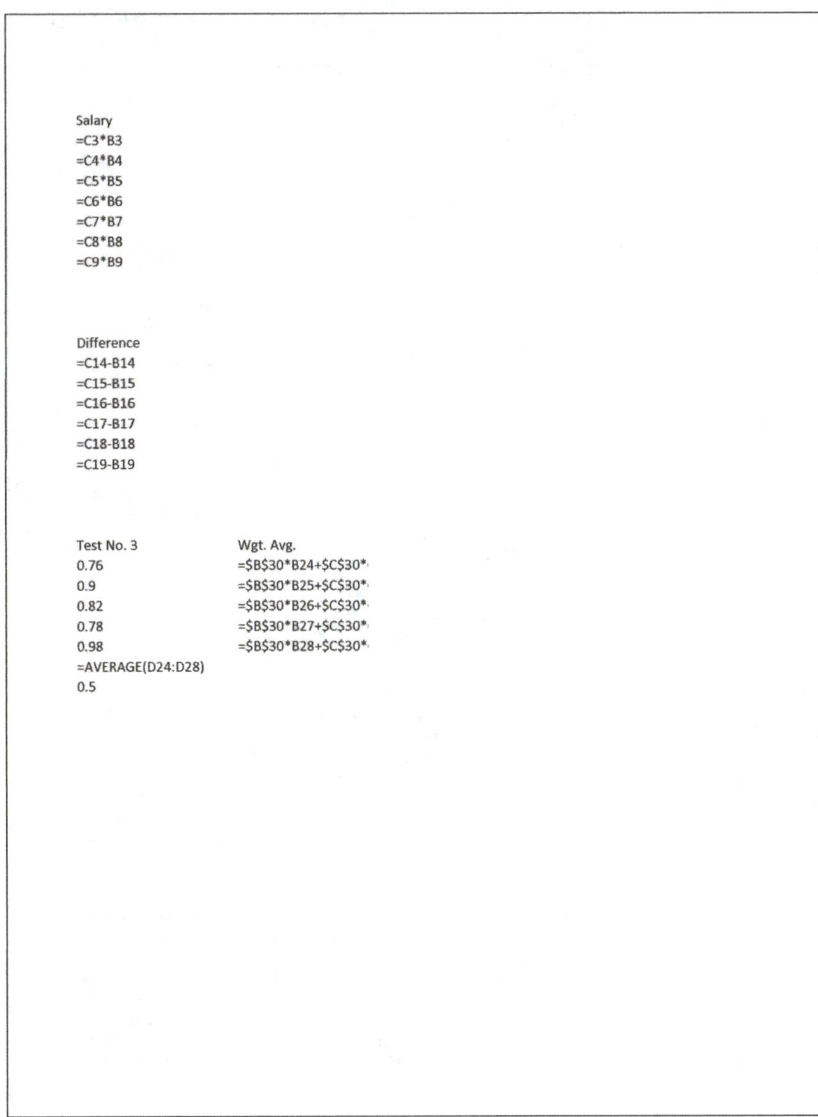

Salary
=C3*B3
=C4*B4
=C5*B5
=C6*B6
=C7*B7
=C8*B8
=C9*B9

Difference
=C14-B14
=C15-B15
=C16-B16
=C17-B17
=C18-B18
=C19-B19

Test No. 3	Wgt. Avg.
0.76	=$B$30*B24+$C$30*
0.9	=$B$30*B25+$C$30*
0.82	=$B$30*B26+$C$30*
0.78	=$B$30*B27+$C$30*
0.98	=$B$30*B28+$C$30*
=AVERAGE(D24:D28)	
0.5	

EL1-C2-VB-Formulas(VB,Step5).xlsx (2 of 2)

Allenmore Auto Sales

February Monthly Sales

Salesperson	Date	Lot No.	Price	Dealer Cost	Gross Profit	Comm %	Total Comm
Arrozo, J.	2/1/2015	14-3291	$ 29,875.00	$ 26,100.00	$ 3,775.00	21%	$ 792.75
Mayfield, L.	2/1/2015	13-2931	26,425.00	23,549.00	2,876.00	22%	632.72
Yamaki, E.	2/4/2015	15-2390	42,399.00	39,999.00	2,400.00	20%	480.00
Parr, G.	2/5/2015	13-3392	19,535.00	16,259.00	3,276.00	22%	720.72
Herzog, W.	2/6/2015	15-1903	50,775.00	46,975.00	3,800.00	20%	760.00
Mayfield, L.	2/7/2015	14-0442	24,955.00	21,100.00	3,855.00	21%	809.55
Yamaki, E.	2/7/2015	14-2119	28,799.00	25,250.00	3,549.00	21%	745.29
Arrozo, J.	2/8/2015	15-2034	52,529.00	49,250.00	3,279.00	20%	655.80
Herzog, W.	2/8/2015	11-2391	9,470.00	5,899.00	3,571.00	23%	821.33
Barstow, A.	2/9/2015	14-2934	18,755.00	16,110.00	2,645.00	21%	555.45
Yamaki, E.	2/9/2015	12-7732	29,585.00	24,900.00	4,685.00	23%	1,077.55
Parr, G.	2/11/2015	13-5583	22,997.00	19,670.00	3,327.00	22%	731.94
Barstow, A.	2/13/2015	15-3443	49,775.00	46,249.00	3,526.00	20%	705.20
Baskins, I.	2/14/2015	10-9034	8,525.00	4,950.00	3,575.00	25%	893.75
Orlinski, P.	2/14/2015	15-2411	35,239.00	31,590.00	3,649.00	20%	729.80
Mayfield, L.	2/15/2015	15-0493	39,772.00	36,129.00	3,643.00	20%	728.60
Orlinski, P.	2/15/2015	10-3881	7,525.00	4,225.00	3,300.00	25%	825.00
Yamaki, E.	2/17/2015	14-2711	19,599.00	16,329.00	3,270.00	21%	686.70
Barstow, A.	2/18/2015	12-6451	11,450.00	8,119.00	3,331.00	23%	766.13
Mayfield, L.	2/20/2015	14-3710	21,755.00	19,079.00	2,676.00	21%	561.96
Arrozo, J.	2/21/2015	14-2238	27,659.00	24,199.00	3,460.00	21%	726.60
Herzog, W.	2/21/2015	11-9005	14,110.00	10,980.00	3,130.00	23%	719.90
Parr, G.	2/21/2015	10-4231	6,320.00	4,199.00	2,121.00	25%	530.25
Baskins, I.	2/22/2015	13-3382	38,655.00	32,775.00	5,880.00	22%	1,293.60
Orlinski, P.	2/22/2015	15-8774	55,095.00	50,979.00	4,116.00	20%	823.20
Arrozo, J.	2/24/2015	10-4999	9,225.00	7,000.00	2,225.00	25%	556.25
Yamaki, E.	2/25/2015	11-3423	13,499.00	10,277.00	3,222.00	23%	741.06
Orlinski, P.	2/27/2015	13-0048	20,957.00	17,900.00	3,057.00	22%	672.54
Herzog, W.	2/28/2015	15-2109	37,655.00	35,009.00	2,646.00	20%	529.20
Mayfield, L.	2/28/2015	14-2200	23,511.00	20,199.00	3,312.00	21%	695.52
Yamaki, E.	2/28/2015	15-1112	44,799.00	40,865.00	3,934.00	20%	786.80
Baskins, I.	2/7/2915	15-0349	43,275.00	40,789.00	2,486.00	20%	497.20

EL1-C2-CS-AASFebSales(CS1).xlsx (1 of 2)

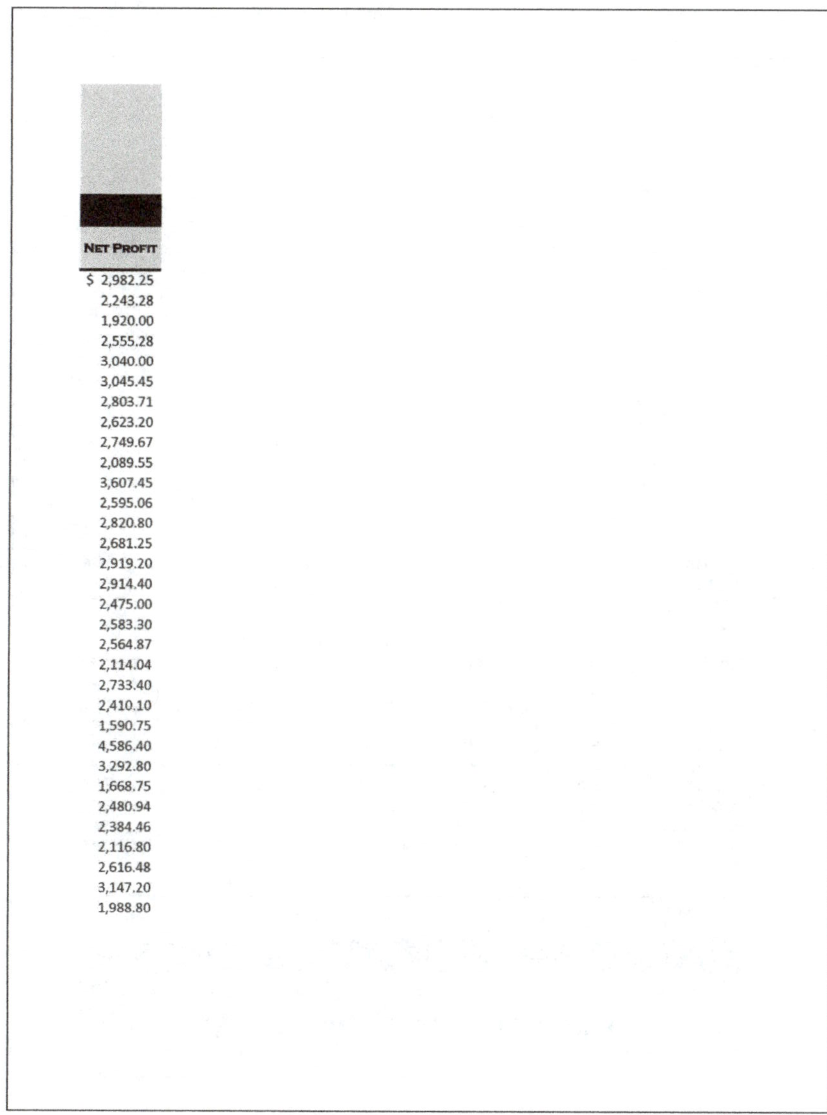

Net Profit
$ 2,982.25
2,243.28
1,920.00
2,555.28
3,040.00
3,045.45
2,803.71
2,623.20
2,749.67
2,089.55
3,607.45
2,595.06
2,820.80
2,681.25
2,919.20
2,914.40
2,475.00
2,583.30
2,564.87
2,114.04
2,733.40
2,410.10
1,590.75
4,586.40
3,292.80
1,668.75
2,480.94
2,384.46
2,116.80
2,616.48
3,147.20
1,988.80

EL1-C2-CS-AASFebSales(CS1).xlsx (2 of 2)

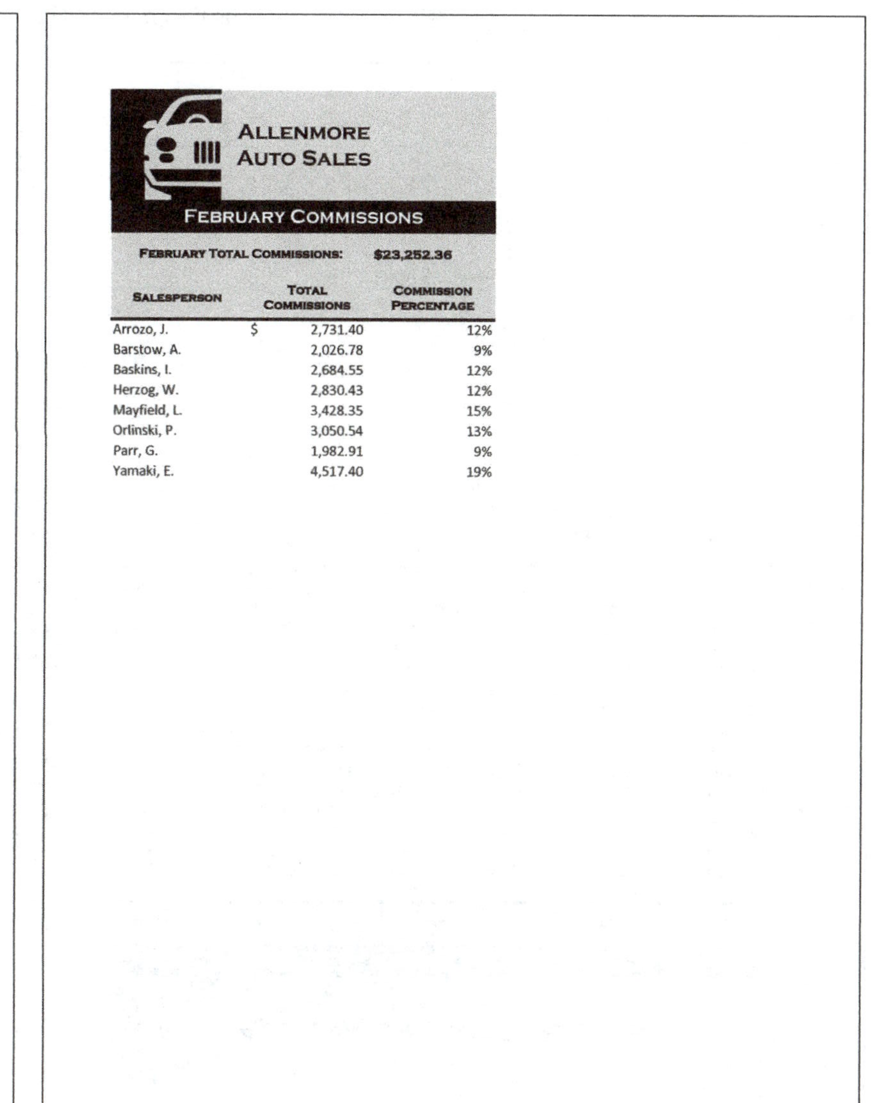

Allenmore Auto Sales

February Commissions

February Total Commissions: $23,252.36

Salesperson	Total Commissions	Commission Percentage
Arrozo, J.	$ 2,731.40	12%
Barstow, A.	2,026.78	9%
Baskins, I.	2,684.55	12%
Herzog, W.	2,830.43	12%
Mayfield, L.	3,428.35	15%
Orlinski, P.	3,050.54	13%
Parr, G.	1,982.91	9%
Yamaki, E.	4,517.40	19%

EL1-C2-CS-AASFebCommissions(CS2).xlsx

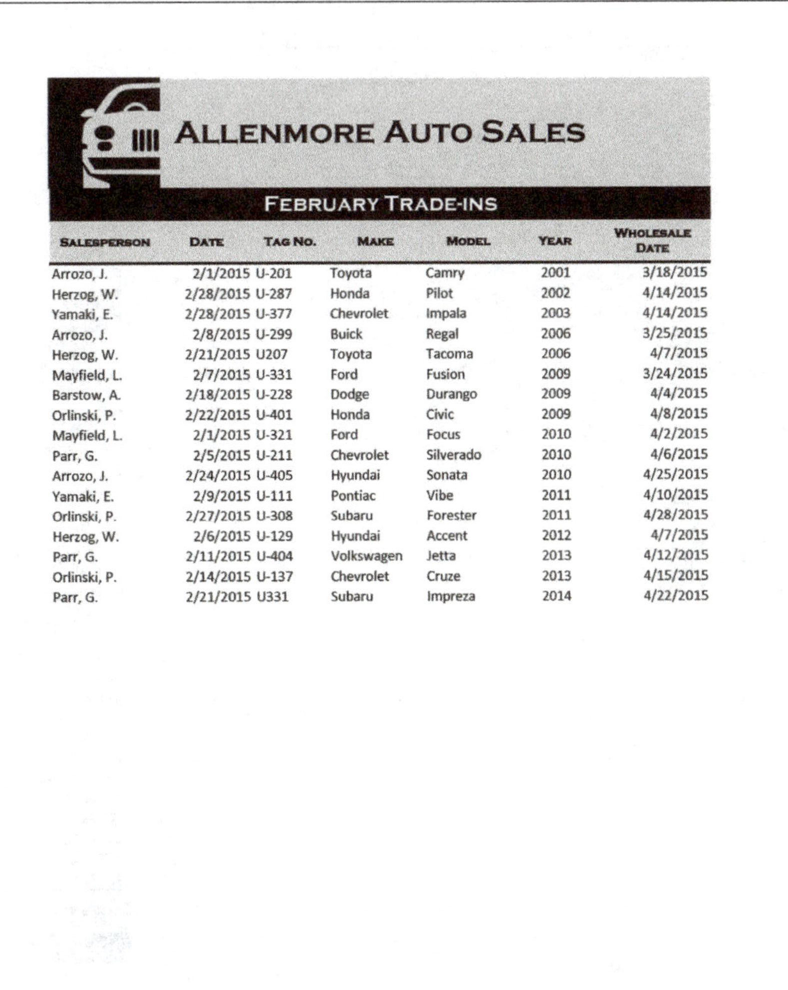

Allenmore Auto Sales

February Trade-Ins

Salesperson	Date	Tag No.	Make	Model	Year	Wholesale Date
Arrozo, J.	2/1/2015	U-201	Toyota	Camry	2001	3/18/2015
Herzog, W.	2/28/2015	U-287	Honda	Pilot	2002	4/14/2015
Yamaki, E.	2/28/2015	U-377	Chevrolet	Impala	2003	4/14/2015
Arrozo, J.	2/8/2015	U-299	Buick	Regal	2006	3/25/2015
Herzog, W.	2/21/2015	U207	Toyota	Tacoma	2006	4/7/2015
Mayfield, L.	2/7/2015	U-331	Ford	Fusion	2009	3/24/2015
Barstow, A.	2/18/2015	U-228	Dodge	Durango	2009	4/4/2015
Orlinski, P.	2/22/2015	U-401	Honda	Civic	2009	4/8/2015
Mayfield, L.	2/1/2015	U-321	Ford	Focus	2010	4/2/2015
Parr, G.	2/5/2015	U-211	Chevrolet	Silverado	2010	4/6/2015
Arrozo, J.	2/24/2015	U-405	Hyundai	Sonata	2010	4/25/2015
Yamaki, E.	2/9/2015	U-111	Pontiac	Vibe	2011	4/10/2015
Orlinski, P.	2/27/2015	U-308	Subaru	Forester	2011	4/28/2015
Herzog, W.	2/6/2015	U-129	Hyundai	Accent	2012	4/7/2015
Parr, G.	2/11/2015	U-404	Volkswagen	Jetta	2013	4/12/2015
Orlinski, P.	2/14/2015	U-137	Chevrolet	Cruze	2013	4/15/2015
Parr, G.	2/21/2015	U331	Subaru	Impreza	2014	4/22/2015

EL1-C2-CS-AASFebTradeIns(CS3).xlsx

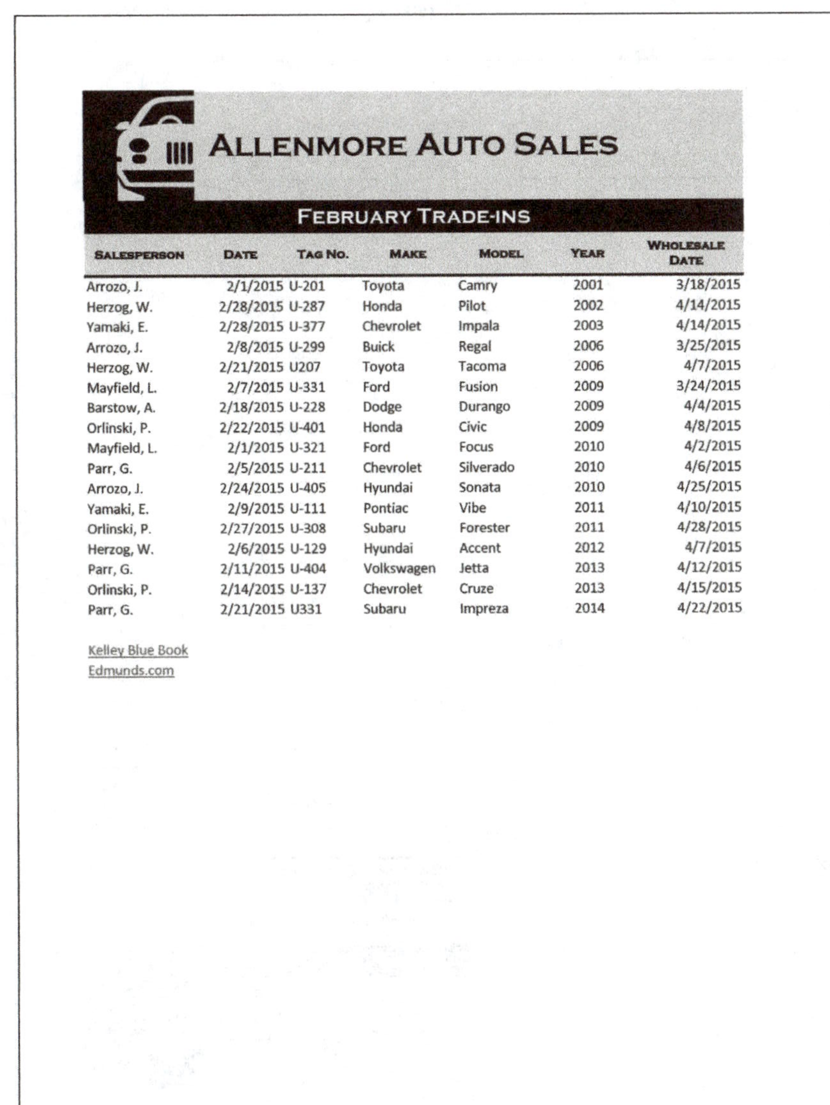

Allenmore Auto Sales

February Trade-Ins

Salesperson	Date	Tag No.	Make	Model	Year	Wholesale Date
Arrozo, J.	2/1/2015	U-201	Toyota	Camry	2001	3/18/2015
Herzog, W.	2/28/2015	U-287	Honda	Pilot	2002	4/14/2015
Yamaki, E.	2/28/2015	U-377	Chevrolet	Impala	2003	4/14/2015
Arrozo, J.	2/8/2015	U-299	Buick	Regal	2006	3/25/2015
Herzog, W.	2/21/2015	U207	Toyota	Tacoma	2006	4/7/2015
Mayfield, L.	2/7/2015	U-331	Ford	Fusion	2009	3/24/2015
Barstow, A.	2/18/2015	U-228	Dodge	Durango	2009	4/4/2015
Orlinski, P.	2/22/2015	U-401	Honda	Civic	2009	4/8/2015
Mayfield, L.	2/1/2015	U-321	Ford	Focus	2010	4/2/2015
Parr, G.	2/5/2015	U-211	Chevrolet	Silverado	2010	4/6/2015
Arrozo, J.	2/24/2015	U-405	Hyundai	Sonata	2010	4/25/2015
Yamaki, E.	2/9/2015	U-111	Pontiac	Vibe	2011	4/10/2015
Orlinski, P.	2/27/2015	U-308	Subaru	Forester	2011	4/28/2015
Herzog, W.	2/6/2015	U-129	Hyundai	Accent	2012	4/7/2015
Parr, G.	2/11/2015	U-404	Volkswagen	Jetta	2013	4/12/2015
Orlinski, P.	2/14/2015	U-137	Chevrolet	Cruze	2013	4/15/2015
Parr, G.	2/21/2015	U331	Subaru	Impreza	2014	4/22/2015

Kelley Blue Book
Edmunds.com

EL1-C2-CS-AASFebTradeIns-2(CS4).xlsx

Excel Level 1, Chapter 3 Model Answers

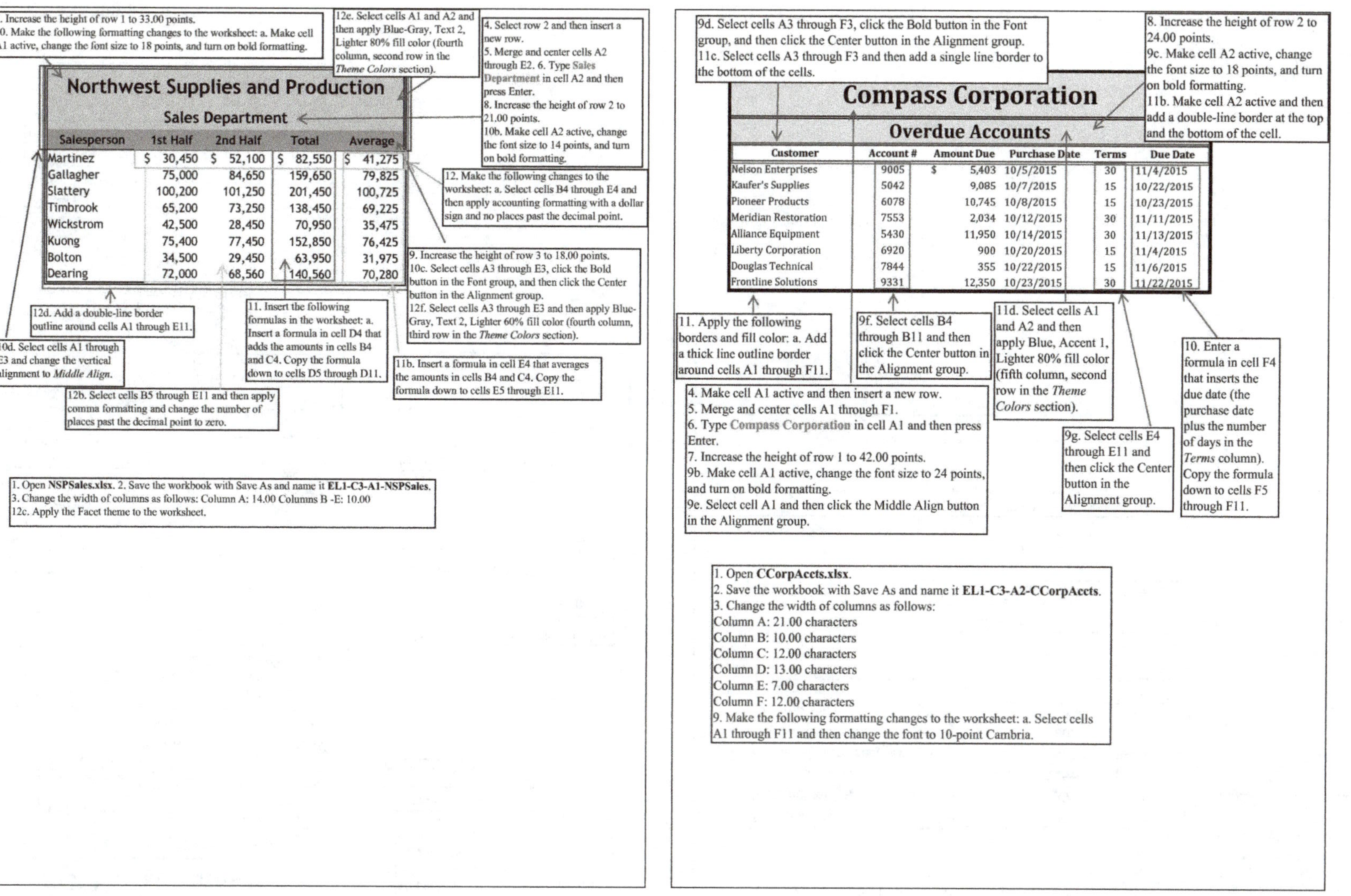

Northwest Supplies and Production				
Sales Department				
Salesperson	1st Half	2nd Half	Total	Average
Martinez	$ 30,450	$ 52,100	$ 82,550	$ 41,275
Gallagher	75,000	84,650	159,650	79,825
Slattery	100,200	101,250	201,450	100,725
Timbrook	65,200	73,250	138,450	69,225
Wickstrom	42,500	28,450	70,950	35,475
Kuong	75,400	77,450	152,850	76,425
Bolton	34,500	29,450	63,950	31,975
Dearing	72,000	68,560	140,560	70,280

Compass Corporation					
Overdue Accounts					
Customer	Account #	Amount Due	Purchase Date	Terms	Due Date
Nelson Enterprises	9005	$ 5,403	10/5/2015	30	11/4/2015
Kaufer's Supplies	5042	9,085	10/7/2015	15	10/22/2015
Pioneer Products	6078	10,745	10/8/2015	15	10/23/2015
Meridian Restoration	7553	2,034	10/12/2015	30	11/11/2015
Alliance Equipment	5430	11,950	10/14/2015	30	11/13/2015
Liberty Corporation	6920	900	10/20/2015	15	11/4/2015
Douglas Technical	7844	355	10/22/2015	15	11/6/2015
Frontline Solutions	9331	12,350	10/23/2015	30	11/22/2015

5. Make cell A1 active and then change the font size to 22 points and turn on bold formatting.
7. Change the height of row 1 to 36.00 points.

3. Select and then merge across cells A1 through D2. ***Hint: Use the* Merge Across *option at the* Merge & Center *button drop-down list.***
4. With cells A1 and A2 selected, click the Middle Align button in the Alignment group and then click the Center button.
17. Add Green, Accent 6, Lighter 80% green fill color (last column, second row in the *Theme Colors* section) to the following cells: A1, A2,

6. Make cell A2 active and then change the font size to 12 points and turn on bold formatting.

11. Make cell B3 active and then apply currency formatting with no places past the decimal point.

O'Rourke Enterprises			
Supplies and Equipment Budget			
Budget Amount	$750,000		
Research and Development			
	Supplies	3.5%	$26,250
	Equipment	22.0%	$165,000
Technical Support			
	Supplies	4.5%	$33,750
	Equipment	19.0%	$142,500
Sales and Marketing			
	Supplies	7.0%	$52,500
	Equipment	14.0%	$105,000
Human Resources			
	Supplies	5.5%	$41,250
	Equipment	10.0%	$75,000
Finances			
	Supplies	4.5%	$33,750
	Equipment	10.0%	$75,000

15. Make cell D8 active and then clear the cell contents. Use the Repeat command, F4, to clear the contents from cells D11, D14, and D17. 16. Select cells A1 through D19, change the font to Constantia, and then change the font color

17. Add Green, Accent 6, Lighter 80% green fill color (last column, second row in the *Theme Colors* section) to the following cells: A1, A2, A5 -D5, A8 - D8, A11 - D11, A14 - D14, and A17 -D17.

12. Select cells C6 through C19 and then apply percentage formatting with one place past the decimal point.

13. Make cell D6 active and then type a formula that multiplies the absolute cell reference $B$3 with the percentage in cell C6. Copy the formula down to cells D7 through D19.
14. With cells D6 through D19 selected, apply currency formatting with no places past the decimal point.

10. Select cells A3 through A17, turn on bold, and then click the Wrap Text button in the Alignment group.

1. Open **OEBudget.xlsx**.
2. Save the workbook with Save As and name it **EL1-C3-A3-OEBudget**.
9. Change the width of column A to 15.00 characters.
18. Automatically adjust the width of column B.

EL1-C3-A3-OEBudget(A3).xlsx

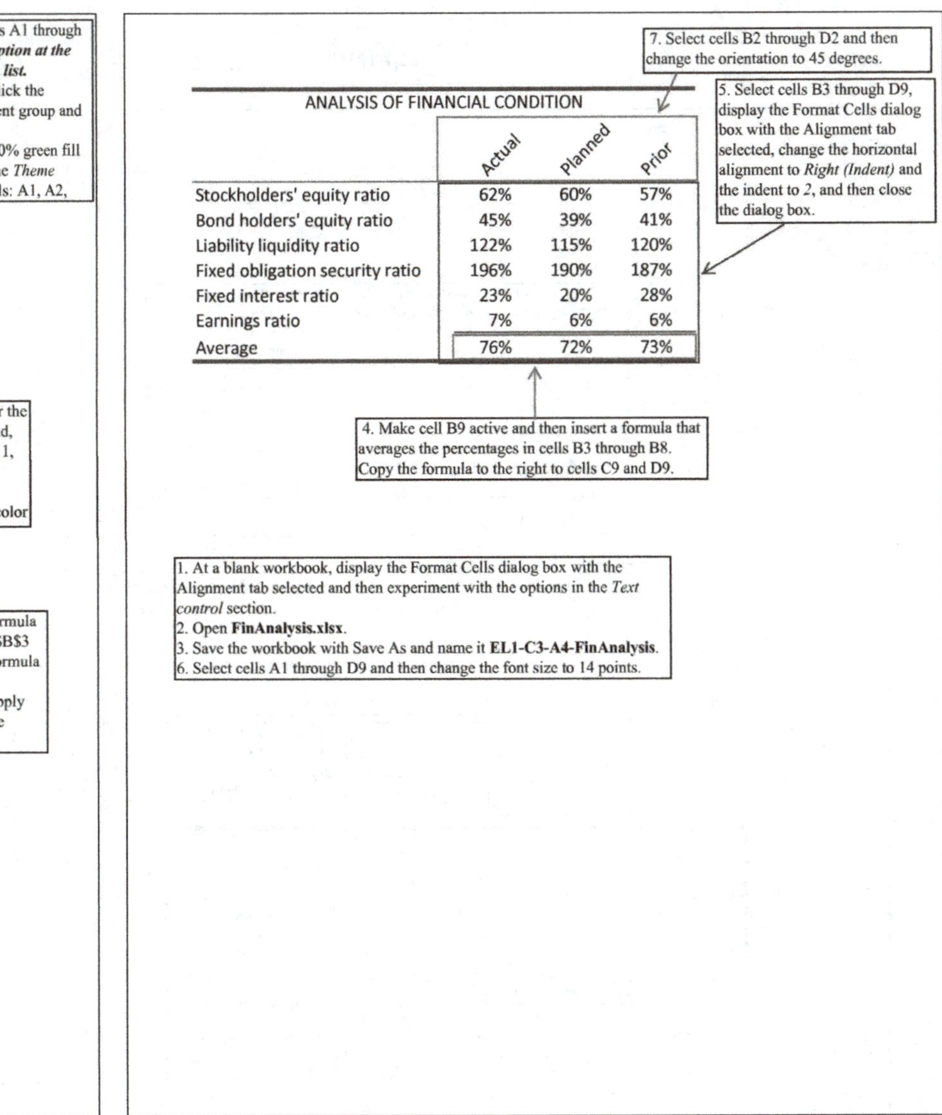
7. Select cells B2 through D2 and then change the orientation to 45 degrees.

5. Select cells B3 through D9, display the Format Cells dialog box with the Alignment tab selected, change the horizontal alignment to *Right (Indent)* and the indent to *2*, and then close the dialog box.

ANALYSIS OF FINANCIAL CONDITION			
	Actual	Planned	Prior
Stockholders' equity ratio	62%	60%	57%
Bond holders' equity ratio	45%	39%	41%
Liability liquidity ratio	122%	115%	120%
Fixed obligation security ratio	196%	190%	187%
Fixed interest ratio	23%	20%	28%
Earnings ratio	7%	6%	6%
Average	76%	72%	73%

4. Make cell B9 active and then insert a formula that averages the percentages in cells B3 through B8. Copy the formula to the right to cells C9 and D9.

1. At a blank workbook, display the Format Cells dialog box with the Alignment tab selected and then experiment with the options in the *Text control* section.
2. Open **FinAnalysis.xlsx**.
3. Save the workbook with Save As and name it **EL1-C3-A4-FinAnalysis**.
6. Select cells A1 through D9 and then change the font size to 14 points.

EL1-C3-A4-FinAnalysis(A4).xlsx

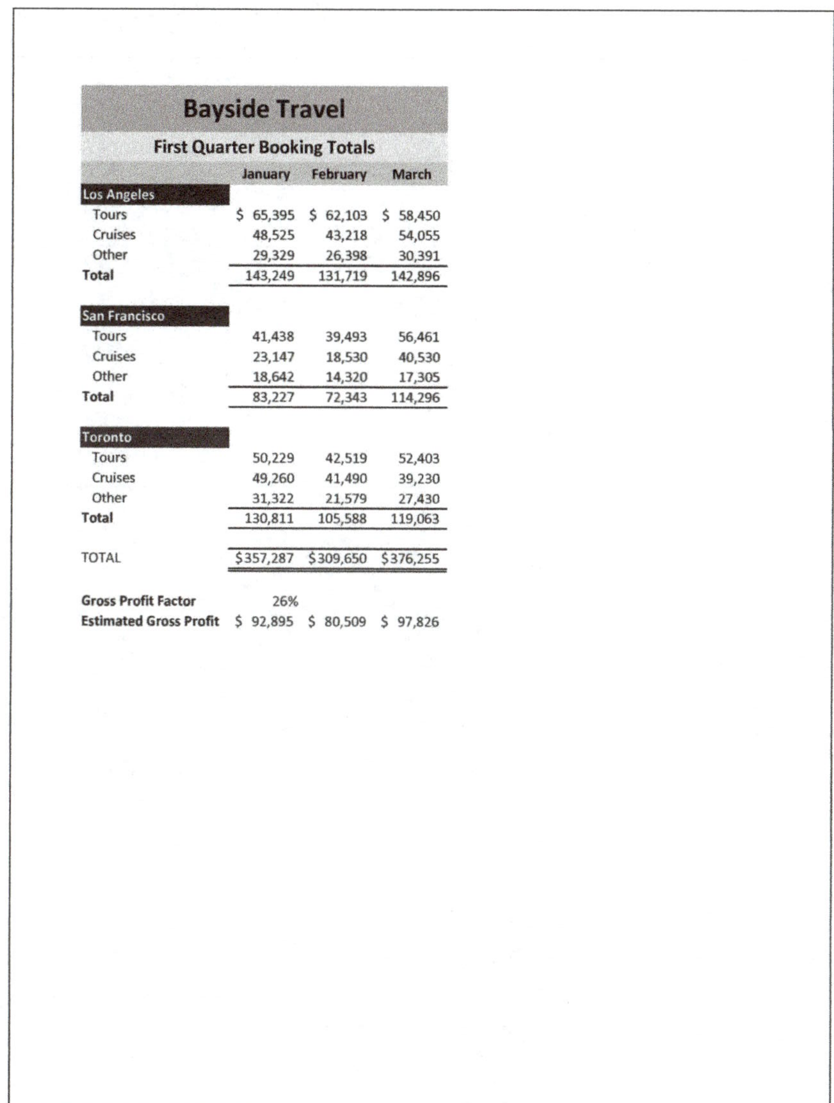

Bayside Travel			
First Quarter Booking Totals			
	January	February	March
Los Angeles			
Tours	$ 65,395	$ 62,103	$ 58,450
Cruises	48,525	43,218	54,055
Other	29,329	26,398	30,391
Total	143,249	131,719	142,896
San Francisco			
Tours	41,438	39,493	56,461
Cruises	23,147	18,530	40,530
Other	18,642	14,320	17,305
Total	83,227	72,343	114,296
Toronto			
Tours	50,229	42,519	52,403
Cruises	49,260	41,490	39,230
Other	31,322	21,579	27,430
Total	130,811	105,588	119,063
TOTAL	$357,287	$309,650	$376,255
Gross Profit Factor	26%		
Estimated Gross Profit	$ 92,895	$ 80,509	$ 97,826

EL1-C3-VB-BTBookings(Step4).xlsx

Bayside Travel		
First Quarter Booking Totals		
	January	February
Los Angeles		
Tours	65395	62103
Cruises	48525	43218
Other	29329	26398
Total	=SUM(B5:B7)	=SUM(C5:C7)
San Francisco		
Tours	41438	39493
Cruises	23147	18530
Other	18642	14320
Total	=SUM(B11:B13)	=SUM(C11:C13)
Toronto		
Tours	50229	42519
Cruises	49260	41490
Other	31322	21579
Total	=SUM(B17:B19)	=SUM(C17:C19)
TOTAL	=B8+B14+B20	=C8+C14+C20
Gross Profit Factor	0.26	
Estimated Gross Profit	=B22*$B24	=C22*$B24

EL1-C3-VB-BTBookings(Step5).xlsx (1 of 2)

March
58450
54055
30391
=SUM(D5:D7)
56461
40530
17305
=SUM(D11:D13)
52403
39230
27430
=SUM(D17:D19)
=D8+D14+D20
=D22*$B24

EL1-C3-VB-BTBookings(Step5).xlsx (2 of 2)

HealthWise Fitness Center			
Plans	*Yearly Dues*	*Quarterly*	*Monthly*
Economy	500.00	125.00	41.67
Standard	550.00	137.50	45.83
Standard Plus	605.00	151.25	50.42
Deluxe	665.50	166.38	55.46
Premium	732.05	183.01	61.00
Ultimate	805.26	201.31	67.10

EL1-C3-CS-HFCDues-1(CS1).xlsx

HealthWise Fitness Center

Plans	Yearly Dues	Quarterly	Late Fees	Monthly	Late Fees
Economy	$ 600.00	$ 150.00	$ 7.50	$ 50.00	$ 3.50
Standard	660.00	165.00	8.25	55.00	3.85
Standard Plus	726.00	181.50	9.08	60.50	4.24
Deluxe	798.60	199.65	9.98	66.55	4.66
Premium	878.46	219.62	10.98	73.21	5.12
Ultimate	$ 966.31	$ 241.58	$ 12.08	$ 80.53	$ 5.64

EL1-C3-CS-HFCDues-2(CS1).xlsx

HealthWise Fitness Center

Weekly Payroll

Employee	Hourly Wage	Hours	Overtime Hours	Overtime Pay	Weekly Salary
Heaton, Kelly	$26.50	40	2	$79.50	$1,139.50
Severson, Joel	$25.00	40	0	$0.00	$1,000.00
Turney, Amanda	$20.00	15	0	$0.00	$300.00
Walters, Leslie	$19.65	30	0	$0.00	$589.50
Overmeyer, Jean	$18.00	20	0	$0.00	$360.00
Haddon, Bonnie	$16.00	40	3	$72.00	$712.00
Baker, Grant	$15.00	40	0	$0.00	$600.00
Calveri, Shannon	$12.00	15	0	$0.00	$180.00
Dugan, Emily	$10.50	40	4	$63.00	$483.00
Joyner, Daniel	$10.50	10	0	$0.00	$105.00
Lee, Alexander	$10.50	10	0	$0.00	$105.00

EL1-C3-CS-HFCPayroll(CS2,FirstPrint).xlsx

HealthWise Fi

Weekly P

Employee	Hourly Wage	Hours
Heaton, Kelly	26.5	40
Severson, Joel	25	40
Turney, Amanda	20	15
Walters, Leslie	19.65	30
Overmeyer, Jean	18	20
Haddon, Bonnie	16	40
Baker, Grant	15	40
Calveri, Shannon	12	15
Dugan, Emily	10.5	40
Joyner, Daniel	10.5	10
Lee, Alexander	10.5	10

EL1-C3-CS-HFCPayroll(CS2,FirstPrint,Formulas).xlsx (1 of 2)

tness Center

'ayroll

Overtime Hours	Overtime Pay	Weekly Salary
2	=D4*(B4*1.5)	=(B4*C4)+E4
0	=D5*(B5*1.5)	=(B5*C5)+E5
0	=D6*(B6*1.5)	=(B6*C6)+E6
0	=D7*(B7*1.5)	=(B7*C7)+E7
0	=D8*(B8*1.5)	=(B8*C8)+E8
3	=D9*(B9*1.5)	=(B9*C9)+E9
0	=D10*(B10*1.5)	=(B10*C10)+E10
0	=D11*(B11*1.5)	=(B11*C11)+E11
4	=D12*(B12*1.5)	=(B12*C12)+E12
0	=D13*(B13*1.5)	=(B13*C13)+E13
0	=D14*(B14*1.5)	=(B14*C14)+E14

EL1-C3-CS-HFCPayroll(CS2,FirstPrint,Formulas).xlsx (2 of 2)

HealthWise Fitness Center

Weekly Payroll

Employee	Hourly Wage	Hours	Overtime Hours	Overtime Pay	Weekly Salary
Heaton, Kelly	$26.50	40	2	$79.50	$1,139.50
Severson, Joel	$25.00	40	0	$0.00	$1,000.00
Turney, Amanda	$22.00	15	0	$0.00	$330.00
Walters, Leslie	$19.65	30	0	$0.00	$589.50
Overmeyer, Jean	$18.00	20	0	$0.00	$360.00
McGuire, Tonya	$17.50	15	0	$0.00	$262.50
Haddon, Bonnie	$16.00	40	3	$72.00	$712.00
Calveri, Shannon	$12.00	15	0	$0.00	$180.00
Dugan, Emily	$10.50	40	4	$63.00	$483.00
Joyner, Daniel	$10.50	20	0	$0.00	$210.00
Lee, Alexander	$10.50	10	0	$0.00	$105.00

EL1-C3-CS-HFCPayroll(CS2,SecondPrint).xlsx

HealthWise Fi

Weekly P

Employee	Hourly Wage	Hours
Heaton, Kelly	26.5	40
Severson, Joel	25	40
Turney, Amanda	22	15
Walters, Leslie	19.65	30
Overmeyer, Jean	18	20
McGuire, Tonya	17.5	15
Haddon, Bonnie	16	40
Calveri, Shannon	12	15
Dugan, Emily	10.5	40
Joyner, Daniel	10.5	20
Lee, Alexander	10.5	10

EL1-C3-CS-HFCPayroll(CS2,SecondPrint,Formulas).xlsx (1 of 2)

tness Center

'ayroll

Overtime Hours	Overtime Pay	Weekly Salary
2	=D4*(B4*1.5)	=(B4*C4)+E4
0	=D5*(B5*1.5)	=(B5*C5)+E5
0	=D6*(B6*1.5)	=(B6*C6)+E6
0	=D7*(B7*1.5)	=(B7*C7)+E7
0	=D8*(B8*1.5)	=(B8*C8)+E8
0	=D9*(B9*1.5)	=(B9*C9)+E9
3	=D10*(B10*1.5)	=(B10*C10)+E10
0	=D11*(B11*1.5)	=(B11*C11)+E11
4	=D12*(B12*1.5)	=(B12*C12)+E12
0	=D13*(B13*1.5)	=(B13*C13)+E13
0	=D14*(B14*1.5)	=(B14*C14)+E14

EL1-C3-CS-HFCPayroll(CS2,SecondPrint,Formulas).xlsx (2 of 2)

HealthWise Fitness Center

New Equipment Costs

Equipment Name	Company	Equipment Model	Price	Quantity	Total Cost
Elliptical Machine					
	Livestrong Fitness	LS8.0E	$799.99	3	$2,399.97
	Sole	E25-2013	999.99	3	2,999.97
Recumbent Bike					
	LifeCore	1050RBs	1,795.00	3	5,385.00
	Spirit	XBR95	1,599.00	3	4,797.00
Upright Bike					
	LeMond	G Force UT	1,969.00	3	5,907.00
	TRUE	CS800	2,695.00	3	8,085.00

EL1-C3-CS-HFCEquip(CS3).xlsx

HealthWise
500 Elliott Avenue
Santa Barbara, CA 93101
January 29, 2012

Craig Fontaine
2263 Ocean Drive
Santa Barbara, CA 93101

Dear Craig Fontaine:

I want to thank you for giving me the opportunity the last time we talked to share the great advantages of a membership with HealthWise. We're confident that a membership will help you in your fitness goals and will tie in seamlessly with the lifestyle that you already enjoy. Here is the cost breakdown of the annual memberships we offer which can be paid in quarterly or monthly installments:

Plans	*Yearly Dues*	*Quarterly*	*Late Fees*	*Monthly*	*Late Fees*
Economy	$ 600.00	$ 150.00	$ 7.50	$ 50.00	$ 3.50
Standard	660.00	165.00	8.25	55.00	3.85
Standard Plus	726.00	181.50	9.08	60.50	4.24
Deluxe	798.60	199.65	9.98	66.55	4.66
Premium	878.46	219.62	10.98	73.21	5.12
Ultimate	$ 966.31	$ 241.58	$ 12.08	$ 80.53	$ 5.64

As you learned when we spoke recently, a membership offers you a number of beneficial features, including:

- State-of-the-art equipment
- Professional and experienced fitness coaches
- Personal trainers
- Various fitness classes for all interests

I'd very much like to discuss further which HealthWise membership would be best for you. If you have any questions and would like to start a FREE 2-week trial membership, you can call me at (310) 555-9964. Thank you for your interest.

Sincerely,

Student Name
Personal Fitness Account Manager

HFCLetter(CS4).xlsx

Excel Level 1, Chapter 4 Model Answers

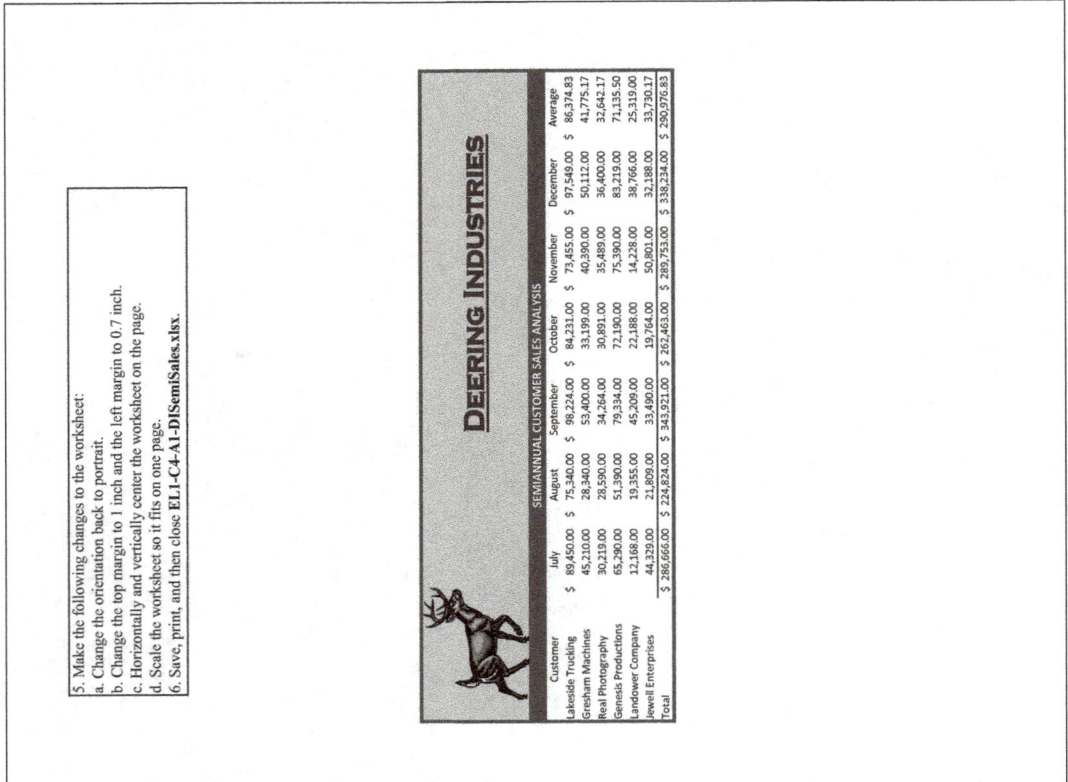

5. Make the following changes to the worksheet:
a. Change the orientation back to portrait.
b. Change the top margin to 1 inch and the left margin to 0.7 inch.
c. Horizontally and vertically center the worksheet on the page.
d. Scale the worksheet so it fits on one page.
6. Save, print, and then close **EL1-C4-A1-DISemiSales.xlsx**.

DEERING INDUSTRIES

SEMIANNUAL CUSTOMER SALES ANALYSIS

Customer	July	August	September	October	November	December	Average
Lakeside Trucking	$ 89,450.00	$ 75,340.00	$ 98,224.00	$ 84,231.00	$ 73,455.00	$ 97,549.00	$ 86,374.83
Gresham Machines	45,210.00	28,340.00	53,400.00	33,199.00	40,390.00	50,112.00	41,775.17
Real Photography	30,219.00	28,590.00	34,264.00	30,891.00	35,489.00	36,400.00	32,642.17
Genesis Productions	65,290.00	51,390.00	79,334.00	72,190.00	75,390.00	83,219.00	71,135.50
Landower Company	12,168.00	19,355.00	45,209.00	22,188.00	14,228.00	38,766.00	25,319.00
Jewell Enterprises	44,329.00	21,809.00	33,490.00	19,764.00	50,801.00	32,188.00	33,730.17
Total	$ 286,666.00	$ 224,824.00	$ 343,921.00	$ 262,463.00	$ 289,753.00	$ 338,234.00	$ 290,976.83

EL1-C4-A1-DISemiSales(A1,Step6).xlsx

1. Open **DISemiSales.xlsx**.
2. Save the workbook with Save As and name it **EL1-C4-A1-DISemiSales**.
3f. Change the orientation of the worksheet to landscape.
3g. Change the top margin to 3 inches and the left margin to 1.5 inches.
4. Save and then print **EL1-C4-A1-DISemiSales.xlsx**.

3. Make the following changes to the worksheet:
a. Insert a formula in cell H4 that averages the amounts in cells B4 through G4.
e. Apply accounting formatting to cell H4.

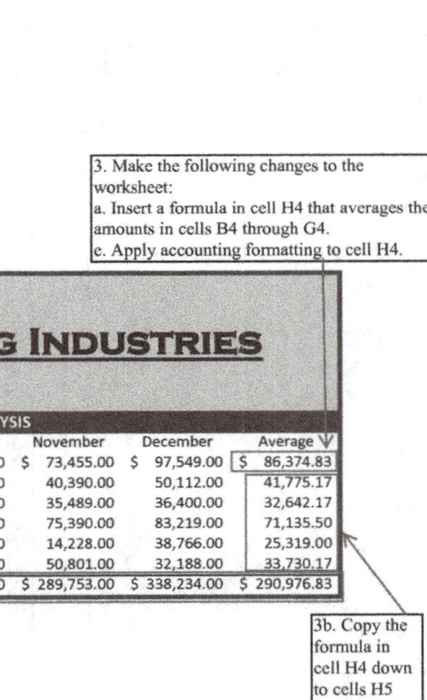

DEERING INDUSTRIES

SEMIANNUAL CUSTOMER SALES ANALYSIS

Customer	July	August	September	October	November	December	Average
Lakeside Trucking	$ 89,450.00	$ 75,340.00	$ 98,224.00	$ 84,231.00	$ 73,455.00	$ 97,549.00	$ 86,374.83
Gresham Machines	45,210.00	28,340.00	53,400.00	33,199.00	40,390.00	50,112.00	41,775.17
Real Photography	30,219.00	28,590.00	34,264.00	30,891.00	35,489.00	36,400.00	32,642.17
Genesis Productions	65,290.00	51,390.00	79,334.00	72,190.00	75,390.00	83,219.00	71,135.50
Landower Company	12,168.00	19,355.00	45,209.00	22,188.00	14,228.00	38,766.00	25,319.00
Jewell Enterprises	44,329.00	21,809.00	33,490.00	19,764.00	50,801.00	32,188.00	33,730.17
Total	$ 286,666.00	$ 224,824.00	$ 343,921.00	$ 262,463.00	$ 289,753.00	$ 338,234.00	$ 290,976.83

3c. Insert a formula in cell B10 that adds the amounts in cells B4 through B9.

d. Copy the formula in cell B10 over to cells C10 through H10. (Click the Auto Fill Options button and then click *Fill Without Formatting* at the dropdown list.)

3b. Copy the formula in cell H4 down to cells H5 through H9.

EL1-C4-A1-DISemiSales(A1,Step4).xlsx

1. Open **CMTests.xlsx**. 2. Save the workbook with Save As and name it **EL1-C4-A2-CMTests**.
3f. Insert a page break between columns G and H.
4. View the worksheet using Page Break Preview.
5. Change back to the Normal view.
9. Display the worksheet in Normal view.
10. Save and then print the worksheet.

1

7. Create a header that prints the page number at the right side of the page.

Clearline Manu

Software Certi

Name	Test 1	Test 2	Test 3	Test 4	Test 5	Test 6
Morris, Eugene	78%	80%	68%	66%	82%	60%
Jiang, Allison	98%	86%	92%	96%	88%	92%
Callahan, Jerome	78%	65%	82%	68%	74%	80%
Longren, Isabella	84%	93%	95%	81%	96%	98%
Soulez, Monica	70%	67%	55%	87%	82%	88%
White, Logan	95%	100%	98%	88%	95%	89%
Howell, Angela	100%	95%	96%	91%	87%	94%
Reed-Carter, Katie	65%	0%	0%	48%	52%	56%
Compton, Aidan	70%	67%	55%	87%	82%	88%
Acosta, Miguel	95%	100%	98%	88%	95%	89%
Potter, Aaron	100%	95%	96%	91%	87%	94%
Rhoden, Christopher	65%	0%	0%	48%	52%	56%
Slater, Chad	80%	82%	88%	79%	83%	76%
Tuell, Paulette	95%	100%	89%	94%	98%	94%
Whitlow, Angelina	82%	72%	85%	83%	71%	73%
Young, Lee	86%	72%	74%	82%	76%	79%
Goldman, Shannon	88%	86%	100%	98%	90%	97%
Bertram, Richard	63%	52%	66%	67%	53%	49%
Average	83%	73%	74%	80%	80%	81%

3c. Type Average in cell A22.

6. Specify that the column titles (A3 through A22) are to print on each page.

3d. Insert a formula in cell B22 that averages the test scores in cells B4 through B21. e. Copy the formula in cell B22 across to cells C22 through N22.

8. Create a footer that prints your name at the left side of the page and the workbook file name at the right side of the page.

Student Name

EL1-C4-A2-CMTests.xlsx

EL1-C4-A2-CMTests(A2,Step10).xlsx (1 of 2)

2

ıfacturing

fication

3. Make the following changes to the worksheet: a. Insert a formula in cell N4 that averages the test scores in cells B4 through M4.

Name	Test 7	Test 8	Test 9	Test 10	Test 11	Test 12	Average
Morris, Eugene	78%	82%	60%	84%	64%	70%	73%
Jiang, Allison	86%	90%	100%	98%	89%	96%	93%
Callahan, Jerome	72%	62%	78%	64%	86%	92%	75%
Longren, Isabella	89%	91%	90%	93%	86%	80%	90%
Soulez, Monica	78%	75%	87%	88%	64%	69%	76%
White, Logan	92%	80%	93%	90%	86%	82%	91%
Howell, Angela	98%	94%	99%	89%	100%	90%	94%
Reed-Carter, Katie	55%	0%	42%	65%	72%	59%	43%
Compton, Aidan	78%	75%	87%	88%	64%	76%	76%
Acosta, Miguel	92%	80%	93%	90%	86%	84%	91%
Potter, Aaron	98%	94%	99%	89%	100%	93%	95%
Rhoden, Christopher	55%	0%	42%	65%	72%	40%	41%
Slater, Chad	78%	69%	83%	87%	84%	69%	80%
Tuell, Paulette	89%	93%	84%	100%	95%	92%	94%
Whitlow, Angelina	78%	73%	81%	82%	67%	69%	76%
Young, Lee	82%	89%	79%	74%	80%	82%	80%
Goldman, Shannon	89%	93%	100%	91%	86%	90%	92%
Bertram, Richard	58%	45%	63%	51%	60%	59%	57%
Average	80%	71%	81%	83%	80%	77%	79%

3b. Copy the formula in cell N4 down to cells N5 through N21.

3e. Copy the formula in cell B22 across to cells C22 through N22.

Student Name

EL1-C4-A2-CMTests.xlsx

EL1-C4-A2-CMTests(A2,Step10).xlsx (2 of 2)

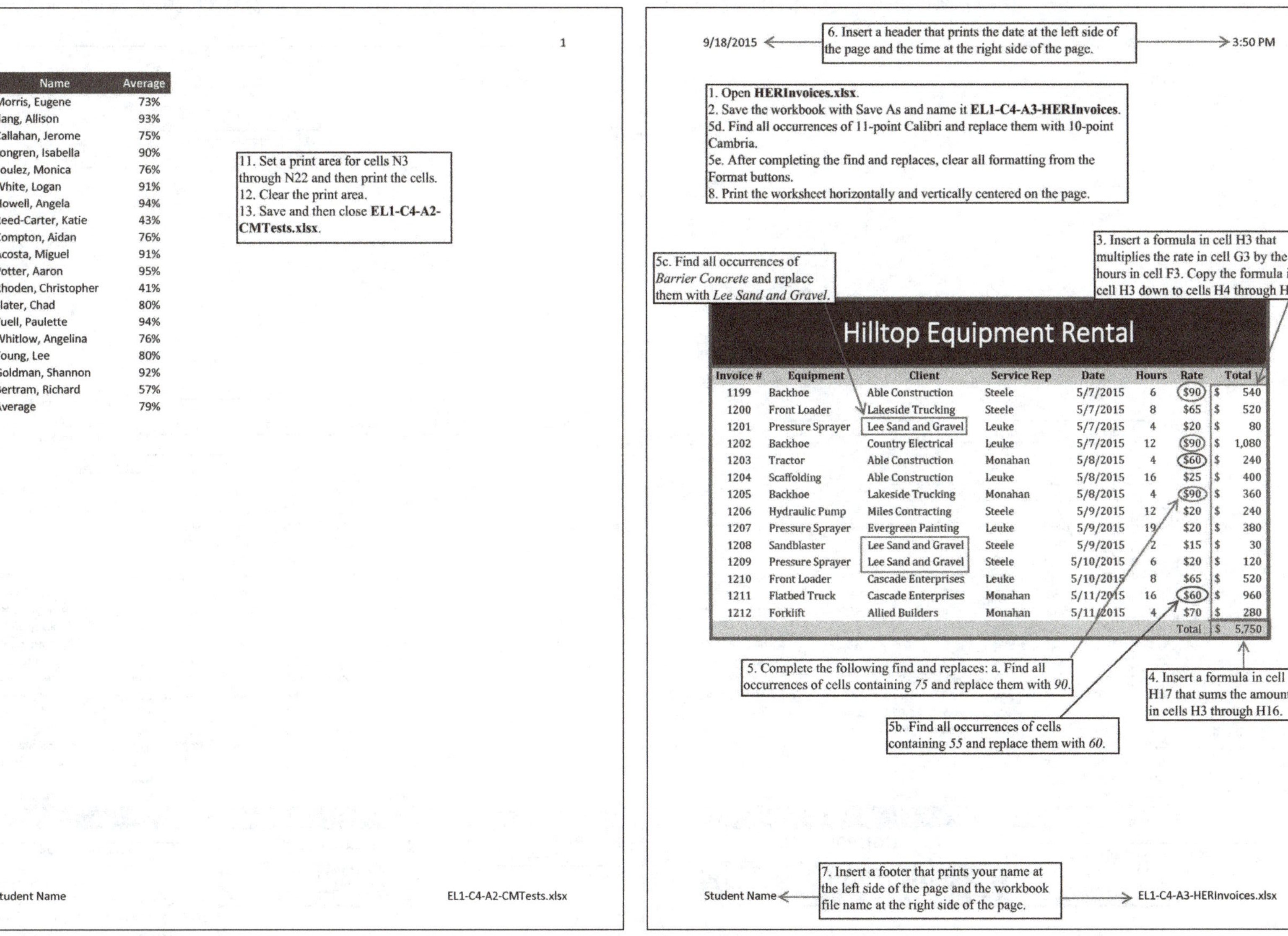

1

Name	Average
Morris, Eugene	73%
Jiang, Allison	93%
Callahan, Jerome	75%
Longren, Isabella	90%
Soulez, Monica	76%
White, Logan	91%
Howell, Angela	94%
Reed-Carter, Katie	43%
Compton, Aidan	76%
Acosta, Miguel	91%
Potter, Aaron	95%
Rhoden, Christopher	41%
Slater, Chad	80%
Tuell, Paulette	94%
Whitlow, Angelina	76%
Young, Lee	80%
Goldman, Shannon	92%
Bertram, Richard	57%
Average	79%

11. Set a print area for cells N3 through N22 and then print the cells.
12. Clear the print area.
13. Save and then close **EL1-C4-A2-CMTests.xlsx**.

Student Name

EL1-C4-A2-CMTests.xlsx

EL1-C4-A2-CMTests(A2,Step11).xlsx

9/18/2015 ← 6. Insert a header that prints the date at the left side of the page and the time at the right side of the page. → 3:50 PM

1. Open **HERInvoices.xlsx**.
2. Save the workbook with Save As and name it **EL1-C4-A3-HERInvoices**.
5d. Find all occurrences of 11-point Calibri and replace them with 10-point Cambria.
5e. After completing the find and replaces, clear all formatting from the Format buttons.
8. Print the worksheet horizontally and vertically centered on the page.

5c. Find all occurrences of *Barrier Concrete* and replace them with *Lee Sand and Gravel*.

3. Insert a formula in cell H3 that multiplies the rate in cell G3 by the hours in cell F3. Copy the formula in cell H3 down to cells H4 through H16.

Hilltop Equipment Rental

Invoice #	Equipment	Client	Service Rep	Date	Hours	Rate	Total
1199	Backhoe	Able Construction	Steele	5/7/2015	6	$90	$ 540
1200	Front Loader	Lakeside Trucking	Steele	5/7/2015	8	$65	$ 520
1201	Pressure Sprayer	Lee Sand and Gravel	Leuke	5/7/2015	4	$20	$ 80
1202	Backhoe	Country Electrical	Leuke	5/7/2015	12	$90	$ 1,080
1203	Tractor	Able Construction	Monahan	5/8/2015	4	$60	$ 240
1204	Scaffolding	Able Construction	Leuke	5/8/2015	16	$25	$ 400
1205	Backhoe	Lakeside Trucking	Monahan	5/8/2015	4	$90	$ 360
1206	Hydraulic Pump	Miles Contracting	Steele	5/9/2015	12	$20	$ 240
1207	Pressure Sprayer	Evergreen Painting	Leuke	5/9/2015	19	$20	$ 380
1208	Sandblaster	Lee Sand and Gravel	Steele	5/9/2015	2	$15	$ 30
1209	Pressure Sprayer	Lee Sand and Gravel	Steele	5/10/2015	6	$20	$ 120
1210	Front Loader	Cascade Enterprises	Leuke	5/10/2015	8	$65	$ 520
1211	Flatbed Truck	Cascade Enterprises	Monahan	5/11/2015	16	$60	$ 960
1212	Forklift	Allied Builders	Monahan	5/11/2015	4	$70	$ 280
						Total	$ 5,750

5. Complete the following find and replaces: a. Find all occurrences of cells containing *75* and replace them with *90*.

4. Insert a formula in cell H17 that sums the amounts in cells H3 through H16.

5b. Find all occurrences of cells containing *55* and replace them with *60*.

Student Name ← 7. Insert a footer that prints your name at the left side of the page and the workbook file name at the right side of the page. → EL1-C4-A3-HERInvoices.xlsx

EL1-C4-A3-HERInvoices(A3).xlsx

1. Open **RPInvoices.xlsx**.
2. Save the workbook with Save As and name it **EL1-C4-A4-RPInvoices**.
11. Center the worksheet horizontally and vertically on the page.
12. Display the worksheet in Normal view.
13. Save and then print **EL1-C4-A4-RPInvoices.xlsx**.

9. Complete a new sort that sorts by date in ascending order (oldest to newest).

7. Sort the records by invoice number in ascending order (smallest to largest).

5. Complete a spelling check on the worksheet.

3. Insert a formula in G4 that multiplies the amount in E4 with the percentage in F4 and then adds the product to cell E4. (If you write the formula correctly, the result in G4 will display as *$488.25*.)

Real Photography

Invoices

Invoice #	Client #	Service	Date	Amount	Tax	Amount Due
1230	10-788	Family Portraits	6/2/2015	$ 450.00	8.5%	$ 488.25
1438	11-279	Wedding Portraits	6/4/2015	$ 1,075.00	8.8%	$ 1,169.60
1129	11-279	Development	6/5/2015	$ 225.00	0.0%	$ 225.00
1326	04-325	Sports Portraits	6/8/2015	$ 750.00	8.5%	$ 813.75
1355	11-279	Development	6/8/2015	$ 350.00	0.0%	$ 350.00
1320	04-325	Sports Portraits	6/12/2015	$ 750.00	8.5%	$ 813.75
1270	04-789	Family Portraits	6/13/2015	$ 560.00	8.8%	$ 609.28
1345	05-335	Development	6/16/2015	$ 400.00	0.0%	$ 400.00
1233	10-455	Sports Portraits	6/19/2015	$ 600.00	8.5%	$ 651.00
1199	03-288	Development	6/20/2015	$ 95.00	0.0%	$ 95.00
1198	11-325	Wedding Portraits	6/20/2015	$ 875.00	8.5%	$ 949.38
1302	10-226	Wedding Portraits	6/23/2015	$ 2,250.00	8.5%	$ 2,441.25
1277	11-005	Business Portrait	6/23/2015	$ 225.00	8.8%	$ 244.80
1144	05-335	Development	6/25/2015	$ 140.00	0.0%	$ 140.00

8. Complete a new sort that sorts the records by client number in ascending order (A to Z).

5. Complete a spelling check on the worksheet.

6. Find all occurrences of *Picture* and replace them with *Portrait*. (Do not type a space after *Picture* or *Portrait* because you want to find occurrences that end with an *s*. Make sure the *Match entire cell contents* check box does not contain a check mark.)

4. Copy the formula in cell G4 down to cells G5 through G17, click the Auto Fill Options button, and then click the *Fill Without Formatting* option.

Student Name ← 10. Insert a footer in the worksheet that prints your name at the left side of the page and the current date at the right side of the page. → 9/18/2015

EL1-C4-A4-RPInvoices(A4,Step13).xlsx

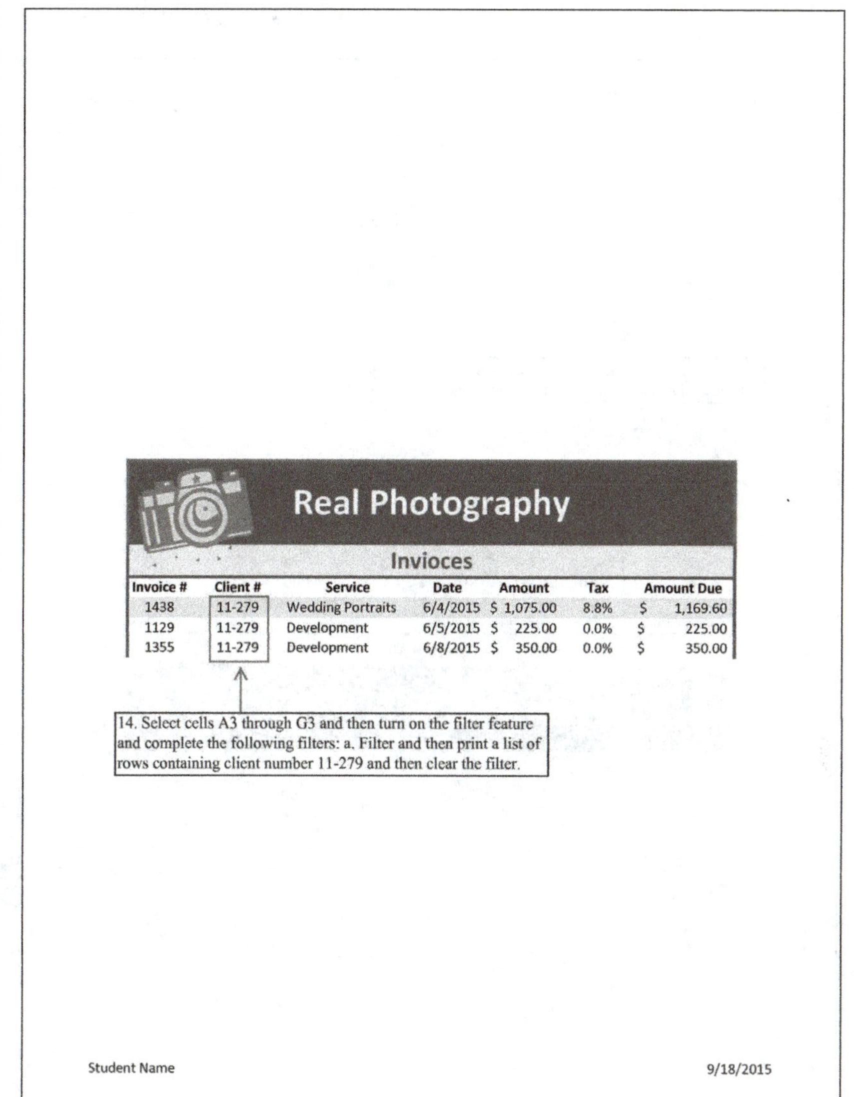

Real Photography

Invioces

Invoice #	Client #	Service	Date	Amount	Tax	Amount Due
1438	11-279	Wedding Portraits	6/4/2015	$ 1,075.00	8.8%	$ 1,169.60
1129	11-279	Development	6/5/2015	$ 225.00	0.0%	$ 225.00
1355	11-279	Development	6/8/2015	$ 350.00	0.0%	$ 350.00

14. Select cells A3 through G3 and then turn on the filter feature and complete the following filters: a. Filter and then print a list of rows containing client number 11-279 and then clear the filter.

Student Name 9/18/2015

EL1-C4-A4-RPInvoices(A4,Step14a).xlsx

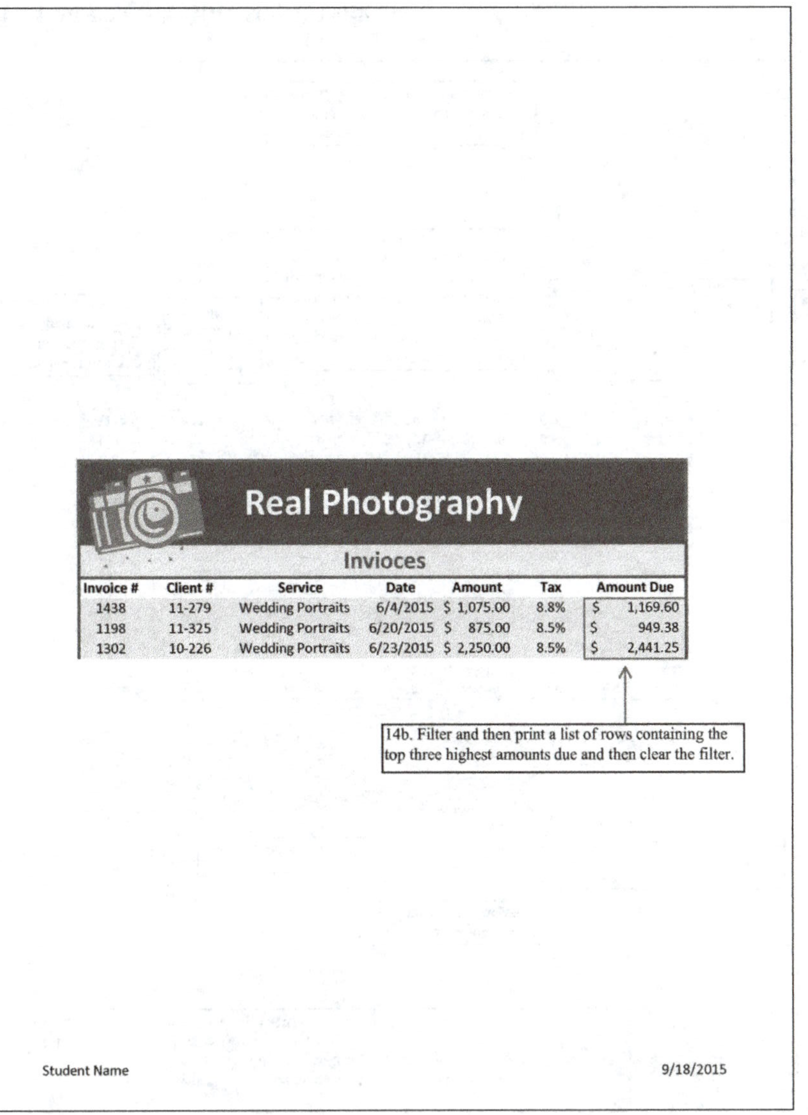

Real Photography

Invioces

Invoice #	Client #	Service	Date	Amount	Tax	Amount Due
1438	11-279	Wedding Portraits	6/4/2015	$ 1,075.00	8.8%	$ 1,169.60
1198	11-325	Wedding Portraits	6/20/2015	$ 875.00	8.5%	$ 949.38
1302	10-226	Wedding Portraits	6/23/2015	$ 2,250.00	8.5%	$ 2,441.25

14b. Filter and then print a list of rows containing the top three highest amounts due and then clear the filter.

Student Name

9/18/2015

EL1-C4-A4-RPInvoices(A4,Step14b).xlsx

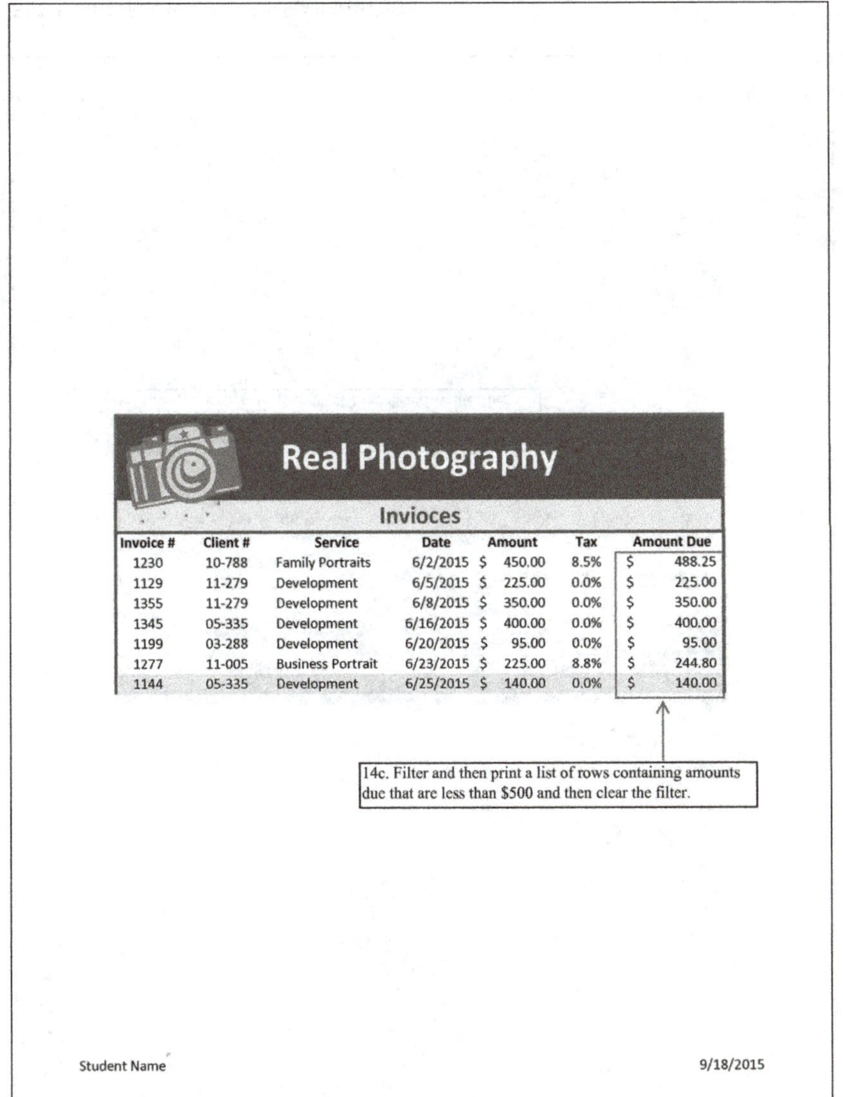

Real Photography

Invioces

Invoice #	Client #	Service	Date	Amount	Tax	Amount Due
1230	10-788	Family Portraits	6/2/2015	$ 450.00	8.5%	$ 488.25
1129	11-279	Development	6/5/2015	$ 225.00	0.0%	$ 225.00
1355	11-279	Development	6/8/2015	$ 350.00	0.0%	$ 350.00
1345	05-335	Development	6/16/2015	$ 400.00	0.0%	$ 400.00
1199	03-288	Development	6/20/2015	$ 95.00	0.0%	$ 95.00
1277	11-005	Business Portrait	6/23/2015	$ 225.00	8.8%	$ 244.80
1144	05-335	Development	6/25/2015	$ 140.00	0.0%	$ 140.00

14c. Filter and then print a list of rows containing amounts due that are less than $500 and then clear the filter.

Student Name

9/18/2015

EL1-C4-A4-RPInvoices(A4,Step14c).xlsx

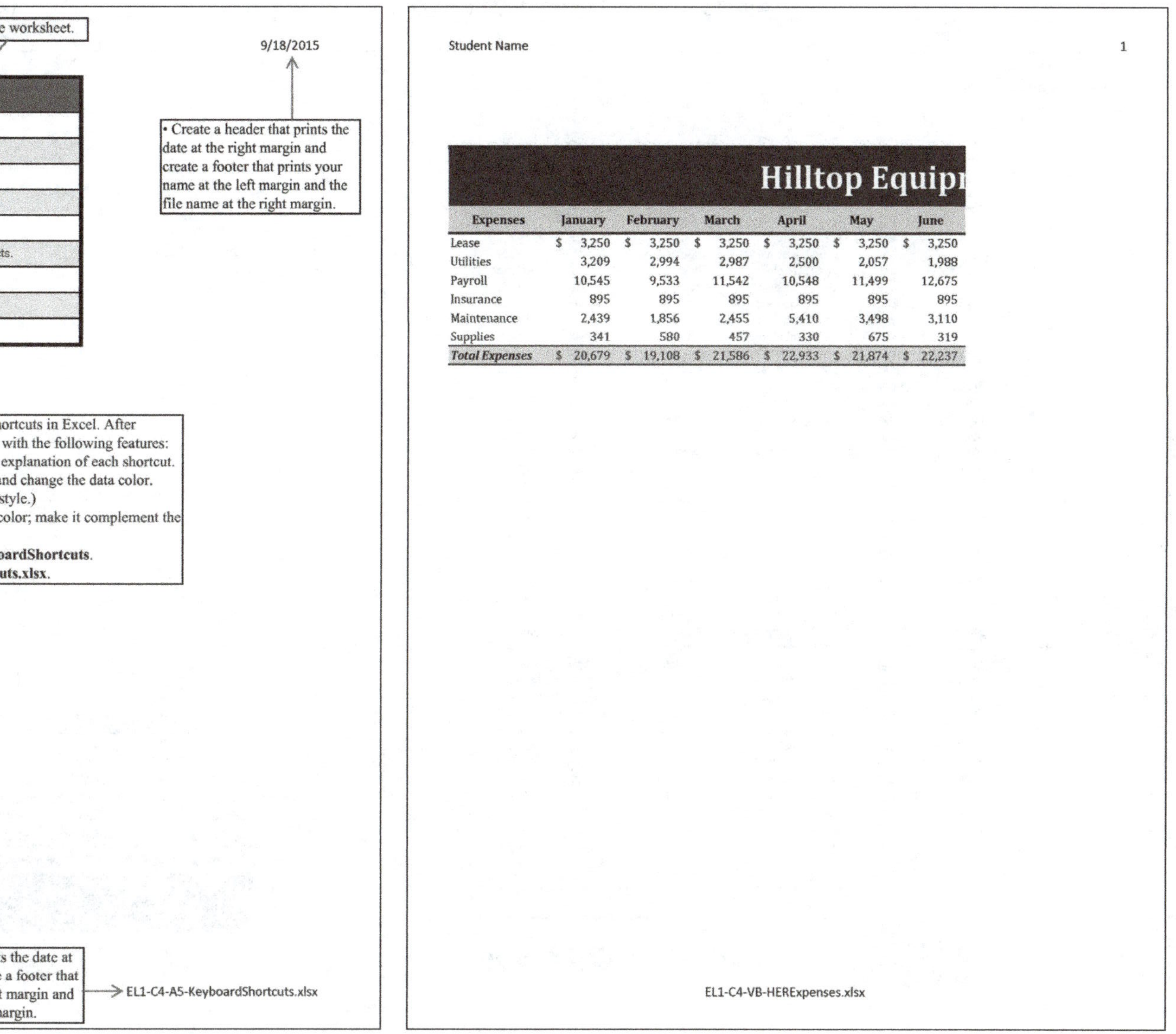

• Create a title for the worksheet.

9/18/2015

Excel Keyboard Shortcuts	
Ctrl+1	Displays the Format Cells dialog box.
Ctrl+2	Applies or removes bold formatting.
Ctrl+3	Applies or removes italic formatting.
Ctrl+4	Applies or removes underlining.
Ctrl+5	Applies or removes strikethrough.
Ctrl+6	Alternates between hiding and displaying objects.
Ctrl+8	Displays or hides the outline symbols.
Ctrl+9	Hides the selected rows.
Ctrl+0	Hides the selected columns.

• Create a header that prints the date at the right margin and create a footer that prints your name at the left margin and the file name at the right margin.

1. Use Excel's Help feature to learn about keyboard shortcuts in Excel. After reading the information presented, create a worksheet with the following features:
• Include at least 10 keyboard shortcuts along with an explanation of each shortcut.
• Set the data in cells in a typeface other than Calibri and change the data color.
• Add borders to the cells. (You determine the border style.)
• Add a color of shading to cells. (You determine the color; make it complement the data color.)
2. Save the workbook and name it **EL1-C4-A5-KeyboardShortcuts**.
3. Print and then close **EL1-C4-A5-KeyboardShortcuts.xlsx**.

Student Name • Create a header that prints the date at the right margin and create a footer that prints your name at the left margin and the file name at the right margin. EL1-C4-A5-KeyboardShortcuts.xlsx

EL1-C4-A5-KeyboardShortcuts(A5).xlsx

Student Name 1

Hilltop Equip

Expenses	January	February	March	April	May	June
Lease	$ 3,250	$ 3,250	$ 3,250	$ 3,250	$ 3,250	$ 3,250
Utilities	3,209	2,994	2,987	2,500	2,057	1,988
Payroll	10,545	9,533	11,542	10,548	11,499	12,675
Insurance	895	895	895	895	895	895
Maintenance	2,439	1,856	2,455	5,410	3,498	3,110
Supplies	341	580	457	330	675	319
Total Expenses	$ 20,679	$ 19,108	$ 21,586	$ 22,933	$ 21,874	$ 22,237

EL1-C4-VB-HERExpenses.xlsx

EL1-C4-VB-HERExpenses(VB).xlsx (1 of 2)

Student Name 2

nent Rental

Expenses	July	August	September	October	November	December	Total
Lease	$ 3,250	$ 3,250	$ 3,250	$ 3,250	$ 3,250	$ 3,250	$ 39,000
Utilities	1,845	1,555	1,890	2,451	2,899	3,005	29,380
Payroll	13,503	13,258	12,475	10,548	10,122	9,359	135,607
Insurance	895	895	895	895	895	895	10,740
Maintenance	2,479	3,100	1,870	6,105	4,220	3,544	40,086
Supplies	451	550	211	580	433	601	5,528
Total Expenses	$ 22,423	$ 22,608	$ 20,591	$ 23,829	$ 21,819	$ 20,654	$ 260,341

EL1-C4-VB-HERExpenses.xlsx

EL1-C4-VB-HERExpenses(VB).xlsx (2 of 2)

9/18/2015 4:12 PM

Macadam Realty

Mortgage Payments

Price of Home	Down Payment %	Down Pay-ment Amount	Loan Amount	Interest Rate	Term of Loan	Monthly Payment
650,000	5%	32,500	617,500	6%	360	3,702
650,000	10%	65,000	585,000	6%	360	3,507
650,000	15%	97,500	552,500	6%	360	3,313
650,000	20%	130,000	520,000	6%	360	3,118
600,000	5%	30,000	570,000	6%	360	3,417
600,000	10%	60,000	540,000	6%	360	3,238
600,000	15%	90,000	510,000	6%	360	3,058
600,000	20%	120,000	480,000	6%	360	2,878
550,000	5%	27,500	522,500	6%	360	3,133
550,000	10%	55,000	495,000	6%	360	2,968
550,000	15%	82,500	467,500	6%	360	2,803
550,000	20%	110,000	440,000	6%	360	2,638
500,000	5%	25,000	475,000	6%	360	2,848
500,000	10%	50,000	450,000	6%	360	2,698
500,000	15%	75,000	425,000	6%	360	2,548
500,000	20%	100,000	400,000	6%	360	2,398
450,000	5%	22,500	427,500	6%	360	2,563
450,000	10%	45,000	405,000	6%	360	2,428
450,000	15%	67,500	382,500	6%	360	2,293
450,000	20%	90,000	360,000	6%	360	2,158
400,000	5%	20,000	380,000	6%	360	2,278
400,000	10%	40,000	360,000	6%	360	2,158
400,000	15%	60,000	340,000	6%	360	2,038
400,000	20%	80,000	320,000	6%	360	1,919
350,000	5%	17,500	332,500	6%	360	1,994
350,000	10%	35,000	315,000	6%	360	1,889
350,000	15%	52,500	297,500	6%	360	1,784
350,000	20%	70,000	280,000	6%	360	1,679
300,000	5%	15,000	285,000	6%	360	1,709
300,000	10%	30,000	270,000	6%	360	1,619
300,000	15%	45,000	255,000	6%	360	1,529
300,000	20%	60,000	240,000	6%	360	1,439
250,000	5%	12,500	237,500	6%	360	1,424
250,000	10%	25,000	225,000	6%	360	1,349
250,000	15%	37,500	212,500	6%	360	1,274
250,000	20%	50,000	200,000	6%	360	1,199
200,000	5%	10,000	190,000	6%	360	1,139
200,000	10%	20,000	180,000	6%	360	1,079
200,000	15%	30,000	170,000	6%	360	1,019
200,000	20%	40,000	160,000	6%	360	959
150,000	5%	7,500	142,500	6%	360	854
150,000	10%	15,000	135,000	6%	360	809
150,000	15%	22,500	127,500	6%	360	764
150,000	20%	30,000	120,000	6%	360	719

Student Name EL1-C4-CS-MRMortgages-01.xlsx

EL1-C4-CS-MRMortgages-01(CS1).xlsx

9/18/2015 4:13 PM

Macadam Realty

Mortgage Payments

Price of Home	Down Payment %	Down Payment Amount	Loan Amount	Interest Rate	Term of Loan	Monthly Payment
$ 150,000	5%	$ 7,500	$ 142,500	7%	360	$ 948
150,000	10%	15,000	135,000	7%	360	898
150,000	15%	22,500	127,500	7%	360	848
150,000	20%	30,000	120,000	7%	360	798
200,000	5%	10,000	190,000	7%	360	1,264
200,000	10%	20,000	180,000	7%	360	1,198
200,000	15%	30,000	170,000	7%	360	1,131
200,000	20%	40,000	160,000	7%	360	1,064
250,000	5%	12,500	237,500	7%	360	1,580
250,000	10%	25,000	225,000	7%	360	1,497
250,000	15%	37,500	212,500	7%	360	1,414
250,000	20%	50,000	200,000	7%	360	1,331
300,000	5%	15,000	285,000	7%	360	1,896
300,000	10%	30,000	270,000	7%	360	1,796
300,000	15%	45,000	255,000	7%	360	1,697
300,000	20%	60,000	240,000	7%	360	1,597
350,000	5%	17,500	332,500	7%	360	2,212
350,000	10%	35,000	315,000	7%	360	2,096
350,000	15%	52,500	297,500	7%	360	1,979
350,000	20%	70,000	280,000	7%	360	1,863
400,000	5%	20,000	380,000	7%	360	2,528
400,000	10%	40,000	360,000	7%	360	2,395
400,000	15%	60,000	340,000	7%	360	2,262
400,000	20%	80,000	320,000	7%	360	2,129
450,000	5%	22,500	427,500	7%	360	2,844
450,000	10%	45,000	405,000	7%	360	2,694
450,000	15%	67,500	382,500	7%	360	2,545
450,000	20%	90,000	360,000	7%	360	2,395
500,000	5%	25,000	475,000	7%	360	3,160
500,000	10%	50,000	450,000	7%	360	2,994
500,000	15%	75,000	425,000	7%	360	2,828
500,000	20%	100,000	400,000	7%	360	2,661
550,000	5%	27,500	522,500	7%	360	3,476
550,000	10%	55,000	495,000	7%	360	3,293
550,000	15%	82,500	467,500	7%	360	3,110
550,000	20%	110,000	440,000	7%	360	2,927
600,000	5%	30,000	570,000	7%	360	3,792
600,000	10%	60,000	540,000	7%	360	3,593
600,000	15%	90,000	510,000	7%	360	3,393
600,000	20%	120,000	480,000	7%	360	3,193
650,000	5%	32,500	617,500	7%	360	4,108
650,000	10%	65,000	585,000	7%	360	3,892
650,000	15%	97,500	552,500	7%	360	3,676
650,000	20%	130,000	520,000	7%	360	3,460

Student Name EL1-C4-CS-MRMortgages-02.xlsx

EL1-C4-CS-MRMortgages-02(CS1).xlsx

1

Maca

2015 Total

	January	February	March	April	May
Lassiter Office					
Sales	$ 1,245,350	$ 957,320	$ 1,453,290	$ 1,735,430	$ 1,643,209
Commissions	$ 112,080	$ 68,525	$ 123,409	$ 158,304	$ 143,248
Prescott Office					
Sales	$ 1,938,432	$ 1,743,096	$ 2,038,342	$ 2,123,945	$ 2,413,048
Commissions	$ 134,230	$ 129,428	$ 141,438	$ 148,430	$ 160,349
Alder Office					
Sales	$ 2,049,390	$ 1,930,291	$ 2,459,309	$ 2,540,590	$ 3,002,938
Commissions	$ 140,005	$ 131,365	$ 162,135	$ 175,430	$ 200,529
Total Sales:	$ 5,233,172	$ 4,630,707	$ 5,950,941	$ 6,399,965	$ 7,059,195
Total Commissions:	$ 386,315	$ 329,318	$ 426,982	$ 482,164	$ 504,126

Student Name

EL1-C4-CS-MRSalesComms(CS2,FirstPrint).jpg (1 of 3)

2

ıdam Realty

Sales and Commissions

	June	July	August	September	October
Lassiter Office					
Sales	$ 1,323,042	$ 1,530,294	$ 1,320,494	$ 1,230,493	$ 1,130,493
Commissions	$ 121,490	$ 127,439	$ 115,342	$ 111,421	$ 100,544
Prescott Office					
Sales	$ 2,139,201	$ 2,034,392	$ 2,212,039	$ 1,937,483	$ 2,234,290
Commissions	$ 150,230	$ 139,438	$ 159,009	$ 133,200	$ 161,328
Alder Office					
Sales	$ 2,930,938	$ 3,093,029	$ 2,879,928	$ 2,708,489	$ 2,630,498
Commissions	$ 195,438	$ 202,545	$ 189,355	$ 182,458	$ 179,511
Total Sales:	$ 6,393,181	$ 6,657,715	$ 6,412,461	$ 5,876,465	$ 5,995,281
Total Commissions:	$ 467,158	$ 469,422	$ 463,706	$ 427,079	$ 441,383

Student Name

EL1-C4-CS-MRSalesComms(CS2,FirstPrint).jpg (2 of 3)

3

	November	December	Total
Lassiter Office			
Sales	$ 1,094,832	$ 967,349	**$ 15,631,596**
Commissions	$ 104,328	$ 88,422	**$ 1,374,552**
Prescott Office			
Sales	$ 1,839,029	$ 1,738,902	**$ 24,392,199**
Commissions	$ 129,432	$ 153,299	**$ 1,739,811**
Alder Office			
Sales	$ 2,455,409	$ 2,203,948	**$ 30,884,757**
Commissions	$ 160,590	$ 138,946	**$ 2,058,307**
Total Sales:	$ 5,389,270	$ 4,910,199	**$ 70,908,552**
Total Commissions:	$ 394,350	$ 380,667	**$ 5,172,670**

Student Name

EL1-C4-CS-MRSalesComms(CS2,FirstPrint).jpg (3 of 3)

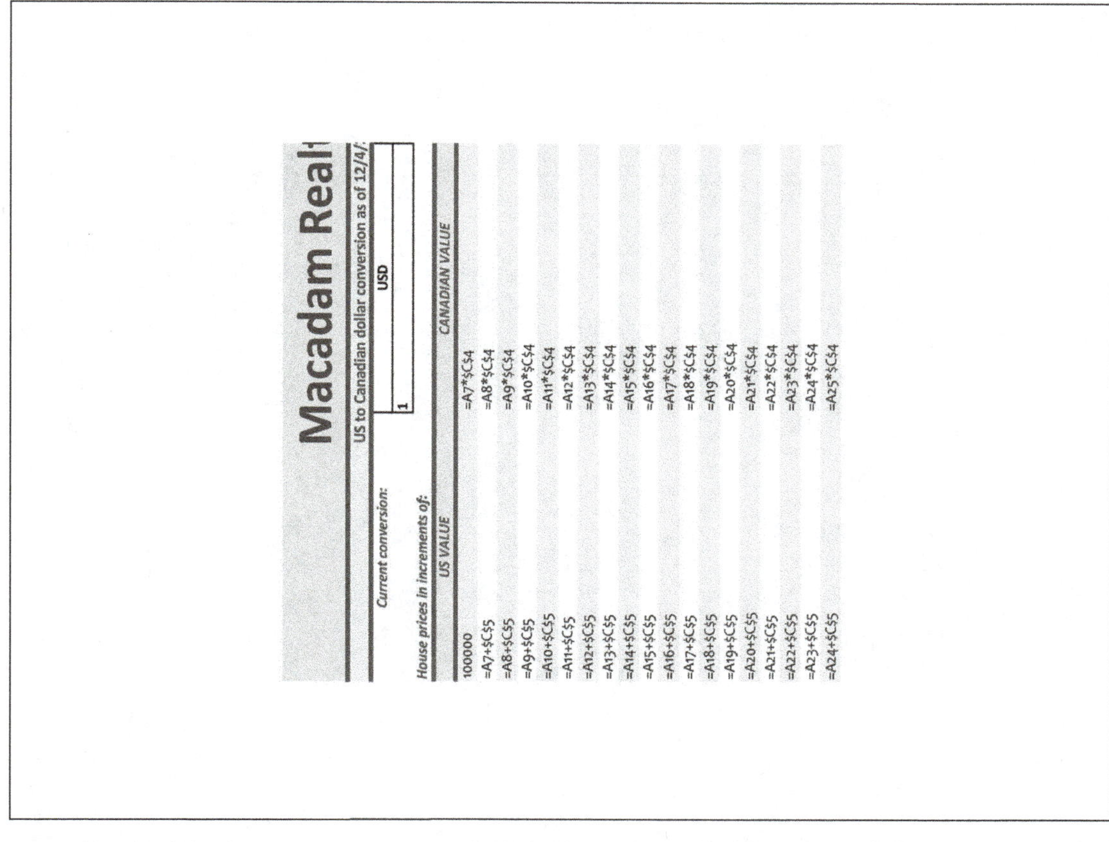

Macadam Realt

US to Canadian dollar conversion as of 12/4/

Current conversion:	1	USD

House prices in increments of:

US VALUE	CANADIAN VALUE
100000	=A7*$C$4
=A7+$C$5	=A8*$C$4
=A8+$C$5	=A9*$C$4
=A9+$C$5	=A10*$C$4
=A10+$C$5	=A11*$C$4
=A11+$C$5	=A12*$C$4
=A12+$C$5	=A13*$C$4
=A13+$C$5	=A14*$C$4
=A14+$C$5	=A15*$C$4
=A15+$C$5	=A16*$C$4
=A16+$C$5	=A17*$C$4
=A17+$C$5	=A18*$C$4
=A18+$C$5	=A19*$C$4
=A19+$C$5	=A20*$C$4
=A20+$C$5	=A21*$C$4
=A21+$C$5	=A22*$C$4
=A22+$C$5	=A23*$C$4
=A23+$C$5	=A24*$C$4
=A24+$C$5	=A25*$C$4

EL1-C4-CS-CanadaPrices(CS3).xlsx (1 of 2)

Macadam Realty

2015 Total Sales and Commissions

	January	February	March	April	May	June	July	August	September	October	November	December	Total
Lassiter Office													
Sales	$ 1,245,350	$ 957,320	$ 1,453,290	$ 1,735,430	$ 1,643,209	$ 1,323,042	$ 1,530,294	$ 1,320,494	$ 1,230,493	$ 1,130,493	$ 1,094,832	$ 967,349	$ 15,631,596
Commissions	$ 112,080	$ 68,525	$ 123,409	$ 158,304	$ 143,248	$ 121,490	$ 127,439	$ 115,342	$ 111,421	$ 100,544	$ 104,328	$ 88,422	$ 1,374,552
Prescott Office													
Sales	$ 1,938,432	$ 1,743,096	$ 2,038,342	$ 2,123,945	$ 2,413,048	$ 2,139,201	$ 2,034,392	$ 2,212,039	$ 1,937,483	$ 2,234,290	$ 1,839,029	$ 1,738,902	$ 24,392,199
Commissions	$ 134,230	$ 129,428	$ 141,438	$ 148,430	$ 160,349	$ 150,230	$ 139,438	$ 159,009	$ 133,200	$ 161,328	$ 129,432	$ 153,299	$ 1,739,811
Alder Office													
Sales	$ 2,049,390	$ 1,930,291	$ 2,459,309	$ 2,540,590	$ 3,002,938	$ 2,930,938	$ 3,093,029	$ 2,879,928	$ 2,708,489	$ 2,630,498	$ 2,455,409	$ 2,203,948	$ 30,884,757
Commissions	$ 140,005	$ 131,365	$ 162,135	$ 175,430	$ 200,529	$ 195,438	$ 202,545	$ 189,355	$ 182,458	$ 179,511	$ 160,590	$ 138,946	$ 2,058,307
Total Sales:	$ 5,233,172	$ 4,630,707	$ 5,950,941	$ 6,399,965	$ 7,059,195	$ 6,393,181	$ 6,657,715	$ 6,412,461	$ 5,876,465	$ 5,995,281	$ 5,389,270	$ 4,910,199	$ 70,908,552
Total Commissions:	$ 386,315	$ 329,318	$ 426,982	$ 482,164	$ 504,126	$ 467,158	$ 469,422	$ 463,706	$ 427,079	$ 441,383	$ 394,350	$ 380,667	$ 5,172,670

9/18/2015

Student Name

EL1-C4-CS-MRSalesComms(CS2,SecondPrint).xlsx

ty

2012
CAD
0.993283
50000
Difference
=A7-B7
=A8-B8
=A9-B9
=A10-B10
=A11-B11
=A12-B12
=A13-B13
=A14-B14
=A15-B15
=A16-B16
=A17-B17
=A18-B18
=A19-B19
=A20-B20
=A21-B21
=A22-B22
=A23-B23
=A24-B24
=A25-B25

EL1-C4-CS-CanadaPrices(CS3).xlsx (2 of 2)

Excel Level 1, Performance Assessment Unit 1 Model Answers

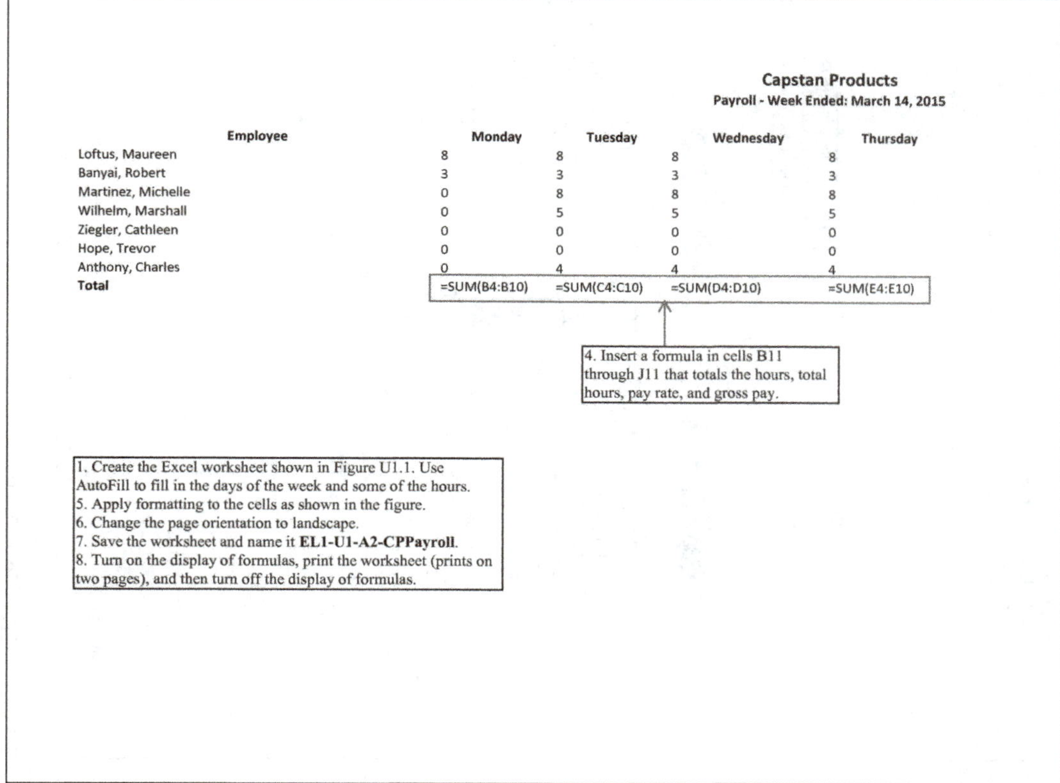

Capstan Products
Payroll - Week Ended: March 14, 2015

Employee	Monday	Tuesday	Wednesday	Thursday
Loftus, Maureen	8	8	8	8
Banyai, Robert	3	3	3	3
Martinez, Michelle	0	8	8	8
Wilhelm, Marshall	0	5	5	5
Ziegler, Cathleen	0	0	0	0
Hope, Trevor	0	0	0	0
Anthony, Charles	0	4	4	4
Total	=SUM(B4:B10)	=SUM(C4:C10)	=SUM(D4:D10)	=SUM(E4:E10)

4. Insert a formula in cells B11 through J11 that totals the hours, total hours, pay rate, and gross pay.

1. Create the Excel worksheet shown in Figure U1.1. Use AutoFill to fill in the days of the week and some of the hours.
5. Apply formatting to the cells as shown in the figure.
6. Change the page orientation to landscape.
7. Save the worksheet and name it **EL1-U1-A2-CPPayroll**.
8. Turn on the display of formulas, print the worksheet (prints on two pages), and then turn off the display of formulas.

EL1-U1-A2-CPPayroll(A2,Step8).xlsx (1 of 2)

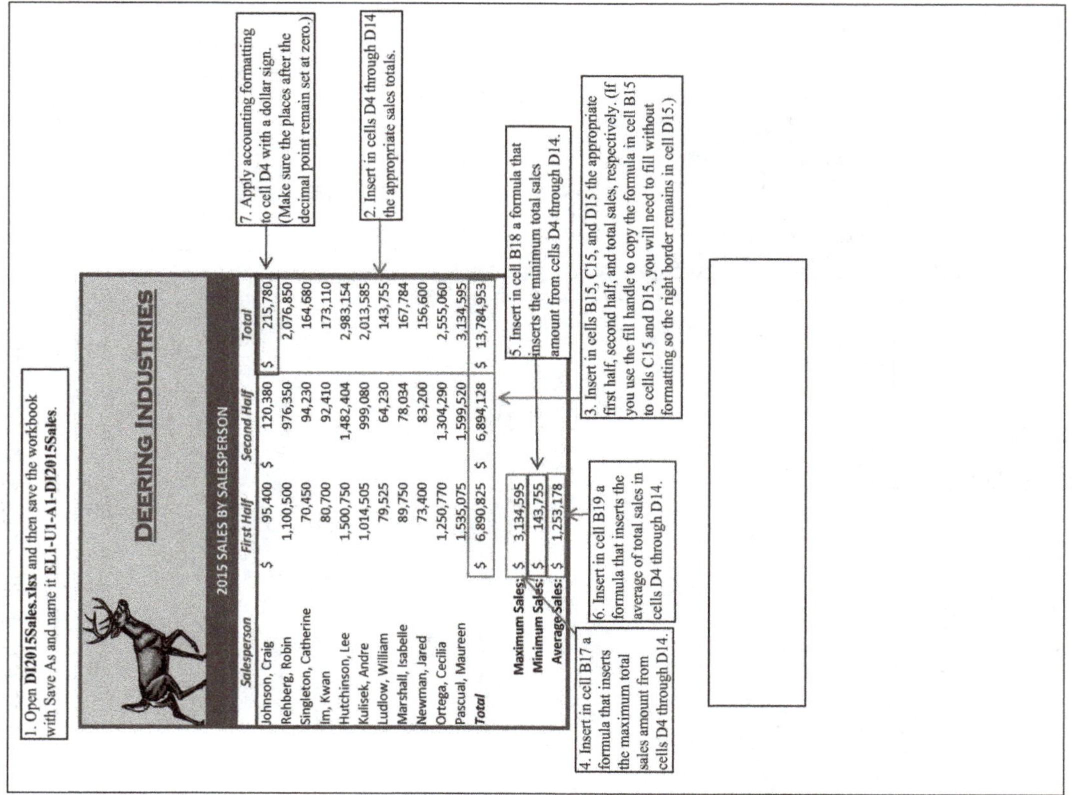

1. Open **DI2015Sales.xlsx** and then save the workbook with Save As and name it **EL1-U1-A1-DI2015Sales**.

DEERING INDUSTRIES

2015 SALES BY SALESPERSON

Salesperson	First Half	Second Half	Total
Johnson, Craig	$ 95,400	$ 120,380	$ 215,780
Rehberg, Robin	1,100,500	976,350	2,076,850
Singleton, Catherine	70,450	94,230	164,680
Im, Kwan	80,700	92,410	173,110
Hutchinson, Lee	1,500,750	1,482,404	2,983,154
Kulisek, Andre	1,014,505	999,080	2,013,585
Ludlow, William	79,525	64,230	143,755
Marshall, Isabelle	89,750	78,034	167,784
Newman, Jared	73,400	83,200	156,600
Ortega, Cecilia	1,250,770	1,304,290	2,555,060
Pascual, Maureen	1,535,075	1,599,520	3,134,595
Total	$ 6,890,825	$ 6,894,128	$ 13,784,953

Maximum Sales:	$ 3,134,595
Minimum Sales:	$ 143,755
Average Sales:	$ 1,253,178

7. Apply accounting formatting to cell D4 with a dollar sign. (Make sure the places after the decimal point remain set at zero.)

2. Insert in cells D4 through D14 the appropriate sales totals.

5. Insert in cell B18 a formula that inserts the minimum total sales amount from cells D4 through D14.

3. Insert in cells B15, C15, and D15 the appropriate first half, second half, and total sales, respectively. (If you use the fill handle to copy the formula in cell B15 to cells C15 and D15, you will need to fill without formatting so the right border remains in cell D15.)

4. Insert in cell B17 a formula that inserts the maximum total sales amount from cells D4 through D14.

6. Insert in cell B19 a formula that inserts the average of total sales in cells D4 through D14.

EL1-U1-A1-DI2015Sales(A1).xlsx

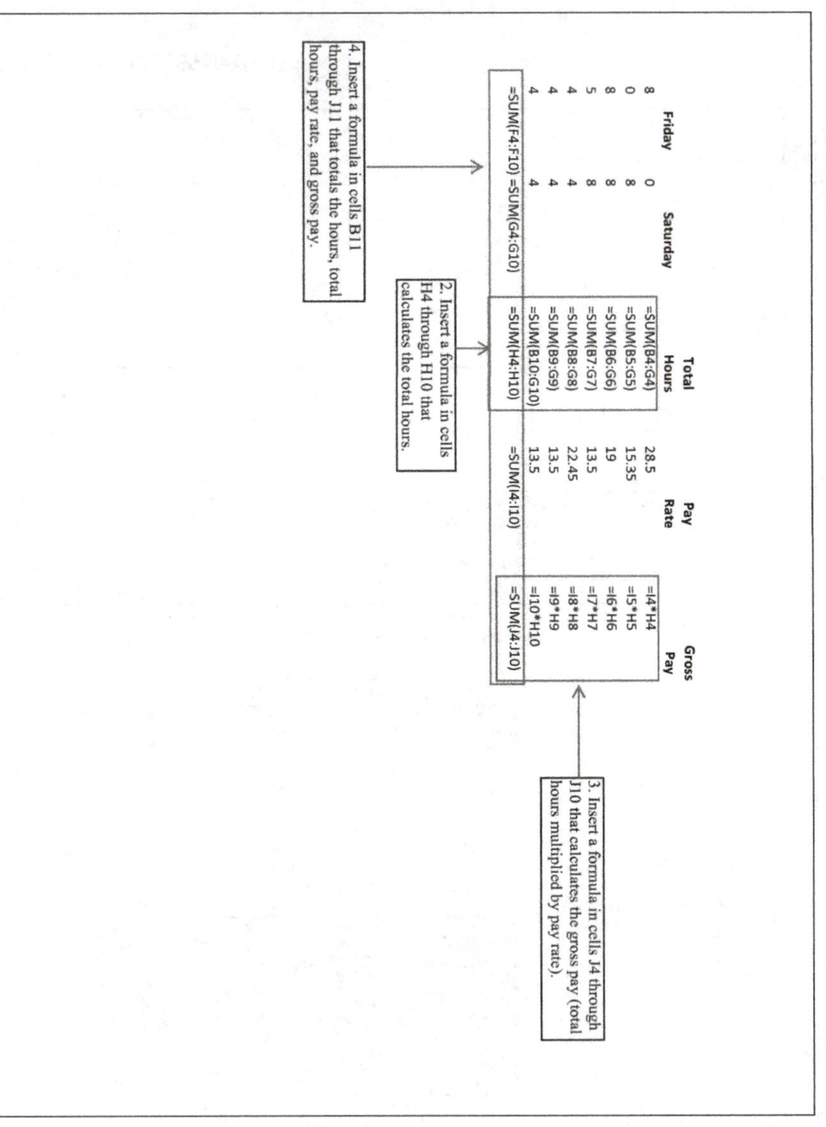

Friday	Saturday	Total Hours	Pay Rate	Gross Pay
8	0	=SUM(B4:G4)	28.5	=I4*H4
0	8	=SUM(B5:G5)	15.35	=I5*H5
8	8	=SUM(B6:G6)	19	=I6*H6
5	8	=SUM(B7:G7)	13.5	=I7*H7
4	4	=SUM(B8:G8)	22.45	=I8*H8
4	4	=SUM(B9:G9)	13.5	=I9*H9
4	4	=SUM(B10:G10)	13.5	=I10*H10
=SUM(F4:F10)	=SUM(G4:G10)	=SUM(H4:H10)	=SUM(I4:I10)	=SUM(J4:J10)

EL1-U1-A2-CPPayroll(A2,Step8).xlsx (2 of 2)

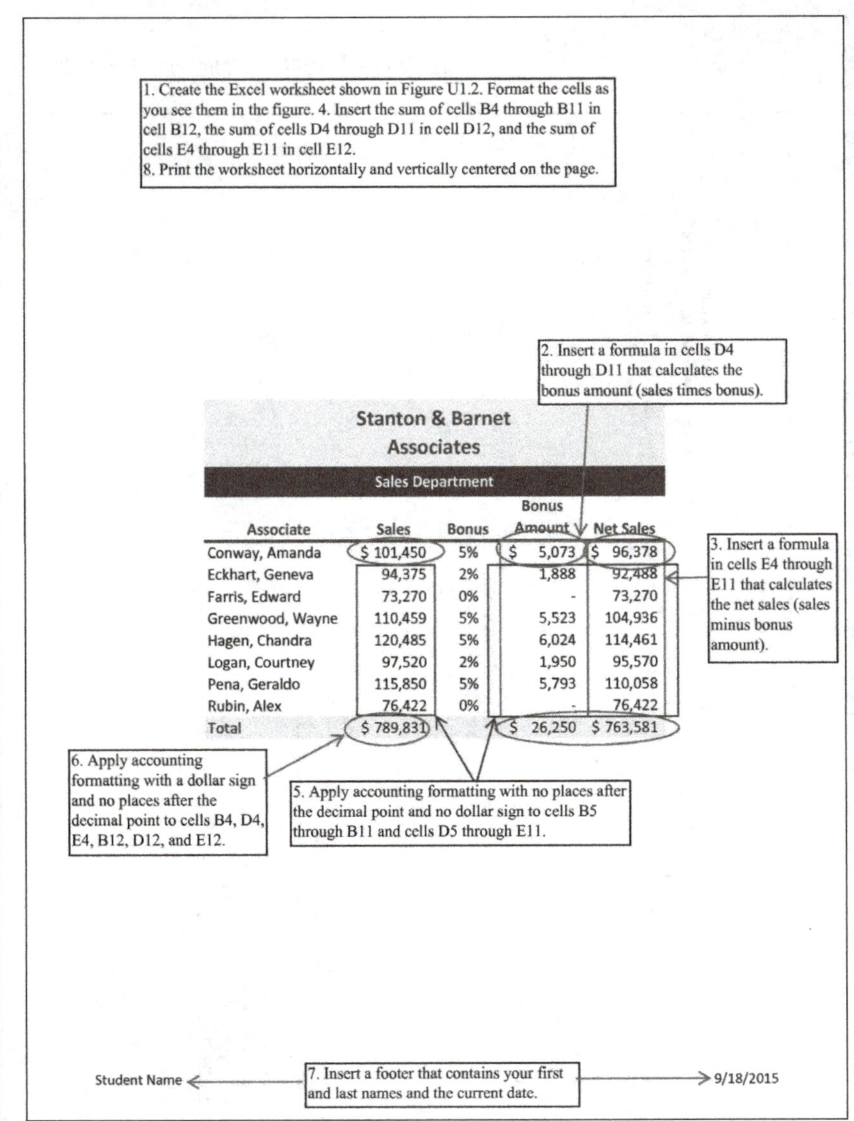

Stanton & Barnet Associates

Sales Department

Associate	Sales	Bonus	Bonus Amount	Net Sales
Conway, Amanda	$ 101,450	5%	$ 5,073	$ 96,378
Eckhart, Geneva	94,375	2%	1,888	92,488
Farris, Edward	73,270	0%	-	73,270
Greenwood, Wayne	110,459	5%	5,523	104,936
Hagen, Chandra	120,485	5%	6,024	114,461
Logan, Courtney	97,520	2%	1,950	95,570
Pena, Geraldo	115,850	5%	5,793	110,058
Rubin, Alex	76,422	0%	-	76,422
Total	$ 789,831		$ 26,250	$ 763,581

EL1-U1-A3-SBASales(A3).xlsx

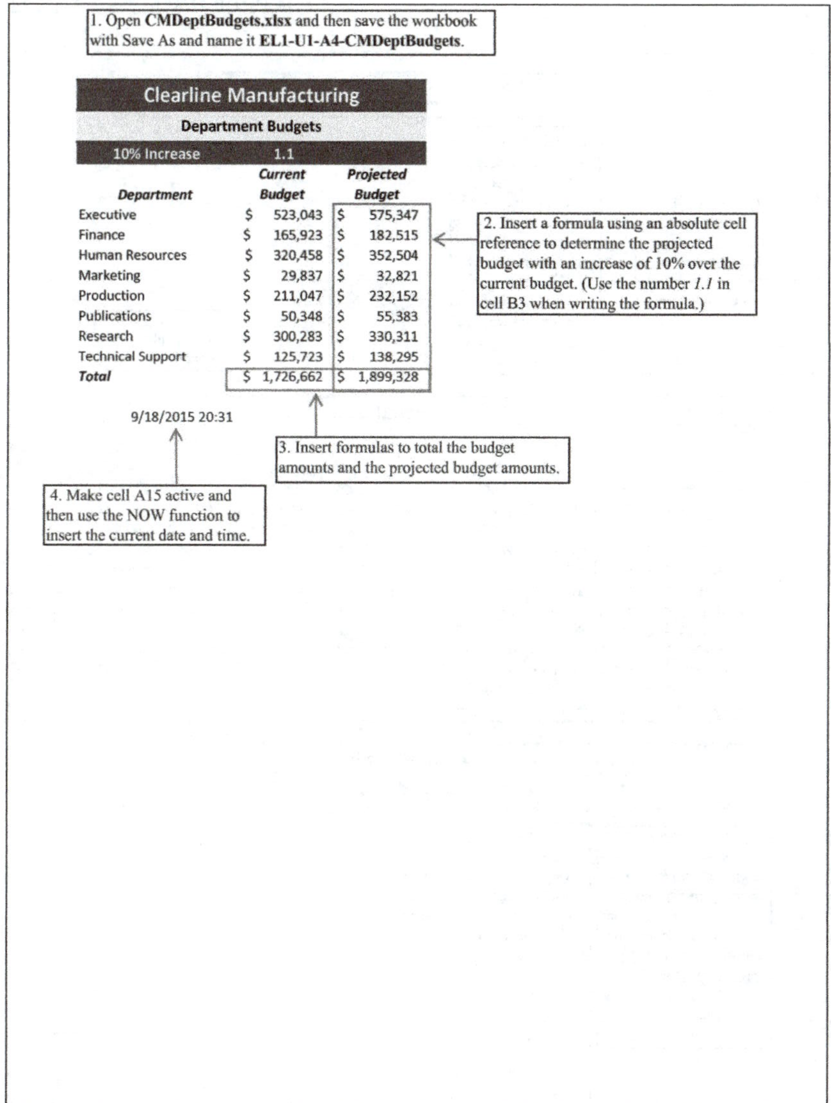

Clearline Manufacturing		
Department Budgets		
10% Increase	1.1	
Department	Current Budget	Projected Budget
Executive	$ 523,043	$ 575,347
Finance	$ 165,923	$ 182,515
Human Resources	$ 320,458	$ 352,504
Marketing	$ 29,837	$ 32,821
Production	$ 211,047	$ 232,152
Publications	$ 50,348	$ 55,383
Research	$ 300,283	$ 330,311
Technical Support	$ 125,723	$ 138,295
Total	$ 1,726,662	$ 1,899,328

EL1-U1-A4-CMDeptBudgets(A4,Step5).xlsx

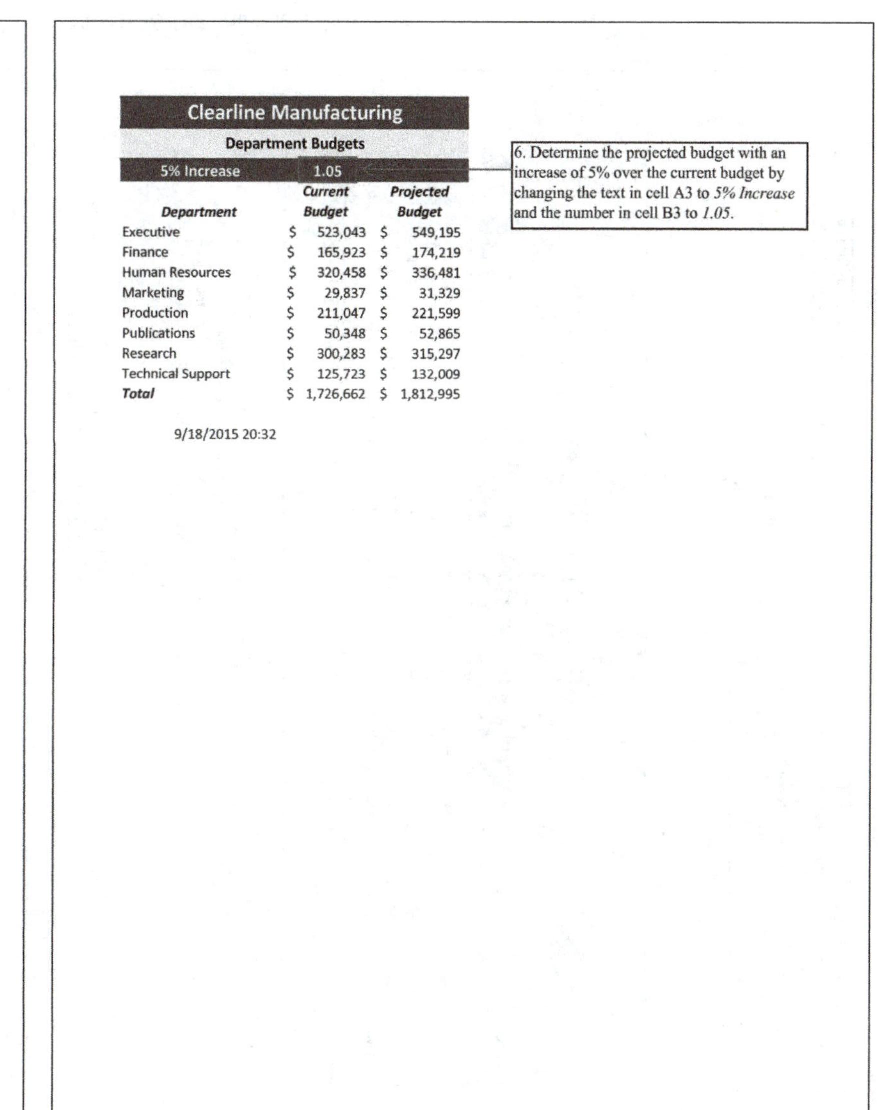

Clearline Manufacturing		
Department Budgets		
5% Increase	1.05	
Department	Current Budget	Projected Budget
Executive	$ 523,043	$ 549,195
Finance	$ 165,923	$ 174,219
Human Resources	$ 320,458	$ 336,481
Marketing	$ 29,837	$ 31,329
Production	$ 211,047	$ 221,599
Publications	$ 50,348	$ 52,865
Research	$ 300,283	$ 315,297
Technical Support	$ 125,723	$ 132,009
Total	$ 1,726,662	$ 1,812,995

EL1-U1-A4-CMDeptBudgets(A4,Step7).xlsx

1. Open **DIAnnualSales.xlsx** and then save the workbook with Save As and name it **EL1-U1-A6-DIAnnualSales**.
4. Change the orientation to landscape.
7. Horizontally and vertically center the worksheet on the page.
8. Specify that the column headings in cells A3 through A12 print on both pages.

5. Insert a header that prints the page number at the right side of the page. → 1

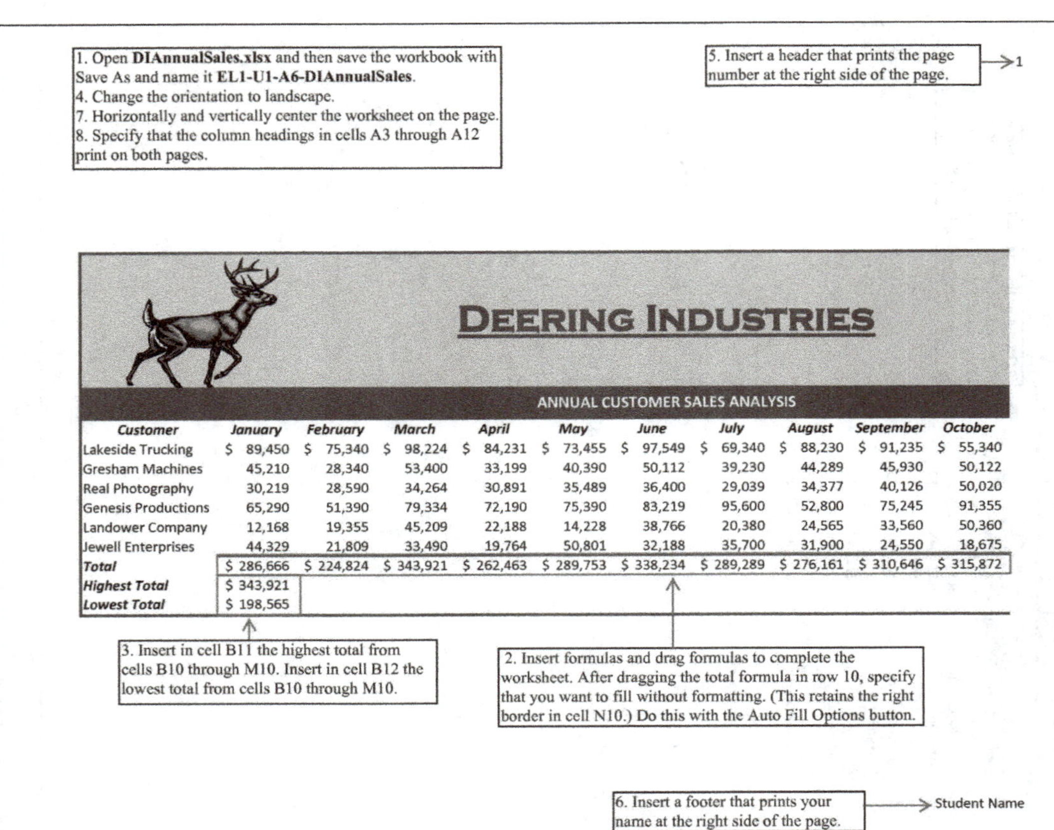

DEERING INDUSTRIES

ANNUAL CUSTOMER SALES ANALYSIS

Customer	January	February	March	April	May	June	July	August	September	October
Lakeside Trucking	$ 89,450	$ 75,340	$ 98,224	$ 84,231	$ 73,455	$ 97,549	$ 69,340	$ 88,230	$ 91,235	$ 55,340
Gresham Machines	45,210	28,340	53,400	33,199	40,390	50,112	39,230	44,289	45,930	50,122
Real Photography	30,219	28,590	34,264	30,891	35,489	36,400	29,039	34,377	40,126	50,020
Genesis Productions	65,290	51,390	79,334	72,190	75,390	83,219	95,600	52,800	75,245	91,355
Landower Company	12,168	19,355	45,209	22,188	14,228	38,766	20,380	24,565	33,560	50,360
Jewell Enterprises	44,329	21,809	33,490	19,764	50,801	32,188	35,700	31,900	24,550	18,675
Total	$ 286,666	$ 224,824	$ 343,921	$ 262,463	$ 289,753	$ 338,234	$ 289,289	$ 276,161	$ 310,646	$ 315,872
Highest Total	$ 343,921									
Lowest Total	$ 198,565									

3. Insert in cell B11 the highest total from cells B10 through M10. Insert in cell B12 the lowest total from cells B10 through M10.

2. Insert formulas and drag formulas to complete the worksheet. After dragging the total formula in row 10, specify that you want to fill without formatting. (This retains the right border in cell N10.) Do this with the Auto Fill Options button.

6. Insert a footer that prints your name at the right side of the page. → Student Name

EL1-U1-A6-DIAnnualSales(A6).xlsx (1 of 2)

1. Open **CCPayroll.xlsx** and then save the workbook with Save As and name it **EL1-U1-A5-CCPayroll.**
7. Center the worksheet horizontally and vertically on the page.

2. Insert a formula in cell E3 that multiplies the hourly rate by the hours and then adds that to the multiplication of the hourly rate by the overtime pay rate (1.5) and then overtime hours. (Use parentheses in the formula and use an absolute cell reference for the overtime pay rate. Refer to Chapter 2, Project 3c.) Copy the formula down to cells E4 through E16.

3. Insert a formula in cell F3 that multiplies the gross pay by the withholding tax rate (W/H Rate). (Use an absolute cell reference for the cell containing the withholding rate. Refer to Chapter 2, Project 3c.) Copy the formula down to cells F4 through F16.

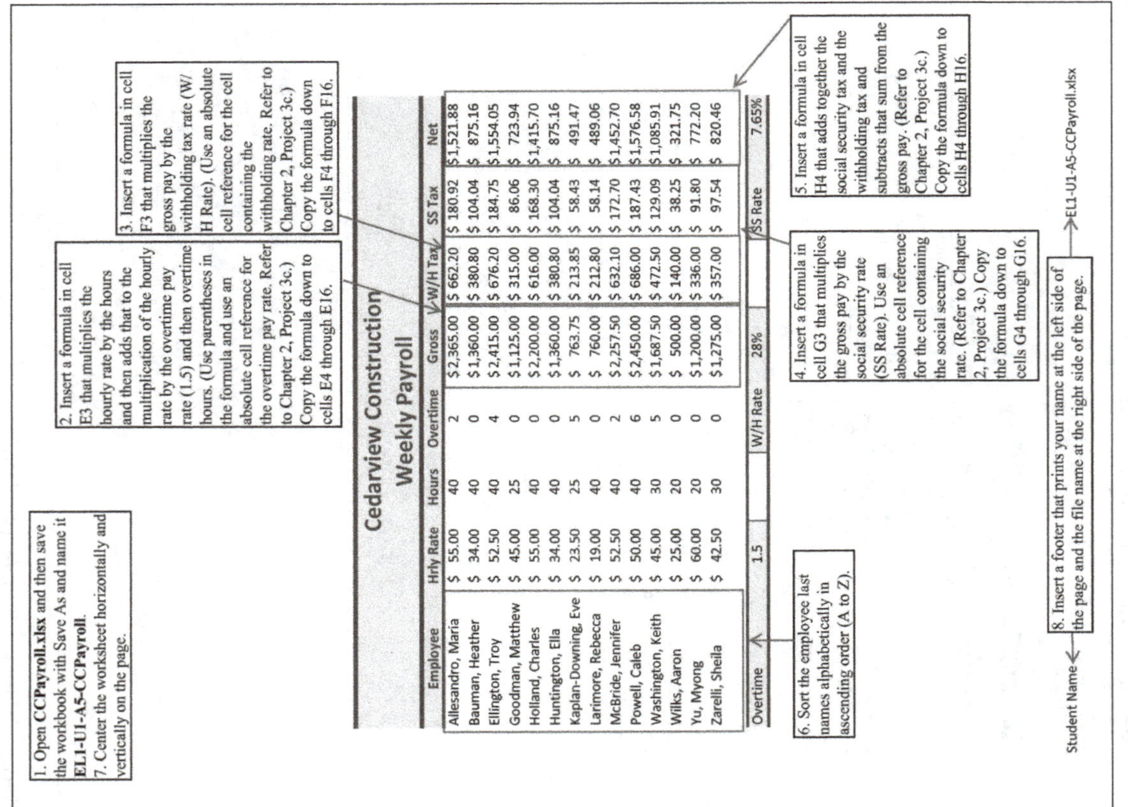

Cedarview Construction
Weekly Payroll

Employee	Hrly Rate	Hours	Overtime	Gross	W/H Tax	SS Tax	Net
Allesandro, Maria	$ 55.00	40	2	$2,365.00	$ 662.20	$ 180.92	$1,521.88
Bauman, Heather	$ 34.00	40	0	$1,360.00	$ 380.80	$ 104.04	$ 875.16
Ellington, Troy	$ 52.50	40	4	$2,415.00	$ 676.20	$ 184.75	$1,554.05
Goodman, Matthew	$ 45.00	25	0	$1,125.00	$ 315.00	$ 86.06	$ 723.94
Holland, Charles	$ 55.00	40	0	$2,200.00	$ 616.00	$ 168.30	$1,415.70
Huntington, Ella	$ 34.00	40	0	$1,360.00	$ 380.80	$ 104.04	$ 875.16
Kaplan-Downing, Eve	$ 23.50	25	5	$ 763.75	$ 213.85	$ 58.43	$ 491.47
Larimore, Rebecca	$ 19.00	40	0	$ 760.00	$ 212.80	$ 58.14	$ 489.06
McBride, Jennifer	$ 52.50	40	2	$2,257.50	$ 632.10	$ 172.70	$1,452.70
Powell, Caleb	$ 50.00	40	6	$2,450.00	$ 686.00	$ 187.43	$1,576.58
Washington, Keith	$ 45.00	30	5	$1,687.50	$ 472.50	$ 129.09	$1,085.91
Wilks, Aaron	$ 25.00	20	0	$ 500.00	$ 140.00	$ 38.25	$ 321.75
Yu, Myong	$ 60.00	20	0	$1,200.00	$ 336.00	$ 91.80	$ 772.20
Zarelli, Sheila	$ 42.50	30	0	$1,275.00	$ 357.00	$ 97.54	$ 820.46
Overtime	1.5		W/H Rate	28%		SS Rate	7.65%

5. Insert a formula in cell H4 that adds together the social security tax and the withholding tax and subtracts that sum from the gross pay. (Refer to Chapter 2, Project 3c.) Copy the formula down to cells H4 through H16.

4. Insert a formula in cell G3 that multiplies the gross pay by the social security rate (SS Rate). Use an absolute cell reference for the cell containing the social security rate. (Refer to Chapter 2, Project 3c.) Copy the formula down to cells G4 through G16.

6. Sort the employee last names alphabetically in ascending order (A to Z).

8. Insert a footer that prints your name at the left side of the page and the file name at the right side of the page.

Student Name ← → EL1-U1-A5-CCPayroll.xlsx

EL1-U1-A5-CPPayroll(A5).xlsx

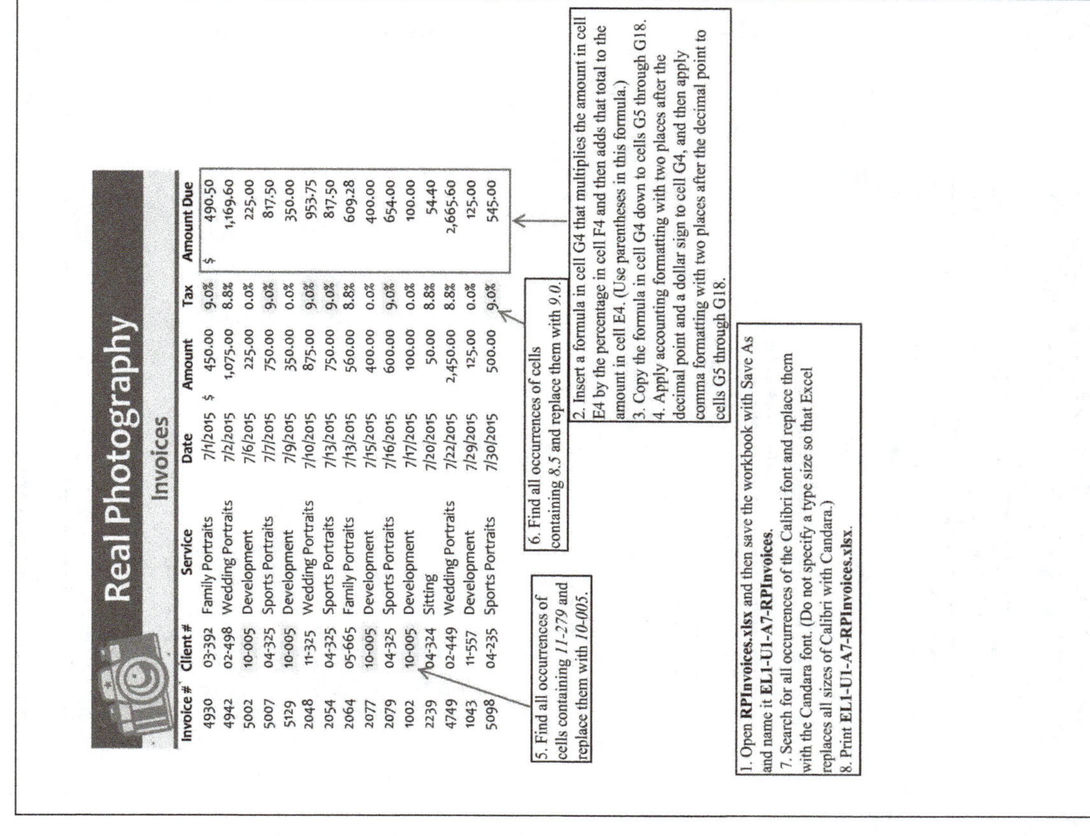

Real Photography

Invoices

Invoice #	Client #	Service	Date	Amount	Tax	Amount Due
4930	03-392	Family Portraits	7/1/2015	$ 450.00	9.0%	$ 490.50
4942	02-498	Wedding Portraits	7/2/2015	1,075.00	8.8%	1,169.60
5002	10-005	Development	7/6/2015	225.00	0.0%	225.00
5007	04-325	Sports Portraits	7/7/2015	750.00	9.0%	817.50
5129	10-005	Development	7/9/2015	350.00	0.0%	350.00
2048	11-325	Wedding Portraits	7/10/2015	875.00	9.0%	953.75
2054	04-325	Sports Portraits	7/13/2015	750.00	9.0%	817.50
2064	05-665	Family Portraits	7/13/2015	560.00	8.8%	609.28
2077	10-005	Development	7/15/2015	400.00	0.0%	400.00
2079	04-325	Sports Portraits	7/16/2015	600.00	9.0%	654.00
1002	10-005	Development	7/17/2015	100.00	0.0%	100.00
2239	04-324	Sitting	7/20/2015	50.00	8.8%	54.40
4749	02-449	Wedding Portraits	7/22/2015	2,450.00	8.8%	2,665.60
1043	11-557	Development	7/29/2015	125.00	0.0%	125.00
5098	04-235	Sports Portraits	7/30/2015	500.00	9.0%	545.00

5. Find all occurrences of cells containing *11-279* and replace them with *10-005*.

6. Find all occurrences of cells containing *8.5* and replace them with *9.0*.

2. Insert a formula in cell G4 that multiplies the amount in cell E4 by the percentage in cell F4 and then adds that total to the amount in cell E4. (Use parentheses in this formula.)
3. Copy the formula in cell G4 down to cells G5 through G18.
4. Apply accounting formatting with two places after the decimal point and a dollar sign to cell G4, and then apply comma formatting with two places after the decimal point to cells G5 through G18.

1. Open **RPInvoices.xlsx** and then save the workbook with Save As and name it **EL1-U1-A7-RPInvoices**.
7. Search for all occurrences of the Calibri font and replace them with the Candara font. (Do not specify a type size so that Excel replaces all sizes of Calibri with Candara.)
8. Print **EL1-U1-A7-RPInvoices.xlsx**.

EL1-U1-A7-RPInvoices(A7,Step8).xlsx

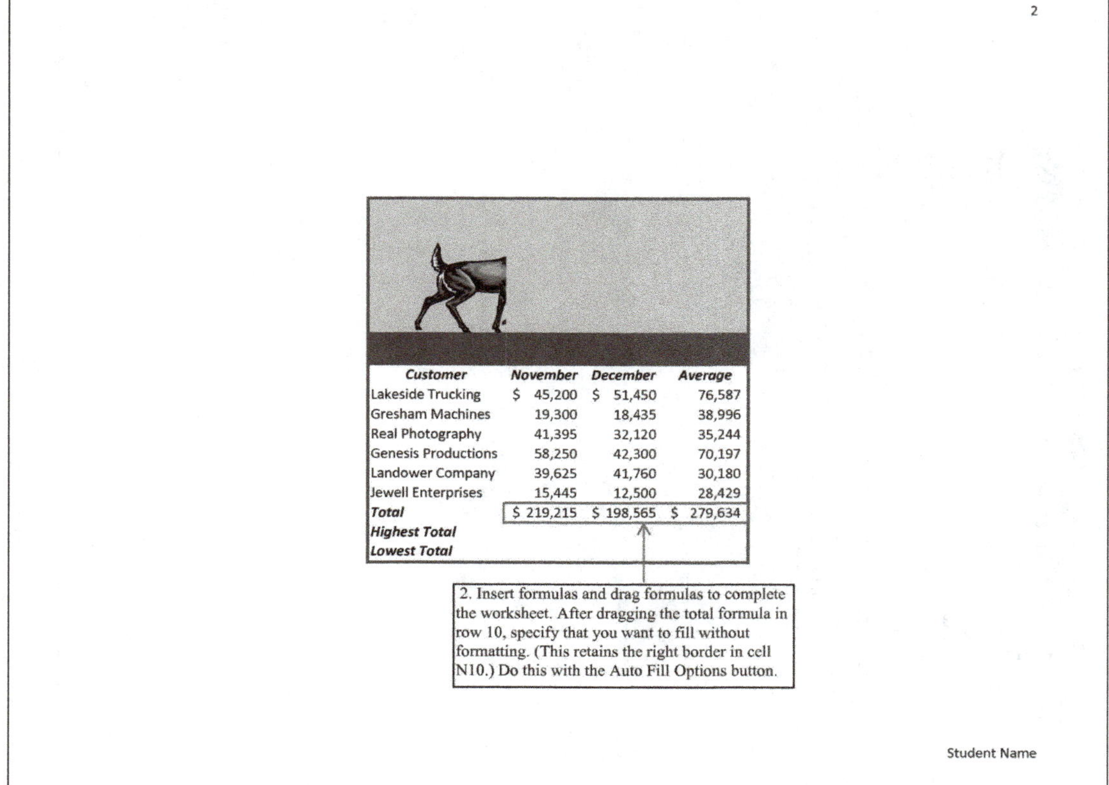

2

Customer	November	December	Average
Lakeside Trucking	$ 45,200	$ 51,450	76,587
Gresham Machines	19,300	18,435	38,996
Real Photography	41,395	32,120	35,244
Genesis Productions	58,250	42,300	70,197
Landower Company	39,625	41,760	30,180
Jewell Enterprises	15,445	12,500	28,429
Total	$ 219,215	$ 198,565	$ 279,634
Highest Total			
Lowest Total			

2. Insert formulas and drag formulas to complete the worksheet. After dragging the total formula in row 10, specify that you want to fill without formatting. (This retains the right border in cell N10.) Do this with the Auto Fill Options button.

Student Name

EL1-U1-A6-DIAnnualSales(A6).xlsx (2 of 2)

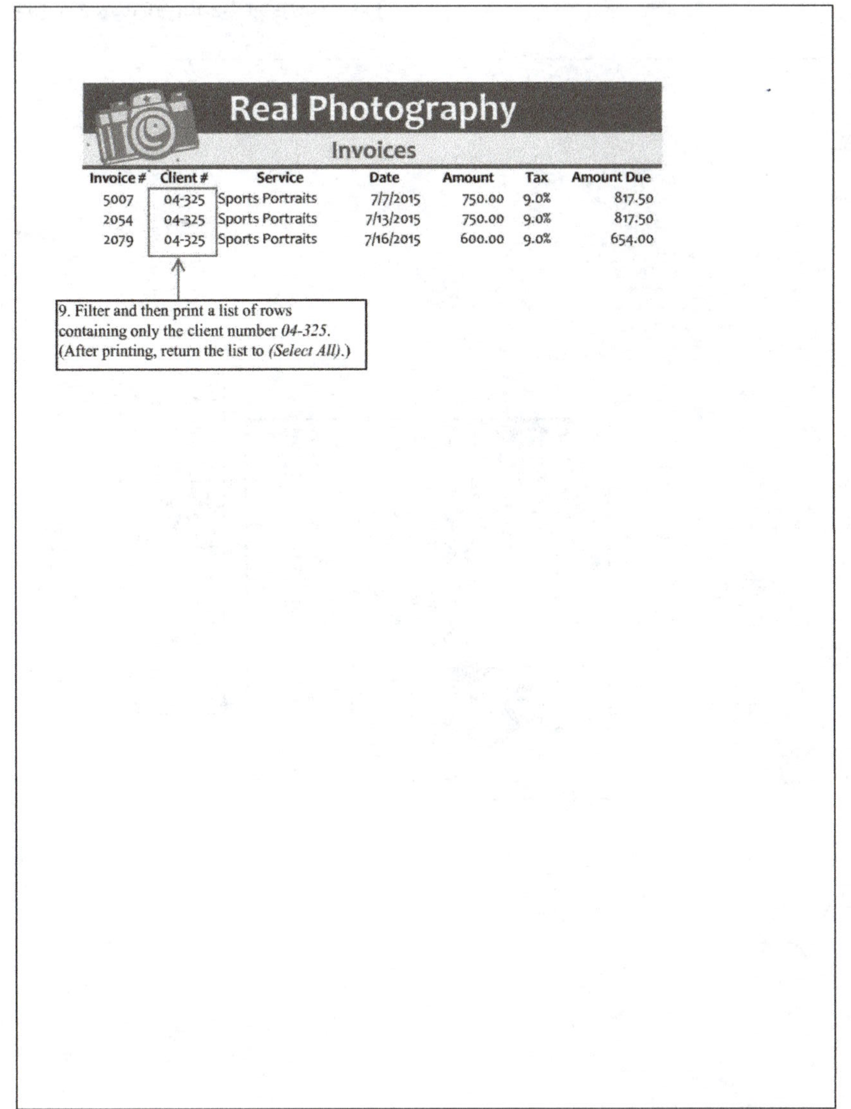

Real Photography

Invoices

Invoice #	Client #	Service	Date	Amount	Tax	Amount Due
5007	04-325	Sports Portraits	7/7/2015	750.00	9.0%	817.50
2054	04-325	Sports Portraits	7/13/2015	750.00	9.0%	817.50
2079	04-325	Sports Portraits	7/16/2015	600.00	9.0%	654.00

9. Filter and then print a list of rows containing only the client number *04-325*. (After printing, return the list to *(Select All)*.)

EL1-U1-A7-RPInvoices(A7,Step9).xlsx

Real Photography

Invoices

Invoice #	Client #	Service	Date	Amount	Tax	Amount Due
5002	10-005	Development	7/6/2015	225.00	0.0%	225.00
5129	10-005	Development	7/9/2015	350.00	0.0%	350.00
2077	10-005	Development	7/15/2015	400.00	0.0%	400.00
1002	10-005	Development	7/17/2015	100.00	0.0%	100.00
1043	11-557	Development	7/29/2015	125.00	0.0%	125.00

10. Filter and then print a list of rows containing only the service *Development*. (After printing, return the list to *(Select All)*.)

EL1-U1-A7-RPInvoices(A7,Step10).xlsx

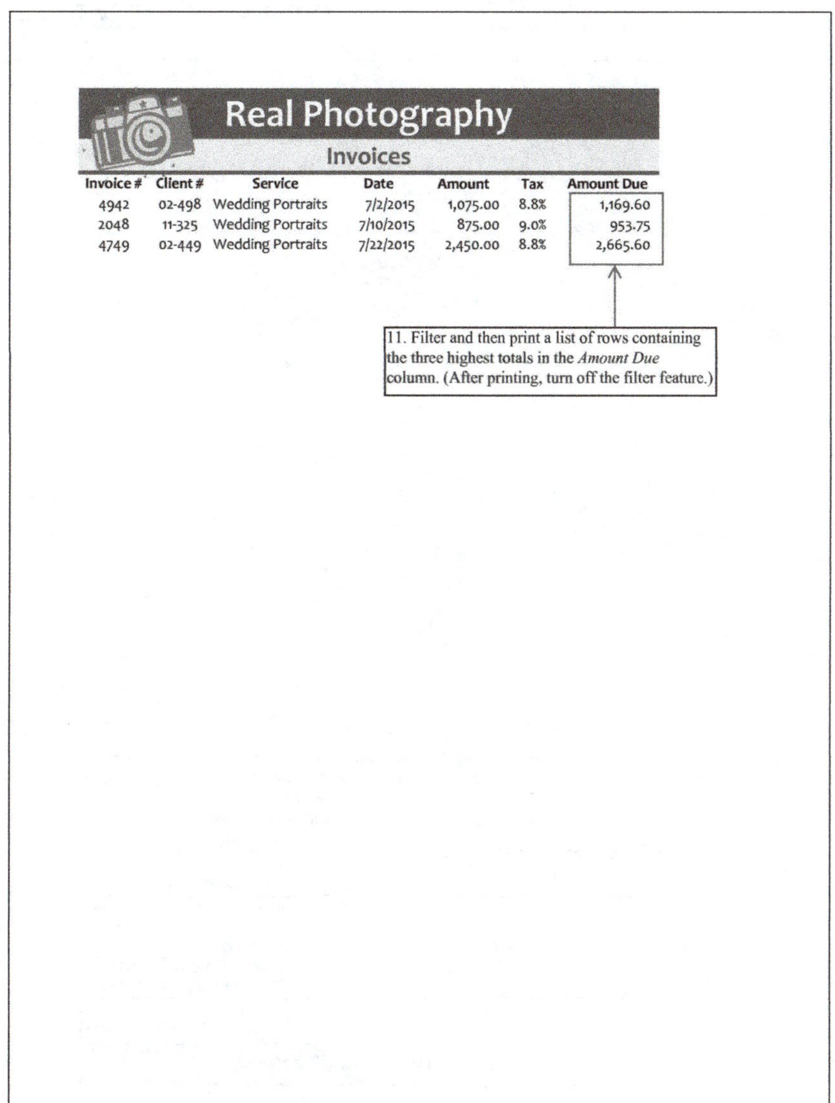

Real Photography

Invoices

Invoice #	Client #	Service	Date	Amount	Tax	Amount Due
4942	02-498	Wedding Portraits	7/2/2015	1,075.00	8.8%	1,169.60
2048	11-325	Wedding Portraits	7/10/2015	875.00	9.0%	953.75
4749	02-449	Wedding Portraits	7/22/2015	2,450.00	8.8%	2,665.60

11. Filter and then print a list of rows containing the three highest totals in the *Amount Due* column. (After printing, turn off the filter feature.)

EL1-U1-A7-RPInvoices(A7,Step11).xlsx

Weekly Order Summary

Product		Total Orders		Average Order Size
Pyramid clock	$	3,050	$	375
Black and gold wall clock	$	2,450	$	125
Dashboard clock	$	2,135	$	230
Traveling alarm clock	$	1,358	$	195
Waterproof watch	$	890	$	90
Gold chain watch	$	755	$	80
Total:	$	10,638	$	1,095

EL1-U1-Act1-OrdersSumm.xlsx

Depreciation Methods

Type	Straight Line
Function	DB
Cost	Initial cost of item
Salvage	Salvage value at end of life of asset
Life	Number of periods over which the asset is depreciated
Period	Period of time you want to calculate depreciation
Months	# of months in first year (assumed 12 If nothing listed)
Type	Double Declining
Function	DDB
Cost	Initial cost of item
Salvage	Salvage value at end of life of asset
Life	Number of periods over which the asset is depreciated
Period	Period of time you want to calculate depreciation
Factor	Rate at which the balance declines (assumed to be 2 if nothing is listed)

EL1-U1-Act2-DepMethods.xlsx

Real Photography

Depreciation

Equipment	Initial Cost	Salvage Value	Life of Asset	Depreciation
Photocopier	$ 5,200.00	$ 1,400.00	8	$249.65
Desktop computer	3,245.00	500.00	4	$298.35
Laptop computer	2,750.00	400.00	4	$247.95
Color laser printer	1,580.00	200.00	4	$135.14
Video camera	875.00	100.00	6	$43.61
Developer	4,210.00	1,250.00	6	$280.44

EL1-U1-Act3-RPDepreciation.xlsx

FINANCIAL REASONS FOR ASSET DEPRECIATION

Depreciation of assets is used because the asset is used for income generation and the item bears wear and tear, eventually becoming destroyed or no longer useful. Instead of writing off the item from the final use of life, businesses can use a partial amount of the asset cost each year. If the item is not written off correctly, the profit for each year would be skewed as a lower profit margin than was actually earned when writing off a large purchase item at the end of its life.

Using different methods impacts the record of a business' profit. There are many different types of depreciations used by businesses in calculating the value of their assets.

STRAIGHT-LINE: The most popular and simplest method of depreciation is the straight-line method. This takes the cost of a new item, reduces the estimated value upon disposal and then is divided by the estimated lifespan. For example, a new computer that costs $5000 will be reduced to a $200 salvage value at the end of 3 years.

The formula for straight-line depreciation would be: ($5000 - $200) / 3 = $1600

The annual depreciation charged for the above computer example is $1600.

DOUBLE-DEPRECIATING: This method is a more exaggerated version of the straight-line method. It determines the percentage of the depreciation in the first year and then doubles it. Each following year, the percentage is multiplied by the depreciating balance until the value is lower than the straight-line charge. At this point, the depreciation method will resume as a straight-line.

Using the above computer example, the formula for double-decline depreciation base would be 66.67%:

(($5000-$200)/3 = $1600) / (($5000-$200) = $4800) = ((33.33%) * 2) = 66.67%

Then:

$4800 * 66.67% = $3200 for the first year's depreciation value.

Then:

((Remaining balance $4800 - $3200) = $1600) / 66.67% = $1066

Although, this new balance dips below the original straight-line depreciation value, so the depreciation formula would now revert to straight-line.

*Information from www.about.com.

EL1-U1-Act3-DepReport.xlsx

MEXICO TRAVEL PLANNING - PUERTO VALLARTA		
February 3 to February 9 - Double Occupancy		
Seattle to Puerto Vallarta	Expedia.com	Travelocity.com
Airfare	$ 581	$ 552
Hotel - Playa Los Arcos	260	325
Estimated Meals	200	200
Entertainment	200	200
Car Rental	50	50
TOTAL per person:	**$ 1,291**	**$ 1,327**
Package Rate (Air + Hotel)	$ 759	$ 827
Estimated Meals	200	200
Entertainment	200	200
Car Rental	50	50
TOTAL per person:	**$ 1,209**	**$ 1,277**
Savings with Package:	82	50

EL1-U1-Act4-TrvlWksht

Excel Level 1, Chapter 5 Model Answers

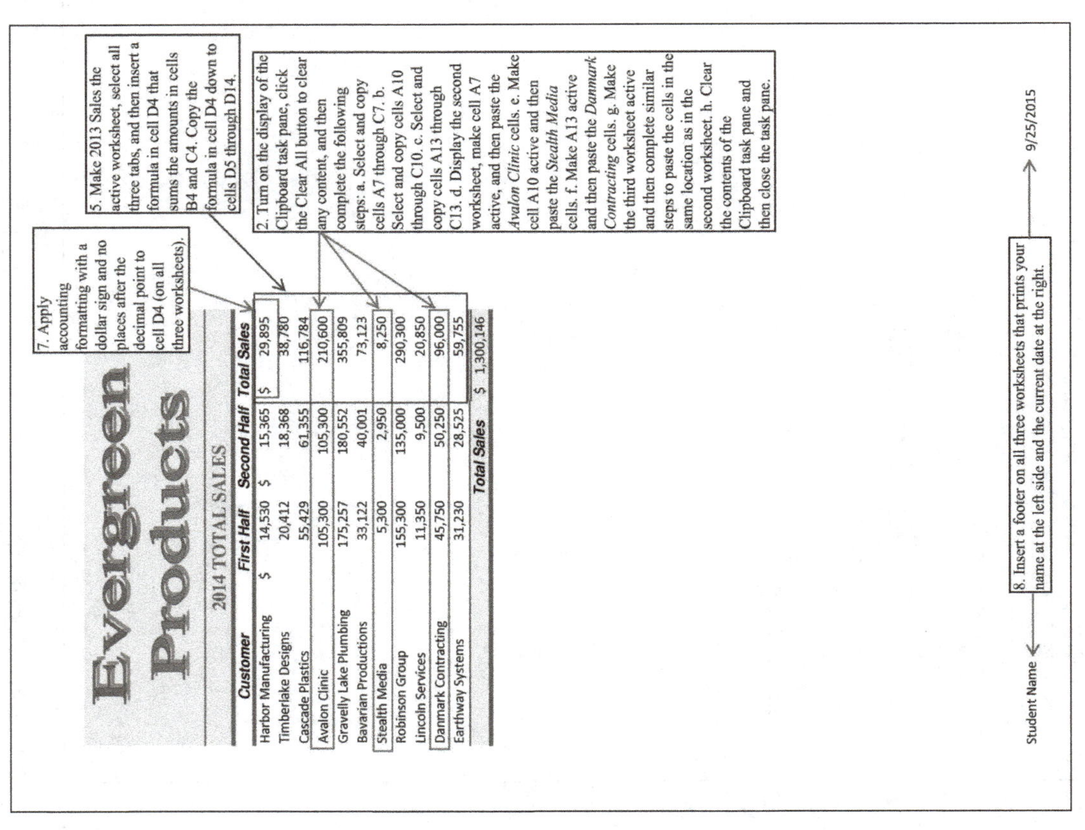

Evergreen Products

2014 TOTAL SALES

Customer	First Half	Second Half	Total Sales
Harbor Manufacturing	$ 14,530	$ 15,365	$ 29,895
Timberlake Designs	20,412	18,368	38,780
Cascade Plastics	55,429	61,355	116,784
Avalon Clinic	105,300	105,300	210,600
Gravelly Lake Plumbing	175,257	180,552	355,809
Bavarian Productions	33,122	40,001	73,123
Stealth Media	5,300	2,950	8,250
Robinson Group	155,300	135,000	290,300
Lincoln Services	11,350	9,500	20,850
Danmark Contracting	45,750	50,250	96,000
Earthway Systems	31,230	28,525	59,755
		Total Sales	$ 1,300,146

7. Apply accounting formatting with a dollar sign and no places after the decimal point to cell D4 (on all three worksheets).

5. Make 2013 Sales the active worksheet, select all three tabs, and then insert a formula in cell D4 that sums the amounts in cells B4 and C4. Copy the formula in cell D4 down to cells D5 through D14.

2. Turn on the display of the Clipboard task pane, click the Clear All button to clear any content, and then complete the following steps: a. Select and copy cells A7 through C7. b. Select and copy cells A10 through C10. c. Select and copy cells A13 through C13. d. Display the second worksheet, make cell A7 active, and then paste the *Avalon Clinic* cells. e. Make cell A10 active and then paste the *Stealth Media* cells. f. Make A13 active and then paste the *Danmark Contracting* cells. g. Make the third worksheet active and then complete similar steps to paste the cells in the same location as in the second worksheet. h. Clear the contents of the Clipboard task pane and then close the task pane.

Student Name ← 8. Insert a footer on all three worksheets that prints your name at the left side and the current date at the right. → 9/25/2015

EL1-C5-A1-EPSales(A1).xlsx (2 of 3)

Evergreen Products

2013 TOTAL SALES

Customer	First Half	Second Half	Total Sales
Harbor Manufacturing	$ 32,500	$ 41,305	$ 73,805
Timberlake Designs	10,200	14,230	24,430
Cascade Plastics	64,230	50,304	114,534
Avalon Clinic	105,300	105,300	210,600
Gravelly Lake Plumbing	200,500	150,700	351,200
Bavarian Productions	45,890	29,405	75,295
Stealth Media	5,300	2,950	8,250
Robinson Group	136,492	144,366	280,858
Lincoln Services	21,890	18,445	40,335
Danmark Contracting	45,750	50,250	96,000
Earthway Systems	35,500	28,750	64,250
		Total Sales	$ 1,339,557

7. Apply accounting formatting with a dollar sign and no places after the decimal point to cell D4 (on all three worksheets).

5. Make 2013 Sales the active worksheet, select all three tabs, and then insert a formula in cell D4 that sums the amounts in cells B4 and C4. Copy the formula in cell D4 down to cells D5 through D14.

2. Turn on the display of the Clipboard task pane, click the Clear All button to clear any content, and then complete the following steps: a. Select and copy cells A7 through C7. b. Select and copy cells A10 through C10. c. Select and copy cells A13 through C13. d. Display the second worksheet, make cell A7 active, and then paste the *Avalon Clinic* cells. e. Make cell A10 active and then paste the *Stealth Media* cells. f. Make A13 active and then paste the *Danmark Contracting* cells. g. Make the third worksheet active and then complete similar steps to paste the cells in the same location as in the second worksheet. h. Clear the contents of the Clipboard task pane and then close the task pane.

6. Make cell D15 active and then insert a formula that sums the amounts in cells D4 through D14.

1. Open **EPSales.xlsx** and then save the workbook with Save As and name it **EL1-C5-A1-EPSales**.
3. Change the name of the Sheet1 tab to *2013 Sales*, the name of the Sheet2 tab to *2014 Sales*, and the name of the Sheet3 tab to *2015 Sales*.
4. Change the color of the 2013 Sales tab to Blue, the color of the 2014 Sales tab to Green, and the color of the 2015 Sales tab to Yellow.

Student Name ← 8. Insert a footer on all three worksheets that prints your name at the left side and the current date at the right. → 9/25/2015

EL1-C5-A1-EPSales(A1).xlsx (1 of 3)

Evergreen Products

2015 TOTAL SALES

Customer	First Half	Second Half	Total Sales
Harbor Manufacturing	$ 15,300	$ 12,600	$ 27,900
Timberlake Designs	6,545	10,590	17,135
Cascade Plastics	42,500	39,500	82,000
Avalon Clinic	105,300	105,300	210,600
Gravelly Lake Plumbing	212,500	230,565	443,065
Bavarian Productions	33,145	45,690	78,835
Stealth Media	5,300	2,950	8,250
Robinson Group	144,500	120,000	264,500
Lincoln Services	8,200	7,950	16,150
Danmark Contracting	45,750	50,250	96,000
Earthway Systems	20,485	24,350	44,835
		Total Sales	$ 1,289,270

7. Apply accounting formatting with a dollar sign and no places after the decimal point to cell D4 (on all three worksheets).

5. Make 2013 Sales the active worksheet, select all three tabs, and then insert a formula in cell D4 that sums the amounts in cells B4 and C4. Copy the formula in cell D4 down to cells D5 through D14.

2. Turn on the display of the Clipboard task pane, click the Clear All button to clear any content, and then complete the following steps: a. Select and copy cells A7 through C7. b. Select and copy cells A10 through C10. c. Select and copy cells A13 through C13. d. Display the second worksheet, make cell A7 active, and then paste the *Avalon Clinic* cells. e. Make cell A10 active and then paste the *Stealth Media* cells. f. Make A13 active and then paste the *Danmark Contracting* cells. g. Make the third worksheet active and then complete similar steps to paste the cells in the same location as in the second worksheet. h. Clear the contents of the Clipboard task pane and then close the task pane.

Student Name ← 8. Insert a footer on all three worksheets that prints your name at the left side and the current date at the right. → 9/25/2015

EL1-C5-A1-EPSales(A1).xlsx (3 of 3)

Student Name   9/25/2015   EL1-C5-A2-CMJanIncome(Assessment2)

7. Insert a custom header on both worksheets that prints your name at the left side, the date in the middle, and the file name at the right side.

Clearline Manufacturing

January - Income Statement

Revenue	
Sales Revenue	$ 85,245
Cost of Sales	32,500
Gross Profit	$ 52,745
Operating Expenses	
Wages and Salaries	$ 23,125
Payroll Taxes	4,625
Lease Payment	5,450
Utilities	905
Supplies	857
Insurance	234
Advertising	2,500
Direct Marketing	4,000
Total Expenses	$ 41,696
Net Profit	$ 11,049

4. Select both sheet tabs and then insert the following formulas: a. Insert a formula in cell B6 that subtracts the cost of sales from the sales revenue (*=B4-B5*).

4b. Insert a formula in cell B16 that sums the amounts in cells B8 through B15.

4c. Insert a formula in cell B17 that subtracts the total expenses from the gross profit (*=B6-B16*).

1. Open **CMJanIncome.xlsx** and then save the workbook with Save As and name it **EL1-C5-A2-CMJanIncome**.
2. Copy cells A1 through B17 in Sheet1 and paste them into Sheet2. (Click the Paste Options button and then click the Keep Source Column Widths button at the drop-down list.)
5. Change the name of the Sheet1 tab to *January* and the name of the Sheet2 tab to *February*.
6. Change the color of the January tab to Blue and the color of the February tab to Red.

EL1-C5-A2-CMJanIncome(A2).xlsx (1 of 2)

Clearline Manufacturing
Software Certification

Name	Test 1	Test 2	Test 3	Test 4	Test 5	Test 6	Test 7	Test 8	Test 9	Test 10	Test 11	Test 12	Average
Arnson, Patrick	89%	65%	76%	89%	98%	65%	76%	87%	55%	78%	67%	69%	76%
Barclay, Jeanine	78%	66%	87%	90%	92%	82%	100%	84%	67%	86%	82%	91%	84%
Calahan, Jack	65%	71%	64%	66%	70%	81%	64%	59%	76%	76%	45%	49%	66%
Cumpston, Kurt	89%	91%	90%	93%	86%	80%	84%	93%	95%	81%	96%	98%	90%
Dimmitt, Marian	78%	73%	81%	82%	67%	69%	82%	72%	85%	83%	71%	73%	76%
Donovan, Nancy	82%	89%	79%	74%	80%	82%	86%	72%	74%	82%	76%	79%	80%
Fisher-Edwards, Teri	89%	93%	100%	91%	86%	90%	88%	86%	100%	98%	90%	97%	92%
Flanery, Stephanie	58%	45%	63%	51%	60%	59%	63%	52%	66%	67%	53%	49%	57%
Heyman, Grover	78%	75%	87%	88%	64%	76%	70%	67%	55%	87%	82%	88%	76%
Herbertson, Wynn	92%	80%	93%	90%	86%	84%	95%	100%	98%	88%	95%	89%	91%
Jewett, Troy	98%	94%	99%	89%	100%	93%	100%	95%	96%	91%	87%	94%	95%
Kwieciak, Kathleen	55%	0%	42%	65%	72%	40%	65%	0%	0%	48%	52%	56%	41%
Leibrand, Maxine	78%	69%	83%	87%	84%	69%	80%	82%	88%	79%	83%	76%	80%
Markovits, Claude	89%	93%	84%	100%	95%	92%	95%	100%	89%	94%	98%	94%	94%
Moonstar, Siana	73%	87%	67%	83%	90%	84%	73%	81%	75%	65%	84%	88%	79%
Nauer, Sheryl	75%	83%	85%	78%	82%	80%	79%	82%	92%	90%	86%	84%	83%
Nunez, James	98%	96%	100%	90%	95%	93%	88%	91%	89%	100%	96%	98%	95%
Nyegaard, Curtis	90%	89%	84%	85%	93%	85%	100%	94%	98%	93%	100%	95%	92%
Oglesbee, Randy	65%	55%	73%	90%	87%	67%	85%	77%	85%	73%	78%	77%	76%
Pherson, Douglas	69%	82%	87%	74%	70%	82%	84%	85%	66%	77%	91%	86%	79%

5. Add two rows immediately above row 18 and then type the following text in the specified cells: A18: Nauer, Sheryl A19: Nunez, James B18: 75 B19: 98 C18: 83 C19: 96 D18: 85 D19: 100 E18: 78 E19: 90 F18: 82 F19: 95 G18: 80 G19: 93 H18: 79 H19: 88 I18: 82 I19: 91 J18: 92 J19: 89 K18: 90 K19: 100 L18: 86 L19: 96 M18: 84 M19: 98

6. Insert a formula in cell N3 that averages the percentages in cells B3 through M3 and then copy the formula down to cells N4 through N22.

1. Open **CMCertTests.xlsx** and then save the workbook with Save As and name it **EL1-C5-A3-CMCertTests**.
2. Make sure cell A1 is active and then split the window by clicking the VIEW tab and then clicking the Split button in the Window group. (This causes the window to split into four panes.)
3. Drag both the horizontal and vertical split lines up and to the left until the horizontal split line is immediately below the second row and the vertical split line is immediately to the right of the first column.
4. Freeze the window panes.
7. Unfreeze the window panes.
8. Remove the split.
9. Change the orientation to landscape and then scale the worksheet to print on one page. ***Hint: Do this with the* Width *option in the Scale to Fit group on the PAGE LAYOUT tab.***

EL1-C5-A3-CMCertTests(A3).xlsx

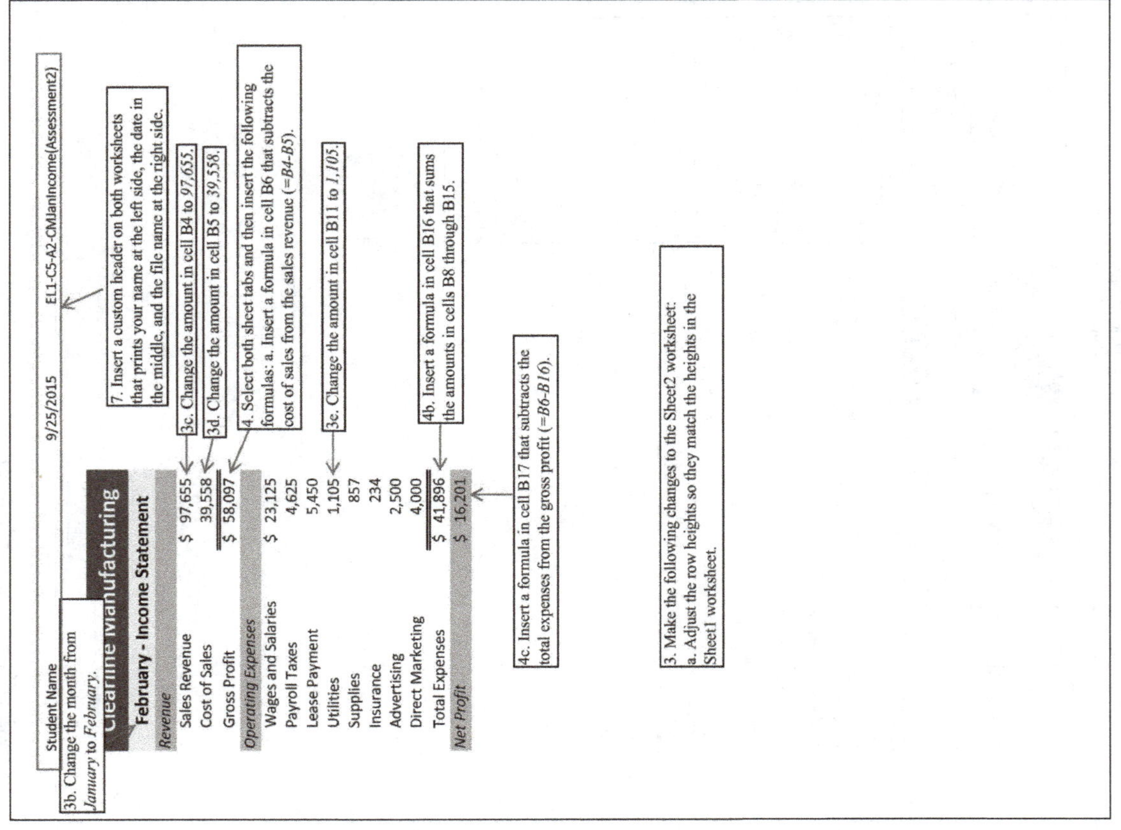

EL1-C5-A2-CMJanIncome(A2).xlsx (2 of 2)

1. Create the worksheet shown in Figure 5.9. (Change the width of column A to 21.00 characters.)
2. Save the workbook and name it **EL1-C5-A4-HCMachRpt**.
3. With **EL1-C5-A4-HCMachRpt.xlsx** open, open **HCEqpRpt.xlsx**.
9. Print the worksheet centered horizontally and vertically on the page.

5. With **EL1-C5-A4-HCMachRpt.xlsx** the active workbook, make cell A1 active and then apply the following formatting:
a. Change the height of row 1 to 25.20 points.
b. Change the font size of the text in cell A1 to 14 points.
c. Apply the Blue, Accent 5, Lighter 80% fill color (ninth column, second row in the *Theme Colors* section) to cell A1.

7. Select cells B2 through G2 and apply the White, Background 1 text color (first column, first row in the *Theme Colors* section). (Make sure the text in the cells is right-aligned.)

6. Select cells A2 through G2 and apply the Blue, Accent 5, Darker 50% fill color (ninth column, last row in the *Theme Colors* section).

8. Select and then apply the Blue, Accent 5, Lighter 80% fill color (ninth column, second row in the *Theme Colors* section) to the following cells: A3 through G3, A7 through G7, and A11 through G11.

EQUIPMENT USAGE REPORT

	January	February	March	April	May	June
Machine #12						
Total hours available	2200	2330	2430	2300	2340	2140
In use	1940	2005	2220	2080	1950	1895
Machine #25						
Total hours available	2100	2240	2450	2105	2390	1950
In use	1800	1935	2110	1750	2215	1645
Machine #30						
Total hours available	2300	2430	2530	2400	2440	2240
In use	2040	2105	2320	2180	2050	1995

4b. Copy cells A10 through G10 in **HCEqpRpt.xlsx** and paste them into **EL1-C5-A4-HCMachRpt.xlsx** beginning with cell A13.

4. Select and copy the following cells from **HCEqpRpt.xlsx** to **EL1-C5-A4-HCMachRpt.xlsx**: a. Copy cells A4 through G4 in **HCEqpRpt.xlsx** and paste them into **EL1-C5-A4-HCMachRpt.xlsx** beginning with cell A12.

EL1-C5-A4-HCMachRpt(A4).xlsx

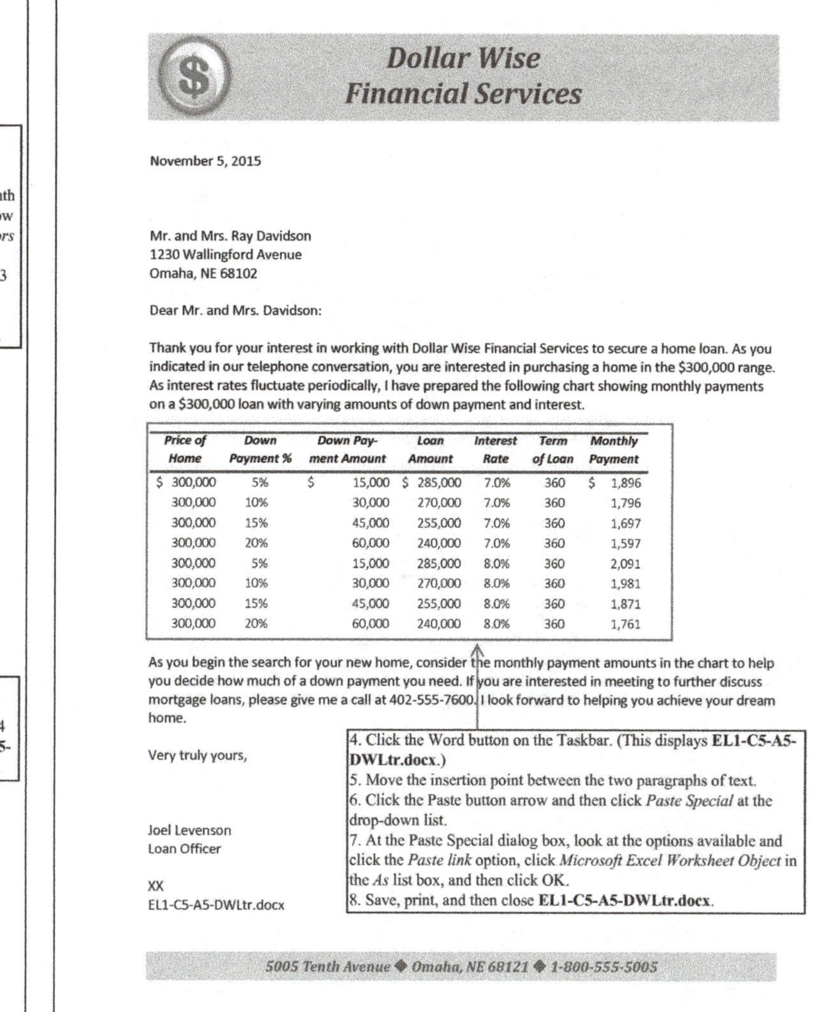

Dollar Wise Financial Services

November 5, 2015

Mr. and Mrs. Ray Davidson
1230 Wallingford Avenue
Omaha, NE 68102

Dear Mr. and Mrs. Davidson:

Thank you for your interest in working with Dollar Wise Financial Services to secure a home loan. As you indicated in our telephone conversation, you are interested in purchasing a home in the $300,000 range. As interest rates fluctuate periodically, I have prepared the following chart showing monthly payments on a $300,000 loan with varying amounts of down payment and interest.

Price of Home	Down Payment %	Down Payment Amount	Loan Amount	Interest Rate	Term of Loan	Monthly Payment
$ 300,000	5%	$ 15,000	$ 285,000	7.0%	360	$ 1,896
300,000	10%	30,000	270,000	7.0%	360	1,796
300,000	15%	45,000	255,000	7.0%	360	1,697
300,000	20%	60,000	240,000	7.0%	360	1,597
300,000	5%	15,000	285,000	8.0%	360	2,091
300,000	10%	30,000	270,000	8.0%	360	1,981
300,000	15%	45,000	255,000	8.0%	360	1,871
300,000	20%	60,000	240,000	8.0%	360	1,761

As you begin the search for your new home, consider the monthly payment amounts in the chart to help you decide how much of a down payment you need. If you are interested in meeting to further discuss mortgage loans, please give me a call at 402-555-7600. I look forward to helping you achieve your dream home.

Very truly yours,

Joel Levenson
Loan Officer

XX
EL1-C5-A5-DWLtr.docx

5005 Tenth Avenue ◆ Omaha, NE 68121 ◆ 1-800-555-5005

4. Click the Word button on the Taskbar. (This displays **EL1-C5-A5-DWLtr.docx**.)
5. Move the insertion point between the two paragraphs of text.
6. Click the Paste button arrow and then click *Paste Special* at the drop-down list.
7. At the Paste Special dialog box, look at the options available and click the *Paste link* option, click *Microsoft Excel Worksheet Object* in the *As* list box, and then click OK.
8. Save, print, and then close **EL1-C5-A5-DWLtr.docx**.

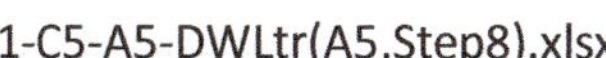

EL1-C5-A5-DWLtr(A5,Step8).xlsx

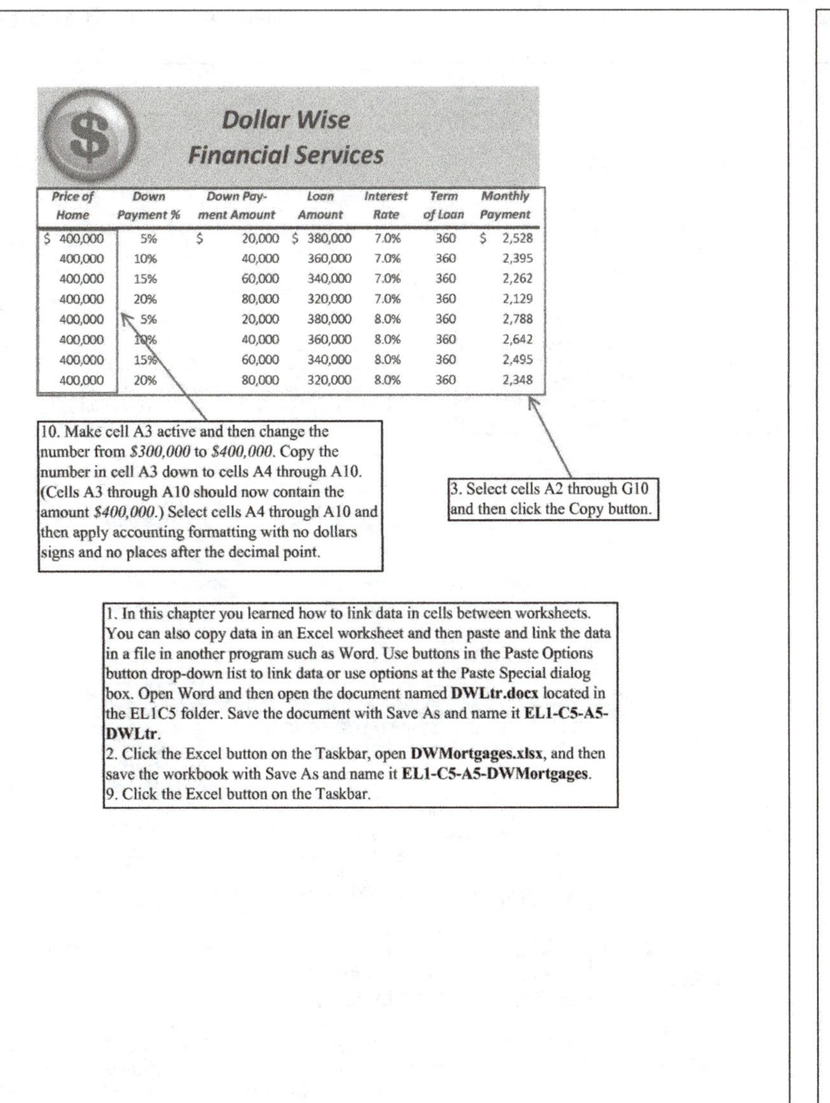

Dollar Wise Financial Services

Price of Home	Down Payment %	Down Payment Amount	Loan Amount	Interest Rate	Term of Loan	Monthly Payment
$ 400,000	5%	$ 20,000	$ 380,000	7.0%	360	$ 2,528
400,000	10%	40,000	360,000	7.0%	360	2,395
400,000	15%	60,000	340,000	7.0%	360	2,262
400,000	20%	80,000	320,000	7.0%	360	2,129
400,000	5%	20,000	380,000	8.0%	360	2,788
400,000	10%	40,000	360,000	8.0%	360	2,642
400,000	15%	60,000	340,000	8.0%	360	2,495
400,000	20%	80,000	320,000	8.0%	360	2,348

10. Make cell A3 active and then change the number from *$300,000* to *$400,000*. Copy the number in cell A3 down to cells A4 through A10. (Cells A3 through A10 should now contain the amount *$400,000*.) Select cells A4 through A10 and then apply accounting formatting with no dollars signs and no places after the decimal point.

3. Select cells A2 through G10 and then click the Copy button.

1. In this chapter you learned how to link data in cells between worksheets. You can also copy data in an Excel worksheet and then paste and link the data in a file in another program such as Word. Use buttons in the Paste Options button drop-down list to link data or use options at the Paste Special dialog box. Open Word and then open the document named **DWLtr.docx** located in the EL1C5 folder. Save the document with Save As and name it **EL1-C5-A5-DWLtr**.
2. Click the Excel button on the Taskbar, open **DWMortgages.xlsx**, and then save the workbook with Save As and name it **EL1-C5-A5-DWMortgages**.
9. Click the Excel button on the Taskbar.

EL1-C5-A5-DWMortgages(A5).xlsx

Dollar Wise Financial Services

November 5, 2015

Mr. and Mrs. Ray Davidson
1230 Wallingford Avenue
Omaha, NE 68102

Dear Mr. and Mrs. Davidson:

Thank you for your interest in working with Dollar Wise Financial Services to secure a home loan. As you indicated in our telephone conversation, you are interested in purchasing a home in the $300,000 range. As interest rates fluctuate periodically, I have prepared the following chart showing monthly payments on a $300,000 loan with varying amounts of down payment and interest.

Price of Home	Down Payment %	Down Payment Amount	Loan Amount	Interest Rate	Term of Loan	Monthly Payment
$400,000	5%	$ 20,000	$380,000	7.0%	360	$ 2,528
$400,000	10%	40,000	360,000	7.0%	360	2,395
$400,000	15%	60,000	340,000	7.0%	360	2,262
$400,000	20%	80,000	320,000	7.0%	360	2,129
$400,000	5%	20,000	380,000	8.0%	360	2,788
$400,000	10%	40,000	360,000	8.0%	360	2,642
$400,000	15%	60,000	340,000	8.0%	360	2,495
$400,000	20%	80,000	320,000	8.0%	360	2,348

As you begin the search for your new home, consider the monthly payment amounts in the chart to help you decide how much of a down payment you need. If you are interested in meeting to further discuss mortgage loans, please give me a call at 402-555-7600. I look forward to helping you achieve your dream home.

Very truly yours,

12. Click the Word button on the Taskbar.
13. Open **EL1-C5-A5-DWLtr.docx**. At the message that displays asking if you want to update the data from the linked files, click Yes.

Joel Levenson
Loan Officer

XX
EL1-C5-A5-DWLtr.docx

5005 Tenth Avenue ◆ Omaha, NE 68121 ◆ 1-800-555-5005

EL1-C5-A5-DWLtr(A5,Step14).xlsx

Clearline Manufacturing

SEMIANNUAL SALES - 2014

Customer	1st Half	2nd Half	Total
Lakeside Trucking	$ 84,300	$ 73,500	$ 157,800
Gresham Machines	33,000	40,500	73,500
Real Photography	30,890	35,465	66,355
Genesis Productions	72,190	75,390	147,580
Landower Company	22,000	15,000	37,000
Jewell Enterprises	19,764	50,801	70,565

EL1-C5-VB-CMSemiSales(VB).xlsx

Student Name 9/25/2015

Gateway Global

January Expenditures

Department	Supplies	Equipment	Total
Production	$ 25,425	$ 135,500	$ 160,925
Technical Support	$ 14,500	$ 65,000	$ 79,500
Finance	$ 5,790	$ 22,000	$ 27,790
Sales and Marketing	$ 35,425	$ 8,525	$ 43,950
Facilities	$ 6,000	$ 1,200	$ 7,200
Total	$ 87,140	$ 232,225	$ 319,365

EL1-C5-CS-GGExp(CS1).xlsx (1 of 4)

Student Name 9/25/2015

Gateway Global

February Expenditures

Department	Supplies	Equipment	Total
Production	$ 38,550	$ 88,500	$ 127,050
Technical Support	$ 14,500	$ 44,250	$ 58,750
Finance	$ 7,500	$ 22,000	$ 29,500
Sales and Marketing	$ 35,425	$ 8,525	$ 43,950
Facilities	$ 6,000	$ 1,200	$ 7,200
Total	$ 101,975	$ 164,475	$ 266,450

EL1-C5-CS-GGExp(CS1).xlsx (2 of 4)

Student Name 9/25/2015

Gateway Global

March Expenditures

Department	Supplies	Equipment	Total
Production	$ 65,000	$ 150,000	$ 215,000
Technical Support	$ 21,750	$ 43,525	$ 65,275
Finance	$ 5,790	$ 22,000	$ 27,790
Sales and Marketing	$ 35,425	$ 8,525	$ 43,950
Facilities	$ 6,000	$ 18,450	$ 24,450
Total	$ 133,965	$ 242,500	$ 376,465

EL1-C5-CS-GGExp(CS1).xlsx (3 of 4)

Student Name 9/25/2015

Gateway Global

Quarterly Expenditures Summary

Month	Supplies	Equipment	Total
January	$ 87,140	$ 232,225	$ 319,365
February	$ 101,975	$ 164,475	$ 266,450
March	$ 133,965	$ 242,500	$ 376,465
Total	$ 323,080	$ 639,200	$ 962,280

EL1-C5-CS-GGExp(CS1).xlsx (4 of 4)

Gateway Global

Blue Team

Monthly Statistics

Player	At Bats	Hits	Walks	Bat. Avg.	On-Base %
Danner, Brenda	8	3	1	0.375	0.444
Sessler, Don	6	4	0	0.667	0.667
Thomas-Main, Gina	8	3	2	0.375	0.500
Devaul, Jay	7	4	1	0.571	0.625
Forbes, Makenzie	4	1	0	0.250	0.250
Kendrick, Jackson	2	2	0	1.000	1.000
Lorenzo, Caitlyn	5	3	0	0.600	0.600
Meyers, Trevor	8	5	2	0.625	0.700
Plemonds, Vicki	9	4	1	0.444	0.500

Student Name 9/25/2015

EL1-C5-CS-GGStats(CS2).xlsx (1 of 2)

Gateway Global

Red Team

Monthly Statistics

Player	At Bats	Hits	Walks	Bat. Avg.	On-Base %
Cook, Kristi	7	4	0	0.571	0.571
Moravek, Ethan	5	2	2	0.400	0.571
Phillips, Sandy	8	5	3	0.625	0.727
Seely, Dylan	6	5	0	0.833	0.833
Golding, Shelley	9	4	2	0.444	0.545
Moeller, Enrique	3	2	0	0.667	0.667
Pastrana, Terra	6	3	1	0.500	0.571
Marshall, Ray	4	3	0	0.750	0.750
Vaita, Danielle	6	4	1	0.667	0.714

Student Name 9/25/2015

EL1-C5-CS-GGStats(CS2).xlsx (2 of 2)

Gateway Global

Metric Conversion Chart

Unit	Conversion
1 inch	2.54 centimeters
1 foot	0.3048 meters
1 yard	0.9144 meters
1 mile	1.609 kilometer

EL1-C5-CS-GGConv(CS3).xlsx (1 of 2)

EL1-C5-CS-GGLtrhd(CS4).xlsx

Gateway Global

Fahrenheit Conversion Chart

F°	C°
0	-18
5	-15
10	-12
15	-9
20	-7
25	-4
30	-1
35	2
40	4
45	7
50	10
55	13
60	16
65	18
70	21
75	24
80	27
85	29
90	32
95	35
100	38

EL1-C5-CS-GGConv(CS3).xlsx (2 of 2)

Gateway Global
2200 North Broad St.
Spokane, WA 99201
Tel 509-555-5289

Gateway Global	
Fahrenheit Conversion Chart	
F°	C°
0	-18
5	-15
10	-12
15	-9
20	-7
25	-4
30	-1
35	2
40	4
45	7
50	10
55	13
60	16
65	18
70	21
75	24
80	27
85	29
90	32
95	35
100	38

EL1-C5-CS-GGConvLtr(CS4).xlsx

Excel Level 1, Chapter 6 Model Answers

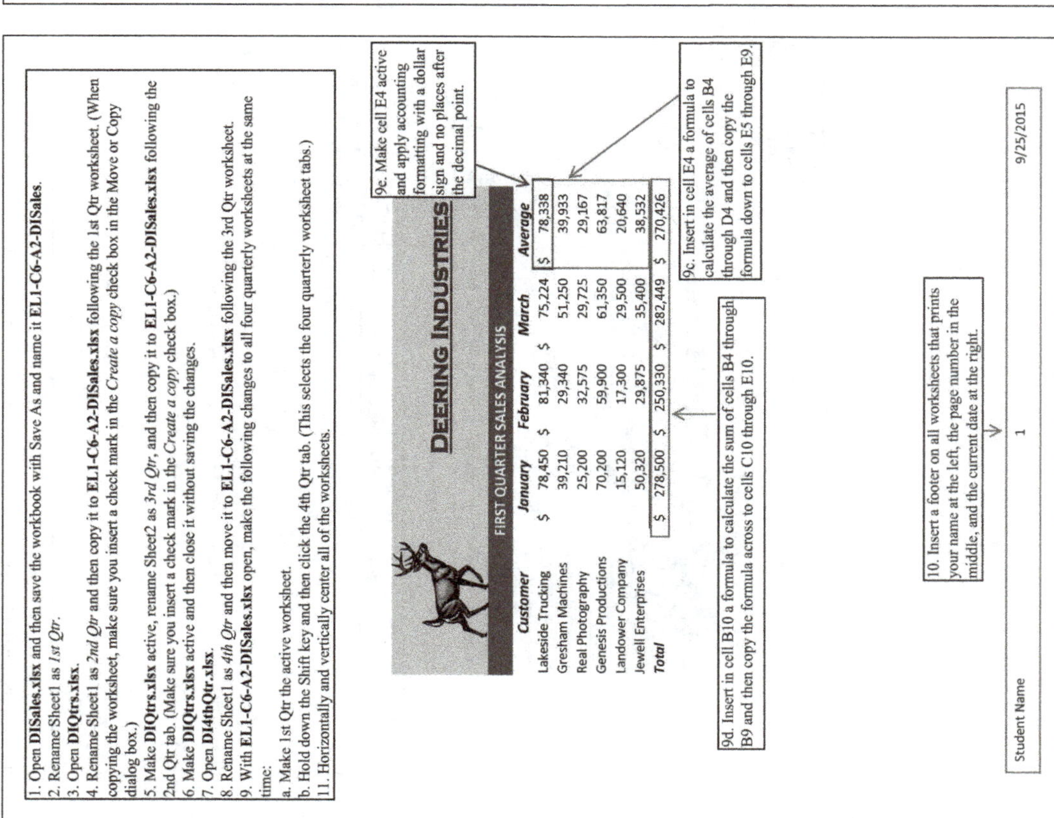

1. Open **DISales.xlsx** and then save the workbook with Save As and name it **EL1-C6-A2-DISales**.
2. Rename Sheet1 as *1st Qtr*.
3. Open **DIQtrs.xlsx**.
4. Rename Sheet1 as *2nd Qtr* and then copy it to **EL1-C6-A2-DISales.xlsx** following the 1st Qtr worksheet. (When copying the worksheet, make sure you insert a check mark in the *Create a copy* check box in the Move or Copy dialog box.)
5. Make **DIQtrs.xlsx** active, rename Sheet2 as *3rd Qtr*, and then copy it to **EL1-C6-A2-DISales.xlsx** following the 2nd Qtr tab. (Make sure you insert a check mark in the *Create a copy* check box.)
6. Make **DIQtrs.xlsx** active and then close it without saving the changes.
7. Open **DI4thQtr.xlsx**.
8. Rename Sheet1 as *4th Qtr* and then move it to **EL1-C6-A2-DISales.xlsx** following the 3rd Qtr worksheet.
9. With **EL1-C6-A2-DISales.xlsx** open, make the following changes to all four quarterly worksheets at the same time:
a. Make 1st Qtr the active worksheet.
b. Hold down the Shift key and then click the 4th Qtr tab. (This selects the four quarterly worksheet tabs.)
11. Horizontally and vertically center all of the worksheets.

DEERING INDUSTRIES

FIRST QUARTER SALES ANALYSIS

Customer	January	February	March	Average
Lakeside Trucking	$ 78,450	$ 81,340	$ 75,224	$ 78,338
Gresham Machines	39,210	29,340	51,250	39,933
Real Photography	25,200	32,575	29,725	29,167
Genesis Productions	70,200	59,900	61,350	63,817
Landower Company	15,120	17,300	29,500	20,640
Jewell Enterprises	50,320	29,875	35,400	38,532
Total	$ 278,500	$ 250,330	$ 282,449	$ 270,426

9e. Make cell E4 active and apply accounting formatting with a dollar sign and no places after the decimal point.

9c. Insert in cell E4 a formula to calculate the average of cells B4 through D4 and then copy the formula down to cells E5 through E9.

9d. Insert in cell B10 a formula to calculate the sum of cells B4 through B9 and then copy the formula across to cells C10 through E10.

10. Insert a footer on all worksheets that prints your name at the left, the page number in the middle, and the current date at the right.

Student Name 1 9/25/2015

EL1-C6-A2-DISales(A2).xlsx (1 of 4)

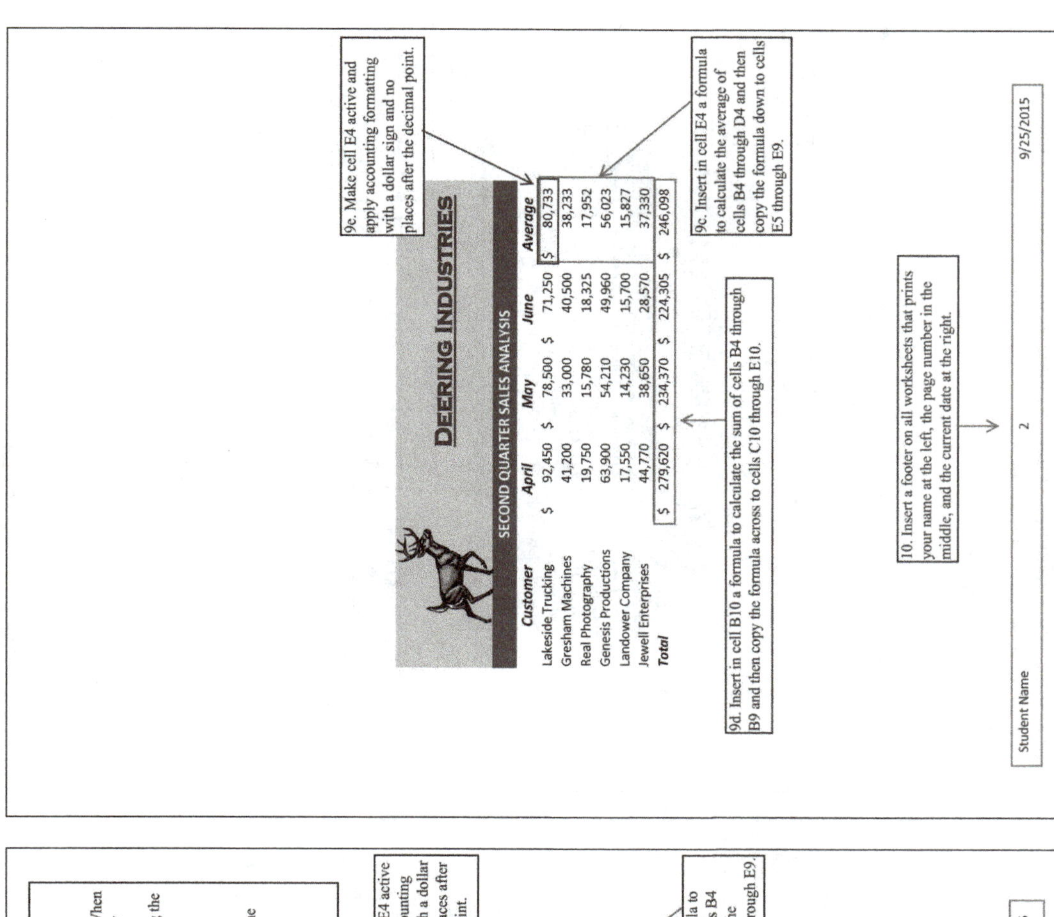

DEERING INDUSTRIES

SECOND QUARTER SALES ANALYSIS

Customer	April	May	June	Average
Lakeside Trucking	$ 92,450	$ 78,500	$ 71,250	$ 80,733
Gresham Machines	41,200	33,000	40,500	38,233
Real Photography	19,750	15,780	18,325	17,952
Genesis Productions	63,900	54,210	49,960	56,023
Landower Company	17,550	14,230	15,700	15,827
Jewell Enterprises	44,770	38,650	28,570	37,330
Total	$ 279,620	$ 234,370	$ 224,305	$ 246,098

9e. Make cell E4 active and apply accounting formatting with a dollar sign and no places after the decimal point.

9c. Insert in cell E4 a formula to calculate the average of cells B4 through D4 and then copy the formula down to cells E5 through E9.

9d. Insert in cell B10 a formula to calculate the sum of cells B4 through B9 and then copy the formula across to cells C10 through E10.

10. Insert a footer on all worksheets that prints your name at the left, the page number in the middle, and the current date at the right.

Student Name 2 9/25/2015

EL1-C6-A2-DISales(A2).xlsx (2 of 4)

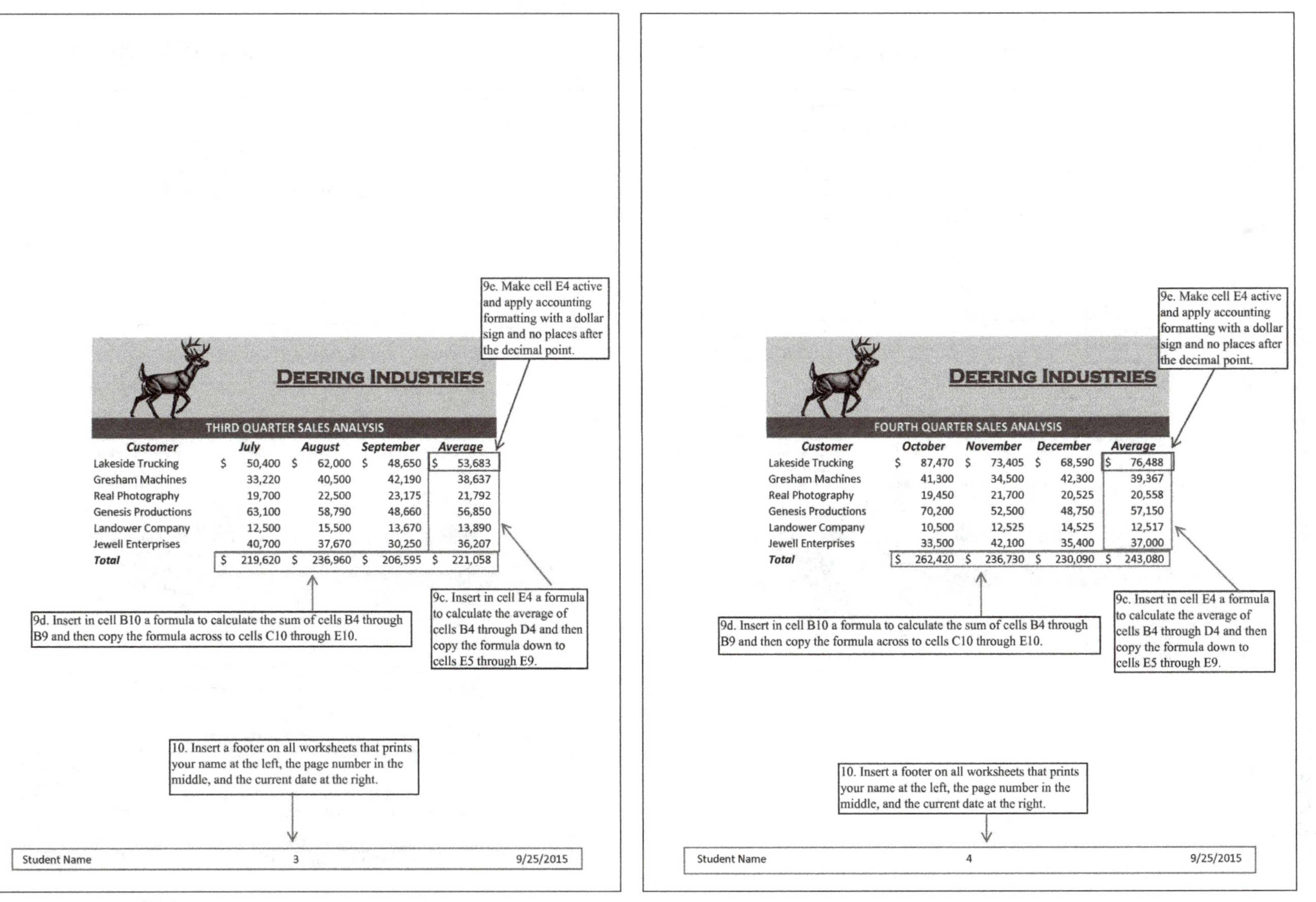

DEERING INDUSTRIES

THIRD QUARTER SALES ANALYSIS

Customer	July	August	September	Average
Lakeside Trucking	$ 50,400	$ 62,000	$ 48,650	$ 53,683
Gresham Machines	33,220	40,500	42,190	38,637
Real Photography	19,700	22,500	23,175	21,792
Genesis Productions	63,100	58,790	48,660	56,850
Landower Company	12,500	15,500	13,670	13,890
Jewell Enterprises	40,700	37,670	30,250	36,207
Total	$ 219,620	$ 236,960	$ 206,595	$ 221,058

EL1-C6-A2-DISales(A2).xlsx (3 of 4)

DEERING INDUSTRIES

FOURTH QUARTER SALES ANALYSIS

Customer	October	November	December	Average
Lakeside Trucking	$ 87,470	$ 73,405	$ 68,590	$ 76,488
Gresham Machines	41,300	34,500	42,300	39,367
Real Photography	19,450	21,700	20,525	20,558
Genesis Productions	70,200	52,500	48,750	57,150
Landower Company	10,500	12,525	14,525	12,517
Jewell Enterprises	33,500	42,100	35,400	37,000
Total	$ 262,420	$ 236,730	$ 230,090	$ 243,080

EL1-C6-A2-DISales(A2).xlsx (4 of 4)

10. Apply the following styles: a. Select cells A1 and A2 and then apply the C06Heading style.

ARMIN ASSOCIATES		
Projected Annual Earnings		
Projected Yearly Income	$ 1,345,800	
Month	Percentage	Earnings
January	8.80%	$ 118,430.40
February	8.30%	111,701.40
March	9.10%	122,467.80
April	8.50%	114,393.00
May	8.60%	115,738.80
June	7.40%	99,589.20
July	6.90%	92,860.20
August	7.80%	104,972.40
September	8.60%	115,738.80
October	9.10%	122,467.80
November	8.50%	114,393.00
December	8.40%	113,047.20

10b. Select cells A5 through C5 and then apply the C06Subheading style.

8. Make cell C6 active and then click the Accounting Number Format button.

7. Make cell C6 active and then insert a formula that multiplies the content of cell B6 by the amount in cell B3. (When writing the formula, identify cell B3 as an absolute reference.) Copy the formula down to cells C7 through C17.

10c. Select cells A6 through A17 and then apply the C06Column style.

1. At a blank worksheet, define a style named *C06Heading* that contains the following formatting: a. Font:14-point Cambria bold in dark blue b. Horizontal alignment: Center alignment c. Borders: Top and bottom in dark blue d. Fill: Light yellow (eighth column, second row)
2. Define a style named *C06Subheading* that contains the following formatting: a. Font: 12-point Cambria bold in dark blue b. Horizontal alignment: Center alignment c. Borders: Top and bottom in dark blue d. Fill: Light green (last column second row)
3. Define a style named *C06Column* that contains the following formatting: a. Number: At the Style dialog box, click the *Number* check box to remove the check mark. b. Font: 12-point Cambria in dark blue c. Fill: Light green (last column second row)
4. Save the workbook and name it **EL1-C6-A3-Styles**.
5. With **EL1-C6-A3-Styles.xlsx** open, open **ProjEarnings.xlsx**.
6. Save the workbook with Save As and name it **EL1-C6-A3-ProjEarnings**.
9. Copy the styles from **EL1-C6-A3-Styles.xlsx** into **EL1-C6-A3-ProjEarnings.xlsx**. ***Hint: Do this at the Merge Styles dialog box.***

EL1-C6-A3-ProjEarnings(A3,Step11).xlsx

12. With **EL1-C6-A3-ProjEarnings.xlsx** open, modify the following styles: a. Modify the C06Heading style so it changes the font color to dark green (last column, sixth row) instead of dark blue, changes the vertical alignment to center alignment, and inserts top and bottom borders in dark green (last column, sixth row) instead of dark blue.

ARMIN ASSOCIATES		
Projected Annual Earnings		
Projected Yearly Income	$ 1,345,800	
Month	Percentage	Earnings
January	8.80%	$ 118,430.40
February	8.30%	111,701.40
March	9.10%	122,467.80
April	8.50%	114,393.00
May	8.60%	115,738.80
June	7.40%	99,589.20
July	6.90%	92,860.20
August	7.80%	104,972.40
September	8.60%	115,738.80
October	9.10%	122,467.80
November	8.50%	114,393.00
December	8.40%	113,047.20

12b. Modify the C06Subheading style so it changes the font color to dark green (last column, sixth row) instead of dark blue and inserts top and bottom borders in dark green (instead of dark blue).

12c. Modify the C06Column style so it changes the font color to dark green (last column, sixth row) instead of dark blue. Do not change any of the other formatting attributes.

EL1-C6-A3-ProjEarnings(A3,Step13).xlsx

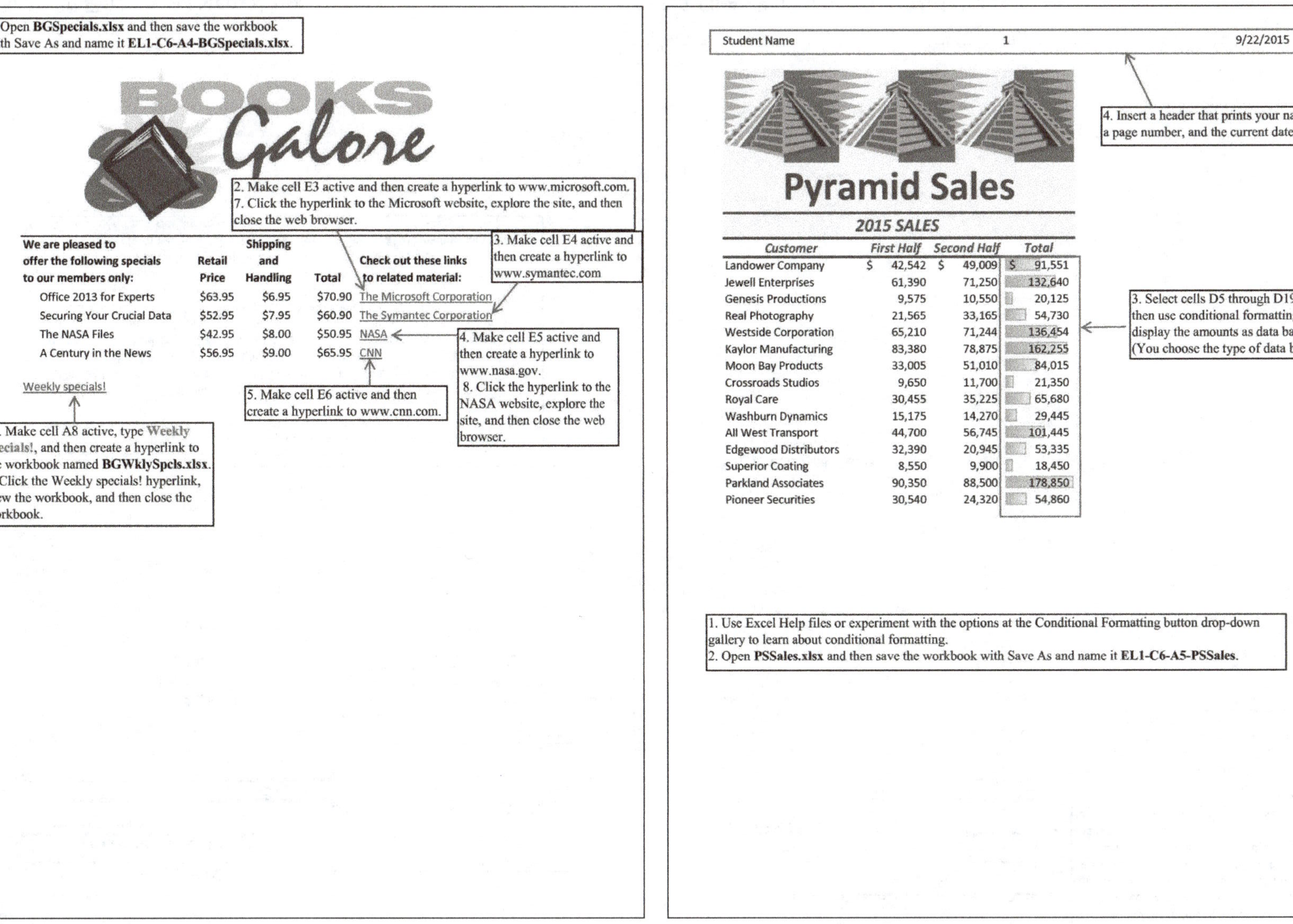

We are pleased to offer the following specials to our members only:	Retail Price	Shipping and Handling	Total	Check out these links to related material:
Office 2013 for Experts	$63.95	$6.95	$70.90	The Microsoft Corporation
Securing Your Crucial Data	$52.95	$7.95	$60.90	The Symantec Corporation
The NASA Files	$42.95	$8.00	$50.95	NASA
A Century in the News	$56.95	$9.00	$65.95	CNN

Weekly specials!

EL1-C6-A4-BGSpecials(A4).xlsx

Customer	First Half	Second Half	Total
Landower Company	$ 42,542	$ 49,009	$ 91,551
Jewell Enterprises	61,390	71,250	132,640
Genesis Productions	9,575	10,550	20,125
Real Photography	21,565	33,165	54,730
Westside Corporation	65,210	71,244	136,454
Kaylor Manufacturing	83,380	78,875	162,255
Moon Bay Products	33,005	51,010	84,015
Crossroads Studios	9,650	11,700	21,350
Royal Care	30,455	35,225	65,680
Washburn Dynamics	15,175	14,270	29,445
All West Transport	44,700	56,745	101,445
Edgewood Distributors	32,390	20,945	53,335
Superior Coating	8,550	9,900	18,450
Parkland Associates	90,350	88,500	178,850
Pioneer Securities	30,540	24,320	54,860

EL1-C6-A5-PSSales(A5).xlsx

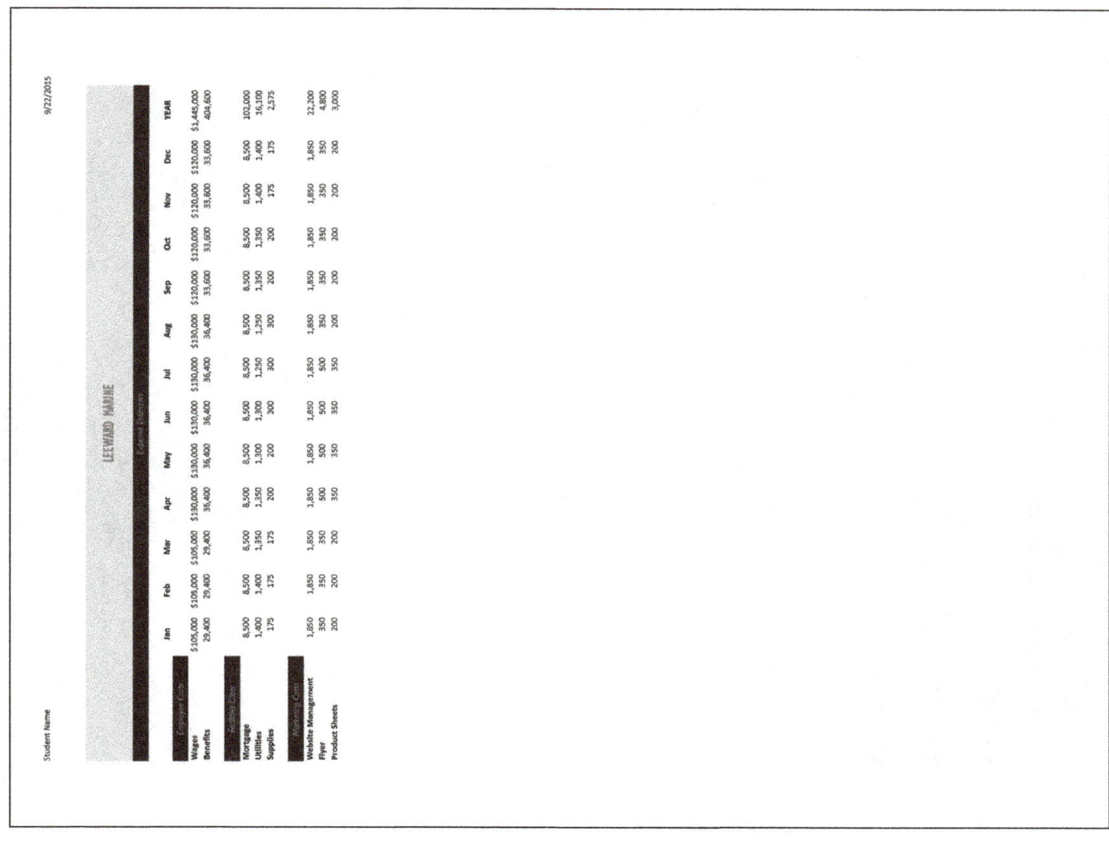

Student Name

9/22/2015

LEEWARD MARINE

	Jan	Feb	Mar	Apr	May	Jun	Jul	Aug	Sep	Oct	Nov	Dec	YEAR
Wages	$105,000	$105,000	$105,000	$130,000	$130,000	$130,000	$130,000	$130,000	$120,000	$120,000	$120,000	$120,000	$1,445,000
Benefits	29,400	29,400	29,400	36,400	36,400	36,400	36,400	36,400	33,600	33,600	33,600	33,600	404,600
Mortgage	8,500	8,500	8,500	8,500	8,500	8,500	8,500	8,500	8,500	8,500	8,500	8,500	102,000
Utilities	1,400	1,400	1,350	1,350	1,300	1,300	1,250	1,250	1,350	1,350	1,400	1,400	16,100
Supplies	175	175	175	200	200	300	300	300	200	200	175	175	2,575
Website Management	1,850	1,850	1,850	1,850	1,850	1,850	1,850	1,850	1,850	1,850	1,850	1,850	22,200
Flyer	350	350	350	500	500	500	500	350	350	350	350	350	4,800
Product Sheets	200	200	200	350	350	350	350	200	200	200	200	200	3,000

EL1-C6-CS-LMExpSummary(CS2).xlsx (1 of 3)

O'Rourke Enterprises

For Office Use Only		

Expense Report

PURPOSE: Advertising Media Conference

STATEMENT NUMBER: 2301

PAY PERIOD: From 10/16/2015 To 10/30/2015

EMPLOYEE INFORMATION:

Name Sophia Constanza

Position Manager

SSN N/A

Department Advertising

Manager Seth Morgenstern

Employee ID 34237

Date	Account	Description	Hotel	Transport	Fuel	Meals	Phone	Entertainment	Misc	Total
22-Oct-15	Advertising	Travel to conference	$ 210.00	$ 358.00		$ 38.75				$ 606.75
23-Oct-15	Advertising	Conference/dinner with client	$ 210.00			$ 53.29		$ 78.50		$ 341.79
24-Oct-15	Advertising	Conference/dinner with client	$ 210.00			$ 68.65				$ 278.65
25-Oct-15	Advertising	Conference	$ 210.00			$ 52.60				$ 262.60
26-Oct-15	Advertising	Conference				$ 40.55				$ 40.55
Total			**$ 840.00**	**$ 358.00**	**$ -**	**$ 253.84**	**$ -**	**$ 78.50**	**$ -**	**$ 1,530.34**
									Subtotal	$ 1,530.34
									Cash Advances	$ 500.00
									Total	$ 1,030.34

APPROVED: Approved by Seth Morgenstern on 10/30/2015

NOTES: Cash advance issued 10/19/2015

Page 1 of 1

EL1-C6-VB-OEExpRpt(VB).xlsx

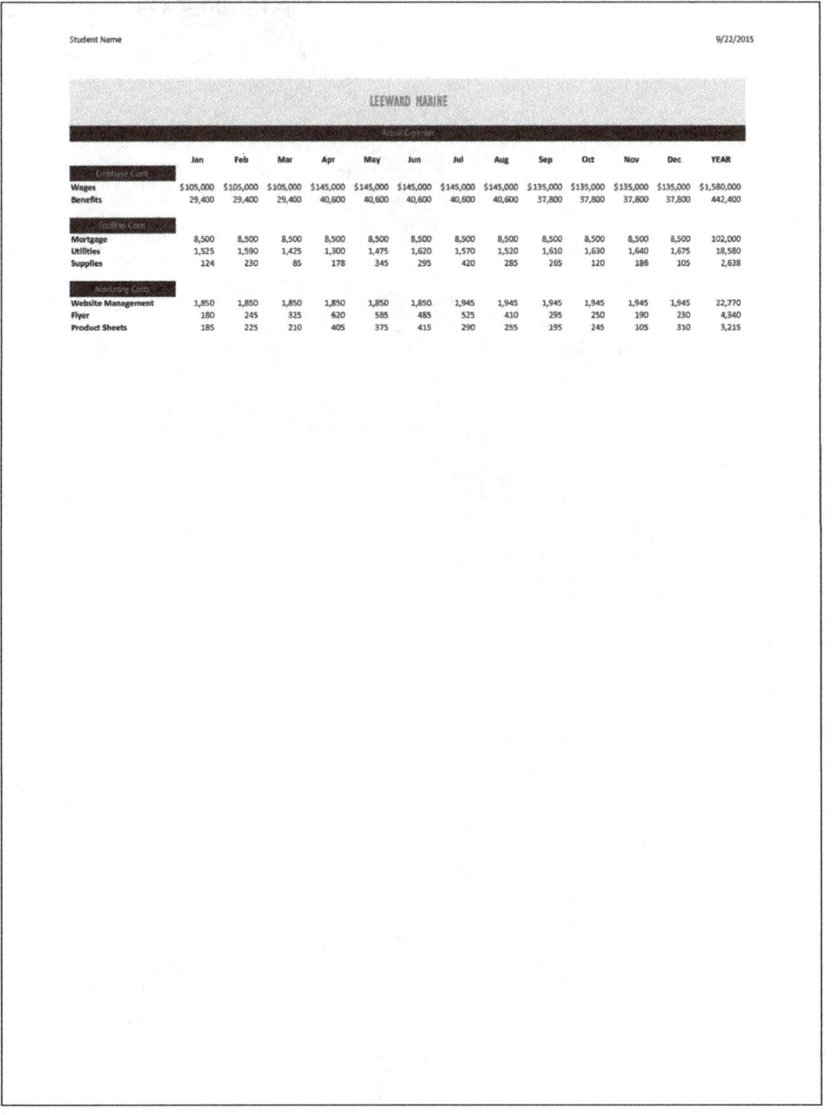

Student Name 9/22/2015

LEEWARD MARINE

Actual Expenses

	Jan	Feb	Mar	Apr	May	Jun	Jul	Aug	Sep	Oct	Nov	Dec	YEAR
Employee Costs													
Wages	$105,000	$105,000	$105,000	$145,000	$145,000	$145,000	$145,000	$145,000	$135,000	$135,000	$135,000	$135,000	$1,580,000
Benefits	29,400	29,400	29,400	40,600	40,600	40,600	40,600	40,600	37,800	37,800	37,800	37,800	442,400
Facilities Costs													
Mortgage	8,500	8,500	8,500	8,500	8,500	8,500	8,500	8,500	8,500	8,500	8,500	8,500	102,000
Utilities	1,525	1,590	1,425	1,300	1,475	1,620	1,570	1,520	1,610	1,630	1,640	1,675	18,580
Supplies	124	230	85	178	345	295	420	285	265	120	186	105	2,638
Marketing Costs													
Website Management	1,850	1,850	1,850	1,850	1,850	1,850	1,945	1,945	1,945	1,945	1,945	1,945	22,770
Flyer	180	245	325	620	585	485	525	410	295	250	190	230	4,340
Product Sheets	185	225	210	405	375	415	290	255	195	245	105	310	3,215

EL1-C6-CS-LMExpSummary(CS2).xlsx (2 of 3)

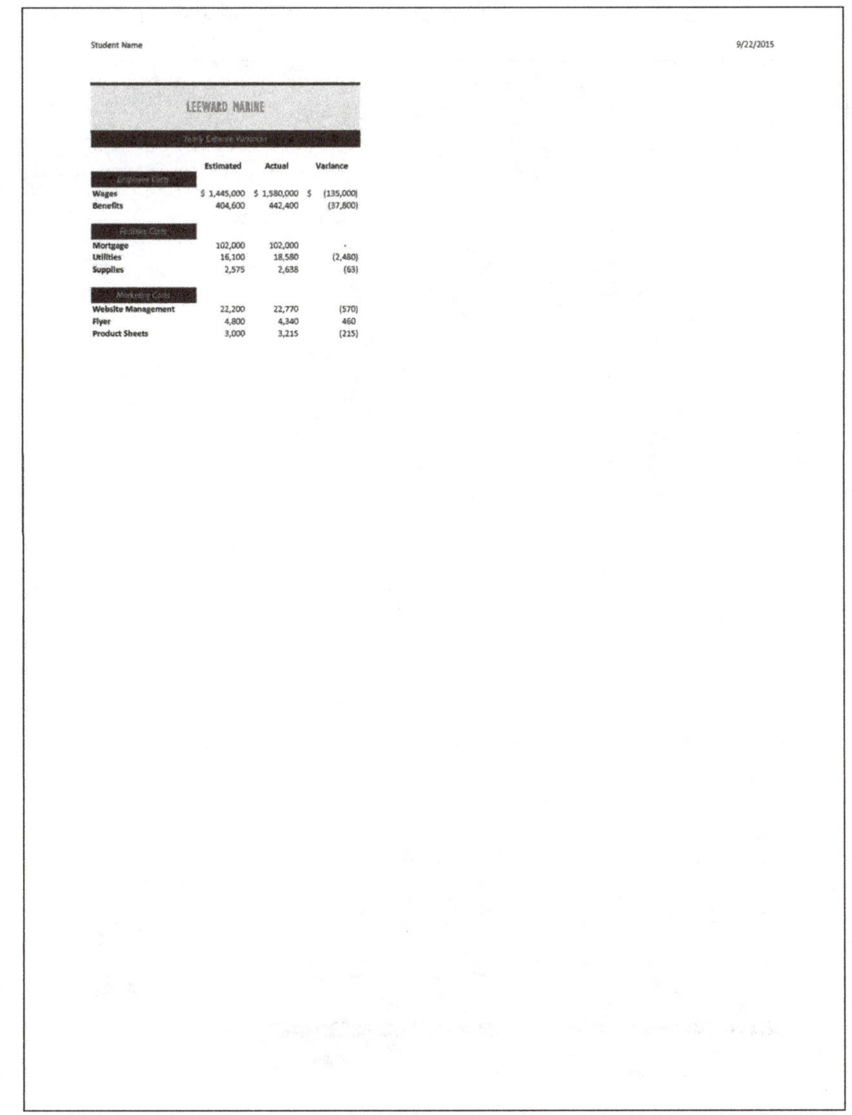

Student Name 9/22/2015

LEEWARD MARINE

Yearly Expense Variances

	Estimated	Actual	Variance
Employee Costs			
Wages	$ 1,445,000	$ 1,580,000	$ (135,000)
Benefits	404,600	442,400	(37,800)
Facilities Costs			
Mortgage	102,000	102,000	-
Utilities	16,100	18,580	(2,480)
Supplies	2,575	2,638	(63)
Marketing Costs			
Website Management	22,200	22,770	(570)
Flyer	4,800	4,340	460
Product Sheets	3,000	3,215	(215)

EL1-C6-CS-LMExpSummary(CS2).xlsx (3 of 3)

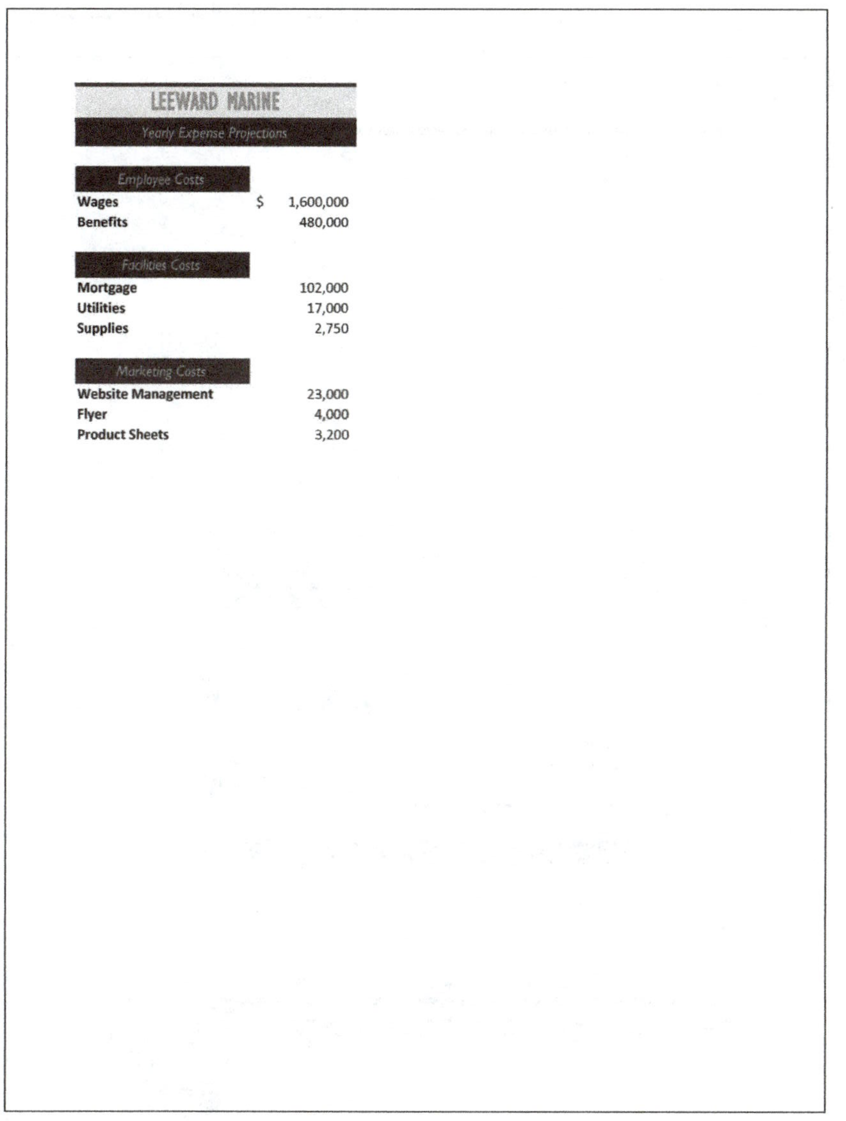

LEEWARD MARINE

Yearly Expense Projections

Employee Costs	
Wages	$ 1,600,000
Benefits	480,000
Facilities Costs	
Mortgage	102,000
Utilities	17,000
Supplies	2,750
Marketing Costs	
Website Management	23,000
Flyer	4,000
Product Sheets	3,200

EL1-C6-CS-LMProjectedExp(CS3).xlsx

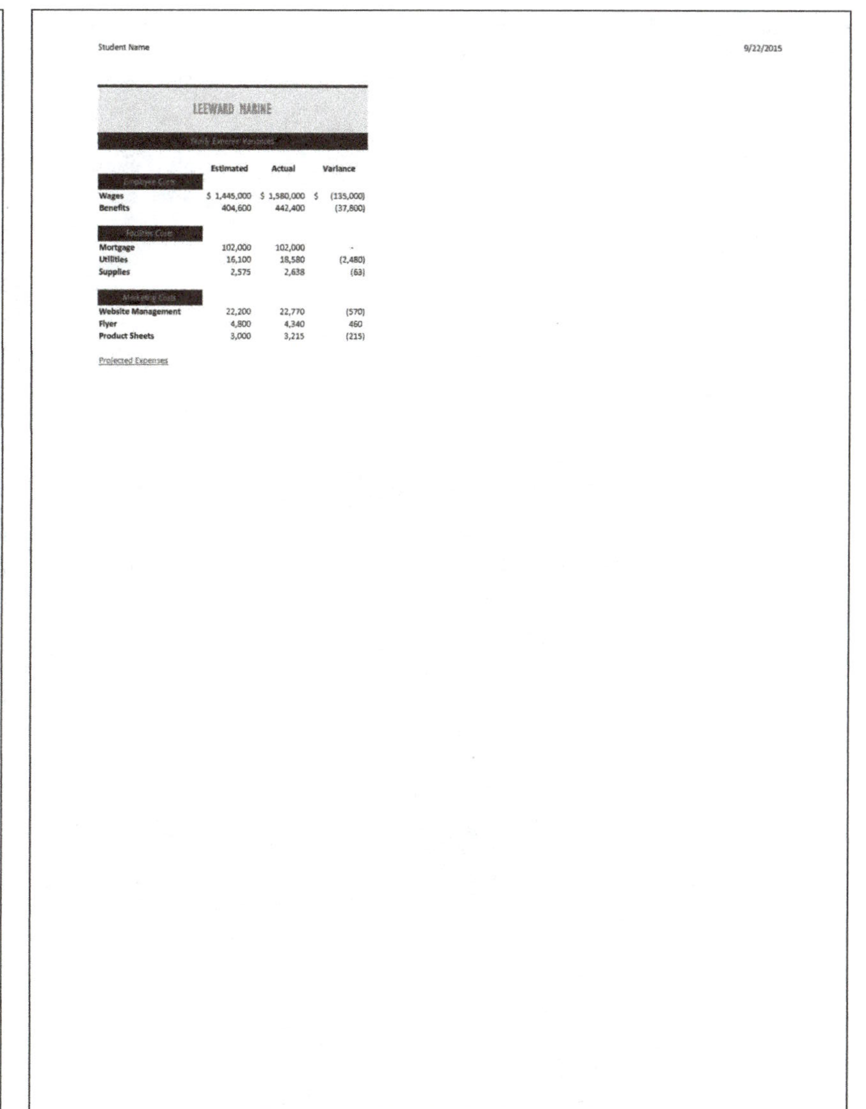

Student Name 9/22/2015

LEEWARD MARINE

Yearly Expense Variances

	Estimated	Actual	Variance
Employee Costs			
Wages	$ 1,445,000	$ 1,580,000	$ (135,000)
Benefits	404,600	442,400	(37,800)
Facilities Costs			
Mortgage	102,000	102,000	-
Utilities	16,100	18,580	(2,480)
Supplies	2,575	2,638	(63)
Marketing Costs			
Website Management	22,200	22,770	(570)
Flyer	4,800	4,340	460
Product Sheets	3,000	3,215	(215)

Projected Expenses

EL1-C6-CS-LMExpSummary(CS3).xlsx

Leeward Marine

4500 Shoreline Drive ♦ Ketchikan, AK 99901 ♦ (907) 555-2200 ♦ www.emcp.com/lmarine

Yearly Expense Variances			
	Estimated	Actual	Variance
Employee Costs			
Wages	$ 1,445,000	$ 1,580,000	$ (135,000)
Benefits	404,600	442,400	(37,800)
Facilities Costs			
Mortgage	102,000	102,000	-
Utilities	16,100	18,580	(2,480)
Supplies	2,575	2,638	(63)
Marketing Costs			
Website Management	22,200	22,770	(570)
Flyer	4,800	4,340	460
Product Sheets	3,000	3,215	(215)

EL1-C6-CS-LMExpSummary(CS4).xlsx

Excel Level 1, Chapter 7 Model Answers

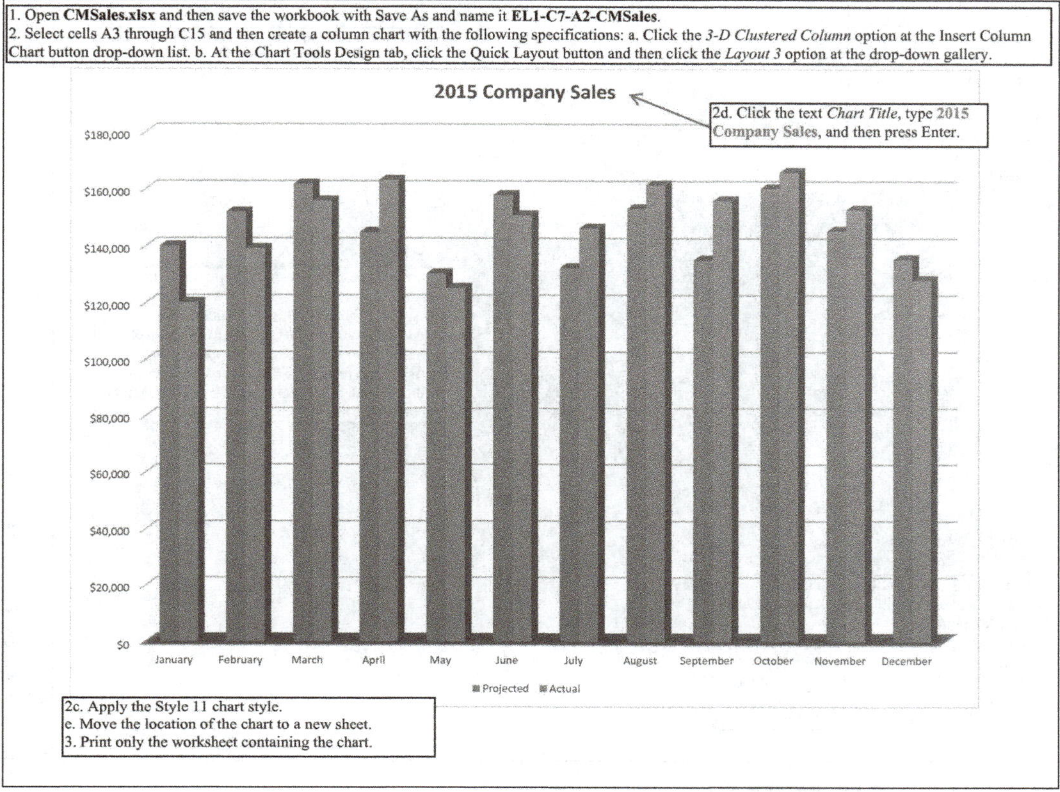

EL1-C7-A2-CMSales(A2).xlsx

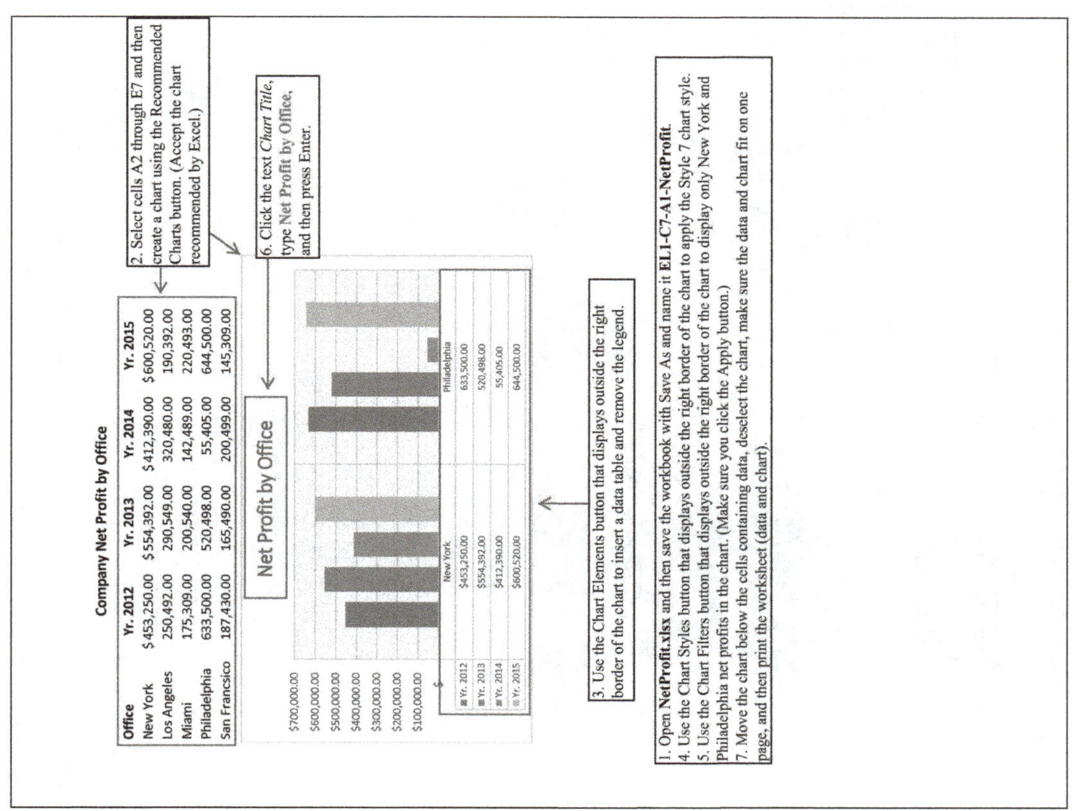

Company Net Profit by Office

Office	Yr. 2012	Yr. 2013	Yr. 2014	Yr. 2015
New York	$453,250.00	$554,392.00	$412,390.00	$600,520.00
Los Angeles	250,492.00	290,549.00	320,480.00	190,392.00
Miami	175,309.00	200,540.00	142,489.00	220,493.00
Philadelphia	633,500.00	520,498.00	55,405.00	644,500.00
San Francisco	187,430.00	165,490.00	200,499.00	145,309.00

EL1-C7-A1-NetProfit(A1).xlsx

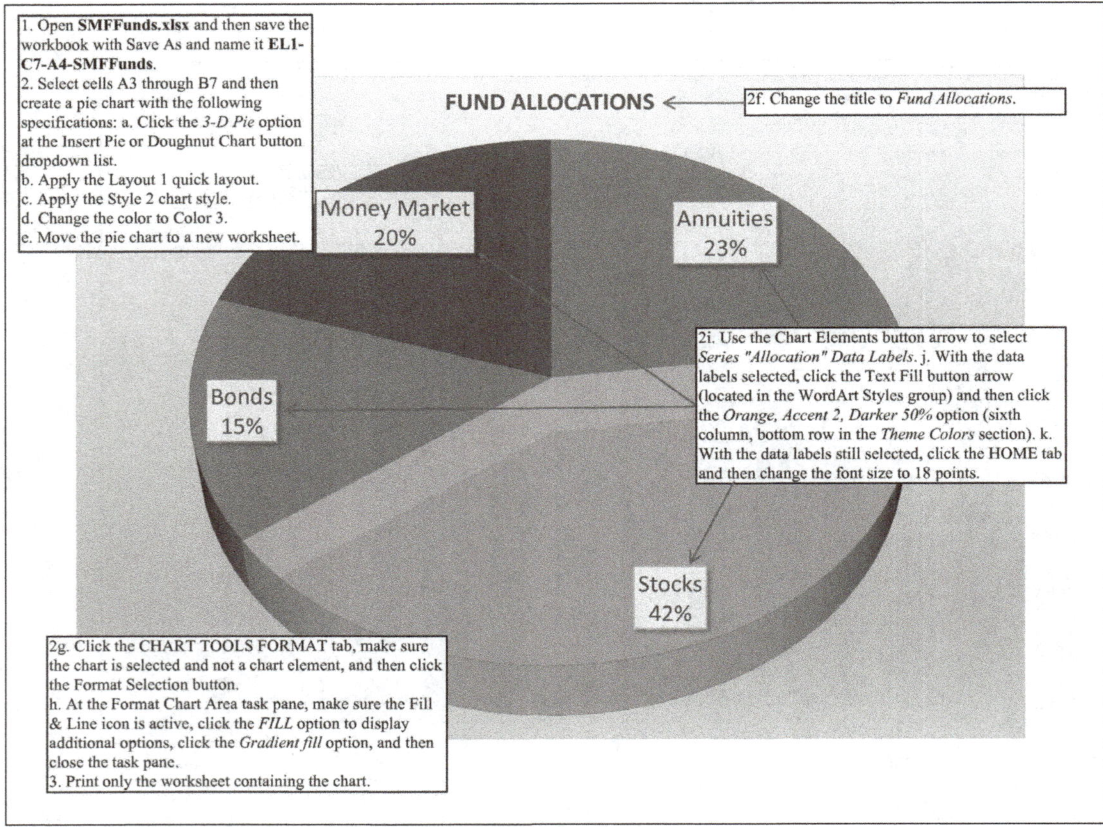

EL1-C7-A4-SMFFunds(A4).xlsx

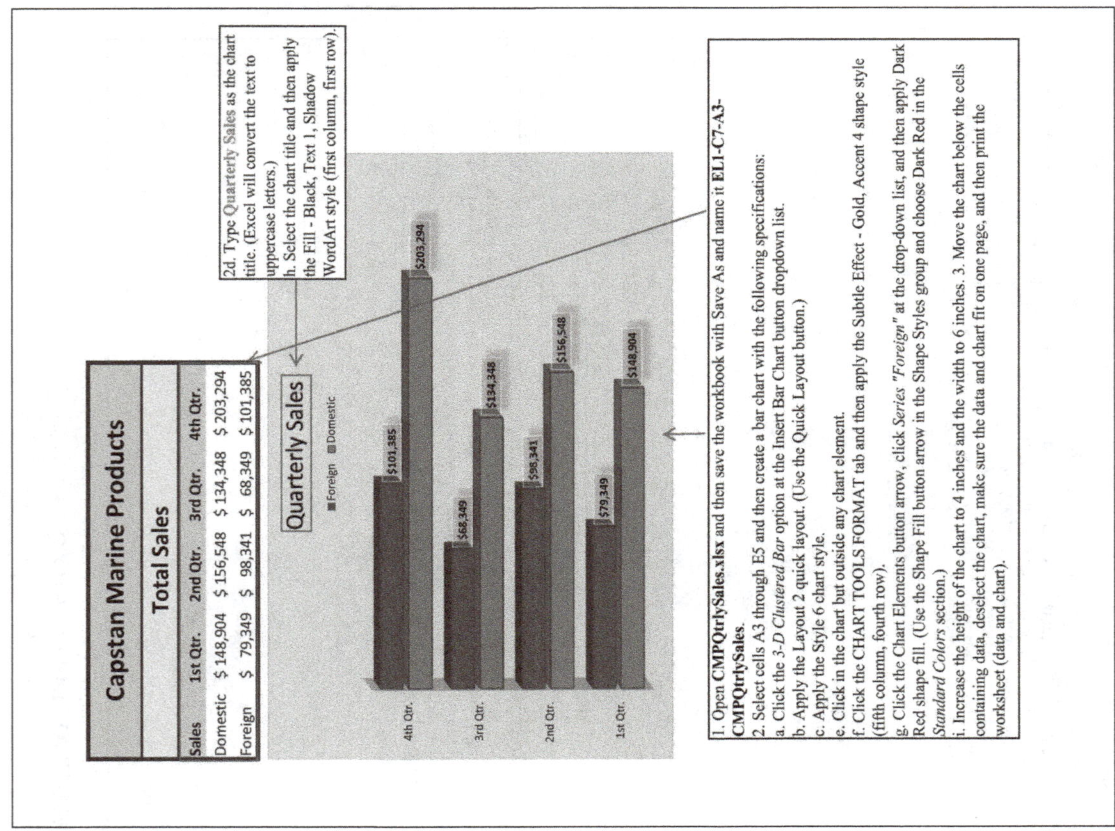

EL1-C7-A3-CMPQtrlySales(A3).xlsx

CLEARLINE MANUFACTURING

Refinance Plan

Lender	Amount	Interest Rate	Term in Months	Monthly Payments
Keystone Mortgage	$ 125,000	7.50%	120	($1,483.77)
Keystone Mortgage	$ 300,000	7.20%	120	($3,514.26)
Willows Credit Union	$ 125,000	7.40%	96	($1,729.20)
Willows Credit Union	$ 300,000	7.10%	96	($4,105.06)

1. Open **CMRefiPlan.xlsx** and then save the workbook with Save As and name it **EL1-C7-A5-CMRefiPlan**.
2. The manager of Clearline Manufacturing is interested in refinancing a loan for either $125,000 or $300,000 and wants to determine the monthly payments.

2. Make cell E4 active and then insert a formula using the PMT function. (For assistance, refer to Project 5a. The monthly payment amounts will display as negative numbers representing outflows of cash.)
3. Copy the formula in cell E4 down to cells E5 through E7.

EL1-C7-A5-CMRefiPlan(A5).xlsx

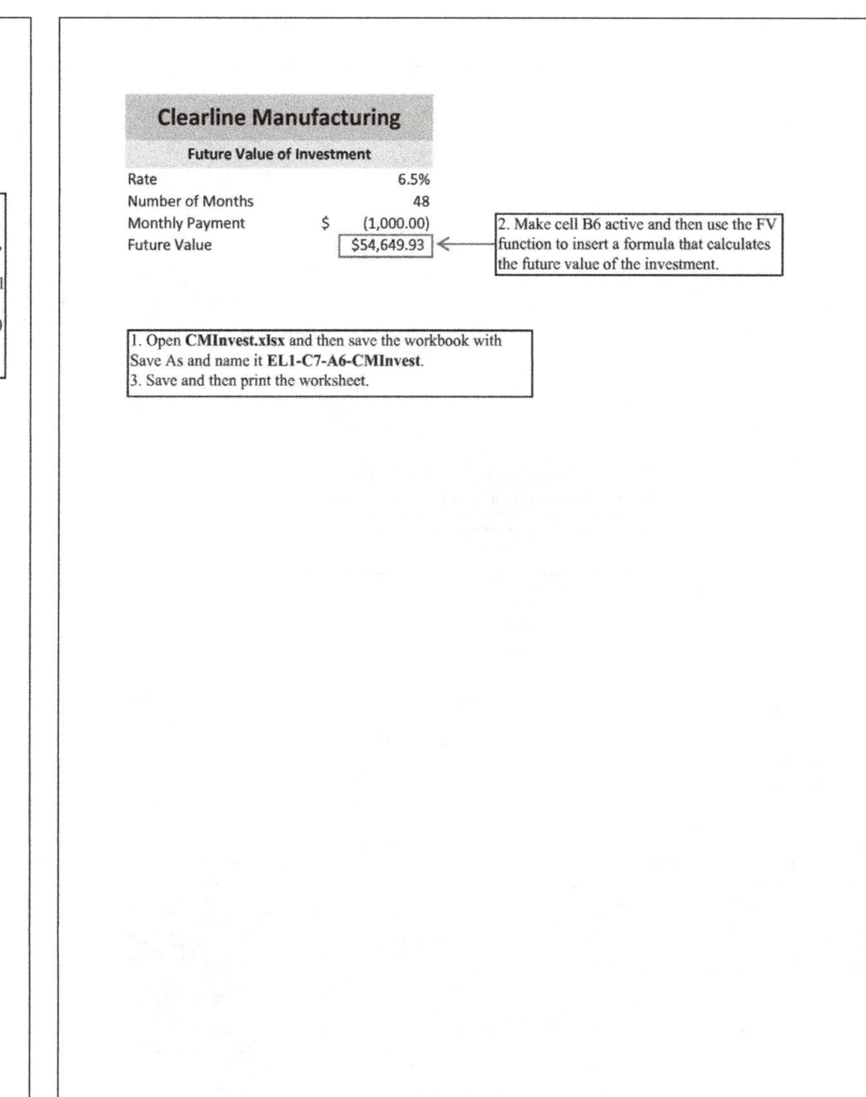

Clearline Manufacturing

Future Value of Investment

Rate		6.5%
Number of Months		48
Monthly Payment	$	(1,000.00)
Future Value		$54,649.93

2. Make cell B6 active and then use the FV function to insert a formula that calculates the future value of the investment.

1. Open **CMInvest.xlsx** and then save the workbook with Save As and name it **EL1-C7-A6-CMInvest**.
3. Save and then print the worksheet.

EL1-C7-A6-CMInvest(A6,Step3).xlsx

Clearline Manufacturing

Future Value of Investment

Rate		8.0%
Number of Months		60
Monthly Payment	$	(500.00)
Future Value		$36,738.43

4. Make the following changes to the worksheet: a. Change the percentage in cell B3 from *6.5%* to *8.0%*.

4b. Change the number in cell B4 from *48* to *60*.

4c. Change the amount in cell B5 from *($1,000)* to *-500*.

EL1-C7-A6-CMInvest(A6,Step5).xlsx

DEERING INDUSTRIES

SEMIANNUAL CUSTOMER SALES ANALYSIS

Salesperson	Sales	Bonus	Amount
Johnson, Craig	$ 115,400	YES	$ 5,770
Rehberg, Robin	98,428	NO	-
Singleton, Catherine	70,450	NO	-
Im, Kwan	80,700	NO	-
Hutchinson, Lee	130,750	YES	6,538
Kulisek, Andre	101,405	YES	5,070
Ludlow, William	79,525	NO	-
Marshall, Isabelle	89,750	NO	-
Newman, Jared	73,400	NO	-
Ortega, Cecilia	190,770	YES	9,539
Pascual, Maureen	145,075	YES	7,254

4. Apply accounting formatting with a dollar sign and no places past the decimal point to cell D4.

3. Make cell D4 active and then insert the formula =IF(C4="YES",B4*0.05,0). If sales are over $99,999, this formula will multiply the sales amount by 5% and then insert the product (result) of the formula in the cell. Copy the formula in cell D4 down to cells D5 through D14.

2. Insert a formula in cell C4 that inserts the word *YES* if the amount in B4 is greater than 99999 and inserts *NO* if the amount is not greater than 99999. Copy the formula in cell C4 down to cells C5 through C14.

1. Open **DISalesBonuses.xlsx** and then save the workbook with Save As and name it **EL1-C7-A7-DISalesBonuses.**
5. Save and then print **EL1-C7-A7-DISalesBonuses.xlsx**.

EL1-C7-A7-DISalesBonuses(A7,Step5).xlsx

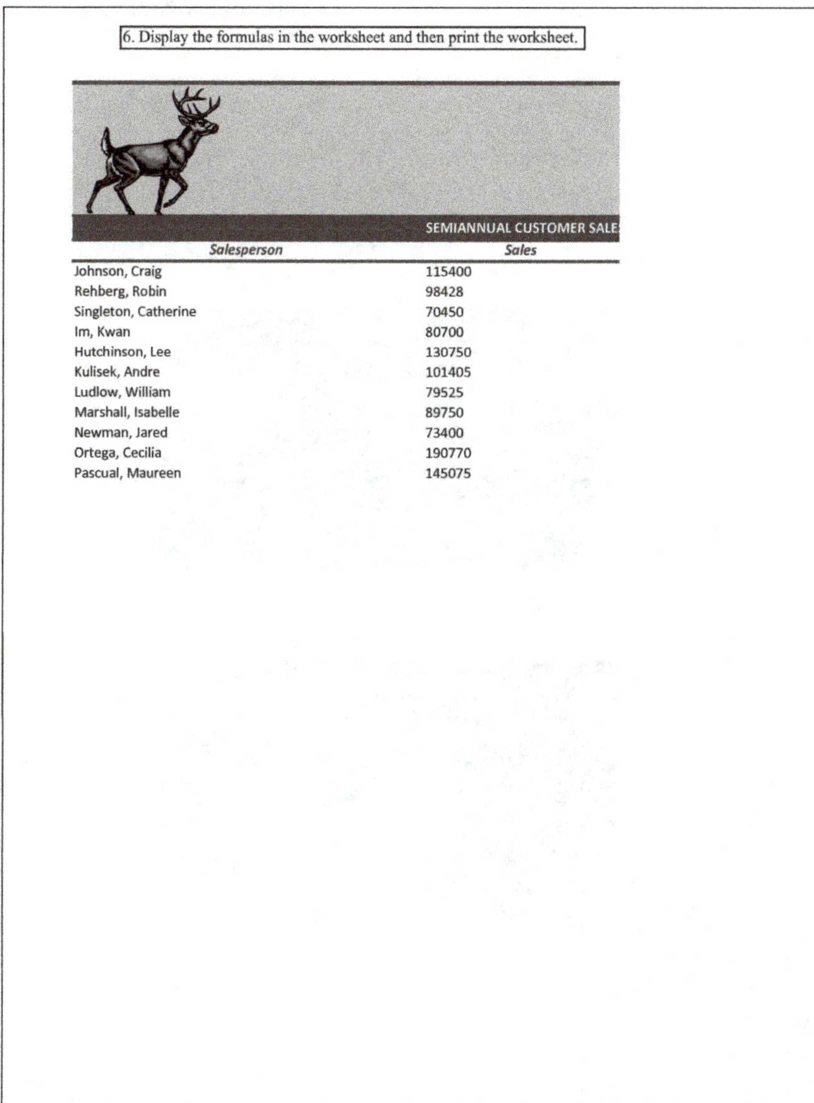

6. Display the formulas in the worksheet and then print the worksheet.

SEMIANNUAL CUSTOMER SALE

Salesperson	Sales
Johnson, Craig	115400
Rehberg, Robin	98428
Singleton, Catherine	70450
Im, Kwan	80700
Hutchinson, Lee	130750
Kulisek, Andre	101405
Ludlow, William	79525
Marshall, Isabelle	89750
Newman, Jared	73400
Ortega, Cecilia	190770
Pascual, Maureen	145075

EL1-C7-A7-DISalesBonuses(A7,Step6).xlsx (1 of 2)

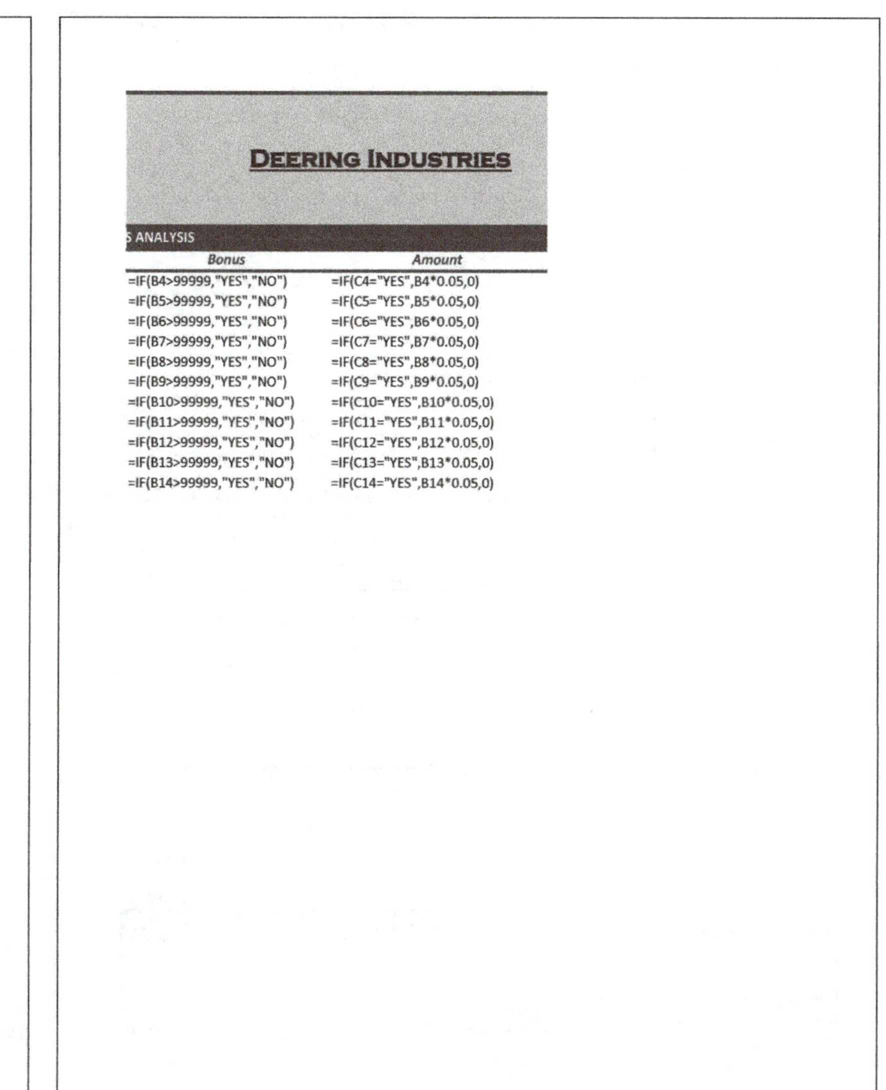

DEERING INDUSTRIES

S ANALYSIS

Bonus	Amount
=IF(B4>99999,"YES","NO")	=IF(C4="YES",B4*0.05,0)
=IF(B5>99999,"YES","NO")	=IF(C5="YES",B5*0.05,0)
=IF(B6>99999,"YES","NO")	=IF(C6="YES",B6*0.05,0)
=IF(B7>99999,"YES","NO")	=IF(C7="YES",B7*0.05,0)
=IF(B8>99999,"YES","NO")	=IF(C8="YES",B8*0.05,0)
=IF(B9>99999,"YES","NO")	=IF(C9="YES",B9*0.05,0)
=IF(B10>99999,"YES","NO")	=IF(C10="YES",B10*0.05,0)
=IF(B11>99999,"YES","NO")	=IF(C11="YES",B11*0.05,0)
=IF(B12>99999,"YES","NO")	=IF(C12="YES",B12*0.05,0)
=IF(B13>99999,"YES","NO")	=IF(C13="YES",B13*0.05,0)
=IF(B14>99999,"YES","NO")	=IF(C14="YES",B14*0.05,0)

EL1-C7-A7-DISalesBonuses(A7,Step6).xlsx (2 of 2)

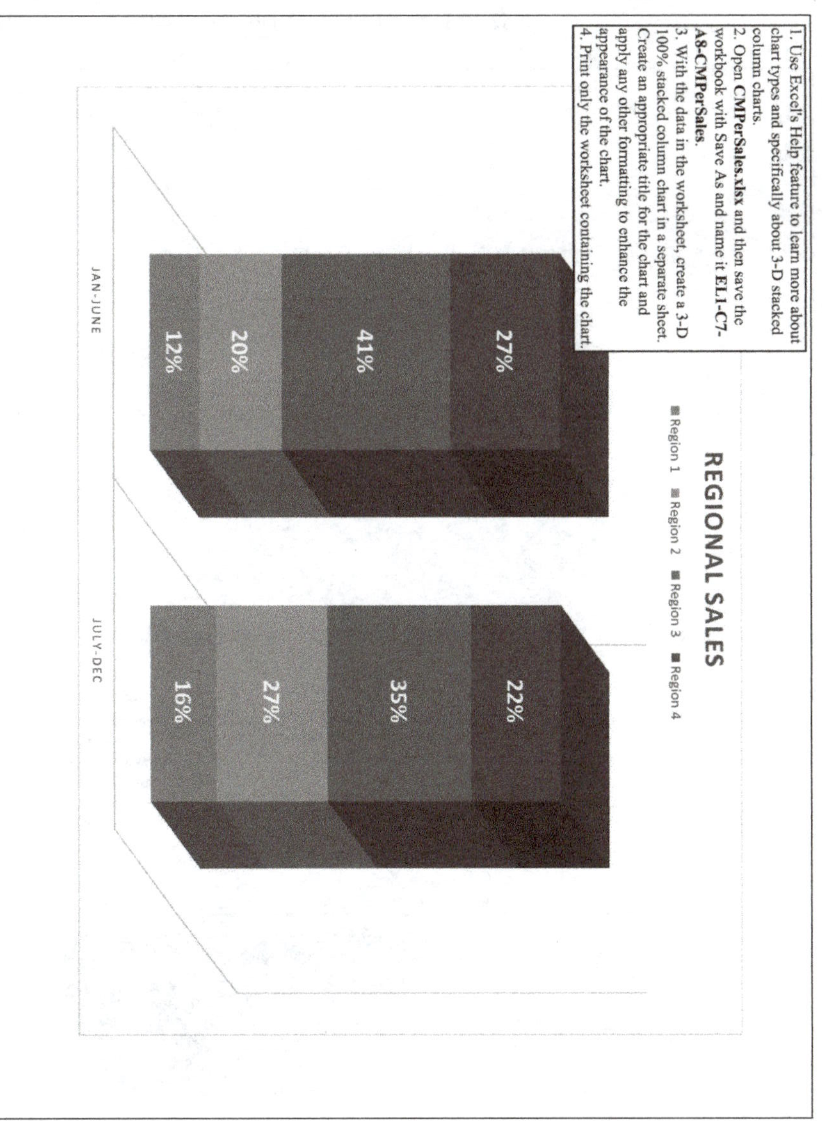

1. Use Excel's Help feature to learn more about chart types and specifically about 3-D stacked column charts.
2. Open **CMPerSales.xlsx** and then save the workbook with Save As and name it **EL1-C7-A8-CMPerSales**.
3. With the data in the worksheet, create a 3-D 100% stacked column chart in a separate sheet. Create an appropriate title for the chart and apply any other formatting to enhance the appearance of the chart.
4. Print only the worksheet containing the chart.

EL1-C7-A8-CMPerSales(A8).xlsx

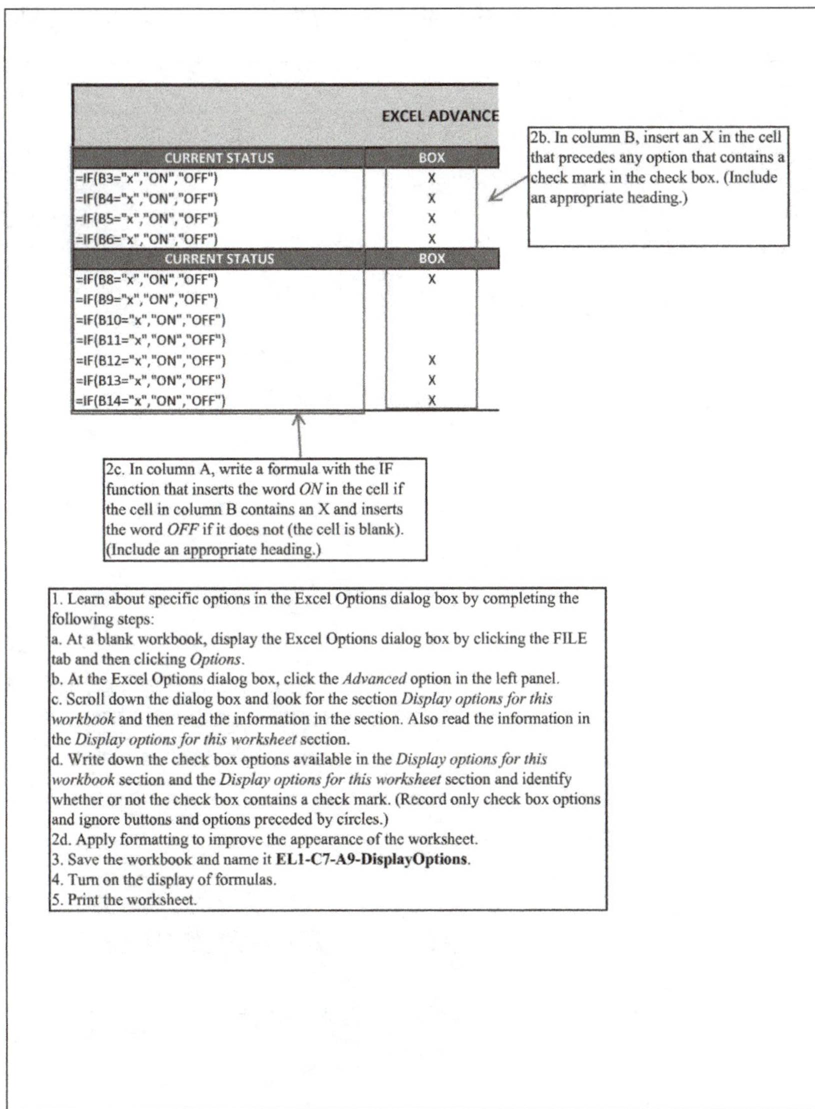

EXCEL ADVANCE	
CURRENT STATUS	BOX
=IF(B3="x","ON","OFF")	X
=IF(B4="x","ON","OFF")	X
=IF(B5="x","ON","OFF")	X
=IF(B6="x","ON","OFF")	X
CURRENT STATUS	BOX
=IF(B8="x","ON","OFF")	X
=IF(B9="x","ON","OFF")	
=IF(B10="x","ON","OFF")	
=IF(B11="x","ON","OFF")	
=IF(B12="x","ON","OFF")	X
=IF(B13="x","ON","OFF")	X
=IF(B14="x","ON","OFF")	X

2b. In column B, insert an X in the cell that precedes any option that contains a check mark in the check box. (Include an appropriate heading.)

2c. In column A, write a formula with the IF function that inserts the word *ON* in the cell if the cell in column B contains an X and inserts the word *OFF* if it does not (the cell is blank). (Include an appropriate heading.)

1. Learn about specific options in the Excel Options dialog box by completing the following steps:
a. At a blank workbook, display the Excel Options dialog box by clicking the FILE tab and then clicking *Options*.
b. At the Excel Options dialog box, click the *Advanced* option in the left panel.
c. Scroll down the dialog box and look for the section *Display options for this workbook* and then read the information in the section. Also read the information in the *Display options for this worksheet* section.
d. Write down the check box options available in the *Display options for this workbook* section and the *Display options for this worksheet* section and identify whether or not the check box contains a check mark. (Record only check box options and ignore buttons and options preceded by circles.)
2d. Apply formatting to improve the appearance of the worksheet.
3. Save the workbook and name it **EL1-C7-A9-DisplayOptions**.
4. Turn on the display of formulas.
5. Print the worksheet.

EL1-C7-A9-DisplayOptions(A9,Step5).xlsx (1 of 2)

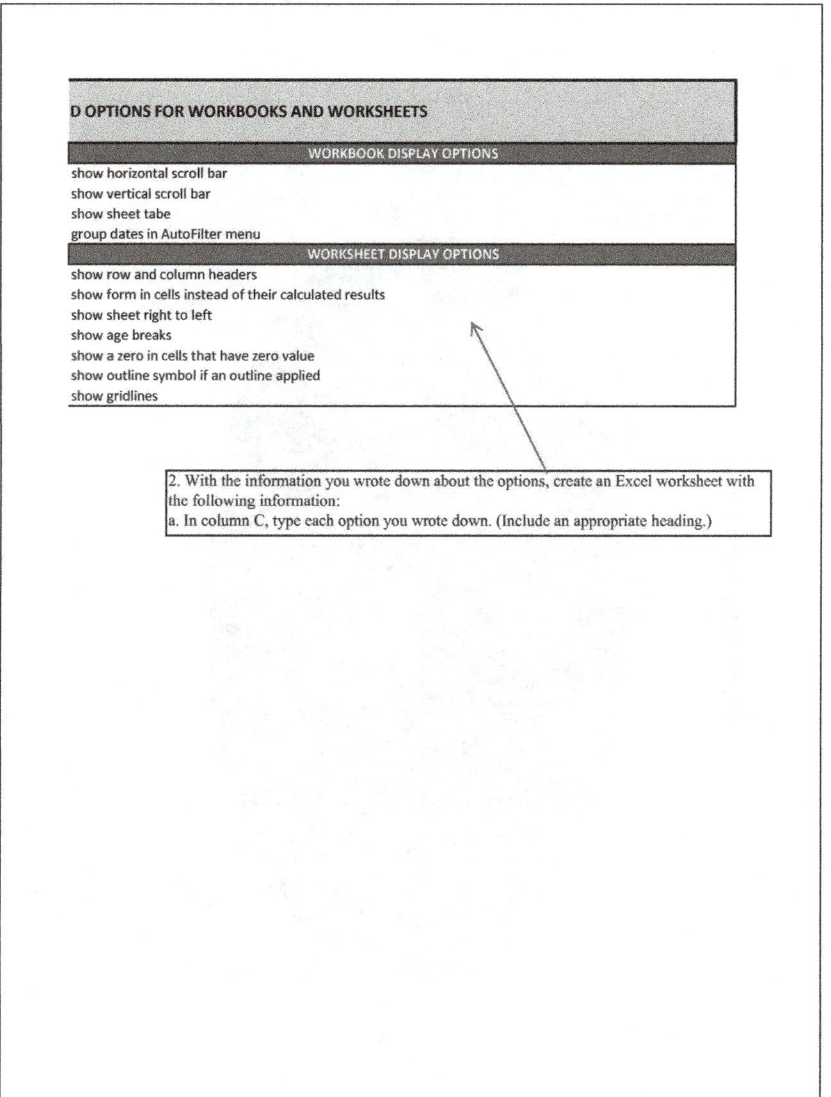

D OPTIONS FOR WORKBOOKS AND WORKSHEETS
WORKBOOK DISPLAY OPTIONS
show horizontal scroll bar
show vertical scroll bar
show sheet tabe
group dates in AutoFilter menu
WORKSHEET DISPLAY OPTIONS
show row and column headers
show form in cells instead of their calculated results
show sheet right to left
show age breaks
show a zero in cells that have zero value
show outline symbol if an outline applied
show gridlines

2. With the information you wrote down about the options, create an Excel worksheet with the following information:
a. In column C, type each option you wrote down. (Include an appropriate heading.)

EL1-C7-A9-DisplayOptions(A9,Step5).xlsx (2 of 2)

6. Turn off the display of formulas.
7. Save, print, and then close **EL1-C7-A9-DisplayOptions.xlsx**.

EXCEL ADVANCED OPTIONS FOR WORKBOOKS AND WORKSHEETS		
CURRENT STATUS	BOX	WORKBOOK DISPLAY OPTIONS
ON	X	show horizontal scroll bar
ON	X	show vertical scroll bar
ON	X	show sheet tabe
ON	X	group dates in AutoFilter menu
CURRENT STATUS	BOX	WORKSHEET DISPLAY OPTIONS
ON	X	show row and column headers
OFF		show form in cells instead of their calculated results
OFF		show sheet right to left
OFF		show age breaks
ON	X	show a zero in cells that have zero value
ON	X	show outline symbol if an outline applied
ON	X	show gridlines

EL1-C7-A9-DisplayOptions(A9,Step7).xlsx

FEBRUARY EXPENSE PERCENTAGES

Supplies	4.1%
Utilities	4.8%
Advertising	5.1%
Marketing	7.1%
Lease	10.2%
Taxes	14.1%
Salaries	54.7%

EL1-C7-VB-CMFebExp(VB).xlsx (2 of 2)

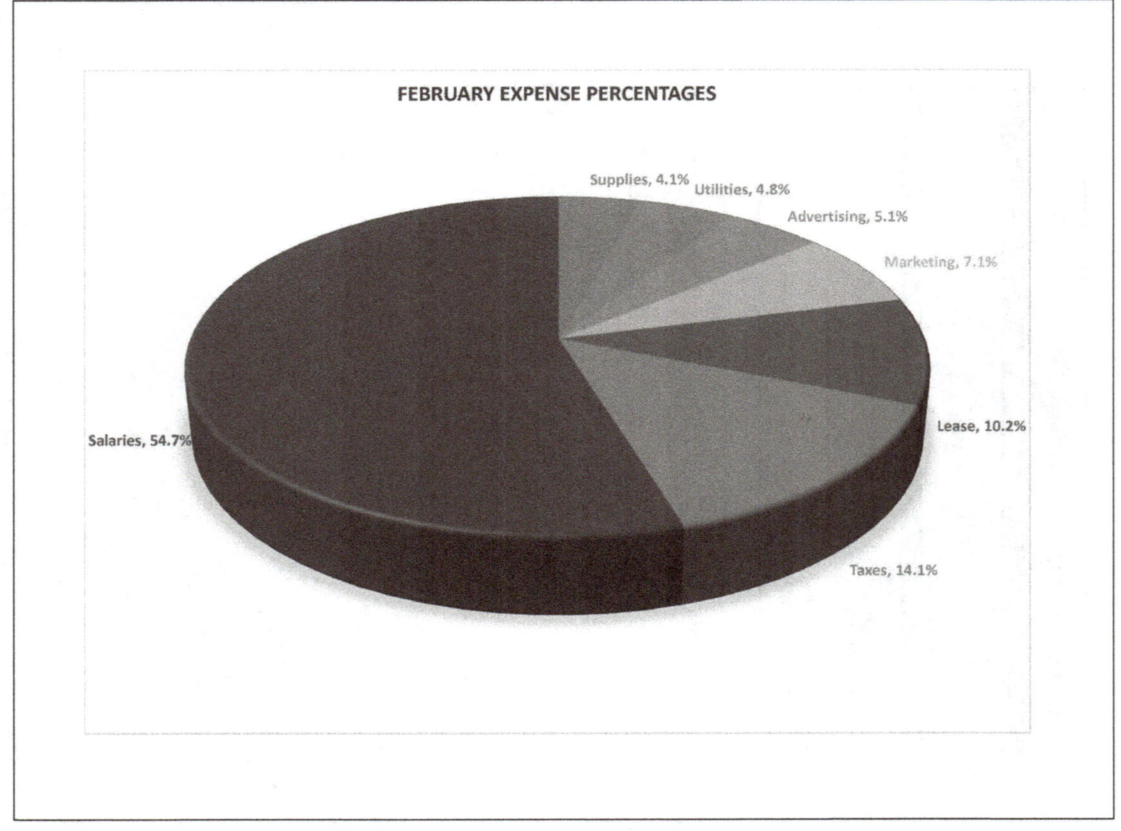

EL1-C7-VB-CMFebExp(VB).xlsx (1 of 2)

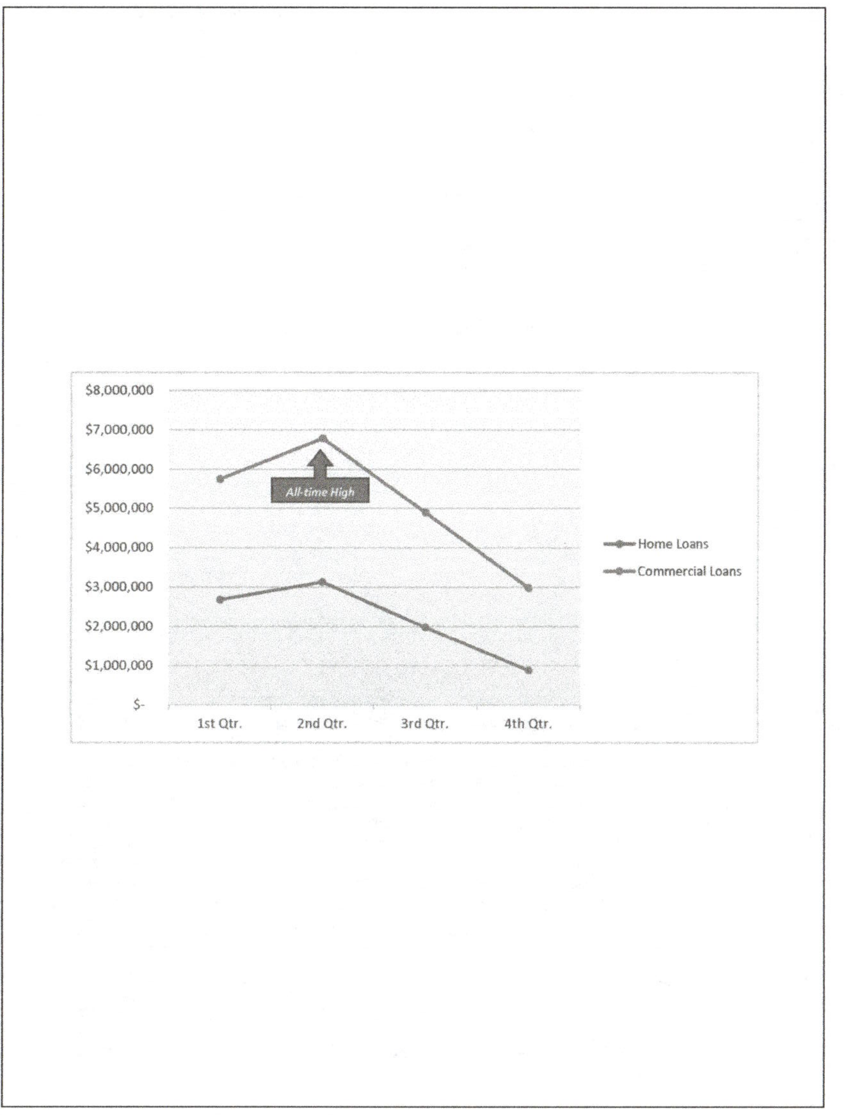

EL1-C7-CS-DWQtrSales(CS1).xlsx

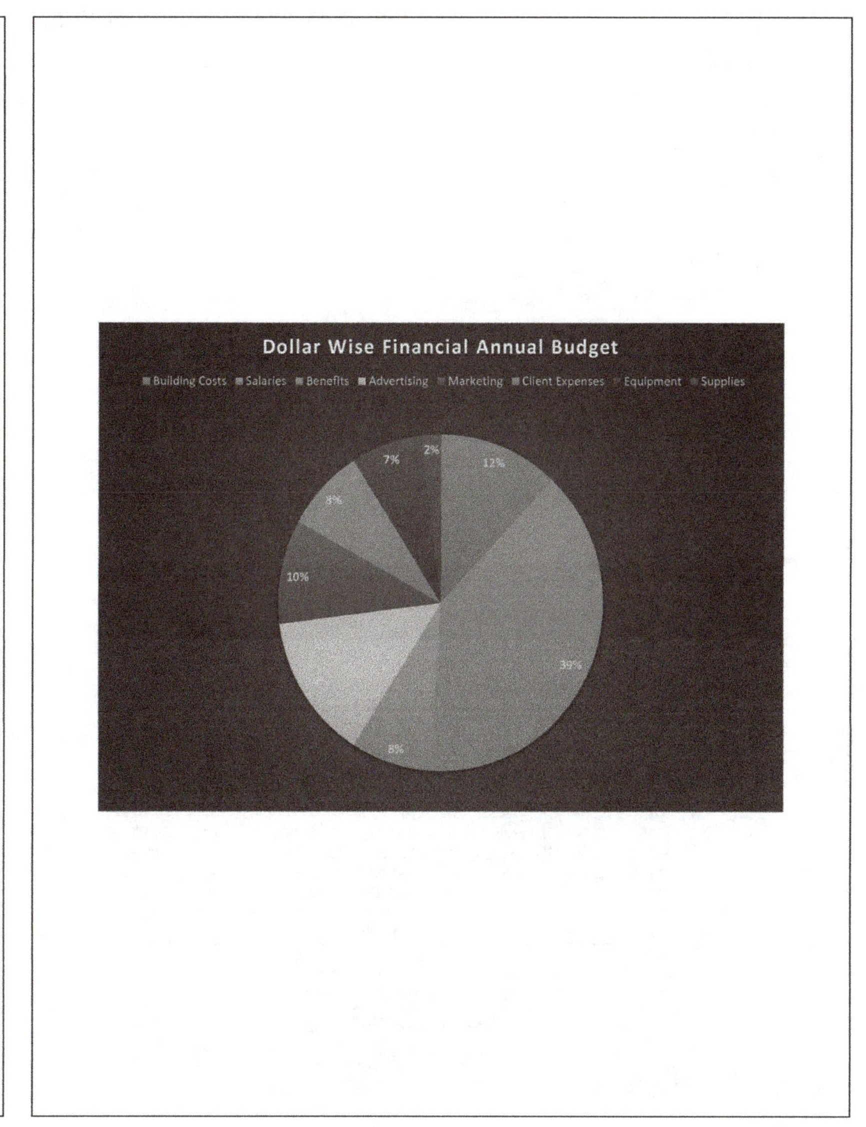

EL1-C7-CS-DWBudget(CS2).xlsx

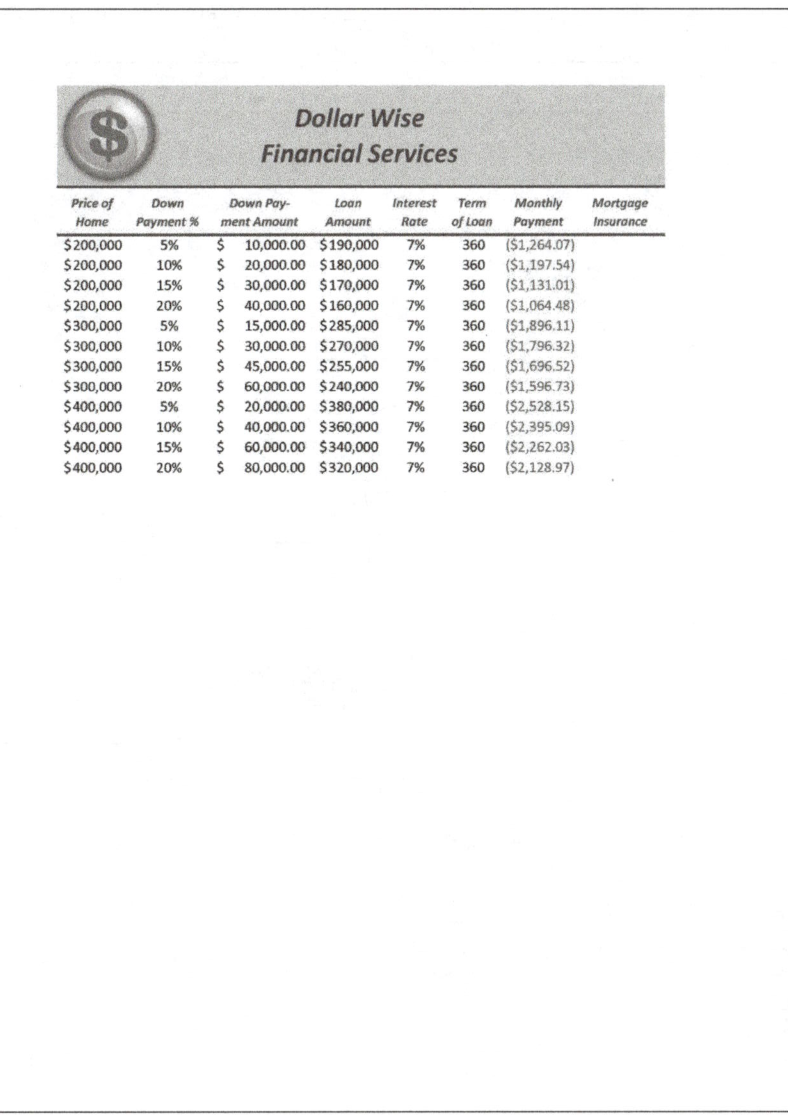

Dollar Wise Financial Services

Price of Home	Down Payment %	Down Payment Amount	Loan Amount	Interest Rate	Term of Loan	Monthly Payment	Mortgage Insurance
$200,000	5%	$ 10,000.00	$190,000	7%	360	($1,264.07)	
$200,000	10%	$ 20,000.00	$180,000	7%	360	($1,197.54)	
$200,000	15%	$ 30,000.00	$170,000	7%	360	($1,131.01)	
$200,000	20%	$ 40,000.00	$160,000	7%	360	($1,064.48)	
$300,000	5%	$ 15,000.00	$285,000	7%	360	($1,896.11)	
$300,000	10%	$ 30,000.00	$270,000	7%	360	($1,796.32)	
$300,000	15%	$ 45,000.00	$255,000	7%	360	($1,696.52)	
$300,000	20%	$ 60,000.00	$240,000	7%	360	($1,596.73)	
$400,000	5%	$ 20,000.00	$380,000	7%	360	($2,528.15)	
$400,000	10%	$ 40,000.00	$360,000	7%	360	($2,395.09)	
$400,000	15%	$ 60,000.00	$340,000	7%	360	($2,262.03)	
$400,000	20%	$ 80,000.00	$320,000	7%	360	($2,128.97)	

EL1-C7-CS-DWMortgageWksht(CS3).xlsx

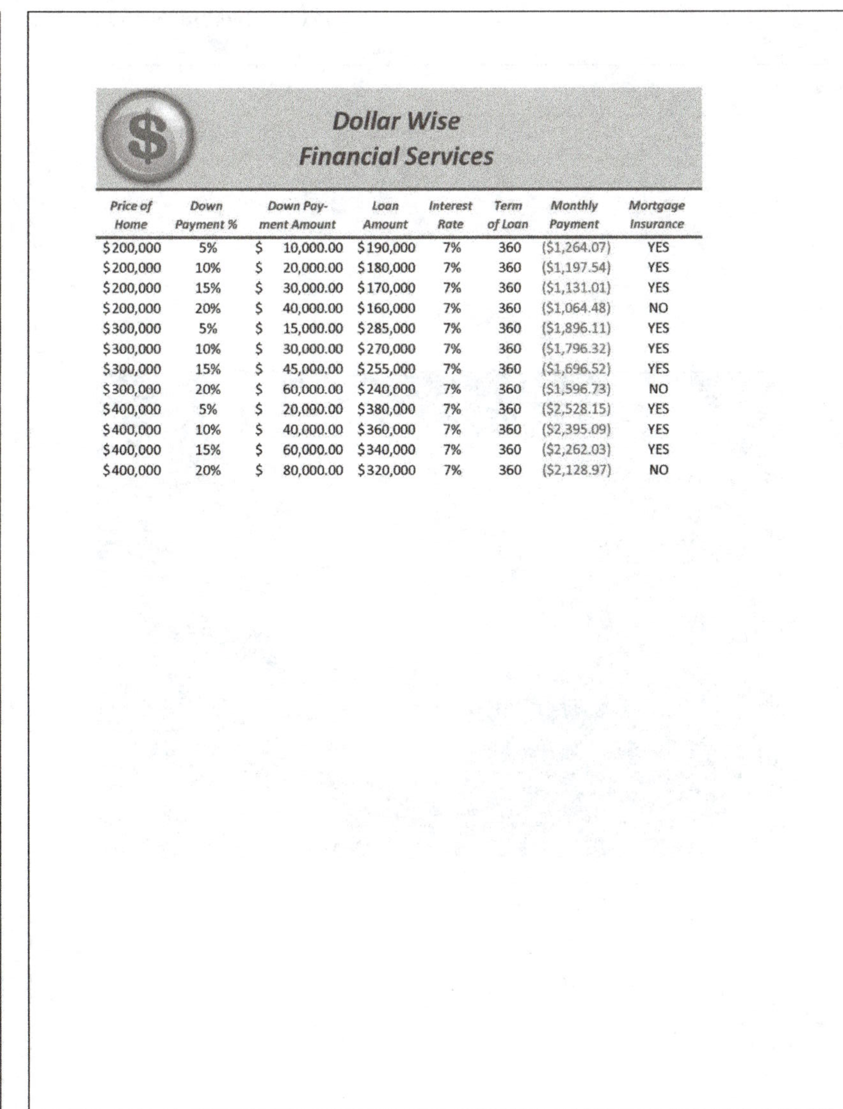

Dollar Wise Financial Services

Price of Home	Down Payment %	Down Payment Amount	Loan Amount	Interest Rate	Term of Loan	Monthly Payment	Mortgage Insurance
$200,000	5%	$ 10,000.00	$190,000	7%	360	($1,264.07)	YES
$200,000	10%	$ 20,000.00	$180,000	7%	360	($1,197.54)	YES
$200,000	15%	$ 30,000.00	$170,000	7%	360	($1,131.01)	YES
$200,000	20%	$ 40,000.00	$160,000	7%	360	($1,064.48)	NO
$300,000	5%	$ 15,000.00	$285,000	7%	360	($1,896.11)	YES
$300,000	10%	$ 30,000.00	$270,000	7%	360	($1,796.32)	YES
$300,000	15%	$ 45,000.00	$255,000	7%	360	($1,696.52)	YES
$300,000	20%	$ 60,000.00	$240,000	7%	360	($1,596.73)	NO
$400,000	5%	$ 20,000.00	$380,000	7%	360	($2,528.15)	YES
$400,000	10%	$ 40,000.00	$360,000	7%	360	($2,395.09)	YES
$400,000	15%	$ 60,000.00	$340,000	7%	360	($2,262.03)	YES
$400,000	20%	$ 80,000.00	$320,000	7%	360	($2,128.97)	NO

EL1-C7-CS-DWMortgageWksht(CS4).xlsx

Average 30-year Fixed Mortgages
2011 to Current

January July

14.00
12.00
10.00
8.00
6.00
4.00
2.00
0.00

2011 2012 2013 2014 2015

EL1-C7-CS-DWRates(CS5).xlsx

Excel Level 1, Chapter 8 Model Answers

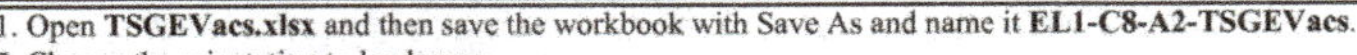

1. Open **TSGEVacs.xlsx** and then save the workbook with Save As and name it **EL1-C8-A2-TSGEVacs**.
5. Change the orientation to landscape.
6. Make sure the data and the airfare information display on one page and then print the worksheet.

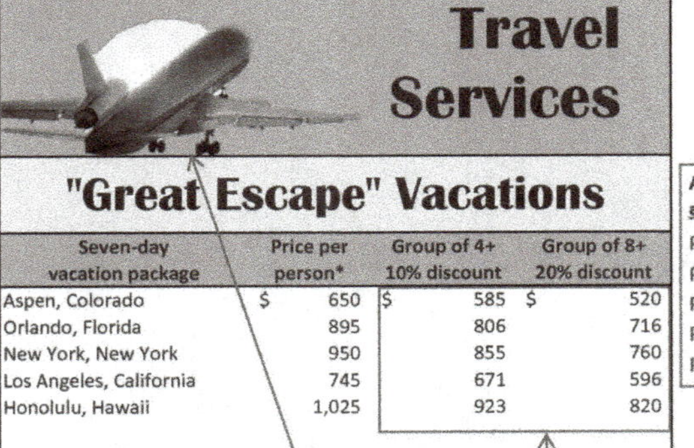

"Great Escape" Vacations

Seven-day vacation package	Price per person*	Group of 4+ 10% discount	Group of 8+ 20% discount
Aspen, Colorado	$ 650	$ 585	$ 520
Orlando, Florida	895	806	716
New York, New York	950	855	760
Los Angeles, California	745	671	596
Honolulu, Hawaii	1,025	923	820

*Prices based on double occupancy and do not include airfare. Taxes extra.
A surcharge will apply for single occupancy.

Airfare from Portland, Oregon, as of today, October 1, 2015

Portland to Aspen, Colorado: $239
Portland to Orlando, Florida: $445
Portland to New York, New York: $519
Portland to Los Angeles, California: $215
Portland to Honolulu, Hawaii: $575

4. Open Word and then open the document named **TSAirfare.docx** located in the EL1C8 folder on your storage medium. Click the Excel button on the Taskbar and then use the Screenshot button (with the *Screen Clipping* option) to select and then insert the airfare information in **EL1-C8-A2-TSGEVacs.xlsx**. Position the information at the right side of the data in

3. Format the image of the airplane and position it as shown in Figure 8.11 with the following specifications:
a. Use the Remove Background button in the Adjust group on the PICTURE TOOLS FORMAT tab to remove a portion of the yellow background so the image displays similar to what you see in the figure.
b. Rotate the image to flip it horizontally.
c. Apply the Brightness: +20% Contrast: +20% correction.
d. Change the height of the image to 1.4 inches and then position the image as shown in the figure.

2. Insert appropriate formulas to calculate the prices based on 10% and 20% discounts and apply the appropriate number formatting. ***Hint: For the 10% discount column, multiply the price per person by 0.90 (which determines 90% of the price) and for the 20% discount column, multiply the price per person by 0.80 (which determines 80% of the price).***

EL1-C8-A2-TSGEVacs(A2).xlsx

1. Open **MSSalesPlans.xlsx** and then save the workbook with Save As and name it **EL1-C8-A1-MSSalesPlans**.
10. Change the worksheet orientation to landscape.

8. Insert the clip art image shown in Figure 8.10 with the following specifications: a. Click the INSERT tab and then click the Online Pictures button. At the Insert Pictures window, search for images related to maple leaves. (The colors of the original clip art image are green and white.) b. Apply the Orange, Accent color 2 Dark clip art image color (third column, second row). c. Apply the Brightness: -20% Contrast: +20% correction (second column, fourth row). d. Apply the Drop Shadow Rectangle picture style (fourth thumbnail). e. Size and move the image so it is positioned as shown in Figure 8.10.

Maplewood Suppliers

Equipment Sales Plans

Equipment	Sale Price	Interest Rate	Term in Months	Monthly Payments	Total Payments	Total Interest
Photocopier, Model C120	$8,500.00	8.80%	60	$175.62	$10,537.33	$2,037.33
Photocopier, Model C150	$12,750.00	8.80%	60	$263.43	$15,805.99	$3,055.99
Photocopier, Model C280	$19,250.00	8.80%	60	$397.73	$23,863.94	$4,613.94

6. Insert a formula in cell G4 that calculates the total amount of interest paid. 7. Copy the formula in cell G4 down to cells G5 and G6.

9. Insert the company name *Maplewood Suppliers* in cell A1 as WordArt with the following specifications: a. Click the WordArt button on the INSERT tab and then click the *Fill - White, Outline - Accent 2, Hard Shadow - Accent 2* image color (fourth column, third row). b. Apply the Orange, Accent 2, Darker 50% text fill (sixth column, bottom row in the *Theme Colors* section). c. Apply the Orange, Accent 2, Lighter 60% text outline (sixth column, third row in the *Theme Colors* section). d. Using the Text Effects button, apply the Square transform text effect. e. Change the width of the WordArt to 5 inches. f. Move the WordArt so it is positioned in cell A1 as shown in Figure 8.10.

2. Insert a formula in cell E4 using the PMT function that calculates monthly payments. (Type a minus sign before the cell designation in the *Pv* text box at the Function Arguments palette.) ***Hint: For assistance, refer to Chapter 7, Project 5a.*** 3. Copy the formula in cell E4 down to cells E5 and E6.

4. Insert a formula in cell F4 that calculates the total amount of the payments. 5. Copy the formula in cell F4 down to cells F5 and F6.

EL1-C8-A1-MSSalesPlans(A1).xlsx

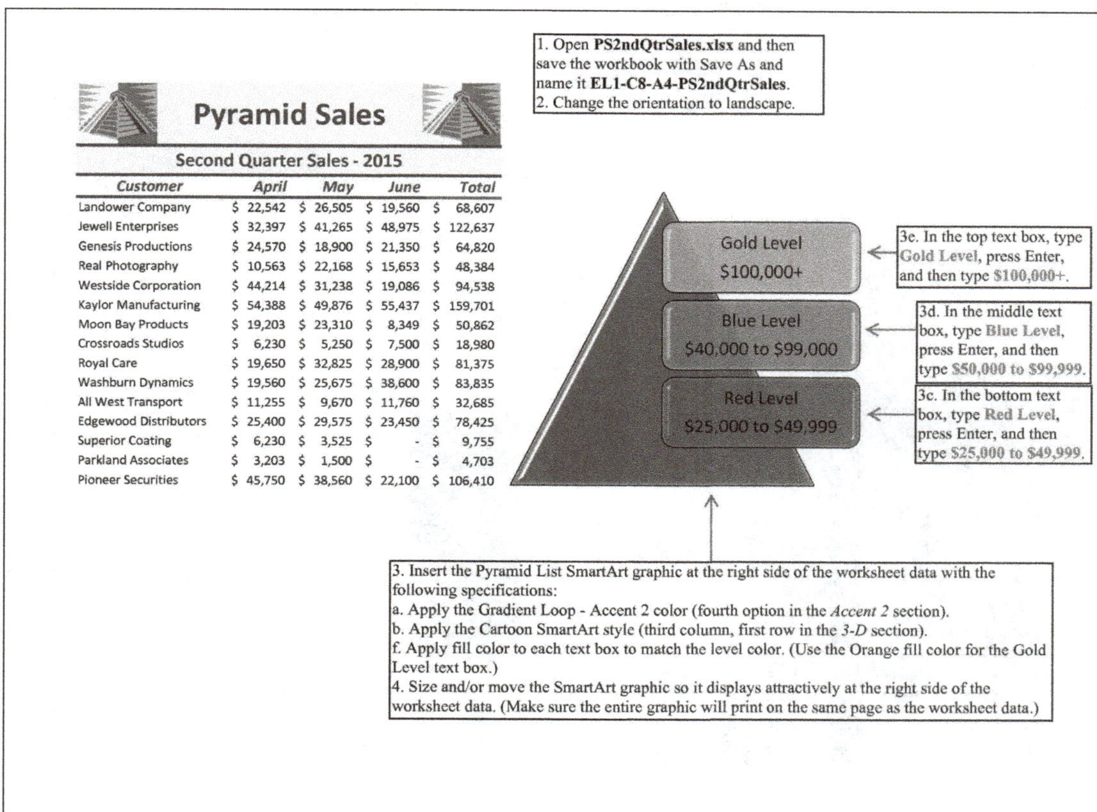

1. Open **PS2ndQtrSales.xlsx** and then save the workbook with Save As and name it **EL1-C8-A4-PS2ndQtrSales**.
2. Change the orientation to landscape.

Pyramid Sales

Second Quarter Sales - 2015

Customer	April	May	June	Total
Landower Company	$ 22,542	$ 26,505	$ 19,560	$ 68,607
Jewell Enterprises	$ 32,397	$ 41,265	$ 48,975	$ 122,637
Genesis Productions	$ 24,570	$ 18,900	$ 21,350	$ 64,820
Real Photography	$ 10,563	$ 22,168	$ 15,653	$ 48,384
Westside Corporation	$ 44,214	$ 31,238	$ 19,086	$ 94,538
Kaylor Manufacturing	$ 54,388	$ 49,876	$ 55,437	$ 159,701
Moon Bay Products	$ 19,203	$ 23,310	$ 8,349	$ 50,862
Crossroads Studios	$ 6,230	$ 5,250	$ 7,500	$ 18,980
Royal Care	$ 19,650	$ 32,825	$ 28,900	$ 81,375
Washburn Dynamics	$ 19,560	$ 25,675	$ 38,600	$ 83,835
All West Transport	$ 11,255	$ 9,670	$ 11,760	$ 32,685
Edgewood Distributors	$ 25,400	$ 29,575	$ 23,450	$ 78,425
Superior Coating	$ 6,230	$ 3,525	$ -	$ 9,755
Parkland Associates	$ 3,203	$ 1,500	$ -	$ 4,703
Pioneer Securities	$ 45,750	$ 38,560	$ 22,100	$ 106,410

3e. In the top text box, type Gold Level, press Enter, and then type $100,000+.

3d. In the middle text box, type Blue Level, press Enter, and then type $50,000 to $99,999.

3c. In the bottom text box, type Red Level, press Enter, and then type $25,000 to $49,999.

3. Insert the Pyramid List SmartArt graphic at the right side of the worksheet data with the following specifications:
a. Apply the Gradient Loop - Accent 2 color (fourth option in the *Accent 2* section).
b. Apply the Cartoon SmartArt style (third column, first row in the *3-D* section).
f. Apply fill color to each text box to match the level color. (Use the Orange fill color for the Gold Level text box.)
4. Size and/or move the SmartArt graphic so it displays attractively at the right side of the worksheet data. (Make sure the entire graphic will print on the same page as the worksheet data.)

EL1-C8-A4-PS2ndQtrSales(A4).xlsx

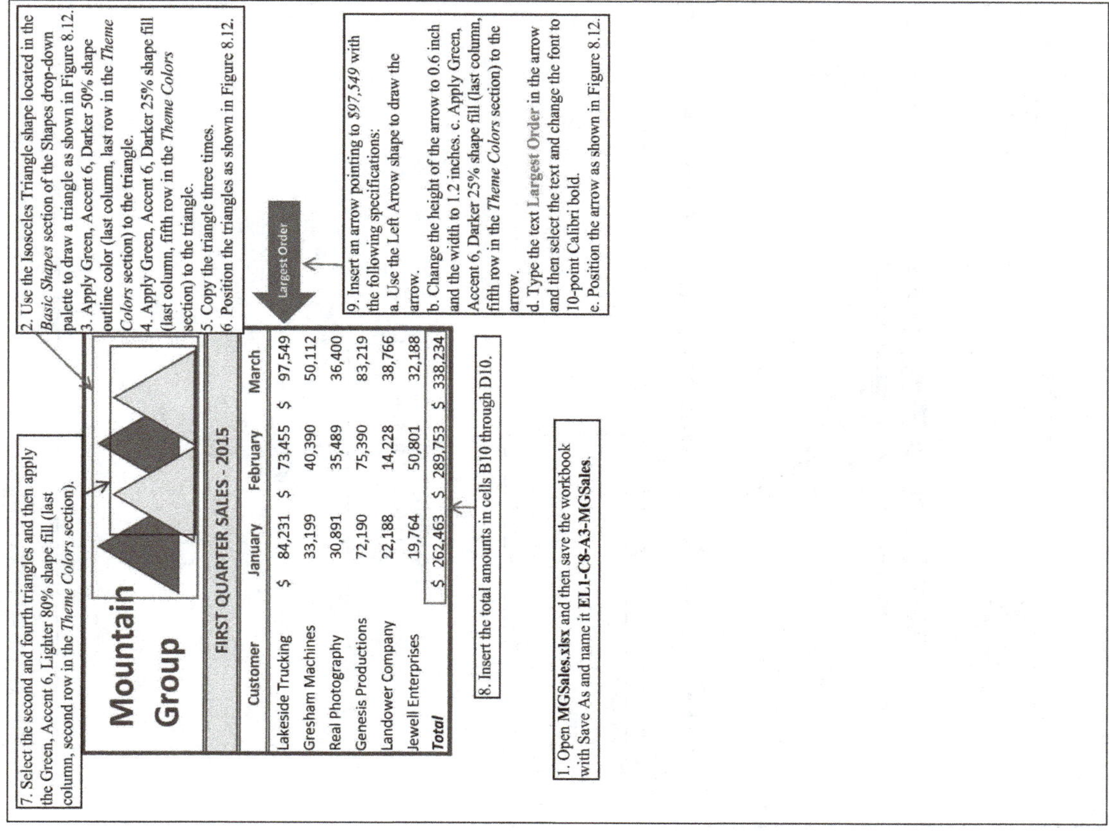

7. Select the second and fourth triangles and then apply the Green, Accent 6, Lighter 80% shape fill (last column, second row in the *Theme Colors* section).

2. Use the Isosceles Triangle shape located in the *Basic Shapes* section of the Shapes drop-down palette to draw a triangle as shown in Figure 8.12.
3. Apply Green, Accent 6, Darker 50% shape outline color (last column, last row in the *Theme Colors* section) to the triangle.
4. Apply Green, Accent 6, Darker 25% shape fill (last column, fifth row in the *Theme Colors* section) to the triangle.
5. Copy the triangle three times.
6. Position the triangles as shown in Figure 8.12.

Mountain Group

FIRST QUARTER SALES - 2015

Customer	January	February	March
Lakeside Trucking	$ 84,231	$ 73,455	$ 97,549
Gresham Machines	33,199	40,390	50,112
Real Photography	30,891	35,489	36,400
Genesis Productions	72,190	75,390	83,219
Landower Company	22,188	14,228	38,766
Jewell Enterprises	19,764	50,801	32,188
Total	$ 262,463	$ 289,753	$ 338,234

9. Insert an arrow pointing to *$97,549* with the following specifications:
a. Use the Left Arrow shape to draw the arrow.
b. Change the height of the arrow to 0.6 inch and the width to 1.2 inches. c. Apply Green, Accent 6, Darker 25% shape fill (last column, fifth row in the *Theme Colors* section) to the arrow.
d. Type the text Largest Order in the arrow and then select the text and change the font to 10-point Calibri bold.
e. Position the arrow as shown in Figure 8.12.

8. Insert the total amounts in cells B10 through D10.

1. Open **MGSales.xlsx** and then save the workbook with Save As and name it **EL1-C8-A3-MGSales**.

EL1-C8-A3-MGSales(A3).xlsx

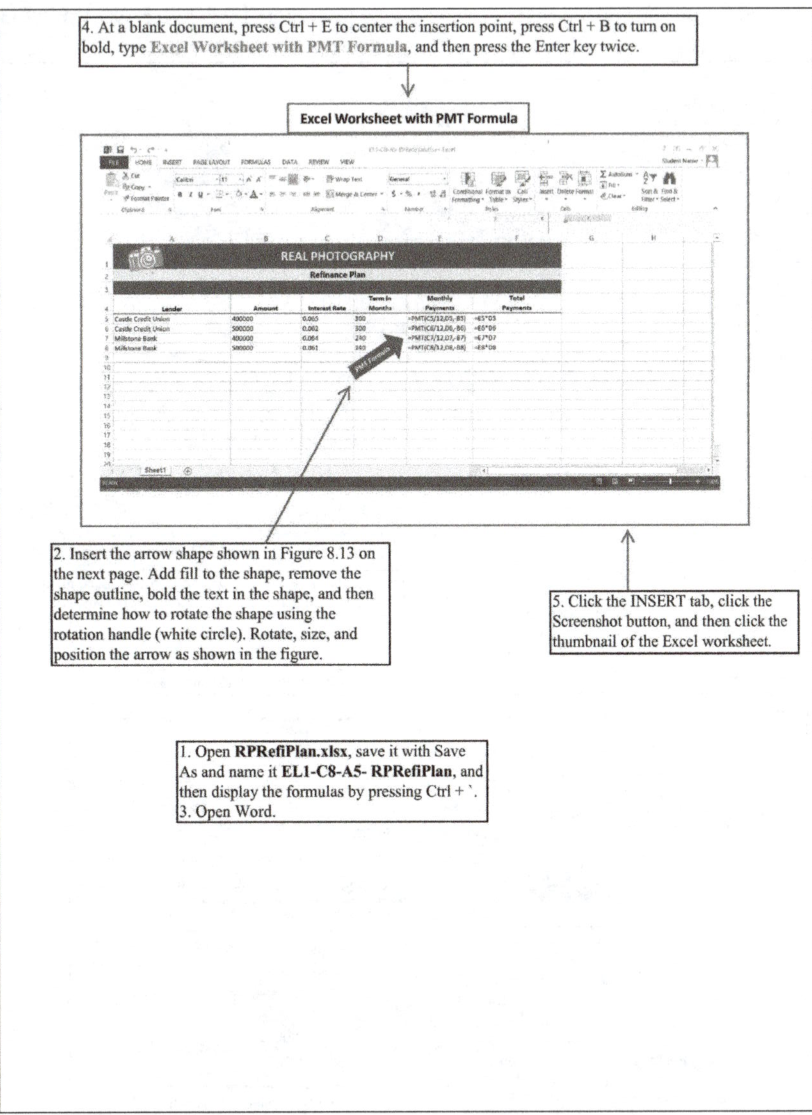

4. At a blank document, press Ctrl + E to center the insertion point, press Ctrl + B to turn on bold, type **Excel Worksheet with PMT Formula**, and then press the Enter key twice.

Excel Worksheet with PMT Formula

2. Insert the arrow shape shown in Figure 8.13 on the next page. Add fill to the shape, remove the shape outline, bold the text in the shape, and then determine how to rotate the shape using the rotation handle (white circle). Rotate, size, and position the arrow as shown in the figure.

5. Click the INSERT tab, click the Screenshot button, and then click the thumbnail of the Excel worksheet.

1. Open **RPRefiPlan.xlsx**, save it with Save As and name it **EL1-C8-A5- RPRefiPlan**, and then display the formulas by pressing Ctrl + `.
3. Open Word.

EL1-C8-A5-PMTFormula(A5).xlsx

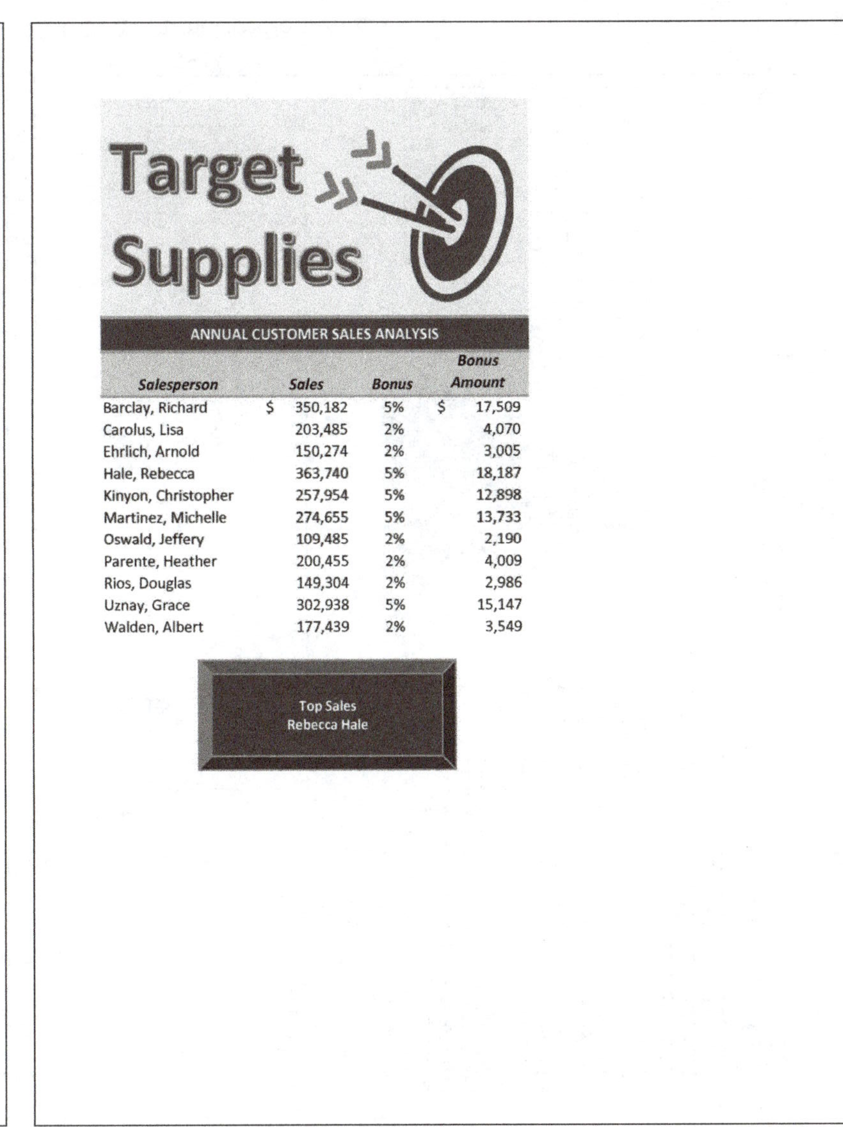

ANNUAL CUSTOMER SALES ANALYSIS

Salesperson	Sales	Bonus	Bonus Amount
Barclay, Richard	$ 350,182	5%	$ 17,509
Carolus, Lisa	203,485	2%	4,070
Ehrlich, Arnold	150,274	2%	3,005
Hale, Rebecca	363,740	5%	18,187
Kinyon, Christopher	257,954	5%	12,898
Martinez, Michelle	274,655	5%	13,733
Oswald, Jeffery	109,485	2%	2,190
Parente, Heather	200,455	2%	4,009
Rios, Douglas	149,304	2%	2,986
Uznay, Grace	302,938	5%	15,147
Walden, Albert	177,439	2%	3,549

Top Sales
Rebecca Hale

EL1-C8-VB-TSYrlySales(VB,Step6).xlsx

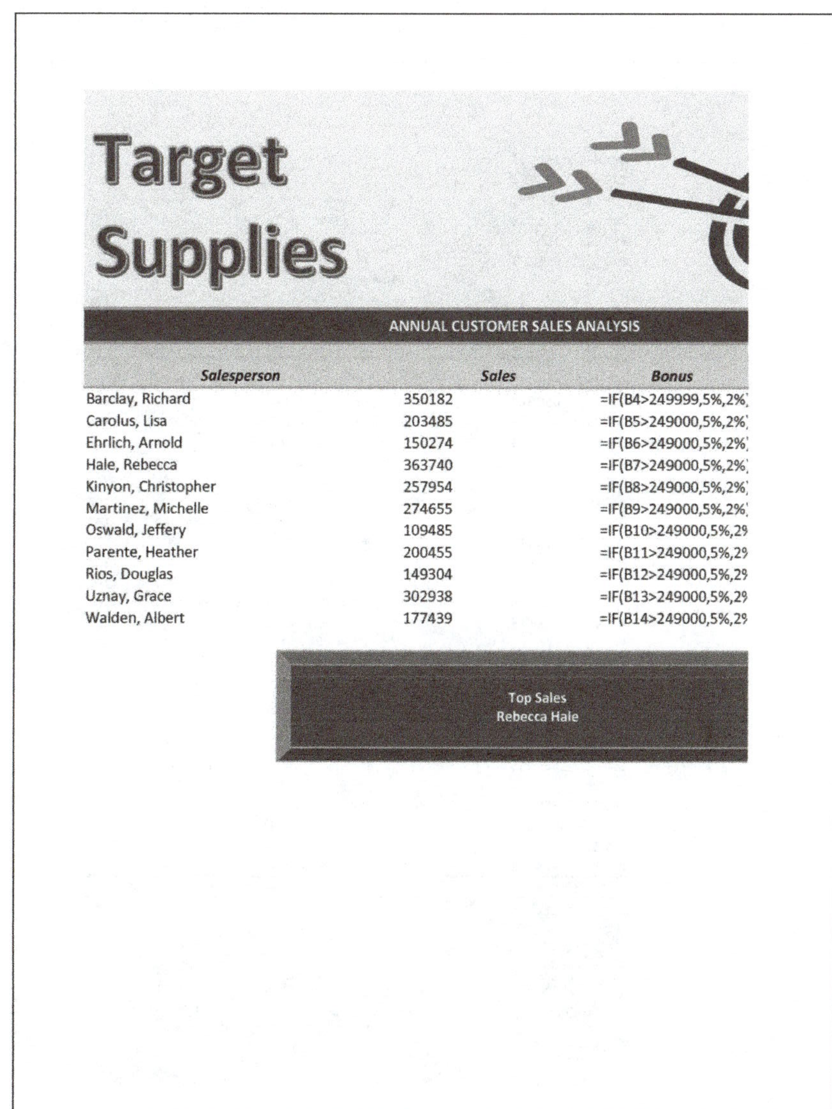

Target Supplies

ANNUAL CUSTOMER SALES ANALYSIS

Salesperson	Sales	Bonus
Barclay, Richard	350182	=IF(B4>249999,5%,2%
Carolus, Lisa	203485	=IF(B5>249000,5%,2%
Ehrlich, Arnold	150274	=IF(B6>249000,5%,2%
Hale, Rebecca	363740	=IF(B7>249000,5%,2%
Kinyon, Christopher	257954	=IF(B8>249000,5%,2%
Martinez, Michelle	274655	=IF(B9>249000,5%,2%
Oswald, Jeffery	109485	=IF(B10>249000,5%,2
Parente, Heather	200455	=IF(B11>249000,5%,2
Rios, Douglas	149304	=IF(B12>249000,5%,2
Uznay, Grace	302938	=IF(B13>249000,5%,2
Walden, Albert	177439	=IF(B14>249000,5%,2

Top Sales
Rebecca Hale

EL1-C8-VB-TSYrlySales(VB,Step7).xlsx (1 of 2)

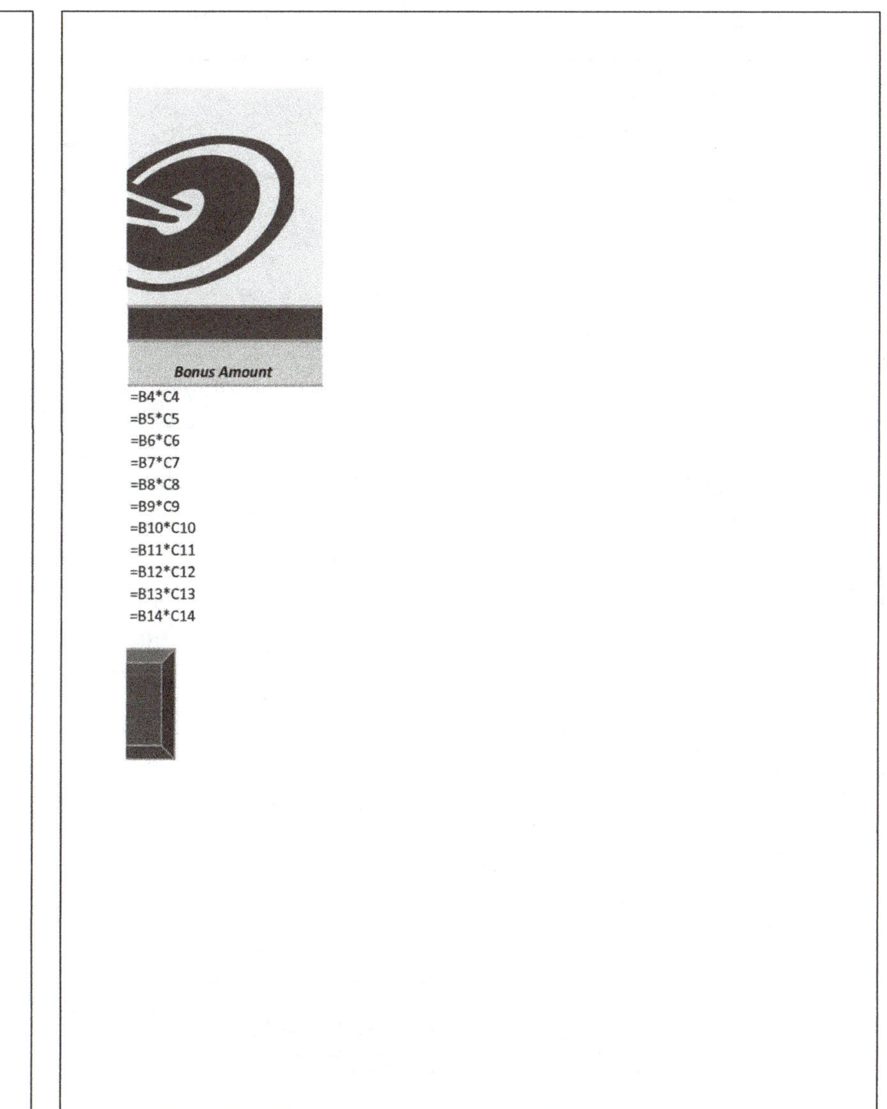

Bonus Amount
=B4*C4
=B5*C5
=B6*C6
=B7*C7
=B8*C8
=B9*C9
=B10*C10
=B11*C11
=B12*C12
=B13*C13
=B14*C14

EL1-C8-VB-TSYrlySales(VB,Step7).xlsx (2 of 2)

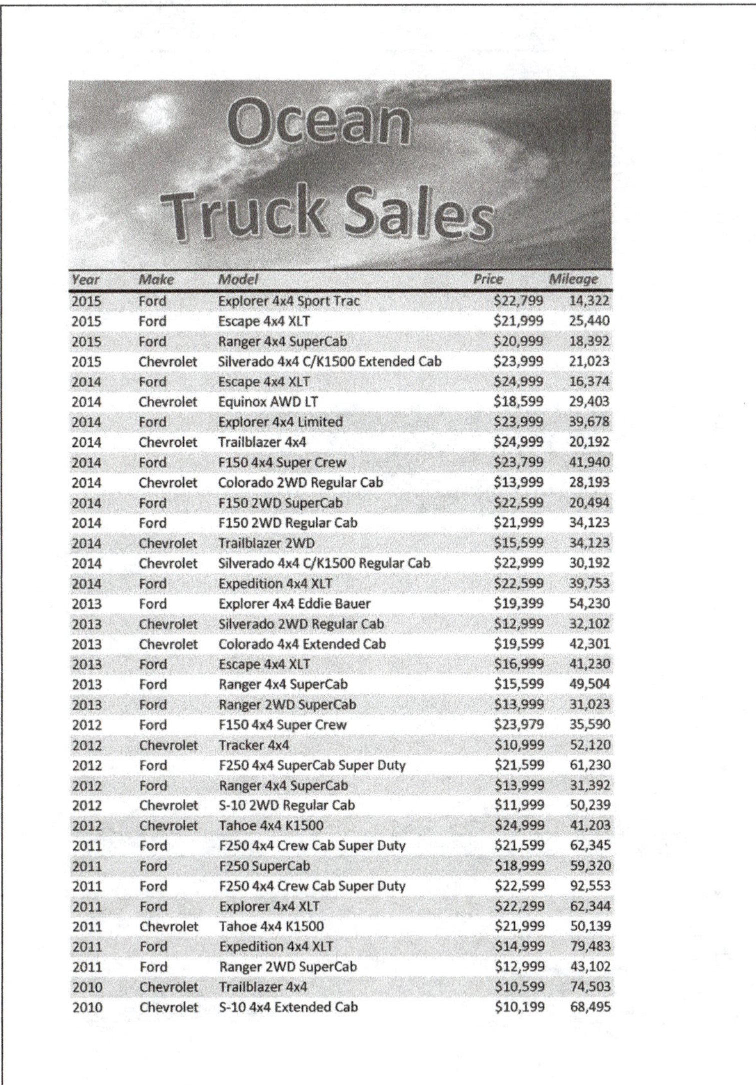

Year	Make	Model	Price	Mileage
2015	Ford	Explorer 4x4 Sport Trac	$22,799	14,322
2015	Ford	Escape 4x4 XLT	$21,999	25,440
2015	Ford	Ranger 4x4 SuperCab	$20,999	18,392
2015	Chevrolet	Silverado 4x4 C/K1500 Extended Cab	$23,999	21,023
2014	Ford	Escape 4x4 XLT	$24,999	16,374
2014	Chevrolet	Equinox AWD LT	$18,599	29,403
2014	Ford	Explorer 4x4 Limited	$23,999	39,678
2014	Chevrolet	Trailblazer 4x4	$24,999	20,192
2014	Ford	F150 4x4 Super Crew	$23,799	41,940
2014	Chevrolet	Colorado 2WD Regular Cab	$13,999	28,193
2014	Ford	F150 2WD SuperCab	$22,599	20,494
2014	Ford	F150 2WD Regular Cab	$21,999	34,123
2014	Chevrolet	Trailblazer 2WD	$15,599	34,123
2014	Chevrolet	Silverado 4x4 C/K1500 Regular Cab	$22,999	30,192
2014	Ford	Expedition 4x4 XLT	$22,599	39,753
2013	Ford	Explorer 4x4 Eddie Bauer	$19,399	54,230
2013	Chevrolet	Silverado 2WD Regular Cab	$12,999	32,102
2013	Chevrolet	Colorado 4x4 Extended Cab	$19,599	42,301
2013	Ford	Escape 4x4 XLT	$16,999	41,230
2013	Ford	Ranger 4x4 SuperCab	$15,599	49,504
2013	Ford	Ranger 2WD SuperCab	$13,999	31,023
2012	Ford	F150 4x4 Super Crew	$23,979	35,590
2012	Chevrolet	Tracker 4x4	$10,999	52,120
2012	Ford	F250 4x4 SuperCab Super Duty	$21,599	61,230
2012	Ford	Ranger 4x4 SuperCab	$13,999	31,392
2012	Chevrolet	S-10 2WD Regular Cab	$11,999	50,239
2012	Chevrolet	Tahoe 4x4 K1500	$24,999	41,203
2011	Ford	F250 4x4 Crew Cab Super Duty	$21,599	62,345
2011	Ford	F250 SuperCab	$18,999	59,320
2011	Ford	F250 4x4 Crew Cab Super Duty	$22,599	92,553
2011	Ford	Explorer 4x4 XLT	$22,299	62,344
2011	Chevrolet	Tahoe 4x4 K1500	$21,999	50,139
2011	Ford	Expedition 4x4 XLT	$14,999	79,483
2011	Ford	Ranger 2WD SuperCab	$12,999	43,102
2010	Chevrolet	Trailblazer 4x4	$10,599	74,503
2010	Chevrolet	S-10 4x4 Extended Cab	$10,199	68,495

EL1-C8-CS-OTSales(CS1).xlsx (1 of 2)

2010	Ford	Explorer 4x4 XLT	$14,599	81,203
2010	Ford	Ranger 2WD Regular Cab	$11,599	34,030
2010	Ford	Explorer 4x4 XLS	$10,299	94,203
2009	Ford	F350 4x4 Crew Cab	$11,999	90,432

EL1-C8-CS-OTSales(CS1).xlsx (2 of 2)

Year	Make	Model	Price	Mileage
2014	Ford	Escape 4x4 XLT	$24,999	16,374
2014	Ford	Explorer 4x4 Limited	$23,999	39,678
2012	Ford	F150 4x4 Super Crew	$23,979	35,590
2014	Ford	F150 4x4 Super Crew	$23,799	41,940
2015	Ford	Explorer 4x4 Sport Trac	$22,799	14,322
2014	Ford	F150 2WD SuperCab	$22,599	20,494
2014	Ford	Expedition 4x4 XLT	$22,599	39,753
2011	Ford	F250 4x4 Crew Cab Super Duty	$22,599	92,553
2011	Ford	Explorer 4x4 XLT	$22,299	62,344
2015	Ford	Escape 4x4 XLT	$21,999	25,440
2014	Ford	F150 2WD Regular Cab	$21,999	34,123
2012	Ford	F250 4x4 SuperCab Super Duty	$21,599	61,230
2011	Ford	F250 4x4 Crew Cab Super Duty	$21,599	62,345
2015	Ford	Ranger 4x4 SuperCab	$20,999	18,392
2013	Ford	Explorer 4x4 Eddie Bauer	$19,399	54,230
2011	Ford	F250 SuperCab	$18,999	59,320
2013	Ford	Escape 4x4 XLT	$16,999	41,230
2013	Ford	Ranger 4x4 SuperCab	$15,599	49,504
2011	Ford	Expedition 4x4 XLT	$14,999	79,483
2010	Ford	Explorer 4x4 XLT	$14,599	81,203
2013	Ford	Ranger 2WD SuperCab	$13,999	31,023
2012	Ford	Ranger 4x4 SuperCab	$13,999	31,392
2011	Ford	Ranger 2WD SuperCab	$12,999	43,102
2009	Ford	F350 4x4 Crew Cab	$11,999	90,432
2010	Ford	Ranger 2WD Regular Cab	$11,599	34,030
2010	Ford	Explorer 4x4 XLS	$10,299	94,203

EL1-C8-CS-OTSalesF&C(CS2).xlsx (2 of 2)

Year	Make	Model	Price	Mileage
2014	Chevrolet	Trailblazer 4x4	$24,999	20,192
2012	Chevrolet	Tahoe 4x4 K1500	$24,999	41,203
2015	Chevrolet	Silverado 4x4 C/K1500 Extended Cab	$23,999	21,023
2014	Chevrolet	Silverado 4x4 C/K1500 Regular Cab	$22,999	30,192
2011	Chevrolet	Tahoe 4x4 K1500	$21,999	50,139
2013	Chevrolet	Colorado 4x4 Extended Cab	$19,599	42,301
2014	Chevrolet	Equinox AWD LT	$18,599	29,403
2014	Chevrolet	Trailblazer 2WD	$15,599	34,123
2014	Chevrolet	Colorado 2WD Regular Cab	$13,999	28,193
2013	Chevrolet	Silverado 2WD Regular Cab	$12,999	32,102
2012	Chevrolet	S-10 2WD Regular Cab	$11,999	50,239
2012	Chevrolet	Tracker 4x4	$10,999	52,120
2010	Chevrolet	Trailblazer 4x4	$10,599	74,503
2010	Chevrolet	S-10 4x4 Extended Cab	$10,199	68,495

EL1-C8-CS-OTSalesF&C(CS2).xlsx (1 of 2)

Small-sized truck: $200

2WD regular cab: $150

SUV 4x4: $100

EL1-C8-CS-OTSalesF&C(CS4).xlsx

Excel Level 1, Performance Assessment Unit 2 Model Answers

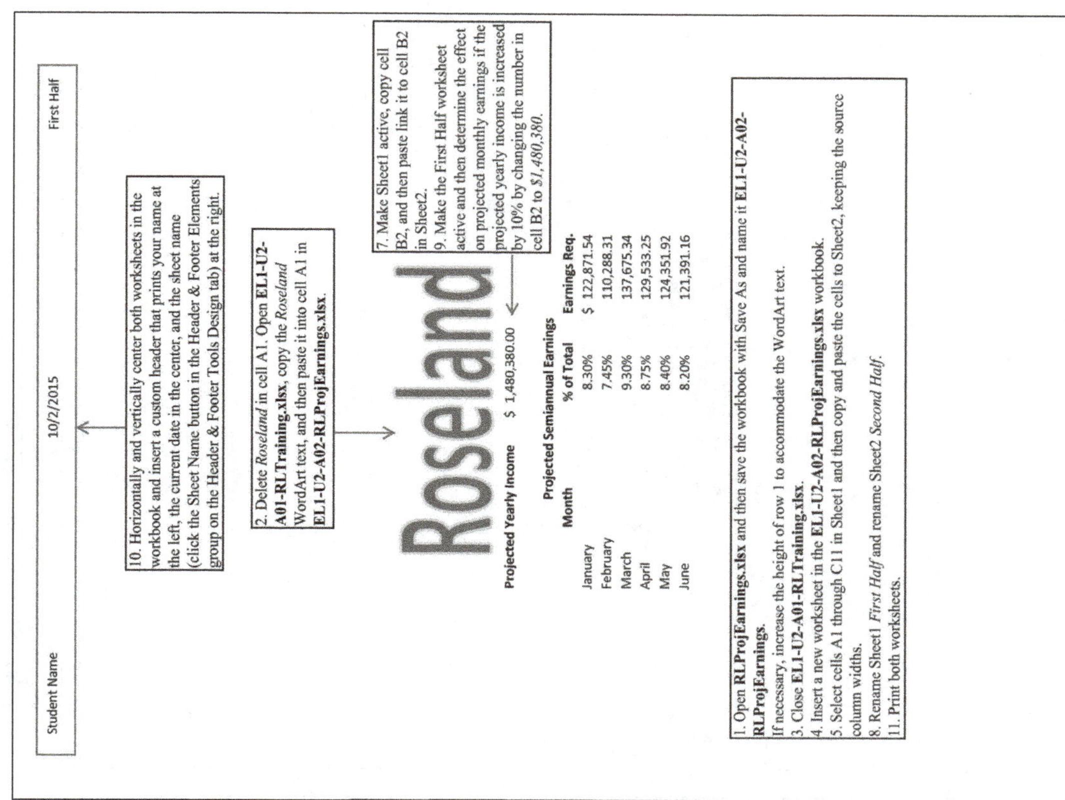

Student Name | 10/2/2015 | First Half

10. Horizontally and vertically center both worksheets in the workbook and insert a custom header that prints your name at the left, the current date in the center, and the sheet name (click the Sheet Name button in the Header & Footer Elements group on the Header & Footer Tools Design tab) at the right.

2. Delete *Roseland* in cell A1. Open **EL1-U2-A01-RLTraining.xlsx**, copy the *Roseland* WordArt text, and then paste it into cell A1 in **EL1-U2-A02-RLProjEarnings.xlsx**.

Roseland

7. Make Sheet1 active, copy cell B2, and then paste link it to cell B2 in Sheet2.
9. Make the First Half worksheet active and then determine the effect on projected monthly earnings if the projected yearly income is increased by 10% by changing the number in cell B2 to *$1,480,380*.

Projected Yearly Income	$ 1,480,380.00	
Projected Semiannual Earnings		
Month	% of Total	Earnings Req.
January	8.30%	$ 122,871.54
February	7.45%	110,288.31
March	9.30%	137,675.34
April	8.75%	129,533.25
May	8.40%	124,351.92
June	8.20%	121,391.16

1. Open **RLProjEarnings.xlsx** and then save the workbook with Save As and name it **EL1-U2-A02-RLProjEarnings.**
If necessary, increase the height of row 1 to accommodate the WordArt text.
3. Close **EL1-U2-A01-RLTraining.xlsx**.
4. Insert a new worksheet in the **EL1-U2-A02-RLProjEarnings.xlsx** workbook.
5. Select cells A1 through C11 in Sheet1 and then copy and paste the cells to Sheet2, keeping the source column widths.
8. Rename Sheet1 *First Half* and rename Sheet2 *Second Half*.
11. Print both worksheets.

EL1-U2-A02-RLProjEarnings(A2,Step11).xlsx (1 of 2)

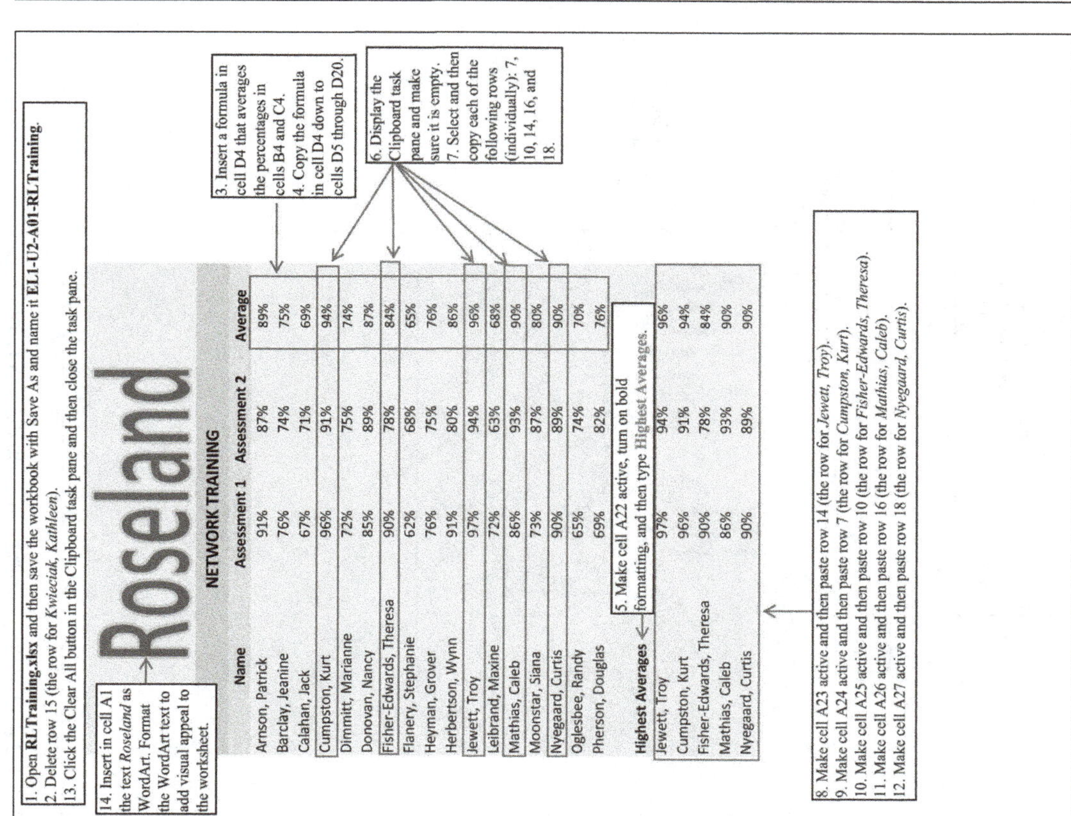

1. Open **RLTraining.xlsx** and then save the workbook with Save As and name it **EL1-U2-A01-RLTraining**.
2. Delete row 15 (the row for *Kwieciak, Kathleen*).
13. Click the Clear All button in the Clipboard task pane and then close the task pane.

14. Insert in cell A1 the text *Roseland* as WordArt. Format the WordArt text to add visual appeal to the worksheet.

Roseland

3. Insert a formula in cell D4 that averages the percentages in cells B4 and C4.
4. Copy the formula in cell D4 down to cells D5 through D20.

6. Display the Clipboard task pane and make sure it is empty.
7. Select and then copy each of the following rows (individually): 7, 10, 14, 16, and 18.

NETWORK TRAINING

Name	Assessment 1	Assessment 2	Average
Arnson, Patrick	91%	87%	89%
Barclay, Jeanine	76%	74%	75%
Calahan, Jack	67%	71%	69%
Cumpston, Kurt	96%	91%	94%
Dimmitt, Marianne	72%	75%	74%
Donovan, Nancy	85%	89%	87%
Fisher-Edwards, Theresa	90%	78%	84%
Flanery, Stephanie	62%	68%	65%
Heyman, Grover	76%	75%	76%
Herbertson, Wynn	91%	80%	86%
Jewett, Troy	97%	94%	96%
Leibrand, Maxine	72%	63%	68%
Mathias, Caleb	86%	93%	90%
Moonstar, Siana	73%	87%	80%
Nyegaard, Curtis	90%	89%	90%
Oglesbee, Randy	65%	74%	70%
Pherson, Douglas	69%	82%	76%
Highest Averages			
Jewett, Troy	97%	94%	96%
Cumpston, Kurt	96%	91%	94%
Fisher-Edwards, Theresa	90%	78%	84%
Mathias, Caleb	86%	93%	90%
Nyegaard, Curtis	90%	89%	90%

5. Make cell A22 active, turn on bold formatting, and then type Highest Averages.

8. Make cell A23 active and then paste row 14 (the row for *Jewett, Troy*).
9. Make cell A24 active and then paste row 7 (the row for *Cumpston, Kurt*).
10. Make cell A25 active and then paste row 10 (the row for *Fisher-Edwards, Theresa*).
11. Make cell A26 active and then paste row 16 (the row for *Mathias, Caleb*).
12. Make cell A27 active and then paste row 18 (the row for *Nyegaard, Curtis*).

EL1-U2-A01-RLTraining(A1).xlsx

Student Name	10/2/2015	Second Half

10. Horizontally and vertically center both worksheets in the workbook and insert a custom header that prints your name at the left, the current date in the center, and the sheet name (click the Sheet Name button in the Header & Footer Elements group on the Header & Footer Tools Design tab) at the right.

6. With Sheet2 displayed, make the following changes:
a. Increase the height of row 1 to accommodate the WordArt text.
b. Delete the contents of cell B2.

Roseland

Projected Yearly Income $ 1,480,380.00

7. Make Sheet1 active, copy cell B2, and then paste link it to cell B2 in Sheet2.

Projected Semiannual Earnings

Month	% of Total	Earnings Req.
July	8.10%	$ 119,910.78
August	7.45%	110,288.31
September	8.70%	128,793.06
October	8.75%	129,533.25
November	8.40%	124,351.92
December	8.20%	121,391.16

6c. Change the contents of the following cells: A6: Change *January* to *July* A7: Change *February* to *August* A8: Change *March* to *September* A9: Change *April* to *October* A10: Change *May* to *November* A11: Change *June* to *December* B6: Change *8.30%* to *8.10%* B8: Change *9.30%* to *8.70%*

EL1-U2-A02-RLProjEarnings(A2,Step11).xlsx (2 of 2)

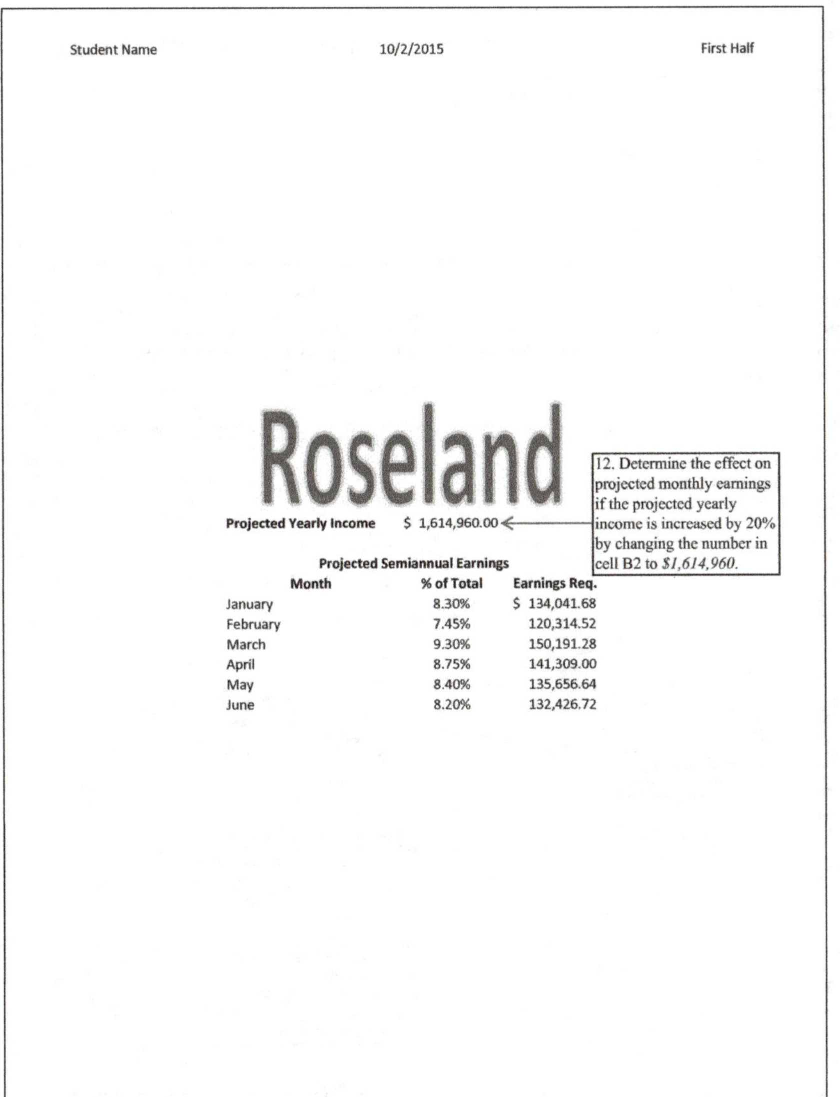

Student Name	10/2/2015	First Half

Roseland

Projected Yearly Income $ 1,614,960.00

12. Determine the effect on projected monthly earnings if the projected yearly income is increased by 20% by changing the number in cell B2 to *$1,614,960.*

Projected Semiannual Earnings

Month	% of Total	Earnings Req.
January	8.30%	$ 134,041.68
February	7.45%	120,314.52
March	9.30%	150,191.28
April	8.75%	141,309.00
May	8.40%	135,656.64
June	8.20%	132,426.72

EL1-U2-A02-RLProjEarnings(A2,Step13).xlsx (1 of 2)

Student Name 10/2/2015 Second Half

Roseland

Projected Yearly Income $ 1,614,960.00

Projected Semiannual Earnings

Month	% of Total	Earnings Req.
July	8.10%	$ 130,811.76
August	7.45%	120,314.52
September	8.70%	140,501.52
October	8.75%	141,309.00
November	8.40%	135,656.64
December	8.20%	132,426.72

EL1-U2-A02-RLProjEarnings(A2,Step13).xlsx (2 of 2)

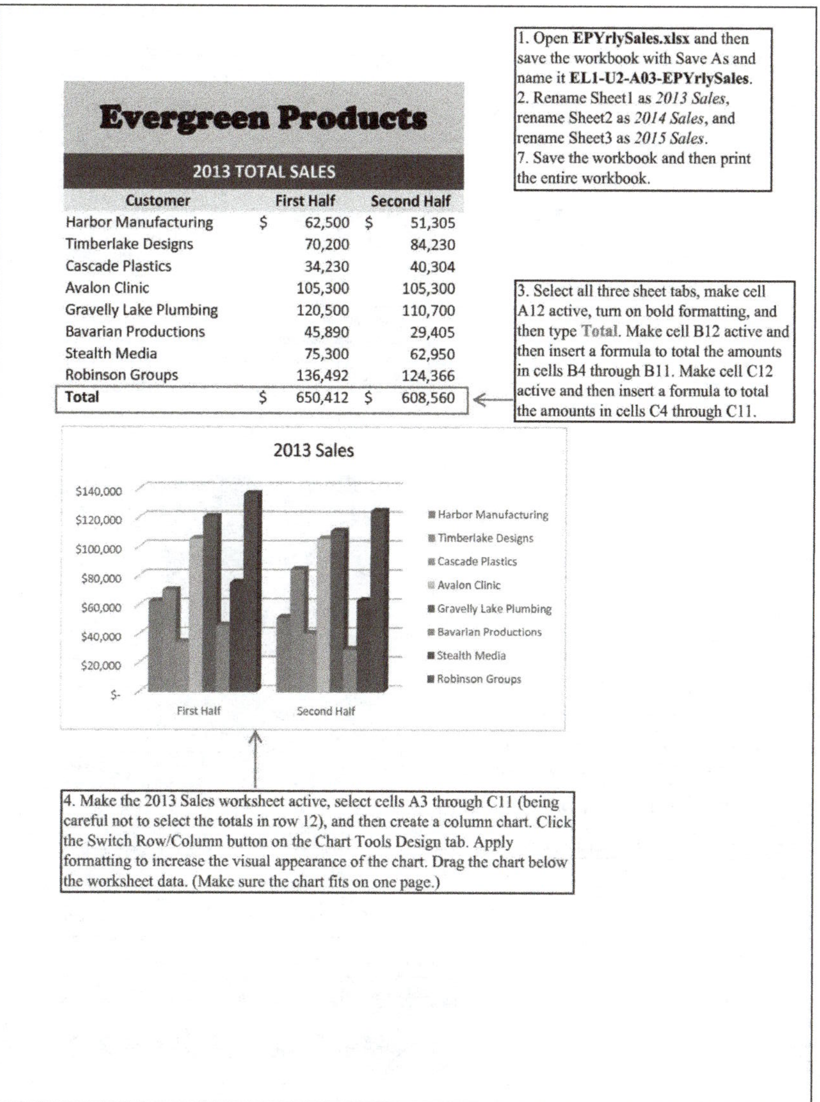

Evergreen Products

2013 TOTAL SALES

Customer	First Half	Second Half
Harbor Manufacturing	$ 62,500	$ 51,305
Timberlake Designs	70,200	84,230
Cascade Plastics	34,230	40,304
Avalon Clinic	105,300	105,300
Gravelly Lake Plumbing	120,500	110,700
Bavarian Productions	45,890	29,405
Stealth Media	75,300	62,950
Robinson Groups	136,492	124,366
Total	$ 650,412	$ 608,560

1. Open **EPYrlySales.xlsx** and then save the workbook with Save As and name it **EL1-U2-A03-EPYrlySales**.
2. Rename Sheet1 as *2013 Sales*, rename Sheet2 as *2014 Sales*, and rename Sheet3 as *2015 Sales*.
7. Save the workbook and then print the entire workbook.

3. Select all three sheet tabs, make cell A12 active, turn on bold formatting, and then type Total. Make cell B12 active and then insert a formula to total the amounts in cells B4 through B11. Make cell C12 active and then insert a formula to total the amounts in cells C4 through C11.

4. Make the 2013 Sales worksheet active, select cells A3 through C11 (being careful not to select the totals in row 12), and then create a column chart. Click the Switch Row/Column button on the Chart Tools Design tab. Apply formatting to increase the visual appearance of the chart. Drag the chart below the worksheet data. (Make sure the chart fits on one page.)

EL1-U2-A03-EPYrlySales(A3).xlsx (1 of 3)

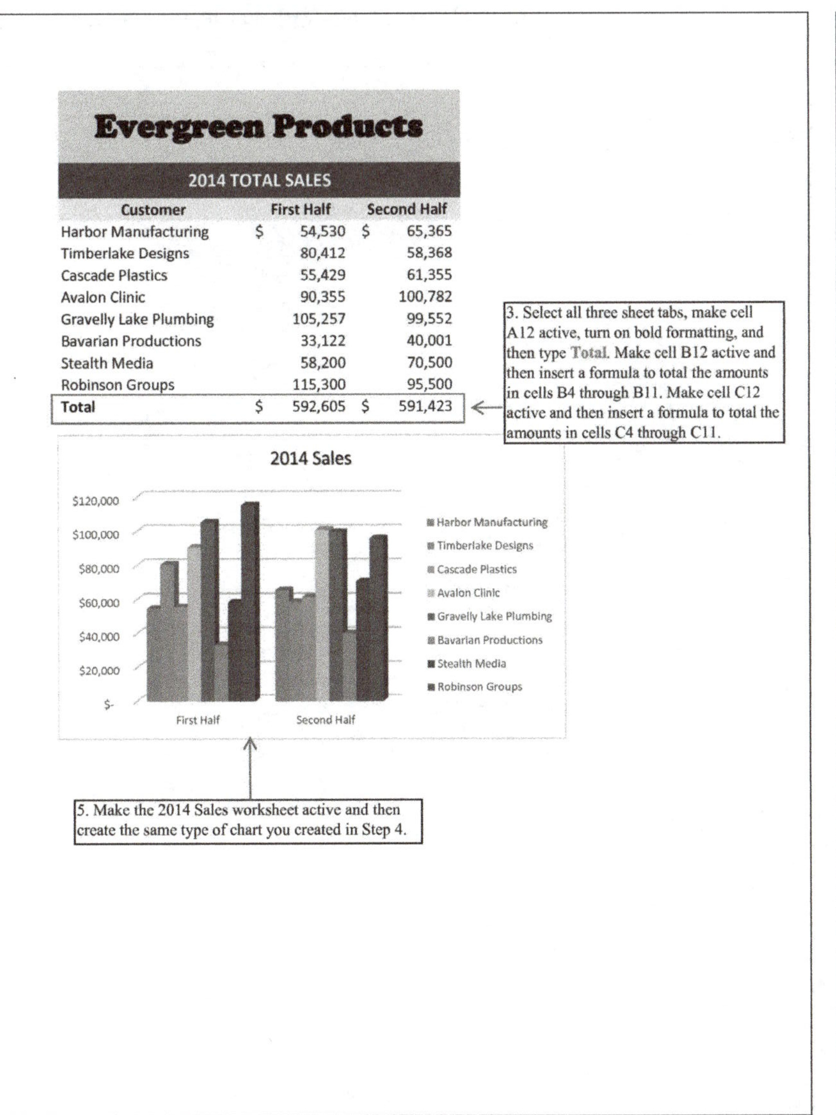

Evergreen Products

2014 TOTAL SALES

Customer	First Half	Second Half
Harbor Manufacturing	$ 54,530	$ 65,365
Timberlake Designs	80,412	58,368
Cascade Plastics	55,429	61,355
Avalon Clinic	90,355	100,782
Gravelly Lake Plumbing	105,257	99,552
Bavarian Productions	33,122	40,001
Stealth Media	58,200	70,500
Robinson Groups	115,300	95,500
Total	$ 592,605	$ 591,423

3. Select all three sheet tabs, make cell A12 active, turn on bold formatting, and then type Total. Make cell B12 active and then insert a formula to total the amounts in cells B4 through B11. Make cell C12 active and then insert a formula to total the amounts in cells C4 through C11.

5. Make the 2014 Sales worksheet active and then create the same type of chart you created in Step 4.

EL1-U2-A03-EPYrlySales(A3).xlsx (2 of 3)

Evergreen Products

2015 TOTAL SALES

Customer	First Half	Second Half
Harbor Manufacturing	$ 55,300	$ 82,600
Timberlake Designs	46,545	60,590
Cascade Plastics	-	-
Avalon Clinic	95,550	86,712
Gravelly Lake Plumbing	112,500	130,565
Bavarian Productions	39,145	45,690
Stealth Media	63,000	49,000
Robinson Groups	104,500	95,000
Total	$ 516,540	$ 550,157

3. Select all three sheet tabs, make cell A12 active, turn on bold formatting, and then type Total. Make cell B12 active and then insert a formula to total the amounts in cells B4 through B11. Make cell C12 active and then insert a formula to total the amounts in cells C4 through C11.

2015 Sales

$100,000
$90,000
$80,000
$70,000
$60,000
$50,000
$40,000
$30,000
$20,000
$10,000
$-
First Half
Second Half
Harbor Manufacturing
Avalon Clinic
Stealth Media

6. Make the 2015 Sales worksheet active and then create the same type of chart you created in Step 4. Filter the records in this chart so that only the following companies display: *Harbor Manufacturing*, *Avalon Clinic*, and *Stealth Media*.

EL1-U2-A03-EPYrlySales(A3).xlsx (3 of 3)

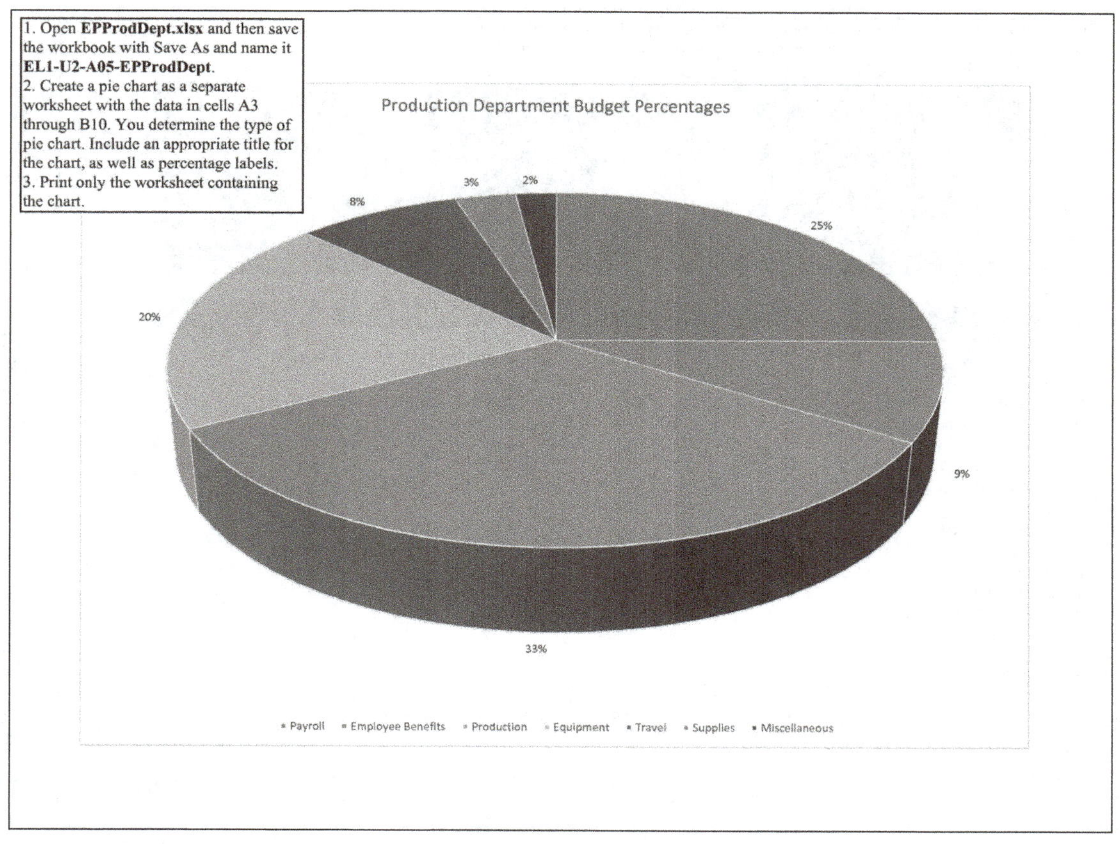

EL1-U2-A05-EPProdDept(A5).xlsx

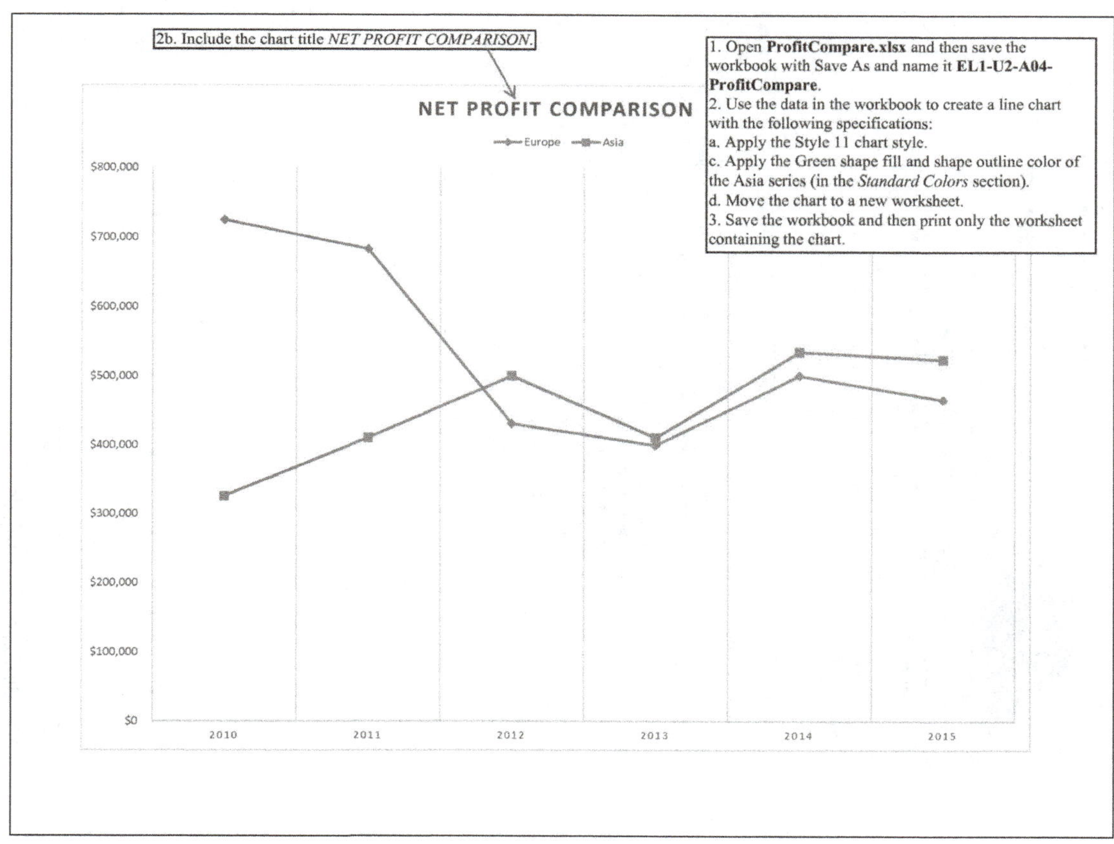

EL1-U2-A04-ProfitCompare(A4).xlsx

1. Open **PSQtrlySales.xlsx** and then save the workbook with Save As and name it **EL1-U2-A07-PSQtrlySales**.
4. Turn on the display of formulas, print the worksheet in landscape orientation, and then turn off the display of formulas. (The worksheet will print on two pages.)

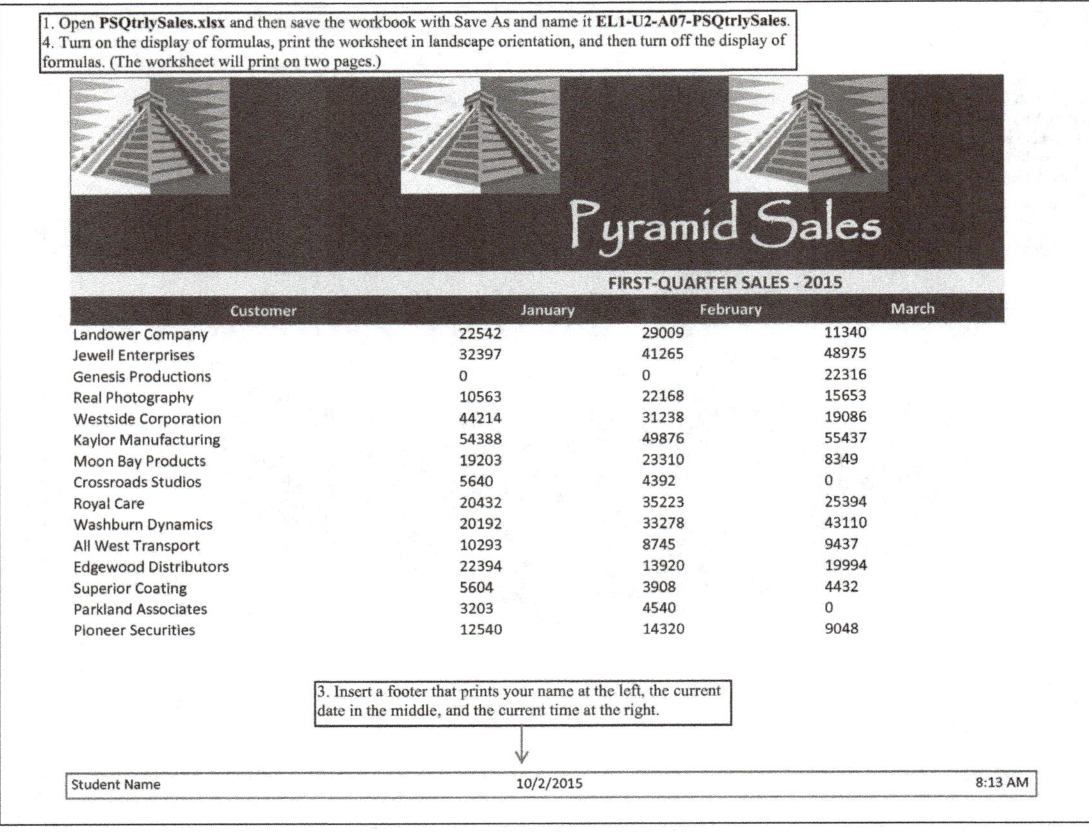

Pyramid Sales

FIRST-QUARTER SALES - 2015

Customer	January	February	March
Landower Company	22542	29009	11340
Jewell Enterprises	32397	41265	48975
Genesis Productions	0	0	22316
Real Photography	10563	22168	15653
Westside Corporation	44214	31238	19086
Kaylor Manufacturing	54388	49876	55437
Moon Bay Products	19203	23310	8349
Crossroads Studios	5640	4392	0
Royal Care	20432	35223	25394
Washburn Dynamics	20192	33278	43110
All West Transport	10293	8745	9437
Edgewood Distributors	22394	13920	19994
Superior Coating	5604	3908	4432
Parkland Associates	3203	4540	0
Pioneer Securities	12540	14320	9048

3. Insert a footer that prints your name at the left, the current date in the middle, and the current time at the right.

Student Name	10/2/2015	8:13 AM

EL1-U2-A07-PSQtrlySales(A7,Step4).xlsx (1 of 2)

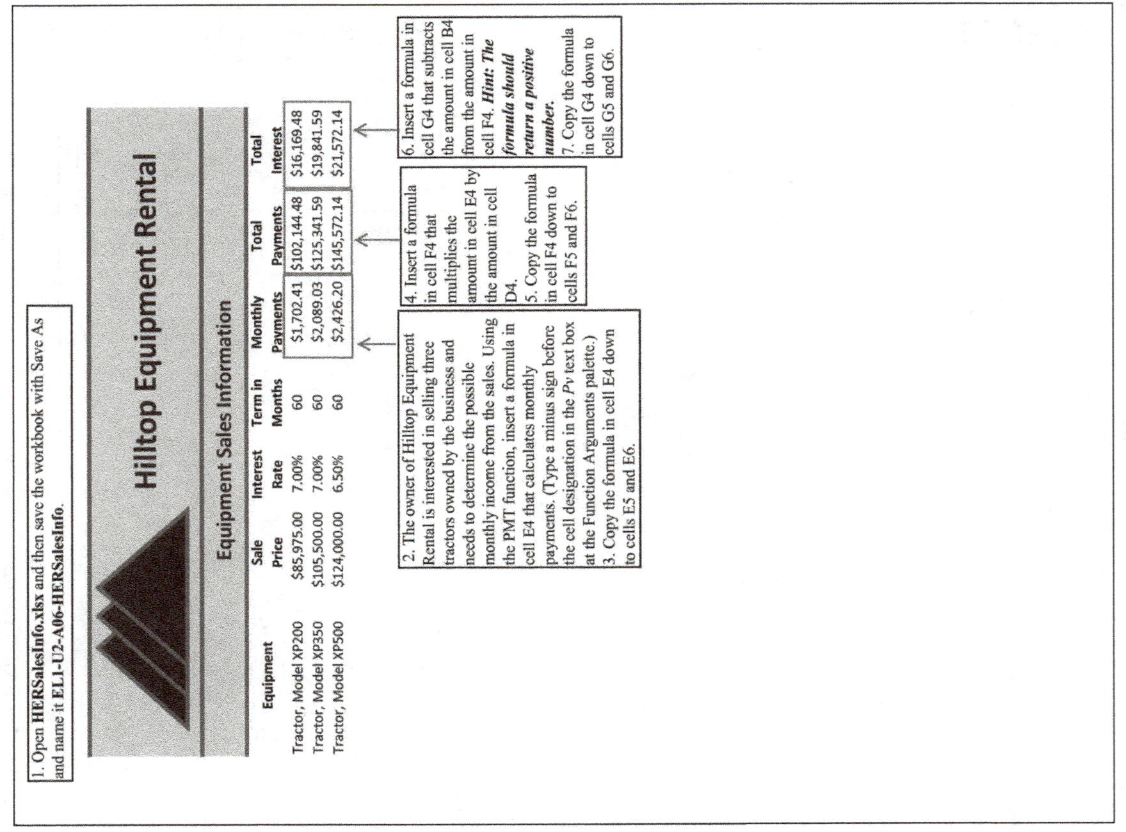

1. Open **HERSalesInfo.xlsx** and then save the workbook with Save As and name it **EL1-U2-A06-HERSalesInfo**.

Hilltop Equipment Rental

Equipment Sales Information

Equipment	Sale Price	Interest Rate	Term in Months	Monthly Payments	Total Payments	Total Interest
Tractor, Model XP200	$85,975.00	7.00%	60	$1,702.41	$102,144.48	$16,169.48
Tractor, Model XP350	$105,500.00	7.00%	60	$2,089.03	$125,341.59	$19,841.59
Tractor, Model XP500	$124,000.00	6.50%	60	$2,426.20	$145,572.14	$21,572.14

2. The owner of Hilltop Equipment Rental is interested in selling three tractors owned by the business and needs to determine the possible monthly income from the sales. Using the PMT function, insert a formula in cell E4 that calculates monthly payments. (Type a minus sign before the cell designation in the *Pv* text box at the Function Arguments palette.)
3. Copy the formula in cell E4 down to cells E5 and E6.

4. Insert a formula in cell F4 that multiplies the amount in cell E4 by the amount in cell D4.
5. Copy the formula in cell F4 down to cells F5 and F6.

6. Insert a formula in cell G4 that subtracts the amount in cell B4 from the amount in cell F4. ***Hint: The formula should return a positive number.***
7. Copy the formula in cell G4 down to cells G5 and G6.

EL1-U2-A06-HERSalesInfo(A6).xlsx

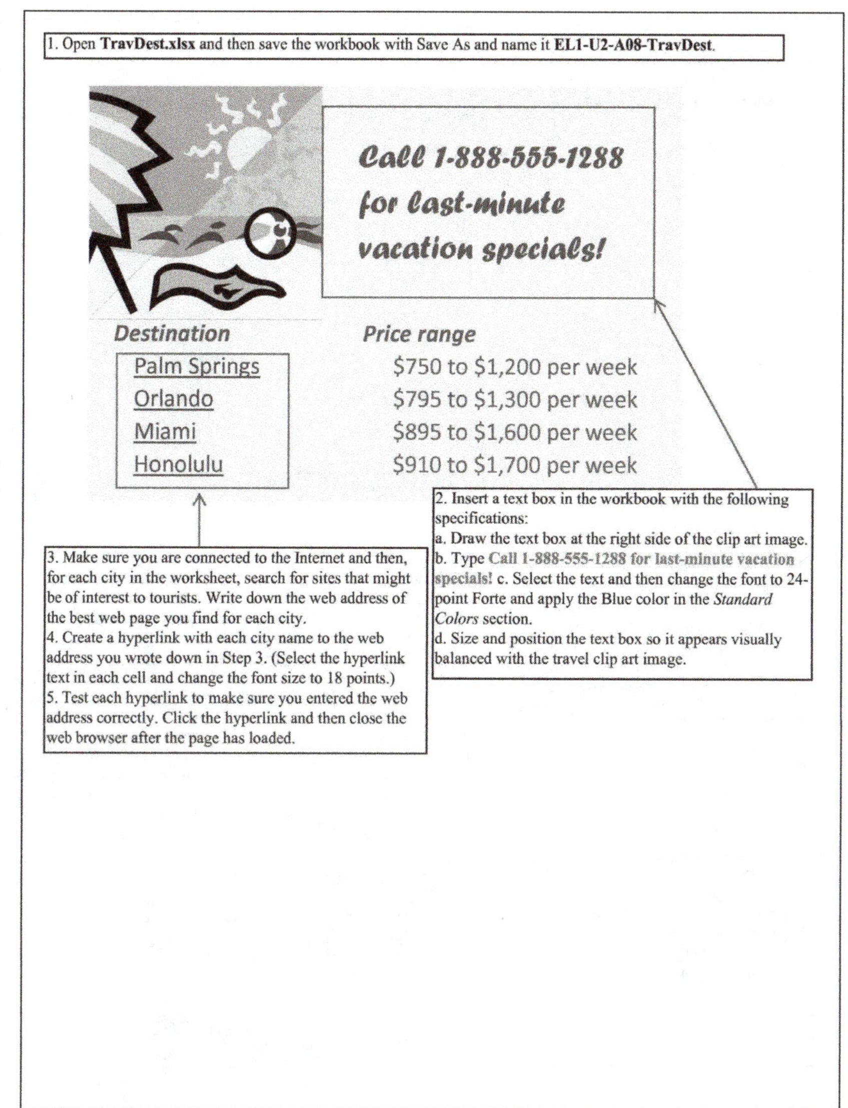

EL1-U2-A08-TravDest(A8).xlsx

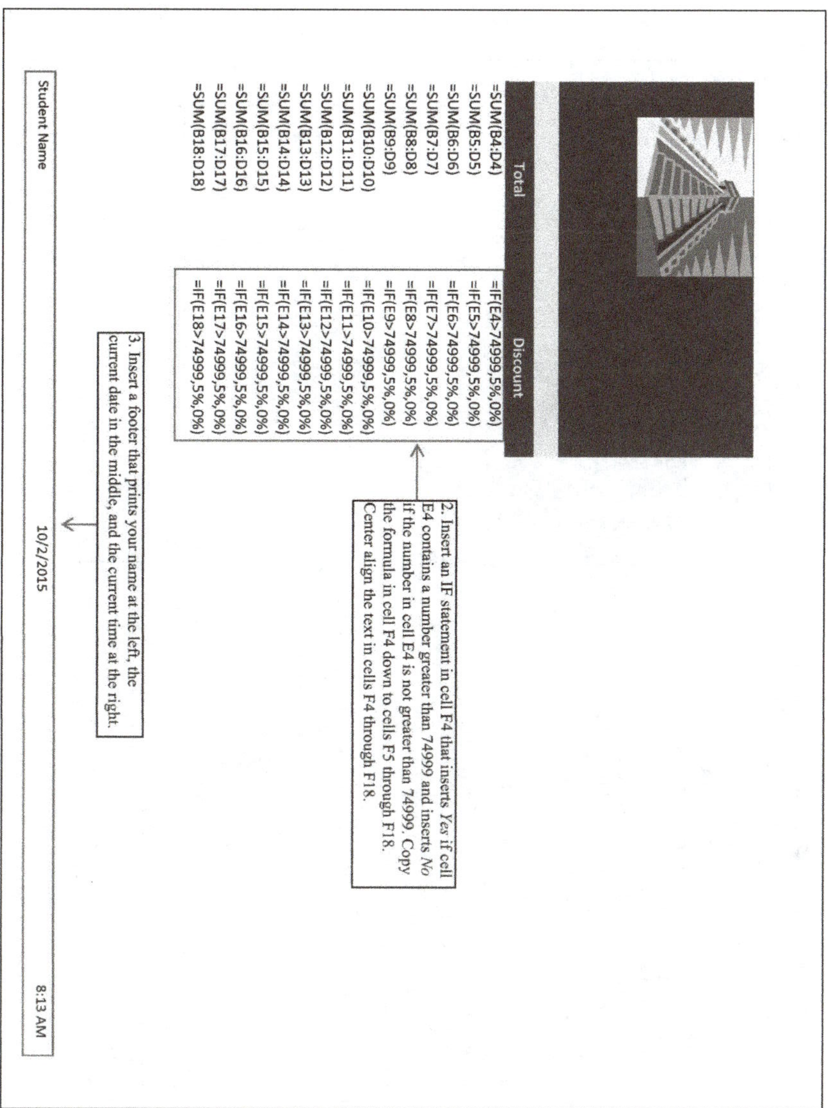

EL1-U2-A07-PSQtrlySales(A7,Step4).xlsx (2 of 2)

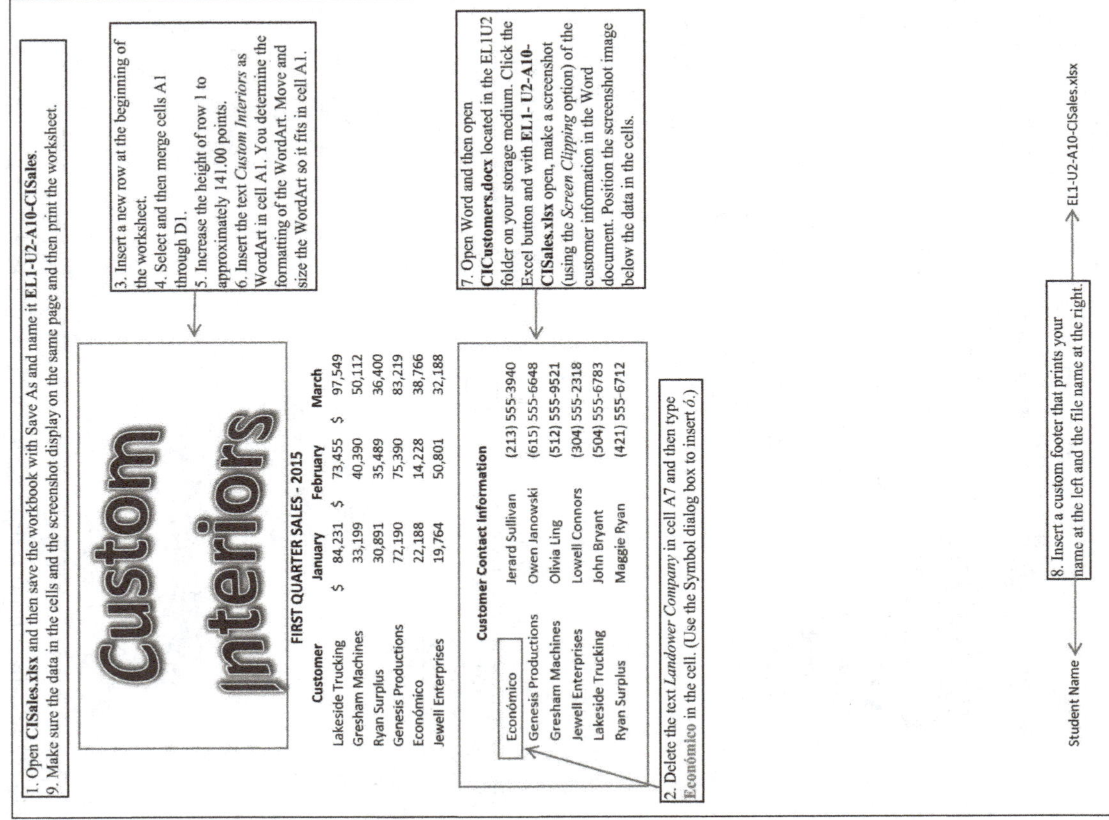
1. Open **CISales.xlsx** and then save the workbook with Save As and name it **EL1-U2-A10-CISales**.
9. Make sure the data in the cells and the screenshot display on the same page and then print the worksheet.

3. Insert a new row at the beginning of the worksheet.
4. Select and then merge cells A1 through D1.
5. Increase the height of row 1 to approximately 141.00 points.
6. Insert the text *Custom Interiors* as WordArt in cell A1. You determine the formatting of the WordArt. Move and size the WordArt so it fits in cell A1.

Custom Interiors

FIRST QUARTER SALES - 2015

Customer	January	February	March
Lakeside Trucking	$ 84,231	$ 73,455	$ 97,549
Gresham Machines	33,199	40,390	50,112
Ryan Surplus	30,891	35,489	36,400
Genesis Productions	72,190	75,390	83,219
Económico	22,188	14,228	38,766
Jewell Enterprises	19,764	50,801	32,188

7. Open Word and then open **CICustomers.docx** located in the EL1U2 folder on your storage medium. Click the Excel button and with **EL1-U2-A10-CISales.xlsx** open, make a screenshot (using the *Screen Clipping* option) of the customer information in the Word document. Position the screenshot image below the data in the cells.

Customer Contact Information

Económico		
Genesis Productions	Jerard Sullivan	(213) 555-3940
Gresham Machines	Owen Janowski	(615) 555-6648
Jewell Enterprises	Olivia Ling	(512) 555-9521
Lakeside Trucking	Lowell Connors	(304) 555-2318
Ryan Surplus	John Bryant	(504) 555-6783
	Maggie Ryan	(421) 555-6712

2. Delete the text *Landower Company* in cell A7 and then type **Económico** in the cell. (Use the Symbol dialog box to insert *ó*.)

8. Insert a custom footer that prints your name at the left and the file name at the right.

Student Name EL1-U2-A10-CISales.xlsx

EL1-U2-A10-CISales(A10).xlsx

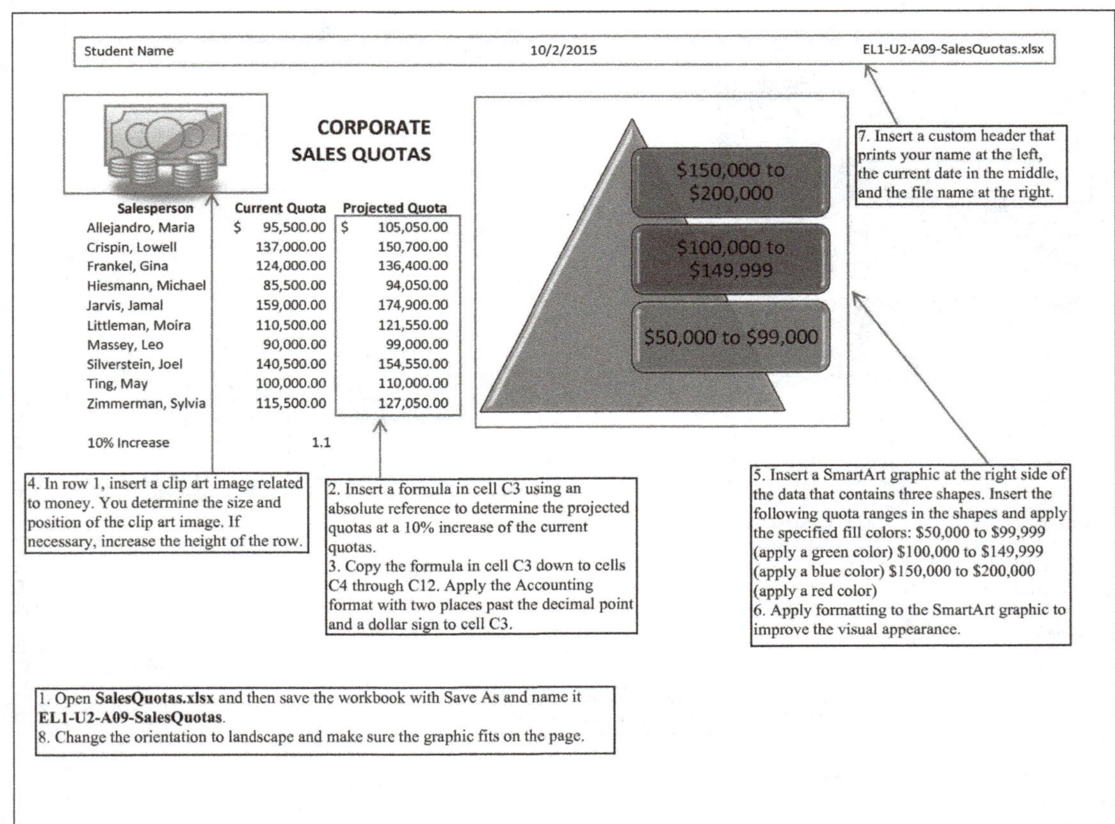
Student Name 10/2/2015 EL1-U2-A09-SalesQuotas.xlsx

CORPORATE SALES QUOTAS

Salesperson	Current Quota	Projected Quota
Allejandro, Maria	$ 95,500.00	$ 105,050.00
Crispin, Lowell	137,000.00	150,700.00
Frankel, Gina	124,000.00	136,400.00
Hiesmann, Michael	85,500.00	94,050.00
Jarvis, Jamal	159,000.00	174,900.00
Littleman, Moira	110,500.00	121,550.00
Massey, Leo	90,000.00	99,000.00
Silverstein, Joel	140,500.00	154,550.00
Ting, May	100,000.00	110,000.00
Zimmerman, Sylvia	115,500.00	127,050.00
10% Increase	1.1	

7. Insert a custom header that prints your name at the left, the current date in the middle, and the file name at the right.

4. In row 1, insert a clip art image related to money. You determine the size and position of the clip art image. If necessary, increase the height of the row.

2. Insert a formula in cell C3 using an absolute reference to determine the projected quotas at a 10% increase of the current quotas.
3. Copy the formula in cell C3 down to cells C4 through C12. Apply the Accounting format with two places past the decimal point and a dollar sign to cell C3.

5. Insert a SmartArt graphic at the right side of the data that contains three shapes. Insert the following quota ranges in the shapes and apply the specified fill colors: $50,000 to $99,999 (apply a green color) $100,000 to $149,999 (apply a blue color) $150,000 to $200,000 (apply a red color)
6. Apply formatting to the SmartArt graphic to improve the visual appearance.

1. Open **SalesQuotas.xlsx** and then save the workbook with Save As and name it **EL1-U2-A09-SalesQuotas**.
8. Change the orientation to landscape and make sure the graphic fits on the page.

EL1-U2-A09-SalesQuotas(A9).xlsx

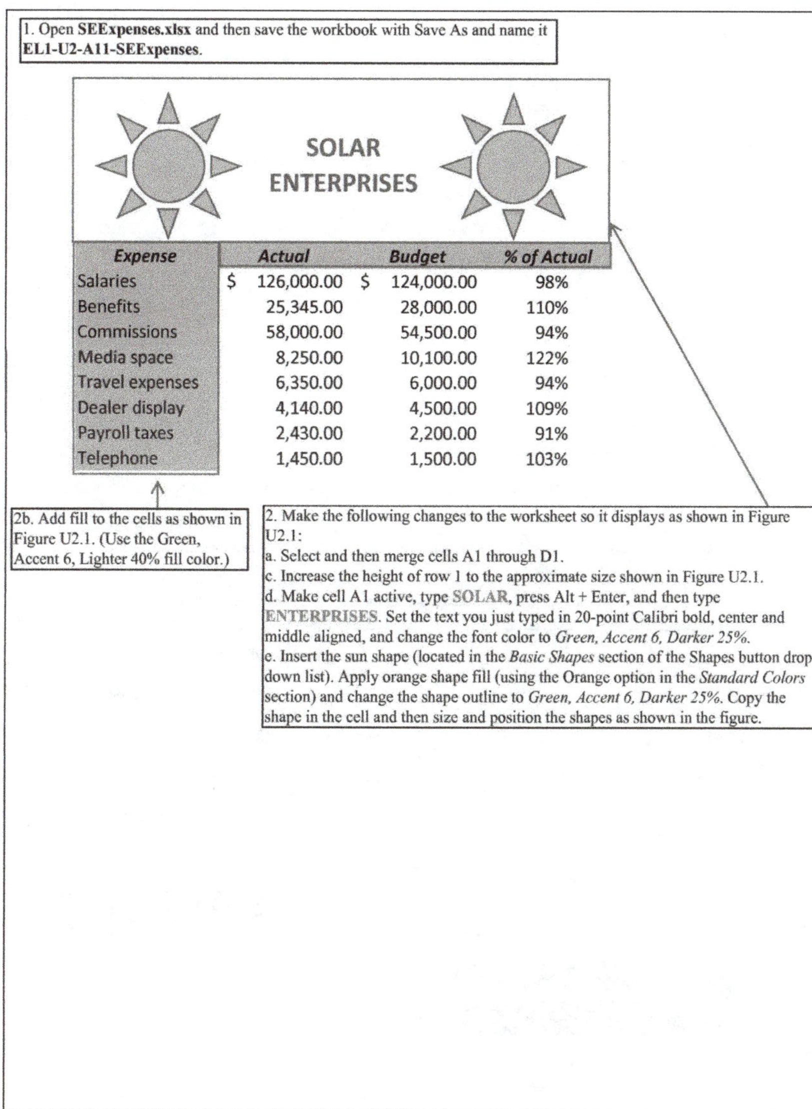

1. Open **SEExpenses.xlsx** and then save the workbook with Save As and name it **EL1-U2-A11-SEExpenses**.

SOLAR ENTERPRISES			
Expense	**Actual**	**Budget**	**% of Actual**
Salaries	$ 126,000.00	$ 124,000.00	98%
Benefits	25,345.00	28,000.00	110%
Commissions	58,000.00	54,500.00	94%
Media space	8,250.00	10,100.00	122%
Travel expenses	6,350.00	6,000.00	94%
Dealer display	4,140.00	4,500.00	109%
Payroll taxes	2,430.00	2,200.00	91%
Telephone	1,450.00	1,500.00	103%

2b. Add fill to the cells as shown in Figure U2.1. (Use the Green, Accent 6, Lighter 40% fill color.)

2. Make the following changes to the worksheet so it displays as shown in Figure U2.1:
a. Select and then merge cells A1 through D1.
c. Increase the height of row 1 to the approximate size shown in Figure U2.1.
d. Make cell A1 active, type SOLAR, press Alt + Enter, and then type ENTERPRISES. Set the text you just typed in 20-point Calibri bold, center and middle aligned, and change the font color to *Green, Accent 6, Darker 25%.*
e. Insert the sun shape (located in the *Basic Shapes* section of the Shapes button drop-down list). Apply orange shape fill (using the Orange option in the *Standard Colors* section) and change the shape outline to *Green, Accent 6, Darker 25%*. Copy the shape in the cell and then size and position the shapes as shown in the figure.

EL1-U2-A11-SEExpenses(A11).xlsx

McCormack Funds		
Projected Annual Budget		
Line Item	*Budget*	*Amount*
Salaries	45%	$ 652,500.00
Benefits	12%	$ 174,000.00
Training	14%	$ 203,000.00
Administrative Costs	10%	$ 145,000.00
Equipment	11%	$ 159,500.00
Supplies	8%	$ 116,000.00
Total Budget allotment:	$ 1,450,000.00	

EL1-U2-Act1-MFBudget.xlsx

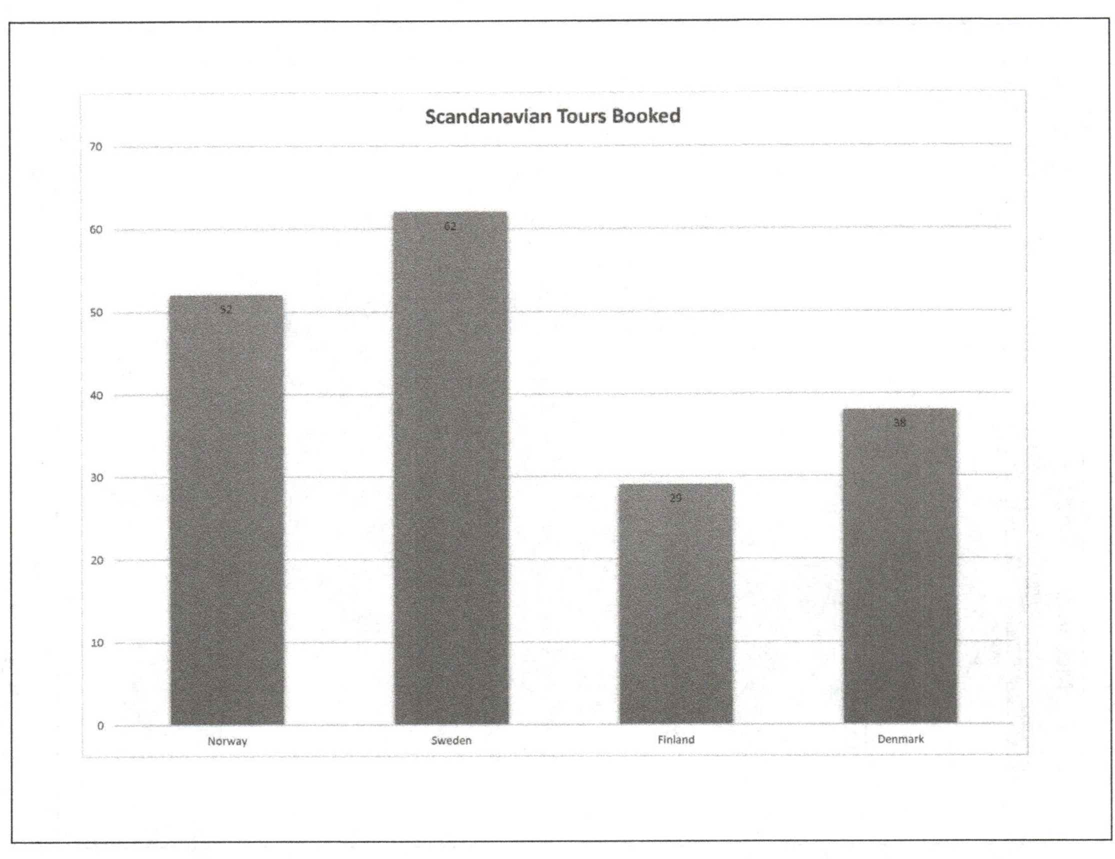

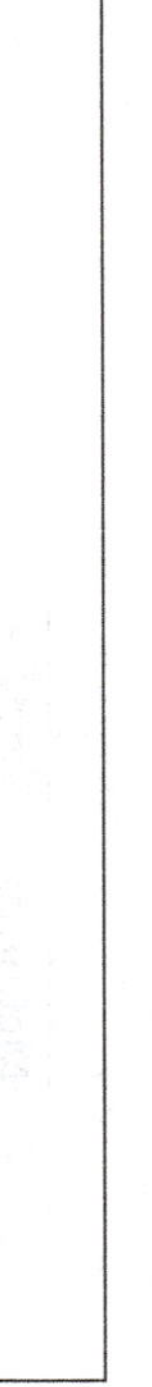

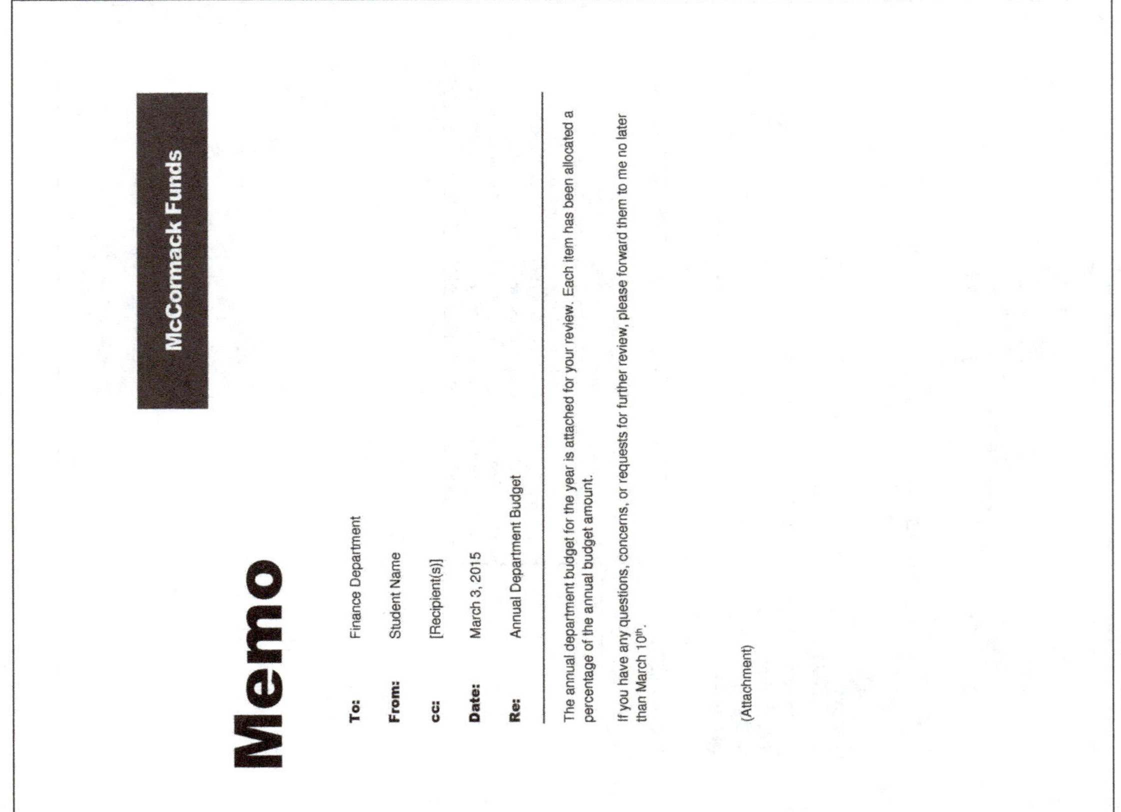

Memo

McCormack Funds

To: Finance Department

From: Student Name

cc: [Recipient(s)]

Date: March 3, 2015

Re: Annual Department Budget

The annual department budget for the year is attached for your review. Each item has been allocated a percentage of the annual budget amount.

If you have any questions, concerns, or requests for further review, please forward them to me no later than March 10th.

(Attachment)

EL1-U2-Act1-MFMemo.xlsx

Carefree Travels	
Whistler Ski Vacation Package	
Round-trip air transportation	$ 395.00
Seven nights' hotel accommodations	1,550.00
Four all-day ski passes	425.00
Compact rental car with unlimited mileage	250.00
Total price of the ski package	**$ 2,620.00**
Book your vacation today at special discount prices.	
Two-for-one discount at many of the local ski resorts.	

EL1-U2-Act3-CTSkiTrips.xlsx

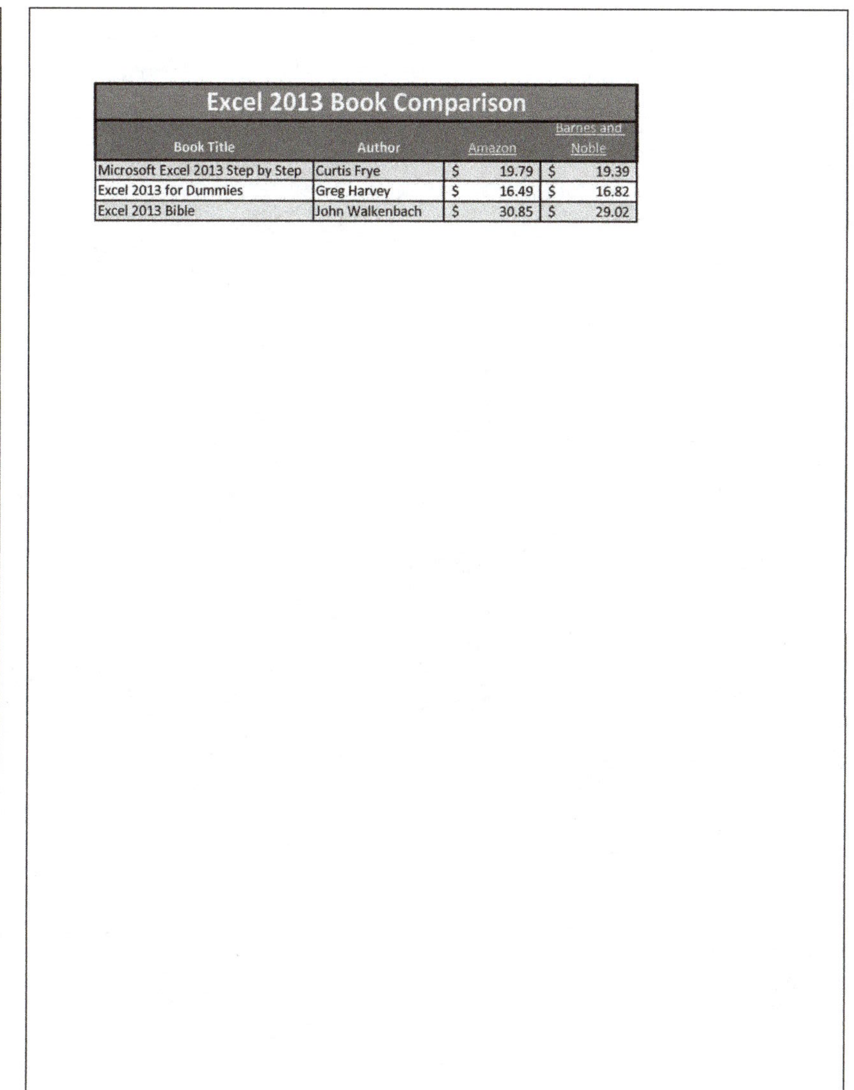

Excel 2013 Book Comparison			
Book Title	Author	Amazon	Barnes and Noble
Microsoft Excel 2013 Step by Step	Curtis Frye	$ 19.79	$ 19.39
Excel 2013 for Dummies	Greg Harvey	$ 16.49	$ 16.82
Excel 2013 Bible	John Walkenbach	$ 30.85	$ 29.02

EL1-U2-IR-Books.xlsx

Landmark Landscaping Company

Employee: Johnathan Holder
Manager: Student Name

Employee phone: (225) 555-3092
Employee email: None

Week ending: ____________

Day		Regular Hours	Overtime	Sick	Vacation	Total
Monday		8.00				8.00
Tuesday		8.00				8.00
Wednesday		8.00	2.00			10.00
Thursday		8.00				8.00
Friday					8.00	8.00
Saturday						
Sunday						
	Total hours	**32.00**	**2.00**		**8.00**	**42.00**
	Rate per hour	$20.00	$30.00			
	Total pay	**$640.00**	**$60.00**			**$700.00**

____________ Employee signature ____________ Date

____________ Manager signature ____________ Date

EL1-U2-JS-TimeCard.xlsx

Excel Level 2, Chapter 1 Model Answers

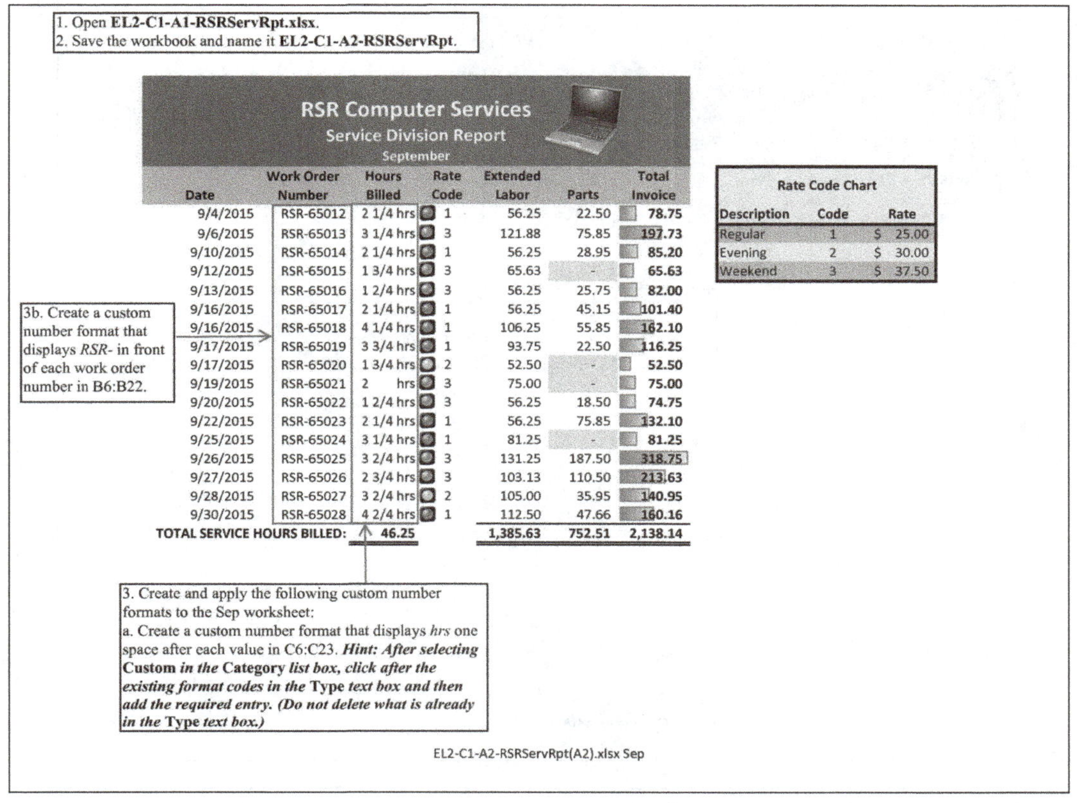

1. Open **EL2-C1-A1-RSRServRpt.xlsx**.
2. Save the workbook and name it **EL2-C1-A2-RSRServRpt**.

RSR Computer Services
Service Division Report
September

Date	Work Order Number	Hours Billed	Rate Code	Extended Labor	Parts	Total Invoice
9/4/2015	RSR-65012	2 1/4 hrs	1	56.25	22.50	78.75
9/6/2015	RSR-65013	3 1/4 hrs	3	121.88	75.85	197.73
9/10/2015	RSR-65014	2 1/4 hrs	1	56.25	28.95	85.20
9/12/2015	RSR-65015	1 3/4 hrs	3	65.63	-	65.63
9/13/2015	RSR-65016	1 2/4 hrs	3	56.25	25.75	82.00
9/16/2015	RSR-65017	2 1/4 hrs	1	56.25	45.15	101.40
9/16/2015	RSR-65018	4 1/4 hrs	1	106.25	55.85	162.10
9/17/2015	RSR-65019	3 3/4 hrs	1	93.75	22.50	116.25
9/17/2015	RSR-65020	1 3/4 hrs	2	52.50	-	52.50
9/19/2015	RSR-65021	2 hrs	3	75.00	-	75.00
9/20/2015	RSR-65022	1 2/4 hrs	3	56.25	18.50	74.75
9/22/2015	RSR-65023	2 1/4 hrs	1	56.25	75.85	132.10
9/25/2015	RSR-65024	3 1/4 hrs	1	81.25	-	81.25
9/26/2015	RSR-65025	3 2/4 hrs	3	131.25	187.50	318.75
9/27/2015	RSR-65026	2 3/4 hrs	3	103.13	110.50	213.63
9/28/2015	RSR-65027	3 2/4 hrs	2	105.00	35.95	140.95
9/30/2015	RSR-65028	4 2/4 hrs	1	112.50	47.66	160.16
TOTAL SERVICE HOURS BILLED:		46.25		1,385.63	752.51	2,138.14

Rate Code Chart

Description	Code	Rate
Regular	1	$ 25.00
Evening	2	$ 30.00
Weekend	3	$ 37.50

3b. Create a custom number format that displays *RSR-* in front of each work order number in B6:B22.

3. Create and apply the following custom number formats to the Sep worksheet:
a. Create a custom number format that displays *hrs* one space after each value in C6:C23. ***Hint: After selecting* Custom *in the* Category *list box, click after the existing format codes in the* Type *text box and then add the required entry. (Do not delete what is already in the* Type *text box.)***

EL2-C1-A2-RSRServRpt(A2).xlsx Sep

EL2-C1-A2-RSRServRpt(A2).xlsx

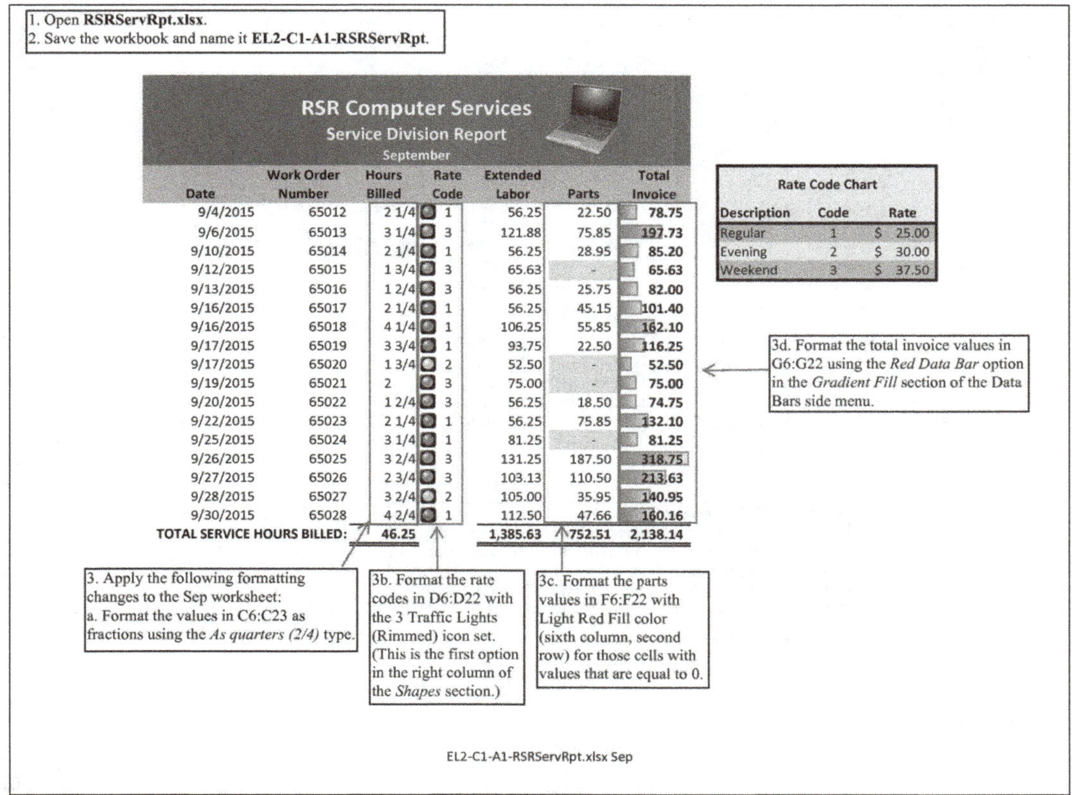

1. Open **RSRServRpt.xlsx**.
2. Save the workbook and name it **EL2-C1-A1-RSRServRpt**.

RSR Computer Services
Service Division Report
September

Date	Work Order Number	Hours Billed	Rate Code	Extended Labor	Parts	Total Invoice
9/4/2015	65012	2 1/4	1	56.25	22.50	78.75
9/6/2015	65013	3 1/4	3	121.88	75.85	197.73
9/10/2015	65014	2 1/4	1	56.25	28.95	85.20
9/12/2015	65015	1 3/4	3	65.63	-	65.63
9/13/2015	65016	1 2/4	3	56.25	25.75	82.00
9/16/2015	65017	2 1/4	1	56.25	45.15	101.40
9/16/2015	65018	4 1/4	1	106.25	55.85	162.10
9/17/2015	65019	3 3/4	1	93.75	22.50	116.25
9/17/2015	65020	1 3/4	2	52.50	-	52.50
9/19/2015	65021	2	3	75.00	-	75.00
9/20/2015	65022	1 2/4	3	56.25	18.50	74.75
9/22/2015	65023	2 1/4	1	56.25	75.85	132.10
9/25/2015	65024	3 1/4	1	81.25	-	81.25
9/26/2015	65025	3 2/4	3	131.25	187.50	318.75
9/27/2015	65026	2 3/4	3	103.13	110.50	213.63
9/28/2015	65027	3 2/4	2	105.00	35.95	140.95
9/30/2015	65028	4 2/4	1	112.50	47.66	160.16
TOTAL SERVICE HOURS BILLED:		46.25		1,385.63	752.51	2,138.14

Rate Code Chart

Description	Code	Rate
Regular	1	$ 25.00
Evening	2	$ 30.00
Weekend	3	$ 37.50

3d. Format the total invoice values in G6:G22 using the *Red Data Bar* option in the *Gradient Fill* section of the Data Bars side menu.

3. Apply the following formatting changes to the Sep worksheet:
a. Format the values in C6:C23 as fractions using the *As quarters (2/4)* type.

3b. Format the rate codes in D6:D22 with the 3 Traffic Lights (Rimmed) icon set. (This is the first option in the right column of the *Shapes* section.)

3c. Format the parts values in F6:F22 with Light Red Fill color (sixth column, second row) for those cells with values that are equal to 0.

EL2-C1-A1-RSRServRpt.xlsx Sep

EL2-C1-A1-RSRServRpt(A1).xlsx

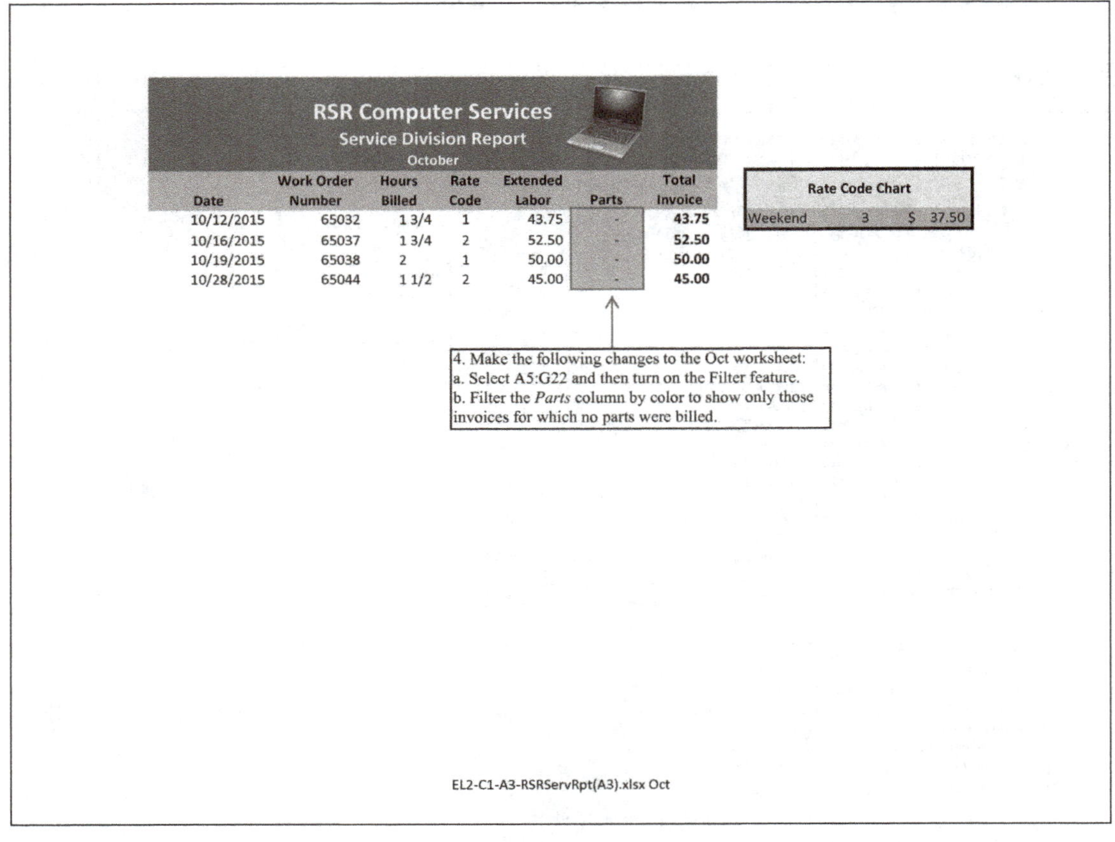

RSR Computer Services

Service Division Report

October

Date	Work Order Number	Hours Billed	Rate Code	Extended Labor	Parts	Total Invoice
10/12/2015	65032	1 3/4	1	43.75	-	**43.75**
10/16/2015	65037	1 3/4	2	52.50	-	**52.50**
10/19/2015	65038	2	1	50.00	-	**50.00**
10/28/2015	65044	1 1/2	2	45.00	-	**45.00**

Rate Code Chart		
Weekend	3	$ 37.50

4. Make the following changes to the Oct worksheet:
a. Select A5:G22 and then turn on the Filter feature.
b. Filter the *Parts* column by color to show only those invoices for which no parts were billed.

EL2-C1-A3-RSRServRpt(A3).xlsx Oct

EL2-C1-A3-RSRServRpt(A3-Oct).xlsx

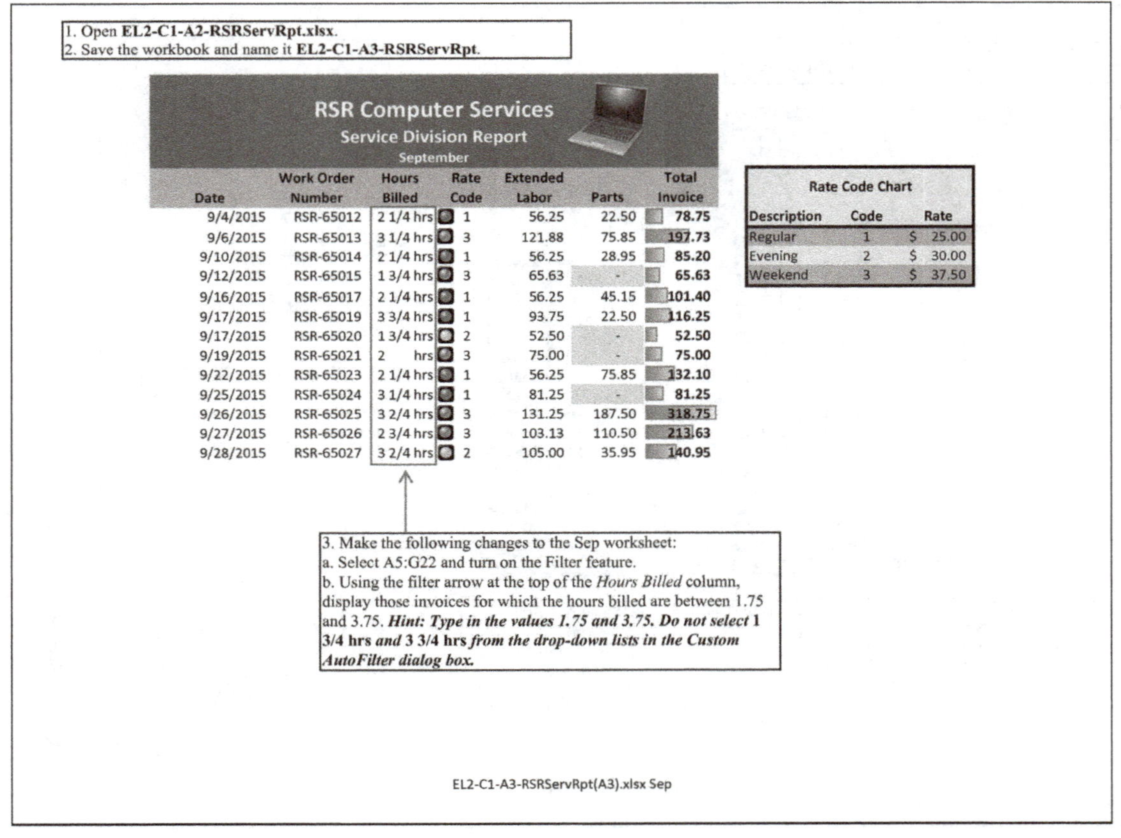

1. Open **EL2-C1-A2-RSRServRpt.xlsx**.
2. Save the workbook and name it **EL2-C1-A3-RSRServRpt**.

RSR Computer Services

Service Division Report

September

Date	Work Order Number	Hours Billed	Rate Code	Extended Labor	Parts	Total Invoice
9/4/2015	RSR-65012	2 1/4 hrs	1	56.25	22.50	**78.75**
9/6/2015	RSR-65013	3 1/4 hrs	3	121.88	75.85	**197.73**
9/10/2015	RSR-65014	2 1/4 hrs	1	56.25	28.95	**85.20**
9/12/2015	RSR-65015	1 3/4 hrs	3	65.63	-	**65.63**
9/16/2015	RSR-65017	2 1/4 hrs	1	56.25	45.15	**101.40**
9/17/2015	RSR-65019	3 3/4 hrs	1	93.75	22.50	**116.25**
9/17/2015	RSR-65020	1 3/4 hrs	2	52.50	-	**52.50**
9/19/2015	RSR-65021	2 hrs	3	75.00	-	**75.00**
9/22/2015	RSR-65023	2 1/4 hrs	1	56.25	75.85	**132.10**
9/25/2015	RSR-65024	3 1/4 hrs	1	81.25	-	**81.25**
9/26/2015	RSR-65025	3 2/4 hrs	3	131.25	187.50	**318.75**
9/27/2015	RSR-65026	2 3/4 hrs	3	103.13	110.50	**213.63**
9/28/2015	RSR-65027	3 2/4 hrs	2	105.00	35.95	**140.95**

Rate Code Chart		
Description	Code	Rate
Regular	1	$ 25.00
Evening	2	$ 30.00
Weekend	3	$ 37.50

3. Make the following changes to the Sep worksheet:
a. Select A5:G22 and turn on the Filter feature.
b. Using the filter arrow at the top of the *Hours Billed* column, display those invoices for which the hours billed are between 1.75 and 3.75. ***Hint: Type in the values 1.75 and 3.75. Do not select* 1 3/4 hrs *and* 3 3/4 hrs *from the drop-down lists in the Custom AutoFilter dialog box.***

EL2-C1-A3-RSRServRpt(A3).xlsx Sep

EL2-C1-A3-RSRServRpt(A3-Sep).xlsx

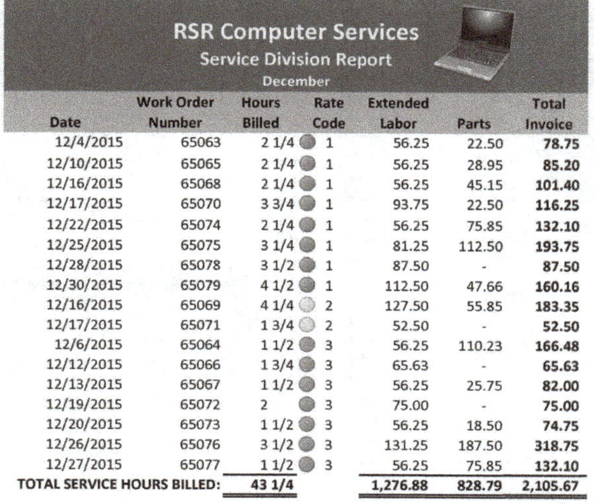

RSR Computer Services
Service Division Report
December

Date	Work Order Number	Hours Billed	Rate Code	Extended Labor	Parts	Total Invoice
12/4/2015	65063	2 1/4	1	56.25	22.50	**78.75**
12/10/2015	65065	2 1/4	1	56.25	28.95	**85.20**
12/16/2015	65068	2 1/4	1	56.25	45.15	**101.40**
12/17/2015	65070	3 3/4	1	93.75	22.50	**116.25**
12/22/2015	65074	2 1/4	1	56.25	75.85	**132.10**
12/25/2015	65075	3 1/4	1	81.25	112.50	**193.75**
12/28/2015	65078	3 1/2	1	87.50	-	**87.50**
12/30/2015	65079	4 1/2	1	112.50	47.66	**160.16**
12/16/2015	65069	4 1/4	2	127.50	55.85	**183.35**
12/17/2015	65071	1 3/4	2	52.50	-	**52.50**
12/6/2015	65064	1 1/2	3	56.25	110.23	**166.48**
12/12/2015	65066	1 3/4	3	65.63	-	**65.63**
12/13/2015	65067	1 1/2	3	56.25	25.75	**82.00**
12/19/2015	65072	2	3	75.00	-	**75.00**
12/20/2015	65073	1 1/2	3	56.25	18.50	**74.75**
12/26/2015	65076	3 1/2	3	131.25	187.50	**318.75**
12/27/2015	65077	1 1/2	3	56.25	75.85	**132.10**
TOTAL SERVICE HOURS BILLED:		**43 1/4**		**1,276.88**	**828.79**	**2,105.67**

Rate Code Chart

Description	Code	Rate
Regular	1	$ 25.00
Evening	2	$ 30.00
Weekend	3	$ 37.50

6. Make the following changes to the Dec worksheet:
a. Remove the filter arrows from the worksheet.
b. Make active any cell within the invoice list.
c. Open the Sort dialog box.
d. Define three sort levels as follows:

Sort by	*Sort On*	*Order*
rate code	cell icon	Red Traffic Light (On Top)
rate code	cell icon	Yellow Traffic Light (On Top)
rate code	cell icon	Green Traffic Light (On Top)

EL2-C1-A3-RSRServRpt(A3).xlsx Dec

EL2-C1-A3-RSRServRpt(A3-Dec).xlsx

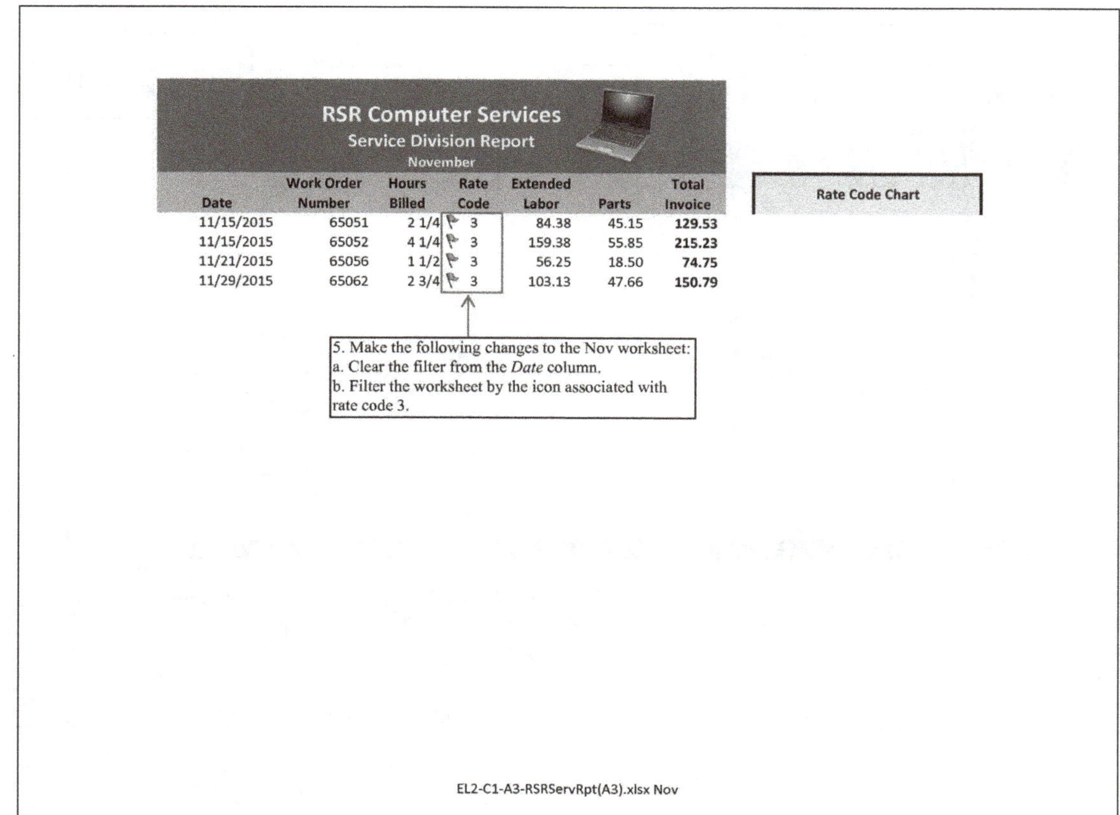

RSR Computer Services
Service Division Report
November

Date	Work Order Number	Hours Billed	Rate Code	Extended Labor	Parts	Total Invoice
11/15/2015	65051	2 1/4	3	84.38	45.15	**129.53**
11/15/2015	65052	4 1/4	3	159.38	55.85	**215.23**
11/21/2015	65056	1 1/2	3	56.25	18.50	**74.75**
11/29/2015	65062	2 3/4	3	103.13	47.66	**150.79**

Rate Code Chart

5. Make the following changes to the Nov worksheet:
a. Clear the filter from the *Date* column.
b. Filter the worksheet by the icon associated with rate code 3.

EL2-C1-A3-RSRServRpt(A3).xlsx Nov

EL2-C1-A3-RSRServRpt(A3-Nov).xlsx

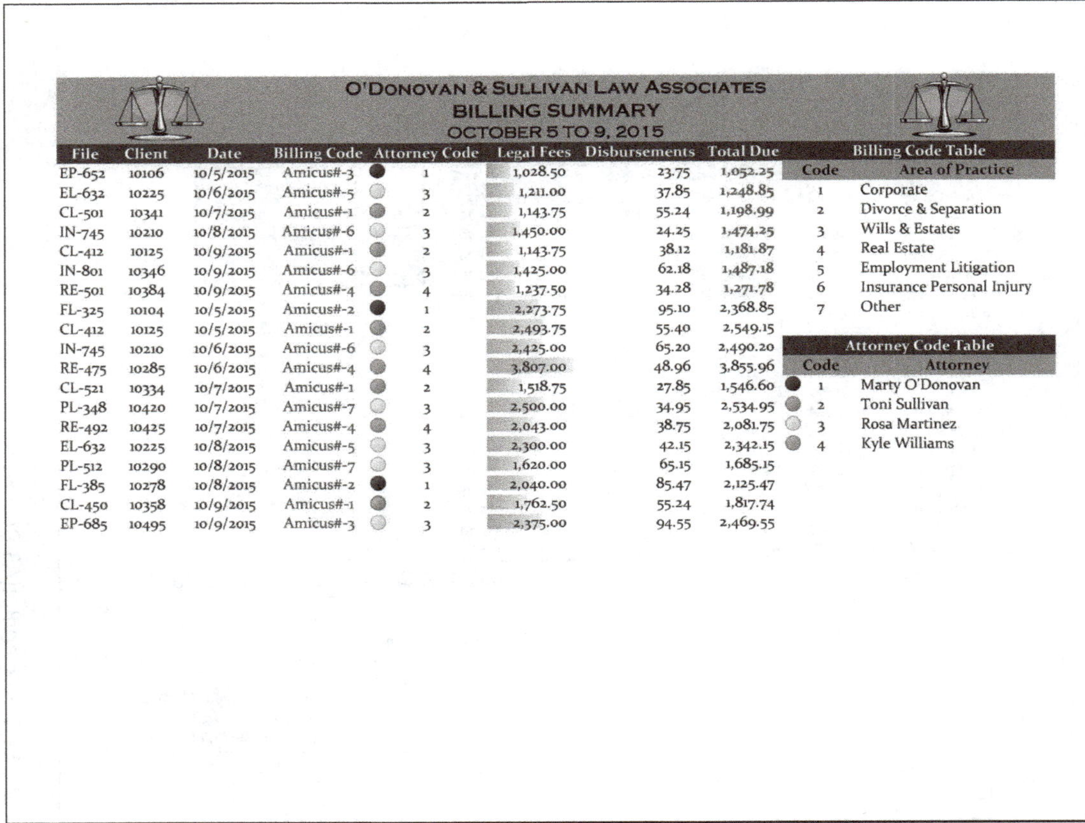

O'DONOVAN & SULLIVAN LAW ASSOCIATES
BILLING SUMMARY
OCTOBER 5 TO 9, 2015

File	Client	Date	Billing Code	Attorney Code	Legal Fees	Disbursements	Total Due
EP-652	10106	10/5/2015	Amicus#-3	1	1,028.50	23.75	1,052.25
EL-632	10225	10/6/2015	Amicus#-5	3	1,211.00	37.85	1,248.85
CL-501	10341	10/7/2015	Amicus#-1	2	1,143.75	55.24	1,198.99
IN-745	10210	10/8/2015	Amicus#-6	3	1,450.00	24.25	1,474.25
CL-412	10125	10/9/2015	Amicus#-1	2	1,143.75	38.12	1,181.87
IN-801	10346	10/9/2015	Amicus#-6	3	1,425.00	62.18	1,487.18
RE-501	10384	10/9/2015	Amicus#-4	4	1,237.50	34.28	1,271.78
FL-325	10104	10/5/2015	Amicus#-2	1	2,273.75	95.10	2,368.85
CL-412	10125	10/5/2015	Amicus#-1	2	2,493.75	55.40	2,549.15
IN-745	10210	10/6/2015	Amicus#-6	3	2,425.00	65.20	2,490.20
RE-475	10285	10/6/2015	Amicus#-4	4	3,807.00	48.96	3,855.96
CL-521	10334	10/7/2015	Amicus#-1	2	1,518.75	27.85	1,546.60
PL-348	10420	10/7/2015	Amicus#-7	3	2,500.00	34.95	2,534.95
RE-492	10425	10/7/2015	Amicus#-4	4	2,043.00	38.75	2,081.75
EL-632	10225	10/8/2015	Amicus#-5	3	2,300.00	42.15	2,342.15
PL-512	10290	10/8/2015	Amicus#-7	3	1,620.00	65.15	1,685.15
FL-385	10278	10/8/2015	Amicus#-2	1	2,040.00	85.47	2,125.47
CL-450	10358	10/9/2015	Amicus#-1	2	1,762.50	55.24	1,817.74
EP-685	10495	10/9/2015	Amicus#-3	3	2,375.00	94.55	2,469.55

Billing Code Table

Code	Area of Practice
1	Corporate
2	Divorce & Separation
3	Wills & Estates
4	Real Estate
5	Employment Litigation
6	Insurance Personal Injury
7	Other

Attorney Code Table

Code	Attorney
1	Marty O'Donovan
2	Toni Sullivan
3	Rosa Martinez
4	Kyle Williams

EL2-C1-VB-BillingsOct5to9(VB).xlsx

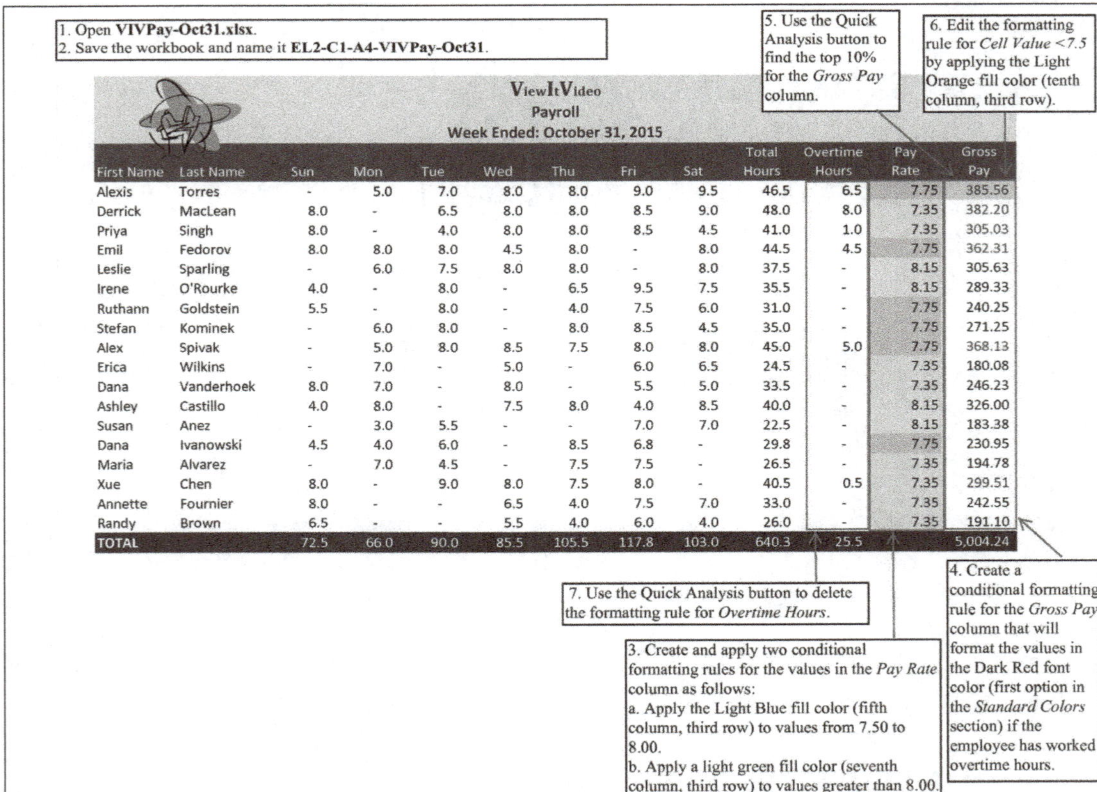

1. Open **VIVPay-Oct31.xlsx**.
2. Save the workbook and name it **EL2-C1-A4-VIVPay-Oct31**.

ViewItVideo
Payroll
Week Ended: October 31, 2015

First Name	Last Name	Sun	Mon	Tue	Wed	Thu	Fri	Sat	Total Hours	Overtime Hours	Pay Rate	Gross Pay
Alexis	Torres	-	5.0	7.0	8.0	8.0	9.0	9.5	46.5	6.5	7.75	385.56
Derrick	MacLean	8.0	-	6.5	8.0	8.0	8.5	9.0	48.0	8.0	7.35	382.20
Priya	Singh	8.0	-	4.0	8.0	8.0	8.5	4.5	41.0	1.0	7.35	305.03
Emil	Fedorov	8.0	8.0	8.0	4.5	8.0	-	8.0	44.5	4.5	7.75	362.31
Leslie	Sparling	-	6.0	7.5	8.0	8.0	-	8.0	37.5	-	8.15	305.63
Irene	O'Rourke	4.0	-	8.0	-	6.5	9.5	7.5	35.5	-	8.15	289.33
Ruthann	Goldstein	5.5	-	8.0	-	4.0	7.5	6.0	31.0	-	7.75	240.25
Stefan	Kominek	-	6.0	8.0	-	8.0	8.5	4.5	35.0	-	7.75	271.25
Alex	Spivak	-	5.0	8.0	8.5	7.5	8.0	8.0	45.0	5.0	7.75	368.13
Erica	Wilkins	-	7.0	-	5.0	-	6.0	6.5	24.5	-	7.35	180.08
Dana	Vanderhoek	8.0	7.0	-	8.0	-	5.5	5.0	33.5	-	7.35	246.23
Ashley	Castillo	4.0	8.0	-	7.5	8.0	4.0	8.5	40.0	-	8.15	326.00
Susan	Anez	-	3.0	5.5	-	-	7.0	7.0	22.5	-	8.15	183.38
Dana	Ivanowski	4.5	4.0	6.0	-	8.5	6.8	-	29.8	-	7.75	230.95
Maria	Alvarez	-	7.0	4.5	-	7.5	7.5	-	26.5	-	7.35	194.78
Xue	Chen	8.0	-	9.0	8.0	7.5	8.0	-	40.5	0.5	7.35	299.51
Annette	Fournier	8.0	-	-	6.5	4.0	7.5	7.0	33.0	-	7.35	242.55
Randy	Brown	6.5	-	-	5.5	4.0	6.0	4.0	26.0	-	7.35	191.10
TOTAL		72.5	66.0	90.0	85.5	105.5	117.8	103.0	640.3	25.5		5,004.24

5. Use the Quick Analysis button to find the top 10% for the *Gross Pay* column.

6. Edit the formatting rule for *Cell Value <7.5* by applying the Light Orange fill color (tenth column, third row).

7. Use the Quick Analysis button to delete the formatting rule for *Overtime Hours*.

3. Create and apply two conditional formatting rules for the values in the *Pay Rate* column as follows:
a. Apply the Light Blue fill color (fifth column, third row) to values from 7.50 to 8.00.
b. Apply a light green fill color (seventh column, third row) to values greater than 8.00.

4. Create a conditional formatting rule for the *Gross Pay* column that will format the values in the Dark Red font color (first option in the *Standard Colors* section) if the employee has worked overtime hours.

EL2-C1-A4-VIVPay-Oct31(A4).xlsx

Two-Year Average Median Household Income by State

Median Income for 2011	
United States	**50,443**
Alabama	42,407
Alaska	58,552
Arizona	48,498
Arkansas	40,553
California	54,681
Colorado	60,381
Connecticut	66,748
Delaware	55,808
District of Columbia	56,988
Florida	45,281
Georgia	45,741
Hawaii	60,232
Idaho	47,997
Illinois	51,483
Indiana	46,020
Iowa	50,391
Kansas	46,827
Kentucky	41,129
Louisiana	40,599
Maine	49,568
Maryland	67,551
Massachusetts	63,085
Michigan	48,308
Minnesota	55,896
Mississippi	40,227
Missouri	46,518
Montana	41,430
Nebraska	54,888
Nevada	49,929
New Hampshire	67,308
New Jersey	63,646
New Mexico	44,270
New York	50,994
North Carolina	45,210
North Dakota	54,488
Ohio	45,991
Oklahoma	46,459
Oregon	51,862
Pennsylvania	49,874
Rhode Island	51,143
South Carolina	41,549
South Dakota	47,003
Tennessee	41,044
Texas	48,902
Utah	56,991
Vermont	54,777
Virginia	62,444
Washington	57,392
West Virginia	42,974
Wisconsin	51,999
Wyoming	54,178

Legend	
Less than 45,000	35,000
Between 45,000 and 55,000	50,000
Greater than 55,000	60,000

Data shown above is the two-year average median for 2010 to 2011. Two-year average median is the sum of two inflation-adjusted single-year medians divided by 2.

Source: U.S. Census Bureau

http://www.census.gov/hhes/www/income/data/statemedian/index.html

EL2-C1-CS-P1-USIncomeStats(P1).xlsx

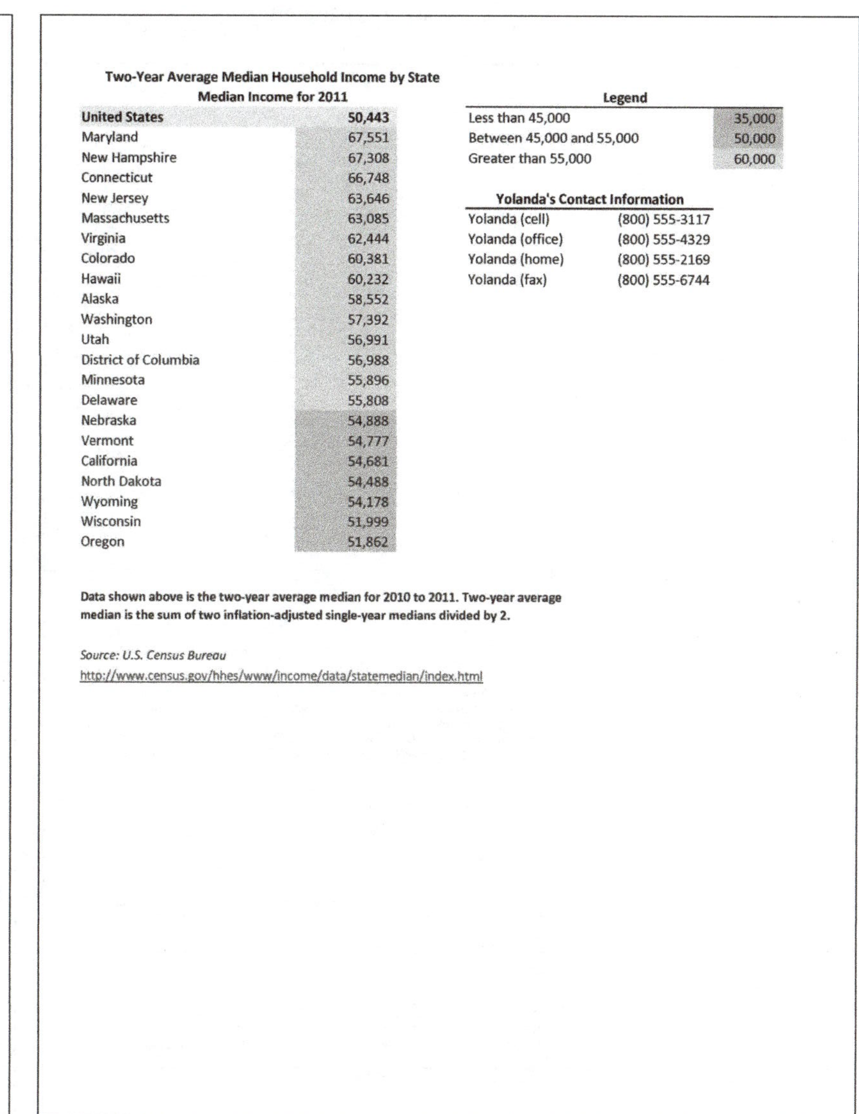

Two-Year Average Median Household Income by State

Median Income for 2011	
United States	**50,443**
Maryland	67,551
New Hampshire	67,308
Connecticut	66,748
New Jersey	63,646
Massachusetts	63,085
Virginia	62,444
Colorado	60,381
Hawaii	60,232
Alaska	58,552
Washington	57,392
Utah	56,991
District of Columbia	56,988
Minnesota	55,896
Delaware	55,808
Nebraska	54,888
Vermont	54,777
California	54,681
North Dakota	54,488
Wyoming	54,178
Wisconsin	51,999
Oregon	51,862

Legend	
Less than 45,000	35,000
Between 45,000 and 55,000	50,000
Greater than 55,000	60,000

Yolanda's Contact Information	
Yolanda (cell)	(800) 555-3117
Yolanda (office)	(800) 555-4329
Yolanda (home)	(800) 555-2169
Yolanda (fax)	(800) 555-6744

Data shown above is the two-year average median for 2010 to 2011. Two-year average median is the sum of two inflation-adjusted single-year medians divided by 2.

Source: U.S. Census Bureau

http://www.census.gov/hhes/www/income/data/statemedian/index.html

EL2-C1-CS-P2-USIncomeStats(P2).xlsx

Two-Year Average Median Household Income by State
Median Income for 2011

United States	**50,443**
Maryland	67,551
New Hampshire	67,308
Connecticut	66,748
New Jersey	63,646
Massachusetts	63,085
Virginia	62,444
Colorado	60,381
Hawaii	60,232
Alaska	58,552
Washington	57,392
Utah	56,991
District of Columbia	56,988
Minnesota	55,896
Delaware	55,808
Nebraska	54,888
Vermont	54,777
California	54,681
North Dakota	54,488
Wyoming	54,178
Wisconsin	51,999
Oregon	51,862

Yolanda's Contact Information	
Yolanda (cell)	(800) 555-3117
Yolanda (office)	(800) 555-4329
Yolanda (home)	(800) 555-2169
Yolanda (fax)	(800) 555-6744

Data shown above is the two-year average median for 2010 to 2011. Two-year average median is the sum of two inflation-adjusted single-year medians divided by 2.

Source: U.S. Census Bureau
http://www.census.gov/hhes/www/income/data/statemedian/index.html

EL2-C1-CS-P3-USIncomeStats(P3).xlsx

Intersting Facts

The U.S. Constitution requires only that the decennial census be a population count. Since the first census in 1790, however, the need for useful information about the United States' population and economy became increasingly evident.

The U.S. government will not release personally identifiable information about an individual to any other individual or agency until 72 years after it is collected for the decennial census.

A permanent Census Office was established in 1902 within the Department of the Interior, becoming the Census Bureau when it moved to the newly created Department of Commerce and Labor in 1903.

The area where the U.S. Census Bureau headquarters is located is named after Col. Samuel Taylor Suit, a nineteenth century businessman and entrepreneur, whose farm, "Suitland," was located near the current intersection of Suitland and Silver Hill Roads.

Herman Hollerith seized on the idea of punch cards, designing a machine that used the location of holes on each card to tally not only overall numbers but also individual characteristics and even cross-tabulations. He tested his new machine in Baltimore in 1887, the same year the hand-counted 1880 census was finally completed, and was successful enough that he won a contract from the Census Office when it reopened for the 1890 census.

Source: U.S. Census Bureau
http://www.census.gov/history/

EL2-C1-CS-P4-USIncomeStats(P4).xlsx

Excel Level 2, Chapter 2 Model Answers

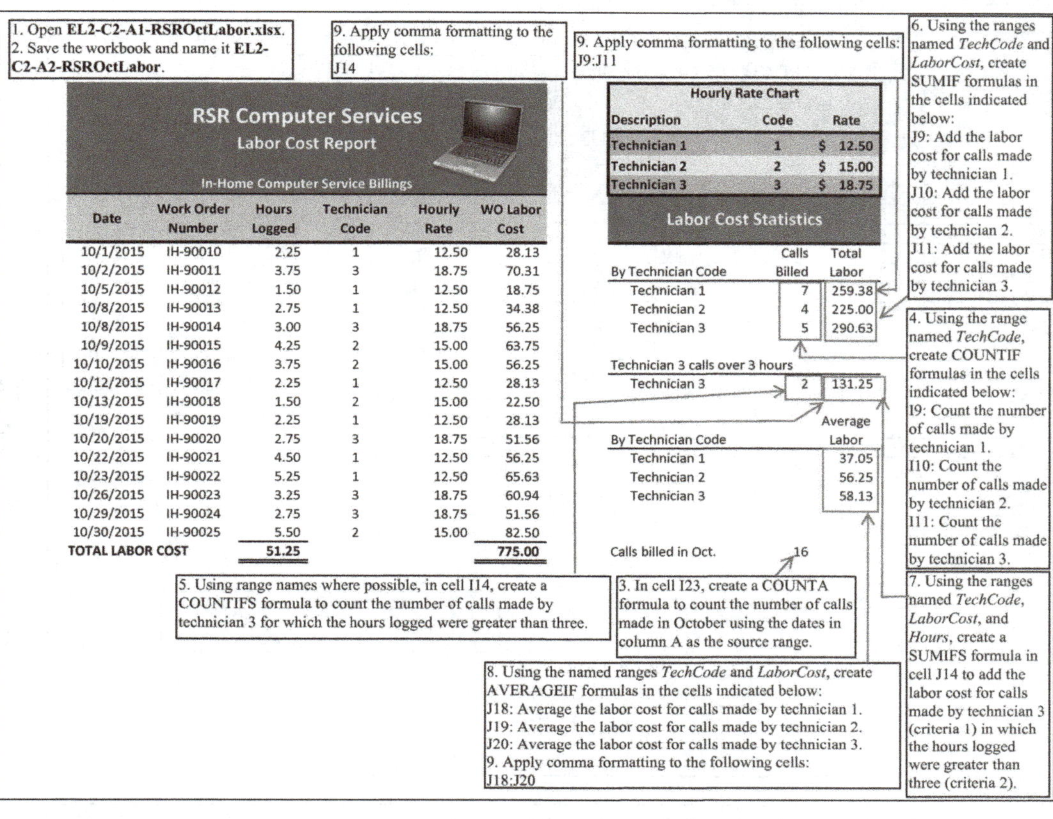

1. Open **EL2-C2-A1-RSROctLabor.xlsx**.
2. Save the workbook and name it **EL2-C2-A2-RSROctLabor**.

9. Apply comma formatting to the following cells: J14

9. Apply comma formatting to the following cells: J9:J11

6. Using the ranges named *TechCode* and *LaborCost*, create SUMIF formulas in the cells indicated below:
J9: Add the labor cost for calls made by technician 1.
J10: Add the labor cost for calls made by technician 2.
J11: Add the labor cost for calls made by technician 3.

RSR Computer Services
Labor Cost Report
In-Home Computer Service Billings

Date	Work Order Number	Hours Logged	Technician Code	Hourly Rate	WO Labor Cost
10/1/2015	IH-90010	2.25	1	12.50	28.13
10/2/2015	IH-90011	3.75	3	18.75	70.31
10/5/2015	IH-90012	1.50	1	12.50	18.75
10/8/2015	IH-90013	2.75	1	12.50	34.38
10/8/2015	IH-90014	3.00	3	18.75	56.25
10/9/2015	IH-90015	4.25	2	15.00	63.75
10/10/2015	IH-90016	3.75	2	15.00	56.25
10/12/2015	IH-90017	2.25	1	12.50	28.13
10/13/2015	IH-90018	1.50	2	15.00	22.50
10/19/2015	IH-90019	2.25	1	12.50	28.13
10/20/2015	IH-90020	2.75	3	18.75	51.56
10/22/2015	IH-90021	4.50	1	12.50	56.25
10/23/2015	IH-90022	5.25	1	12.50	65.63
10/26/2015	IH-90023	3.25	3	18.75	60.94
10/29/2015	IH-90024	2.75	3	18.75	51.56
10/30/2015	IH-90025	5.50	2	15.00	82.50
TOTAL LABOR COST		51.25			775.00

Hourly Rate Chart		
Description	Code	Rate
Technician 1	1	$ 12.50
Technician 2	2	$ 15.00
Technician 3	3	$ 18.75

Labor Cost Statistics

By Technician Code	Calls Billed	Total Labor
Technician 1	7	259.38
Technician 2	4	225.00
Technician 3	5	290.63
Technician 3 calls over 3 hours		
Technician 3	2	131.25

By Technician Code	Average Labor
Technician 1	37.05
Technician 2	56.25
Technician 3	58.13

Calls billed in Oct. 16

4. Using the range named *TechCode*, create COUNTIF formulas in the cells indicated below:
I9: Count the number of calls made by technician 1.
I10: Count the number of calls made by technician 2.
I11: Count the number of calls made by technician 3.

5. Using range names where possible, in cell I14, create a COUNTIFS formula to count the number of calls made by technician 3 for which the hours logged were greater than three.

3. In cell I23, create a COUNTA formula to count the number of calls made in October using the dates in column A as the source range.

7. Using the ranges named *TechCode*, *LaborCost*, and *Hours*, create a SUMIFS formula in cell J14 to add the labor cost for calls made by technician 3 (criteria 1) in which the hours logged were greater than three (criteria 2).

8. Using the named ranges *TechCode* and *LaborCost*, create AVERAGEIF formulas in the cells indicated below:
J18: Average the labor cost for calls made by technician 1.
J19: Average the labor cost for calls made by technician 2.
J20: Average the labor cost for calls made by technician 3.
9. Apply comma formatting to the following cells: J18:J20

EL2-C2-A2-RSROctLabor(A2).xlsx

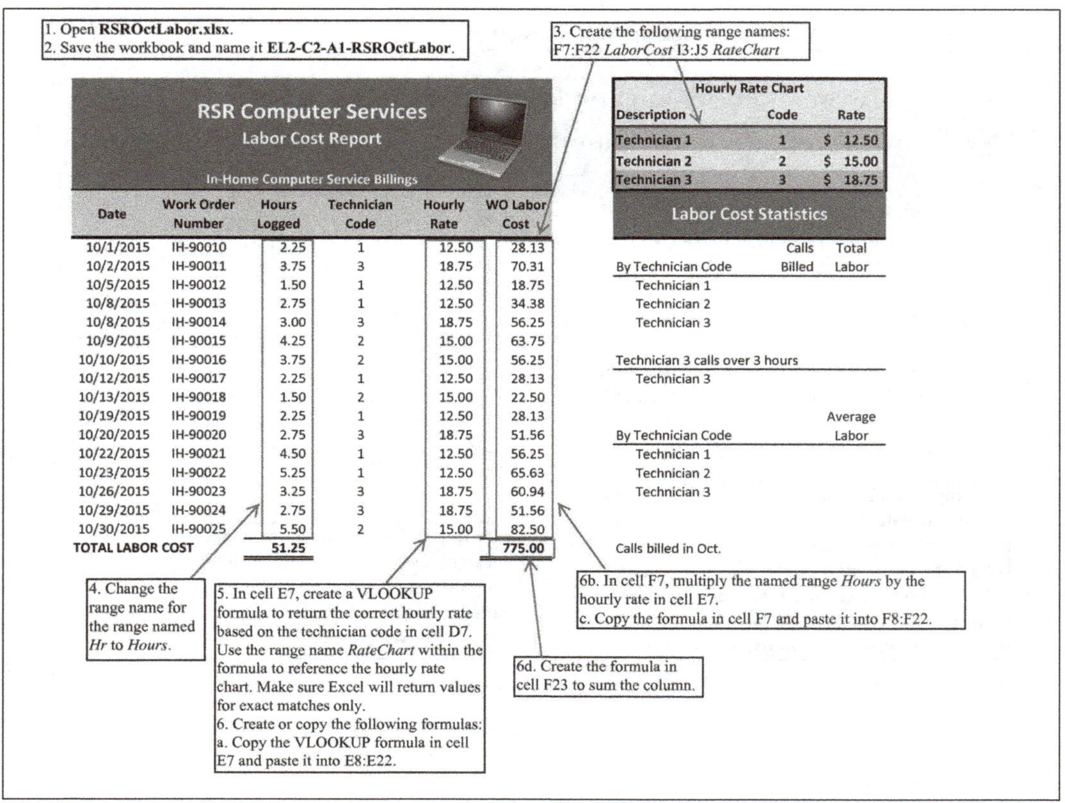

1. Open **RSROctLabor.xlsx**.
2. Save the workbook and name it **EL2-C2-A1-RSROctLabor**.

3. Create the following range names:
F7:F22 *LaborCost* I3:J5 *RateChart*

RSR Computer Services
Labor Cost Report
In-Home Computer Service Billings

Date	Work Order Number	Hours Logged	Technician Code	Hourly Rate	WO Labor Cost
10/1/2015	IH-90010	2.25	1	12.50	28.13
10/2/2015	IH-90011	3.75	3	18.75	70.31
10/5/2015	IH-90012	1.50	1	12.50	18.75
10/8/2015	IH-90013	2.75	1	12.50	34.38
10/8/2015	IH-90014	3.00	3	18.75	56.25
10/9/2015	IH-90015	4.25	2	15.00	63.75
10/10/2015	IH-90016	3.75	2	15.00	56.25
10/12/2015	IH-90017	2.25	1	12.50	28.13
10/13/2015	IH-90018	1.50	2	15.00	22.50
10/19/2015	IH-90019	2.25	1	12.50	28.13
10/20/2015	IH-90020	2.75	3	18.75	51.56
10/22/2015	IH-90021	4.50	1	12.50	56.25
10/23/2015	IH-90022	5.25	1	12.50	65.63
10/26/2015	IH-90023	3.25	3	18.75	60.94
10/29/2015	IH-90024	2.75	3	18.75	51.56
10/30/2015	IH-90025	5.50	2	15.00	82.50
TOTAL LABOR COST		51.25			775.00

Hourly Rate Chart		
Description	Code	Rate
Technician 1	1	$ 12.50
Technician 2	2	$ 15.00
Technician 3	3	$ 18.75

Labor Cost Statistics

By Technician Code	Calls Billed	Total Labor
Technician 1		
Technician 2		
Technician 3		
Technician 3 calls over 3 hours		
Technician 3		

By Technician Code	Average Labor
Technician 1	
Technician 2	
Technician 3	

Calls billed in Oct.

4. Change the range name for the range named *Hr* to *Hours*.

5. In cell E7, create a VLOOKUP formula to return the correct hourly rate based on the technician code in cell D7. Use the range name *RateChart* within the formula to reference the hourly rate chart. Make sure Excel will return values for exact matches only.
6. Create or copy the following formulas:
a. Copy the VLOOKUP formula in cell E7 and paste it into E8:E22.

6b. In cell F7, multiply the named range *Hours* by the hourly rate in cell E7.
c. Copy the formula in cell F7 and paste it into F8:F22.

6d. Create the formula in cell F23 to sum the column.

EL2-C2-A1-RSROctLabor(A1).xlsx

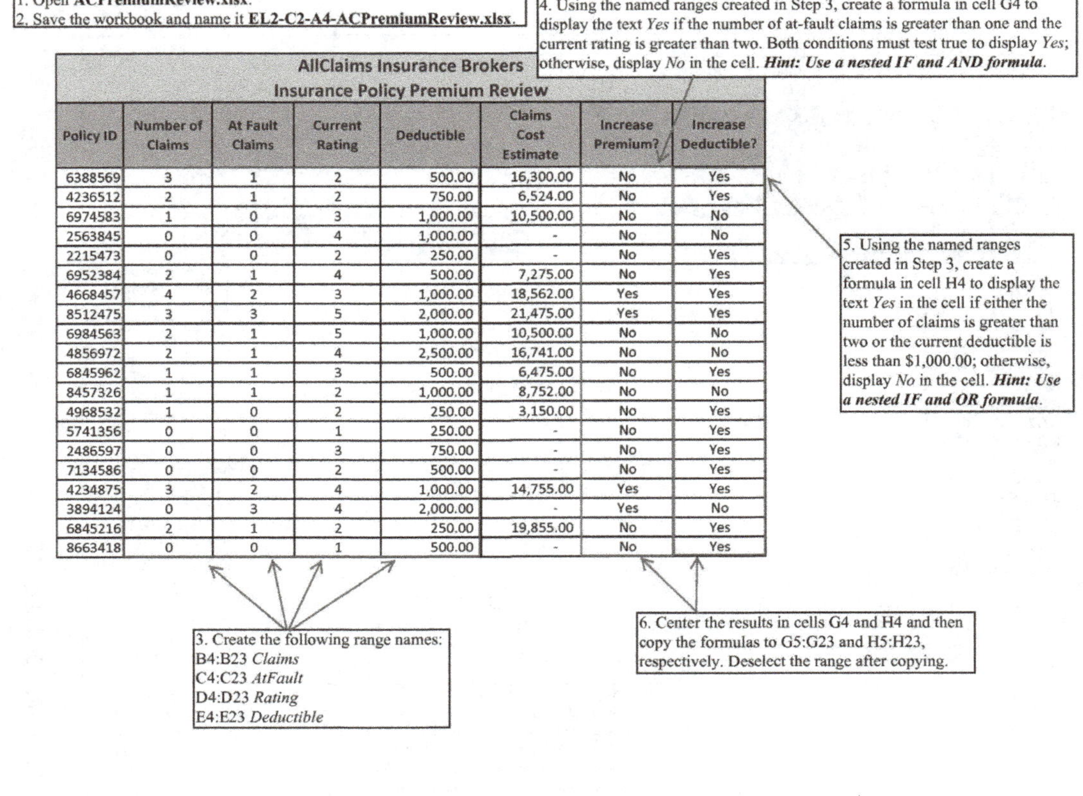

1. Open **ACPremiumReview.xlsx**.
2. Save the workbook and name it **EL2-C2-A4-ACPremiumReview.xlsx**.

AllClaims Insurance Brokers
Insurance Policy Premium Review

Policy ID	Number of Claims	At Fault Claims	Current Rating	Deductible	Claims Cost Estimate	Increase Premium?	Increase Deductible?
6388569	3	1	2	500.00	16,300.00	No	Yes
4236512	2	1	2	750.00	6,524.00	No	Yes
6974583	1	0	3	1,000.00	10,500.00	No	No
2563845	0	0	4	1,000.00	-	No	No
2215473	0	0	2	250.00	-	No	Yes
6952384	2	1	4	500.00	7,275.00	No	Yes
4668457	4	2	3	1,000.00	18,562.00	Yes	Yes
8512475	3	3	5	2,000.00	21,475.00	Yes	Yes
6984563	2	1	5	1,000.00	10,500.00	No	No
4856972	2	1	4	2,500.00	16,741.00	No	No
6845962	1	1	3	500.00	6,475.00	No	Yes
8457326	1	1	2	1,000.00	8,752.00	No	No
4968532	1	0	2	250.00	3,150.00	No	Yes
5741356	0	0	1	250.00	-	No	Yes
2486597	0	0	3	750.00	-	No	Yes
7134586	0	0	2	500.00	-	No	Yes
4234875	3	2	4	1,000.00	14,755.00	Yes	Yes
3894124	0	3	4	2,000.00	-	Yes	No
6845216	2	1	2	250.00	19,855.00	No	Yes
8663418	0	0	1	500.00	-	No	Yes

3. Create the following range names:
B4:B23 *Claims*
C4:C23 *AtFault*
D4:D23 *Rating*
E4:E23 *Deductible*

4. Using the named ranges created in Step 3, create a formula in cell G4 to display the text *Yes* if the number of at-fault claims is greater than one and the current rating is greater than two. Both conditions must test true to display *Yes*; otherwise, display *No* in the cell. ***Hint: Use a nested IF and AND formula.***

5. Using the named ranges created in Step 3, create a formula in cell H4 to display the text *Yes* in the cell if either the number of claims is greater than two or the current deductible is less than $1,000.00; otherwise, display *No* in the cell. ***Hint: Use a nested IF and OR formula.***

6. Center the results in cells G4 and H4 and then copy the formulas to G5:G23 and H5:H23, respectively. Deselect the range after copying.

EL2-C2-A4-ACPremiumReview(A4).xlsx

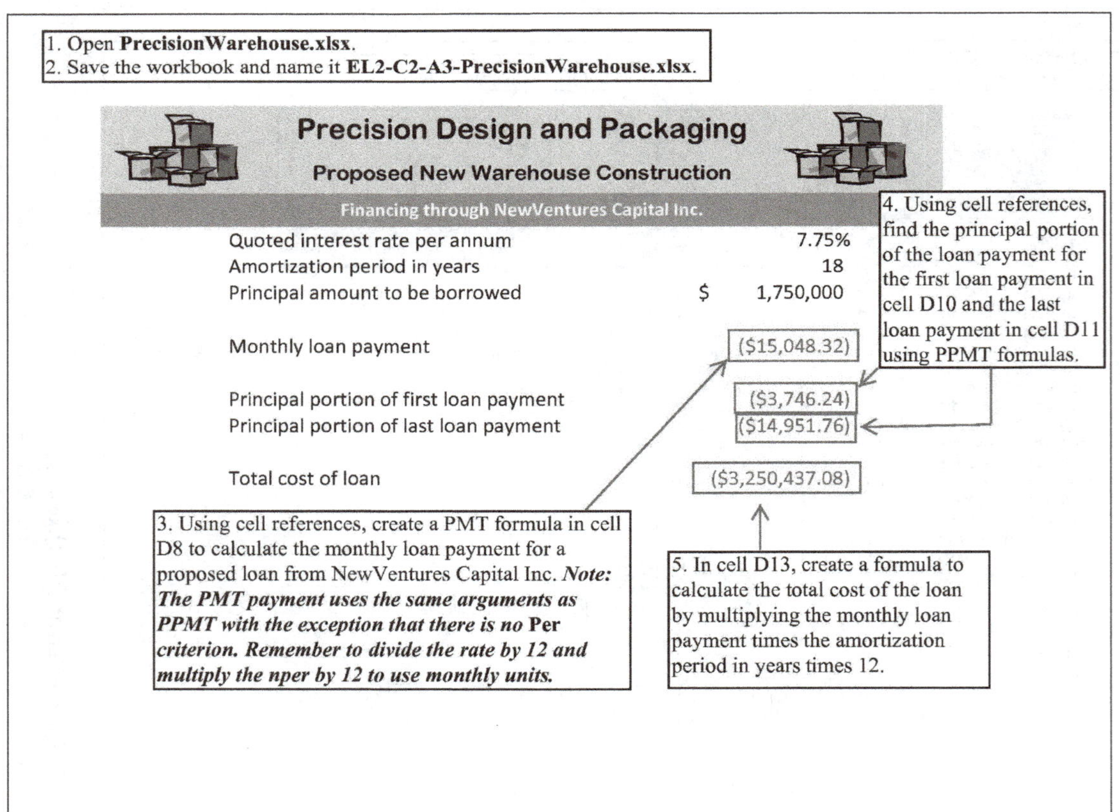

1. Open **PrecisionWarehouse.xlsx**.
2. Save the workbook and name it **EL2-C2-A3-PrecisionWarehouse.xlsx**.

Quoted interest rate per annum	7.75%
Amortization period in years	18
Principal amount to be borrowed	$ 1,750,000
Monthly loan payment	($15,048.32)
Principal portion of first loan payment	($3,746.24)
Principal portion of last loan payment	($14,951.76)
Total cost of loan	($3,250,437.08)

3. Using cell references, create a PMT formula in cell D8 to calculate the monthly loan payment for a proposed loan from NewVentures Capital Inc. ***Note: The PMT payment uses the same arguments as PPMT with the exception that there is no* Per *criterion. Remember to divide the rate by 12 and multiply the nper by 12 to use monthly units.***

4. Using cell references, find the principal portion of the loan payment for the first loan payment in cell D10 and the last loan payment in cell D11 using PPMT formulas.

5. In cell D13, create a formula to calculate the total cost of the loan by multiplying the monthly loan payment times the amortization period in years times 12.

EL2-C2-A3-PrecisionWarehouse(A3).xlsx

O'DONOVAN & SULLIVAN LAW ASSOCIATES
BILLING SUMMARY
OCTOBER 5 TO 9, 2015

File	Client	Date	Attorney Code	Billable Hours	Hourly Rate	Legal Fees
FL-325	10104	10/5/2015	1	26.75	85.00	2,273.75
EP-652	10106	10/5/2015	1	12.10	85.00	1,028.50
CL-412	10125	10/5/2015	2	33.25	75.00	2,493.75
IN-745	10210	10/6/2015	3	24.25	100.00	2,425.00
EL-632	10225	10/6/2015	3	12.11	100.00	1,211.00
RE-475	10285	10/6/2015	4	42.30	90.00	3,807.00
CL-501	10341	10/7/2015	2	15.25	75.00	1,143.75
CL-521	10334	10/7/2015	2	20.25	75.00	1,518.75
PL-348	10420	10/7/2015	3	25.00	100.00	2,500.00
RE-492	10425	10/7/2015	4	22.70	90.00	2,043.00
EL-632	10225	10/8/2015	3	23.00	100.00	2,300.00
PL-512	10290	10/8/2015	3	16.20	100.00	1,620.00
IN-745	10210	10/8/2015	3	14.50	100.00	1,450.00
FL-385	10278	10/8/2015	1	24.00	85.00	2,040.00
CL-412	10125	10/9/2015	2	15.25	75.00	1,143.75
CL-450	10358	10/9/2015	2	23.50	75.00	1,762.50
IN-801	10346	10/9/2015	3	14.25	100.00	1,425.00
EP-685	10495	10/9/2015	3	23.75	100.00	2,375.00
RE-501	10384	10/9/2015	4	13.75	90.00	1,237.50
			TOTAL	402.16	TOTAL	$ 35,798.25

Billing Statistics

Total Legal Fees Billed by Attorney

1	Marty O'Donovan	$ 5,342.25
2	Toni Sullivan	$ 8,062.50
3	Rosa Martinez	$ 15,306.00
4	Kyle Williams	$ 7,087.50
	TOTAL	$ 35,798.25

Average Billable Hours by Attorney

1	Marty O'Donovan	20.95
2	Toni Sullivan	21.50
3	Rosa Martinez	19.13
4	Kyle Williams	26.25

Attorney Code Table

Code	Attorney	Hourly Rate
1	Marty O'Donovan	85.00
2	Toni Sullivan	75.00
3	Rosa Martinez	100.00
4	Kyle Williams	90.00

EL2-C2-VB1-BillHrsOct5to9(VB1).xlsx

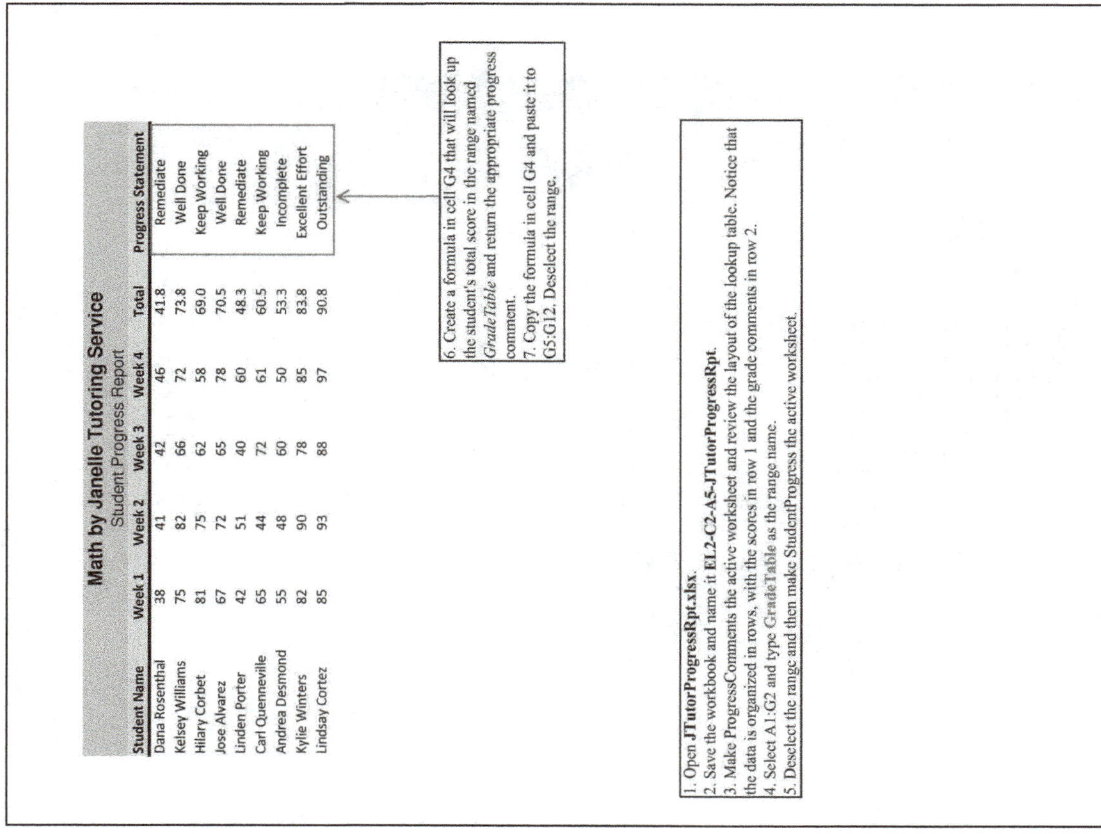

Math by Janelle Tutoring Service
Student Progress Report

Student Name	Week 1	Week 2	Week 3	Week 4	Total	Progress Statement
Dana Rosenthal	38	41	42	46	41.8	Remediate
Kelsey Williams	75	82	66	72	73.8	Well Done
Hilary Corbet	81	75	62	58	69.0	Keep Working
Jose Alvarez	67	72	65	78	70.5	Well Done
Linden Porter	42	51	40	60	48.3	Remediate
Carl Quenneville	65	44	72	61	60.5	Keep Working
Andrea Desmond	55	48	60	50	53.3	Incomplete
Kylie Winters	82	90	78	85	83.8	Excellent Effort
Lindsay Cortez	85	93	88	97	90.8	Outstanding

6. Create a formula in cell G4 that will look up the student's total score in the range named *GradeTable* and return the appropriate progress comment.
7. Copy the formula in cell G4 and paste it to G5:G12. Deselect the range.

1. Open **JTutorProgressRpt.xlsx**.
2. Save the workbook and name it **EL2-C2-A5-JTutorProgressRpt**.
3. Make ProgressComments the active worksheet and review the layout of the lookup table. Notice that the data is organized in rows, with the scores in row 1 and the grade comments in row 2.
4. Select A1:G2 and type GradeTable as the range name.
5. Deselect the range and then make StudentProgress the active worksheet.

EL2-C2-A5-JTutorProgressRpt(A5).xlsx

Pizza by Mario 2015 Franchise Sales

Store	City	State	Year Est.	Sales	Royalty %	Royalty Fee
101	Detroit	Michigan	2002	652,458		
102	Detroit	Michigan	2002	466,153		
103	Flint	Michigan	2003	324,965		
104	Ann Arbor	Michigan	2004	652,146		
105	Ann Arbor	Michigan	2004	378,458		
106	Kalamazoo	Michigan	2004	528,346		
107	Port Huron	Michigan	2004	345,892		
108	Toledo	Ohio	2004	653,485		
109	Toledo	Ohio	2005	354,268		
110	Toledo	Ohio	2005	554,213		
111	Akron	Ohio	2005	461,853		
112	Cincinnati	Ohio	2006	512,463		
113	Madison	Wisconsin	2006	325,496		
114	Madison	Wisconsin	2006	745,865		
115	Milwaukee	Wisconsin	2007	451,236		
116	Milwaukee	Wisconsin	2007	554,168		
117	Milwaukee	Wisconsin	2007	653,856		
118	Cedar Rapids	Iowa	2008	541,285		
119	Cedar Rapids	Iowa	2008	347,856		
120	Cedar Rapids	Iowa	2009	568,457		
121	Des Moines	Iowa	2009	641,257		
122	Lansing	Michigan	2010	347,865		
123	Green Bay	Wisconsin	2010	401,588		
124	Columbus	Ohio	2011	504,796		
125	Davenport	Iowa	2011	310,496		
126	Livonia	Michigan	2014	314,698		
	TOTAL SALES AND ROYALTY FEES			12,593,619		-

Franchise Statistics Section	
# of stores with sales > 500,000	13
# of Michigan stores with sales > 500,000	3
Average sales for Detroit, MI stores	559,306
Average Sales for Michigan stores established prior to 2004	481,192
Total Sales for stores established prior to 2010	10,714,176
Total Sales for Michigan stores established prior to 2010	3,348,418

Franchise Royalty Rate Table	
Royalty payment to head office based on sales	
300,000	1%
400,000	2%
500,000	3%
600,000	4%
700,000	5%
800,000	6%

Franchisees pay a royalty fee calculated as a percent of sales. The percentage charged is the rate that is closest to the sales value without going over.
Example:
Gross Sales = 530,000; Royalty is 3% of 530,000.

EL2-C2-CS-P1-PBMSales(P1).xlsx

Wellington Park Medical Center

Division of Cardiology
Adult Cardiac Surgery Costs

Month: October Surgeon: Novak

Patient Number	Patient Last Name	Patient First Name	Surgery Code	Days in Hospital	Surgery Fee	Valve Cost	Postoperative Hospital Cost	Total Cost
60334124	Wagner	Sara	MRP	7	$ 5,325.00	$ -	$ 6,317.50	$ 11,642.50
60334567	Gonzalez	Hector	ARP	10	4,876.00	-	9,025.00	13,901.00
60398754	Vezina	Paula	ABP	5	4,820.00	-	4,512.50	9,332.50
60347821	Dowling	Jager	MRT	11	6,240.00	775.00	9,927.50	16,942.50
60328192	Ashman	Carl	ARP	4	4,876.00	-	3,610.00	8,486.00
60321349	Kaiser	Lana	ART	12	6,190.00	775.00	10,830.00	17,795.00
60398545	Van Bomm	Emile	ABP	7	4,820.00	-	6,317.50	11,137.50
60342548	Youngblood	Frank	ABP	6	4,820.00	-	5,415.00	10,235.00
60331569	Lorimar	Hannah	MRT	8	6,240.00	775.00	7,220.00	14,235.00
60247859	Peterson	Mark	ART	9	6,190.00	775.00	8,122.50	15,087.50
60158642	O'Connor	Terry	ABP	7	4,820.00	-	6,317.50	11,137.50
60458962	Jenkins	Esther	MRP	9	5,325.00	-	8,122.50	13,447.50
68521245	Norfolk	Leslie	ABP	8	4,820.00	-	7,220.00	12,040.00
63552158	Adams-Wiley	Susan	MRT	6	6,240.00	775.00	5,415.00	12,430.00
68451278	Estevez	Stefan	ARP	6	4,876.00	-	5,415.00	10,291.00
				Total Cost:	$ 80,478.00	$ 3,875.00	$ 103,787.50	$ 188,140.50

Postoperative hospital cost per day: $ 902.50
Aortic or mitral valve cost: $ 775.00

Surgery Code	Surgery Fee	Surgery Procedure
ABP	4,820	Artery Bypass
ARP	4,876	Aortic Valve Repair
ART	6,190	Aortic Valve Replacement
MRP	5,325	Mitral Valve Repair
MRT	6,240	Mitral Valve Replacement

EL2-C2-VB2-WPMCCardioCosts(VB2).xlsx

Store	City	State	Year Est.	Sales
101	Detroit	Michigan	2002	652,458
102	Detroit	Michigan	2002	466,153
103	Flint	Michigan	2003	324,965
104	Ann Arbor	Michigan	2004	652,146
105	Ann Arbor	Michigan	2004	378,458
106	Kalamazoo	Michigan	2004	528,346
107	Port Huron	Michigan	2004	345,892
108	Toledo	Ohio	2004	653,485
109	Toledo	Ohio	2005	354,268
110	Toledo	Ohio	2005	554,213
111	Akron	Ohio	2005	461,853
112	Cincinnati	Ohio	2006	512,463
113	Madison	Wisconsin	2006	325,496
114	Madison	Wisconsin	2006	745,865
115	Milwaukee	Wisconsin	2007	451,236
116	Milwaukee	Wisconsin	2007	554,168
117	Milwaukee	Wisconsin	2007	653,856
118	Cedar Rapids	Iowa	2008	541,285
119	Cedar Rapids	Iowa	2008	347,856
120	Cedar Rapids	Iowa	2009	568,457
121	Des Moines	Iowa	2009	641,257
122	Lansing	Michigan	2010	347,865
123	Green Bay	Wisconsin	2010	401,588
124	Columbus	Ohio	2011	504,796
125	Davenport	Iowa	2011	310,496
126	Livonia	Michigan	2014	314,698
	TOTAL SALES AND ROYALTY FEES			12,593,619

Franchise Statistics Section	
Average Sales	484,370
Maximum Sales	745,865
Minimum Sales	310,496
Median Sales	485,475
Standard deviation of sales	129045.6042

The median sales of 486,475 means that half of the stores sales were greater than 486,475 and half were lower.

The standard deviation of sales is 129,045.6042 and shows how widely sales are dispersed from the average sales of 484,370.

EL2-C2-CS-P3-PBMSales(P3).xlsx

Pizza by Mario 2015 Franchise Sales

Store	City	State	Year Est.	Sales	Royalty %	Royalty Fee
101	Detroit	Michigan	2002	652,458	4%	26,098.32
102	Detroit	Michigan	2002	466,153	2%	9,323.06
103	Flint	Michigan	2003	324,965	1%	3,249.65
104	Ann Arbor	Michigan	2004	652,146	4%	26,085.84
105	Ann Arbor	Michigan	2004	378,458	1%	3,784.58
106	Kalamazoo	Michigan	2004	528,346	3%	15,850.38
107	Port Huron	Michigan	2004	345,892	1%	3,458.92
108	Toledo	Ohio	2004	653,485	4%	26,139.40
109	Toledo	Ohio	2005	354,268	1%	3,542.68
110	Toledo	Ohio	2005	554,213	3%	16,626.39
111	Akron	Ohio	2005	461,853	2%	9,237.06
112	Cincinnati	Ohio	2006	512,463	3%	15,373.89
113	Madison	Wisconsin	2006	325,496	1%	3,254.96
114	Madison	Wisconsin	2006	745,865	5%	37,293.25
115	Milwaukee	Wisconsin	2007	451,236	2%	9,024.72
116	Milwaukee	Wisconsin	2007	554,168	3%	16,625.04
117	Milwaukee	Wisconsin	2007	653,856	4%	26,154.24
118	Cedar Rapids	Iowa	2008	541,285	3%	16,238.55
119	Cedar Rapids	Iowa	2008	347,856	1%	3,478.56
120	Cedar Rapids	Iowa	2009	568,457	3%	17,053.71
121	Des Moines	Iowa	2009	641,257	4%	25,650.28
122	Lansing	Michigan	2010	347,865	1%	3,478.65
123	Green Bay	Wisconsin	2010	401,588	2%	8,031.76
124	Columbus	Ohio	2011	504,796	3%	15,143.88
125	Davenport	Iowa	2011	310,496	1%	3,104.96
126	Livonia	Michigan	2014	314,698	1%	3,146.98
	TOTAL SALES AND ROYALTY FEES			12,593,619		346,449.71

Franchise Statistics Section	
# of stores with sales > 500,000	13
# of Michigan stores with sales > 500,000	3
Average sales for Detroit, MI stores	559,306
Average Sales for Michigan stores established prior to 2004	481,192
Total Sales for stores established prior to 2010	10,714,176
Total Sales for Michigan stores established prior to 2010	3,348,418

Franchise Royalty Rate Table Royalty payment to head office based on sales	
300,000	1%
400,000	2%
500,000	3%
600,000	4%
700,000	5%
800,000	6%

Franchisees pay a royalty fee calculated as a percent of sales. The percentage charged is the rate that is closest to the sales value without going over.
Example:
Gross Sales = 530,000; Royalty is 3% of 530,000.

EL2-C2-CS-P2-PBMSales(P2).xlsx

Pizza by Mario New Franchise Possibilities

City	State	Population	Mean Household Income
Indianapolis	Indiana	820,445	59,149
Fort Wayne	Indiana	253,691	57,233
Minneapolis	Minnesota	382,578	68,190
Saint Paul	Minnesota	285,068	63,520

Source: American Fact Finder
http://factfinder2.census.gov/legacy/aff_sunset.html?_lang=en

EL2-C2-CS-P4-PBMSales(P4).xlsx

Excel Level 2, Chapter 3 Model Answers

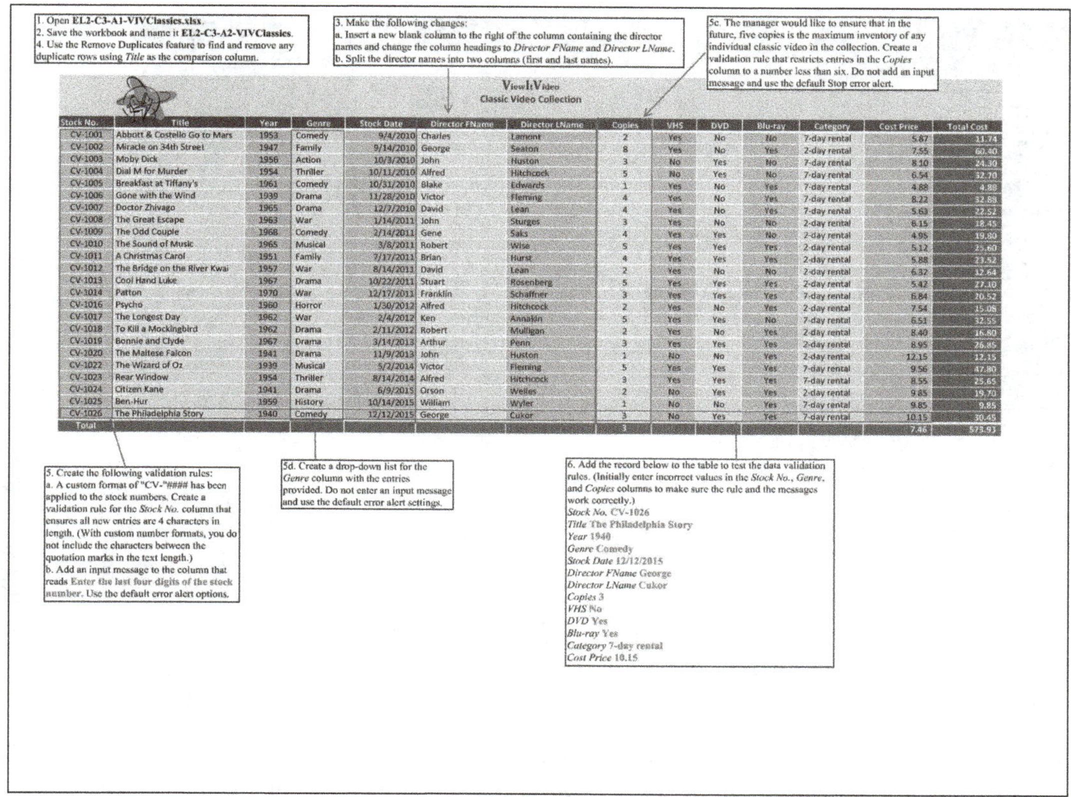

1. Open **EL2-C3-A1-VIVClassics.xlsx**.
2. Save the workbook and name it **EL2-C3-A2-VIVClassics**.
4. Use the Remove Duplicates feature to find and remove any duplicate rows using *Title* as the comparison column.

3. Make the following changes:
a. Insert a new blank column to the right of the column containing the director names and change the column headings to *Director FName* and *Director LName*.
b. Split the director names into two columns (first and last names).

5c. The manager would like to ensure that in the future, five copies is the maximum inventory of any individual classic video in the collection. Create a validation rule that restricts entries in the *Copies* column to a number less than six. Do not add an input message and use the default Stop error alert.

ViewItVideo
Classic Video Collection

Stock No.	Title	Year	Genre	Stock Date	Director FName	Director LName	Copies	VHS	DVD	Blu-ray	Category	Cost Price	Total Cost
CV-1001	Abbott & Costello Go to Mars	1953	Comedy	9/4/2010	Charles	Lamont	2	Yes	No	No	7-day rental	5.87	11.74
CV-1002	Miracle on 34th Street	1947	Family	9/14/2010	George	Seaton	8	Yes	No	Yes	2-day rental	7.55	60.40
CV-1003	Moby Dick	1956	Action	10/3/2010	John	Huston	3	No	Yes	No	7-day rental	8.10	24.30
CV-1004	Dial M for Murder	1954	Thriller	10/11/2010	Alfred	Hitchcock	5	No	Yes	No	7-day rental	6.54	32.70
CV-1005	Breakfast at Tiffany's	1961	Comedy	10/31/2010	Blake	Edwards	1	Yes	No	Yes	7-day rental	4.88	4.88
CV-1006	Gone with the Wind	1939	Drama	11/28/2010	Victor	Fleming	4	Yes	No	Yes	7-day rental	8.22	32.88
CV-1007	Doctor Zhivago	1965	Drama	12/7/2010	David	Lean	4	Yes	No	Yes	7-day rental	5.63	22.52
CV-1008	The Great Escape	1963	War	1/14/2011	John	Sturges	3	Yes	No	No	2-day rental	6.15	18.45
CV-1009	The Odd Couple	1968	Comedy	2/14/2011	Gene	Saks	4	Yes	Yes	No	2-day rental	4.95	19.80
CV-1010	The Sound of Music	1965	Musical	3/8/2011	Robert	Wise	5	Yes	Yes	Yes	2-day rental	5.12	25.60
CV-1011	A Christmas Carol	1951	Family	7/17/2011	Brian	Hurst	4	Yes	Yes	Yes	2-day rental	5.88	23.52
CV-1012	The Bridge on the River Kwai	1957	War	8/14/2011	David	Lean	2	Yes	No	No	2-day rental	6.32	12.64
CV-1013	Cool Hand Luke	1967	Drama	10/22/2011	Stuart	Rosenberg	5	Yes	Yes	Yes	2-day rental	5.42	27.10
CV-1014	Patton	1970	War	12/17/2011	Franklin	Schaffner	3	Yes	Yes	Yes	7-day rental	6.84	20.52
CV-1016	Psycho	1960	Horror	1/30/2012	Alfred	Hitchcock	2	Yes	No	Yes	2-day rental	7.54	15.08
CV-1017	The Longest Day	1962	War	2/4/2012	Ken	Annakin	5	Yes	Yes	No	7-day rental	6.51	32.55
CV-1018	To Kill a Mockingbird	1962	Drama	2/11/2012	Robert	Mulligan	2	Yes	No	Yes	2-day rental	8.40	16.80
CV-1019	Bonnie and Clyde	1967	Drama	3/14/2013	Arthur	Penn	3	Yes	Yes	Yes	2-day rental	8.95	26.85
CV-1020	The Maltese Falcon	1941	Drama	11/9/2013	John	Huston	1	No	No	Yes	2-day rental	12.15	12.15
CV-1022	The Wizard of Oz	1939	Musical	5/2/2014	Victor	Fleming	5	Yes	Yes	Yes	7-day rental	9.56	47.80
CV-1023	Rear Window	1954	Thriller	8/14/2014	Alfred	Hitchcock	3	Yes	Yes	Yes	7-day rental	8.55	25.65
CV-1024	Citizen Kane	1941	Drama	6/9/2015	Orson	Welles	2	No	Yes	Yes	2-day rental	9.85	19.70
CV-1025	Ben-Hur	1959	History	10/14/2015	William	Wyler	1	No	No	Yes	7-day rental	9.85	9.85
CV-1026	The Philadelphia Story	1940	Comedy	12/12/2015	George	Cukor	3	No	Yes	Yes	7-day rental	10.15	30.45
Total							3					7.46	573.93

5. Create the following validation rules:
a. A custom format of "CV-"#### has been applied to the stock numbers. Create a validation rule for the *Stock No.* column that ensures all new entries are 4 characters in length. (With custom number formats, you do not include the characters between the quotation marks in the text length.)
b. Add an input message to the column that reads Enter the last four digits of the stock number. Use the default error alert options.

5d. Create a drop-down list for the *Genre* column with the entries provided. Do not enter an input message and use the default error alert settings.

6. Add the record below to the table to test the data validation rules. (Initially enter incorrect values in the *Stock No.*, *Genre*, and *Copies* columns to make sure the rule and the messages work correctly.)
Stock No. CV-1026
Title The Philadelphia Story
Year 1940
Genre Comedy
Stock Date 12/12/2015
Director FName George
Director LName Cukor
Copies 3
VHS No
DVD Yes
Blu-ray Yes
Category 7-day rental
Cost Price 10.15

EL2-C3-A2-VIVClassics(A2).xlsx

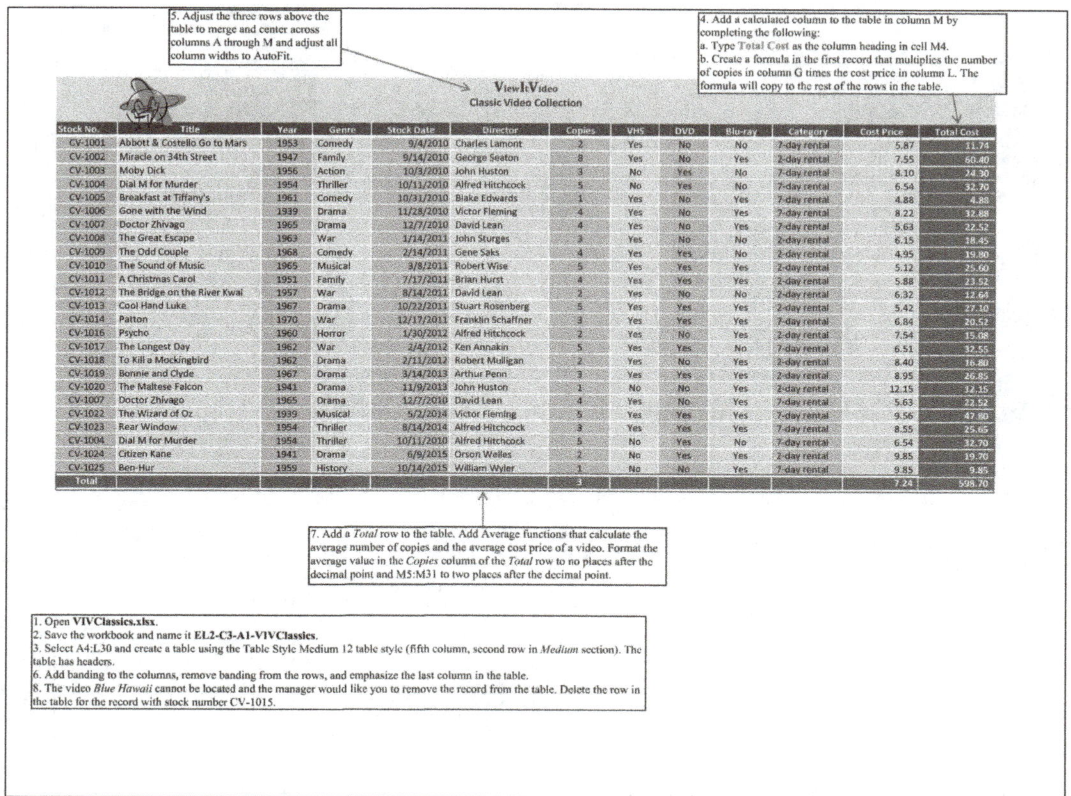

5. Adjust the three rows above the table to merge and center across columns A through M and adjust all column widths to AutoFit.

4. Add a calculated column to the table in column M by completing the following:
a. Type Total Cost as the column heading in cell M4.
b. Create a formula in the first record that multiplies the number of copies in column G times the cost price in column L. The formula will copy to the rest of the rows in the table.

ViewItVideo
Classic Video Collection

Stock No.	Title	Year	Genre	Stock Date	Director	Copies	VHS	DVD	Blu-ray	Category	Cost Price	Total Cost
CV-1001	Abbott & Costello Go to Mars	1953	Comedy	9/4/2010	Charles Lamont	2	Yes	No	No	7-day rental	5.87	11.74
CV-1002	Miracle on 34th Street	1947	Family	9/14/2010	George Seaton	8	Yes	No	Yes	2-day rental	7.55	60.40
CV-1003	Moby Dick	1956	Action	10/3/2010	John Huston	3	No	Yes	No	7-day rental	8.10	24.30
CV-1004	Dial M for Murder	1954	Thriller	10/11/2010	Alfred Hitchcock	5	No	Yes	No	7-day rental	6.54	32.70
CV-1005	Breakfast at Tiffany's	1961	Comedy	10/31/2010	Blake Edwards	1	Yes	No	Yes	7-day rental	4.88	4.88
CV-1006	Gone with the Wind	1939	Drama	11/28/2010	Victor Fleming	4	Yes	No	Yes	7-day rental	8.22	32.88
CV-1007	Doctor Zhivago	1965	Drama	12/7/2010	David Lean	4	Yes	No	Yes	7-day rental	5.63	22.52
CV-1008	The Great Escape	1963	War	1/14/2011	John Sturges	3	Yes	No	No	2-day rental	6.15	18.45
CV-1009	The Odd Couple	1968	Comedy	2/14/2011	Gene Saks	4	Yes	Yes	No	2-day rental	4.95	19.80
CV-1010	The Sound of Music	1965	Musical	3/8/2011	Robert Wise	5	Yes	Yes	Yes	2-day rental	5.12	25.60
CV-1011	A Christmas Carol	1951	Family	7/17/2011	Brian Hurst	4	Yes	Yes	Yes	2-day rental	5.88	23.52
CV-1012	The Bridge on the River Kwai	1957	War	8/14/2011	David Lean	2	Yes	No	No	2-day rental	6.32	12.64
CV-1013	Cool Hand Luke	1967	Drama	10/22/2011	Stuart Rosenberg	5	Yes	Yes	Yes	2-day rental	5.42	27.10
CV-1014	Patton	1970	War	12/17/2011	Franklin Schaffner	3	Yes	Yes	Yes	7-day rental	6.84	20.52
CV-1016	Psycho	1960	Horror	1/30/2012	Alfred Hitchcock	2	Yes	No	Yes	2-day rental	7.54	15.08
CV-1017	The Longest Day	1962	War	2/4/2012	Ken Annakin	5	Yes	Yes	No	7-day rental	6.51	32.55
CV-1018	To Kill a Mockingbird	1962	Drama	2/11/2012	Robert Mulligan	2	Yes	No	Yes	2-day rental	8.40	16.80
CV-1019	Bonnie and Clyde	1967	Drama	3/14/2013	Arthur Penn	3	Yes	Yes	Yes	2-day rental	8.95	26.85
CV-1020	The Maltese Falcon	1941	Drama	11/9/2013	John Huston	1	No	No	Yes	2-day rental	12.15	12.15
CV-1007	Doctor Zhivago	1965	Drama	12/7/2010	David Lean	4	Yes	No	Yes	7-day rental	5.63	22.52
CV-1022	The Wizard of Oz	1939	Musical	5/2/2014	Victor Fleming	5	Yes	Yes	Yes	7-day rental	9.56	47.80
CV-1023	Rear Window	1954	Thriller	8/14/2014	Alfred Hitchcock	3	Yes	Yes	Yes	7-day rental	8.55	25.65
CV-1004	Dial M for Murder	1954	Thriller	10/11/2010	Alfred Hitchcock	5	No	Yes	No	7-day rental	6.54	32.70
CV-1024	Citizen Kane	1941	Drama	6/9/2015	Orson Welles	2	No	Yes	Yes	2-day rental	9.85	19.70
CV-1025	Ben-Hur	1959	History	10/14/2015	William Wyler	1	No	No	Yes	7-day rental	9.85	9.85
Total						3					7.24	598.70

7. Add a *Total* row to the table. Add Average functions that calculate the average number of copies and the average cost price of a video. Format the average value in the *Copies* column of the *Total* row to no places after the decimal point and M5:M31 to two places after the decimal point.

1. Open **VIVClassics.xlsx**.
2. Save the workbook and name it **EL2-C3-A1-VIVClassics**.
3. Select A4:L30 and create a table using the Table Style Medium 12 table style (fifth column, second row in *Medium* section). The table has headers.
6. Add banding to the columns, remove banding from the rows, and emphasize the last column in the table.
8. The video *Blue Hawaii* cannot be located and the manager would like you to remove the record from the table. Delete the row in the table for the record with stock number CV-1015.

EL2-C3-A1-VIVClassics(A1).xlsx

Wellington Park Medical Center

Nursing Division Casual Relief Call List

Payroll No.	First Name	Last Name	Designation	Hire Date	Telephone	OR Exp?	Day Shift Only?	Night Shift Only?	Either Shift?	Hourly Rate	Shift Cost
19658	Paula	Sanderson	RN	4/28/2000	555-3485	No	No	No	Yes	38.50	**308.00**
38642	Tania	Ravi	RN	6/22/2002	555-6969	Yes	Yes	No	Weekends only	38.50	**308.00**
78452	Terry	Mason	RN	10/8/2015	555-1279	Yes	No	Yes	No	38.50	**308.00**
96523	Lynn	Pietre	RN	10/22/1998	555-2548	Yes	Yes	No	Weekends only	35.00	**280.00**
45968	David	Featherstone	RN	9/9/2001	555-5961	No	No	No	Yes	35.00	**280.00**
46956	Orlando	Zambian	RN	11/10/2001	555-1186	No	Yes	No	No	35.00	**280.00**
56983	Amanda	Sanchez	RN	4/27/1999	555-4896	Yes	No	Yes	No	33.00	**264.00**
68429	Rene	Quenneville	RN	8/15/2003	555-4663	Yes	Yes	No	Weekends only	22.50	**180.00**
69417	Denis	LaPierre	RN	8/23/2003	555-8643	No	No	Yes	No	22.50	**180.00**
37944	Fernando	Este	RN	7/18/2005	555-4545	No	No	No	Yes	22.50	**180.00**
78647	Jay	Bjorg	RN	5/14/2007	555-6598	No	No	No	Yes	22.50	**180.00**
95558	Sam	Vargas	RN	3/2/2009	555-4571	No	No	No	Yes	22.50	**180.00**
98731	Zail	Singh	RN	5/6/2011	555-3561	Yes	Yes	No	No	22.50	**180.00**
58612	Savana	Ruiz	RN	4/15/2012	555-8457	Yes	No	Yes	Weekends only	22.50	**180.00**
96721	Noreen	Kalir	RN	4/3/2009	555-1876	Yes	Yes	No	No	21.50	**172.00**
89367	Xiu	Zheng	LPN	4/23/2006	555-7383	Yes	Yes	No	No	18.75	**150.00**
14586	Alma	Fernandez	LPN	8/3/1997	555-7412	Yes	No	No	Yes	16.75	**134.00**
48652	Dana	Casselman	LPN	10/15/1997	555-6325	Yes	No	No	Yes	16.75	**134.00**
85412	Kelly	Lund	LPN	11/19/1998	555-3684	No	Yes	No	Weekends only	15.75	**126.00**
98364	Lana	Bourne	LPN	7/15/2008	555-9012	Yes	Yes	No	No	15.50	**124.00**
90467	Nadir	Abouzeen	LPN	8/12/2008	555-9023	No	No	No	Yes	14.50	**116.00**
68475	Kelly	O'Brien	LPN	1/20/2012	555-6344	No	Yes	No	Weekends only	13.75	**110.00**
								Average Hourly Rate and Shift Cost:		**24.74**	**197.91**

EL2-C3-VB1-WPMCallList(VB1).xlsx

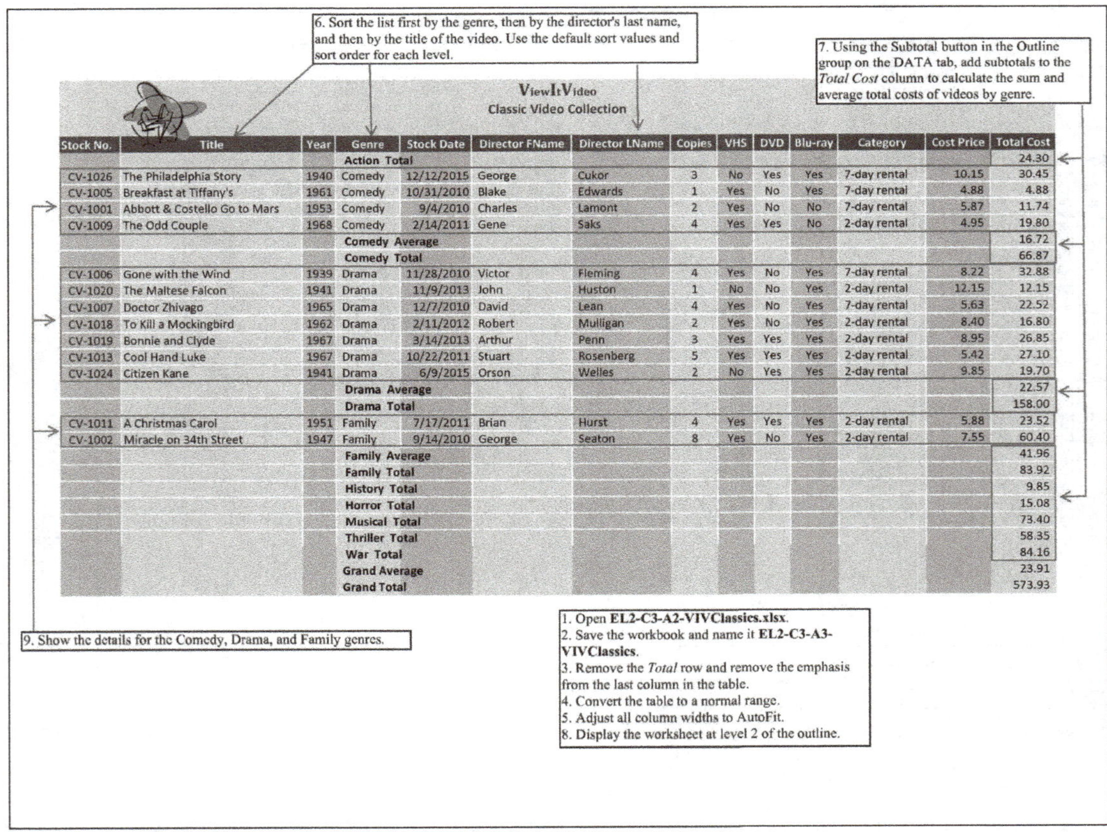

6. Sort the list first by the genre, then by the director's last name, and then by the title of the video. Use the default sort values and sort order for each level.

7. Using the Subtotal button in the Outline group on the DATA tab, add subtotals to the *Total Cost* column to calculate the sum and average total costs of videos by genre.

ViewItVideo

Classic Video Collection

Stock No.	Title	Year	Genre	Stock Date	Director FName	Director LName	Copies	VHS	DVD	Blu-ray	Category	Cost Price	Total Cost
			Action Total										24.30
CV-1026	The Philadelphia Story	1940	Comedy	12/12/2015	George	Cukor	3	No	Yes	Yes	7-day rental	10.15	30.45
CV-1005	Breakfast at Tiffany's	1961	Comedy	10/31/2010	Blake	Edwards	1	Yes	No	Yes	7-day rental	4.88	4.88
CV-1001	Abbott & Costello Go to Mars	1953	Comedy	9/4/2010	Charles	Lamont	2	Yes	No	No	7-day rental	5.87	11.74
CV-1009	The Odd Couple	1968	Comedy	2/14/2011	Gene	Saks	4	Yes	Yes	No	2-day rental	4.95	19.80
			Comedy Average										16.72
			Comedy Total										66.87
CV-1006	Gone with the Wind	1939	Drama	11/28/2010	Victor	Fleming	4	Yes	No	Yes	7-day rental	8.22	32.88
CV-1020	The Maltese Falcon	1941	Drama	11/9/2013	John	Huston	1	No	No	Yes	2-day rental	12.15	12.15
CV-1007	Doctor Zhivago	1965	Drama	12/7/2010	David	Lean	4	Yes	No	Yes	7-day rental	5.63	22.52
CV-1018	To Kill a Mockingbird	1962	Drama	2/11/2012	Robert	Mulligan	2	Yes	No	Yes	2-day rental	8.40	16.80
CV-1019	Bonnie and Clyde	1967	Drama	3/14/2013	Arthur	Penn	3	Yes	Yes	Yes	2-day rental	8.95	26.85
CV-1013	Cool Hand Luke	1967	Drama	10/22/2011	Stuart	Rosenberg	5	Yes	Yes	Yes	2-day rental	5.42	27.10
CV-1024	Citizen Kane	1941	Drama	6/9/2015	Orson	Welles	2	No	Yes	Yes	2-day rental	9.85	19.70
			Drama Average										22.57
			Drama Total										158.00
CV-1011	A Christmas Carol	1951	Family	7/17/2011	Brian	Hurst	4	Yes	Yes	Yes	2-day rental	5.88	23.52
CV-1002	Miracle on 34th Street	1947	Family	9/14/2010	George	Seaton	8	Yes	No	Yes	2-day rental	7.55	60.40
			Family Average										41.96
			Family Total										83.92
			History Total										9.85
			Horror Total										15.08
			Musical Total										73.40
			Thriller Total										58.35
			War Total										84.16
			Grand Average										23.91
			Grand Total										573.93

9. Show the details for the Comedy, Drama, and Family genres.

1. Open **EL2-C3-A2-VIVClassics.xlsx**.
2. Save the workbook and name it **EL2-C3-A3-VIVClassics**.
3. Remove the *Total* row and remove the emphasis from the last column in the table.
4. Convert the table to a normal range.
5. Adjust all column widths to AutoFit.
8. Display the worksheet at level 2 of the outline.

EL2-C3-A3-VIVClassics(A3).xlsx

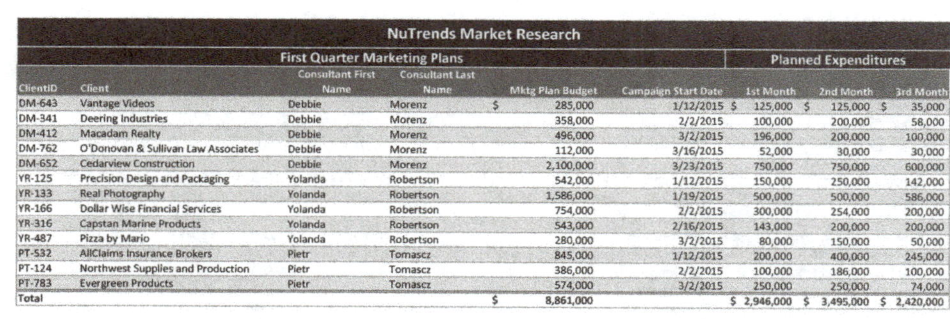

NuTrends Market Research											
First Quarter Marketing Plans							Planned Expenditures				
ClientID	Client	Consultant First Name	Consultant Last Name		Mktg Plan Budget	Campaign Start Date		1st Month		2nd Month		3rd Month
DM-643	Vantage Videos	Debbie	Morenz	$	285,000	1/12/2015	$	125,000	$	125,000	$	35,000
DM-341	Deering Industries	Debbie	Morenz		358,000	2/2/2015		100,000		200,000		58,000
DM-412	Macadam Realty	Debbie	Morenz		496,000	3/2/2015		196,000		200,000		100,000
DM-762	O'Donovan & Sullivan Law Associates	Debbie	Morenz		112,000	3/16/2015		52,000		30,000		30,000
DM-652	Cedarview Construction	Debbie	Morenz		2,100,000	3/23/2015		750,000		750,000		600,000
YR-125	Precision Design and Packaging	Yolanda	Robertson		542,000	1/12/2015		150,000		250,000		142,000
YR-133	Real Photography	Yolanda	Robertson		1,586,000	1/19/2015		500,000		500,000		586,000
YR-166	Dollar Wise Financial Services	Yolanda	Robertson		754,000	2/2/2015		300,000		254,000		200,000
YR-316	Capstan Marine Products	Yolanda	Robertson		543,000	2/16/2015		143,000		200,000		200,000
YR-487	Pizza by Mario	Yolanda	Robertson		280,000	3/2/2015		80,000		150,000		50,000
PT-532	AllClaims Insurance Brokers	Pietr	Tomascz		845,000	1/12/2015		200,000		400,000		245,000
PT-124	Northwest Supplies and Production	Pietr	Tomascz		386,000	2/2/2015		100,000		186,000		100,000
PT-783	Evergreen Products	Pietr	Tomascz		574,000	3/2/2015		250,000		250,000		74,000
Total				$	8,861,000		$	2,946,000	$	3,495,000	$	2,420,000

EL2-C3-CS-P1-NuTrendsMktPlans(P1).xlsx

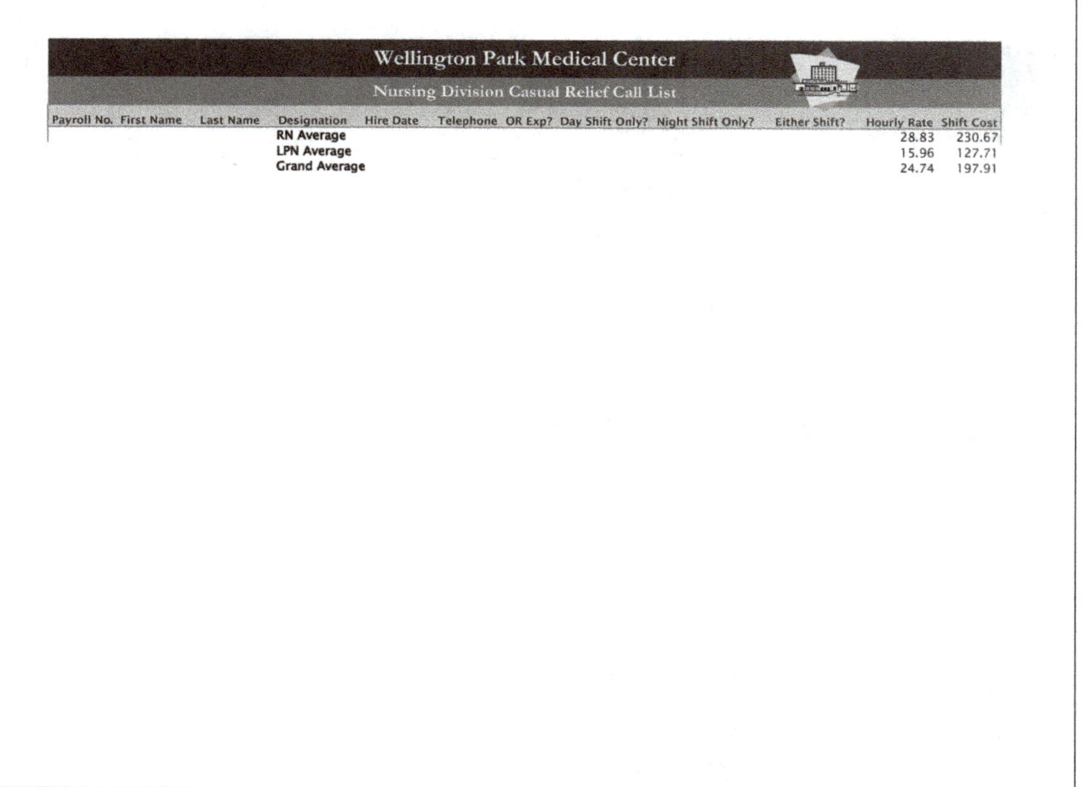

Wellington Park Medical Center											
Nursing Division Casual Relief Call List											
Payroll No.	First Name	Last Name	Designation	Hire Date	Telephone	OR Exp?	Day Shift Only?	Night Shift Only?	Either Shift?	Hourly Rate	Shift Cost
			RN Average							28.83	230.67
			LPN Average							15.96	127.71
			Grand Average							24.74	197.91

EL2-C3-VB2-WPMCallList(VB2).xlsx

EL2-C3-CS-P3-NuTrendsMktPlans(P3).xlsx

ClientID	Client	Consultant	Mktg Plan Budget	Campaign Start Date	1st Month	2nd Month	3rd Month
				>01/31/2015			

NuTrends Market Research							
First Quarter Marketing Plans					Planned Expenditures		
ClientID	**Client**	**Consultant**	**Mktg Plan Budget**	**Campaign Start Date**	**1st Month**	**2nd Month**	**3rd Month**
DM-341	Deering Industries	Debbie Morenz	358,000	2/2/2015	100,000	200,000	58,000
YR-125	Precision Design and Packaging	Yolanda Robertson	542,000	1/12/2015	150,000	250,000	142,000
YR-133	Real Photography	Yolanda Robertson	1,586,000	1/19/2015	500,000	500,000	586,000
YR-166	Dollar Wise Financial Services	Yolanda Robertson	754,000	2/2/2015	300,000	254,000	200,000
DM-412	Macadam Realty	Debbie Morenz	496,000	3/2/2015	196,000	200,000	100,000
DM-652	Cedarview Construction	Debbie Morenz	2,100,000	3/23/2015	750,000	750,000	600,000
YR-316	Capstan Marine Products	Yolanda Robertson	543,000	2/16/2015	143,000	200,000	200,000
PT-124	Northwest Supplies and Production	Pietr Tomascz	386,000	2/2/2015	100,000	186,000	100,000
PT-783	Evergreen Products	Pietr Tomascz	574,000	3/2/2015	250,000	250,000	74,000
DM-643	Vantage Videos	Debbie Morenz	285,000	1/12/2015	125,000	125,000	35,000
PT-532	AllClaims Insurance Brokers	Pietr Tomascz	845,000	1/12/2015	200,000	400,000	245,000
YR-487	Pizza by Mario	Yolanda Robertson	280,000	3/2/2015	80,000	150,000	50,000
DM-762	O'Donovan & Sullivan Law Associates	Debbie Morenz	112,000	3/16/2015	52,000	30,000	30,000

NuTrends Market Research Campaigns Starting After January 31, 2015							
ClientID	**Client**	**Consultant**	**Mktg Plan Budget**	**Campaign Start Date**	**1st Month**	**2nd Month**	**3rd Month**
DM-341	Deering Industries	Debbie Morenz	358,000	2/2/2015	100,000	200,000	58,000
YR-166	Dollar Wise Financial Services	Yolanda Robertson	754,000	2/2/2015	300,000	254,000	200,000
DM-412	Macadam Realty	Debbie Morenz	496,000	3/2/2015	196,000	200,000	100,000
DM-652	Cedarview Construction	Debbie Morenz	2,100,000	3/23/2015	750,000	750,000	600,000
YR-316	Capstan Marine Products	Yolanda Robertson	543,000	2/16/2015	143,000	200,000	200,000
PT-124	Northwest Supplies and Production	Pietr Tomascz	386,000	2/2/2015	100,000	186,000	100,000
PT-783	Evergreen Products	Pietr Tomascz	574,000	3/2/2015	250,000	250,000	74,000
YR-487	Pizza by Mario	Yolanda Robertson	280,000	3/2/2015	80,000	150,000	50,000
DM-762	O'Donovan & Sullivan Law Associates	Debbie Morenz	112,000	3/16/2015	52,000	30,000	30,000

EL2-C3-CS-P2-NuTrendsMktPlans(P2).xlsx

NuTrends Market Research								
First Quarter Marketing Plans						Planned Expenditures		
ClientID	Client	Consultant First Name	Consultant Last Name	Mktg Plan Budget	Campaign Start Date	1st Month	2nd Month	3rd Month
			Morenz Average	670,200		244,600	261,000	164,600
			Morenz Total	3,351,000		1,223,000	1,305,000	823,000
			Robertson Average	741,000		234,600	270,800	235,600
			Robertson Total	3,705,000		1,173,000	1,354,000	1,178,000
			Tomascz Average	601,667		183,333	278,667	139,667
			Tomascz Total	1,805,000		550,000	836,000	419,000
			Grand Average	681,615		226,615	268,846	186,154
			Grand Total	8,861,000		2,946,000	3,495,000	2,420,000

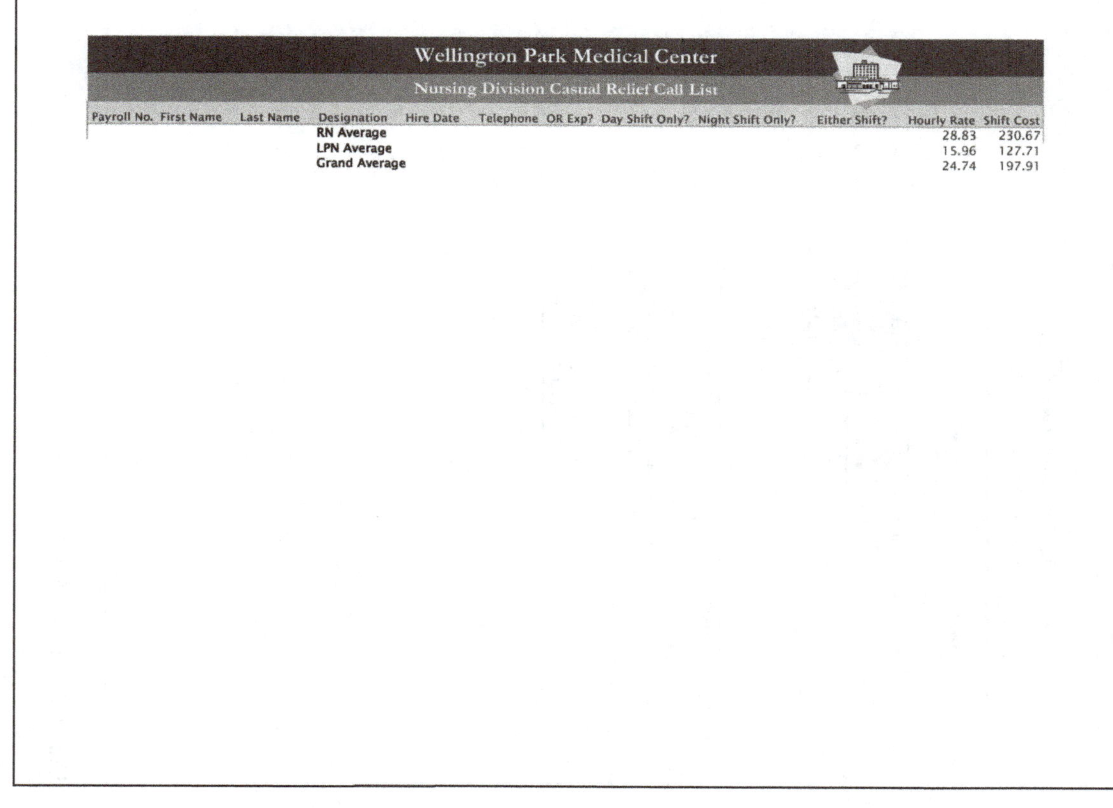

Wellington Park Medical Center

Nursing Division Casual Relief Call List

Payroll No.	First Name	Last Name	Designation	Hire Date	Telephone	OR Exp?	Day Shift Only?	Night Shift Only?	Either Shift?	Hourly Rate	Shift Cost
			RN Average							28.83	230.67
			LPN Average							15.96	127.71
			Grand Average							24.74	197.91

EL2-C3-CS-P4-NuTrendsSalaryAnalysis(P4).xlsx

Excel Level 2, Chapter 4 Model Answers

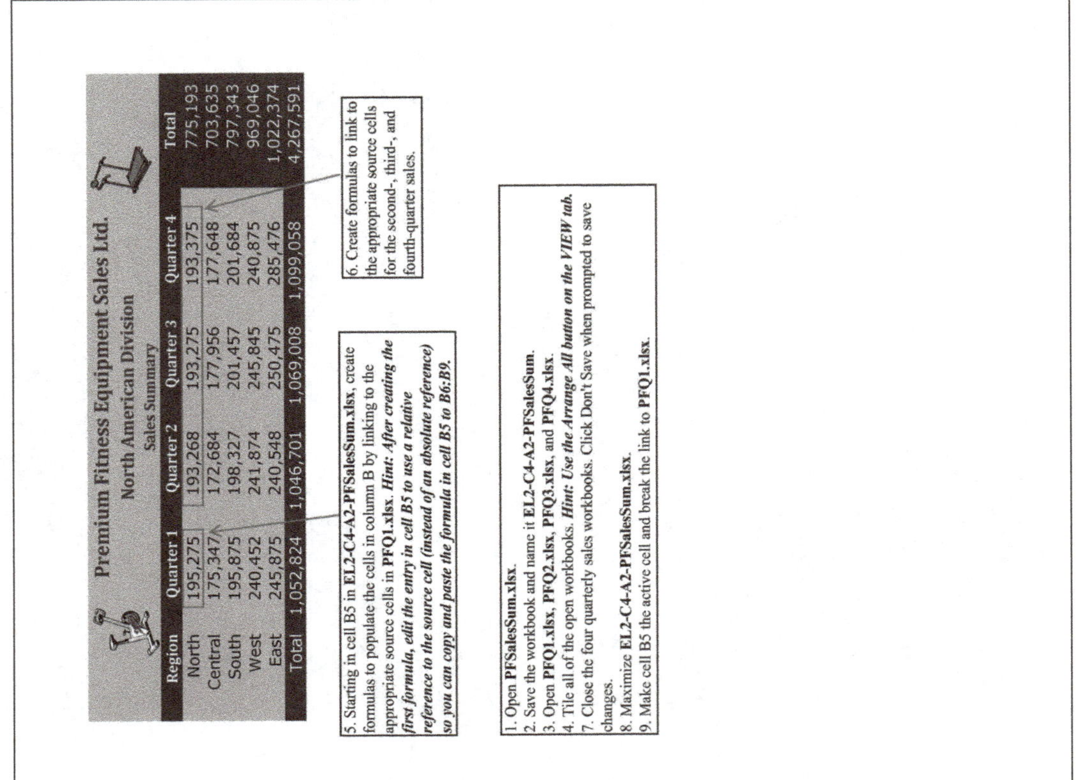

Premium Fitness Equipment Sales Ltd.
North American Division
Sales Summary

Region	Quarter 1	Quarter 2	Quarter 3	Quarter 4	Total
North	195,275	193,268	193,275	193,375	775,193
Central	175,347	172,684	177,956	177,648	703,635
South	195,875	198,327	201,457	201,684	797,343
West	240,452	241,874	245,845	240,875	969,046
East	245,875	240,548	250,475	285,476	1,022,374
Total	1,052,824	1,046,701	1,069,008	1,099,058	4,267,591

5. Starting in cell B5 in **EL2-C4-A2-PFSalesSum.xlsx**, create formulas to populate the cells in column B by linking to the appropriate source cells in **PFQ1.xlsx**. ***Hint: After creating the first formula, edit the entry in cell B5 to use a relative reference to the source cell (instead of an absolute reference) so you can copy and paste the formula in cell B5 to B6:B9.***

6. Create formulas to link to the appropriate source cells for the second-, third-, and fourth-quarter sales.

1. Open **PFSalesSum.xlsx**.
2. Save the workbook and name it **EL2-C4-A2-PFSalesSum**.
3. Open **PFQ1.xlsx**, **PFQ2.xlsx**, **PFQ3.xlsx**, and **PFQ4.xlsx**.
4. Tile all of the open workbooks. ***Hint: Use the Arrange All button on the VIEW tab.***
7. Close the four quarterly sales workbooks. Click Don't Save when prompted to save changes.
8. Maximize **EL2-C4-A2-PFSalesSum.xlsx**.
9. Make cell B5 the active cell and break the link to **PFQ1.xlsx**.

EL2-C4-A2-PFSalesSum(A2).xlsx

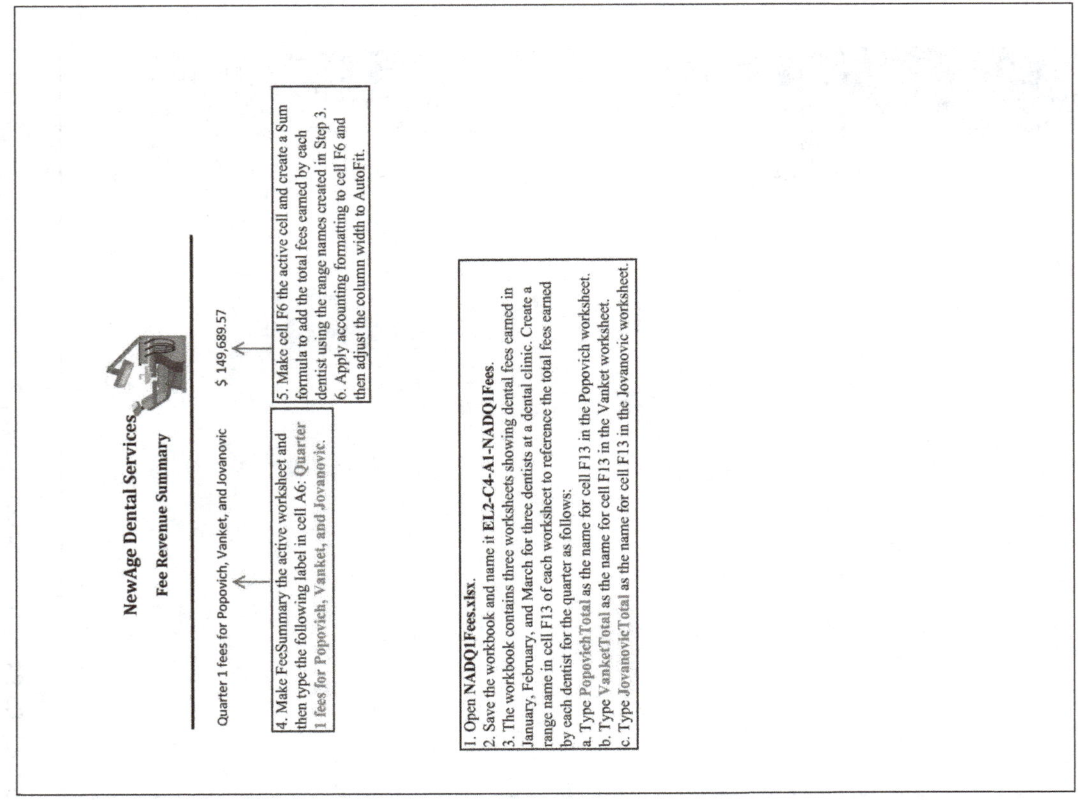

NewAge Dental Services
Fee Revenue Summary

Quarter 1 fees for Popovich, Vanket, and Jovanovic $ 149,689.57

4. Make FeeSummary the active worksheet and then type the following label in cell A6: **Quarter 1 fees for Popovich, Vanket, and Jovanovic**.

5. Make cell F6 the active cell and create a Sum formula to add the total fees earned by each dentist using the range names created in Step 3.
6. Apply accounting formatting to cell F6 and then adjust the column width to AutoFit.

1. Open **NADQ1Fees.xlsx**.
2. Save the workbook and name it **EL2-C4-A1-NADQ1Fees**.
3. The workbook contains three worksheets showing dental fees earned in January, February, and March for three dentists at a dental clinic. Create a range name in cell F13 of each worksheet to reference the total fees earned by each dentist for the quarter as follows:
a. Type **PopovichTotal** as the name for cell F13 in the Popovich worksheet.
b. Type **VanketTotal** as the name for cell F13 in the Vanket worksheet.
c. Type **JovanovicTotal** as the name for cell F13 in the Jovanovic worksheet.

EL2-C4-A1-NADQ1Fees(A1).xlsx

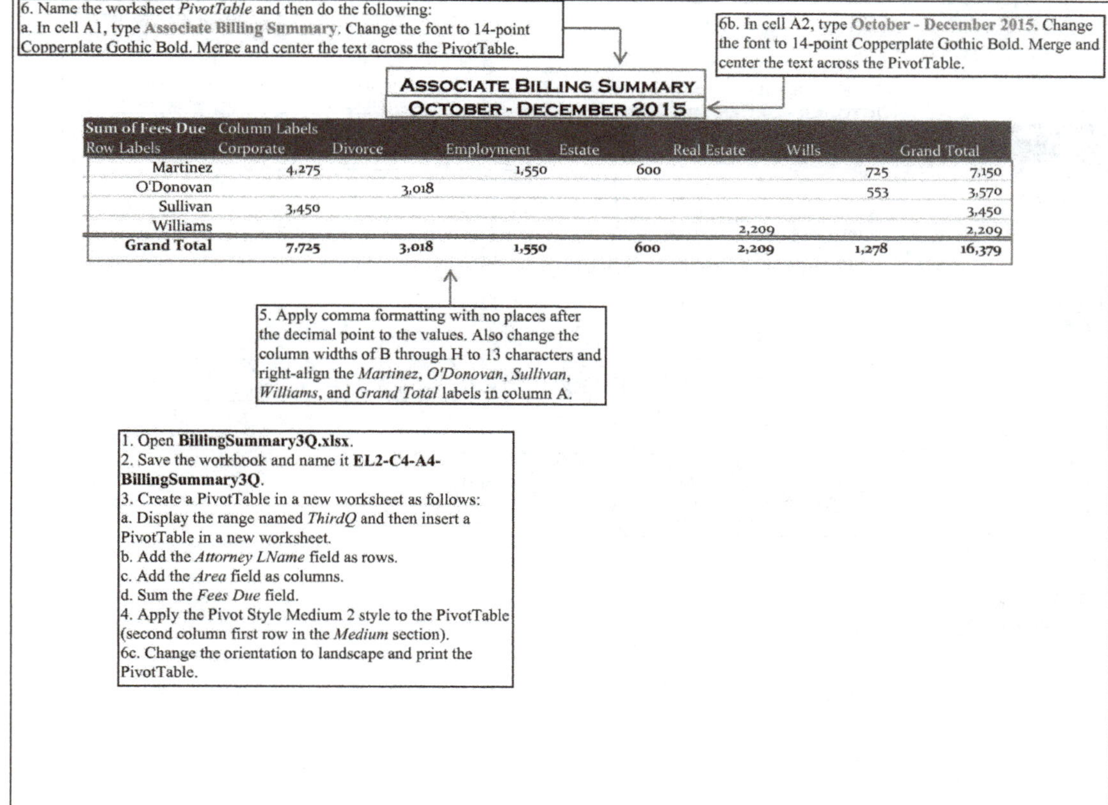

6. Name the worksheet *PivotTable* and then do the following:
a. In cell A1, type **Associate Billing Summary**. Change the font to 14-point Copperplate Gothic Bold. Merge and center the text across the PivotTable.

6b. In cell A2, type **October - December 2015**. Change the font to 14-point Copperplate Gothic Bold. Merge and center the text across the PivotTable.

ASSOCIATE BILLING SUMMARY
OCTOBER - DECEMBER 2015

Sum of Fees Due	Column Labels						
Row Labels	Corporate	Divorce	Employment	Estate	Real Estate	Wills	Grand Total
Martinez	4,275		1,550	600		725	7,150
O'Donovan		3,018				553	3,570
Sullivan	3,450						3,450
Williams					2,209		2,209
Grand Total	7,725	3,018	1,550	600	2,209	1,278	16,379

5. Apply comma formatting with no places after the decimal point to the values. Also change the column widths of B through H to 13 characters and right-align the *Martinez, O'Donovan, Sullivan, Williams,* and *Grand Total* labels in column A.

1. Open **BillingSummary3Q.xlsx**.
2. Save the workbook and name it **EL2-C4-A4-BillingSummary3Q**.
3. Create a PivotTable in a new worksheet as follows:
a. Display the range named *ThirdQ* and then insert a PivotTable in a new worksheet.
b. Add the *Attorney LName* field as rows.
c. Add the *Area* field as columns.
d. Sum the *Fees Due* field.
4. Apply the Pivot Style Medium 2 style to the PivotTable (second column first row in the *Medium* section).
6c. Change the orientation to landscape and print the PivotTable.

EL2-C4-A4-BillingSummary3Q(A4,Step6).xlsx

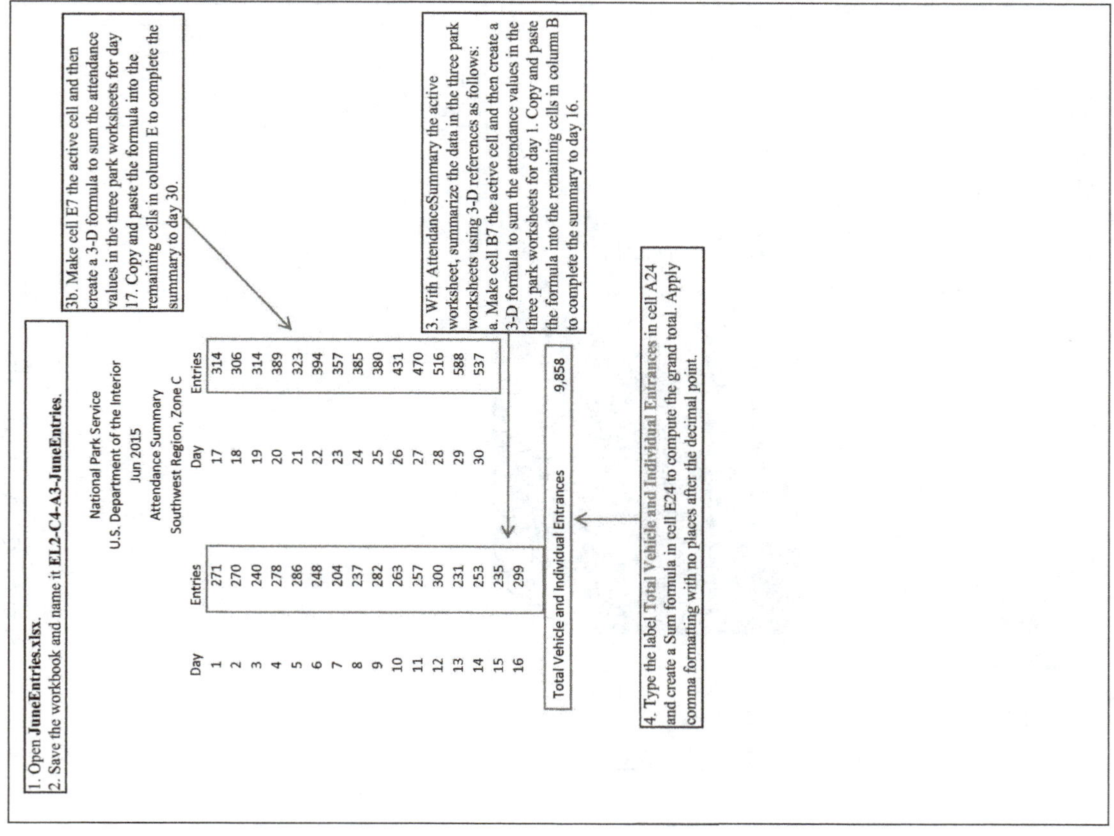

1. Open **JuneEntries.xlsx**.
2. Save the workbook and name it **EL2-C4-A3-JuneEntries**.

National Park Service
U.S. Department of the Interior
Jun 2015
Attendance Summary
Southwest Region, Zone C

Day	Entries	Day	Entries
1	271	17	314
2	270	18	306
3	240	19	314
4	278	20	389
5	286	21	323
6	248	22	394
7	204	23	357
8	237	24	385
9	282	25	380
10	263	26	431
11	257	27	470
12	300	28	516
13	231	29	588
14	253	30	537
15	235		
16	299		

Total Vehicle and Individual Entrances 9,858

3b. Make cell E7 the active cell and then create a 3-D formula to sum the attendance values in the three park worksheets for day 17. Copy and paste the formula into the remaining cells in column E to complete the summary to day 30.

3. With AttendanceSummary the active worksheet, summarize the data in the three park worksheets using 3-D references as follows:
a. Make cell B7 the active cell and then create a 3-D formula to sum the attendance values in the three park worksheets for day 1. Copy and paste the formula into the remaining cells in column B to complete the summary to day 16.

4. Type the label **Total Vehicle and Individual Entrances** in cell A24 and create a Sum formula in cell E24 to compute the grand total. Apply comma formatting with no places after the decimal point.

EL2-C4-A3-JuneEntries(A3).xlsx

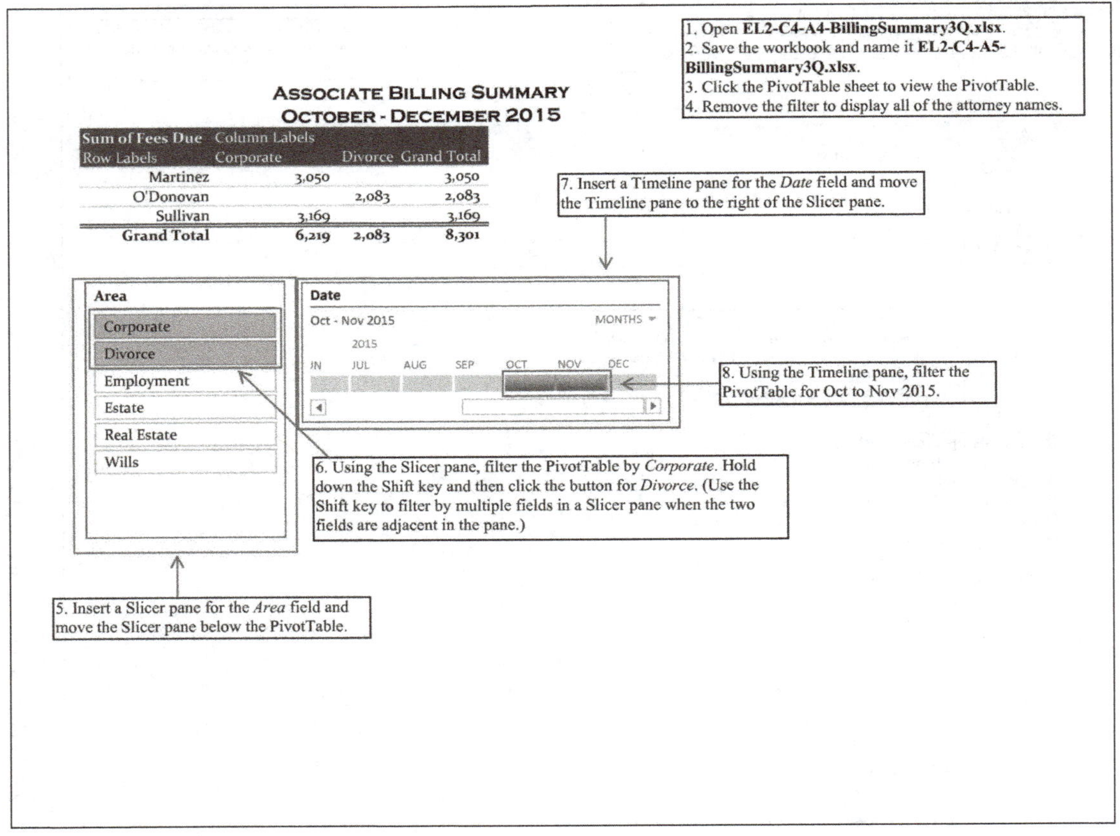

EL2-C4-A5-BillingSummary3Q(A5).xlsx

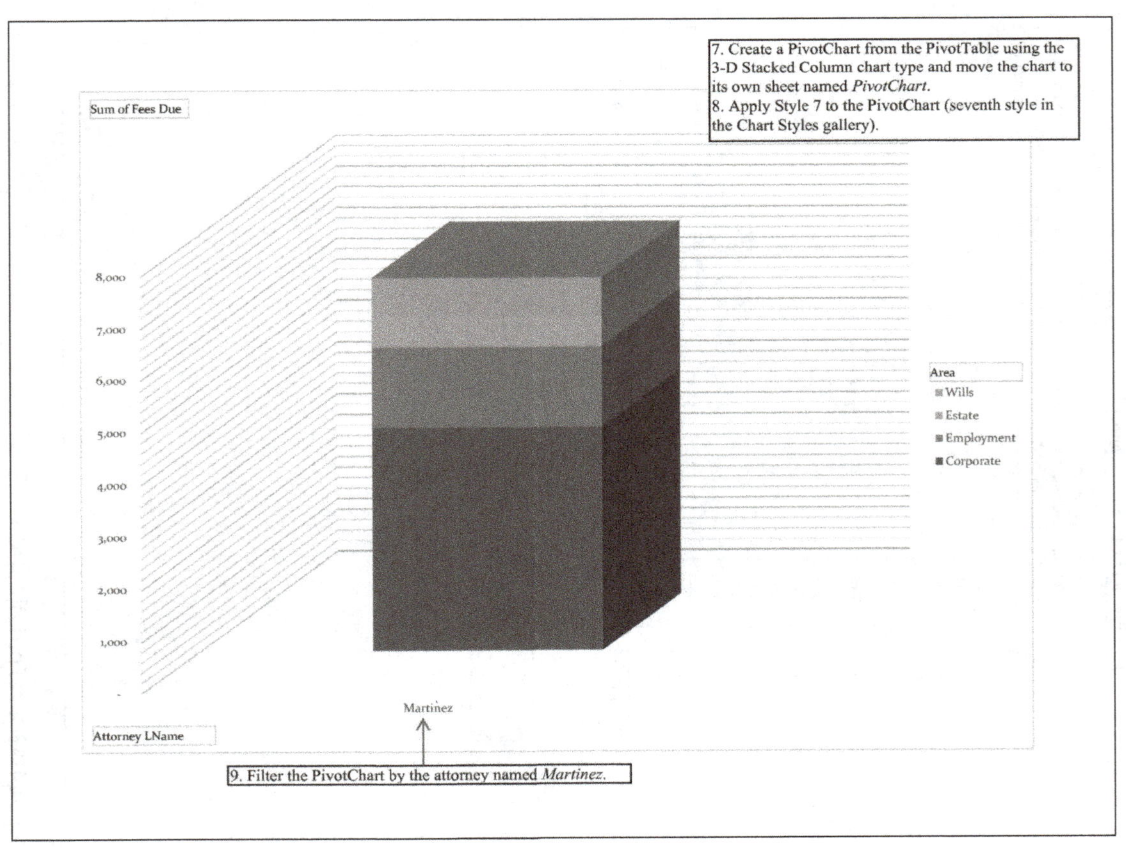

EL2-C4-A4-BillingSummary3Q(A4,Step10).xlsx

Hillsdale Realtors

October Sales

Sum of Sale Price	Column Labels			
Row Labels	Condominium	Single family home	Townhome	Grand Total
Chandler	$ 610,900	$ 325,500	$ 952,100	$ 1,888,500
Glendale	640,400	881,375		1,521,775
Mesa	275,800	846,750	165,800	1,288,350
Phoenix	695,000	2,148,100	174,900	3,018,000
Grand Total	**$ 2,222,100**	**$ 4,201,725**	**$ 1,292,800**	**$ 7,716,625**

EL2-C4-VB-HROctSales(VB,PivotTable).xlsx

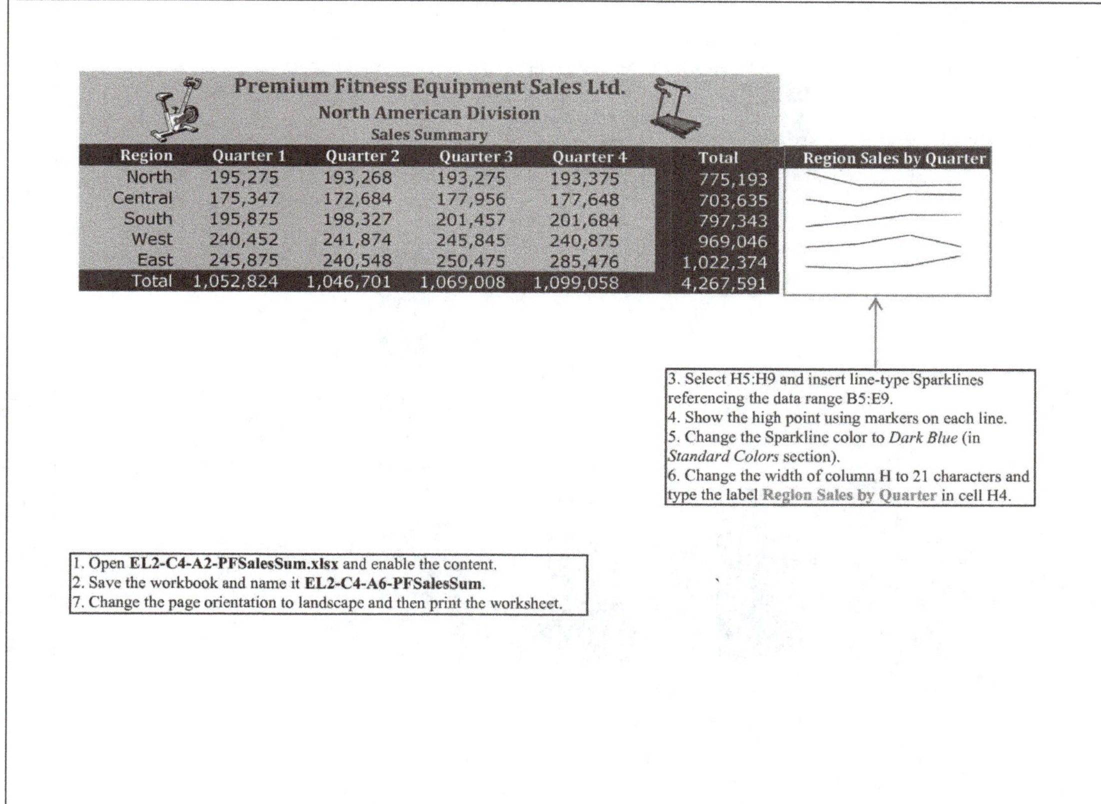

Premium Fitness Equipment Sales Ltd.
North American Division
Sales Summary

Region	Quarter 1	Quarter 2	Quarter 3	Quarter 4	Total	Region Sales by Quarter
North	195,275	193,268	193,275	193,375	775,193	
Central	175,347	172,684	177,956	177,648	703,635	
South	195,875	198,327	201,457	201,684	797,343	
West	240,452	241,874	245,845	240,875	969,046	
East	245,875	240,548	250,475	285,476	1,022,374	
Total	1,052,824	1,046,701	1,069,008	1,099,058	4,267,591	

3. Select H5:H9 and insert line-type Sparklines referencing the data range B5:E9.
4. Show the high point using markers on each line.
5. Change the Sparkline color to *Dark Blue* (in *Standard Colors* section).
6. Change the width of column H to 21 characters and type the label **Region Sales by Quarter** in cell H4.

1. Open **EL2-C4-A2-PFSalesSum.xlsx** and enable the content.
2. Save the workbook and name it **EL2-C4-A6-PFSalesSum**.
7. Change the page orientation to landscape and then print the worksheet.

EL2-C4-A6-PFSalesSum(A6).xlsx

Row Labels	Average of Gross Sales	Average of Net Income
Iowa	**$ 481,870.20**	**$ 113,941.00**
Cedar Rapids	485,866.00	120,365.67
Davenport	310,496.00	53,370.00
Des Moines	641,257.00	155,238.00
Michigan	**445,664.56**	**107,262.44**
Ann Arbor	515,302.00	129,330.00
Detroit	559,305.50	136,327.50
Flint	324,965.00	82,375.00
Kalamazoo	528,346.00	130,250.00
Lansing	347,865.00	66,370.00
Livonia	314,698.00	66,087.00
Port Huron	345,892.00	88,965.00
Ohio	**506,846.33**	**121,750.33**
Akron	461,853.00	110,258.00
Cincinatti	512,463.00	117,653.00
Columbus	504,796.00	111,055.00
Toledo	520,655.33	130,512.00
Wisconsin	**522,034.83**	**126,215.67**
Green Bay	401,588.00	66,200.00
Madison	535,680.50	138,042.50
Milwaukee	553,086.67	138,336.33
Grand Total	$ 484,369.96	$ 116,263.96

EL2-C4-CS-P1-PBMRpt(P1).xlsx

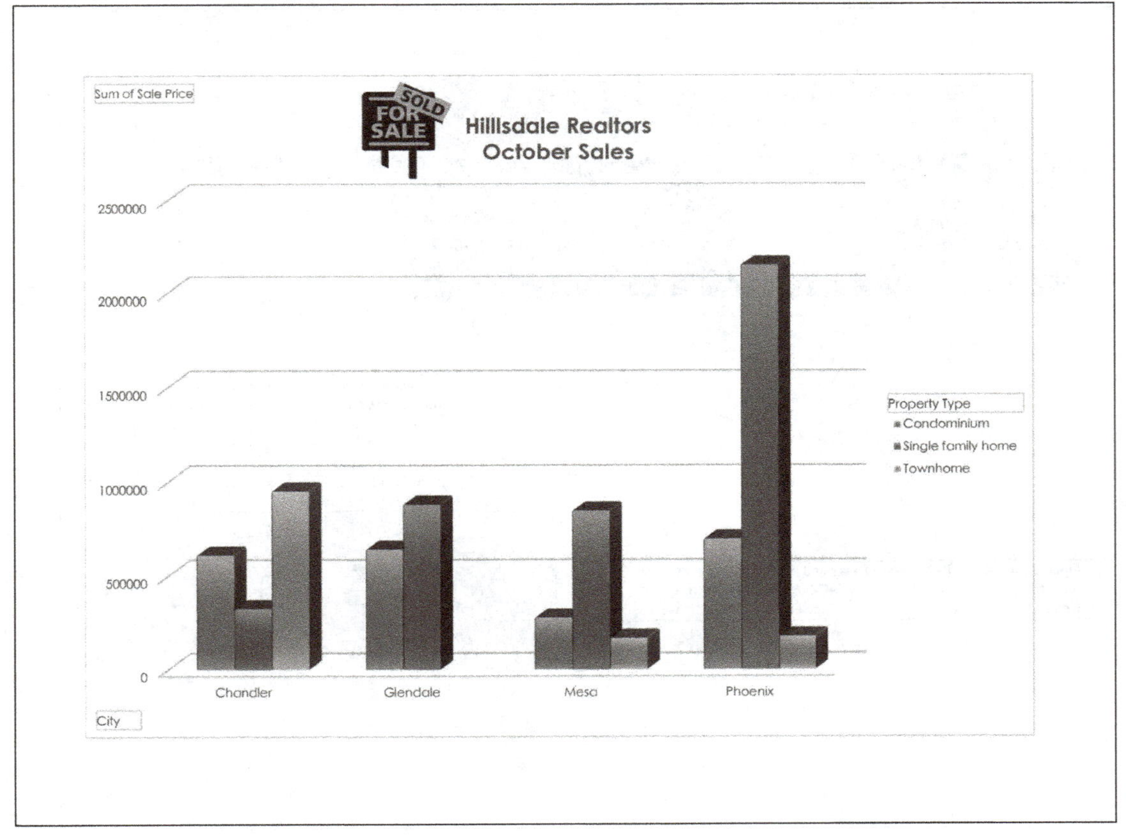

EL2-C4-VB-HROctSales(VB,PivotChart).xlsx

Row Labels	Average of Gross Sales
Iowa	
Cedar Rapids	2.00
Davenport	3.00
Des Moines	1.00
Michigan	
Ann Arbor	3.00
Detroit	1.00
Flint	6.00
Kalamazoo	2.00
Lansing	4.00
Livonia	7.00
Port Huron	5.00
Ohio	
Akron	4.00
Cincinatti	2.00
Columbus	3.00
Toledo	1.00
Wisconsin	
Green Bay	3.00
Madison	2.00
Milwaukee	1.00

EL2-C4-CS-P3-PBMRpt(P3).xlsx

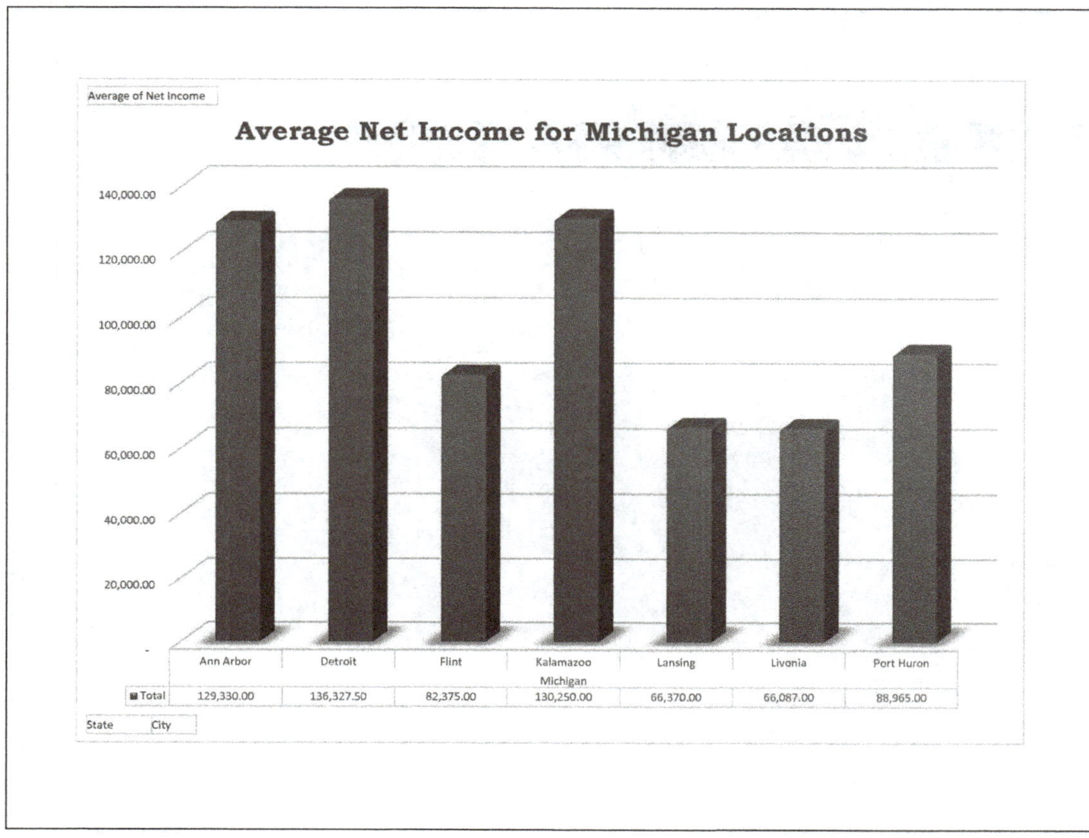

EL2-C4-CS-P2-PBMRpt(P2).xlsx

	Pizza By Mario		Dominos	
Row Labels	Sum of Gross Sales	Sum of Net Income	Sum of Gross Sales	Sum of Net Income
Grand Total	$ 12,593,619	$ 3,022,863	$ 1,680,000,000	$ 501,340,000

Source: Market Watch
http://www.marketwatch.com/investing/stock/dpz/financials

EL2-C4-CS-P4-PizzaFranchiseComparison(P4).xlsx

Excel Level 2, Performance Assessment Unit 1 Model Answers

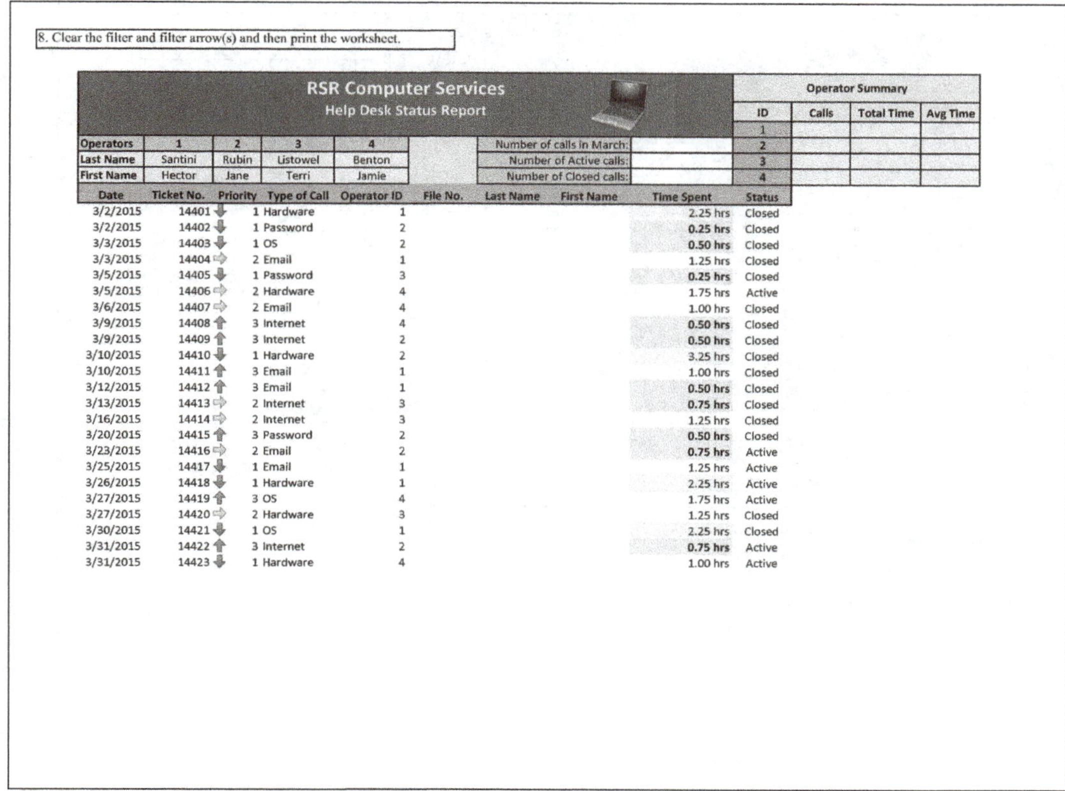

8. Clear the filter and filter arrow(s) and then print the worksheet.

RSR Computer Services
Help Desk Status Report

Operators	1	2	3	4
Last Name	Santini	Rubin	Listowel	Benton
First Name	Hector	Jane	Terri	Jamie

Number of calls in March:	
Number of Active calls:	
Number of Closed calls:	

Operator Summary			
ID	Calls	Total Time	Avg Time
1			
2			
3			
4			

Date	Ticket No.	Priority	Type of Call	Operator ID	File No.	Last Name	First Name	Time Spent	Status
3/2/2015	14401	1	Hardware	1				2.25 hrs	Closed
3/2/2015	14402	1	Password	2				0.25 hrs	Closed
3/3/2015	14403	1	OS	2				0.50 hrs	Closed
3/3/2015	14404	2	Email	1				1.25 hrs	Closed
3/5/2015	14405	1	Password	3				0.25 hrs	Closed
3/5/2015	14406	2	Hardware	4				1.75 hrs	Active
3/6/2015	14407	2	Email	4				1.00 hrs	Closed
3/9/2015	14408	3	Internet	4				0.50 hrs	Closed
3/9/2015	14409	3	Internet	2				0.50 hrs	Closed
3/10/2015	14410	1	Hardware	2				3.25 hrs	Closed
3/10/2015	14411	3	Email	1				1.00 hrs	Closed
3/12/2015	14412	3	Email	1				0.50 hrs	Closed
3/13/2015	14413	2	Internet	3				0.75 hrs	Closed
3/16/2015	14414	2	Internet	3				1.25 hrs	Closed
3/20/2015	14415	3	Password	2				0.50 hrs	Closed
3/23/2015	14416	2	Email	2				0.75 hrs	Active
3/25/2015	14417	1	Email	1				1.25 hrs	Active
3/26/2015	14418	1	Hardware	1				2.25 hrs	Active
3/27/2015	14419	3	OS	4				1.75 hrs	Active
3/27/2015	14420	2	Hardware	3				1.25 hrs	Closed
3/30/2015	14421	1	OS	1				2.25 hrs	Closed
3/31/2015	14422	3	Internet	2				0.75 hrs	Active
3/31/2015	14423	1	Hardware	4				1.00 hrs	Active

EL2-U1-A1-RSRHelpDesk(A1,Step8).xlsx

RSR Computer Services
Help Desk Status Report

Operators	1	2	3	4
Last Name	Santini	Rubin	Listowel	Benton
First Name	Hector	Jane	Terri	Jamie

Number of calls in March:	
Number of Active calls:	
Number of Closed calls:	

Operator Summary			
ID	Calls	Total Time	Avg Time
1			
2			
3			
4			

Date	Ticket No.	Priority	Type of Call	Operator ID	File No.	Last Name	First Name	Time Spent	Status
3/2/2015	14401	1	Hardware	1				2.25 hrs	Closed
3/10/2015	14410	1	Hardware	2				3.25 hrs	Closed
3/26/2015	14418	1	Hardware	1				2.25 hrs	Active
3/30/2015	14421	1	OS	1				2.25 hrs	Closed

EL2-U1-A1-RSRHelpDesk(A1,Step7).xlsx

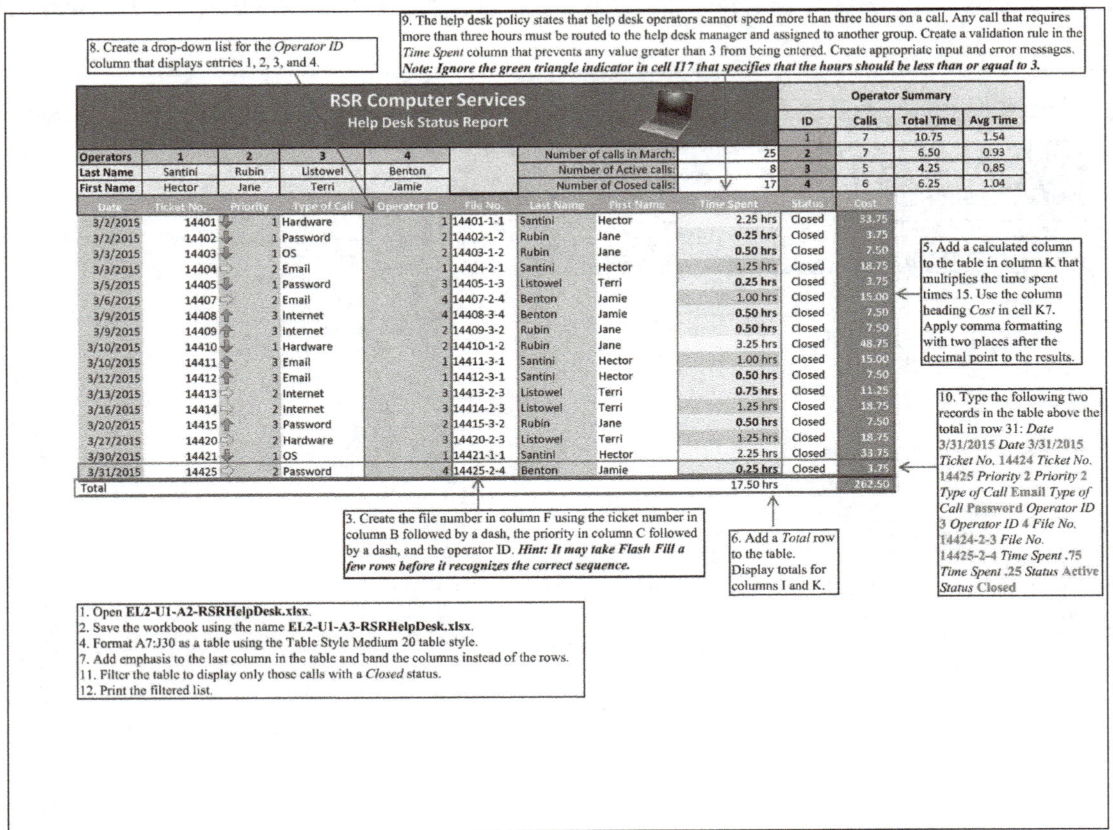

8. Create a drop-down list for the *Operator ID* column that displays entries 1, 2, 3, and 4.

9. The help desk policy states that help desk operators cannot spend more than three hours on a call. Any call that requires more than three hours must be routed to the help desk manager and assigned to another group. Create a validation rule in the *Time Spent* column that prevents any value greater than 3 from being entered. Create appropriate input and error messages. ***Note: Ignore the green triangle indicator in cell I17 that specifies that the hours should be less than or equal to 3.***

RSR Computer Services
Help Desk Status Report

Operators	1	2	3	4
Last Name	Santini	Rubin	Listowel	Benton
First Name	Hector	Jane	Terri	Jamie

Number of calls in March:	25
Number of Active calls:	8
Number of Closed calls:	17

Operator Summary			
ID	Calls	Total Time	Avg Time
1	7	10.75	1.54
2	7	6.50	0.93
3	5	4.25	0.85
4	6	6.25	1.04

Date	Ticket No.	Priority	Type of Call	Operator ID	File No.	Last Name	First Name	Time Spent	Status	Cost
3/2/2015	14401	1	Hardware	1	14401-1-1	Santini	Hector	2.25 hrs	Closed	33.75
3/2/2015	14402	1	Password	2	14402-1-2	Rubin	Jane	0.25 hrs	Closed	3.75
3/3/2015	14403	1	OS	2	14403-1-2	Rubin	Jane	0.50 hrs	Closed	7.50
3/3/2015	14404	2	Email	1	14404-2-1	Santini	Hector	1.25 hrs	Closed	18.75
3/5/2015	14405	1	Password	3	14405-1-3	Listowel	Terri	0.25 hrs	Closed	3.75
3/6/2015	14407	2	Email	4	14407-2-4	Benton	Jamie	1.00 hrs	Closed	15.00
3/9/2015	14408	3	Internet	4	14408-3-4	Benton	Jamie	0.50 hrs	Closed	7.50
3/9/2015	14409	3	Internet	2	14409-3-2	Rubin	Jane	0.50 hrs	Closed	7.50
3/10/2015	14410	1	Hardware	2	14410-1-2	Rubin	Jane	3.25 hrs	Closed	48.75
3/10/2015	14411	3	Email	1	14411-3-1	Santini	Hector	1.00 hrs	Closed	15.00
3/12/2015	14412	3	Email	1	14412-3-1	Santini	Hector	0.50 hrs	Closed	7.50
3/13/2015	14413	2	Internet	3	14413-2-3	Listowel	Terri	0.75 hrs	Closed	11.25
3/16/2015	14414	2	Internet	3	14414-2-3	Listowel	Terri	1.25 hrs	Closed	18.75
3/20/2015	14415	3	Password	2	14415-3-2	Rubin	Jane	0.50 hrs	Closed	7.50
3/27/2015	14420	2	Hardware	3	14420-2-3	Listowel	Terri	1.25 hrs	Closed	18.75
3/30/2015	14421	1	OS	1	14421-1-1	Santini	Hector	2.25 hrs	Closed	33.75
3/31/2015	14425	2	Password	4	14425-2-4	Benton	Jamie	0.25 hrs	Closed	3.75
Total								17.50 hrs		262.50

5. Add a calculated column to the table in column K that multiplies the time spent times 15. Use the column heading *Cost* in cell K7. Apply comma formatting with two places after the decimal point to the results.

10. Type the following two records in the table above the total in row 31: *Date* 3/31/2015 *Date* 3/31/2015 *Ticket No.* 14424 *Ticket No.* 14425 *Priority* 2 *Priority* 2 *Type of Call* Email *Type of Call* Password *Operator ID* 3 *Operator ID* 4 *File No.* 14424-2-3 *File No.* 14425-2-4 *Time Spent* .75 *Time Spent* .25 *Status* Active *Status* Closed

3. Create the file number in column F using the ticket number in column B followed by a dash, the priority in column C followed by a dash, and the operator ID. ***Hint: It may take Flash Fill a few rows before it recognizes the correct sequence.***

6. Add a *Total* row to the table. Display totals for columns I and K.

1. Open **EL2-U1-A2-RSRHelpDesk.xlsx**.
2. Save the workbook using the name **EL2-U1-A3-RSRHelpDesk.xlsx**.
4. Format A7:J30 as a table using the Table Style Medium 20 table style.
7. Add emphasis to the last column in the table and band the columns instead of the rows.
11. Filter the table to display only those calls with a *Closed* status.
12. Print the filtered list.

EL2-U1-A3-RSRHelpDesk(A3,.Step12).xlsx

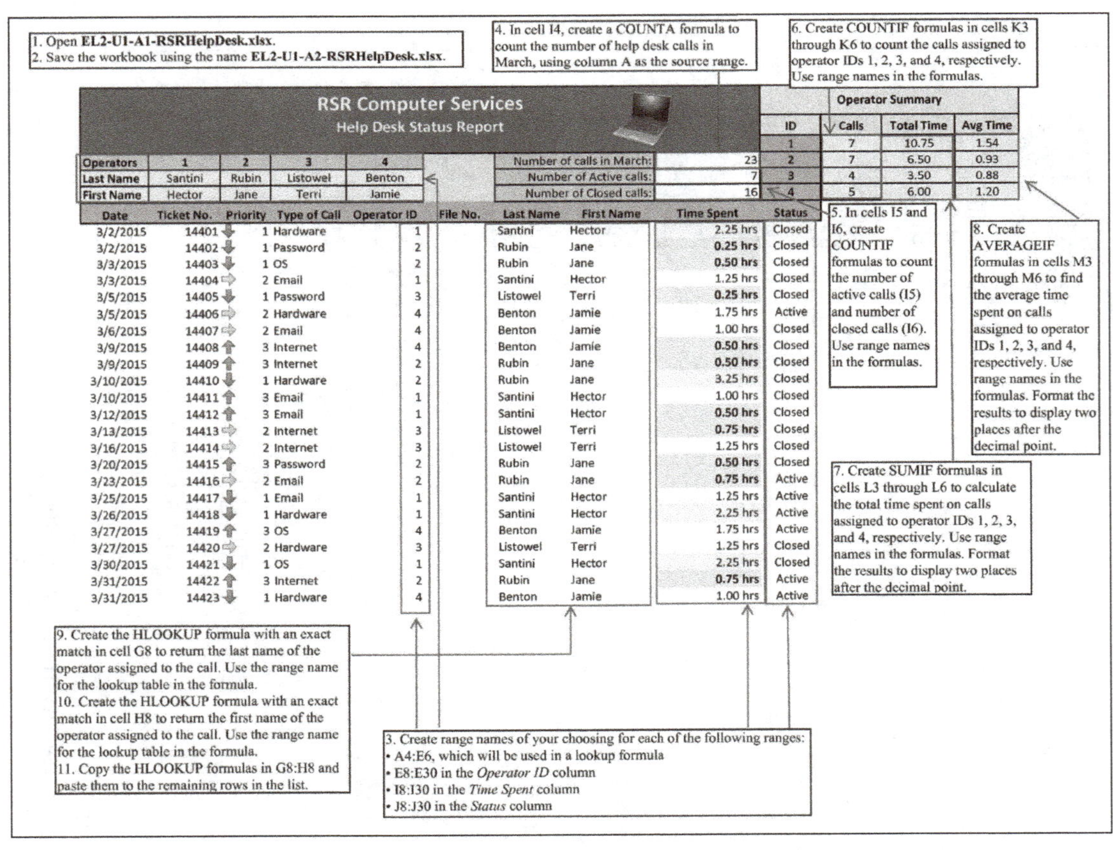

1. Open **EL2-U1-A1-RSRHelpDesk.xlsx**.
2. Save the workbook using the name **EL2-U1-A2-RSRHelpDesk.xlsx**.

4. In cell I4, create a COUNTA formula to count the number of help desk calls in March, using column A as the source range.

6. Create COUNTIF formulas in cells K3 through K6 to count the calls assigned to operator IDs 1, 2, 3, and 4, respectively. Use range names in the formulas.

RSR Computer Services
Help Desk Status Report

Operators	1	2	3	4
Last Name	Santini	Rubin	Listowel	Benton
First Name	Hector	Jane	Terri	Jamie

Number of calls in March:	23
Number of Active calls:	7
Number of Closed calls:	16

Operator Summary			
ID	Calls	Total Time	Avg Time
1	7	10.75	1.54
2	7	6.50	0.93
3	4	3.50	0.88
4	5	6.00	1.20

Date	Ticket No.	Priority	Type of Call	Operator ID	File No.	Last Name	First Name	Time Spent	Status
3/2/2015	14401	1	Hardware	1		Santini	Hector	2.25 hrs	Closed
3/2/2015	14402	1	Password	2		Rubin	Jane	0.25 hrs	Closed
3/3/2015	14403	1	OS	2		Rubin	Jane	0.50 hrs	Closed
3/3/2015	14404	2	Email	1		Santini	Hector	1.25 hrs	Closed
3/5/2015	14405	1	Password	3		Listowel	Terri	0.25 hrs	Closed
3/5/2015	14406	2	Hardware	4		Benton	Jamie	1.75 hrs	Active
3/6/2015	14407	2	Email	4		Benton	Jamie	1.00 hrs	Closed
3/9/2015	14408	3	Internet	4		Benton	Jamie	0.50 hrs	Closed
3/9/2015	14409	3	Internet	2		Rubin	Jane	0.50 hrs	Closed
3/10/2015	14410	1	Hardware	2		Rubin	Jane	3.25 hrs	Closed
3/10/2015	14411	3	Email	1		Santini	Hector	1.00 hrs	Closed
3/12/2015	14412	3	Email	1		Santini	Hector	0.50 hrs	Closed
3/13/2015	14413	2	Internet	3		Listowel	Terri	0.75 hrs	Closed
3/16/2015	14414	2	Internet	3		Listowel	Terri	1.25 hrs	Closed
3/20/2015	14415	3	Password	2		Rubin	Jane	0.50 hrs	Closed
3/23/2015	14416	2	Email	2		Rubin	Jane	0.75 hrs	Active
3/25/2015	14417	1	Email	1		Santini	Hector	1.25 hrs	Active
3/26/2015	14418	1	Hardware	1		Santini	Hector	2.25 hrs	Active
3/27/2015	14419	3	OS	4		Benton	Jamie	1.75 hrs	Active
3/27/2015	14420	2	Hardware	3		Listowel	Terri	1.25 hrs	Closed
3/30/2015	14421	1	OS	1		Santini	Hector	2.25 hrs	Closed
3/31/2015	14422	3	Internet	2		Rubin	Jane	0.75 hrs	Active
3/31/2015	14423	1	Hardware	4		Benton	Jamie	1.00 hrs	Active

5. In cells I5 and I6, create COUNTIF formulas to count the number of active calls (I5) and number of closed calls (I6). Use range names in the formulas.

8. Create AVERAGEIF formulas in cells M3 through M6 to find the average time spent on calls assigned to operator IDs 1, 2, 3, and 4, respectively. Use range names in the formulas. Format the results to display two places after the decimal point.

7. Create SUMIF formulas in cells L3 through L6 to calculate the total time spent on calls assigned to operator IDs 1, 2, 3, and 4, respectively. Use range names in the formulas. Format the results to display two places after the decimal point.

9. Create the HLOOKUP formula with an exact match in cell G8 to return the last name of the operator assigned to the call. Use the range name for the lookup table in the formula.
10. Create the HLOOKUP formula with an exact match in cell H8 to return the first name of the operator assigned to the call. Use the range name for the lookup table in the formula.
11. Copy the HLOOKUP formulas in G8:H8 and paste them to the remaining rows in the list.

3. Create range names of your choosing for each of the following ranges:
- A4:E6, which will be used in a lookup formula
- E8:E30 in the *Operator ID* column
- I8:I30 in the *Time Spent* column
- J8:J30 in the *Status* column

15. Clear both filters.
16. Save, print, and then close **EL2-U1-A3-RSRHelpDesk.xlsx**.

RSR Computer Services
Help Desk Status Report

Operator Summary			
ID	Calls	Total Time	Avg Time
1	7	10.75	1.54
2	7	6.50	0.93
3	5	4.25	0.85
4	6	6.25	1.04

Operators	1	2	3	4
Last Name	Santini	Rubin	Listowel	Benton
First Name	Hector	Jane	Terri	Jamie

Number of calls in March:	25
Number of Active calls:	8
Number of Closed calls:	17

Date	Ticket No.	Priority	Type of Call	Operator ID	File No.	Last Name	First Name	Time Spent	Status	Cost
3/2/2015	14401	1	Hardware	1	14401-1-1	Santini	Hector	2.25 hrs	Closed	33.75
3/2/2015	14402	1	Password	2	14402-1-2	Rubin	Jane	0.25 hrs	Closed	3.75
3/3/2015	14403	1	OS	2	14403-1-2	Rubin	Jane	0.50 hrs	Closed	7.50
3/3/2015	14404	2	Email	1	14404-2-1	Santini	Hector	1.25 hrs	Closed	18.75
3/5/2015	14405	1	Password	3	14405-1-3	Listowel	Terri	0.25 hrs	Closed	3.75
3/5/2015	14406	2	Hardware	4	14406-2-4	Benton	Jamie	1.75 hrs	Active	26.25
3/6/2015	14407	2	Email	4	14407-2-4	Benton	Jamie	1.00 hrs	Closed	15.00
3/9/2015	14408	3	Internet	4	14408-3-4	Benton	Jamie	0.50 hrs	Closed	7.50
3/9/2015	14409	3	Internet	2	14409-3-2	Rubin	Jane	0.50 hrs	Closed	7.50
3/10/2015	14410	1	Hardware	2	14410-1-2	Rubin	Jane	3.25 hrs	Closed	48.75
3/10/2015	14411	3	Email	1	14411-3-1	Santini	Hector	1.00 hrs	Closed	15.00
3/12/2015	14412	3	Email	1	14412-3-1	Santini	Hector	0.50 hrs	Closed	7.50
3/13/2015	14413	2	Internet	3	14413-2-3	Listowel	Terri	0.75 hrs	Closed	11.25
3/16/2015	14414	2	Internet	3	14414-2-3	Listowel	Terri	1.25 hrs	Closed	18.75
3/20/2015	14415	3	Password	2	14415-3-2	Rubin	Jane	0.50 hrs	Closed	7.50
3/23/2015	14416	2	Email	2	14416-2-2	Rubin	Jane	0.75 hrs	Active	11.25
3/25/2015	14417	1	Email	1	14417-1-1	Santini	Hector	1.25 hrs	Active	18.75
3/26/2015	14418	1	Hardware	1	14418-1-1	Santini	Hector	2.25 hrs	Active	33.75
3/27/2015	14419	3	OS	4	14419-3-4	Benton	Jamie	1.75 hrs	Active	26.25
3/27/2015	14420	2	Hardware	3	14420-2-3	Listowel	Terri	1.25 hrs	Closed	18.75
3/30/2015	14421	1	OS	1	14421-1-1	Santini	Hector	2.25 hrs	Closed	33.75
3/31/2015	14422	3	Internet	2	14422-3-2	Rubin	Jane	0.75 hrs	Active	11.25
3/31/2015	14423	1	Hardware	4	14423-1-4	Benton	Jamie	1.00 hrs	Active	15.00
3/31/2015	14424	2	Email	3	14424-2-3	Listowel	Terri	0.75 hrs	Active	11.25
3/31/2015	14425	2	Password	4	14425-2-4	Benton	Jamie	0.25 hrs	Closed	3.75
Total								27.75 hrs		416.25

EL2-U1-A3-RSRHelpDesk(A3,.Step16).xlsx

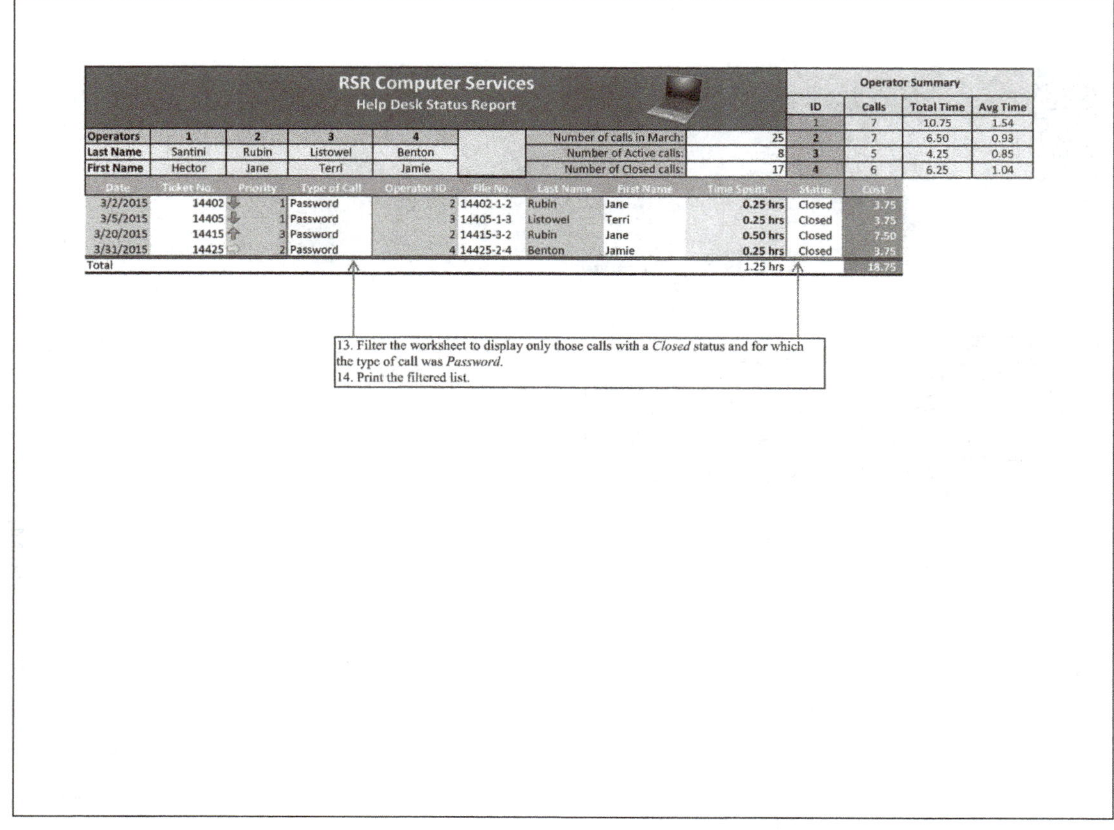

RSR Computer Services
Help Desk Status Report

Operator Summary			
ID	Calls	Total Time	Avg Time
1	7	10.75	1.54
2	7	6.50	0.93
3	5	4.25	0.85
4	6	6.25	1.04

Operators	1	2	3	4
Last Name	Santini	Rubin	Listowel	Benton
First Name	Hector	Jane	Terri	Jamie

Number of calls in March:	25
Number of Active calls:	8
Number of Closed calls:	17

Date	Ticket No.	Priority	Type of Call	Operator ID	File No.	Last Name	First Name	Time Spent	Status	Cost
3/2/2015	14402	1	Password	2	14402-1-2	Rubin	Jane	0.25 hrs	Closed	3.75
3/5/2015	14405	1	Password	3	14405-1-3	Listowel	Terri	0.25 hrs	Closed	3.75
3/20/2015	14415	3	Password	2	14415-3-2	Rubin	Jane	0.50 hrs	Closed	7.50
3/31/2015	14425	2	Password	4	14425-2-4	Benton	Jamie	0.25 hrs	Closed	3.75
Total								1.25 hrs		18.75

EL2-U1-A3-RSRHelpDesk(A3,.Step14).xlsx

8. Display the outlined worksheet at level 3 and then print the worksheet.

RSR Computer Services
Help Desk Status Report

Operators	1	2	3	4
Last Name	Santini	Rubin	Listowel	Benton
First Name	Hector	Jane	Terri	Jamie

Number of calls in March:	25
Number of Active calls:	8
Number of Closed calls:	17

Operator Summary			
ID	Calls	Total Time	Avg Time
1	7	10.75	1.54
2	7	6.50	0.93
3	5	4.25	0.85
4	6	6.25	1.04

Date	Ticket No.	Priority	Type of Call	Operator ID	File No.	Last Name	First Name	Time Spent	Status	Cost
3/31/2015	14423	1	Hardware	4	14423-1-4	Benton	Jamie	1.00 hrs	Active	15.00
3/6/2015	14407	2	Email	4	14407-2-4	Benton	Jamie	1.00 hrs	Closed	15.00
3/5/2015	14406	2	Hardware	4	14406-2-4	Benton	Jamie	1.75 hrs	Active	26.25
3/31/2015	14425	2	Password	4	14425-2-4	Benton	Jamie	0.25 hrs	Closed	3.75
3/9/2015	14408	3	Internet	4	14408-3-4	Benton	Jamie	0.50 hrs	Closed	7.50
3/27/2015	14419	3	OS	4	14419-3-4	Benton	Jamie	1.75 hrs	Active	26.25
						Benton Total				93.75
3/5/2015	14405	1	Password	3	14405-1-3	Listowel	Terri	0.25 hrs	Closed	3.75
3/31/2015	14424	2	Email	3	14424-2-3	Listowel	Terri	0.75 hrs	Active	11.25
3/27/2015	14420	2	Hardware	3	14420-2-3	Listowel	Terri	1.25 hrs	Closed	18.75
3/13/2015	14413	2	Internet	3	14413-2-3	Listowel	Terri	0.75 hrs	Closed	11.25
3/16/2015	14414	2	Internet	3	14414-2-3	Listowel	Terri	1.25 hrs	Closed	18.75
						Listowel Total				63.75
3/10/2015	14410	1	Hardware	2	14410-1-2	Rubin	Jane	3.25 hrs	Closed	48.75
3/3/2015	14403	1	OS	2	14403-1-2	Rubin	Jane	0.50 hrs	Closed	7.50
3/2/2015	14402	1	Password	2	14402-1-2	Rubin	Jane	0.25 hrs	Closed	3.75
3/23/2015	14416	2	Email	2	14416-2-2	Rubin	Jane	0.75 hrs	Active	11.25
3/9/2015	14409	3	Internet	2	14409-3-2	Rubin	Jane	0.50 hrs	Closed	7.50
3/31/2015	14422	3	Internet	2	14422-3-2	Rubin	Jane	0.75 hrs	Active	11.25
3/20/2015	14415	3	Password	2	14415-3-2	Rubin	Jane	0.50 hrs	Closed	7.50
						Rubin Total				97.50
3/25/2015	14417	1	Email	1	14417-1-1	Santini	Hector	1.25 hrs	Active	18.75
3/2/2015	14401	1	Hardware	1	14401-1-1	Santini	Hector	2.25 hrs	Closed	33.75
3/26/2015	14418	1	Hardware	1	14418-1-1	Santini	Hector	2.25 hrs	Active	33.75
3/30/2015	14421	1	OS	1	14421-1-1	Santini	Hector	2.25 hrs	Closed	33.75
3/3/2015	14404	2	Email	1	14404-2-1	Santini	Hector	1.25 hrs	Closed	18.75
3/10/2015	14411	3	Email	1	14411-3-1	Santini	Hector	1.00 hrs	Closed	15.00
3/12/2015	14412	3	Email	1	14412-3-1	Santini	Hector	0.50 hrs	Closed	7.50
						Santini Total				161.25
						Grand Total				416.25

EL2-U1-A4-RSRHelpDesk(A4,.Step8).xlsx

RSR Computer Services
Help Desk Status Report

Operators	1	2	3	4
Last Name	Santini	Rubin	Listowel	Benton
First Name	Hector	Jane	Terri	Jamie

Number of calls in March:	25
Number of Active calls:	8
Number of Closed calls:	17

Operator Summary			
ID	Calls	Total Time	Avg Time
1	7	10.75	1.54
2	7	6.50	0.93
3	5	4.25	0.85
4	6	6.25	1.04

Date	Ticket No.	Priority	Type of Call	Operator ID	File No.	Last Name	First Name	Time Spent	Status	Cost
						Benton Total				93.75
						Listowel Total				63.75
						Rubin Total				97.50
						Santini Total				161.25
						Grand Total				416.25

1. Open **EL2-U1-A3-RSRHelpDesk.xlsx**.
2. Save the workbook using the name **EL2-U1-A4-RSRHelpDesk**.
3. Remove the *Total* row from the table.
4. Convert the table to a normal range.
5. Sort the list first by the operator's last name, then by the operator's first name, then by the call priority, and finally by the type of call --all in ascending order.
6. Add a subtotal to the list at each change in operator last name to calculate the total cost of calls by each operator.
7. Display the outlined worksheet at level 2 and then print the worksheet.

EL2-U1-A4-RSRHelpDesk(A4,.Step7).xlsx

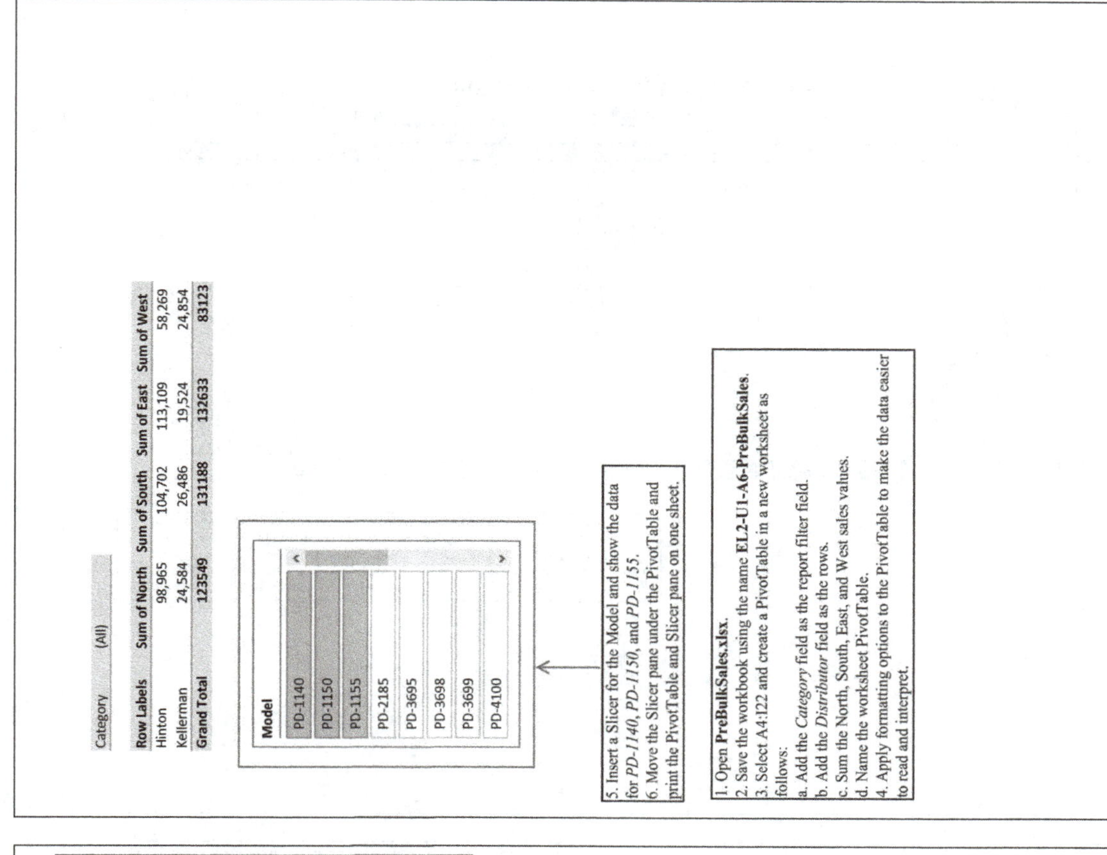

EL2-U1-A6-PreBulkSales(A6,Step6).xlsx

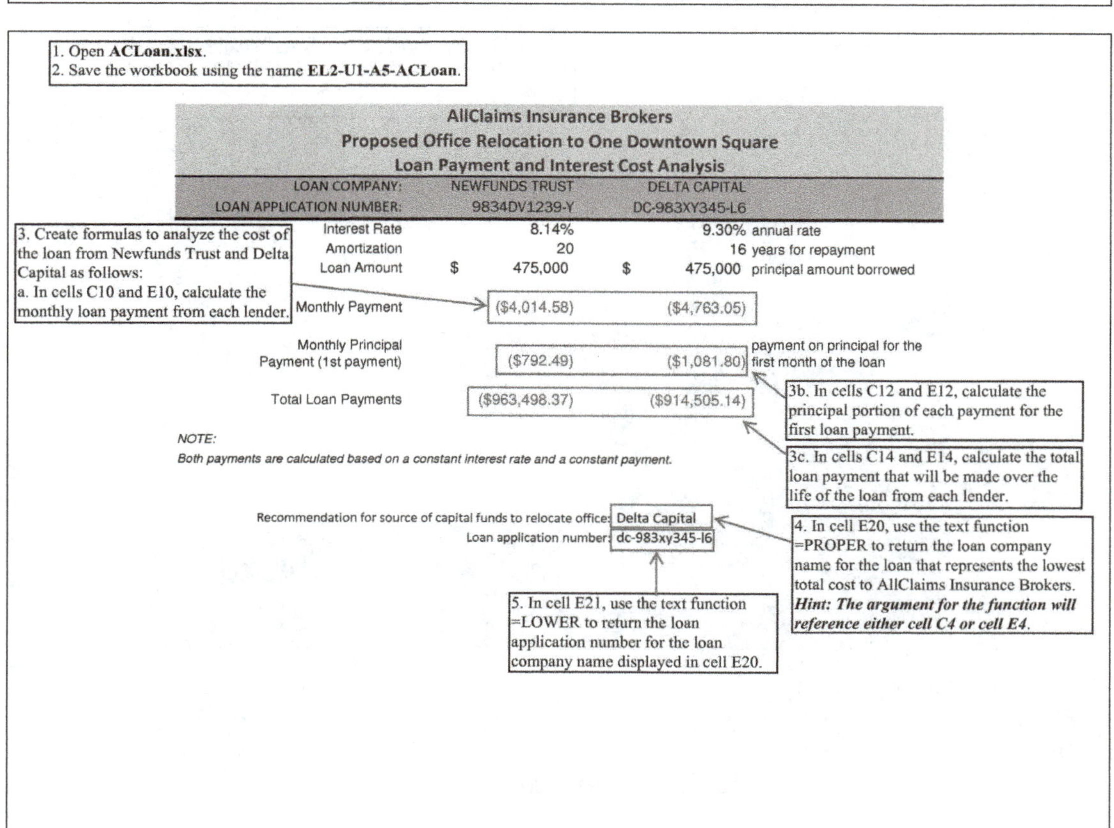

EL2-U1-A5-ACLoan(A5).xlsx

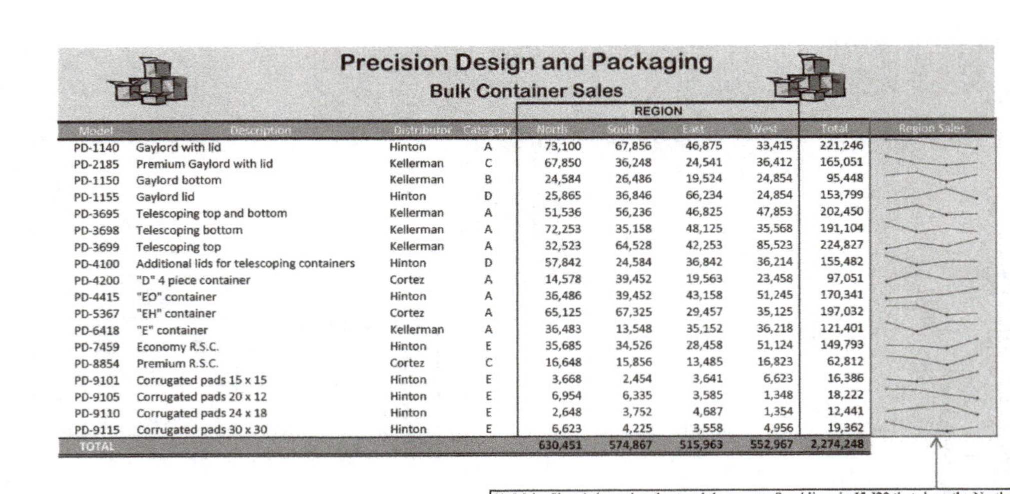

Precision Design and Packaging
Bulk Container Sales

Model	Description	Distributor	Category	North	South	East	West	Total	Region Sales
				REGION					
PD-1140	Gaylord with lid	Hinton	A	73,100	67,856	46,875	33,415	221,246	
PD-2185	Premium Gaylord with lid	Kellerman	C	67,850	36,248	24,541	36,412	165,051	
PD-1150	Gaylord bottom	Kellerman	B	24,584	26,486	19,524	24,854	95,448	
PD-1155	Gaylord lid	Hinton	D	25,865	36,846	66,234	24,854	153,799	
PD-3695	Telescoping top and bottom	Kellerman	A	51,536	56,236	46,825	47,853	202,450	
PD-3698	Telescoping bottom	Kellerman	A	72,253	35,158	48,125	35,568	191,104	
PD-3699	Telescoping top	Kellerman	A	32,523	64,528	42,253	85,523	224,827	
PD-4100	Additional lids for telescoping containers	Hinton	D	57,842	24,584	36,842	36,214	155,482	
PD-4200	"D" 4 piece container	Cortez	A	14,578	39,452	19,563	23,458	97,051	
PD-4415	"EO" container	Hinton	A	36,486	39,452	43,158	51,245	170,341	
PD-5367	"EH" container	Cortez	A	65,125	67,325	29,457	35,125	197,032	
PD-6418	"E" container	Kellerman	A	36,483	13,548	35,152	36,218	121,401	
PD-7459	Economy R.S.C.	Hinton	E	35,685	34,526	28,458	51,124	149,793	
PD-8854	Premium R.S.C.	Cortez	C	16,648	15,856	13,485	16,823	62,812	
PD-9101	Corrugated pads 15 x 15	Hinton	E	3,668	2,454	3,641	6,623	16,386	
PD-9105	Corrugated pads 20 x 12	Hinton	E	6,954	6,335	3,585	1,348	18,222	
PD-9110	Corrugated pads 24 x 18	Hinton	E	2,648	3,752	4,687	1,354	12,441	
PD-9115	Corrugated pads 30 x 30	Hinton	E	6,623	4,225	3,558	4,956	19,362	
TOTAL				630,451	574,867	515,963	552,967	2,274,248	

11. Make Sheet1 the active sheet and then create Sparklines in J5:J22 that show the North, South, East, and West sales in a line chart. Set the width of column J to 18 characters. Customize the Sparklines by changing the Sparkline color and adding data points. (You determine which data point to show and what color to make the points.) Type an appropriate label in cell J4 and add other formatting that will improve the appearance of the worksheet.

EL2-U1-A6-PreBulkSales(A6,Step12).xlsx

7. Create a PivotChart and move it to a separate sheet named PivotChart that graphs the data from the PivotTable in a 3-D Clustered Column chart.
9. Apply the Style 3 format to the chart.
10. Print the chart.

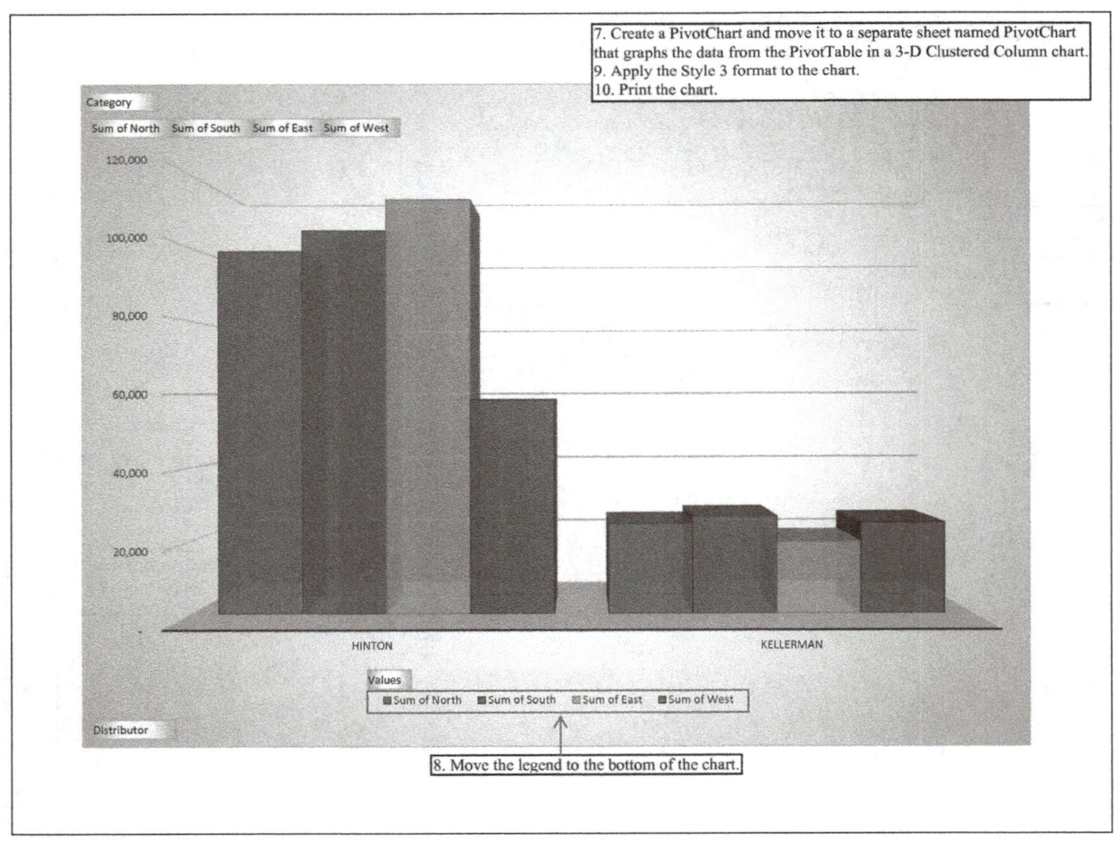

8. Move the legend to the bottom of the chart.

EL2-U1-A6-PreBulkSales(A6,Step10).xlsx

14. Type TOTALS in cell B10 and then create formulas in cells D10 and H10 to calculate the total sales and total payments, respectively. Format the totals and adjust column widths as necessary.

Precision Design and Packaging

Distributor Payments

Distributors	Total Sales	Payment
Cortez	356,895	3,568.95
Hinton	917,072	18,341.44
Kellerman	1,000,281	40,011.24
TOTALS	$ 2,274,248	$ 61,921.63

=GETPIVOTDATA("Total",'[EL2-U1-A7-PreSource(A7).xlsx]PivotTable'!$A$3,"Distributor","Cortez")

8. Create linked external references starting in cell D6 in **EL2-U1-A7- PreDistPymnt.xlsx** to the appropriate source cells in the PivotTable in **EL2-U1-A7-PreSource.xlsx** so that the distributor payment worksheet displays the total sales for each distributor. ***Note: Since you are linking to a PivotTable, Excel automatically generates a GETPIVOTDATA function formula in each linked cell.***
11. Apply comma formatting with no places after the decimal point to D6:D8.

12. Precision Design and Packaging pays each distributor a percentage of sales depending on the total sales achieved. The percentage for each category of sales is shown in the following chart: **Sales Percentage** Less than $600,000 1% Greater than or equal to $600,000 but less than $1,000,000 2% $1,000,000 and above 4% Calculate the payment owed for the distributors in H6:H8. Perform the calculation using one of the following two methods. (Choose the method that you find easiest to understand.)
• Create a nested IF statement.
• Create a lookup table in the worksheet that contains the sale ranges and three percentage values.
Next, add a column next to each distributor with a lookup formula to return the correct percentage and then calculate the payment using total sales times the percentage value.
13. Apply comma formatting with two places after the decimal point to H6:H8.

15. Write the GETPIVOTDATA formula for cell D6 at the bottom of the printout.

1. Open **PreDistPymnt.xlsx**.
2. Save the workbook using the name **EL2-U1-A7-PreDistPymnt**.
3. Open **EL2-U1-A6-PreBulkSales.xlsx**.
4. Save the workbook using the name **EL2-U1-A7-PreSource**.
5. Make the PivotTable worksheet active, remove any filters, delete the Slicer pane, and then edit the PivotTable Fields so that *Sum of Total* is the only numeric field displayed in the table.
6. Save **EL2-U1-A7-PreSource.xlsx**.
7. Arrange the display of the two workbooks vertically.
9. Close **EL2-U1-A7-PreSource.xlsx**.
10. Maximize **EL2-U1-A7-PreDistPymnt.xlsx**.
15. Print the worksheet.

EL2-U1-A7-PreDistPymnt(A7,Step15).xlsx

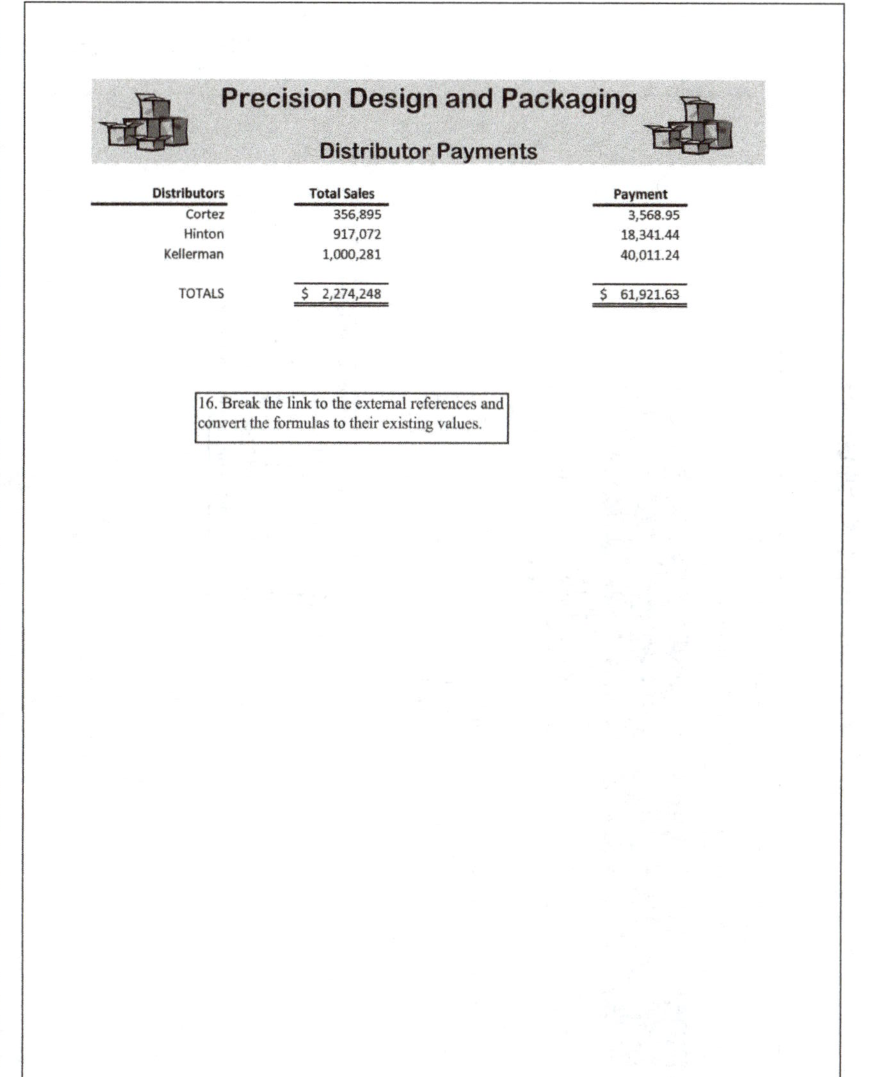

Precision Design and Packaging

Distributor Payments

Distributors	Total Sales	Payment
Cortez	356,895	3,568.95
Hinton	917,072	18,341.44
Kellerman	1,000,281	40,011.24
TOTALS	$ 2,274,248	$ 61,921.63

16. Break the link to the external references and convert the formulas to their existing values.

EL2-U1-A7-PreDistPymnt(A7,Step17).xlsx

Excel Level 2, Chapter 5 Model Answers

1. Open **NationalBdgt.xlsx**.
2. Save the workbook and name it **EL2-C5-A2-NationalBdgt**.

National Online Marketing Inc.

Computing Services Department

	Current budget	Projected increase	New budget
Wages and benefits	371,875	8,230	380,105
Computer supplies	150,350	2,255	152,605
Training and development	63,850	6,385	70,235
Other administrative costs	49,576	2,479	52,055
Total costs:	**635,651**		**655,000**

3. Make cell D8 the active cell and open the Goal Seek dialog box.
4. Find the projected increase for wages and benefits that will make the total cost of the new budget equal $655,000.
5. Accept the solution Goal Seek calculates.

EL2-C5-A2-NationalBdgt(A2).xlsx

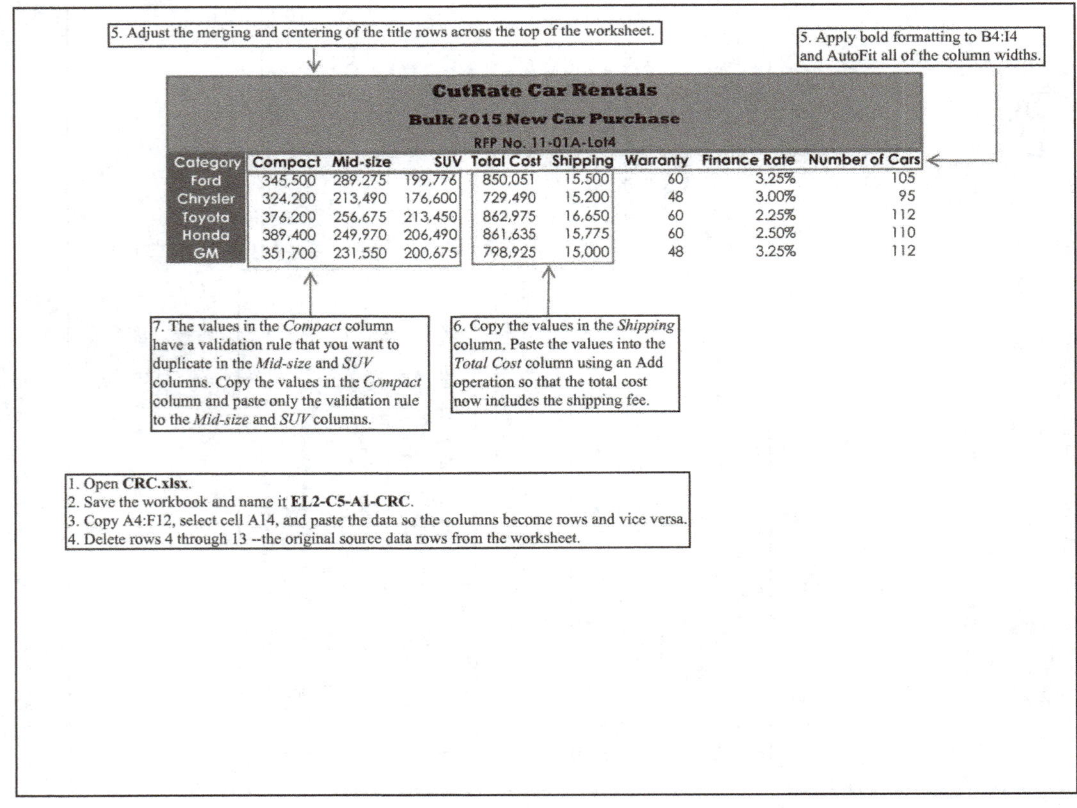

5. Adjust the merging and centering of the title rows across the top of the worksheet.

5. Apply bold formatting to B4:I4 and AutoFit all of the column widths.

CutRate Car Rentals

Bulk 2015 New Car Purchase

RFP No. 11-01A-Lot4

Category	Compact	Mid-size	SUV	Total Cost	Shipping	Warranty	Finance Rate	Number of Cars
Ford	345,500	289,275	199,776	850,051	15,500	60	3.25%	105
Chrysler	324,200	213,490	176,600	729,490	15,200	48	3.00%	95
Toyota	376,200	256,675	213,450	862,975	16,650	60	2.25%	112
Honda	389,400	249,970	206,490	861,635	15,775	60	2.50%	110
GM	351,700	231,550	200,675	798,925	15,000	48	3.25%	112

7. The values in the *Compact* column have a validation rule that you want to duplicate in the *Mid-size* and *SUV* columns. Copy the values in the *Compact* column and paste only the validation rule to the *Mid-size* and *SUV* columns.

6. Copy the values in the *Shipping* column. Paste the values into the *Total Cost* column using an Add operation so that the total cost now includes the shipping fee.

1. Open **CRC.xlsx**.
2. Save the workbook and name it **EL2-C5-A1-CRC**.
3. Copy A4:F12, select cell A14, and paste the data so the columns become rows and vice versa.
4. Delete rows 4 through 13 --the original source data rows from the worksheet.

EL2-C5-A1-CRC(A1).xlsx

Scenario Summary	Current Values:	OriginalTarget	LowSales	HighSales
Changing Cells:				
East	0.20	0.30	0.20	0.36
West	0.32	0.45	0.32	0.58
Ontario	0.48	0.65	0.48	0.77
Quebec	0.37	0.50	0.37	0.63
Result Cells:				
$H$18	97.78	105.20	97.78	111.36

Notes: Current Values column represents values of changing cells at time Scenario Summary Report was created. Changing cells for each scenario are highlighted in gray.

5. Create a scenario summary report displaying cell H18 as the result cell.

EL2-C5-A3-PreCdnTarget(A3,Step6).xlsx

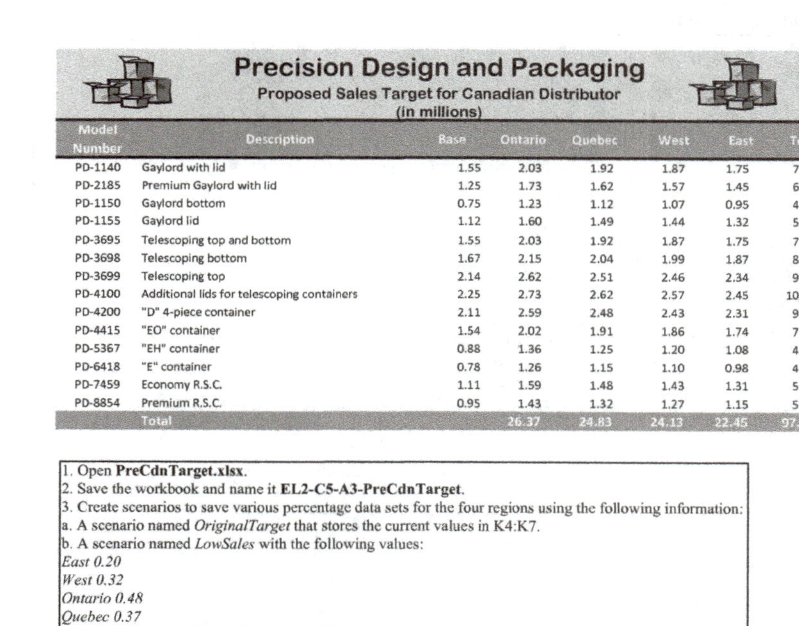

Precision Design and Packaging

Proposed Sales Target for Canadian Distributor

(in millions)

Model Number	Description	Base	Ontario	Quebec	West	East	Total
PD-1140	Gaylord with lid	1.55	2.03	1.92	1.87	1.75	7.57
PD-2185	Premium Gaylord with lid	1.25	1.73	1.62	1.57	1.45	6.37
PD-1150	Gaylord bottom	0.75	1.23	1.12	1.07	0.95	4.37
PD-1155	Gaylord lid	1.12	1.60	1.49	1.44	1.32	5.85
PD-3695	Telescoping top and bottom	1.55	2.03	1.92	1.87	1.75	7.57
PD-3698	Telescoping bottom	1.67	2.15	2.04	1.99	1.87	8.05
PD-3699	Telescoping top	2.14	2.62	2.51	2.46	2.34	9.93
PD-4100	Additional lids for telescoping containers	2.25	2.73	2.62	2.57	2.45	10.37
PD-4200	"D" 4-piece container	2.11	2.59	2.48	2.43	2.31	9.81
PD-4415	"EO" container	1.54	2.02	1.91	1.86	1.74	7.53
PD-5367	"EH" container	0.88	1.36	1.25	1.20	1.08	4.89
PD-6418	"E" container	0.78	1.26	1.15	1.10	0.98	4.49
PD-7459	Economy R.S.C.	1.11	1.59	1.48	1.43	1.31	5.81
PD-8854	Premium R.S.C.	0.95	1.43	1.32	1.27	1.15	5.17
	Total		26.37	24.83	24.13	22.45	97.78

Sales Target Assumptions	
East	0.20
West	0.32
Ontario	0.48
Quebec	0.37

4. Show the LowSales scenario and then print the worksheet.

1. Open **PreCdnTarget.xlsx**.
2. Save the workbook and name it **EL2-C5-A3-PreCdnTarget**.
3. Create scenarios to save various percentage data sets for the four regions using the following information:
a. A scenario named *OriginalTarget* that stores the current values in K4:K7.
b. A scenario named *LowSales* with the following values:
East 0.20
West 0.32
Ontario 0.48
Quebec 0.37
c. A scenario named *HighSales* with the following values:
East 0.36
West 0.58
Ontario 0.77
Quebec 0.63

EL2-C5-A3-PreCdnTarget(A3,Step4).xlsx

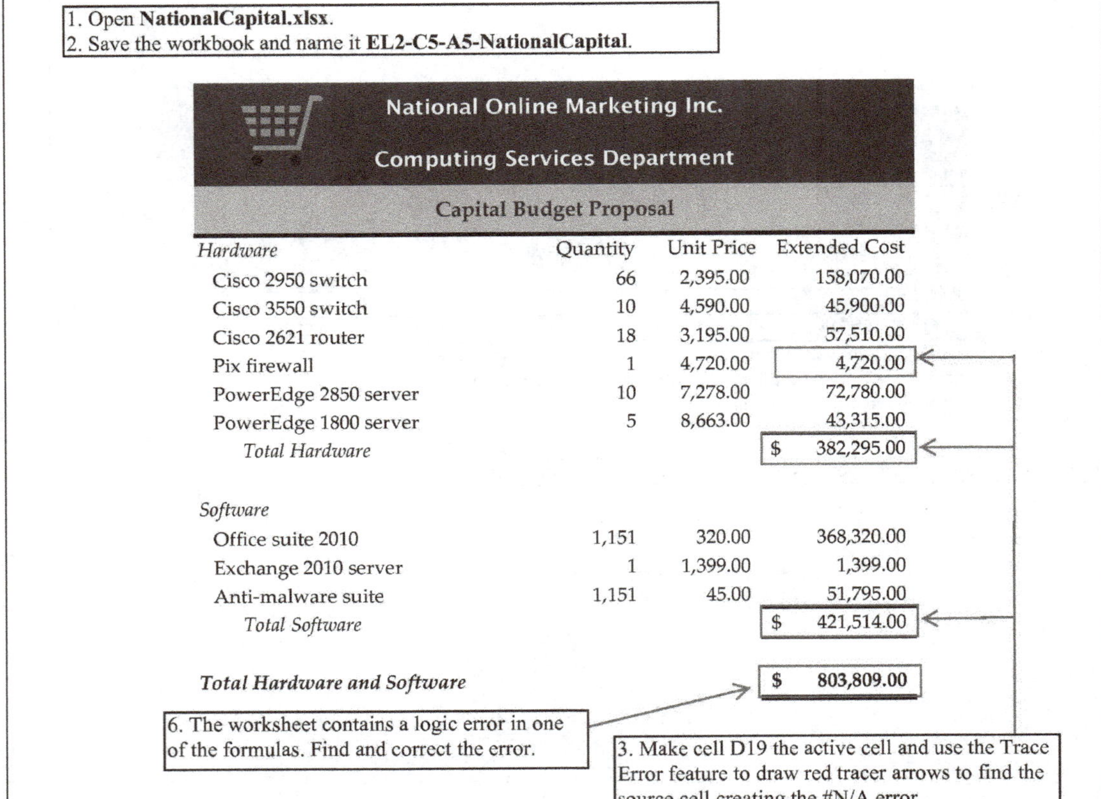

1. Open **NationalCapital.xlsx**.
2. Save the workbook and name it **EL2-C5-A5-NationalCapital**.

National Online Marketing Inc.

Computing Services Department

Capital Budget Proposal

Hardware	Quantity	Unit Price	Extended Cost
Cisco 2950 switch	66	2,395.00	158,070.00
Cisco 3550 switch	10	4,590.00	45,900.00
Cisco 2621 router	18	3,195.00	57,510.00
Pix firewall	1	4,720.00	4,720.00
PowerEdge 2850 server	10	7,278.00	72,780.00
PowerEdge 1800 server	5	8,663.00	43,315.00
Total Hardware			$ 382,295.00
Software			
Office suite 2010	1,151	320.00	368,320.00
Exchange 2010 server	1	1,399.00	1,399.00
Anti-malware suite	1,151	45.00	51,795.00
Total Software			$ 421,514.00
Total Hardware and Software			**$ 803,809.00**

6. The worksheet contains a logic error in one of the formulas. Find and correct the error.

3. Make cell D19 the active cell and use the Trace Error feature to draw red tracer arrows to find the source cell creating the #N/A error.

EL2-C5-A5-NationalCapital(A5).xlsx

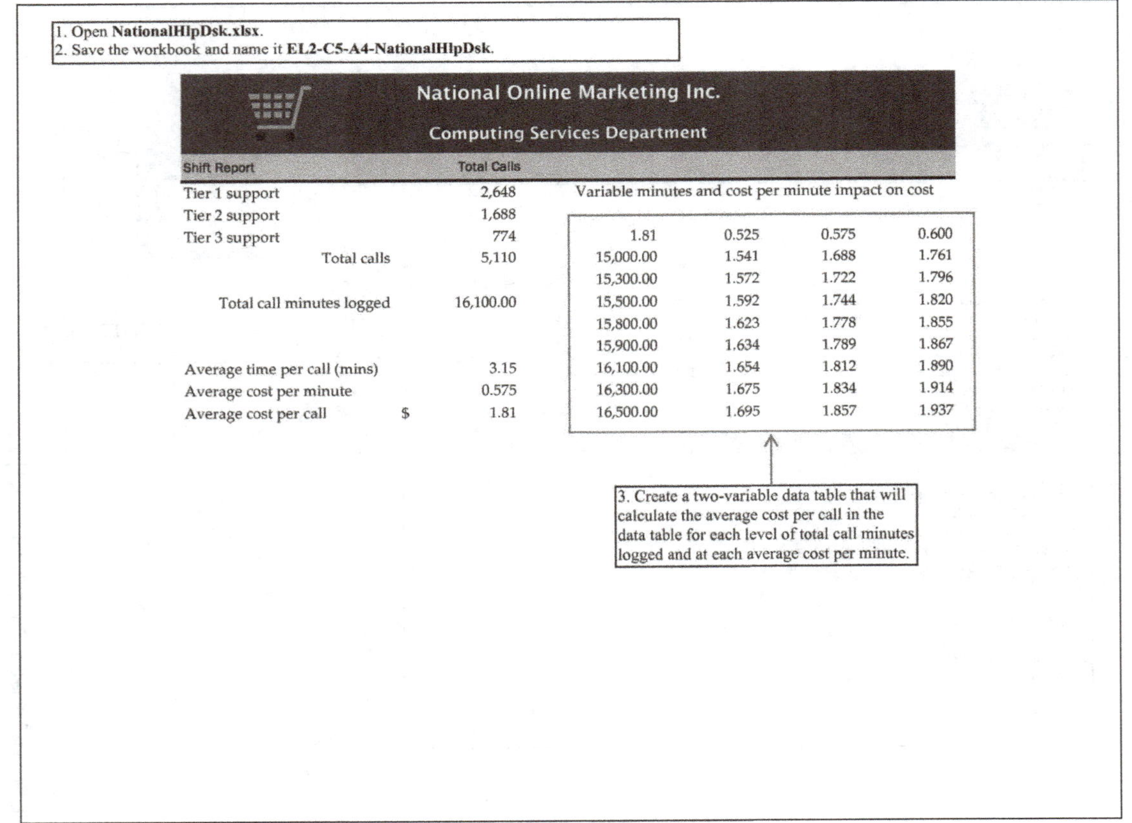

1. Open **NationalHlpDsk.xlsx**.
2. Save the workbook and name it **EL2-C5-A4-NationalHlpDsk**.

National Online Marketing Inc.

Computing Services Department

Shift Report		Total Calls
Tier 1 support		2,648
Tier 2 support		1,688
Tier 3 support		774
Total calls		5,110
Total call minutes logged		16,100.00
Average time per call (mins)		3.15
Average cost per minute		0.575
Average cost per call	$	1.81

Variable minutes and cost per minute impact on cost

1.81	0.525	0.575	0.600
15,000.00	1.541	1.688	1.761
15,300.00	1.572	1.722	1.796
15,500.00	1.592	1.744	1.820
15,800.00	1.623	1.778	1.855
15,900.00	1.634	1.789	1.867
16,100.00	1.654	1.812	1.890
16,300.00	1.675	1.834	1.914
16,500.00	1.695	1.857	1.937

3. Create a two-variable data table that will calculate the average cost per call in the data table for each level of total call minutes logged and at each average cost per minute.

EL2-C5-A4-NationalHlpDsk(A4).xlsx

Scenario Summary				
	Current Values:	Low Rate Increase	Mid Rate Increase	High Rate Increase
Changing Cells:				
BaseRate	18.00	20.00	22.00	24.00
Result Cells:	***Monthly revenue for each lesson assuming no change in number of registered students***			
BasicTheory	180.00	200.00	220.00	240.00
BegRock	270.00	300.00	330.00	360.00
IntRock	176.00	192.00	208.00	224.00
AdvRock	104.00	112.00	120.00	128.00
BegJazz	324.00	360.00	396.00	432.00
DevJazz	220.00	240.00	260.00	280.00
SinglePedalBeats	396.00	440.00	484.00	528.00
SinglePedalFills	270.00	300.00	330.00	360.00
BassDoubles	352.00	384.00	416.00	448.00
MonthlyRevTota	**2,292.00**	**2,528.00**	**2,764.00**	**3,000.00**

Notes: Current Values column represents values of changing cells at time Scenario Summary Report was created. Changing cells for each scenario are highlighted in green.

EL2-C5-VB2-Lessons(VB2).xlsx

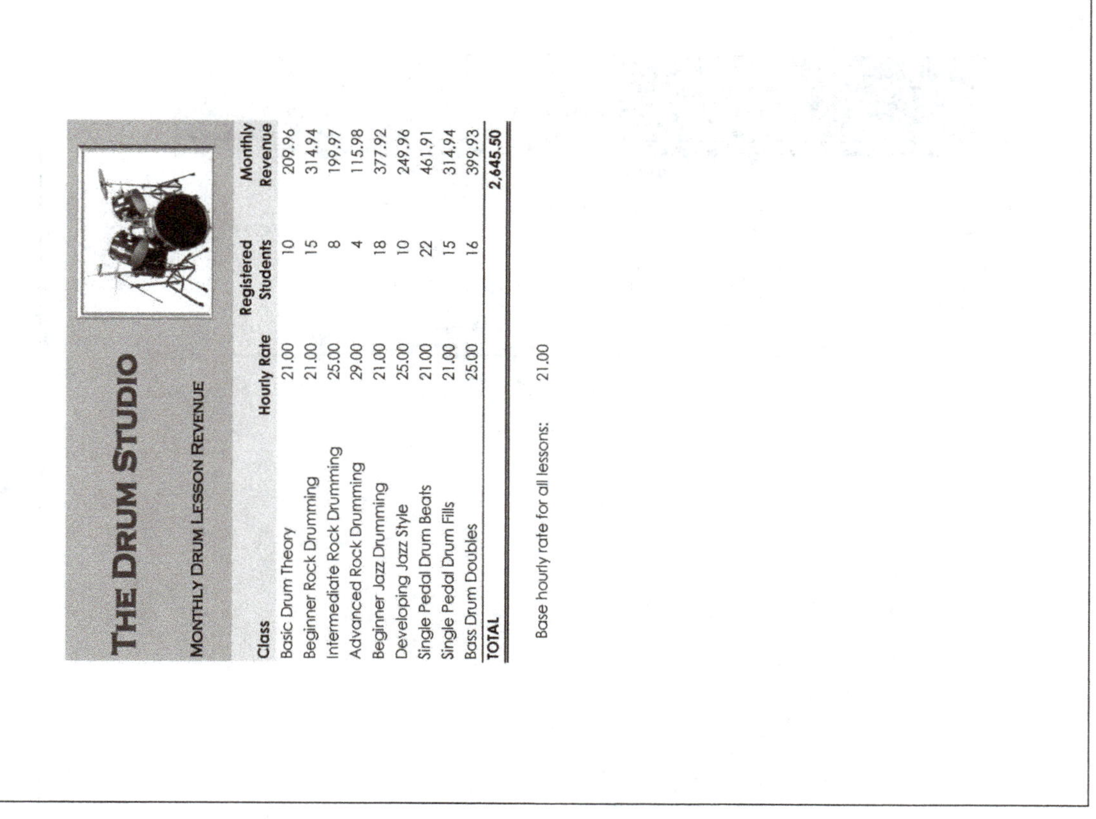

THE DRUM STUDIO

MONTHLY DRUM LESSON REVENUE

Class	Hourly Rate	Registered Students	Monthly Revenue
Basic Drum Theory	21.00	10	209.96
Beginner Rock Drumming	21.00	15	314.94
Intermediate Rock Drumming	25.00	8	199.97
Advanced Rock Drumming	29.00	4	115.98
Beginner Jazz Drumming	21.00	18	377.92
Developing Jazz Style	25.00	10	249.96
Single Pedal Drum Beats	21.00	22	461.91
Single Pedal Drum Fills	21.00	15	314.94
Bass Drum Doubles	25.00	16	399.93
TOTAL			**2,645.50**

Base hourly rate for all lessons: 21.00

EL2-C5-VB1-Lessons(VB1).xlsx

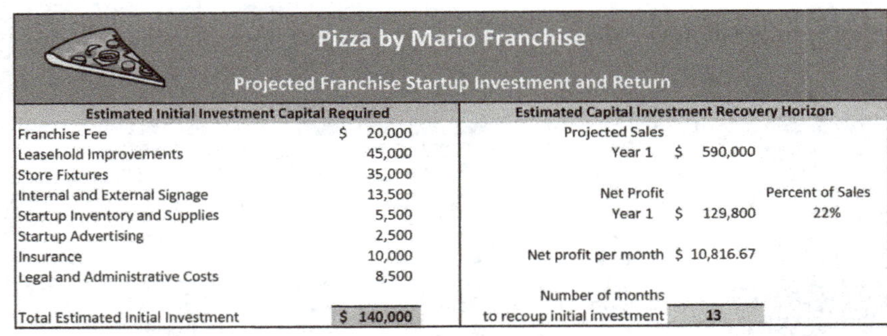

Pizza by Mario Franchise

Projected Franchise Startup Investment and Return

Estimated Initial Investment Capital Required		Estimated Capital Investment Recovery Horizon		
Franchise Fee	$ 20,000	Projected Sales		
Leasehold Improvements	45,000	Year 1	$ 590,000	
Store Fixtures	35,000			
Internal and External Signage	13,500	Net Profit		Percent of Sales
Startup Inventory and Supplies	5,500	Year 1	$ 129,800	22%
Startup Advertising	2,500			
Insurance	10,000	Net profit per month	$ 10,816.67	
Legal and Administrative Costs	8,500			
		Number of months		
Total Estimated Initial Investment	$ 140,000	to recoup initial investment	13	

EL2-C5-CS-P2-PBMStartup(P2-LowestValue).xlsx

Pizza by Mario Franchise

Projected Franchise Startup Investment and Return

Estimated Initial Investment Capital Required		Estimated Capital Investment Recovery Horizon		
Franchise Fee	$ 20,000	Projected Sales		
Leasehold Improvements	45,000	Year 1	$ 699,971	
Store Fixtures	35,000			
Internal and External Signage	13,500	Net Profit		Percent of Sales
Startup Inventory and Supplies	5,500	Year 1	$ 139,994	20%
Startup Advertising	2,500			
Insurance	10,000	Net profit per month	$ 11,666.18	
Legal and Administrative Costs	8,500			
		Number of months		
Total Estimated Initial Investment	$ 140,000	to recoup initial investment	12	

EL2-C5-CS-P1-PBMStartup(P1).xlsx

Pizza by Mario Franchise

Projected Franchise Startup Investment and Return

Estimated Initial Investment Capital Required		Estimated Capital Investment Recovery Horizon		
Franchise Fee	$ 20,000	Projected Sales		
Leasehold Improvements	45,000	Year 1	$ 590,000	
Store Fixtures	35,000			
Internal and External Signage	13,500	Net Profit		Percent of Sales
Startup Inventory and Supplies	5,500	Year 1	$ 129,800	22%
Startup Advertising	2,500			
Insurance	10,000	Net profit per month	$ 10,816.67	
Legal and Administrative Costs	8,500			
		Number of months		
Total Estimated Initial Investment	$ 140,000	to recoup initial investment	13	

Find & Select - Formulas or
Go To Special - Formulas

EL2-C5-CS-P3-PBMStartup(P3).xlsx

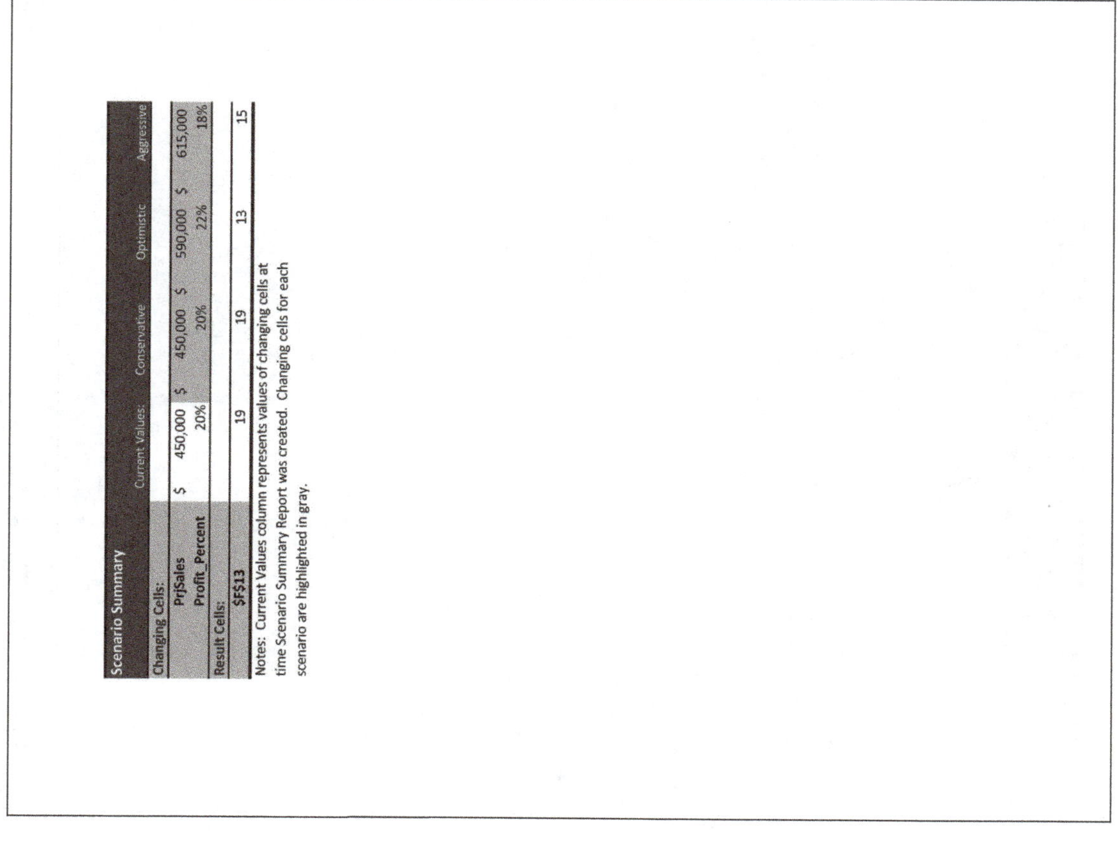

Scenario Summary

	Current Values:	Conservative	Optimistic	Aggressive
Changing Cells:				
PrjSales	$ 450,000	$ 450,000	$ 590,000	$ 615,000
Profit_Percent	20%	20%	22%	18%
Result Cells:				
$F$13	19	19	13	15

Notes: Current Values column represents values of changing cells at time Scenario Summary Report was created. Changing cells for each scenario are highlighted in gray.

EL2-C5-CS-P2-PBMStartup(P2-SummaryReport).xlsx

Pizza by Mario Franchise

Monthly Loan Payment

Bank	TD Canada Trust	
URL	http://www.tdcanadatrust.com/products-services/banking/personal-credit/loans.jsp	
TD Prime Rate		3.0%
Risk %		2.0%
Total Interest Rate		5.0%
Total Estimated Initial investment	$	140,000
Term (years)		5
Monthly Loan Payment		($2,641.97)

EL2-C5-CS-P4-PBMStartup(P4).xlsx

Excel Level 2, Chapter 6 Model Answers

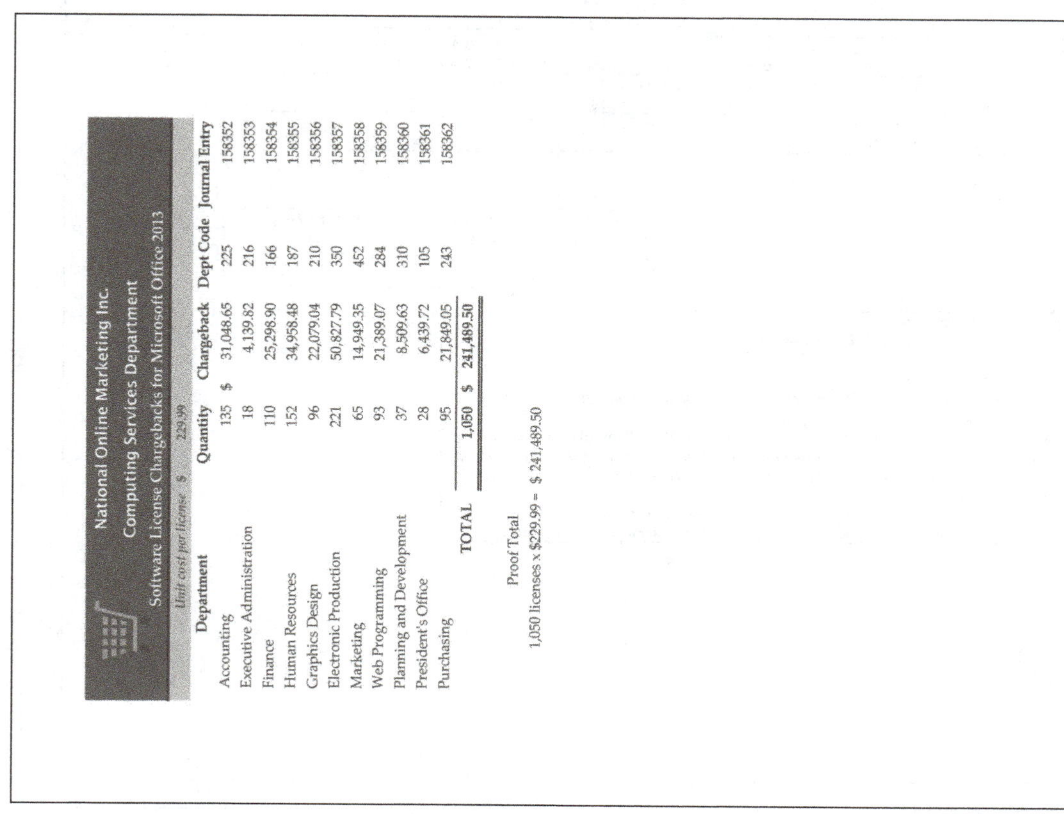

National Online Marketing Inc.
Computing Services Department
Software License Chargebacks for Microsoft Office 2013

Unit cost per license	$ 229.99			
Department	**Quantity**	**Chargeback**	**Dept Code**	**Journal Entry**
Accounting	135	$ 31,048.65	225	158352
Executive Administration	18	4,139.82	216	158353
Finance	110	25,298.90	166	158354
Human Resources	152	34,958.48	187	158355
Graphics Design	96	22,079.04	210	158356
Electronic Production	221	50,827.79	350	158357
Marketing	65	14,949.35	452	158358
Web Programming	93	21,389.07	284	158359
Planning and Development	37	8,509.63	310	158360
President's Office	28	6,439.72	105	158361
Purchasing	95	21,849.05	243	158362
TOTAL	1,050	$ 241,489.50		

Proof Total
1,050 licenses x $229.99 = $ 241,489.50

EL2-C6-A1-NationalLicenses(A1,Step12).xlsx (1 of 2)

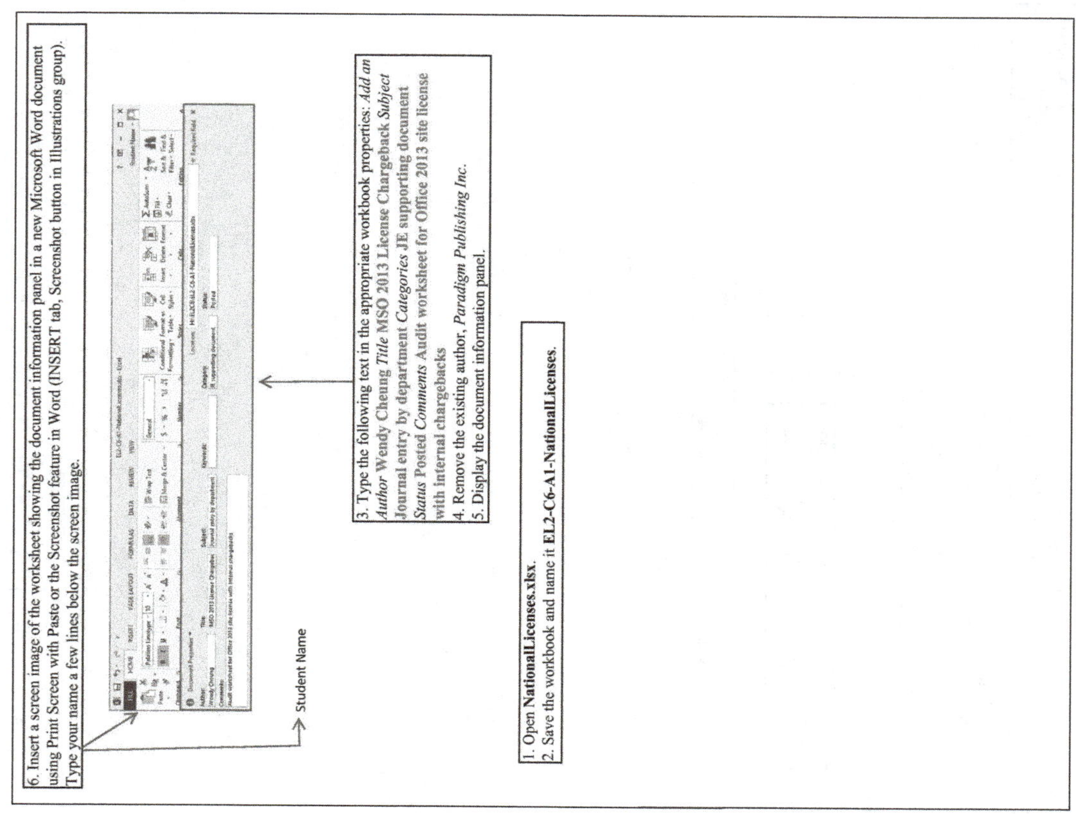

EL2-C6-A1-NationalLicenses(A1,Step8).xlsx

4. Change the user name to *Lorne Moir* and then edit the following cells:
C11: from *4,352* to *5520*
C18: from *15,241* to *15960*

Action Number	Date	Time	Who	Change	Sheet	Range	New Value	Old Value	Action Type	Losing Action
1	4/4/2013	6:54 PM	Lorne Moir	Cell Change	Sheet1	C11	5,520.00	4,352.00		
2	4/4/2013	6:54 PM	Lorne Moir	Cell Change	Sheet1	C18	15,960.00	15,241.00		
3	4/4/2013	6:58 PM	Gerri Gonzales	Cell Change	Sheet1	F4	5,126.00	3,845.00		
4	4/4/2013	6:58 PM	Gerri Gonzales	Cell Change	Sheet1	F9	9,320.00	7,745.00		

The history ends with the changes saved on 4/4/2013 at 6:58 PM.

7. Change the user name to *Gerri Gonzales,* open **EL2-C6-A2-PreMfgTargets.xlsx**, and then edit the following cells:
F4: from *3,845* to *5126*
F9: from *7,745* to *9320*

1. Open **PreMfgTargets.xlsx**.
2. Save the workbook and name it **EL2-C6-A2-PreMfgTargets**.
3. Share the workbook.
5. Save the workbook.
6. Open a new instance of Excel. ***Note: Refer to Project 2c to open a new instance of Excel.***
8. Save the workbook.
9. Create a history sheet with a record of the changes made to the data by all of the users.
10. Print the history sheet. ***Note: If you submit your assignment work electronically, create a copy of the history sheet in a new workbook, since the history sheet is automatically deleted when the file is saved.***
11. Save and then close both instances of **EL2-C6-A2-PreMfgTargets.xlsx**.
12. Change the user name back to the original user name for the computer you are using.

EL2-C6-A2-PreMfgTargets(A2,Step10).xlsx

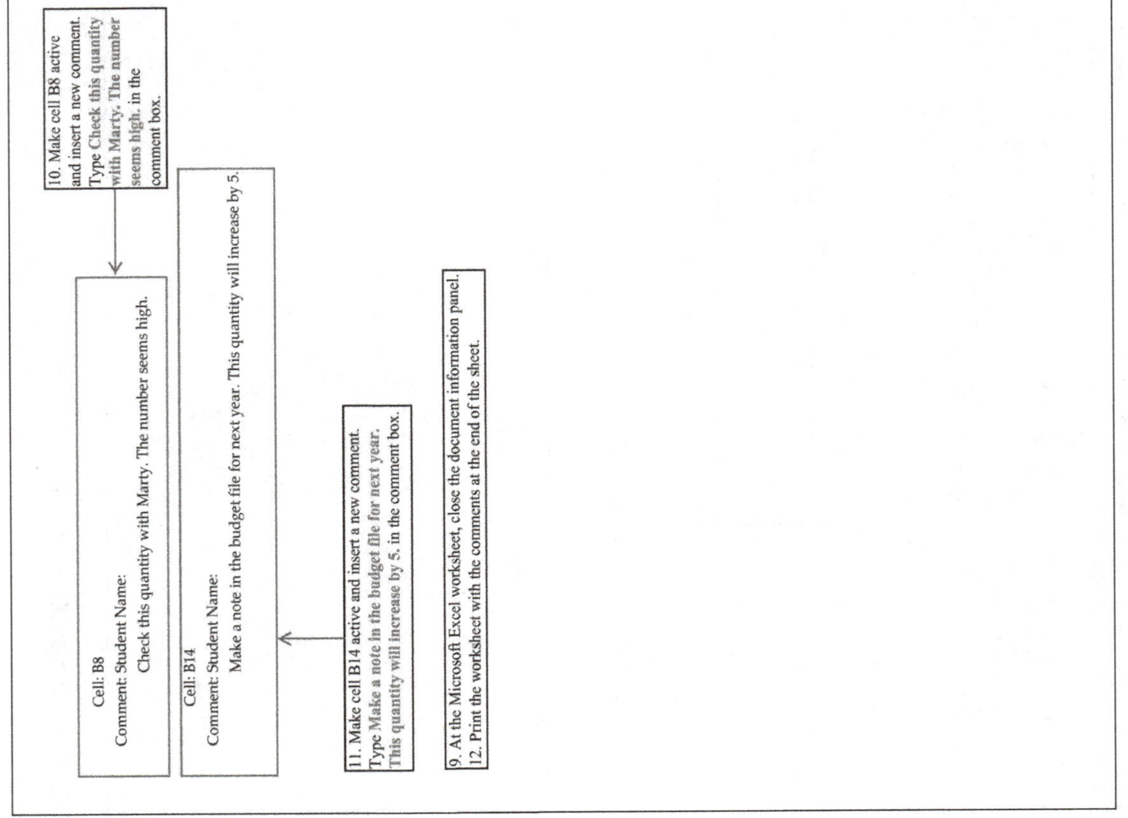

EL2-C6-A1-NationalLicenses(A1,Step12).xlsx (2 of 2)

10. Print the 2015MfgTargets worksheet.

Precision Design and Packaging

Bulk Container 2015 Manufacturing Units (in thousands)

Model Number	Description	East	West	North	South	Total
PD-1140	Gaylord with lid	2,531	3,755	4,215	3,845	14,346
PD-2185	Premium Gaylord with lid	2,251	3,157	4,185	3,214	12,807
PD-1150	Gaylord bottom	5,234	5,584	6,145	4,832	21,795
PD-1155	Gaylord lid	5,234	5,584	6,145	4,832	21,795
PD-3695	Telescoping top and bottom	10,253	12,458	11,254	14,853	48,818
PD-3698	Telescoping bottom	8,532	8,863	9,145	7,745	34,285
PD-3699	Telescoping top	7,541	8,651	8,842	7,652	32,686
PD-4100	Additional lids for telescoping containers	4,352	3,487	3,417	4,832	16,088
PD-4200	"D" 4-piece container	3,475	4,278	5,513	4,862	18,128
PD-4415	"EO" container	3,251	4,577	5,914	5,142	18,884
PD-5367	"EH" container	2,534	3,014	4,437	5,684	15,669
PD-6418	"E" container	6,523	6,988	7,214	6,348	27,073
PD-7459	Economy R.S.C.	6,325	6,942	6,845	6,512	26,624
PD-8854	Premium R.S.C.	5,214	5,748	6,145	6,327	23,434
PD-9101	Corrugated pads 15 x 15	15,241	18,241	16,854	17,458	67,794
PD-9105	Corrugated pads 20 x 12	16,325	19,652	22,418	20,463	78,858
PD-9110	Corrugated pads 24 x 18	12,453	15,874	17,698	18,496	64,521
PD-9115	Corrugated pads 30 x 30	8,653	8,846	9,154	7,763	34,416
	Total	125,922	145,699	155,540	150,860	578,021

Proof of Total 578,021

EL2-C6-A6-PreMfgTargets(A6,Step10).xlsx

5. Change the user name to *Grant Antone* and then edit the following cells:
D4: from *3,251* to *3755*
D17: from *5,748* to *6176*

Action Number	Date	Time	Who	Change	Sheet	Range	New Value	Old Value	Action Type	Losing Action
1	4/4/2013	7:39 PM	Grant Antone	Cell Change	2015MfgTargets	D4	3,755.00	3,251.00		
2	4/4/2013	7:39 PM	Grant Antone	Cell Change	2015MfgTargets	D17	6,176.00	5,748.00		
3	4/4/2013	7:39 PM	Jean Kocsis	Cell Change	2015MfgTargets	E6	5,748.00	6,145.00		
4	4/4/2013	7:39 PM	Jean Kocsis	Cell Change	2015MfgTargets	E11	3,417.00	2,214.00		

The history ends with the changes saved on 4/4/2013 at 7:39 PM.

6. Save the workbook, change the user name to *Jean Kocsis*, and then edit the following cells:
E6: from *6,145* to *5748*
E11: from *2,214* to *3417*

1. Open **EL2-C6-A5-PreMfgTargets.xlsx**.
2. Save the workbook and name it **EL2-C6-A6-PreMfgTargets.**
3. Unprotect the workbook structure so that new sheets can be added, deleted, renamed, or copied.
4. Turn on the Track Changes feature.
7. Save the workbook and then change the user name back to the original user name for the computer you are using.
8. Accept and Reject the changes in the cells as follows: D4: Accept
D17: Reject
E6: Reject
E11: Accept
9. Create and print a history sheet of the changes made to the worksheet. ***Note: If you submit your assignment work electronically, create a copy of the history sheet in a new workbook, since the history sheet is automatically deleted when the file is saved.***

EL2-C6-A6-PreMfgTargets(A6,Step9).xlsx

Action Number	Date	Time	Who	Change	Sheet	Range	New Value	Old Value	Action Type
1	11/11/2015	4:06 PM	Erin Haviland	Cell Change	Sheet1	C4	$17.25	$16.50	
2	11/11/2015	4:06 PM	Erin Haviland	Cell Change	Sheet1	C7	$8.50	$8.25	
3	11/11/2015	4:06 PM	Erin Haviland	Cell Change	Sheet1	C10	$22.50	$20.00	
4	11/11/2015	4:06 PM	Erin Haviland	Cell Change	Sheet1	C14	$27.50	$28.50	
5	11/11/2015	4:06 PM	Erin Haviland	Cell Change	Sheet1	B7	25 minute trail walk	30 minute trail walk	

The history ends with the changes saved on 11/11/2015 at 4:06 PM.

EL2-C6-VB-PawsParadise(VB,Step5).xlsx (1 of 2)

Action Number	Date	Time	Who	Change	Sheet	Range	New Value	Old Value	Action Type	Losing Action
1	11/11/2015	4:03 PM	Erin Haviland	Cell Change	Sheet1	C4	$17.25	$16.50		
2	11/11/2015	4:03 PM	Erin Haviland	Cell Change	Sheet1	C7	$8.50	$8.25		
3	11/11/2015	4:03 PM	Erin Haviland	Cell Change	Sheet1	C10	$22.50	$20.00		
4	11/11/2015	4:03 PM	Erin Haviland	Cell Change	Sheet1	C14	$27.50	$28.50		
5	11/11/2015	4:03 PM	Erin Haviland	Cell Change	Sheet1	B7	25 minute trail walk	30 minute trail walk		

The history ends with the changes saved on 11/11/2015 at 4:03 PM.

EL2-C6-VB-PawsParadise(VB,History).xlsx

Action Number	Date	Time	Who	Change	Sheet	Range	New Value	Old Value	Action Type	Losing Action
1	6/25/2013	8:25 AM	Yolanda	Cell Change	Sheet1	E7	Jae-Dong Han	Perry Thibeault		
2	6/25/2013	8:25 AM	Yolanda	Cell Change	Sheet1	E18	Leslie Posno	Kayla Racicot		
3	6/25/2013	8:25 AM	Nicola	Cell Change	Sheet1	D4	February	January		
4	6/25/2013	8:25 AM	Nicola	Cell Change	Sheet1	D10	December	June		

The history ends with the changes saved on 6/25/2013 at 8:25 AM.

EL2-C6-CS-P2-PBMNewFranchises(P2-HistorySheet).xlsx

Losing Action

EL2-C6-VB-PawsParadise(VB,Step5).xlsx (2 of 2)

Pizza by Mario Franchise

Target Franchise Startups for 2015 by State

City	State	Store	Month	Prospective Franchisee
Chicago	Illinois	135	February	Doranda Pepelassis
Chicago	Illinois	136	March	Adrian Vosburg
Peoria	Illinois	137	May	Ana Peterson
Rockford	Illinois	138	July	Jae-Dong Han
Ft. Wayne	Indiana	139	January	Corporate-owned
Indianapolis	Indiana	140	March	Dario Galiano
Indianapolis	Indiana	141	December	Gordon Lesniewski
Lexington	Kentucky	142	February	Steve Cummings
Lexington	Kentucky	143	June	Antonio Barbosa
Louisville	Kentucky	144	May	Terri Enriquez
Louisville	Kentucky	145	September	Keith Lawrence
St. Louis	Missouri	146	January	Corporate-owned
St. Louis	Missouri	147	October	Tori Scarpelli
Springfield	Missouri	148	February	Alice Wexler
Bloomington	Minnesota	149	January	Leslie Posno
Bloomington	Minnesota	150	July	Corporate-owned
Minneapolis	Minnesota	151	August	Art Mickolwin
Minneapolis	Minnesota	152	September	Amanda Gourdreau
St. Paul	Minnesota	153	October	Gina Carvalo
St. Paul	Minnesota	154	November	George Lazenby

EL2-C6-CS-P2-PBMNewFranchises(P2-TrackedChanges).xlsx

Pizza by Mario Franchise

Target Franchise Startups for 2015 by State

City	State	Store	Month	Prospective Franchisee
Chicago	Illinois	135	February	[illegible]
Chicago	Illinois	136	March	Ad
Peoria	Illinois	137	May	Ar
Rockford	Illinois	138	July	Ja
Ft. Wayne	Indiana	139	January	Corporate-owned
Indianapolis	Indiana	140	March	Dario Galiano
Indianapolis	Indiana	141	December	Gordon Lesniewski
Lexington	Kentucky	142	February	Steve Cummings
Lexington	Kentucky	143	June	[illegible]
Louisville	Kentucky	144	May	Te
Louisville	Kentucky	145	September	Ke
St. Louis	Missouri	146	January	Co
St. Louis	Missouri	147	October	Tori Scarpelli
Springfield	Missouri	148	February	Alice Wexler
Bloomington	Minnesota	149	January	Leslie Posno
Bloomington	Minnesota	150	July	Corporate-owned
Minneapolis	Minnesota	151	August	[illegible]
Minneapolis	Minnesota	152	September	Ar
St. Paul	Minnesota	153	October	Gi
St. Paul	Minnesota	154	November	Ge

Leonard Scriver: Opening a second store in Chicago is more likely to occur in April.

Leonard Scriver: Move the opening to June, as resources at the head office will be stretched in May.

Leonard Scriver: Try to open this franchise at the same time as store 151.

EL2-C6-CS-P3-PBM-LScriver(P3).xlsx

Excel Level 2, Chapter 7 Model Answers

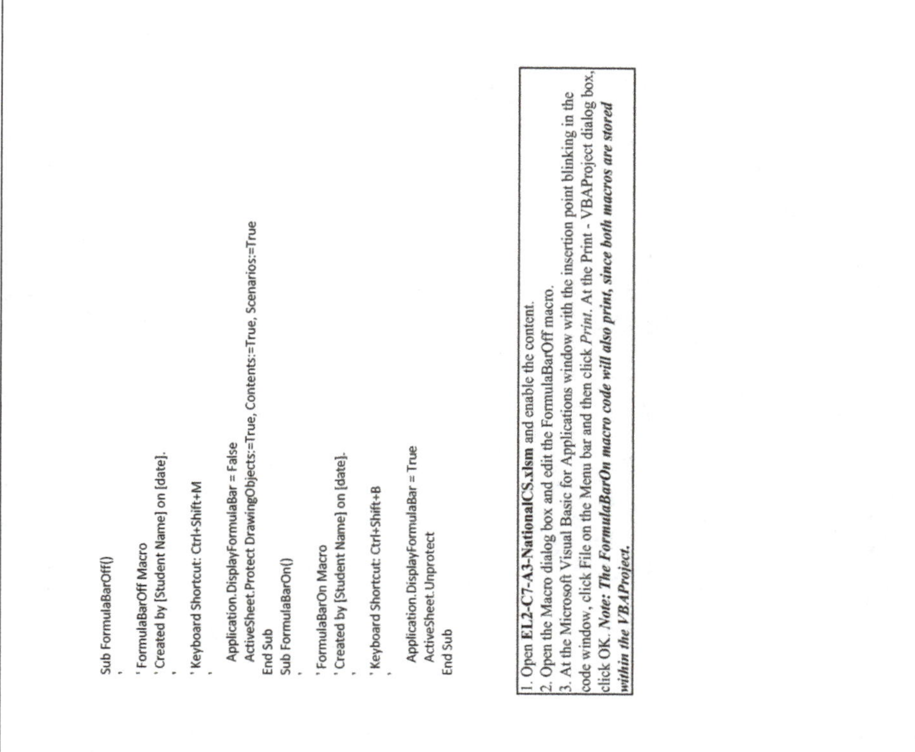

```
Sub FormulaBarOff()
'
' FormulaBarOff Macro
' Created by [Student Name] on [date].
'
' Keyboard Shortcut: Ctrl+Shift+M
'
    Application.DisplayFormulaBar = False
    ActiveSheet.Protect DrawingObjects:=True, Contents:=True, Scenarios:=True
End Sub
Sub FormulaBarOn()
'
' FormulaBarOn Macro
' Created by [Student Name] on [date].
'
' Keyboard Shortcut: Ctrl+Shift+B
'
    Application.DisplayFormulaBar = True
    ActiveSheet.Unprotect
End Sub
```

1. Open **EL2-C7-A3-NationalCS.xlsm** and enable the content.
2. Open the Macro dialog box and edit the FormulaBarOff macro.
3. At the Microsoft Visual Basic for Applications window with the insertion point blinking in the code window, click File on the Menu bar and then click *Print*. At the Print - VBAProject dialog box, click OK. ***Note: The FormulaBarOn macro code will also print, since both macros are stored within the VBAProject.***

EL2-C7-A4-NationalCS(A4,Step3).xlsx

National Online Marketing Inc.

Accounting Department

General Ledger Journal Entry Documentation

Internal Chargeback for Computing Services Department

Batch Technical Service Requests (TSRs)

	Parts	Labor	Total	CSDept-TSR	Dept Code	GL Account Number	Journal Entry Number
Accounting	$ 557.45	$ 820.00	$ 1,377.45	CS-4020	225	010501	159021
Executive Administration	1,057.45	1,550.00	2,607.45	CS-4021	216	010510	159022
Finance	355.22	225.00	580.22	CS-4022	166	010542	159023
Human Resources	187.42	85.50	272.92	CS-4023	187	010553	159024
Graphics Design	637.54	265.75	903.29	CS-4024	210	010555	159025
Electronic Production	857.00	355.00	1,212.00	CS-4025	350	010560	159026
Marketing	14.00	275.50	289.50	CS-4026	452	010575	159027
Web Programming	72.47	65.75	138.22	CS-4027	284	010582	159028
Planning and Development	65.84	55.50	121.34	CS-4028	310	010585	159029
President's Office	154.75	65.50	220.25	CS-4029	105	010590	159030
Purchasing	346.85	255.50	602.35	CS-4030	243	010596	159031
			$ 8,324.99				

1. Open **NationalCS.xlsx**.
2. Save the workbook and name it **EL2-C7-A2-NationalCS**.
3. Press Ctrl + T to run the Ion macro.
4. Press Ctrl + Shift + Q to run the Landscape macro.

EL2-C7-A2-NationalCS(A2).xlsx

4. Click File on the Menu bar and then click *Close and Return to Microsoft Excel.*
5. Close **EL2-C7-A3-NationalCS.xlsm**.
6. Open **MyMacros-StudentName.xlsm** and enable the content.
7. Open the Macro dialog box and edit the Landscape macro.
8. At the Microsoft Visual Basic for Applications window with the insertion point blinking in the code window, click File on the Menu bar and then click *Print*. At the Print - VBAProject dialog box, click OK. ***Note: The Ion macro code will also print, since both macros are stored within the VBAProject.***

```
Sub Landscape()
'
' Landscape Macro
' Created by [Student Name] on [date].
'
' Keyboard Shortcut: Ctrl+Shift+Q
'
    Application.PrintCommunication = False
    With ActiveSheet.PageSetup
        .PrintTitleRows = ""
        .PrintTitleColumns = ""
    End With
    Application.PrintCommunication = True
    ActiveSheet.PageSetup.PrintArea = ""
    Application.PrintCommunication = False
    With ActiveSheet.PageSetup
        .LeftHeader = ""
        .CenterHeader = ""
        .RightHeader = ""
        .LeftFooter = ""
        .CenterFooter = ""
        .RightFooter = ""
        .LeftMargin = Application.InchesToPoints(0.5)
        .RightMargin = Application.InchesToPoints(0.5)
        .TopMargin = Application.InchesToPoints(1)
        .BottomMargin = Application.InchesToPoints(0.5)
        .HeaderMargin = Application.InchesToPoints(0.3)
        .FooterMargin = Application.InchesToPoints(0.3)
        .PrintHeadings = False
        .PrintGridlines = False
        .PrintComments = xlPrintNoComments
        .PrintQuality = 600
        .CenterHorizontally = True
        .CenterVertically = False
        .Orientation = xlLandscape
        .Draft = False
        .PaperSize = xlPaperLetter
        .FirstPageNumber = xlAutomatic
        .Order = xlDownThenOver
        .BlackAndWhite = False
        .Zoom = 100
        .PrintErrors = xlPrintErrorsDisplayed
        .OddAndEvenPagesHeaderFooter = False
        .DifferentFirstPageHeaderFooter = False
        .ScaleWithDocHeaderFooter = True
        .AlignMarginsHeaderFooter = True
        .EvenPage.LeftHeader.Text = ""
        .EvenPage.CenterHeader.Text = ""
```

EL2-C7-A4-MyMacros-StudentName(A4,Step8).xlsx (1 of 2)

```
        .EvenPage.RightHeader.Text = ""
        .EvenPage.LeftFooter.Text = ""
        .EvenPage.CenterFooter.Text = ""
        .EvenPage.RightFooter.Text = ""
        .FirstPage.LeftHeader.Text = ""
        .FirstPage.CenterHeader.Text = ""
        .FirstPage.RightHeader.Text = ""
        .FirstPage.LeftFooter.Text = ""
        .FirstPage.CenterFooter.Text = ""
        .FirstPage.RightFooter.Text = ""
    End With
    Application.PrintCommunication = True
End Sub
Sub Ion()
'
' Ion Macro
' Created by [Student Name] on [date].
'
' Keyboard Shortcut: Ctrl+t
'
    ActiveWorkbook.ApplyTheme ( _
        "C:\Program Files (x86)\Microsoft Office\Document Themes 15\Ion.thmx")
    ActiveWindow.DisplayGridlines = False
End Sub
```

EL2-C7-A4-MyMacros-StudentName(A4,Step8).xlsx (2 of 2)

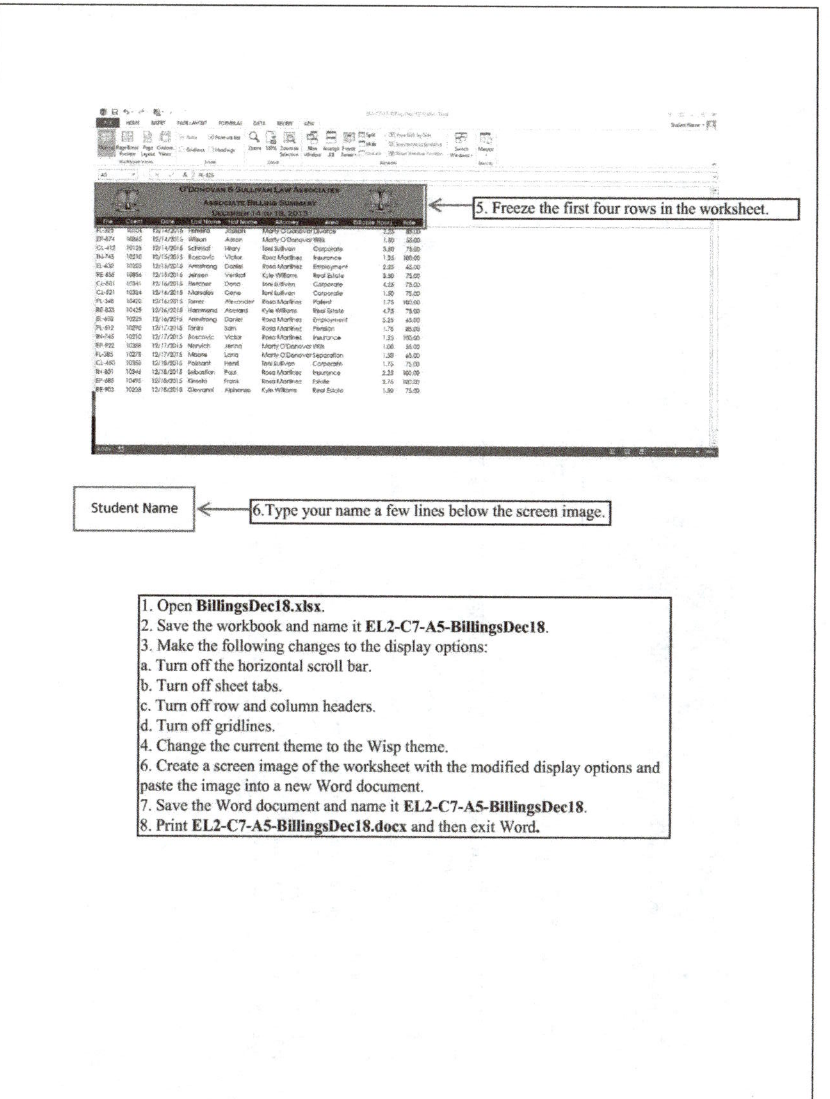

EL2-C7-A5-BillingsDec18(A5).xlsx

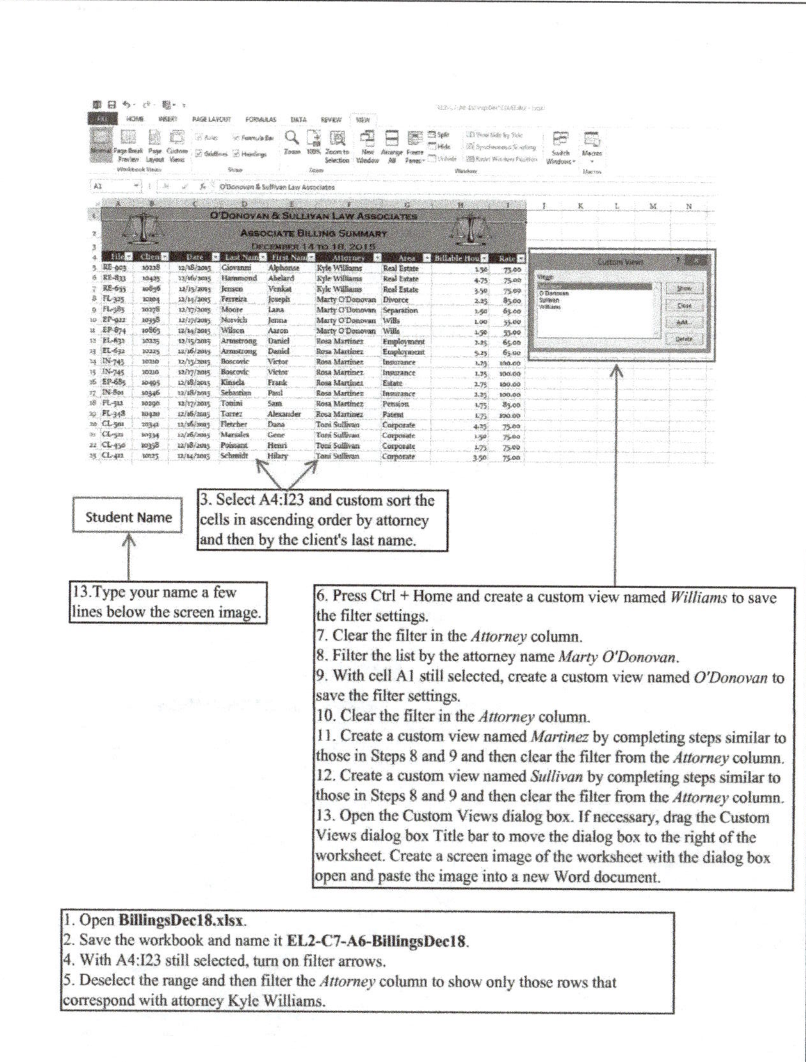

EL2-C7-A6-BillingsDec18(A6).xlsx

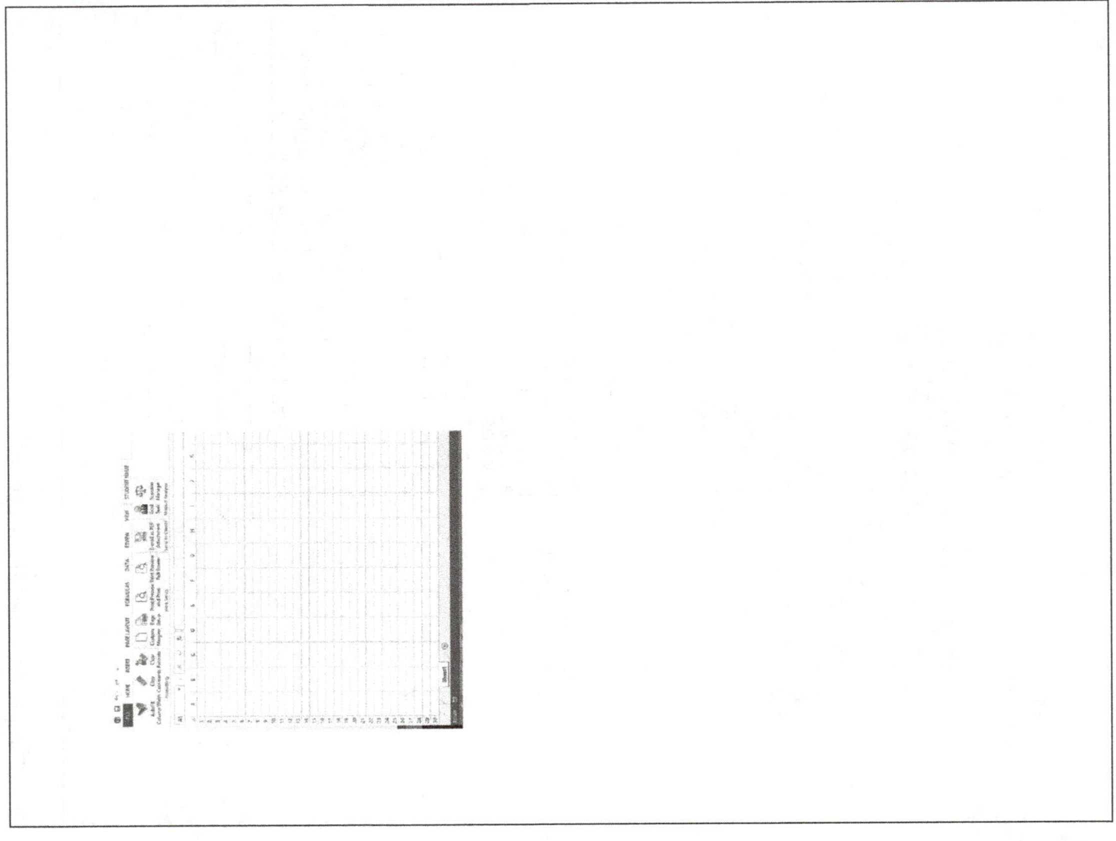

EL2-C7-VB1-MyRibbon(VB1).docx

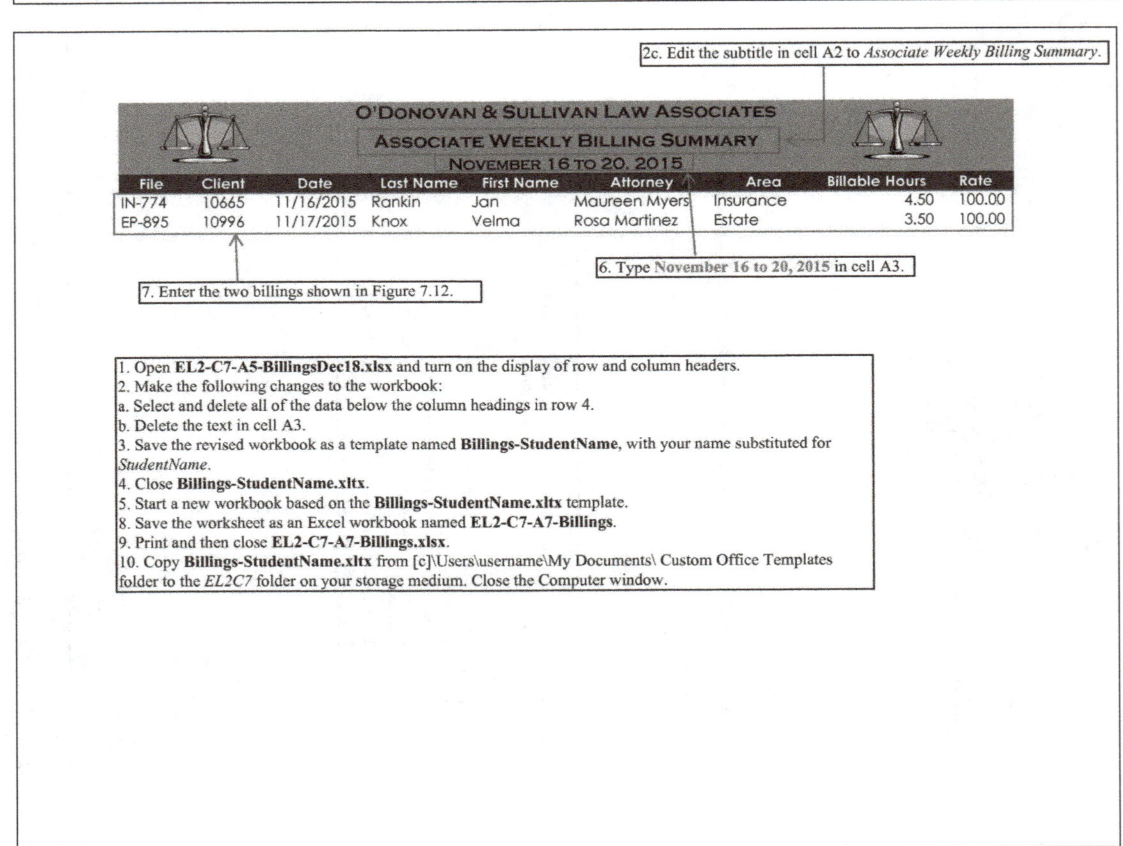

2c. Edit the subtitle in cell A2 to *Associate Weekly Billing Summary*.

O'DONOVAN & SULLIVAN LAW ASSOCIATES

ASSOCIATE WEEKLY BILLING SUMMARY

NOVEMBER 16 TO 20, 2015

File	Client	Date	Last Name	First Name	Attorney	Area	Billable Hours	Rate
IN-774	10665	11/16/2015	Rankin	Jan	Maureen Myers	Insurance	4.50	100.00
EP-895	10996	11/17/2015	Knox	Velma	Rosa Martinez	Estate	3.50	100.00

6. Type November 16 to 20, 2015 in cell A3.

7. Enter the two billings shown in Figure 7.12.

1. Open **EL2-C7-A5-BillingsDec18.xlsx** and turn on the display of row and column headers.
2. Make the following changes to the workbook:
a. Select and delete all of the data below the column headings in row 4.
b. Delete the text in cell A3.
3. Save the revised workbook as a template named **Billings-StudentName**, with your name substituted for *StudentName*.
4. Close **Billings-StudentName.xltx**.
5. Start a new workbook based on the **Billings-StudentName.xltx** template.
8. Save the worksheet as an Excel workbook named **EL2-C7-A7-Billings**.
9. Print and then close **EL2-C7-A7-Billings.xlsx**.
10. Copy **Billings-StudentName.xltx** from [c]\Users\username\My Documents\ Custom Office Templates folder to the *EL2C7* folder on your storage medium. Close the Computer window.

EL2-C7-A7-Billings(A7).xlsx

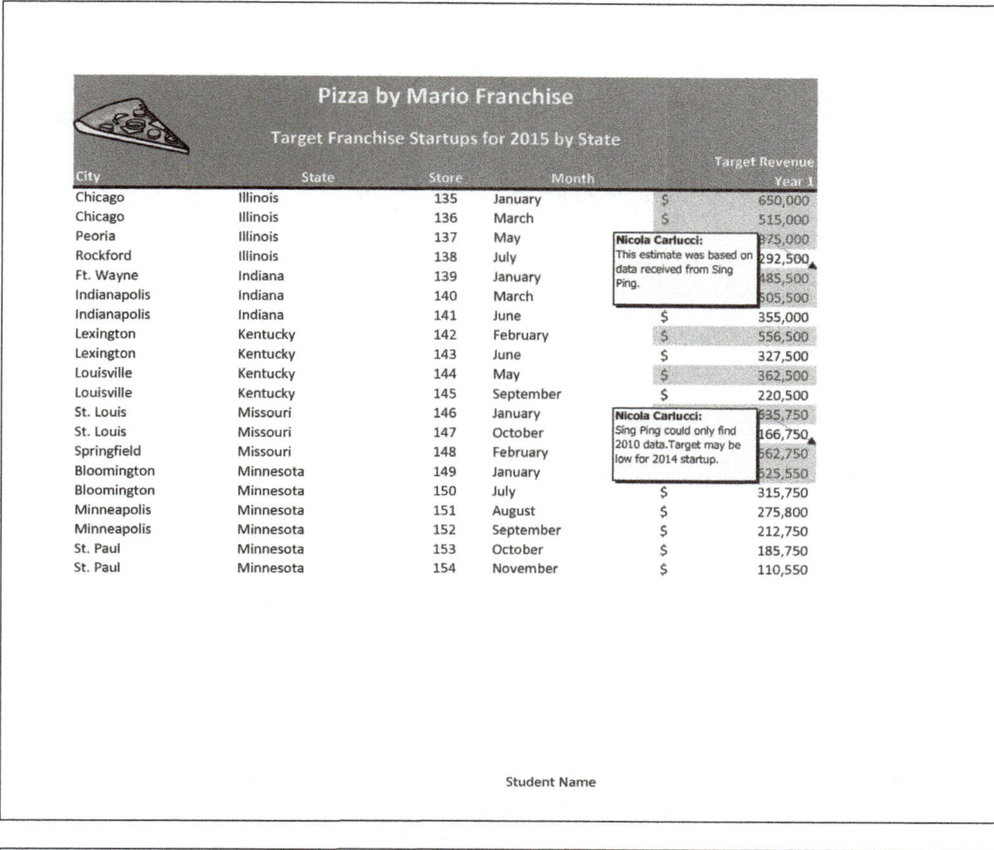

Pizza by Mario Franchise

Target Franchise Startups for 2015 by State

City	State	Store	Month	Target Revenue Year 1
Chicago	Illinois	135	January	$ 650,000
Chicago	Illinois	136	March	$ 515,000
Peoria	Illinois	137	May	75,000
Rockford	Illinois	138	July	292,500
Ft. Wayne	Indiana	139	January	85,500
Indianapolis	Indiana	140	March	05,500
Indianapolis	Indiana	141	June	$ 355,000
Lexington	Kentucky	142	February	$ 556,500
Lexington	Kentucky	143	June	$ 327,500
Louisville	Kentucky	144	May	$ 362,500
Louisville	Kentucky	145	September	$ 220,500
St. Louis	Missouri	146	January	35,750
St. Louis	Missouri	147	October	166,750
Springfield	Missouri	148	February	62,750
Bloomington	Minnesota	149	January	25,550
Bloomington	Minnesota	150	July	$ 315,750
Minneapolis	Minnesota	151	August	$ 275,800
Minneapolis	Minnesota	152	September	$ 212,750
St. Paul	Minnesota	153	October	$ 185,750
St. Paul	Minnesota	154	November	$ 110,550

Nicola Carlucci: This estimate was based on data received from Sing Ping.

Nicola Carlucci: Sing Ping could only find 2010 data.Target may be low for 2014 startup.

Student Name

EL2-C7-CS-P2-PBMNewFranchiseRev(P2).xlsx

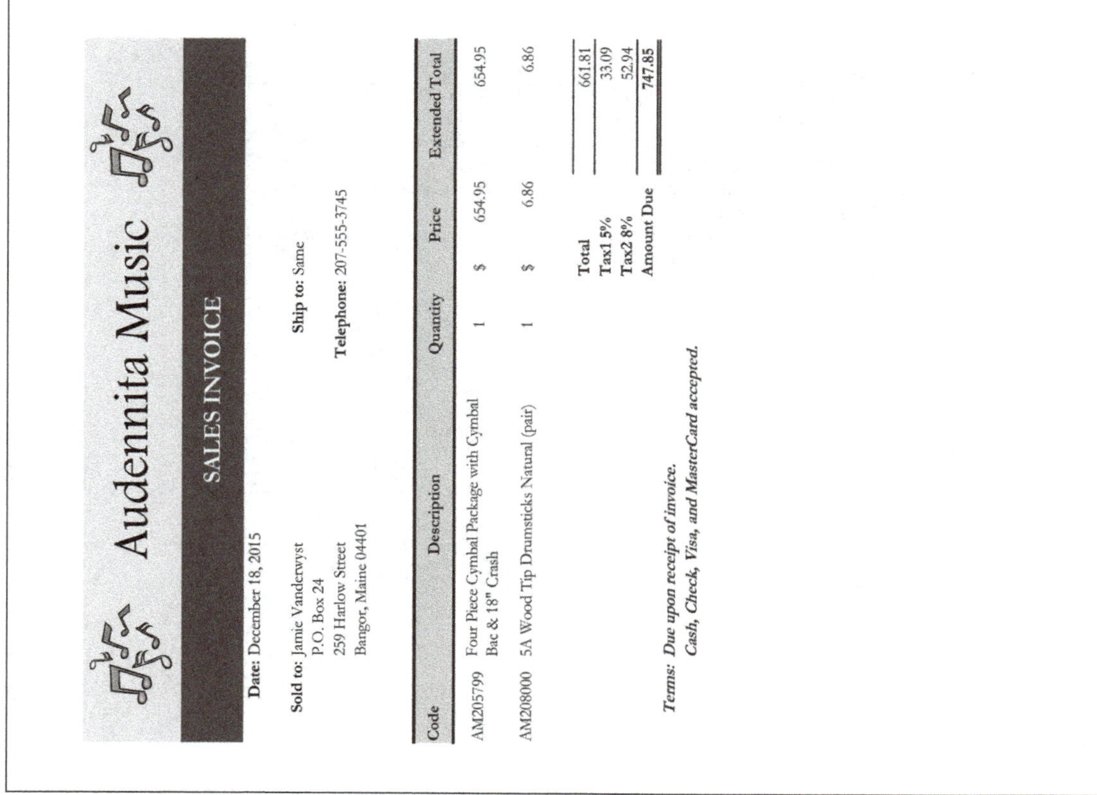

Audennita Music

SALES INVOICE

Date: December 18, 2015

Sold to: Jamie Vanderwyst
P.O. Box 24
259 Harlow Street
Bangor, Maine 04401

Ship to: Same

Telephone: 207-555-3745

Code	Description	Quantity	Price	Extended Total
AM205799	Four Piece Cymbal Package with Cymbal Bac & 18" Crash	1	$ 654.95	654.95
AM208000	5A Wood Tip Drumsticks Natural (pair)	1	$ 6.86	6.86
			Total	661.81
			Tax1 5%	33.09
			Tax2 8%	52.94
			Amount Due	747.85

Terms: Due upon receipt of invoice.
Cash, Check, Visa, and MasterCard accepted.

EL2-C7-VB2-AudennitaInvtoVanderwyst(VB2).xlsx

Macro Name	Shortcut Keys	Description
OrganicTheme	Ctrl + Shift + O	Apply the Organic theme and show all comments
ColumnWidth	Ctrl + Shift + W	Set the active column's width to 20 characters
TopTen	Ctrl + Shift + T	Apply conditional formatting to highlight the top 10 in a selected list. Accept defualt formatting options.
Accounting	Ctrl + Shift + A	Apply the Accounting format with no places after the decimal point
Footer	Ctrl + Shift + F	Create a footer that prints your name centered at the bottom of the worksheet

EL2-C7-CS-P2-NuTrendMacros.xlsm

Excel Level 2, Chapter 8 Model Answers

6. Make UIRateMI the active worksheet.
7. Make cell A6 active. Import the comma delimited text file named ***UIRateMI.csv***.
9. Print the UIRateMI worksheet.

8. Make the following changes to the data:
a. Change the width of column B to 8 characters.
b. Change the width of columns C to F to 15 characters.

Hillsdale Financial Services

Research Services Department

Three-year unemployment data for the State of Michigan

http://data.bls.gov/cgi-bin/surveymost?r5

Series ID LASST26000003

Year	Period	State	Labor Force	Employment	Unemployment	Jobless Rate
2012	Sep	Michigan	4,666,000	4,233,000	432,000	9.3
2012	Aug	Michigan	4,659,000	4,222,000	437,000	9.4
2012	Jul	Michigan	4,661,000	4,239,000	421,000	9
2012	Jun	Michigan	4,663,000	4,261,000	402,000	8.6
2012	May	Michigan	4,664,000	4,269,000	395,000	8.5
2012	Apr	Michigan	4,659,000	4,270,000	389,000	8.3
2012	Mar	Michigan	4,656,000	4,259,000	397,000	8.5
2012	Feb	Michigan	4,647,000	4,238,000	409,000	8.8
2012	Jan	Michigan	4,633,000	4,216,000	417,000	9
2011	Dec	Michigan	4,630,000	4,199,000	431,000	9.3
2011	Nov	Michigan	4,636,000	4,192,000	444,000	9.6
2011	Oct	Michigan	4,642,000	4,183,000	459,000	9.9
2011	Sep	Michigan	4,648,000	4,175,000	473,000	10.2
2011	Aug	Michigan	4,653,000	4,167,000	486,000	10.4
2011	Jul	Michigan	4,658,000	4,164,000	493,000	10.6
2011	Jun	Michigan	4,662,000	4,167,000	495,000	10.6
2011	May	Michigan	4,667,000	4,174,000	493,000	10.6
2011	Apr	Michigan	4,670,000	4,179,000	491,000	10.5
2011	Mar	Michigan	4,673,000	4,181,000	493,000	10.5
2011	Feb	Michigan	4,675,000	4,176,000	499,000	10.7
2011	Jan	Michigan	4,678,000	4,168,000	511,000	10.9
2010	Dec	Michigan	4,684,000	4,158,000	526,000	11.2
2010	Nov	Michigan	4,694,000	4,151,000	543,000	11.6
2010	Oct	Michigan	4,706,000	4,146,000	560,000	11.9
2010	Sep	Michigan	4,718,000	4,145,000	574,000	12.2
2010	Aug	Michigan	4,732,000	4,146,000	586,000	12.4
2010	Jul	Michigan	4,746,000	4,149,000	597,000	12.6
2010	Jun	Michigan	4,760,000	4,152,000	608,000	12.8
2010	May	Michigan	4,772,000	4,153,000	620,000	13
2010	Apr	Michigan	4,782,000	4,151,000	631,000	13.2
2010	Mar	Michigan	4,787,000	4,146,000	642,000	13.4
2010	Feb	Michigan	4,789,000	4,138,000	651,000	13.6
2010	Jan	Michigan	4,789,000	4,130,000	659,000	13.8
2009	Dec	Michigan	4,790,000	4,126,000	664,000	13.9
2009	Nov	Michigan	4,795,000	4,126,000	669,000	14
2009	Oct	Michigan	4,806,000	4,131,000	675,000	14.1
2009	Sep	Michigan	4,821,000	4,139,000	682,000	14.1
2009	Aug	Michigan	4,837,000	4,151,000	685,000	14.2

EL2-C8-A1-HRS(A1,Step9).xlsx (1 of 2)

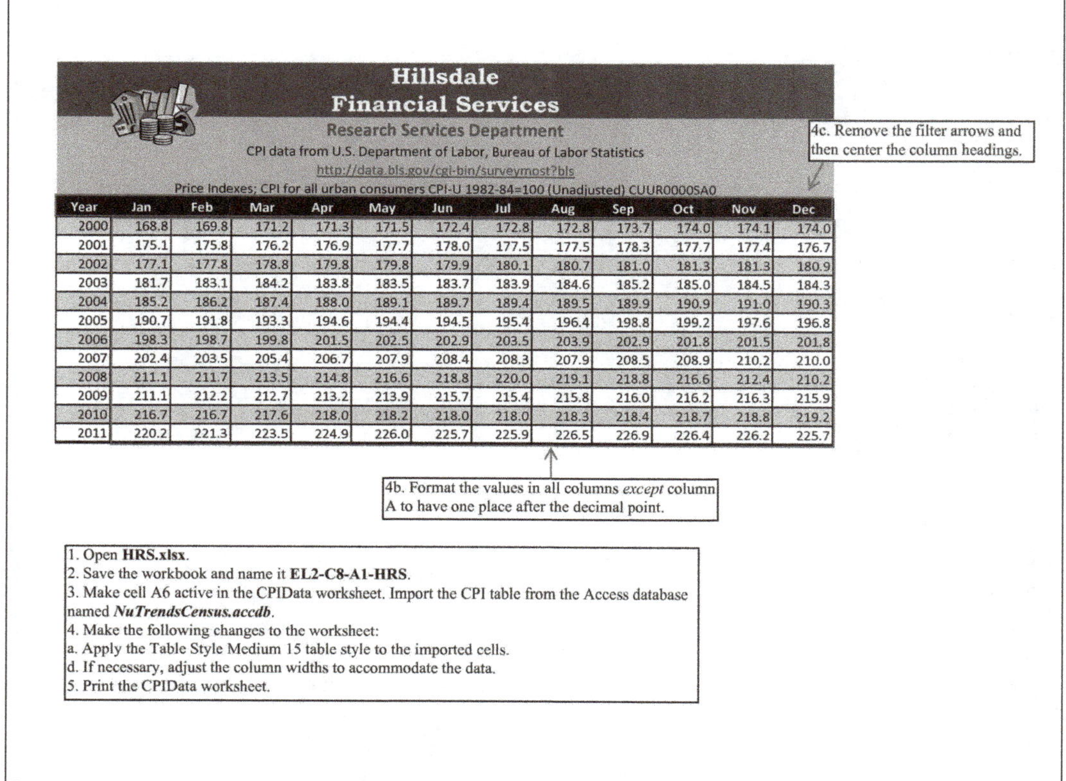

Hillsdale Financial Services

Research Services Department

CPI data from U.S. Department of Labor, Bureau of Labor Statistics

http://data.bls.gov/cgi-bin/surveymost?bls

Price Indexes; CPI for all urban consumers CPI-U 1982-84=100 (Unadjusted) CUUR0000SA0

Year	Jan	Feb	Mar	Apr	May	Jun	Jul	Aug	Sep	Oct	Nov	Dec
2000	168.8	169.8	171.2	171.3	171.5	172.4	172.8	172.8	173.7	174.0	174.1	174.0
2001	175.1	175.8	176.2	176.9	177.7	178.0	177.5	177.5	178.3	177.7	177.4	176.7
2002	177.1	177.8	178.8	179.8	179.8	179.9	180.1	180.7	181.0	181.3	181.3	180.9
2003	181.7	183.1	184.2	183.8	183.5	183.7	183.9	184.6	185.2	185.0	184.5	184.3
2004	185.2	186.2	187.4	188.0	189.1	189.7	189.4	189.5	189.9	190.9	191.0	190.3
2005	190.7	191.8	193.3	194.6	194.4	194.5	195.4	196.4	198.8	199.2	197.6	196.8
2006	198.3	198.7	199.8	201.5	202.5	202.9	203.5	203.9	202.9	201.8	201.5	201.8
2007	202.4	203.5	205.4	206.7	207.9	208.4	208.3	207.9	208.5	208.9	210.2	210.0
2008	211.1	211.7	213.5	214.8	216.6	218.8	220.0	219.1	218.8	216.6	212.4	210.2
2009	211.1	212.2	212.7	213.2	213.9	215.7	215.4	215.8	216.0	216.2	216.3	215.9
2010	216.7	216.7	217.6	218.0	218.2	218.0	218.0	218.3	218.4	218.7	218.8	219.2
2011	220.2	221.3	223.5	224.9	226.0	225.7	225.9	226.5	226.9	226.4	226.2	225.7

4c. Remove the filter arrows and then center the column headings.

4b. Format the values in all columns *except* column A to have one place after the decimal point.

1. Open **HRS.xlsx**.
2. Save the workbook and name it **EL2-C8-A1-HRS**.
3. Make cell A6 active in the CPIData worksheet. Import the CPI table from the Access database named ***NuTrendsCensus.accdb***.
4. Make the following changes to the worksheet:
a. Apply the Table Style Medium 15 table style to the imported cells.
d. If necessary, adjust the column widths to accommodate the data.
5. Print the CPIData worksheet.

EL2-C8-A1-HRS(A1,Step5).xlsx

2009 Jul	Michigan	4,852,000	4,169,000	683,000	14.1
2009 Jun	Michigan	4,866,000	4,190,000	676,000	13.9
2009 May	Michigan	4,877,000	4,215,000	662,000	13.6
2009 Apr	Michigan	4,887,000	4,243,000	643,000	13.2
2009 Mar	Michigan	4,894,000	4,276,000	618,000	12.6
2009 Feb	Michigan	4,901,000	4,313,000	589,000	12
2009 Jan	Michigan	4,909,000	4,354,000	556,000	11.3

EL2-C8-A1-HRS(A1,Step9).xlsx (2 of 2)

Hillsdale Realtors

October Sales Report

October was another record-breaking month for Hillsdale Realtors. Sales exceeded the target by 8% and if the trend continues, our annual sales will surpass last year by over $1 million! Below is an itemized list of sales by date for the month.

7. Change the value in cell F4 to *525000*. 8. Change the value in cell F5 to *212000*.

Sale Date	Listing #	Agent Last Name	Property Type	City	Sale Price	Commission
10/1/2015	282715	Fernandez	Single family home	Phoenix	$ 525,000	$ 18,375.00
10/2/2015	315825	O'Brien	Townhome	Phoenix	$ 212,000	$ 7,420.00
10/5/2015	458215	O'Brien	Single family home	Mesa	$ 225,500	$ 7,892.50
10/7/2015	351245	Youngblood	Single family home	Chandler	$ 325,500	$ 11,392.50
10/9/2015	312548	Williamson	Townhome	Mesa	$ 165,800	$ 5,803.00
10/9/2015	291524	Fernandez	Single family home	Phoenix	$ 425,800	$ 14,903.00
10/12/2015	263412	Youngblood	Single family home	Phoenix	$ 375,800	$ 13,153.00
10/14/2015	254853	O'Brien	Townhome	Chandler	$ 341,500	$ 11,952.50
10/15/2015	302154	Fernandez	Townhome	Chandler	$ 225,600	$ 7,896.00
10/15/2015	311452	Youngblood	Condominium	Phoenix	$ 349,900	$ 12,246.50
10/19/2015	302785	O'Brien	Single family home	Glendale	$ 425,675	$ 14,898.63
10/19/2015	268457	O'Brien	Condominium	Glendale	$ 225,400	$ 7,889.00
10/21/2015	316548	Youngblood	Condominium	Phoenix	$ 345,100	$ 12,078.50
10/21/2015	315863	Fernandez	Single family home	Glendale	$ 455,700	$ 15,949.50
10/22/2015	294563	O'Brien	Condominium	Glendale	$ 415,000	$ 14,525.00
10/23/2015	288451	Fernandez	Townhome	Chandler	$ 385,000	$ 13,475.00
10/23/2015	275143	Fernandez	Single family home	Mesa	$ 275,500	$ 9,642.50
10/26/2015	311148	Youngblood	Single family home	Mesa	$ 345,750	$ 12,101.25
10/26/2015	325984	Youngblood	Condominium	Chandler	$ 285,900	$ 10,006.50
10/29/2015	246845	Youngblood	Single family home	Phoenix	$ 545,200	$ 19,082.00
10/29/2015	334567	O'Brien	Single family home	Phoenix	$ 475,800	$ 16,653.00
10/30/2015	266845	Fernandez	Condominium	Chandler	$ 325,000	$ 11,375.00
10/30/2015	254836	Youngblood	Condominium	Mesa	$ 275,800	$ 9,653.00
			Total Sales and Commissions		$ 7,953,225	$278,362.88

1. Open **HROctSalesByDateByRep.xlsx**.
2. Save the workbook and name it **EL2-C8-A2-HROctSalesByDateByRep**.
3. With SalesByDate the active worksheet, link A3:G27 at the end of the Word document named **HROctRpt.docx**.
4. Change the margins in the Word document to *Narrow* (top, bottom, left, and right to 0.5 inch).
5. Use Save As to name the revised Word document **EL2-C8-A2-HROctRpt.docx**.
6. Switch to Excel and then press Esc to remove the scrolling marquee and then deselect the range.
9. Save **EL2-C8-A2-HROctSalesByDateByRep.xlsx**.
10. Switch to Word, right-click the linked object, and then click *Update Link* at the shortcut menu.
11. Print the Word document.
12. Break the link in the Word document.

EL2-C8-A2-HROctRpt(A2,Step11).xlsx

1. Open **HROctSalesByDateByRep.xlsx**.
2. Save the workbook and name it **EL2-C8-A3-HROctSalesByDateByRep**.
3. Make SalesByRep the active worksheet.
4. Display the worksheet at outline level 2 so that only the sales agent names, sale prices, and commissions display.
5. Create a column chart in a separate sheet to graph the sales commissions earned by each sales agent. You determine an appropriate chart style, title, and other chart elements.
6. Start PowerPoint and open **HROctRpt.pptx**.
7. Save the presentation with Save As and name it **EL2-C8-A3-HROctRpt**.
9. Print the presentation as Handouts with three slides per page.

11/3/2015

HILLSDALE REALTORS

NEW SALES RECORD

- 23 properties sold!
- Value of properties sold = $7.7 million
- Total commission income = $270,082

COMMISSIONS BY SALES AGENT

8. Embed the chart created in Step 5 on Slide 3 of the presentation. Resize the chart if necessary.

1

EL2-C8-A3-HROctRpt(A3).pptx

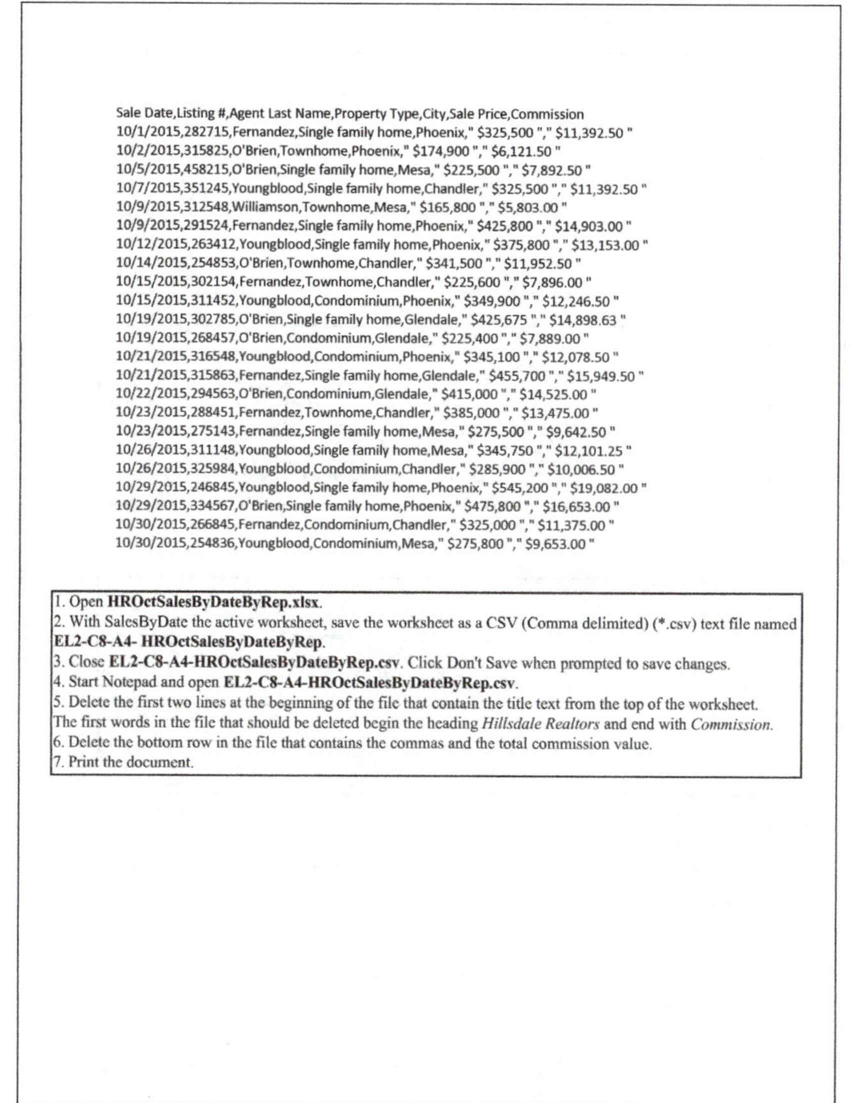

Sale Date,Listing #,Agent Last Name,Property Type,City,Sale Price,Commission
10/1/2015,282715,Fernandez,Single family home,Phoenix," $325,500 "," $11,392.50 "
10/2/2015,315825,O'Brien,Townhome,Phoenix," $174,900 "," $6,121.50 "
10/5/2015,458215,O'Brien,Single family home,Mesa," $225,500 "," $7,892.50 "
10/7/2015,351245,Youngblood,Single family home,Chandler," $325,500 "," $11,392.50 "
10/9/2015,312548,Williamson,Townhome,Mesa," $165,800 "," $5,803.00 "
10/9/2015,291524,Fernandez,Single family home,Phoenix," $425,800 "," $14,903.00 "
10/12/2015,263412,Youngblood,Single family home,Phoenix," $375,800 "," $13,153.00 "
10/14/2015,254853,O'Brien,Townhome,Chandler," $341,500 "," $11,952.50 "
10/15/2015,302154,Fernandez,Townhome,Chandler," $225,600 "," $7,896.00 "
10/15/2015,311452,Youngblood,Condominium,Phoenix," $349,900 "," $12,246.50 "
10/19/2015,302785,O'Brien,Single family home,Glendale," $425,675 "," $14,898.63 "
10/19/2015,268457,O'Brien,Condominium,Glendale," $225,400 "," $7,889.00 "
10/21/2015,316548,Youngblood,Condominium,Phoenix," $345,100 "," $12,078.50 "
10/21/2015,315863,Fernandez,Single family home,Glendale," $455,700 "," $15,949.50 "
10/22/2015,294563,O'Brien,Condominium,Glendale," $415,000 "," $14,525.00 "
10/23/2015,288451,Fernandez,Townhome,Chandler," $385,000 "," $13,475.00 "
10/23/2015,275143,Fernandez,Single family home,Mesa," $275,500 "," $9,642.50 "
10/26/2015,311148,Youngblood,Single family home,Mesa," $345,750 "," $12,101.25 "
10/26/2015,325984,Youngblood,Condominium,Chandler," $285,900 "," $10,006.50 "
10/29/2015,246845,Youngblood,Single family home,Phoenix," $545,200 "," $19,082.00 "
10/29/2015,334567,O'Brien,Single family home,Phoenix," $475,800 "," $16,653.00 "
10/30/2015,266845,Fernandez,Condominium,Chandler," $325,000 "," $11,375.00 "
10/30/2015,254836,Youngblood,Condominium,Mesa," $275,800 "," $9,653.00 "

1. Open **HROctSalesByDateByRep.xlsx**.
2. With SalesByDate the active worksheet, save the worksheet as a CSV (Comma delimited) (*.csv) text file named **EL2-C8-A4- HROctSalesByDateByRep**.
3. Close **EL2-C8-A4-HROctSalesByDateByRep.csv**. Click Don't Save when prompted to save changes.
4. Start Notepad and open **EL2-C8-A4-HROctSalesByDateByRep.csv**.
5. Delete the first two lines at the beginning of the file that contain the title text from the top of the worksheet. The first words in the file that should be deleted begin the heading *Hillsdale Realtors* and end with *Commission*.
6. Delete the bottom row in the file that contains the commas and the total commission value.
7. Print the document.

EL2-C8-A4-HROctSalesByDateByRep(A4).csv

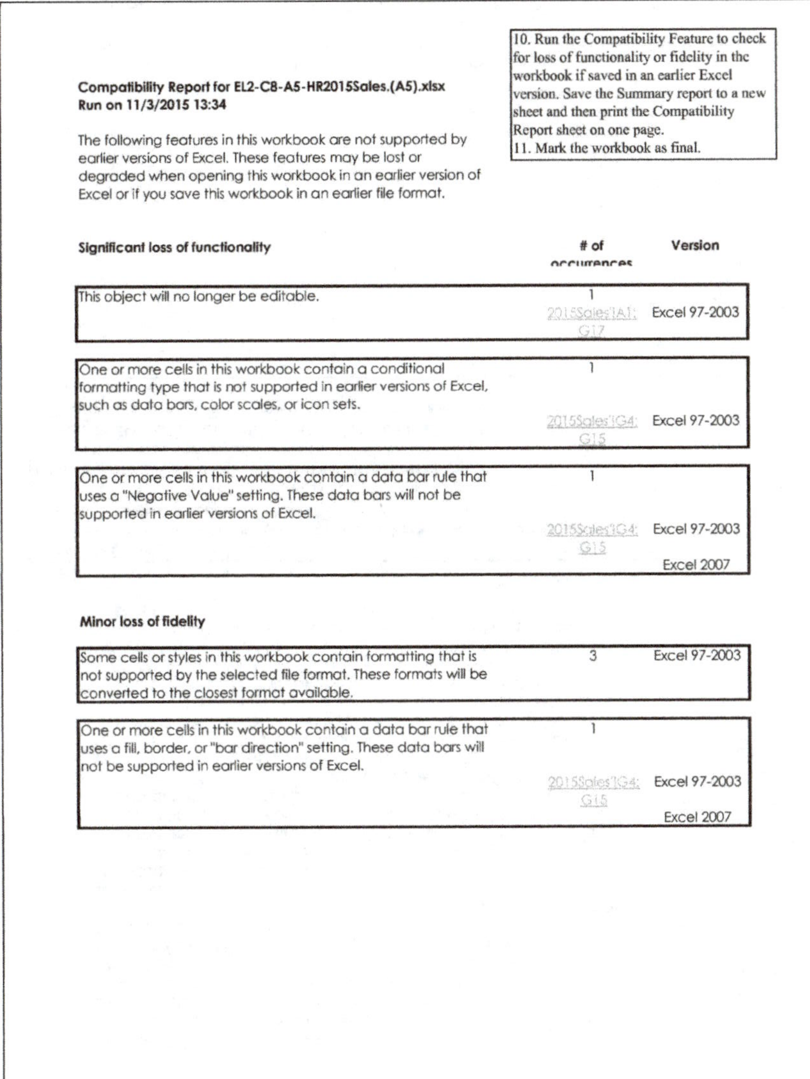

Student Name

9. Click the FILE tab. With the Info backstage area displayed showing all properties, paste a screen image into a new Word document using the Print Screen with Paste or the Screenshot feature. Type your name a few lines below the screen image. Print the Word document and then exit Word without saving.

1. Open **HR2015Sales.xlsx**.
2. Save the workbook and name it **EL2-C8-A5-HR2015Sales**.
3. Display the Info backstage area and show all properties. Read the information in the *Author*, *Title*, and *Subject* property text boxes. Open the Properties dialog box (by clicking *Advanced Properties* from the Properties button drop-down list) and read the information in the Statistics and Custom tabs. Close the Properties dialog box. Click the Back button and click the REVIEW tab.
4. Turn on the display of all comments and then read the comments that appear.
5. Change to Page Layout view and check for a header or footer in the workbook.
6. Use the Document Inspector feature to check the workbook for private and hidden information. Leave all options selected at the Document Inspector dialog box.
7. Remove all items that display with red exclamation marks and then close the dialog box.
8. Click the REVIEW tab, turn off the Show All Comments feature, and switch to Normal view.

EL2-C8-A5-HR2015Sales(A5,Step9).xlsx

Compatibility Report for EL2-C8-A5-HR2015Sales.(A5).xlsx
Run on 11/3/2015 13:34

The following features in this workbook are not supported by earlier versions of Excel. These features may be lost or degraded when opening this workbook in an earlier version of Excel or if you save this workbook in an earlier file format.

10. Run the Compatibility Feature to check for loss of functionality or fidelity in the workbook if saved in an earlier Excel version. Save the Summary report to a new sheet and then print the Compatibility Report sheet on one page.
11. Mark the workbook as final.

Significant loss of functionality	**# of occurrences**	**Version**
This object will no longer be editable.	1 2015Sales!A1:G17	Excel 97-2003
One or more cells in this workbook contain a conditional formatting type that is not supported in earlier versions of Excel, such as data bars, color scales, or icon sets.	1 2015Sales!G4:G15	Excel 97-2003
One or more cells in this workbook contain a data bar rule that uses a "Negative Value" setting. These data bars will not be supported in earlier versions of Excel.	1 2015Sales!G4:G15	Excel 97-2003 Excel 2007

Minor loss of fidelity		
Some cells or styles in this workbook contain formatting that is not supported by the selected file format. These formats will be converted to the closest format available.	3	Excel 97-2003
One or more cells in this workbook contain a data bar rule that uses a fill, border, or "bar direction" setting. These data bars will not be supported in earlier versions of Excel.	1 2015Sales!G4:G15	Excel 97-2003 Excel 2007

EL2-C8-A5-HR2015Sales.(A5,Step10).xlsx

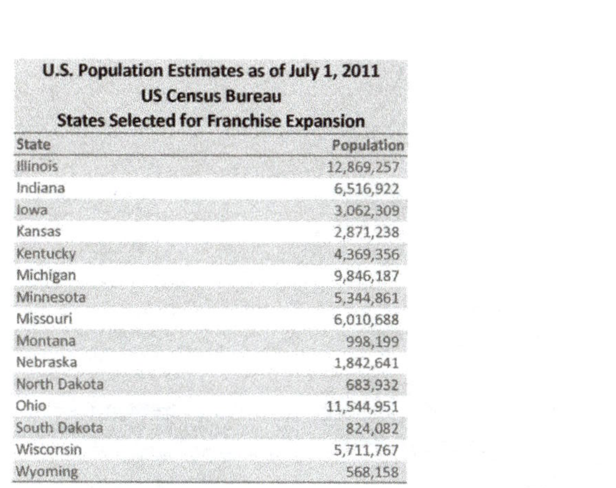

U.S. Population Estimates as of July 1, 2011
US Census Bureau
States Selected for Franchise Expansion

State	Population
Illinois	12,869,257
Indiana	6,516,922
Iowa	3,062,309
Kansas	2,871,238
Kentucky	4,369,356
Michigan	9,846,187
Minnesota	5,344,861
Missouri	6,010,688
Montana	998,199
Nebraska	1,842,641
North Dakota	683,932
Ohio	11,544,951
South Dakota	824,082
Wisconsin	5,711,767
Wyoming	568,158

EL2-C8-VB-PBMReport(VB,Step2).xlsx

Pizza by Mario

Franchise Expansion Marketing Report

By: Student Name

EL2-C8-VB-PBMReport(VB,Step5).docx (1 of 2)

Pizza by Mario Franchise Expansion

Selected States for New Franchises

The states selected for franchise expansions are located geographically adjacent to states in which existing franchises are located. This decision was made in consultation with the NuTrends Market Research consultant for the following reasons:

- Minimize travel area for head office personnel
- Provide for lower distribution costs of supplies from the head office warehouse
- Lower cost of travel for franchisees to training and meetings at head office

NuTrends Market Research provided the latest population estimates from the U.S. Census Bureau for the target states. The following chart depicts these estimates.

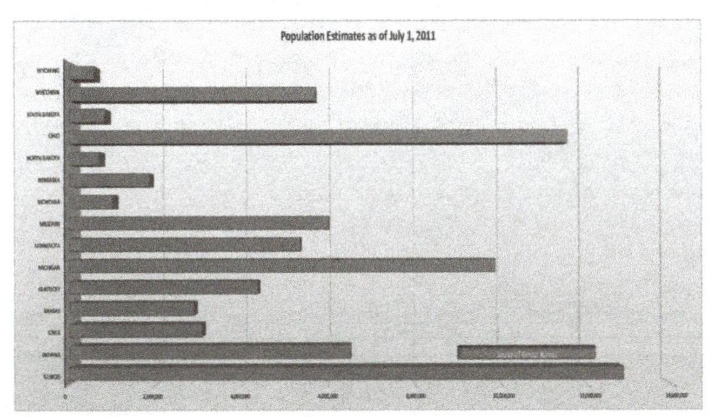

New franchises have been planned in Illinois, Indiana, and Kentucky. Based on the state populations shown in the chart, the writer recommends that Pizza by Mario consider actively recruiting new franchises within Ohio, Michigan, Indiana, and Illinois.

EL2-C8-VB-PBMReport(VB,Step5).docx (2 of 2)

NuTrends Market Research
Data from U.S. Census Bureau

People QuickFacts	Illinois	USA
Population, 2012 estimate	12,875,255	313,914,040
Population, 2010 (April 1) estimates base	12,830,632	308,747,508
Population, percent change, April 1, 2010 to July 1, 2012	0.30%	1.70%
Population, 2010	12,830,632	308,745,538
Persons under 5 years, percent, 2011	6.40%	6.50%
Persons under 18 years, percent, 2011	24.10%	23.70%
Persons 65 years and over, percent, 2011	12.70%	13.30%
Female persons, percent, 2011	50.90%	50.80%
White persons, percent, 2011 (a)	78.00%	78.10%
Black persons, percent, 2011 (a)	14.80%	13.10%
American Indian and Alaska Native persons, percent, 2011 (a)	0.60%	1.20%
Asian persons, percent, 2011 (a)	4.80%	5.00%
Native Hawaiian and Other Pacific Islander persons, percent, 2011 (a)	0.10%	0.20%
Persons reporting two or more races, percent, 2011	1.70%	2.30%
Persons of Hispanic or Latino Origin, percent, 2011 (b)	16.20%	16.70%
White persons not Hispanic, percent, 2011	63.30%	63.40%
Living in same house 1 year & over, percent, 2007-2011	86.70%	84.60%
Foreign born persons, percent, 2007-2011	13.70%	12.80%
Language other than English spoken at home, percent age 5+, 2007-2011	22.00%	20.30%
High school graduate or higher, percent of persons age 25+, 2007-2011	86.60%	85.40%
Bachelor's degree or higher, percent of persons age 25+, 2007-2011	30.70%	28.20%
Veterans, 2007-2011	770,388	22,215,303
Mean travel time to work (minutes), workers age 16+, 2007-2011	28.1	25.4
Housing units, 2011	5,297,318	132,312,404
Homeownership rate, 2007-2011	68.70%	66.10%
Housing units in multi-unit structures, percent, 2007-2011	32.90%	25.90%
Median value of owner-occupied housing units, 2007-2011	$198,500	$186,200
Households, 2007-2011	4,773,002	114,761,359
Persons per household, 2007-2011	2.62	2.6
Per capita money income in the past 12 months (2011 dollars), 2007-2011	$29,376	$27,915
Median household income, 2007-2011	$56,576	$52,762
Persons below poverty level, percent, 2007-2011	13.10%	14.30%

EL2-C8-CS-P1-PBMResearch(P1-Illinois).xlsx

NuTrends Market Research
Data from U.S. Census Bureau

People QuickFacts	Indiana	USA
Population, 2012 estimate	6,537,334	313,914,040
Population, 2010 (April 1) estimates base	6,483,800	308,747,508
Population, percent change, April 1, 2010 to July 1, 2012	0.80%	1.70%
Population, 2010	6,483,802	308,745,538
Persons under 5 years, percent, 2011	6.60%	6.50%
Persons under 18 years, percent, 2011	24.50%	23.70%
Persons 65 years and over, percent, 2011	13.20%	13.30%
Female persons, percent, 2011	50.80%	50.80%
White persons, percent, 2011 (a)	86.80%	78.10%
Black persons, percent, 2011 (a)	9.40%	13.10%
American Indian and Alaska Native persons, percent, 2011 (a)	0.40%	1.20%
Asian persons, percent, 2011 (a)	1.70%	5.00%
Native Hawaiian and Other Pacific Islander persons, percent, 2011 (a)	0.10%	0.20%
Persons reporting two or more races, percent, 2011	1.70%	2.30%
Persons of Hispanic or Latino Origin, percent, 2011 (b)	6.20%	16.70%
White persons not Hispanic, percent, 2011	81.30%	63.40%
Living in same house 1 year & over, percent, 2007-2011	84.40%	84.60%
Foreign born persons, percent, 2007-2011	4.50%	12.80%
Language other than English spoken at home, percent age 5+, 2007-2011	7.90%	20.30%
High school graduate or higher, percent of persons age 25+, 2007-2011	86.60%	85.40%
Bachelor's degree or higher, percent of persons age 25+, 2007-2011	22.70%	28.20%
Veterans, 2007-2011	478,030	22,215,303
Mean travel time to work (minutes), workers age 16+, 2007-2011	23.1	25.4
Housing units, 2011	2,800,614	132,312,404
Homeownership rate, 2007-2011	71.10%	66.10%
Housing units in multi-unit structures, percent, 2007-2011	18.50%	25.90%
Median value of owner-occupied housing units, 2007-2011	$123,300	$186,200
Households, 2007-2011	2,472,870	114,761,359
Persons per household, 2007-2011	2.53	2.6
Per capita money income in the past 12 months (2011 dollars), 2007-2011	$24,497	$27,915
Median household income, 2007-2011	$48,393	$52,762
Persons below poverty level, percent, 2007-2011	14.10%	14.30%

EL2-C8-CS-P1-PBMResearch(P1-Indiana).xlsx

NuTrends Market Research
Data from U.S. Census Bureau

People QuickFacts	Kentucky	USA
Population, 2012 estimate	4,380,415	313,914,040
Population, 2010 (April 1) estimates base	4,339,357	308,747,508
Population, percent change, April 1, 2010 to July 1, 2012	0.90%	1.70%
Population, 2010	4,339,367	308,745,538
Persons under 5 years, percent, 2011	6.40%	6.50%
Persons under 18 years, percent, 2011	23.40%	23.70%
Persons 65 years and over, percent, 2011	13.50%	13.30%
Female persons, percent, 2011	50.80%	50.80%
White persons, percent, 2011 (a)	88.90%	78.10%
Black persons, percent, 2011 (a)	8.00%	13.10%
American Indian and Alaska Native persons, percent, 2011 (a)	0.30%	1.20%
Asian persons, percent, 2011 (a)	1.20%	5.00%
Native Hawaiian and Other Pacific Islander persons, percent, 2011 (a)	0.10%	0.20%
Persons reporting two or more races, percent, 2011	1.60%	2.30%
Persons of Hispanic or Latino Origin, percent, 2011 (b)	3.20%	16.70%
White persons not Hispanic, percent, 2011	86.10%	63.40%
Living in same house 1 year & over, percent, 2007-2011	84.70%	84.60%
Foreign born persons, percent, 2007-2011	3.10%	12.80%
Language other than English spoken at home, percent age 5+, 2007-2011	4.70%	20.30%
High school graduate or higher, percent of persons age 25+, 2007-2011	81.70%	85.40%
Bachelor's degree or higher, percent of persons age 25+, 2007-2011	20.60%	28.20%
Veterans, 2007-2011	323,823	22,215,303
Mean travel time to work (minutes), workers age 16+, 2007-2011	22.6	25.4
Housing units, 2011	1,932,599	132,312,404
Homeownership rate, 2007-2011	69.50%	66.10%
Housing units in multi-unit structures, percent, 2007-2011	17.80%	25.90%
Median value of owner-occupied housing units, 2007-2011	$118,700	$186,200
Households, 2007-2011	1,681,085	114,761,359
Persons per household, 2007-2011	2.49	2.6
Per capita money income in the past 12 months (2011 dollars), 2007-2011	$23,033	$27,915
Median household income, 2007-2011	$42,248	$52,762
Persons below poverty level, percent, 2007-2011	18.10%	14.30%

EL2-C8-CS-P1-PBMResearch(P1-Kentucky).xlsx

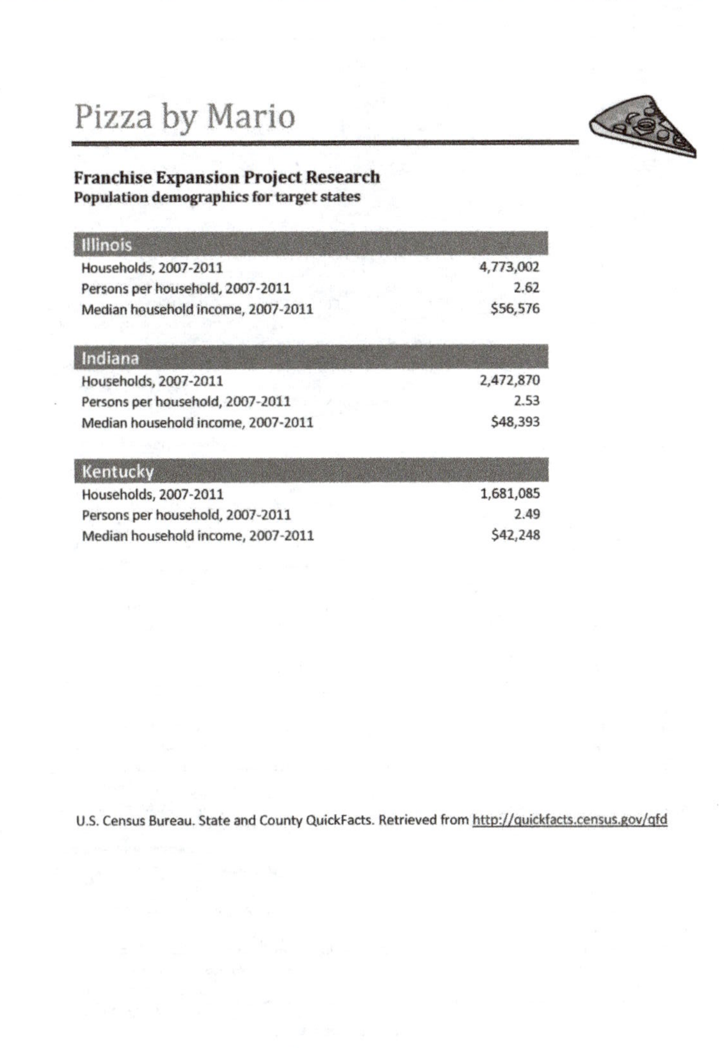

Pizza by Mario

Franchise Expansion Project Research
Population demographics for target states

Illinois	
Households, 2007-2011	4,773,002
Persons per household, 2007-2011	2.62
Median household income, 2007-2011	$56,576

Indiana	
Households, 2007-2011	2,472,870
Persons per household, 2007-2011	2.53
Median household income, 2007-2011	$48,393

Kentucky	
Households, 2007-2011	1,681,085
Persons per household, 2007-2011	2.49
Median household income, 2007-2011	$42,248

U.S. Census Bureau. State and County QuickFacts. Retrieved from http://quickfacts.census.gov/qfd

EL2-C8-CS-P2-PBMExpansionResearch.docx

Excel Level 2, Performance Assessment Unit 2 Model Answers

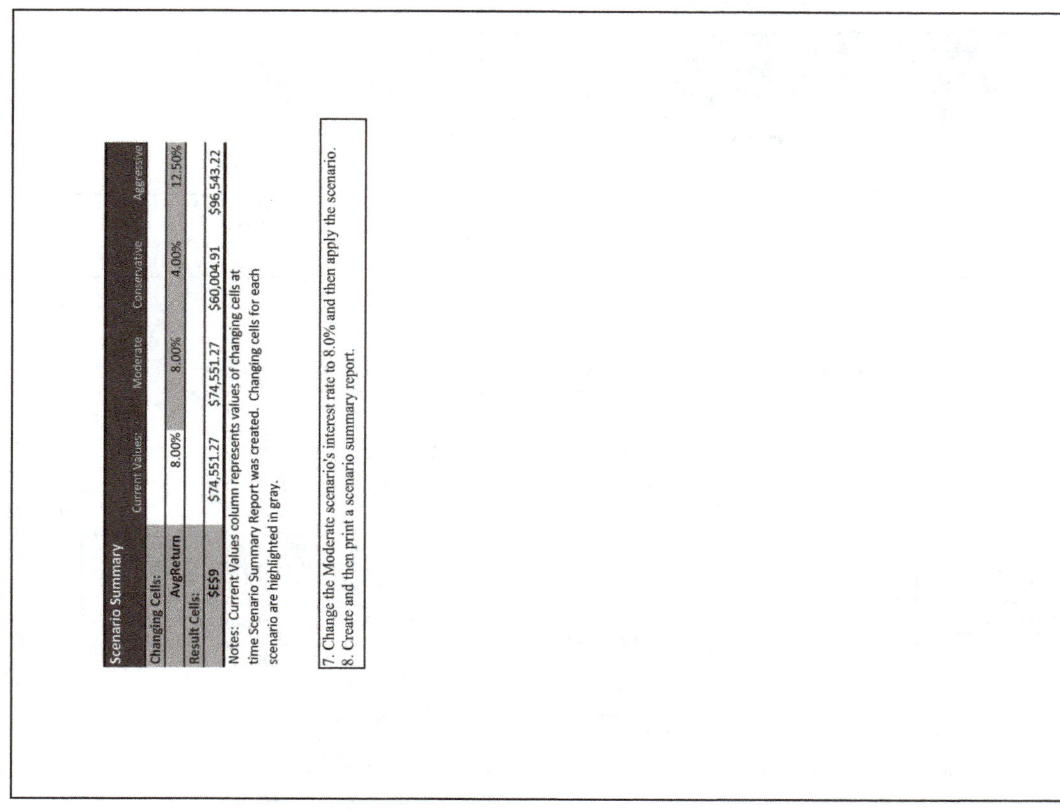

Scenario Summary

	Current Values:	Moderate	Conservative	Aggressive
Changing Cells:				
AvgReturn	8.00%	8.00%	4.00%	12.50%
Result Cells:				
$E$9	$74,551.27	$74,551.27	$60,004.91	$96,543.22

Notes: Current Values column represents values of changing cells at time Scenario Summary Report was created. Changing cells for each scenario are highlighted in gray.

7. Change the Moderate scenario's interest rate to 8.0% and then apply the scenario.
8. Create and then print a scenario summary report.

EL2-U2-A1-HillsInvtPlan(A1,Step8).xlsx

Hillsdale Financial Services

Investment Proposal

Client: Lou McAllister — Risk tolerance score: 18

Advisor: Nadia Forrester — Portfolio recommendation: Moderate

Investment Plan

Monthly contribution	$ (407.50)
Number of years to invest	10
Forecasted annual interest rate	12.50%
Projected value of plan at end of term	$96,543.22

Assumptions

No change in payment amount.

Annual interest rate is average rate over the life of the plan.

No withdrawals during the investment period.

4. Assign the range name *AvgReturn* to cell E8.
5. Create three scenarios for changing cell E8 as follows:
Moderate 5.5%
Conservative 4.0%
Aggressive 12.5%

1. Open **HillsInvtPlan.xlsx**.
2. Save the workbook and name it **EL2-U2-A1-HillsInvtPlan**.
3. Use Goal Seek to find the monthly contribution amount the client must make to increase the projected value of the plan to $65,000 at the end of the term. Accept the solution Goal Seek calculates.
6. Apply the Aggressive scenario and then print the worksheet.

EL2-U2-A1-HillsInvtPlan(A1,Step6).xlsx

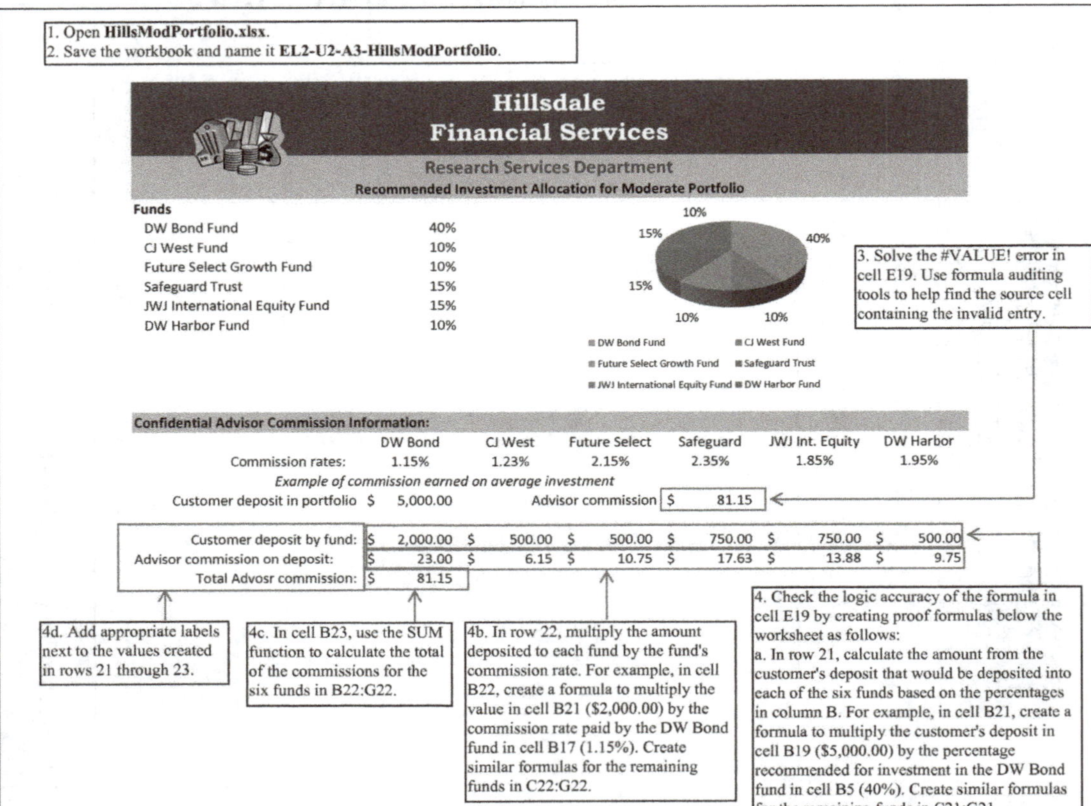

EL2-U2-A3-HillsModPortfolio(A3).xlsx

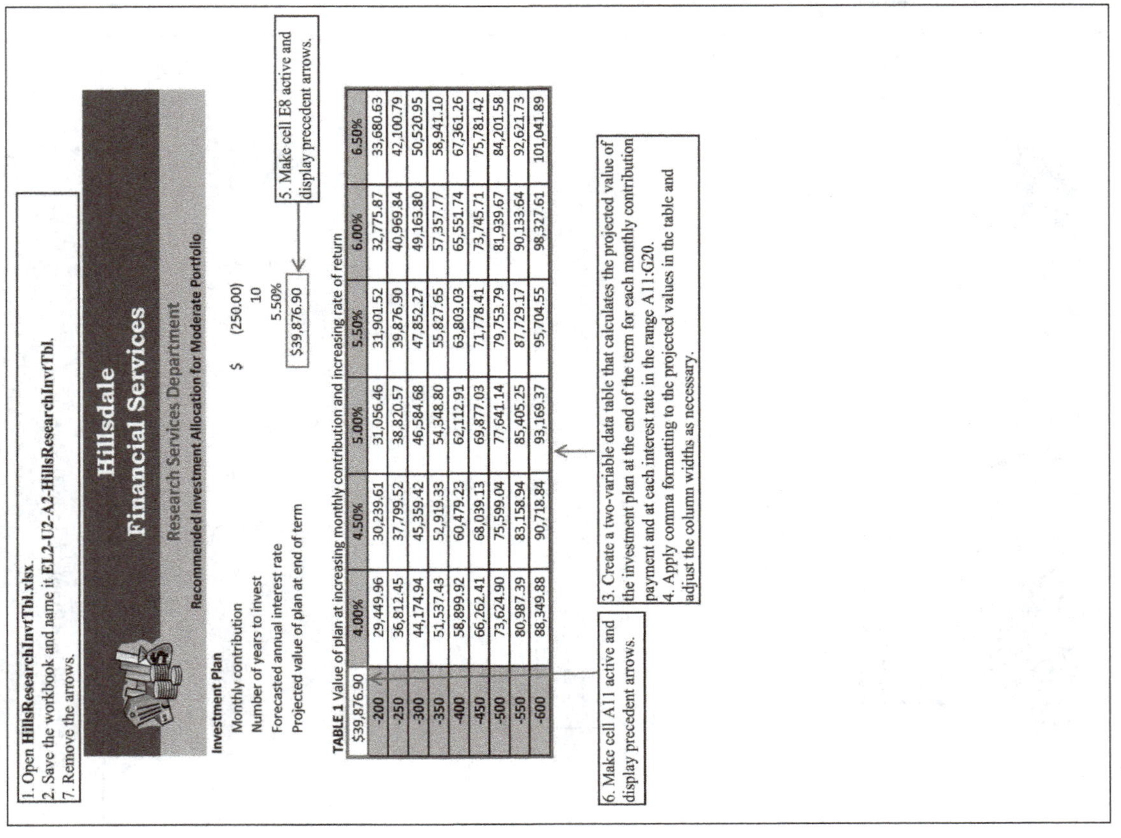

TABLE 1 Value of plan at increasing monthly contribution and increasing rate of return

$39,876.90	4.00%	4.50%	5.00%	5.50%	6.00%	6.50%
-200	29,449.96	30,239.61	31,056.46	31,901.52	32,775.87	33,680.63
-250	36,812.45	37,799.52	38,820.57	39,876.90	40,969.84	42,100.79
-300	44,174.94	45,359.42	46,584.68	47,852.27	49,163.80	50,520.95
-350	51,537.43	52,919.33	54,348.80	55,827.65	57,357.77	58,941.10
-400	58,899.92	60,479.23	62,112.91	63,803.03	65,551.74	67,361.26
-450	66,262.41	68,039.13	69,877.03	71,778.41	73,745.71	75,781.42
-500	73,624.90	75,599.04	77,641.14	79,753.79	81,939.67	84,201.58
-550	80,987.39	83,158.94	85,405.25	87,729.17	90,133.64	92,621.73
-600	88,349.88	90,718.84	93,169.37	95,704.55	98,327.61	101,041.89

EL2-U2-HillsResearchInvtTbl(A2).xlsx

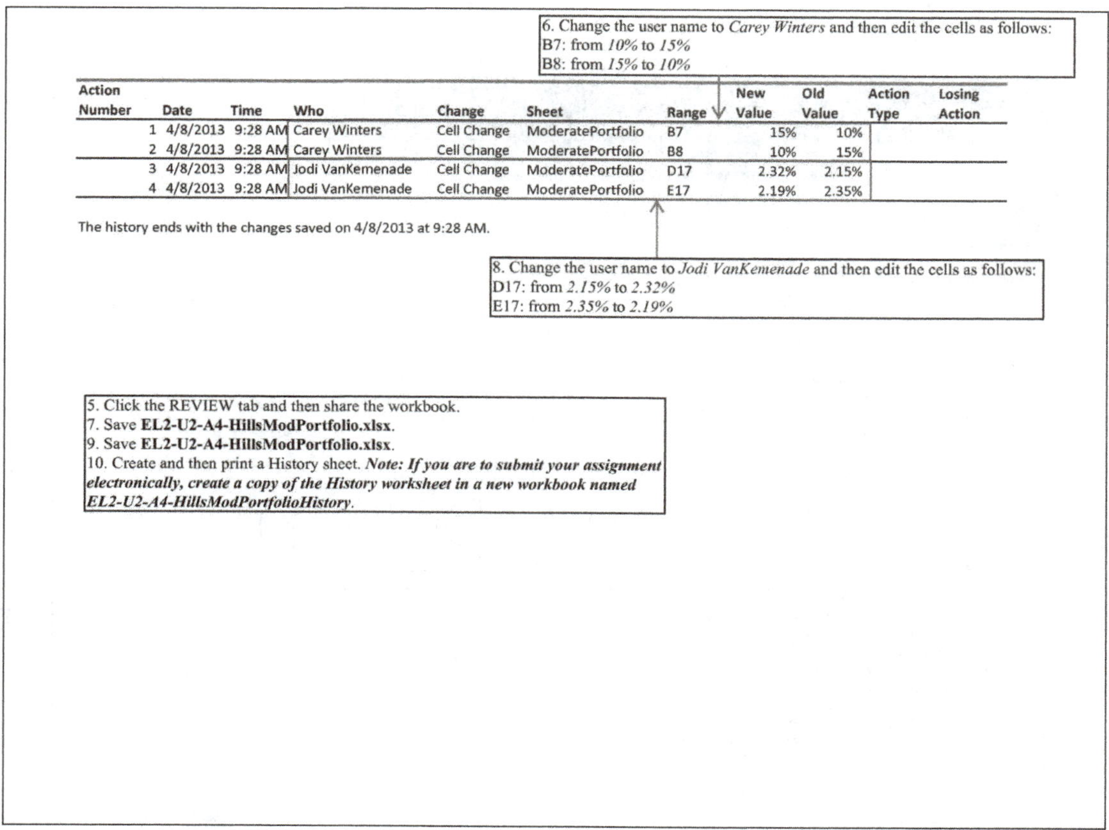

6. Change the user name to *Carey Winters* and then edit the cells as follows:
B7: from *10%* to *15%*
B8: from *15%* to *10%*

Action Number	Date	Time	Who	Change	Sheet	Range	New Value	Old Value	Action Type	Losing Action
1	4/8/2013	9:28 AM	Carey Winters	Cell Change	ModeratePortfolio	B7	15%	10%		
2	4/8/2013	9:28 AM	Carey Winters	Cell Change	ModeratePortfolio	B8	10%	15%		
3	4/8/2013	9:28 AM	Jodi VanKemenade	Cell Change	ModeratePortfolio	D17	2.32%	2.15%		
4	4/8/2013	9:28 AM	Jodi VanKemenade	Cell Change	ModeratePortfolio	E17	2.19%	2.35%		

The history ends with the changes saved on 4/8/2013 at 9:28 AM.

8. Change the user name to *Jodi VanKemenade* and then edit the cells as follows:
D17: from *2.15%* to *2.32%*
E17: from *2.35%* to *2.19%*

5. Click the REVIEW tab and then share the workbook.
7. Save **EL2-U2-A4-HillsModPortfolio.xlsx**.
9. Save **EL2-U2-A4-HillsModPortfolio.xlsx**.
10. Create and then print a History sheet. ***Note: If you are to submit your assignment electronically, create a copy of the History worksheet in a new workbook named EL2-U2-A4-HillsModPortfolioHistory.***

EL2-U2-A4-HillsModPortfolio(A4,Step10).xlsx

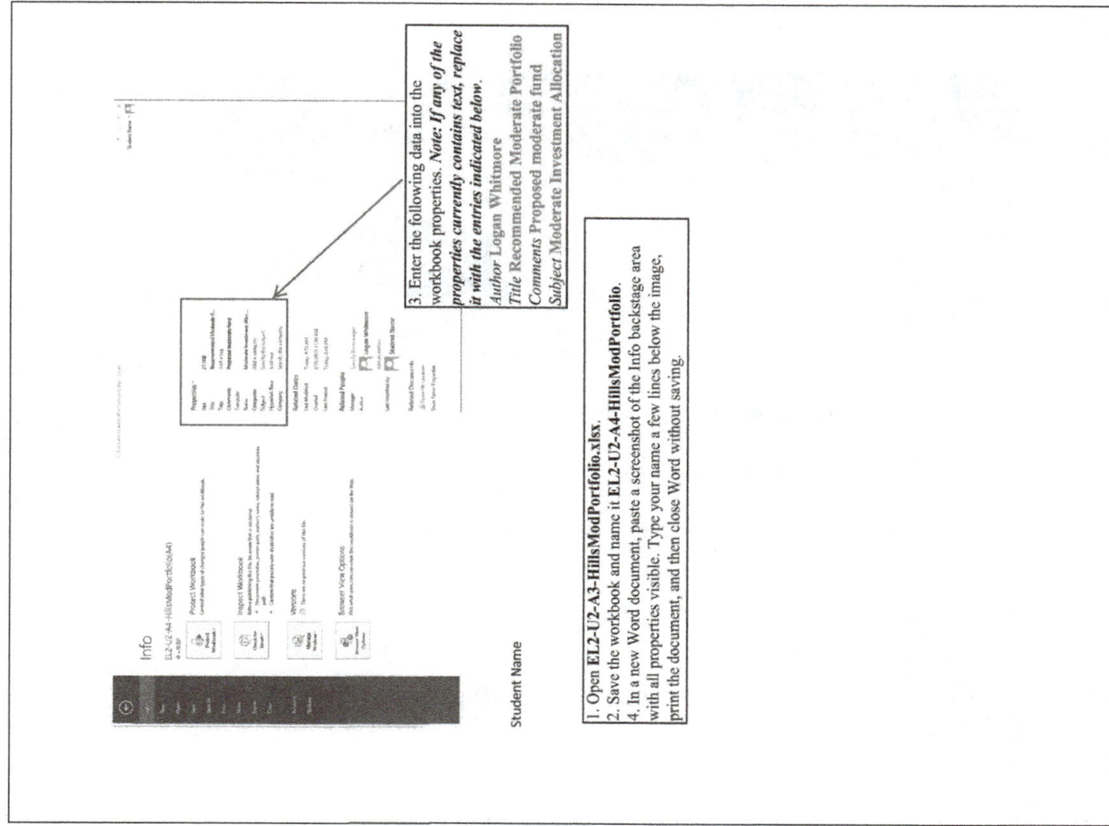

EL2-U2-A4-HillsModPortfolio(A4,Step4).xlsx

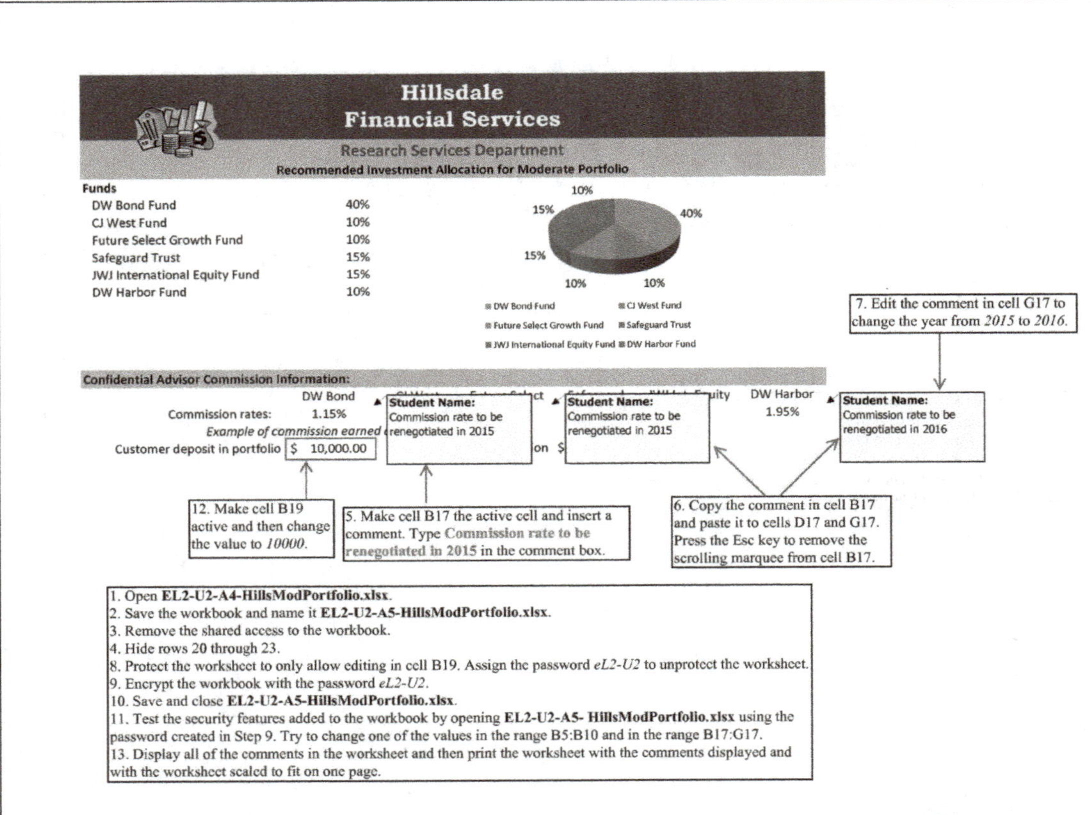

EL2-U2-A5-HillsModPortfolio(A5,Step13).xlsx

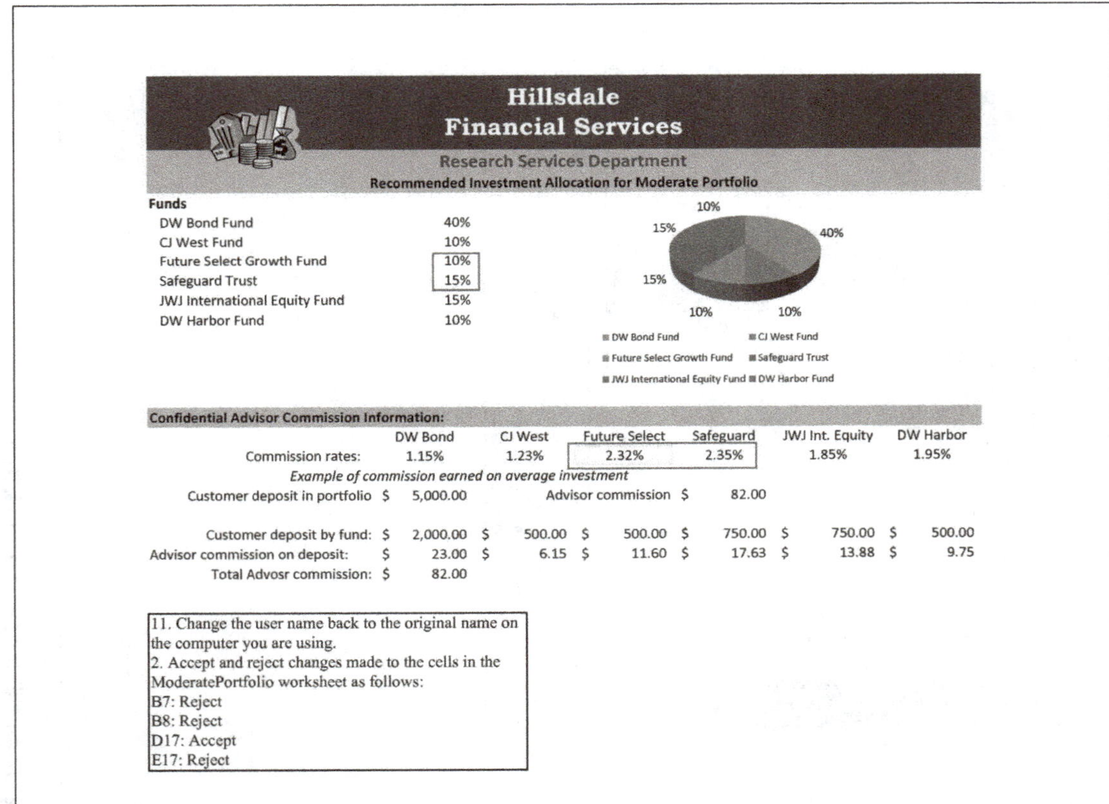

EL2-U2-A4-HillsModPortfolio(A4,Step13).xlsx

```
Sub CustomHeader()
'
' CustomHeader Macro
' Created by [Student Name] on [date].
'
' Keyboard Shortcut: Ctrl+Shift+H
'
    Application.PrintCommunication = False
    With ActiveSheet.PageSetup
        .PrintTitleRows = ""
        .PrintTitleColumns = ""
    End With
    Application.PrintCommunication = True
    ActiveSheet.PageSetup.PrintArea = ""
    Application.PrintCommunication = False
    With ActiveSheet.PageSetup
        .LeftHeader = "Private and Confidential"
        .CenterHeader = ""
        .RightHeader = ""
        .LeftFooter = ""
        .CenterFooter = ""
        .RightFooter = ""
        .LeftMargin = Application.InchesToPoints(0.7)
        .RightMargin = Application.InchesToPoints(0.7)
        .TopMargin = Application.InchesToPoints(0.75)
        .BottomMargin = Application.InchesToPoints(0.75)
        .HeaderMargin = Application.InchesToPoints(0.3)
        .FooterMargin = Application.InchesToPoints(0.3)
        .PrintHeadings = False
        .PrintGridlines = False
        .PrintComments = xlPrintInPlace
        .PrintQuality = 600
        .CenterHorizontally = True
        .CenterVertically = False
        .Orientation = xlLandscape
        .Draft = False
        .PaperSize = xlPaperLetter
        .FirstPageNumber = xlAutomatic
        .Order = xlDownThenOver
        .BlackAndWhite = False
        .Zoom = False
        .FitToPagesWide = 1
        .FitToPagesTall = 1
        .PrintErrors = xlPrintErrorsDisplayed
        .OddAndEvenPagesHeaderFooter = False
        .DifferentFirstPageHeaderFooter = False
        .ScaleWithDocHeaderFooter = True
        .AlignMarginsHeaderFooter = True
```

EL2-U2-A6-HillsModPortfolio(A6,Step6).vba (1 of 2)

```
        .EvenPage.LeftHeader.Text = ""
        .EvenPage.CenterHeader.Text = ""
        .EvenPage.RightHeader.Text = ""
        .EvenPage.LeftFooter.Text = ""
        .EvenPage.CenterFooter.Text = ""
        .EvenPage.RightFooter.Text = ""
        .FirstPage.LeftHeader.Text = ""
        .FirstPage.CenterHeader.Text = ""
        .FirstPage.RightHeader.Text = ""
        .FirstPage.LeftFooter.Text = ""
        .FirstPage.CenterFooter.Text = ""
        .FirstPage.RightFooter.Text = ""
    End With
    Application.PrintCommunication = True
End Sub
Sub CustomView()
'
' CustomView Macro
' Created by [Student Name] on [date].
'
' Keyboard Shortcut: Ctrl+Shift+T
'
    ActiveWorkbook.ApplyTheme ( _
        "C:\Users\Student\AppData\Roaming\Microsoft\Templates\LiveContent\15\User\Document
Themes\1033\Metropolitan.thmx" _
        )
    With ActiveWindow
        .DisplayGridlines = False
        .DisplayHeadings = False
    End With
End Sub
```

1. Open **EL2-U2-A5-HillsModPortfolio.xlsx**.
2. Unprotect the worksheet, turn off the display of all comments, and then delete the comments in cells B17, D17, and G17.
3. Display the Custom Views dialog box. When a workbook has been shared, Excel automatically creates a custom view (with the label *Personal View*) for each person who accessed the file and for the original worksheet state before sharing was enabled. Delete all of the custom views in the dialog box and then add a new custom view named *ModeratePortfolioOriginalView*.
4. Create two macros to be stored in the active workbook as follows:
a. Create a macro named *CustomDisplay* that applies the Metropolitan theme and turns off the display of gridlines and row and column headers in the current worksheet. Assign the macro to the shortcut key Ctrl + Shift + T. Enter an appropriate description that includes your name and the date the macro was created.
b. Create a macro named *CustomHeader* that prints the text *Private and Confidential* at the left margin in the header. Assign the macro to the shortcut key Ctrl + Shift + H. Enter an appropriate description that includes your name and the date the macro was created.
5. Test the macros by opening **EL2-U2-A1-HillsInvtPlan.xlsx**. Make InvestmentPlanProposal the active worksheet and then run the two macros created in Step 4. View the worksheet in the Print backstage area. Close the Print backstage area and then close **EL2-U2-A1-HillsInvtPlan.xlsx** without saving the changes.
6. Print the VBA program code for the two macros and then close the Microsoft Visual Basic for Applications window and return to Excel.

EL2-U2-A6-HillsModPortfolio(A6,Step6).vba (2 of 2)

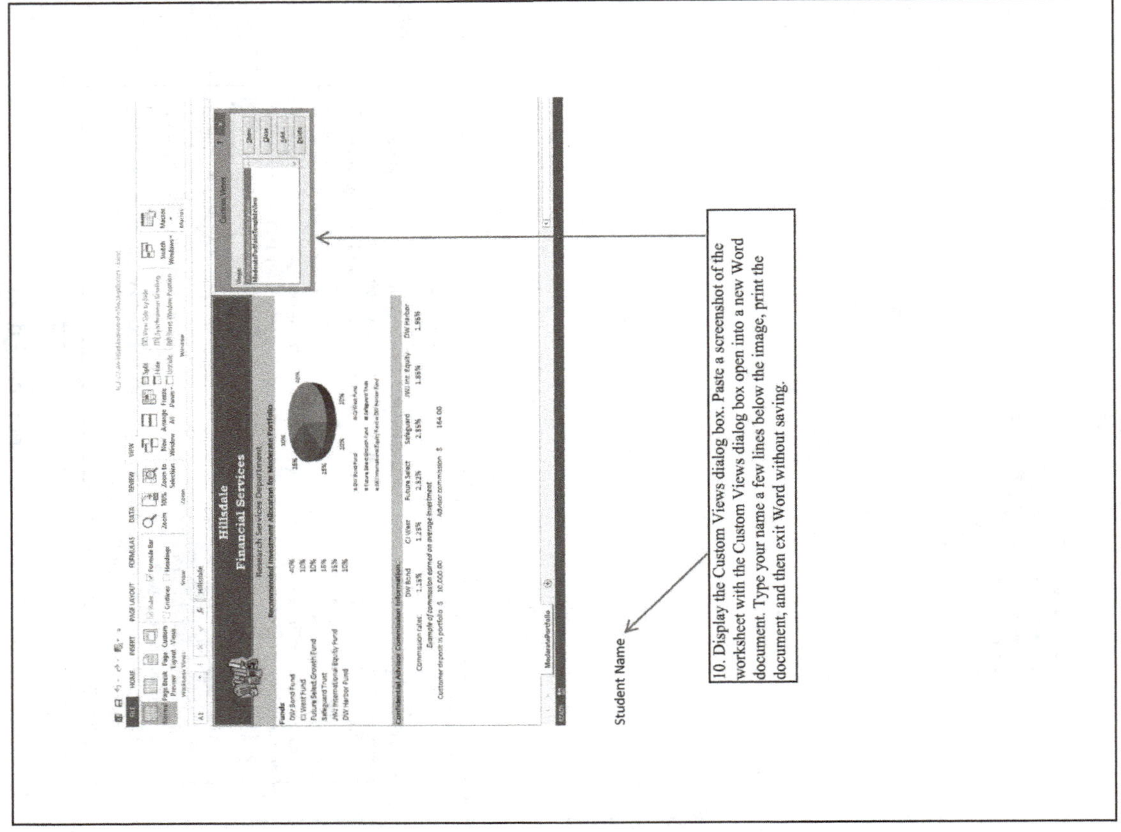

EL2-U2-A6-HillsModPortfolio(A6,Step10).docx

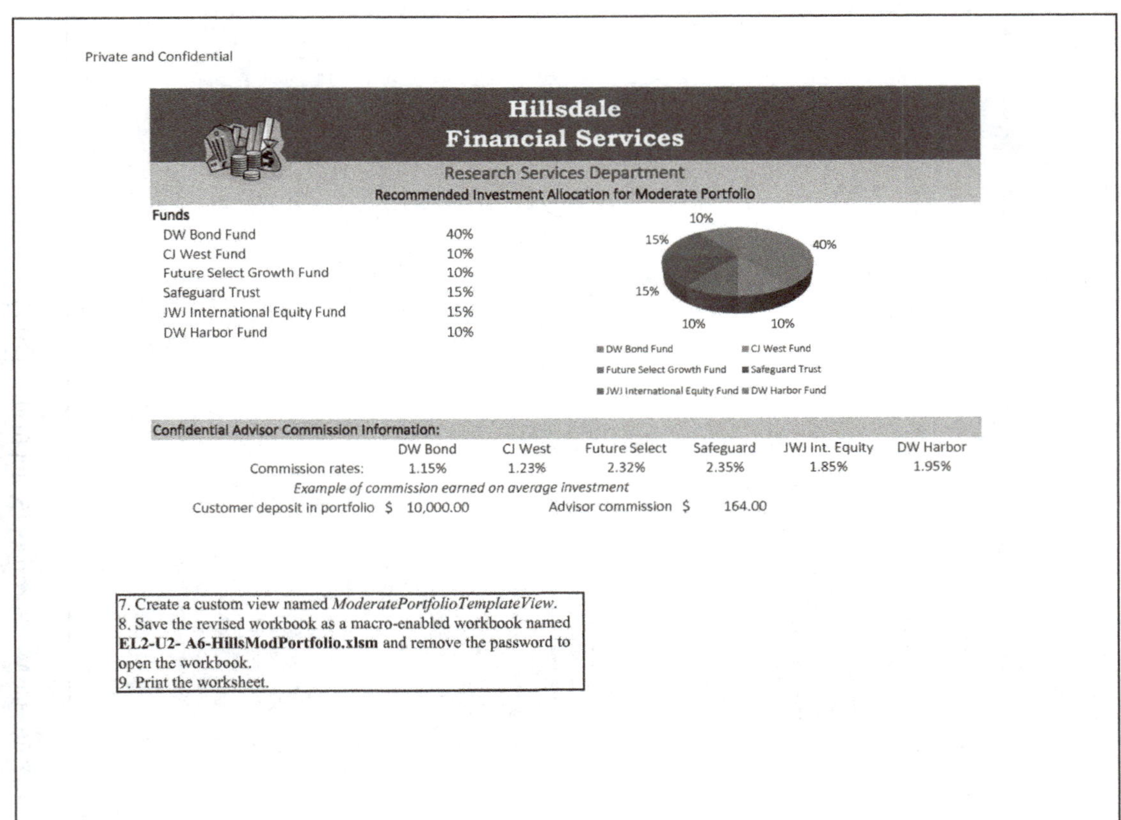

Private and Confidential

Hillsdale
Financial Services

Research Services Department

Recommended Investment Allocation for Moderate Portfolio

Funds	
DW Bond Fund	40%
CJ West Fund	10%
Future Select Growth Fund	10%
Safeguard Trust	15%
JWJ International Equity Fund	15%
DW Harbor Fund	10%

Confidential Advisor Commission Information:

	DW Bond	CJ West	Future Select	Safeguard	JWJ Int. Equity	DW Harbor
Commission rates:	1.15%	1.23%	2.32%	2.35%	1.85%	1.95%

Example of commission earned on average investment

Customer deposit in portfolio $ 10,000.00 Advisor commission $ 164.00

7. Create a custom view named *ModeratePortfolioTemplateView*.
8. Save the revised workbook as a macro-enabled workbook named **EL2-U2- A6-HillsModPortfolio.xlsm** and remove the password to open the workbook.
9. Print the worksheet.

EL2-U2-A6-HillsModPortfolio(A6,Step9).xlsm

1. Open **EL2-U2-A2-HillsResearchInvtTbl.xlsx**.

Hillsdale Financial Services

Research Services Department

Investment Planner

2a. Change the label in cell A3 to *Investment Planner*.

Investment Plan

Monthly contribution	$ (475.00)
Number of years to invest	5
Forecasted annual interest rate	4.75%
Projected value of plan at end of term	$32,097.68

6. Type the following information in the appropriate cells:
Monthly contribution: -475
Number of years to invest: 5
*Forecasted annual interest rate:*4.75%

TABLE 1 Value of plan at increasing monthly contribution and increasing rate of return

	4.00%	4.50%	5.00%	5.50%	6.00%	6.50%
-200	13,259.80	13,429.11	13,601.22	13,776.16	13,954.01	14,134.79
-250	16,574.74	16,786.39	17,001.52	17,220.21	17,442.51	17,668.49
-300	19,889.69	20,143.67	20,401.82	20,664.25	20,931.01	21,202.19
-350	23,204.64	23,500.94	23,802.13	24,108.29	24,419.51	24,735.89
-400	26,519.59	26,858.22	27,202.43	27,552.33	27,908.01	28,269.59
-450	29,834.54	30,215.50	30,602.74	30,996.37	31,396.51	31,803.29
-500	33,149.49	33,572.78	34,003.04	34,440.41	34,885.02	35,336.98
-550	36,464.44	36,930.05	37,403.35	37,884.45	38,373.52	38,870.68
-600	39,779.39	40,287.33	40,803.65	41,328.49	41,862.02	42,404.38

2b. Change the font color of cell A11 to white. This will make the cell appear to be empty. (You want to disguise the entry in this cell because you think displaying the value at the top left of the data table will confuse Hillsdale customers.)

2. Make the following changes to the worksheet:
c. Clear the contents of E5:E7.
d. Protect the worksheet so that editing is allowed only in E5:E7. Assign the password *eL2-U2* to unprotect the worksheet.
3. Save the revised workbook as a template named **HillsInvPlan-StudentName** with your name substituted for *StudentName*.
4. Close **HillsInvPlan-StudentName.xltx**.
5. Start a new workbook based on the **HillsInvPlan-StudentName.xltx** template.
7. Save the workbook as an Excel workbook named **EL2-U2-A7-HillsInvPlan**.
8. Print and then close **EL2-U2-A7-HillsInvPlan.xlsx**.
9. Copy the template created in this assessment to the EL2U2 folder on your storage medium.

EL2-U2-A7-HillsInvPlan(A7).xlsx

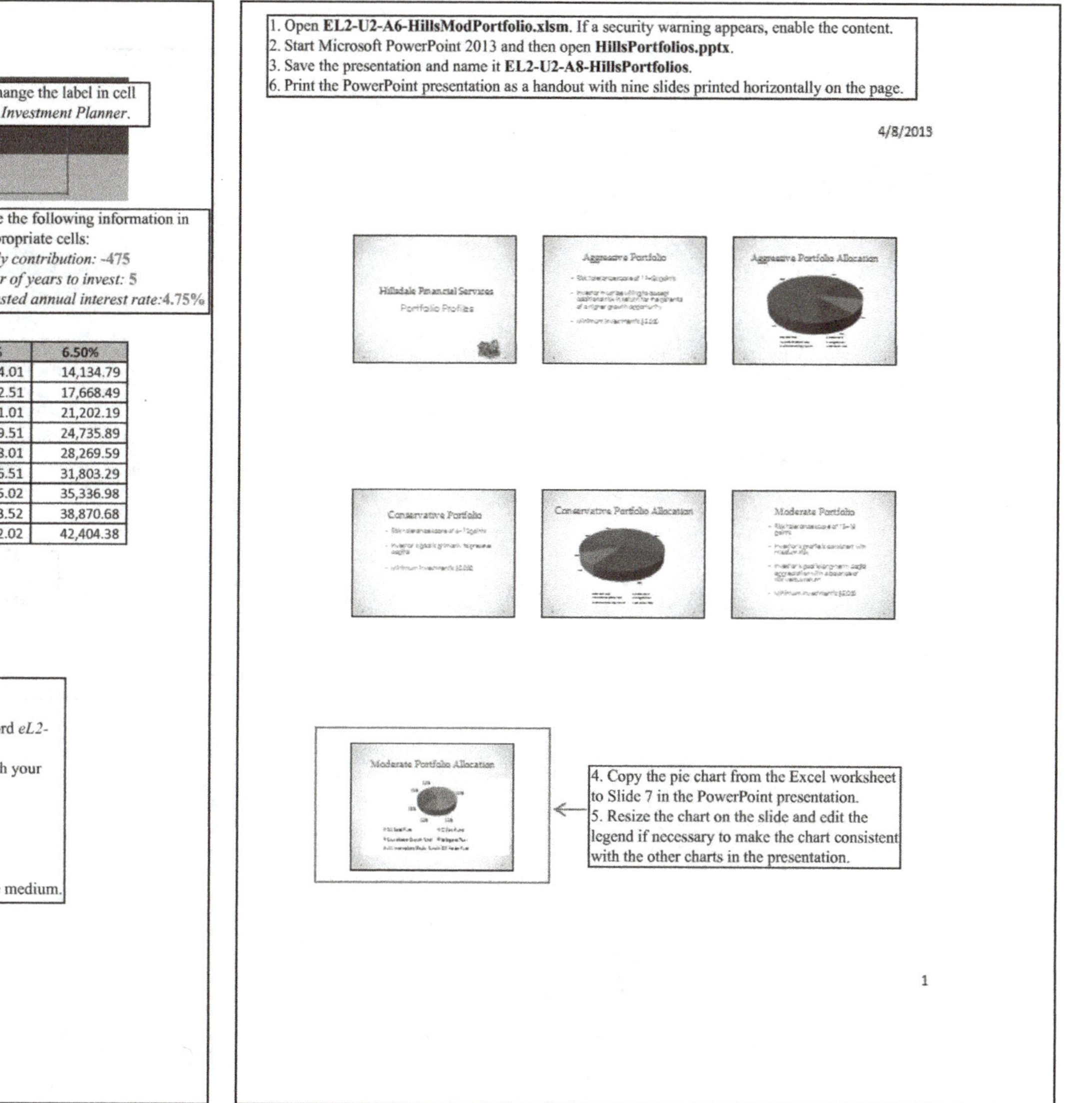

1. Open **EL2-U2-A6-HillsModPortfolio.xlsm**. If a security warning appears, enable the content.
2. Start Microsoft PowerPoint 2013 and then open **HillsPortfolios.pptx**.
3. Save the presentation and name it **EL2-U2-A8-HillsPortfolios**.
6. Print the PowerPoint presentation as a handout with nine slides printed horizontally on the page.

4/8/2013

4. Copy the pie chart from the Excel worksheet to Slide 7 in the PowerPoint presentation.
5. Resize the chart on the slide and edit the legend if necessary to make the chart consistent with the other charts in the presentation.

1

EL2-U2-A8-HillsPortfolios(A8,Step6).pptx

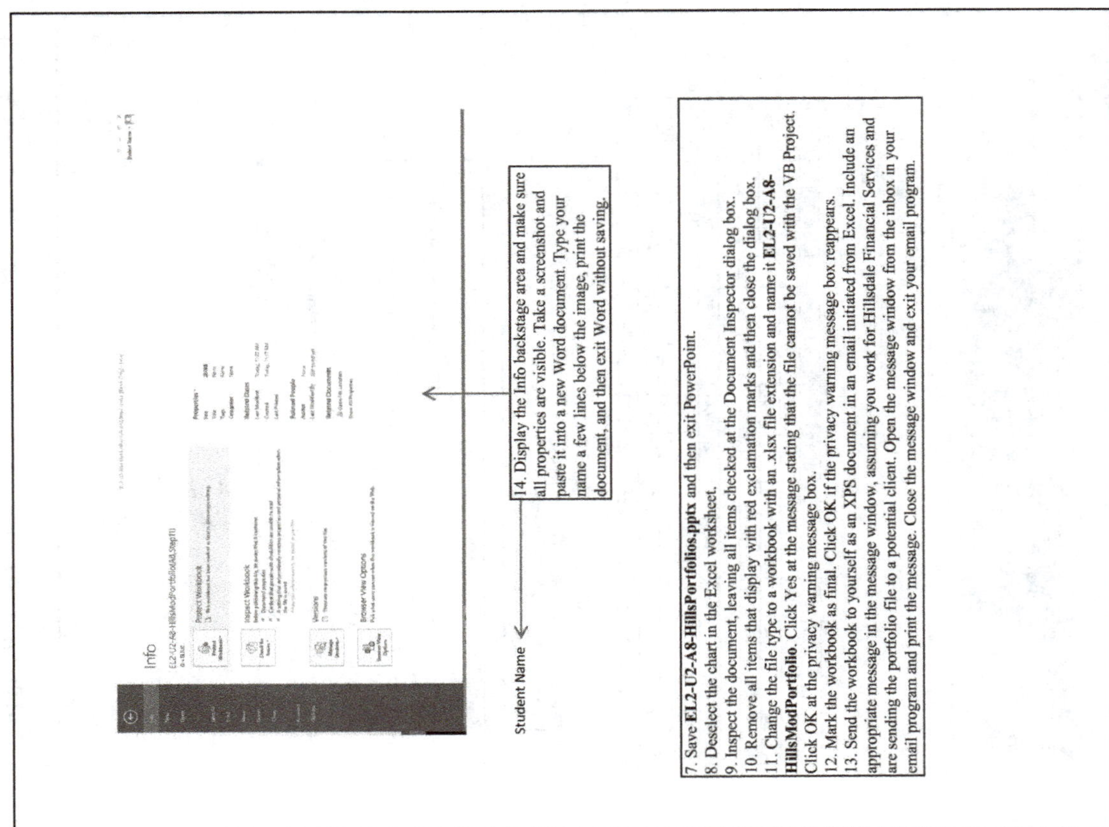

EL2-U2-A8-HillsPortfolios(A8,Step14).docx

Rubrics

Benchmark Excel 2013 Level 1, Chapter 1

Note that the following are suggested rubrics. Instructors should feel free to customize the rubric to suit their grading standards and/or to adjust the point values.

Suggested Scoring Distribution: Above average = student completes 80% or more of task(s); average = student completes 70–79% of task(s); below average = student completes 69% or less of task(s)

Skills Check

Assessment 1: Create a Worksheet using AutoComplete
File: **EL1-C1-A1-Plan.xlsx**

Steps	Tasks	Criteria	Value	Score
1	Typing, Accuracy, Formatting	At a blank workbook, create worksheet shown in Fig. 1.12 as follows: a. To create © symbol in A1, type **(c)**. b. Type misspelled words as shown, letting AutoCorrect correct them; then use AutoComplete to insert second occurrence of *Category, Available,* and *Balance.* c. Merge and center A1 and B1.	7	
2-3	Organization, Finishing	Save as **EL1-C1-A1-Plan.xlsx**, print, then close workbook.	3	
		TOTAL POINTS	10	

Assessment 2: Create and Format a Worksheet
File: **EL1-C1-A2-Exp.xlsx**

Steps	Tasks	Criteria	Value	Score
1	Typing, Formatting, Formulas	At a blank workbook, create worksheet shown in Fig. 1.13 as follows: a. Merge and center A1 through C1. b. After typing, automatically adjust width of column A. c. Insert in B8 sum of B3 through B7, and in C8 sum of C3 through C7. d. Apply *Accounting Number Format* style, decrease decimal point by two positions in B3, C3, B8, and C8. e. Apply *Comma Style, decrease decimal point* two times in B4 through C7. f. For number amounts shown as (###), automatically adjust width of appropriate columns.	7	
2-3	Organization, Finishing	Save as **EL1-C1-A2-Exp**, print, then close workbook.	3	
		TOTAL POINTS	10	

Assessment 3: Create a Worksheet Using the Fill Handle
File: **EL1-C1-A3-Invest.xlsx**

Steps	Tasks	Criteria	Value	Score
1	Typing, Accuracy, Formatting	At a blank workbook, create worksheet shown in Fig. 1.14 as follows: a. Type **Monday** in B2, then use fill handle to fill in remaining days of week. b. Type **350** in B3, then use fill handle to fill in remaining numbers in row. c. Merge and center A1 through G1.	3	
2	Formulas	Insert in G3 the sum of cells B3 through F3, insert in G4 the sum of B4 through F4.	2	
3-4	Formatting	After typing the data, select B3 through G4; then change to *Accounting Number Format, two decimal points*. If necessary, adjust column widths.	2	
5-6	Organization, Finishing	Save as **EL1-C1-A3-Invest**, print, then close workbook.	3	
		TOTAL POINTS	**10**	

Assessment 4: Insert Formulas in a Worksheet
File: **EL1-C1-A4-DIAnalysis.xlsx**

Steps	Tasks	Criteria	Value	Score
1	Organization, Accuracy	Open **DIAnalysis.xlsx**, Save As **EL1-C1-A4-DIAnalysis.xlsx.**	3	
2	Formulas	Insert formula in B15 that totals amounts in B4 through B14.	4	
3-5	Editing	Use fill handle to copy relatively formula in cell B15 to cell C15 and to copy relatively formula in cell D4 down to cells D5 through D14. Insert a formula in cell D4 that finds the average of the amounts in cell B4 and C4.	3	
6	Formatting	Select D5 through D14, then apply Comma Style with zero decimals.	2	
7	Organization, Finishing	Resave, print, then close workbook.	3	
		TOTAL POINTS	**15**	

Visual Benchmark

Create, Format, and Insert Formulas in a Worksheet
File: **EL1-C1-VB-PersExps.xlsx**

Steps	Tasks	Criteria	Value	Score
1	Typing, Editing, Formulas, Formatting	At a blank workbook, create worksheet shown in Fig. 1.15 as follows: a. Type data as shown in the figure. Use fill handle when appropriate, merge and center *Personal Expenses – July through December*, automatically adjust column widths. b. Insert formulas to determine averages and totals. c. Apply *Accounting Number Format* style, *zero decimal places*, to amounts in B4 through H4 and B12 through H12. d. Apply Comma Style, zero decimals, to amounts in B5 through H11.	7	
2-3	Organization, Finishing	Save as **EL1-C1-VB-PersExps**, print, then close workbook.	3	
		TOTAL POINTS	**10**	

Case Study

Part 1
File: **EL1-C1-CS-DICalendar.xlsx**

Steps	Tasks	Criteria	Value	Score
1	Organization, Typing, Editing	Open **DICalendar.xlsx**, then do the following: • Type text *November, 2015* in cell A2, then days of the week (*Sunday*, *Monday*, *Tuesday*, *Wednesday*, *Thursday*, *Friday*, and *Saturday*) in A3 through G3. (Fill handle may be used.) • Insert number *1 through 7* in A4 through G4. • Insert in the calendar the remaining numbers of the days • If fill handle used, fill should not have formatting. • Insert text *Excel training will be held Thursday, November 5 from 9-11 a.m.* in cell E5, using Alt + Enter to put on two lines. • Insert text *A staff meeting is held the second and fourth Monday of each month from 9-10 a.m.* in cells B7 and B11. • Insert text *Time cards are due the first and third Fridays of the month* in cells F5 and F9. • Insert text *A production team meeting is scheduled for Tuesday, November 24, from 1-3 p.m.* in cell C11.	12	
2	Organization, Finishing	Save as **EL1-C1-CS-DICalendar**, print, then close workbook.	3	
		TOTAL POINTS	**15**	

Part 2
File: **EL1-C1-CS-DIExpenditures.xlsx**

Steps	Tasks	Criteria	Value	Score
1	Accuracy, Typing, Formulas	Open **DIExpenditures.xlsx**, insert data shown in Fig. 1.16, then insert formulas to calculate averages and totals. Apply the comma style formatting to cells F5 through F8.	7	
2	Organization, Finishing	Save workbook as **EL1-C1-CS-DIExpenditures**, print, then close.	3	
		TOTAL POINTS	10	

Part 3
File: **EL1-C1-CS-DIExpenditures.xlsx and EL1-C1-CS-DINotetoJS.docx**

Steps	Tasks	Criteria	Value	Score
1	Typing	In Word, type a note to Jennifer Strauss explaining an Excel worksheet has been prepared with Purchasing Department expenditures. Included are cells from the worksheet containing the expenditure information.	6	
2	Organization, Editing, Formatting	In Excel, open **EL1-C1-CS-DIExpenditures.xlsx**, copy cells A3 through F9, then paste them in Word document. Make corrections to the table so information is readable.	5	
3	Organization, Finishing	Save document as **EL1-C1-CS-DINotetoJS.docx**, print, then close. Close **EL1-C1-CS-DIExpenditures.xlsx**.	4	
		TOTAL POINTS	15	

Part 4
File: **EL1-C1-CS-DICopiers.xlsx**

Steps	Tasks	Criteria	Value	Score
1	Research, Typing	After using the Internet to research three companies that sell copiers (different copier models), open **DICopiers.xlsx**, then type the companies, model numbers, and prices in the designated cells.	7	
2	Organization, Finishing	Save as **EL1-C1-CS-DICopiers.xlsx**, print, then close workbook.	3	
		TOTAL POINTS	10	

Benchmark Excel 2013 Level 1, Chapter 2

Skills Check

Assessment 1: Insert AVERAGE, MAX, and MIN Functions
File: **EL1-C2-A1-DISalesAnalysis.xlsx**

Steps	Tasks	Criteria	Value	Score
1-2	Organization, Accuracy	Open **DISalesAnalysis.xlsx**, Save As **EL1-C2-A1-DISalesAnalysis.**	3	
3-7	Functions, Formulas	3. Use AVERAGE function to determine monthly sales (H4 through H9). 4. Format cell H4 with the accounting number format with no places past the decimal point. 5. Total each monthly column including Average column (B10 through H10). 6. Use *MAX* function to determine highest monthly total (for B10 through G10), then insert amount in B11. 7. Use *MIN* function to determine lowest monthly total (for B10 through G10), then insert amount in B12.	10	
8	Organization, Finishing	Save, print, then close workbook **EL1-C2-A1-DISalesAnalysis.xlsx**	2	
		TOTAL POINTS	**15**	

Assessment 2: Insert the Sum Function and Enter Formulas with Mathematical Operators
File: **EL1-C2-A2-CMQrtlyIncome.xlsx**

Steps	Tasks	Criteria	Value	Score
1-2	Organization, Accuracy	Open **CMQrtlyIncome.xlsx**, Save As **EL1-C2-A2-CMQrtlyIncome.**	3	
3	Functions, Editing	Insert the following formulas: a. In cell B7, insert a formula (=B5-B6) b. In cell B12, insert a formula (=SUM(B9:B11) c. In cell B14 insert a formula (=B7-B12) d. In cell B15 enter a formula (=B14-(B14*22%)	5	
4	Formulas	Use Relative Copying: the formulas in column B to columns C and D using the fill handle.	2	
5-7	Formulas, Formatting	Insert the total in cell E5 using the *AutoSum* button to add the range B5:D5. Fill the *SUM function* in cell E5 to the range E6:E15 Apply the *accounting number format* with a dollar sign and one place past the decimal point to cells B5 through E5.	2	
8-9	Organization, Finishing	Insert a *TODAY* function in cell A18. Save, print, then close workbook **EL1-C2-A2-CMQrtlyIncome.xlsx**	3	
		TOTAL POINTS	**15**	

Assessment 3: Write Formulas with Absolute Cell References
File: **EL1-C2-A3-CCQuotas.xlsx**

Steps	Tasks	Criteria	Value	Score
1-2	Organization, Accuracy	Open **CCQuotas.xlsx**, Save As **EL1-C2-A3-CCQuotas.**	3	
3	Formatting, Typing, Function	a. Insert a formula using absolute reference to determine the projected quotas with a 10% increase from the current quota. b. Save and then print **EL1-C2-A3-CCQuotas** **c.** Determine the projected quotas with a 15% increase from the current quota by changing cell A15 to *15% Increase* and cell B15 *to 1.15.* d. Save and then print **EL1-C2-A3-CCQuotas.xlsx.** e. Determine the projected quotas with a 20% increase from the current quota.	4	
4-5	Formatting, Organization, Finishing	Format cell C4 with the accounting number format with no places after the decimal point. Save, print, then close workbook **EL1-C2-A3-CCQuotas.xlxs.**	3	
		TOTAL POINTS	**10**	

Assessment 4: Write Formulas with Mixed Cell References
File: **EL1-C2-A4-AASMileageChart.xlsx**

Steps	Tasks	Criteria	Value	Score
1-2	Organization, Accuracy	Open **AASMileageChart.xlsx**, Save As **EL1-C2-A4-AASMileageChart.xlsx.**	3	
3	Functions, Editing, Formulas	Insert formulas that determine the mileage range of vehicles that have differing mile per gallon and fuel tank capacities in Cell C5 (=B5*C4); change cell references in the formula (absolute) to correctly multiply the correct values in the chart. Use the fill handle to complete the chart (fill without formatting)	14	
4	Finishing	Save, print and close **EL1-C2-A4-AASMileageChart.xlsx**	3	
		TOTAL POINTS	**20**	

Assessment 5: Use Help to Learn about Excel Options
File: **EL1-C2-A5-ParenFormulas.xlsx**

Steps	Tasks	Criteria	Value	Score
1	Using Help	Open blank workbook, use the Help feature and a. Search for "overview of formulas". b. Click Overview of formulas article hyperlink, scroll down to heading "Use of parentheses" c. Read information d. Close the Excel Help feature.	3	
2-3	Opening, Finishing	Open the ParenFormulas.xlsx, save the workbook as **EL1-C2-A5-ParenFormulas**	2	

Steps	Tasks	Criteria	Value	Score
4-7	Formatting, Editing Formulas	Change the results of the formulas individually (do not use the fill handle) in the range B6:B10 by editing the formulas to include parentheses. Edit formulas and compare the new results to the values in Column C. (Yes displays in Column D for each formula) Turn on display of formulas.	8	
8	Finishing	Save, print and then close workbook **EL1-C2-A5-ParenFormulas.xlsx.**	2	
		TOTAL POINTS	15	

Visual Benchmark

Create a Worksheet and Insert Formulas

File: **EL1-C2-VB-Formulas.xlsx**

Steps	Tasks	Criteria	Value	Score
1	Typing, Accuracy, Formulas	At a blank workbook, type the data indicated in Fig. 2.4, but **not** in following cells—instead insert formulas as indicated (results of formulas should match results seen in the figure): • In D3 through D9, insert formula that calculates salary. • In D14 through D19, insert formula that calculates differences. • In B29 through D29, insert formulas that calculates the averages • In E24 through E28, insert formula that calculates the weighted averages of test scores. • *Results should match results in figure 2.4.*	12	
2	Formatting	Apply any other formatting so worksheet looks similar to the one shown in Fig. 2.4.	3	
3-4	Organization, Finishing	Save workbook as **EL1-C2-VB-Formulas**, then print.	2	
5-6	Editing, Finishing, Organization	Display formulas in worksheet, print, turn off the display of formulas, then close workbook **EL1-C2-VB-Formulas.xlsx**.	3	
		TOTAL POINTS	20	

Case Study

Part 1

File: **EL1-C2-CS-AASFebSales.xlsx**

Steps	Tasks	Criteria	Value	Score
1	Organization, Typing, Editing	Open **AASFebSales.xlsx**, then save the workbook with the name **EL1-C2-CS-AASFebSales**: • Column F, insert formula that displays the gross profit • Column H, insert formula that displays the gross profit by the commission percentage • Column I, insert a formula that displays the net profit • Change accounting number format with dollar signs for cells D4, E4, F4, H4, and I4	8	
2	Organization, Finishing	Save as **EL1-C2-CS-AASFebSales.xlsx**.	2	
		TOTAL POINTS	**10**	

Part 2

File: **EL1-C2-CS-AASFebCommissions.xlsx**

Steps	Tasks	Criteria	Value	Score
1	Formulas, Accuracy	Open **AASFebCommissions.xlsx**. Save As **EL1-C2-CS-AASFebCommissions.xlsx.** Insert a formula in Cell C5 that divides B5 by Cell C3. (use absolute cell reference for cell C3). Copy the formula down to cells C6 through C12.	7	
2	Organization, Finishing	Save, print the workbook **AASFebCommissions.xlsx** then close.	3	
		TOTAL POINTS	**10**	

Part 3

File: **EL1-C2-CS-AASFebTradeIns.xlsx**

Steps	Tasks	Criteria	Value	Score
1	Research, Editing	Create a worksheet for automobile trade-ins for the month of February. Any used automobile older than 2010 to be wholesaled after 45 days and any automobile newer than 2009 to be wholesaled after 60 days. Column G: Insert a formula for trade-ins older than 2010, add 45 days to the date in column B. Column G: Insert a formula in to add 45 days to trade-ins 2009 and older and add 60 days to trade-ins 2010 and newer	7	
2	Organization, Finishing	Save the workbook **EL1-C2-CS-AAFebTradeIns.xlsx** then print.	3	
		TOTAL POINTS	**10**	

Part 4

File: **EL1-C2-CS-AASFebTradeIns-2.xlsx**

Steps	Tasks	Criteria	Value	Score
1	Research, Typing, Accuracy	Use the internet to locate at least two websites that provide estimates on the value of used automobiles (such as Kelly Blue Book (kbb.com) and Edmunds.com. Add two hyperlinks to the February trade-ins workbook for these two sites so sales staff can open and review the current sales information.	7	
2	Organization, Finishing	Save print workbook **EL1-C2-CS-AAFebTradeIns-2**. Close.	3	
		TOTAL POINTS	**10**	

Part 5

File: **EL1-C2-CS-DWLetter.docx**

Steps	Tasks	Criteria	Value	Score
1	Feature, Typing, Editing, Accuracy	Use letter template in Word to create a letter to be sent to client to tell client loan has been approved. Copy and link data from **EL1-C2-CS-DWMortgage.xlsx** worksheet to the letter.	7	
2	Organization, Finishing	Save document as **DWLetter**, print, then close.	3	
		TOTAL POINTS	**10**	

Benchmark Excel 2013 Level 1, Chapter 3

Skills Check

Assessment 1: Format a Sales and Bonuses Worksheet

File: **EL1-C3-A1-NSPSales.xlsx**

Steps	Tasks	Criteria	Value	Score
1-2	Organization, Accuracy	Open **NSPSales.xlsx**, Save As **EL1-C3-A1-NSPSales.**	3	
3-5, 7-10	Formatting	3. Change the width of columns as follows: Column A = 14.00, Columns B–E = 10.00, 4. Select row 2 and then insert a new row 5. Merge and center A2 through E2. 7–9. Increase height of row 1 to 33.00, row 2 to 21.00, and row 3 to 18.00. 10. Make formatting changes to worksheet: a. In A1, change font size to 18 points, bold. b. In A2, change font size to 14 points, bold. c. Select A3 through E3, click Bold, then click Center. d. Select A1 through E3, change vertical alignment to Middle Align.	12	

Steps	Tasks	Criteria	Value	Score
6	Typing	Type **Sales Department** in A2 and then press Enter.	2	
11	Formulas	Insert the following formulas: a. In D4, a formula that adds amounts in B4 and C4, then copy it down to D5 through D11. b. In E4, a formula that averages amounts in B4 and C4, then copy it down to E5 through E11.	7	
12	Formatting	Make the following changes to the worksheet: a. Select B4 through E4, apply the accounting number format with a dollar sign, no decimal point b. Select B5 through E11, then apply the Comma Style format and change the number of places past the decimal point to zero. c. Apply the Facet theme to the worksheet. d. Add double-line border around A1 through E11. e. Select A1 and A2, then apply *Blue-Gray, Text 2, Lighter 80%* fill color (fourth column, second row in the *Theme Colors* section) f. Select A3 through E3, then apply *Blue-Gray*, *Text 2*, *Lighter 60%* fill color, (fourth column, third row in the *Theme Colors* section.).	7	
13	Organization, Finishing	Save, print, and close **EL1-C3-A1-NSPSales.xlsx**.	4	
		TOTAL POINTS	**35**	

Assessment 2: Format an Overdue Accounts Worksheet
File: **EL1-C3-A2-CCorpAccts.xlsx**

Steps	Tasks	Criteria	Value	Score
1-2	Organization, Accuracy	Open **CCorpAccts.xlsx**, Save As **EL1-C3-A2-CCorpAccts.**	3	
3-9,	Formatting, Accuracy, Typing	3. Change the width of columns as follows: Column A = 21.00; Column B = 10.00; Column C = 12.00; Column D = 13.00; Column E = 7.00; Column F = 12.00 4. Make cell A1 active, then insert a new row. 5. Merge and center A1 through F1. 6. Type **Compass Corporation** in A1, press Enter. 7–8. Increase height of row 1 to 42.00, then height of row 2 to 24.00. 9a–9c. Select A1 through F11, then change font to *10*-point *Cambria*; make A1 active, change font size to 24 points, turn on bold; make A2 active, change font size to 18 points, turn on bold. d. Select A3 through F3, click Bold button, then click Center button in Alignment group. e. Select A1 , click Middle Align button. f–g. Select B4 through B11, then click Center; select E4 through E11 and then click Center button.	24	

Steps	Tasks	Criteria	Value	Score
10-11	Functions, Formulas	10. Enter a formula in cell F4 that inserts the due date (purchase date plus the number of days in the *Terms* column) Copy the formula down to cells F5 through F11 11. Apply the following borders and fill color: a. Add a thick line outline border around cells A1 through F11. b. Make cell A2 active, add a double-line border at the top and the bottom of the cell. c. Select cells A3 through F3, add a single line border to the bottom of the cells d. Select cells A1 and A2, apply *Blue, Accent 1, Lighter 80%* fill color (fifth column, second row in the *Theme* Colors section)	10	
12	Finishing	Save, print, then close **EL1-C3-A2-CCorpAccts.xlsx** workbook.	3	
		TOTAL POINTS	**40**	

Assessment 3: Format a Supplies and Equipment Worksheet
File: **EL1-C3-A3-OEBudget.xlsx**

Steps	Tasks	Criteria	Value	Score
1-2	Organization, Accuracy	Open **OEBudget.xlsx**, Save As **EL1-C3-A3-OEBudget.**	3	
3-4 10-12 14-17	Formatting	3. Select and then merge across A1 through D2. 4. With A1 and A2 selected, click Middle Align button, then click Center button. 10. Select A3 through A17, turn on bold, then click Wrap Text button. 11. Cell B3, apply currency formatting with no decimal places. 12. Cells C6 through C19, apply percent formatting with one decimal point. 14. D6 through D19, apply currency formatting with no decimal points. 15. D8: clear cell contents. Use F4 to repeat, clear the contents from cells D11- D14, and D17. 16. A1 through D19, change the font to *Constantia*, change the font color to *Dark Blue* (*Standard Colors* section) 17. Cells A1, A2, A5-D5, A8-D8, A11-D11, A14- D14, and A17-D17: Add *Green, Accent 6, Lighter 80% green* fill color (last column, second row in the *Theme Colors* section)	13	
5-6	Formatting, Font sizes	5–6. Make A1 active, then change font size to 22 points and turn on bold; make A2 active, then change font size to 12 points and turn on bold.	4	
7-9 18	Formatting, change height and widths	7–8. Change height of row 1 to 36.00; change height of row 2 to 21.00. 9. Change width of column A to 15.00. 18. Adjust width of Column B	3	

Steps	Tasks	Criteria	Value	Score
13	Formulas	13. Make cell D6 active, type formula that multiplies the absolute cell reference $B$3 with the percentage in cell C6. Copy the formula down to cells D7through D19	4	
19	Saving, Finishing	Save, print, close **EL1-C3-A3-OEBudget.xlsx**	3	
		TOTAL POINTS	**30**	

Assessment 4: Format a Financial Analysis Worksheet
File: **EL1-C3-A4-FinAnalysis.xlsx**

Steps	Tasks	Criteria	Value	Score
1	Research	At a blank workbook, display Format Cells dialog box with Alignment tab selected, then experiment with options in *Text control* section.	3	
2-3	Organization, Accuracy	Open **FinAnalysis.xlsx**, Save As **EL1-C3-A4-FinAnalysis.xlsx.**	3	
4	Formulas, Editing	Make B9 active, then insert formula that averages percentages in B3 through B8. Copy formula to C9 and D9.	4	
5-7	Formatting	5. Select B3 through D9, display Format dialog box, Alignment tab, change horizontal alignment to *Right (Indent)* and indent to 2, then close dialog box. 6–7. Select A1 through D9, then change font size to 14; select B2 through D2, then change orientation to 45 degrees. .	7	
8	Organization, Finishing	Save, print, then close workbook **EL1-C3-A4-FinAnalysis.xlsx**	3	
		TOTAL POINTS	**20**	

Visual Benchmark

Create a Worksheet and Insert Formulas
File: **EL1-C3-VB-BTBookings.xlsx**

Steps	Tasks	Criteria	Value	Score
1	Typing, Accuracy, Formulas	At a blank workbook, type data indicated in Fig. 3.11, but **not** in following cells: B8:D8, B14:D14, B20:D20, B22:D22, and B25:D25—instead *insert formulas* as indicated (results of formulas should match results seen in figure):	12	
2	Formatting	Apply formatting so worksheet looks similar to Fig. 3.11.	3	
3-4	Organization, Finishing	Save as **EL1-C3-VB-BTBookings**, then print.	2	
5-6	Editing, Finishing, Organization	Display formulas in worksheet, print, turn off display of formulas, then close workbook.	3	
		TOTAL POINTS	**20**	

Case Study

Part 1

File: **EL1-C3-CS-HFCDues-1.xlsx** and **EL1-C3-CS-HFCDues-2.xlsx**

Steps	Tasks	Criteria	Value	Score
1	Organization	Open **HFCDues.xlsx**, Save As **EL1-C3-CS-HFCDues-1.xlsx**.	3	
2	Formatting, Typing, Formulas, Editing	Select B3 through D8, apply accounting number formatting, two decimal places, and dollar sign. • In B3, insert *500.00.* • In B4, insert formula that adds amount in B3 with product (multiplication) of B3 multiplied by 10%. (Formula looks like this: **=B3+(B3*10%)**). Copy formula in B4 down to B5 through B8. • Insert formula in C3 that divides amount in B3 by 4, then copy formula down to C4 through C8. • Insert formula in D3 that divides amount in B3 by 12, then copy formula down to D4 through D8. • Apply formatting to enhance visual display of worksheet.	12	
3	Organization, Finishing	Resave, then print worksheet.	2	
4	Organization	With **EL1-C3-CS-HFCDues-1.xlsx** open, *Save As* **EL1-C3-CS-HFCDues-2.xlsx**.	3	
5	Formatting, Typing, Formulas, Editing	• Cell B3: change to $600. • Add late fee information to the worksheet by inserting new column to right of Column C, typing **Late Fees** in D2 and F2. • Insert formula in D3 that multiplies amount in C3 by 5%. Copy formula down to D4 through D8. • Insert formula in F3 that multiplies amount in E3 by 7%, then copy formula down to F4 through F8. (If necessary, change number formatting for F3 through F8 to Accounting with two decimal places and dollar sign.) • Cells B3 through F3, and Cells B8 through F8, change the Accounting format to include dollar signs. • Apply any additional formatting to enhance visual display of worksheet.	7	
6	Organization, Finishing	Save, print, then close worksheet **EL1-C3-CS-HFCDues-2.xlsx**.	3	
		TOTAL POINTS	**30**	

Part 2

File: **EL1-C3-CS-HFCPayroll.xlsx**

Steps	Tasks	Criteria	Value	Score
1	Typing, Accuracy	At a blank workbook, prepare a payroll worksheet using the information in Figure 3.12. Include information as follows.	5	

Steps	Tasks	Criteria	Value	Score
2	Formulas, Formatting, Finishing, Editing	Insert formulas: • *OvertimePay* column that multiplies hourly wage by overtime rate of 1.5. Multiply that amount by the number of overtime hours. • *Weekly Salary Column*: Insert a formula that multiplies the hourly wage by the number of hours plus the overtime pay. • Apply formatting to enhance visual display of worksheet. • Save as **EL1-C3-CS-HFCPayroll**, then print. • Turn on display of formulas, print worksheet again, then turn off display of formulas.	10	
3	Typing, Editing	Make following changes to worksheet: Change hourly wage for **Amanda Turney** to *$22.00;* increase hours for **Daniel Joyner** to *20*; remove row for **Grant Baker**; insert row between **Jean Overmeyer** and **Bonnie Haddon**, type following in cells in new row: Employee: **Tonya McGuire**; Hourly Wage: **$17.50**; Hours: **15**. Overtime hours: 0	6	
4	Editing, Finishing, Organization	Resave and print worksheet **EL1-C3-CS-HFCPayroll.xlsx**. Turn on display of formulas, print worksheet again, then turn off display of formulas. Save, Print and Close workbook, **EL1-C3-CS-HFCPayroll.xlsx**.	4	
		TOTAL POINTS	**25**	

Part 3

File: **EL1-C3-CS-HFCEquip.xlsx**

Steps	Tasks	Criteria	Value	Score
1	Research, Writing	Create a Worksheet using the information from searching the Internet for: • **Elliptical machines** for sale, locating two different models and, and if possible, at least two companies that sell each model. Make a note of company names, model numbers, and prices. • **Recumbent bikes** for sale, locating two different models and if possible, at least two companies that sell each model. Make notes as above. • **Upright bikes** for sale, locating two different models and if possible, at least two companies that sell each model. Make notes as above.	10	
2	Typing, Formulas, Formatting	Prepare an Excel worksheet with the following information: • Company Name, Equipment name; Equipment model; Price • A column that multiplies the price by the number required (which is 3). Include fitness center name, HealthWise Fitness Center, and any other information determined necessary. Apply formatting to enhance visual display of worksheet.	7	
3	Organization, Finishing	Save as **EL1-C3-CS-HFCEquip**, print, then close.	3	
		TOTAL POINTS	**20**	

Part 4
File: **EL1-C3-CS-HFCLetter.docx**

Steps	Tasks	Criteria	Value	Score
1	Feature, Typing, Editing, Accuracy	Use *letter template* in Word to create a letter to be sent to prospective client (user-chosen) on information about the fitness center, plans offered, and dues amounts. Copy data from **EL1-C2-CS-HFCDues-02.xlsx** worksheet to the letter. Make any formatting changes to make data more readable.	7	
2	Organization, Finishing	Save document as **HFCLetter**, print, then close.	3	
		TOTAL POINTS	10	

Benchmark Excel 2013 Level 1, Chapter 4

Skills Check

Assessment 1: Format a Data Analysis Worksheet
File: **EL1-C4-A1-DISemiSales.xlsx**

Steps	Tasks	Criteria	Value	Score
1-2	Organization, Accuracy	Open **DISemiSales.xlsx**, Save As **EL1-C4-A1-DISemiSales.**	3	
3	Formulas, Formatting, Editing	Make changes to worksheet: a. **Cell H4**: Insert formula that averages amounts in cells B4 through G4. b. **Cell H4:** Copy formula down to H5 through H9. c. **Cell B10**: Insert formula adding amounts in B4 through B9. d. **Cell B10**: Copy formula over to cells C10 through H10. (Use *Fill Without Formatting*.) e. **Cell H4**: Apply *Accounting Number* Format style. f. Change orientation of worksheet to *landscape*. g. Change *top margin* to 3 inches, *left margin* to 1.5 inches.	8	
4	Organization, Finishing	Save and print with changes in step 3: **EL1-C4-A1-DISemiSales.xlsx**	4	
5, 6	Formatting	Make additional changes: • Orientation to portrait. • Change top margin to 1 inch, left margin to 0.7 inch. • Horizontally and vertically center worksheet on the page. • Scale worksheet so it fits on one page. • Save, print and close worksheet: **EL1-C4-A1-DISemiSales.xlxs**	5	
		TOTAL POINTS	20	

Assessment 2: Format a Test Results Worksheet
File: **EL1-C4-A2-CMTests.xlsx**

Steps	Tasks	Criteria	Value	Score
1-2	Organization, Accuracy	Open **CMTests.xlsx**, Save As **EL1-C4-A2-CMTests.**	**3**	
3	Formulas, Editing, Typing, Formatting	3a–3f. **Cell N4**: Insert a formula that averages test scores in B4 through M4. **Cell N4**: Copy formula to N5 through N21. **Cell A22**: Type **Average** **Cell B22**: Insert formula that averages test scores in B4 through B21. **Cell B22**: Copy formula to C22 through N22. Insert a page break between columns G and H.	**9**	
4-6	Finishing, Organization	4–5. View worksheet in Page Break Preview, then change back to Normal view. 6. Specify column titles (A3 through A22) to print on each page.	**4**	
7-8		Create header that prints page number at right side of page. Create footer that prints student name at left side of page and workbook file name at right side of page.	**3**	
9-11		9. Display worksheet in Normal view 10. Save, print worksheet 11-12. Set print area for N3 through N22, then print those cells, clear print area.	**4**	
12	Organization, Finishing	Save, then close workbook **EL1-C4-A2-CMTests.xlsx.**	**2**	
		TOTAL POINTS	**25**	

Assessment 3: Format an Equipment Rental Worksheet
File: **EL1-C4-A3-HERInvoices.xlsx**

Steps	Tasks	Criteria	Value	Score
1-2	Organization, Accuracy	Open **HERInvoices.xlsx**, Save As **EL1-C4-A3-HERInvoices.**	**3**	
3-4	Formulas, Editing	**Cell H3**: Insert formula that multiplies rate in cell G3 by hours in F3. Copy formula down to cells H4 through H16. **Cell H17**: Insert formula that sums amounts in H3 through H16.	**5**	
5	Editing	Complete the following find and replaces: a. Find all occurrences of cells containing *75*, replace with *90*. b. Find all occurrences of cells containing *55*, replace with *60*. c. Find all occurrences of *Barrier Concrete*, replace with *Lee Sand and Gravel*. d. Find all occurrences of 11-point Calibri, replace with 10-point Cambria. After completing, clear all formatting from Format buttons.	**5**	

Steps	Tasks	Criteria	Value	Score
6-7	Formatting	Insert header that prints date at left side of page and time at right side of page, then insert footer that prints student name at left side of page and workbook file name at right side of page.	4	
8-9	Organization, Finishing	Print the worksheet horizontally and vertically centered on the page. Save, print, then close workbook **EL1-C4-A3-HERInvoices.xlsx.**	3	
		TOTAL POINTS	**20**	

Assessment 4: Format an Invoices Worksheet
File: **EL1-C4-A4-RPInvoices.xlsx**

Steps	Tasks	Criteria	Value	Score
1-2	Organization, Accuracy	Open **RPInvoices.xlsx**, Save As **EL1-C4-A4-RPInvoices.**	3	
3-9	Formulas, Editing	3–4. **Cell G4**: Insert formula that multiplies amount in E4 with percentage in F4, then adds product to E4. (Result should display as *$488.25*.) Copy formula in G4 down to G5 through G17, click Auto Fill Options button, then click *Fill Without Formatting*. 5. Complete a spelling check. 6. Find all occurrences of *Picture* and replace with *Portrait*. (Goal is to find occurrences that end with an *s*. *Match entire contents* check box should not contain check mark.) 7–9. Sort records by invoice number in ascending order (smallest to largest); complete new sort that sorts records by client number in ascending order (A to Z); complete new sort that sorts date in ascending order (oldest to newest).	12	
10-11	Formatting	10. Insert footer in the worksheet that prints student name at left side of page and current date at right side. 11. Center worksheet horizontally and vertically. 12. Display worksheet in Normal View.	5	
13	Organization, Finishing	Save, then print **EL1-C4-A4-RPInvoices.xlsx**	2	
14	Enhancement	Select cells A3 through G3, then turn on filter feature and complete following filters: a. Filter, then print list of rows containing client number 11-279, then clear the filter. b. Filter, then print list of rows containing top three highest amounts due, then clear the filter. c. Filter, then print list of rows containing amounts due that are less than $500, then clear the filter.	6	
15	Organization, Finishing	Save, then close workbook **EL1-C4-A4-RPInvoices.xlsx.**	2	
		TOTAL POINTS	**30**	

Assessment 5: Create a Worksheet Containing Keyboard Shortcuts

File: **EL1-C4-A5-KeyboardShortcuts.xlsx**

Steps	Tasks	Criteria	Value	Score
1	Research, Typing, Formatting	After using Excel Help feature to learn about keyboard shortcuts, create a worksheet with the following features: • A worksheet title. • Include at least 10 keyboard shortcuts along with an explanation of each shortcut. • Set the data in cells in a typeface other than Calibri and change the data color. • Add borders to cells, add color shading (both are user-selected, shading should be complementary to data color.) • Create header that prints date at right margin; create footer that prints student name at left margin and file name at right margin.	12	
2-3	Organization, Finishing	Save as **EL1-C4-A5-KeyboardShortcuts.xlsx**, print, then close.	3	
		TOTAL POINTS	15	

Visual Benchmark

Create and Format an Expense Worksheet

File: **EL1-C4-VB-HEREexpenses.xlsx**

Steps	Tasks	Criteria	Value	Score
1	Typing, Accuracy, Formulas	At a blank workbook, type data indicated in Fig. 4.13, but **not** in following cells—instead insert formulas as indicated (results of formulas should match results seen in figure). In **N3 through N8**, insert formula that sums monthly expenses for the year. In **B9 through N9**, insert formula that sums the monthly expenses for each month and for entire year.	10	
2-3	Formatting	2. Change left and right margins to 0.45, and change top margin to 1.5. 3. Apply formatting so worksheet looks similar to the one shown in figure (heading in 26-point Cambria, remaining data in 10-point Cambria, bold formatting as shown.)	5	
4, 6-7	Organization, Finishing	After Step 3, Save as **EL1-C4-VB-HEREexpenses**. After Step 5, resave, print, then close (should be on 2 pages).	5	
5	Formatting	After examining Fig. 4.14, make following changes: Insert page break between columns G and H; insert headers and footer as shown; specify column titles print on second page as shown in Fig. 4.14.	5	
		TOTAL POINTS	25	

Case Study

Part 1

File: **EL1-C4-CS-MRMortgages-01.xlsx** and **EL1-C4-CS-MRMortgages-02.xlsx**

Steps	Tasks	Criteria	Value	Score
1	Organization	Open **MRMortgages.xlsx**, Save As **EL1-C4-CS-MRMortgages-01.xlsx**.	3	
2	Formulas, Functions, Formatting, Editing	• In **column C**, insert formula that determines down payment amount; in **column D**, insert formula that determines loan amount; in **column G**, drag formula in G4 down to cells G5 through G47.- • Insert date and time as a header, student name and workbook name as footer. • Find 11-point Calibri formatting and replace with 11-point Candara. • Scale the worksheet so it prints on one page.	12	
3	Organization, Finishing	Resave, then print worksheet **EL1-C4-CS-MRMortgages-01.xlsx.**	2	
4	Editing, Typing, Formatting	• Sort the *Price of Home* column from smallest to largest. • Change percentage amount in column E from 6% to *7%.* • Shade cells in row 4 in *light gold color* that matches the fill in A2. Copy shading to every other row of cells in worksheet (stopping at row 46).	4	
5	Typing, Organization, Finishing	Save As **EL1-C4-CS-MRMortgages-02**. Edit the footer to reflect workbook name change. Resave, print, then close (print on one page).	4	
		TOTAL POINTS	**25**	

Part 2

File: **EL1-C4-CS-MRSalesComms.xlsx**

Steps	Tasks	Criteria	Value	Score
1	Organization	Open **MRSalesComms.xlsx**, Save As **EL1-C4-CS-MRSalesComms.xlsx**.	3	
2	Formulas, Functions, Editing, Formatting, Typing	Make the following changes to the worksheet: • Calculate the sales and commissions, insert totals in the appropriate locations in the worksheet. • Calculate the total sales and total commissions, insert totals in appropriate locations in worksheet. • Apply appropriate number formatting. • Apply formatting similar to worksheet prepared in Part 1. • Change left margin to 1.2 inches, top margin to 1.5 inches • Include a header that prints the page number and a footer that prints student's name.	16	
3	Organization, Finishing	Save, then print (row titles print on both pages).	2	

Steps	Tasks	Criteria	Value	Score
4	Editing, Formatting	Make additional changes: • Remove the header containing page number. Edit footer so date prints at left margin and name prints at the right. • Change orientation to landscape • Scale worksheet so it prints on one page.	7	
5	Organization, Finishing	Save As **EL1-C4-CS-MRSalesComms.xlsx**.	2	
		TOTAL POINTS	**30**	

Part 3

File: **EL1-C4-CS-CanadaPrices.xlsx**

Steps	Tasks	Criteria	Value	Score
1	Research, Writing, Accuracy, Typing, Formatting, Formulas, Functions	Use Internet to search for MS MoneyCentral Investor Currency Rate site, determining current exchange rate for Canada, then create a worksheet with following specs: • Apply formatting similar to formatting in first two parts of case study. • Create the following columns: Column for home price in American dollars that begin with $100,000, increment every $50,000 and end with $1,000,000. Column for home price converted to Canadian dollars. • Apply any additional formatting to improve visual appeal.	25	
2	Organization, Editing, Finishing	Save as **EL1-C4-CS-CanadaPrices.** Display formulas, then print. Redisplay formulas, then close workbook.	5	
		TOTAL POINTS	**30**	

Benchmark Excel 2013 Level 1, Unit 1 Performance Assessment

Assessing Proficiency

Assessment 1: Calculate Total, Maximum, Minimum, and Average Yearly Sales

File: **EL1-U1-A1-DI2015Sales.xlsx**

Steps	Tasks	Criteria	Value	Score
1	Organizing	Open **DI2015Sales.xlsx**. Save as **EL1-U1-A1-DI2015Sales**	2	

Steps	Tasks	Criteria	Value	Score
2-6	Functions, Formulas	2. Cells D4 through D14: Insert appropriate sales totals 3. Cells B15, C15, D15: Insert the appropriate first half, second half, and total sales, respectively. 4. Cell B17: Insert a formula that calculates the maximum total sales amount from cells D4 through D14. 5. Cell B18: Insert a formula that calculates the minimum total sales amount from cells D4through D14. 6. Cell B19: insert a formula that calculates the average of total sales in cells D4 through D14.	11	
7	Formatting, Editing	Apply accounting formatting to Cell D4 with a dollar sign with zero decimal places.	4	
8	Finishing, Organization	Save, print worksheet **EL1-U1-A1-DI2015Sales.xlsx**.	3	
		TOTAL POINTS	**20**	

Assessment 2: Create Worksheet with AutoFill and Calculate Hours and Gross Pay
File: **EL1-U1-A2-CPPayroll.xlsx**

Steps	Tasks	Criteria	Value	Score
1	Organization, Accuracy	Create the Excel worksheet as in Figure U1.1. Use AutoFill to fill in the days of the week, hours	3	
2-4	Formulas	2. Insert formula in cell H4 through H10 that calculates the total hours. 3. Insert formula in J4 through J10 that calculates the gross pay (total hours multiplied by pay rate) 4. Insert formula in cells B11 through J11 that totals the hours, total hours, pay rate, and gross pay.	11	
5-6	Formatting	Apply formatting to cells as shown in figure. Change the orientation to landscape.	4	
7-9	Finishing, Organization	Save worksheet as **EL1-U1-A2-CPPayroll.** Turn on the display of formulas, print the worksheet (prints on two pages) and then turn off the display of formulas. Save and then close **EL1-U1-A2-CPPayroll.xlsx.**	2	
		TOTAL POINTS	**20**	

Assessment 3: Sales Bonuses Workbook
File: **EL1-U1-A3-SBASales.xlsx**

Steps	Tasks	Criteria	Value	Score
1	Organization, Accuracy	**Create the spreadsheet as in Figure U1.2. Format appropriately.**	3	

Steps	Tasks	Criteria	Value	Score
2-4	Functions, Formulas, Editing	2. Insert a formula in Cells D4 through D11 that calculates the bonus amount (sales times bonus). 3. Insert a formula in cells E4 through E11 that calculates the net sales (sales minus bonus amount). 4. Cell B12: Insert the sum of cells B4 through B11; Cell D12: the sum of cells D4 through D11 Cell E12: the sum of cells E4 through E11	12	
5-6	Formatting	Cells B5 through B11 and Cells D5 through D11: Apply accounting formatting with no decimal places, no dollar sign Cells B4, D4, E4, B12, D12, and E12: Apply accounting formatting with a dollar sign, no decimal places	2	
7	Organization, Finishing	Insert a footer that contains your first and last names and the current date Print the worksheet horizontally, vertically centered on the page Save as **EL1-U1-A3-SBASales.xlsx** and close.	3	
		TOTAL POINTS	**20**	

Assessment 4: Format First Quarter Sales Workbook
File: **EL1-U1-A4-CMDeptBudgets.xlsx**

Steps	Tasks	Criteria	Value	Score
1	Organization, Accuracy	Open **CMDeptBudgets.xlsx**, Save As **EL1-U1-A4-CMDeptBudgets.**	3	
2-4	Formulas	2. Insert formula using absolute reference to determine the projected budget with an increase of 10% over the current budget. 3. Insert formulas to total the budget amounts and the projected budget amounts. 4. Cell A15: Use the NOW function to insert the current date and time.	11	
5	Finishing	Save and print the worksheet.	3	
6	Formulas	Cell A3: Determine the projected budget with an increase of 5% over the current budget by changing the text in to 5% *Increase Cell B3:* change the number to 1.05.	5	
7	Finishing, Organization	Save, print and then close **EL1-U1-A4-CMDeptBudgets.xlsx**	3	
		TOTAL POINTS	**25**	

Assessment 5: Format Weekly Payroll Workbook
File: **EL1-U1-A5-CCPayroll.xlsx**

Steps	Tasks	Criteria	Value	Score
1	Organization, Accuracy	Open **CCPayroll.xlsx**, Save As **EL1-U1-A5-CCPayroll.**	3	
2-5	Formulas, Editing	2. E3: Insert formula that multiplies hourly rate by hours, then adds that to multiplication of hourly rate by overtime pay rate (1.5), then overtime hours. (Use parentheses in formula and use an absolute reference for overtime pay rate (1.5). Refer to Chapter 2, Project 5c.) Copy formula down to cells E4 through E16. 3. Cell F3: Insert formula that multiplies gross pay by withholding tax rate (W/H Rate). (Use an absolute reference for containing withholding rate. Refer to Chapter 2, Project 5c.) Copy formula down to cells F4 through F16. 4. Cell G3: Insert formula that multiplies gross pay by Social Security rate (SS Rate). Use an absolute reference for cells containing Social Security rate. (Refer to Chapter 2, Project 5c.) Copy formula down to cells G4 through G16. 5. Cell H4: Insert formula that adds together Social Security tax and withholding tax and subtracts that from gross pay. (Refer to Chapter 2, Project 5c.) Copy formula down to cells H4 through H16.	18	
6, 8	Editing	6. Sort employee last names alphabetically in ascending order (A to Z). 8. Insert footer that prints student name at left side of page and file name at right side.	4	
7	Formatting	Center worksheet horizontally and vertically on page.	2	
9	Organization, Finishing	Resave, print, then close workbook **EL1-U1-A5-CCPayroll.xlsx**	3	
		TOTAL POINTS	**30**	

Assessment 6: Format Customer Sales Analysis Workbook
File: **EL1-U1-A6-DIAnnualSales.xlsx**

Steps	Tasks	Criteria	Value	Score
1	Organization, Accuracy	Open **DIAnnualSales.xlsx**, Save As **EL1-U1-A6-DIAnnualSales.**	3	
2-3	Formulas, Editing, Accuracy, Functions	2. Insert formulas and drag them to complete worksheet. After dragging total formula in row 10, specify to fill without formatting. (This retains right border in N10.) Use AutoFill Options button. 3. Cell B11: Insert formula that calculates the highest total from cells B10 through M10, Cell B12: Insert formula that calculates the lowest total from cells B10 through M10.	8	
4, 7	Formatting	4. Change orientation to landscape. 7. Horizontally and vertically center worksheet.	2	

Steps	Tasks	Criteria	Value	Score
5-6, 8	Editing	5–6. Insert header that prints page number at right side of page, then a footer that prints student name at right side. 8. Specify that column headings in A3 through A12 print on both pages.	4	
9	Organization, Finishing	Resave, print, then close workbook **EL1-U1-A6-DIAnnualSales.xlsx.**	3	
		TOTAL POINTS	**20**	

Assessment 7: Format Invoices Workbook
File: **EL1-U1-A7-RPInvoices.xlsx**

Steps	Tasks	Criteria	Value	Score
1	Organization, Accuracy	Open **RPInvoices.xlsx**, Save As **EL1-U1-A7-RPInvoices.**	3	
2-3	Formulas	Cell G4: Insert formula that multiplies amount in E4 by percentage in F4, then adds that total to amount in E4. (Use parentheses in formula.) Copy the formula in cell G4 down to cells G5 through G18.	4	
4-7	Editing	4. Cell G4: Apply *accounting* number format with two decimal places and a dollar sign Cells G5 through G18: apply *Comma style* formatting with two decimal places 5-7. Find all occurrences of cells containing *11-279* and replace with *10*-005; then find all occurrences of cells containing *8.5* and replace with *9.0*. Search for *Calibri* font, then replace with Candara font. (Font size not specified.)	5	
8-11	Enhancement, Finishing	8. Print worksheet EL1-U1-A7-RPInvoices.xlsx. 9–11. Filter, then print list of rows containing only client number 04-*325*. (After printing, return to *(Select All)*.) Filter, then print list of rows containing only service *Development*. (Return to *(Select All)*.) Filter, then print list of rows containing top three highest totals in *Amount Due* column, and after printing, turn off filter feature.	6	
12	Organization	Resave, then close workbook **EL1-U1-A7-RPInvoices.xlsx.**	2	
		TOTAL POINTS	**20**	

Writing Activities

Activity 1: Plan and Prepare Orders Summary Workbook
File: **EL1-U1-Act1-OrdersSumm.xlsx**

Steps	Tasks	Criteria	Value	Score
1	Accuracy, Typing, Formatting	Plan and prepare worksheet with the information shown in Fig. U1.3. Apply formatting (user-chosen) to worksheet.	12	

Steps	Tasks	Criteria	Value	Score
2	Organization, Finishing	Save as **EL1-U1-Act1-OrdersSumm.xlxs**, print, then close.	3	
		TOTAL POINTS	15	

Activity 2: Prepare Depreciation Workbook
File: **EL1-U1-Act2-DepMethods.xlsx**

Steps	Tasks	Criteria	Value	Score
1	Research, Typing, Functions, Formatting	Use Excel Help feature to learn about depreciation methods—straight-line, fixed-declining and double-declining (Financial Category) Create an Excel worksheet with following information: • An appropriate title • A heading for straight-line depreciation, and one for the straight-line depreciation function • The name and description for each straight-line depreciation function argument category • A heading for double-declining depreciation, double-declining depreciation function, and name and description for each double-declining depreciation function argument category Apply formatting (user-chosen) to worksheet.	11	
2	Organization, Finishing	Save as **EL1-U1-Act2-DepMethods**, print (with worksheet horizontally/vertically/centered on page), then close.	4	
		TOTAL POINTS	15	

Activity 3: Insert Straight-Line Depreciation Formula
File: **EL1-U1-Act3-RPDepreciation.xlsx** and **EL1-U1-Act3-DepReport.docx**

Steps	Tasks	Criteria	Value	Score
1	Organization, Accuracy	Open **RPDepreciation.xlsx**, Save As **EL1-U1-Act3-RPDepreciation.**	3	
2	Functions, Editing, Formatting	E4: Insert function to determine straight-line depreciation. Copy formula down to E5 through E9. Apply formatting (user-chosen) to worksheet.	5	
3	Finishing, Organization	Save as **EL1-U1-Act3-RPDepreciation.xlsx**, print (worksheet horizontally/vertically/centered on page), then close.	4	
4	Research, Writing	[**OPTIONAL EXERCISE**] Use Internet or school library to research topic of straight-line and double-declining depreciation, to learn why businesses depreciate their assets. What purpose does it serve? Use Word 2010 to write a half-page, single-spaced report explaining financial reasons for using depreciation methods.	10	
5	Organization, Finishing	[**OPTIONAL EXERCISE**] Save document as **EL1-U1-Act3-DepReport**, print, then close.	3	
		TOTAL POINTS	25	

Internet Research

Activity 4: Create a Travel Planning Worksheet
File: **EL1-U1-Act4-TrvWksht.xlsx**

Steps	Tasks	Criteria	Value	Score
1	Research, Typing, Formulas, Formatting	After using Internet (user-chosen search engine) to research info on traveling to specific country of interest, find sites providing cost info for airlines, hotels, meals, entertainment, and car rentals. Create travel planning worksheet for country chosen that includes: • An appropriate title and appropriate headings • Airline costs, hotel costs (off-season and in-season rates if available), estimated meal costs, entertainment costs, and car rental costs.	12	
3	Organization, Finishing	Save as **EL1-U1-Act4-TrvlWksht**, print, then close.	3	
		TOTAL POINTS	15	

Benchmark Excel 2013 Level 1, Chapter 5

Skills Check

Assessment 1: Copy and Paste Data Between Worksheets in a Sales Workbook
File: **EL1-C5-A1-EPSales.xlsx**

Steps	Tasks	Criteria	Value	Score
1	Organization, Accuracy	Open **EPSales.xlsx**, Save As **EL1-C5-A1-EPSales.xlsx**.	3	
2-3	Editing, Accuracy, Typing	2. Turn on display of the Clipboard task pane, click Clear All button, then complete the following: a–c. Select and copy cells A7 through C7; select and copy A10 through C10; then select and copy A13 through C13. d–f. Display second worksheet, make A7 active, then paste the *Avalon Clinic* cells; make A10 active, then paste *Stealth Media* cells; then make A13 active and paste the *Danmark Contracting* cells. g. Make the third worksheet active, then complete similar steps to paste the cells in same location as second worksheet. h. Clear contents of Clipboard task pane, then close. 3. Change names of Sheet1 tab to *2013 Sales*, Sheet2 tab to *2014 Sales*, and Sheet3 tab to *2015 Sales*.	18	
4	Formatting	4. Change colors of **2013** Sales tab to *blue*, **2014** Sales tab to *green*, and **2015** Sales tab to *yellow*.	3	
5-6	Formulas	5. Display 2013 Sales worksheet, select all three tabs, then insert a formula in *D4* that sums amounts in cells B4 and C4. Copy formula down to cells D5 through D14. 6. Make D15 active, then insert a formula that sums amounts in cells D4 through D14.	4	

Steps	Tasks	Criteria	Value	Score
7-8	Formatting, Editing	7. Apply *accounting* formatting with a dollar sign and no decimal places to Cell D4 (on all three worksheets) 8. Insert footer on all three worksheets that prints student name at left side and current date at right.	4	
9-10	Organization, Finishing	Resave, print all 3 worksheets, then close **workbook EL1-C5-A1-EPSales.xlsx.**	3	
		TOTAL POINTS	**35**	

Assessment 2: Copy, Paste, and Format Worksheets in an Income Statement Workbook

File: **EL1-C5-A2-CMJanIncome.xlsx**

Steps	Tasks	Criteria	Value	Score
1	Organization, Accuracy	Open **CMJanIncome.xlsx**, Save As **EL1-C5-A2-CMJanIncome.xlsx.**	3	
2	Editing	Copy cells A1 through B17 in Sheet1, paste into Sheet2. (Using Paste Options button, keep Source Column Widths.)	3	
3	Formatting, Typing	Make changes to the Sheet2 worksheet: a. Adjust row heights so they match heights in Sheet1. b. Change the month from January to February. c–e. Change amount in B4 to 97,655; the amount in B5 to 39,558; then the amount in B11 to *1,105*.	4	
4	Formulas	Select both sheet tabs, insert the following formulas: A formula in B6 that subtracts *Cost of Sales* from *Sales Revenue* **(=*B4-B5*)**; a formula in B16 that sums amounts in B8 through B15; then a formula in B17 that subtracts *Total Expenses* from the *Gross Profit* **(=*B6-B16*).**	5	
5-6	Formatting, Typing	5. Change name of Sheet1 tab to *January* and name of Sheet2 tab to February. 6. Change color of *January tab to blue* and *color of February tab to red.*	4	
7	Editing	Insert custom header on both worksheets that prints student name at left, date in the middle, and file name at right.	3	
8	Organization, Finishing	Resave, print, then close workbook **EL1-C5-A2-CMJanIncome.xlsx**	3	
		TOTAL POINTS	**25**	

Assessment 3: Freeze and Unfreeze Window Panes in a Test Scores Workbook

File: **EL1-C5-A3-CMCertTests.xlsx**

Steps	Tasks	Criteria	Value	Score
1	Organization, Accuracy	Open **CMCertTests.xlsx**, Save As **EL1-C5-A3-CMCertTests.xlsx.**	3	
2-4	Customization, Accuracy	2. Make cell A1 active, split window by clicking View tab, then clicking Split button in Window group. (Window splits into four panes.) 3. Drag horizontal and vertical gray lines up and to left until horizontal gray line is immediately below second row and vertical gray line is immediately to right of first column. 4. Freeze window panes.	4	
5	Editing, Typing	Add two rows immediately above row 18, then type text shown (in Step 5, on page 181) in specified cells.	8	
6	Formulas, Editing	Insert formula in cell N3 that averages percentages in cells B3 through M3; copy down to N4 through N22.	3	
7-8	Formatting	Unfreeze window panes, remove split.	2	
9	Formatting	Change orientation to *Landscape,* then scale worksheet to print on one page (using *Width* option in the Scale to Fit group in Page Layout tab).	2	
10	Organization, Finishing	Resave, print, then close workbook **EL1-C5-A3-CMCertTests.xlsx.**	3	
		TOTAL POINTS	**25**	

Assessment 4: Create, Copy, Paste, and Format Cells in an Equipment Usage Workbook

File: **EL1-C5-A4-HCMachRpt.xlsx**

Steps	Tasks	Criteria	Value	Score
1-2	Typing, Formatting, Organization	At a blank workbook, create worksheet shown in Fig. 5.10, changing width of column A to 21. Save as **EL1-C5-A4-HCMachRpt**.	5	
3-4	Organization, Editing	3. With EL1**-C5-A4-HCMachRpt.xlsx** open, open **HCEqpRpt.xlsx**. 4. Select and copy following cells from **HCEqpRpt.xlsx** to **EL1-C5-A4-HCMachRpt.xlsx**: a–b. Copy A4 through G4 in **HCEqpRpt.xlsx**, paste into **EL1-C5-A4-**HCMachRpt**.xlsx** beginning with cell A12; copy A10 through G10 in **HCEqpRpt.xlsx**, paste into **EL1-C5-A4-HCMachRpt.xlsx** beginning with cell A13.	5	

Steps	Tasks	Criteria	Value	Score
5-9	Formatting, Finishing	5. With **EL1-C5-A4-HCMachRpt.xlsx** active, make cell A1 active, then apply following formatting: a. Change height of row 1 to *25.20*. b. Change font size of text in cell A1 to *14 points*. c. Cell A1: Apply the *Blue, Accent 5, Lighter 80% fill color* (ninth column, second row in the Theme Colors section) 6. Select cells A2 through G2, apply the *Blue, Accent 5, Darker 50% fill color* (ninth column, last row in the *Theme Colors* section). 7. Select B2 through G2, apply *white, Background 1 text color* (first column, first row in the *Theme Colors* section) (Make sure the text in the cells is right-aligned) 8. Select A3 through G3, A7 through G7, A11 through G11: : apply the *Blue, Accent 5, Lighter 80% fill color* (ninth column, second row in the Theme Colors section) 9.Print worksheet centered horizontally and vertically.	12	
10-11	Organization, Finishing	Save, then close workbook. Close **EL1-C5-A4-HCMachRpt.xlsx**. Close **HCEqpRpt.xlsx**	3	
		TOTAL POINTS	25	

Assessment 5: Copying and Linking Data in a Word Document
File: **EL1-C5-A5-DWLtr.docx** and **EL1-C5-A5-DWMortgages.xlsx**

Steps	Tasks	Criteria	Value	Score
1-2	Organization, Accuracy	In Word, open **DWLtr.docx**, Save As **EL1-C5-A5-DWLtr**. In Excel, open **DWMortgages.xlsx**, Save As **EL1-C5-A5-DWMortgages**.	6	
3	Formulas, Functions, Formatting	Copy cells A2 through G10	4	
4-7	Editing, Accuracy	4–8. Click Word button on Taskbar, move insertion point between two paragraphs of text, click Paste button arrow, then click *Paste Special* at drop-down list; at Paste Special dialog box, click *Paste link* option, click *Microsoft Excel Worksheet Object* in *As* list box, then click OK.	6	
8	Formatting	Save, print, close EL1-C5-A5-DWLtr.docx	2	
9-15	Organization, Finishing	9-11. Open Excel. Cell A3: change number from $300,000 to $400,000. Copy A3 ($400,000) down to cells A4 through A10 and then apply accounting number format (no dollar signs, no decimal places). Save, print, close **EL1-C5-A5-DWMortgages.xlsx** 12-14. Open Word EL1-C5-A5-DWLtr.docx from taskbar and update data from linked files. Save, print, then close **EL1-C5-A5-DWLtr.docx**.	12	
		TOTAL POINTS	30	

Visual Benchmark

Create and Format a Sales Worksheet Using Formulas

File: **EL1-C5-VB-CMSemiSales.xlsx**

Steps	Tasks	Criteria	Value	Score
1	Typing, Editing, Formulas, Formatting	At a blank workbook, create worksheet shown in Fig. 5.10 as follows: • Do not type data in cells D4 through D9; instead enter a formula that totals first-half and second-half yearly sales. • Apply formatting shown in the figure, including changing font sizes, column widths, row heights, shading, and borders. • Rename sheet tab, change tab color as shown in figure.	12	
2	Editing	Copy A1 through D9, then paste the cells in Sheet2.	3	
3	Editing, Typing, Formatting	Edit the cells and apply formatting, matching worksheet shown in Fig. 5.11. Rename sheet tab and change tab color as shown in the figure.	5	
4-6	Organization, Finishing	Save completed workbook as **EL1-C5-VB-CMSemiSales**. Print both worksheets, then close **EL1-C5-VB-CMSemiSales.xlsx**.	5	
		TOTAL POINTS	25	

Case Study

Part 1

File: **EL1-C5-CS-GGExp.xlsx**

Steps	Tasks	Criteria	Value	Score
1	Typing, Editing, Formatting, Formulas	At a blank workbook, create a worksheet as follows: • Company name is Gateway Global and the title is *January Expenditures*. • Create columns and type info Figure 5.12 • Insert formula in Total column that sums amounts in supplies and equipment columns, then insert formula in total row that sums supplies amounts, equipment amounts, and total amounts. • Apply formatting (fill color, borders, font color, shading) to enhance visual appeal of worksheet.	15	

Steps	Tasks	Criteria	Value	Score
2	Editing, Typing	After creating and formatting worksheet, do the following: • Insert a new worksheet and then copy the data from Sheet 1 to Sheet 2. • Insert a new worksheet and then copy the data in Sheet1 to Sheet 3. Make following changes to data in Sheet2: • Change *January Expenditures* to *February Expenditures*. • Change Production department supplies to *$38,550* and equipment amount to *$88,500.* • Change Technical Support department equipment amount to *$44,250* and Finance department supplies to *$7,500.* Make the following changes to data in Sheet3: • Change *January Expenditures* to *March Expenditure.* • Change Production department supplies amount supplies to *$65,000* and equipment amount to *$150,000.* • Change Technical Support department supplies amount to *$21,750* and equipment amount to *$43,525.* Change Facilities department equipment amount to *$18,450.*	10	
3	Typing, Formatting, Editing	Create a new worksheet that summarizes supplies and equipment totals for January, February, and March. Apply same formatting to worksheet as applied to other three. Change tab name for Sheet1 to *Jan. Expenditures*, for Sheet2 to *Feb. Expenditures*, for Sheet3 to *Mar. Expenditures*, and for Sheet4 to *Qtr. Summary.* Change color of each tab (user-determined). Insert header that prints student name at left side of each worksheet and current date at right side.	7	
4	Organization, Finishing	Save as **EL1-C5-CS-GGExp**, print, then close workbook.	3	
		TOTAL POINTS	**35**	

Part 2
File: **EL1-C5-CS-GGStats.xlsx**

Steps	Tasks	Criteria	Value	Score
1	Formulas, Typing, Formatting, Editing	Open **CGStats.xlsx**, change both worksheets as follows: • Insert formula that calculates a player's batting average (Hits ÷ At Bats); then a formula that calculates player's on-base percentage: (Walks + Hits) ÷ (At Bats + Walks). • Select E5 through F15, then specify three decimal places. • Insert company name. • Apply formatting to enhance visual appeal of worksheets; then horizontally and vertically center worksheets. • Insert footer that prints on both worksheets, with student name at left of worksheet and date at right.	12	
2	Research, Enhancement	After using Help feature and/or experimenting, apply *Good* cell style to any cell in *Batting Average* column with average over .400; apply same style to cells in both worksheets.	5	

Steps	Tasks	Criteria	Value	Score
3	Organization, Finishing	Save, print, then close workbook EL1-C5-CS-GGStats.xlsx	3	
		TOTAL POINTS	**20**	

Part 3

File: **EL1-C5-CS-GGConv.xlsx**

Steps	Tasks	Criteria	Value	Score
1	Research, Typing, Accuracy	After using the Internet for research, create a conversion worksheet in a blank workbook as follows: • Include length conversions: 1 inch to centimeters; 1 foot to centimeters; 1 yard to meters; 1 mile to kilometers.	15	
2	Research, Formulas, Editing	Locate a site on the Internet that provides formula for converting Fahrenheit temperatures to Celsius, then create another worksheet in workbook with the following: Insert Fahrenheit temperatures beginning with zero, continuing to 100, and incrementing by 5 (for example, 0, 5, 10, 15); then insert formula converting Fahrenheit temperatures to Celsius.	8	
3	Typing, Formatting	Include company name *Gateway Global* in both worksheets. Apply additional formatting to improve the visual appeal of worksheets. Rename both sheet names, then apply a color to each tab (name and color are user-chosen).	8	
4	Organization, Finishing	Save as **EL1-C5-CS-GGConv**. Print both worksheets centered horizontally and vertically, then close the workbook.	4	
		TOTAL POINTS	**35**	

Part 4

File: **EL1-C5-CS-GGLtrhd.docx** and **EL1-C5-CS-GGConvLtr.docx**

Steps	Tasks	Criteria	Value	Score
1	Typing, Formatting, Organization	At a blank document in Word, create letterhead containing the following: The company name *Gateway Global*, the address including street address, city, state, and ZIP code, or street address, city, province, and postal code (user-determined); and the telephone number (user-determined). Apply formatting to improve visual appeal of the letterhead. Save as **EL1-C5-CS-GGLtrhd**; then save again as **EL1-C5-CS-GGConvLtr**.	10	
2	Organization, Editing, Formatting	In Excel, open **EL1-C5-CS-GGConv.xlsx**. In first worksheet, copy the cells containing data, then paste into **EL1-C5-CS-GGConvLtr.docx** as a picture object. Center the picture object between left and right margins.	5	
3	Organization, Finishing	Save, print, then close **EL1-C5-CS-ConvLtr.docx**. Exit Word, then in Excel, close **EL1-C5-CS-GGConv.xlsx**.	5	
		TOTAL POINTS	**20**	

Benchmark Excel 2013 Level 1, Chapter 6

Skills Check

Assessment 1: Manage Workbooks

File: **N/A**

Steps	Tasks	Criteria	Value	Score
1-7	Folder and Workbook Management, Accuracy	1. Display Open dialog box with EL1C6 folder as the active folder. 2–6. Create new folder named *O'Rourke* in the EL1C6 folder. Copy **OEBudget.xlsx**, **OEPayroll.xlsx**, and **OEPlans.xlsx** to O'Rourke folder. Display contents of O'Rourke folder, rename **OEBudget.xlsx** to **OEEquipBudget.xlsx**; then rename **OEPlans.xlsx** to **OEPurchasePlans.xlsx**. Change the active folder back to EL1C6. 7. Close Open dialog box.	10	
		TOTAL POINTS	10	

Assessment 2: Move and Copy Worksheets Between Sales Analysis Workbooks

File: **EL1-C6-A2-DISales.xlsx**

Steps	Tasks	Criteria	Value	Score
1-2	Organization, Accuracy	Open **DISales.xlsx**, Save As **EL1-C6-A2-DISales.xlsx**; Rename Sheet 1 as 1st Qtr.	2	
3-6	Editing, Copying	From **DIQtrs.xlsx:** Rename Sheet1 as *2nd Qtr* and then copy it to **EL1-C6-A2-DISales.xlsx** following the 1st Qtr worksheet. (*When copying the worksheet, insert a check mark in the* ***Create a copy*** *check box in the Move or Copy dialog box)* Make **DIQtrs.xlsx** active, rename Sheet2 as *3rd Qtr*, and then copy it to **EL1-C6-A2-DISales.xlsx** following the 2nd Qtr tab. Close without saving changes.	9	
7-8		Open **DI4thQtr.xlsx.** Rename Sheet 1 as 4th Qtr and copy into the 4th Qtr worksheet of **EL1-C6-A2-DISlaes.xlsx**	2	
9	Editing, Formulas, Formatting	With **EL1-C6-A2-DISales.xlsx** open, make the following changes to all four quarterly worksheets at same time: a–b. Make 1st Qtr active worksheet, then hold down Shift key and click 4th Qtr tab (selecting all four worksheets). c–d. Insert in cell E4 a formula to calculate average of cells B4 through D4, then copy formula down to cells E5 through E9. Insert in B10 formula to calculate sum of cells B4 through B9, then copy formula to C10 through E10. e. Make E4 active, apply Accounting *Number Format* with no decimal places.	8	
10-11	Editing, Formatting	10. Insert footer on all worksheets that prints student name at left, page number in middle, current date at right. 11. Horizontally and vertically center all worksheets.	5	
12-13	Organization, Finishing	Resave, print all four worksheets, then close workbook **EL1-C6-A2-DISales.xlsx.**	4	

Steps	Tasks	Criteria	Value	Score
		TOTAL POINTS	**30**	

Assessment 3: Define and Apply Styles to a Projected Earnings Workbook
File: **EL1-C6-A3-Styles.xlsx** and **EL1-C6-A3-ProjEarnings.xlsx**

Steps	Tasks	Criteria	Value	Score
1-3	Organization, Formatting, Enhancement	1. At a blank worksheet, define a style named *C06Heading* with following formatting: a–d. 14-point Cambria bold in *dark blue* color; *horizontal alignment* of *Center*; top and bottom border in *dark blue* color; and *light yellow* fill. 2. Define a style named *C06Subheading* that contains following formatting: a–d. *12-point Cambria* bold in *dark blue* color; *horizontal alignment* of *Center*; top and bottom border in *dark blue* color; and *light green* fill. 3. Define style named *C06Column* with the following formatting: a–c. At Style dialog box, click *Number* check box to remove check mark; *12-point Cambria* in *dark blue color*; and *light green fill*.	**13**	
4-6, 9, 11	Organization	4. Save workbook and name it **EL1-C6-A3-Styles**. 5–6. With **EL1-C6-A3-Styles.xlsx** open, open **ProjEarnings.xlsx**, Save As **EL1-C6-A3-ProjEarnings**. 9. Copy styles from **EL1-C6-A3-Styles.xlsx** into **EL1-C6-A3-ProjEarnings.xlsx**. 11. Save again, then print **EL1-C6-A3-ProjEarnings.xlsx**.	**10**	
7	Formulas	Make C6 active, insert a formula that multiplies content of B6 with amount in B3. (Cell B3 is an absolute reference.) Copy formula down to cells C7 through C17.	**3**	
8, 10	Formatting, Enhancement	8. Make C6 active, click *Accounting Number* Format. 10. Apply following styles: a–c. Select A1 and A2, apply *C06Heading* style; select A5 through C5, apply *C06Subheading* style; then select A6 through A17, apply *C06Column* style.	**4**	
12	Formatting, Enhancement	With **EL1-C6-A3-ProjEarnings.xlsx** open, modify styles: a–c. Modify *C06Heading* so it changes font color to *dark green* (last column, sixth row) , *vertical alignment* to *Center*, and inserts top and bottom border in *dark green*.(last column, sixth row) Modify *C06Subheading* so it changes font color to *dark green* (last column, sixth row) and inserts a top and bottom border in *dark green*. Modify *C06Column* so it changes font color to *dark green* (last column, sixth row) but leaves all of other formatting attributes.	**6**	
13-14	Organization, Finishing	Resave, print **EL1-C6-A3-ProjEarnings**, then close all other open workbooks without saving them.	**4**	
		TOTAL POINTS	**40**	

Assessment 4: Insert Hyperlinks in a BookStore Workbook
File: **EL1-C6-A4-BGSpecials.xlsx**

Steps	Tasks	Criteria	Value	Score
1	Organization, Accuracy	Open **BGSpecials.xlsx**, Save As **EL1-C6-A4-BGSpecials.xlsx**.	3	
2-6	Editing, Typing, Accuracy	Make cell **E3** active, then hyperlink it to www.microsoft.com; Make **E4** active, then hyperlink to www.symantec.com; Make **E5** active, then hyperlink to www.nasa.gov; Make **E6** active, hyperlink to www.cnn.com website. Make **A8** active, type **Weekly specials!** then create a hyperlink to workbook named **BGWklySpcls.xlsx**.	10	
7-9	Accuracy, Research	Click hyperlink to the Microsoft website, explore the site, then close the web browser. Click hyperlink to NASA site, explore it, then close browser. Click the **Weekly specials!** hyperlink, view workbook, then close workbook.	4	
10	Organization, Finishing	Resave, print, then close original workbook **EL1-C6-A4-BGSpecials.xlsx.**	3	
		TOTAL POINTS	**20**	

Assessment 5: Apply Conditional Formatting to a Sales Workbook
File: **EL1-C6-A5-PSSales.docx**

Steps	Tasks	Criteria	Value	Score
1-2	Research, Organization, Accuracy	After using Excel Help feature to learn about conditional formatting or after experimenting, open **PSSales.xlsx**, then Save As **EL1-C6-A5-PSSales**.	5	
3	Enhancement	Select cells D5 through D19, then use conditional formatting to display amounts as data bars.	3	
4	Editing	Insert header that prints student name, page number, and current date.	3	
5	Organization, Accuracy	Resave, print, then close workbook **EL1-C6-A5-PSSales.xlsx.**	4	
		TOTAL POINTS	**15**	

Visual Benchmark

Fill In an Expense Report Form
File: **EL1-C6-VB-OEExpRpt.xlsx**

Steps	Tasks	Criteria	Value	Score
1	Accuracy	Display New tab Backstage view, click Sample templates button, then double-click *Expense Report* template.	3	
2-3, 5	Enhancement	2. With the expense report open, apply the *Retrospect* theme. 3, 5. Select J1 through L1, then apply *Note cell* style. Make L18 active and apply *Bad* cell style.	4	
4	Typing, Accuracy	4. Type information in cells as indicated in Fig. 6.9.	10	
6-7	Organization, Finishing	Save as **EL1-C6-VB-OEExpRpt**, print, then close.	3	
		TOTAL POINTS	**20**	

Case Study

Part 1
File: **EL1-C6-CS-LMExpSummary.xlsx**

Steps	Tasks	Criteria	Value	Score
1	Organization, Accuracy	Open **LMEstExp.xlsx**, Save As **EL1-C6-CS-LMExpSummary.xlsx**. Open **LMActExp.xlsx**.	4	
2	Editing, Organization	With **LMActExp.xlsx** open, copy the worksheet into **EL1-C6-CS-LMExpSummary.xlsx**, make **LMActExp.xlsx** the active workbook, then close.	4	
3	Formatting, Typing, Enhancement	Apply appropriate *formatting* to numbers, insert necessary formulas in each worksheet. (Use Clear to clear contents of cells N8, N9, N13, N14 in both worksheets.) Include company name *Leeward Marine* in worksheets. Create styles, then apply the styles to cells in each worksheet to maintain consistent formatting. Automatically adjust widths of columns to accommodate the longest entry.	15	
4	Organization	Save **EL1-C6-CS-LMExpSummary**.**xlsx** workbook.	2	
		TOTAL POINTS	**25**	

Part 2

File: **EL1-C6-CS-LMExpSummary.xlsx**

Steps	Tasks	Criteria	Value	Score
1	Organization, Editing, Accuracy	With **EL1-C6-CS-LMExpSummary.xlsx** open, open **LMExpVar.xlsx**, then copy worksheet into **EL1-C6-CS-LMExpSummary.xlsx**. Make **LMExpVar.xlsx** the active workbook, then close.	5	
2	Editing, Typing, Formatting	Rename sheet tab containing estimated expenses to *Estimated Exp*, rename tab with actual expenses to *Actual Exp*, rename tab containing variances to *Summary*. *Recolor* the tabs for the renamed sheets. Select yearly estimated expense amounts (column N) in Estimated Exp, then paste amounts in appropriate cells in Summary worksheet; click Paste Options button, then click Values & Number Formatting button in *Paste Values* section of drop-down list. Select yearly actual expense amounts (column N) in Actual Exp worksheet, then paste amounts in appropriate cells in Summary worksheet; click Paste Options button, then click Values & Number Formatting button in *Paste Values* section of drop-down list.	12	
3	Formatting, Formulas, Enhancement	Apply appropriate formatting to numbers, then insert a formula that calculates the variances (differences) of estimated and actual expenses. Clear contents of cells D8, D9, D13, D14. Apply styles to Summary worksheet so formatting is similar to Estimated Exp and Actual Exp worksheets.	10	
4	Editing, Formatting	Insert an appropriate header or footer in each worksheet. Scale worksheets so each prints on one page.	4	
5	Organization, Finishing	Save, print all worksheets, then close workbook **EL1-C6-CS-LMExpSummary.xlsx**	4	
		TOTAL POINTS	**35**	

Part 3

File: **EL1-C6-CS-LMExpSummary.xlsx and EL1-C6-CS-LMProjectedExp.xlsx**

Steps	Tasks	Criteria	Value	Score
1	Research, Accuracy, Typing	Open **LMProjectedExp.xlsx** then Save As **EL1-C6-CS-LMProjectedExp.** Format similar to **EL1-C6-CS-LMExpSummary.xlsx** using the styles created.	12	
2	Organization, Finishing	Save as **EL1-C6-CS-LMProjectedExp.xlsx**, then close. Open **EL1-C6-CS-LMExpSummary.xlsx** and insert a hyperlink to the **EL1-C6-CS-LMProjectedExp.xlsx** workbook**.** User determines the cell location and hyperlink text for the hyperlink. Save **EL1-C6-CS-LMESummary.xlsx.** Print only the Summary worksheet.	3	
		TOTAL POINTS	**15**	

Part 4
File: **EL1-C6-CS-LMExpSummary.xlsx**

Steps	Tasks	Criteria	Value	Score
1	Organization, Typing, Editing	In Word, open **LMLtrd.docx**. Press Enter two times. Make Excel active program, then open **EL1-C6-CS-LMExpSummary.xlsx**. Copy cells containing information on the yearly expense variances, then paste them into **LMLtrhd.docx** as a picture object.	7	
2	Organization, Finishing	Save document as **EL1-C6-CS-LMExpSummary.docx**, print, then close. Close Excel document.	3	
		TOTAL POINTS	**10**	

Benchmark Excel 2013 Level 1, Chapter 7

Skills Check

Assessment 1: Create a Net Profit Chart
File: **EL1-C7-A1-NetProfit.xlsx**

Steps	Tasks	Criteria	Value	Score
1	Organization, Accuracy	Open **NetProfit.xlsx**, Save As **EL1-C7-A1-NetProfit.xlsx**.	2	
2	Graphing, Formatting	Select cells A23 through E7, then create a chart using the Recommended Charts button. (Accept the chart recommended by Excel).	4	
3-5	Finishing, Organization	Use *Chart Elements* button to insert a data table, remove legend. Use *Chart Styles* button and apply the Style 7 chart style. Use the *Chart Filters* button to display only New York and Philadelphia net profits in the chart.	7	
6-8	Editing, Closing	Change Chart Title to **Net Profit by Office**, press Enter Move the chart below the cells containing data, make formatting changes to reveal data and chart to fit on one page. Print worksheet (data and chart) Save, close **EL1-C7-A1-NetProfit.xlsx**	7	
		TOTAL POINTS	**20**	

Assessment 2: Create a Company Sales Column Chart
File: **EL1-C7-A2-CMSales.xlsx**

Steps	Tasks	Criteria	Value	Score
1	Organization, Accuracy	Open **CMSales.xlsx**, Save As **EL1-C7-A2-CMSales.xlsx**.	3	
2	Graphing, Formatting	Select A3 through E5, then create *Column* chart with following: a. Click *3-D Clustered Column* option at Insert Column Chart button drop-down list. b. CHART TOOLS DESIGN: Apply *Layout 3.* c. Apply *Style 11* chart styles. d. *Chart Title:* type **2015 Company Sales,** press Enter. e. Move location of the chart to a new sheet.	14	
3-4	Organization, Finishing	Print only the worksheet containing the chart. Save, close **EL1-C7-A2-CMSales.xlsx**	3	
		TOTAL POINTS	20	

Assessment 3: Create Quarterly Domestic and Foreign Sales Bar Chart
File: **EL1-C7-A3-CMPQtrlySales.xlsx**

Steps	Tasks	Criteria	Value	Score
1	Organization, Accuracy	Open **CMPQtrlySales.xlsx**, Save As **EL1-C7-A3-CMPQtrlySales.xlsx**.	3	
2	Graphing, Formatting, Accuracy	Select cells A3- through E5 and then create a bar chart with the following specs: a. Select *3-D Clustered Bar* at the Insert Bar Chart b. Apply *Layout 2* quick layout c. Apply *Style 6* chart style d. **Chart Title**: ***Quarterly Sales*** (will convert to upper case) e. Click outside of chart element f. **CHART TOOLS FORMAT**: Apply the *Subtle Effect – Gold, Accent 4 shape style* (fifth column, fourth row) g. **Chart Elements** button: select *Series "Foreign"*, apply *Dark Red shape fill (Standard Colors* section*)* h. **Chart Title**: apply the *Fill – Black, Text 1, Shadow WordArt style* (first column, first row) i. Increase chart *height to 4-inches*; *Width to 6-inches*	9	
3-4	Organization, Finishing	*Move* the chart below the cells containing data, deselect chart, fit to one page, print worksheet (data and chart) Save then close workbook **EL1-C7-A3-CMPQtrlySales.xlsx**	3	
		TOTAL POINTS	15	

Assessment 4: Create a Fund Allocations Pie Chart

File: **EL1-C7-A4-SMFFunds.xlsx**

Steps	Tasks	Criteria	Value	Score
1-2	Typing, Accuracy, Formatting	Open **SMFFunds.xlsx**, Save As **EL1-C7-A4-SMFFunds.xlsx.** **Select cells** ***A3- B7,*** create a pie chart with the following specs: a. *3-DPie* option b. Apply the *Layout 1 quick layout* c. Apply *Style 2* Chart style d. Change the color to *Color 3* e. *Move* the pie chart to new worksheet f. Change title to ***Fund Allocations*** g. **CHART TOOLS FORMAT** tab: select *chart, Format Selection* h. Format Chart Area, (make Fill & Line icon active) select *Fill* option, Select *the Gradient fill* option, close. i. **Chart Elements**: select *Series "Allocation" Data Labels.* j. **Data Labels**: select the *Text Fill button* (WordArt Styles group) select *Orange, Accent 2, Darker 50%* (sixth column, bottom row in *Theme Colors* section) k. **Data Labels:** HOME, change the font size *to 18 points.*	12	
3	Printing	Print only the worksheet containing the chart.	1	
4	Organization, Finishing	Save as **EL1-C7-A4-SMFFunds.xlsx**.	2	
		TOTAL POINTS	15	

Assessment 5: Write a Formula with the PMT Function

File: **EL1-C7-A5-CMRefiPlan.xlsx**

Steps	Tasks	Criteria	Value	Score
1	Organization, Accuracy	Open **CMRefiPlan.xlsx**, Save As **EL1-C7-A5-CMRefiPlan.xlsx**.	3	
2-3	Graphing, Formatting, Enhancement	**Cell E4**: Insert a *PMT function* to calculate refinancing a loan for either $125,000 or $300,000 to determine the monthly payments. Copy the formula down to cells E5 through E7.	9	
4	Organization, Finishing	Save, print, then close workbook **EL1-C7-A5-CMRefiPlan.xlsx.**	3	
		TOTAL POINTS	15	

Assessment 6: Write a Formula with the FV Function
File: **EL1-C7-A6-CMInvest.xlsx**

Steps	Tasks	Criteria	Value	Score
1-2	Research, Typing, Graphing, Formatting	Open **CMInvest.xlsx**, Save As **EL1-C7-A6-CMInvest.xlsx** **Cell B6:** Insert a formula that calculates the future value of the investment using the *FV function.*	5	
3	Organization, Finishing	Save and print the worksheet **EL1-C7-A6-CMInvest.xlsx**	2	
4-5		Make the following changes: a. **Cell B3**: change percentage to *8.0%* b. **Cell B4**: change to *60* c. **Cell B5**: change to *-500 (negative 500)* Save, print and close **EL1-C7-A6-CMInvest.xlsx**	3	
		TOTAL POINTS	10	

Assessment 7: Write a Formula with the IF Function
File: **EL1-C7-A7-DISalesBonuses.xlsx**

Steps	Tasks	Criteria	Value	Score
1-2	Research, Typing, Graphing, Formatting	Open **DISalesBonuses.xlsx**, Save As **EL1-C7-A7-DISalesBonuses.xlsx** **Cell B4:** Insert a formula that inserts the word ***YES*** if the amount in B4 is greater than 99999 and inserts the word ***NO*** if the amount is not greater than 99999. Copy the formula down to Cells *C5 through C14.*	6	
3-5	Organization, Finishing	**Cell D4**:insert a formula =IF(C4=”YES”,B4*0.05,0) Copy the formula in cell D4 down to cells *D5 through D14.* Apply accounting formatting with a dollar sign and no decimal places to cell D4. Save and print the worksheet **EL1-C7-A7-DISalesBonuses.xlsx**	6	
6-8		Display the formulas and print the worksheet. Turn off display formulas. Save, close **EL1C7-A7-DISalesBonuses.xlsx**	3	
		TOTAL POINTS	15	

Assessment 8: Create a Stacked Cylinder Chart
File: **EL1-C7-A8-CMPerSales.xlsx**

Steps	Tasks	Criteria	Value	Score
1-2	Research,	Use Excel’s Help to learn more about chart types specifically about 3-D stacked column charts. Open **CMPerSales.xlsx** and Save As **EL1-C7-A8-CMPerSales.xlsx**	4	

Steps	Tasks	Criteria	Value	Score
3-4	Organization,	Using the data in the worksheet, create a *3-D 100% stacked* column chart in a separate sheet. Create a *Title* and apply other formatting to enhance the chart. Print only the worksheet containing the chart.	5	
5	Finishing	Close **EL1-C7-A8-CMPerSales.xlsx**	1	
		TOTAL POINTS	**10**	

Assessment 9: Learn About Excel Options
File: **EL1-C7-A9-DisplayOptions.xlsx**

Steps	Tasks	Criteria	Value	Score
1	Research, Typing, Formatting	Learn about Excel options by completing the following: a. Open a Blank workbook, display Excel Options under FILE tab, selecting *Options*. b. **Excel Options**, select the *Advanced* option c. Scroll to *Display options for this workbook*; read section and Read *Display option* for this worksheet section d. *Write down* the check box options available in the *Display options for this workbook* section and the *Display options for this worksheet* section and identify whether or not the check box contains a check mark.	5	
2	Creating a spreadsheet, Formulas, Formatting	With the information, create a spreadsheet with the following specs: a. **Column C**: type each option you wrote from previous step; include an appropriate heading b. **Column B**: Insert an X in the cell that precedes any option that contains a check mark; include an appropriate heading c. **Column A**: write an ***IF statement*** that inserts the word *ON* in the cell if the cell in column B contains an X and inserts the word *OFF* if it does not; include an appropriate heading. d. Apply formatting to improve appearance	8	
3-7	Finishing	Save the workbook as **EL1-C7-A9-DisplayOptions** Turn on the display of formulas and print the worksheet Turn off the display of formulas. Save, print and close **EL1C7-A9-DisplayOptions.xlsx.**	2	
		TOTAL POINTS:	**15**	

Visual Benchmark

Create and Format a Pie Chart

File: **EL1-C7-VB-CMFebExp.xlsx**

Steps	Tasks	Criteria	Value	Score
1	Typing, Graphing, Accuracy, Formatting	At a blank workbook, enter data, then create a pie chart in a separate sheet as shown in Fig. 7.12, using the information shown in the pie chart to create the data. Format and edit chart so it appears similar to the figure.	7	
2-4	Organization, Finishing	Save as **EL1-C7-VB-CMFebExp**, print both worksheets, then close the workbook.	3	
		TOTAL POINTS	**10**	

Case Study

Part 1

File: **EL1-C7-CS-DWQtrSales.xlsx**

Steps	Tasks	Criteria	Value	Score
1	Typing, Graphing, Enhancement	At a blank workbook, create two charts based on data provided (shown in Part 1 on page 269). (Type and style of chart, layout, formatting, are user-chosen.) In Commercial Loans chart containing the text *All-time High,* insert a shape pointing to the second quarter amount (*$6,785,250*).	12	
2	Organization, Finishing	Save as **EL1-C7-CS-DWQtrSales**, print only the chart, then close workbook.	3	
		TOTAL POINTS	**15**	

Part 2

File: **EL1-C7-CS-DWBudget.xlsx**

Steps	Tasks	Criteria	Value	Score
1	Typing, Accuracy, Formulas, Graphing	At a blank workbook, using the information provided (see Part 2 page 269), calculate the percentage of the budget for each item, then create a pie chart with it. (Chart style, layout, and formatting is user-determined.)	12	
2	Organization, Finishing	Save as **EL1-C7-CS-DWBudget.xlsx**, print only the chart, then close workbook.	3	
		TOTAL POINTS	**15**	

Part 3

File: **EL1-C7-CS-DWMortgageWksht.xlsx**

Steps	Tasks	Criteria	Value	Score
1	Formulas, Typing	Open **DWMortgageWksht.xlsx** worksheet. Create a worksheet showing the monthly payments on various priced homes with varying interest rates by inserting the following formulas: **Cells A11 through A14**: Insert $400,000 as home price; create a formula that calculates payment with a down payment of: 5%, 10%, 15%, and 20%. **Column C**: formula that determines the down payment amount **Column D**: formula that determines the loan amount **Column G**: formula using the PMT function (will display a negative number)	7	
2	Organization, Finishing	Save as **EL1-C7-CS-DWMortgageWksht**, then close workbook.	3	
		TOTAL POINTS	**10**	

Part 4

File: **EL1-C7-CS-DWMortgageWksht.xlsx**

Steps	Tasks	Criteria	Value	Score
1	Typing, Formulas,	Create a worksheet using an **IF Statement in Column H** that inserts the word *NO* if the percentage in column B is equal to or greater than 20% and inserts the word *YES* if the percentage in column B is less than 20%.	12	
2	Organization, Finishing	Save document as **EL1-C7-CS-DWMortgageWksht.xlsx**, print, then close..	3	
		TOTAL POINTS	**15**	

Part 5

File: **EL1-C7-CS-DWRates.xlsx.**

Steps	Tasks	Criteria	Value	Score
1-3	Research, Typing, Formulas,	Research the Internet to search for historical data on the national average for mortgage interest rates. With the research create a spreadsheet using a formula that determines the average mortgage rate or a 30-year FRM (Fixed rate mortgage) for each January and July beginning with the year 2012 through the current year. Include the current average interest rate. Use the information to create a chart.	12	
2	Organization, Finishing	Save document as **EL1-C7-CS-DWRates.xlsx**, print only the chart, then close.	3	
		TOTAL POINTS	**15**	

Benchmark Excel 2013 Level 1, Chapter 8

Skills Check

Assessment 1: Insert a Clip Art Image and WordArt in an Equipment Sales Workbook

File: **EL1-C8-A1-MSSalesPlans.xlsx**

Steps	Tasks	Criteria	Value	Score
1	Organization, Accuracy	Open **MSSalesPlans.xlsx**, Save As **EL1-C8-A1-MSSalesPlans.xlsx**.	3	
2-7	Formulas, Functions, Editing	2–3.Insert formula in E4 using **PMT** function that calculates monthly payments. *Hint*: Refer to Chapter 7, Project 5a. Copy formula in cell E4 down to cells E5 and E6. 4–5. Insert formula in *F4* that calculates total amount of payments, then copy it to F5 and F6. 6–7. Insert a formula in cell *G4* that calculates total amount of interest paid, then copy it to G5 and G6.	9	
8-9	Formatting	**8**. Insert clip art image shown in Fig. 8.10 with the following specifications: a. Search for it using search word *maple leaves*. (Colors of this clip art image are green and white.) b. Apply the *Orange, Accent color 2 Dark* clip art image color (third column, second row) c-d. Apply *Brightness: -20% Contrast: +20%*, correction (second column, fourth row) then apply *Drop Shadow Rectangle* picture style. (fourth thumbnail) e. Size and move image to position as shown in the figure 8.10. **9**. Insert company name *Maplewood Suppliers* in *A1* as WordArt. a. Use *Fill - White, Outline – Accent 2, Hard Shadow – Accent 2 image color* (fourth column, third row) b. Apply the *Orange, Accent 2, Darker 50% text fill* (sixth column, bottom row in the *Theme Colors* section). c. Apply the *Orange, Accent 2, Lighter 60% text outline* (sixth column, third row I the *Theme Colors* section). d. Use the Text Effects, apply the *Square transform text* effect. e. WordArt: change width to *5-inches* f. Move the WordArt so it is positioned in cell *A1*, (see Figure 8.10)	10	
10-11	Finishing, Organization	Change worksheet orientation to *landscape*. Save, print, then close workbook **EL1-C8-A1-MSSalesPlans.xlsx**	3	
		TOTAL POINTS	**25**	

Assessment 2: Insert Formulas and Format a Travel Company Workbook
File: **EL1-C8-A2-TSGEVacs.xlsx**

Steps	Tasks	Criteria	Value	Score
1	Organization, Accuracy	Open **TSGEVacs.xlsx**, Save As **EL1-C8-A2-TSGEVacs.xlsx**.	3	
2-6	Formatting, Editing	2. Insert appropriate formulas to calculate the prices based on 10% and 20% discounts, apply appropriate number formatting. 3. *Format image* of airplane position as shown in figure, with following specs: a. Use *Remove Background* button in the Adjust group on the **PICTURE TOOLS FORMAT** tab to remove a portion of yellow background so image displays similar to figure. b. *Rotate* image and *flip* it horizontally. c. Apply *Brightness: +20%, Contrast: +20%* correction. d. **Image**: change the height of the image to *1.4-inches* and then position the image as shown in the figure. 4. Open Word file: **TSAirfare.docx** located in EL1C8 folder on the storage medium. Insert the airfare information in **EL1-C8-A2-TSGEVacs.xlsx,** position on the right side of the data in the worksheet. 5. Change orientation to *landscape*. 6. Edit the information if necessary to display the airfare information on one page; print the worksheet.	19	
7	Organization	Save, close **EL1-C8-A2-TSGEVacs.xlsx**	2	
8	Finishing	Close **TSAirfare.docx**.	1	
		TOTAL POINTS	25	

Assessment 3: Insert and Format Shapes in a Company Sales Workbook
File: **EL1-C8-A3-MGSales.xlsx**

Steps	Tasks	Criteria	Value	Score
1	Organization, Accuracy	Open **MGSales.xlsx**, Save As **EL1-C8-A3-MGSales.xlsx**.	3	
2-8	Typing, Formatting, Editing	2. Use the **Isosceles Triangle** shape, in *Basic Shapes* section to draw a triangle as shown in Figure 8.12. 3. Apply *Green, Accent 6, Darker 50% shape* outline color (last column, last row in the *Theme Colors* section) to the triangle. 4. Apply *Green, Accent 6, Darker 25% shape* fill (last column, fifth row in the *Theme Colors* section) to the triangle. 5-6. Copy the triangle three times and position as shown in figure 8.12. 7. Select the second and fourth triangles and apply *Green, Accent 6, Lighter 80% shape* fill (last column, second row in the *Theme Colors* section). 8. Insert the total amounts in cells *B10 through D10*.	10	

Steps	Tasks	Criteria	Value	Score
9	Enhancement, Formatting	9. Insert an arrow pointing to *$97,549* with the following specifications: a. Insert the *Left Arrow* shape to draw the arrow. b. Change the height of the arrow to *0.6 inch* and the width *to 1.2 inches*. c. Apply *Green, Accent 6, Darker 25% shape* fill (last column, fifth row in the Theme Colors section) to the arrow. d. Type the text **Largest Order** in the arrow and then select the text and change the font to *10-Point Calibri bold.* e. Position the arrow as shown in Figure 8.12.	10	
10	Finishing	Save, print close **EL1-C8-A3-MGSales.xlsx**	2	
		TOTAL POINTS	25	

Assessment 4: Insert and Format a SmartArt Graphic in a Sales Workbook
File: **EL1-C8-A4-PS2ndQtrSales.xlsx**

Steps	Tasks	Criteria	Value	Score
1	Organization, Accuracy	Open **PS2ndQtrSales.xlsx**, Save As **EL1-C8-A4- PS2ndQtrSales.xlsx.**	3	
2-4	Enhancement, Typing, Formatting	2. Change orientation to landscape. 3. Insert a pyramid shape at right side of worksheet data using *Pyramid List SmartArt graphic* with the following specs: a. Change color to *Gradient Loop - Accent 2.* b. Apply *Cartoon* SmartArt style. c–e. In bottom text box, type **Red Level**, press Enter, then type **$25,000 to $49,999**. In middle text box, type **Blue Level**, press Enter, then type **$50,000 to $99,999**. In top text box, type **Gold Level**, press Enter, then type **$100,000+**. f. Apply *fill* to each text box to match level color. (use *Orange* for the Gold level) 4. Size and/or move SmartArt graphic so it displays attractively at right side of worksheet data. (Make sure entire graphic will print on same page as worksheet data.)	14	
5	Organization, Finishing	Save, print, and then close workbook **EL1-C8-A4-PS2ndQtrSales.xlsx.**	3	
		TOTAL POINTS	20	

Assessment 5: Create and Insert a Screenshot
File: **EL1-C8-A5-RPRefiPlan.xlsx**

Steps	Tasks	Criteria	Value	Score
1	Organization, Accuracy	Open **RPRefiPlan.xlsx**, Save As **EL1-C8-A5-RPRefiPlan**, then then display formulas (Ctrl + `).	3	
2	Enhancement, Formatting	Insert arrow shape shown in Fig. 8.13, then *add fill* to shape, remove shape outline, *bold text* in shape, then figure out how to rotate it using the rotation handle. Rotate, size, and position arrow as shown in figure.	8	

Steps	Tasks	Criteria	Value	Score
3-4	Organization, Editing	Open Word. At a blank document, press **Ctrl + E** to center insertion point, press **Ctrl + B** to turn on bold, type **Excel Worksheet with PMT Formula**, and then press Enter twice.	6	
5	Enhancement	Click Insert tab, click Screenshot button, and then click the thumbnail of the Excel worksheet.	4	
6-8	Organization, Finishing	Save Word document as **EL1-C8-A5-PMTFormula**, print, then close, exit Word. In Excel, close **EL-C8-A5-RPRefiPlan.xlsx** without saving changes.	4	
		TOTAL POINTS	25	

Visual Benchmark

Insert Formulas, WordArt, and Clip Art in a Worksheet
File: **EL1-C8-VB-TSYrlySales.xlsx**

Steps	Tasks	Criteria	Value	Score
1	Organization, Accuracy	Open **TSYrlySales.xlsx**, Save As **EL1-C8-VB- TSYrlySales.xlsx**.	3	
2	Formulas, Functions	Insert following formulas, as indicated in Fig. 8.14: (*Do not* type data in following cells—insert formulas instead. Results of formulas should match results in figure.) • **Cells C4 through C14**: Insert formula with *IF function* that inserts *5%* if amount in cell in column B is greater than $249,999 or *2%* if amount is not greater than $249,999. • **Cells D4 through D14**: Insert formula that multiplies amount in column B with amount in column C. • **Cell D4:** Apply *Accounting formatting* with a dollar sign, no decimal places	6	

Steps	Tasks	Criteria	Value	Score
3-5	Enhancement, Typing, Formatting	3. Insert company name *Target Supplies* as WordArt with following specifications: • Use *Fill – Black, Text 1, Outline – Background 1, Hard Shadow – Accent 1 option (second column, third row),* • To type WordArt text, press Ctrl + L (this changes to left text alignment), type **Target**, press Enter, type **Supplies**. • Apply color to *Orange, Accent 2, Darker 50%* text fill color • Apply *Orange, Accent 2, Lighter 40% text outline* color in the *Theme Colors* section). • Move WordArt to position as shown in the figure. 4. Insert target clip art image (use words *archery, arrows, target* to search) with following specs: • Apply *Orange, Accent color 2 light* color • Apply *brightness: 20% Contrast: -20% correction* • Size and position the clip art as shown in figure. 5. Draw shape displaying below data with following specs: • Use *Bevel* shape. • Type text in shape, apply *bold*, change to *center* and *middle alignment.* • Apply *Orange, Accent 2, Darker 50% shape fill* color in the *Theme Colors* section) • Apply *Orange, Accent 2* shape outline color	17	
6-8	Organization, Finishing	Save and then print worksheet. Press Ctrl + ` to turn on display of formulas, print worksheet again. Turn off display of formulas, close workbook.	4	
		TOTAL POINTS	**30**	

Case Study

Part 1

File: **EL1-C8-CS-OTSales.xlsx**

Steps	Tasks	Criteria	Value	Score
1	Organization, Accuracy	Open **OTSales.xlsx**, Save As **EL1-C8-CS-OTSales.xlsx**.	3	
2	Formatting	Apply formatting to improve appearance of the worksheet, then insert at least one clip art (use *truck* or *ocean*).	9	
3	Organization, Finishing	Resave, then print worksheet.	3	
		TOTAL POINTS	**15**	

Part 2
File: **EL1-C8-CS-OTSalesF&C.xlsx**

Steps	Tasks	Criteria	Value	Score
1	Organization, Accuracy	With **EL1-C8-CS-OTSales.xlsx** open, Save As **EL1-C8-CS-OTSalesF&C.xlsx**	3	
2	Editing	Divide workbook into two worksheets with one worksheet containing all Ford vehicles, the other containing all Chevrolets. Rename worksheet tabs to reflect contents. Sort each worksheet by price, most expensive to least.	6	
3	Enhancement	Insert in first worksheet a SmartArt graphic (user-chosen) that contains the following information: Small-sized truck = $200 2WD Regular Cab = $150 SUV 4x4 = $100	4	
4	Editing, Formatting	Copy graphic in first worksheet, then paste into the second one. Change the orientation to landscape.	3	
5	Organization, Finishing	Save, print, and then close workbook **EL1-C8-CS-OTSalesF&C.xlsx.**	4	
		TOTAL POINTS	**20**	

Part 3
File: **EL1-C8-CS-OTSales-WebPage.mht**

Steps	Tasks	Criteria	Value	Score
1	Organization, Accuracy	Open **EL1-C8-CS-OTSales.xlsx**. Display Save As dialog box, click *Save as type* option, determine how to save the workbook as a single file web page (*.mht, *.mhtml), then save as one with the name **EL1-C8-CS-OTSales-WebPage.**	6	
2	Accuracy	Open Internet browser, then open the web page. Look at the information in the file, then close the Internet browser.	4	
		TOTAL POINTS	**10**	

Part 4
File: **N/A**

Steps	Tasks	Criteria	Value	Score
1	Organization, Accuracy	Open **EL1-C8-CS-OTSalesF&C.xlsx,** then open PowerPoint.	3	
2	Formatting, Editing	Change slide layout in PowerPoint to Blank. Copy graphic in first worksheet, then paste it into the PowerPoint blank slide. Increase and/or move graphic so it better fills slide.	4	
3	Finishing, Organization	Print the slide, then close PowerPoint without saving the presentation. Close **EL1-C8-CS-OTSalesF&C.xlsx**.	3	
		TOTAL POINTS	**10**	

Benchmark Excel 2013 Level 1, Unit 2
Performance Assessment

Assessing Proficiency

Assessment 1: Copy and Paste Data and Insert WordArt in a Training Scores Workbook
File: **EL1-U2-A01-RLTraining.xlsx**

Steps	Tasks	Criteria	Value	Score
1	Organization, Accuracy	Open **RLTraining.xlsx**, Save As **EL1-U2-A01-RLTraining.**	3	
2-13	Editing, Typing	2. Delete row 15. 3-4. Cell D4: insert a formula that averages the percentages in cells B4 and C4; copy formula to cells D5 through D20. 5. Cell A22: Bolded, text =**Highest Averages.** 6. Clear the Clipboard task pane 7. Select then copy each of following rows (individually): row 7, 10, 14, 16, 18. 8–12. Cell A23: paste row 14 (*Jewett, Troy*); Cell A24: paste row 7 (*Cumpston, Kurt*); Cell A25 paste row 10 (*Fisher-Edwards, Theresa*); Cell A26: paste row 16 (*Mathias, Caleb*); Cell A27: paste row 18 (the row for *Nyegaard, Curtis*). 13. Click Clear All in Clipboard task pane, then close it.	16	
14	Enhancement, Formatting	Cell A1: insert text *Roseland* as WordArt. Format the WordArt to add visual appeal to worksheet.	3	
15	Organization, Finishing	Save, print, then close workbook **EL1-U2-A01-RLTraining.xlsx**	3	
		TOTAL POINTS	25	

Assessment 2: Manage Multiple Worksheets in a Projected Earnings Workbook
File: **EL1-U2-A02-RLProjEarnings.xlsx**

Steps	Tasks	Criteria	Value	Score
1	Organization, Accuracy	Open **RLProjEarnings.xlsx**, Save As **EL1-U2-A02-RLProjEarnings.**	3	

Steps	Tasks	Criteria	Value	Score
2- 11	Editing, Formatting, Typing	2. Cell A1: Delete *Roseland*. Open **EL1-U2-A01-RLTraining. xlsx**, then copy the *Rosel* WordArt text and paste it into A1 in **EL1-U2-A02-RLProjEarnings.xlsx**. If necessary, increase height of row 1 to accommodate the WordArt. 3. Close EL1-U2-A01-RLTraining workbook. 4. Insert a new worksheet in the EL1-U2-A02-RLProjEarnings. Xlsx 5. Select cells A1 through C11, then copy and paste to Sheet2, keeping source column widths. 6. With Sheet2 displayed, make following changes: a. Increase height of row 1 to accommodate WordArt. b. Delete contents of cell B2. c. Change contents of following cells: A6: Change *January* to *July;* A7: Change *February* to *August;* A8: Change *March* to *September;* A9: Change *April* to *October;* A10: Change *May* to *November;* A11: Change *June* to *December;* B6: Change *8.30%* to *8.10%;* B8: Change *9.30%* to *8.70%.* 7. Sheet1: copy cell B2 and paste (linking it) to cell B2 in Sheet2. 8. Rename Sheet1 to *First Half* and rename Sheet2 to *Second Half.* 9. First Half worksheet, determine effect on projected monthly earnings if projected yearly income is increased by 10% by changing number in B2 to *$1,480,380.* 10. Horizontally and vertically center both worksheets. Insert a custom header with student name at left, current date in center, and sheet name (use Sheet Name button) at right. 11. Print both worksheets. 12. Determine effect on projected monthly earnings if projected yearly income is increased by 20%, by changing number in cell B2 to *$1,614,960.*	23	
13-14	Finishing, Organization	Save, print both worksheets again, and then close workbook **EL1-U2-A02-RPLProjEarnings.xlsx.**	4	
		TOTAL POINTS	**30**	

Assessment 3: Create Charts in Worksheets in a Sales Totals Workbook
File: **EL1-U2-A03-EPYrlySales.xlsx**

Steps	Tasks	Criteria	Value	Score
1	Organization, Accuracy	Open **EPYrlySales.xlsx**, Save As **EL1-U2-A03-EPYrlySales.**	3	
2	Editing, Accuracy	Sheet 1: Rename to *2013 Sales*, Sheet2 to *2014 Sales*, and Sheet3 to *2015 Sales*.	3	
3	Formatting, Typing, Formulas	Select all three sheet tabs, make cell A12 active, click Bold, then type **Total**. In B12, insert formula to total amounts in B4 through B11. In C12, insert formula to total amounts in C4 through C11.	5	

Steps	Tasks	Criteria	Value	Score
4-6	Graphing, Formatting	**2013 Sales** worksheet: select cells A3 through C11 (not the totals in row 12), then create a *column chart.* Click Switch Row/Column button at Chart Tools Design tab. Apply formatting to increase visual appeal of chart, then drag it below worksheet data. (Fit on one page.) **2014 Sales** worksheet: create the same type of chart completed in 2013 worksheet. **2015** Sales worksheet: create same type of chart you created in previous steps.	16	
7-8	Organization, Finishing	Resave, print entire workbook **EL1-U2-A03-EPYrlySales.xlsx,** and then close.	3	
		TOTAL POINTS	30	

Assessment 4: Create and Format a Line Chart
File: **EL1-U2-A04-ProfitCompare.xlsx**

Steps	Tasks	Criteria	Value	Score
1	Typing, Accuracy	Open **ProfitCompare.xlsx**, Save As **EL1-U2-A04-ProfitCompare.xlsx**	5	
2	Graphing, Formatting	2. Using data in workbook, create line chart with the following specs: a. Apply Style 11 chart style b. Chart Title: *NET PROFIT COMPARISON.* c. Apply *Green shape fill* and shape outline color of the Asia series (Standard colors section) d. Move chart to a new sheet.	10	
3-4,	Organization, Finishing	3. Save, print only the sheet containing chart, then close workbook **EL1-U2-A04-ProfitCompare.xlsx.**	5	
		TOTAL POINTS	20	

Assessment 5: Create and Format a Pie Chart
File: EL1-U2-A05-EPProdDept.xlsx

Steps	Tasks	Criteria	Value	Score
1	Organization, Accuracy	Open **EPProdDept.xlsx**, Save As **EL1-U2-A05-EPProdDept.**	3	
2	Graphing, Formatting	*Cells A3 through B10:* Create a pie chart from these cells as a separate sheet. Student determines type of pie. Include an appropriate title and percentage labels.	9	
3-4	Organization, Finishing	Print only the worksheet containing the chart. Save, close workbook **EL1-U2-A05-EPProdDept.xlsx**	3	
		TOTAL POINTS	15	

Assessment 6: Use the PMT Function and Apply Formatting to a Workbook
File: EL1-U2-A06-HERSalesInfo.xlsx

Steps	Tasks	Criteria	Value	Score
1	Organization, Accuracy	Open **HERSalesInfo.xlsx**, Save As **EL1-U2-A06-HERSalesInfo.**	2	
2-3	Formulas	**Cell E4**: Insert a formula that calculates monthly payment using PMT function. (use minus sign before cell designation) Copy formula down to Cells E5 and E6.	7	
4-5	Formulas	**Cell F4:** insert a formula that multiplies the amount in cell E4 by the amount in Cell D4. Copy the formula down to cells F5 and F6.	7	
6-7	Formulas	**Cell G4:** Insert a formula that subtracts the amount in cell B4 from the amount in cell F4. (positive number) Copy the formula down to cells G5 and G6.	7	
8	Organization, Finishing	Save, print and close **EL1-U2-A06-HERSalesInfo.xlsx**	2	
		TOTAL POINTS	**25**	

Assessment 7: Use the IF Function and Apply Formatting to a Workbook
File: EL1-U2-A07-PSQtrlySales.xlsx

Steps	Tasks	Criteria	Value	Score
1	Organization, Accuracy	Open **PSQtrlySales.xlsx**, Save As **EL1-U2-A07-PSQtrlySales.**	3	
2	Formulas, Formatting	**Cell F4:** Insert an *IF statement* that inserts *YES* if cell E4 contains a number greater than 74999 and inserts *No* if the number in cell E4 is not greater than 74999. Copy the formula down to cells F5 through F18. *Center the text* in cells F4 through F18.	9	
3-4	Formatting, Enhancement	3. *Insert a footer* that prints name at left, current date in the center, current time at right. 4. Print the worksheet with the display of formulas, landscape orientation (then turn of the display of formulas. (printing will be two pages)	5	
5	Finishing	Save, print, close **EL1-U2-A07-PSQtrlySales.xlsx**	3	
		TOTAL POINTS	**20**	

Assessment 8: Insert a Text Box and Hyperlinks in a Travel Workbook
File: EL1-U2-A08-TravDest.xlsx

Steps	Tasks	Criteria	Value	Score
1	Organization, Accuracy	Open **TravDest.xlsx**, Save As **EL1-U2-A08-TravDest.**	3	

Steps	Tasks	Criteria	Value	Score
2	Editing, Typing, Accuracy	Insert a text box with the following specs: a. Draw a text box at the right side of the clip art image. b. Insert the text **Call 1-888-555-1288 for last minute vacation specials!** c. Change the font to 24-point Forte and apply the Blue color in the Standard Colors section. d. Size and position the text box so it appears visually balanced with the travel clip art image.	4	
3-4	Formatting, Enhancement	Internet Search for Cities in Worksheet: *Search for sites* that may be of interest to tourists. Write down website address for the best website for each city. *Create a hyperlink* with each city name to the web address you wrote down. Change the font size to *18 points.*	7	
5	Editing	*Test and edit* the hyperlinks	3	
6	Finishing	Save, print close **EL1-U2-A08-TravDest.xlsx**	3	
		TOTAL POINTS	20	

Assessment 9: Insert an Image and a SmartArt Graphic in a Workbook File: EL1-U2-A09-SalesQuotas.xlsx

Steps	Tasks	Criteria	Value	Score
1	Organization, Accuracy	Open **SalesQuotas.xlsx**, Save As **EL1-U2-A09-SalesQuotas.**	3	
2-3	Editing, Formatting, Typing, Accuracy, Enhancement	**Cell C3**: Insert a formula using an absolute reference that calculates the projected quotas at a 10% increase above the current quotas. Copy the formula down to cells C4 through C12. **Cell C3**: Apply the Accounting format with two decimal places and a dollar sign	6	
4	Editing	**Row 1**: *Insert a clip art image* related to money. User determines the size and position of the clip art image. If necessary increase the height of the row.	4	
5-6	SmartArt Graphic, Typing, Formatting	*Insert* a SmartArt graphic at the right side of the data that contains three shapes. *Insert* the following quota ranges in the shapes and apply the fill colors as follows: $50,000 to $99,000 (apply a green color) $100,000 to $149,999 (apply a blue color) $150,000 to $200,000 (apply a red color) *Apply formatting* to improve visual appearance.	6	
7	Editing	Insert a *custom header* that prints name at left, current date in center and file name at right.	3	
8-9	Formatting, Finishing	Change to *Landscape* Orientation, graphic should fit on page. Save, print and close **EL1-U2-A09-SalesQuotas.xlsx**	3	
		TOTAL POINTS	25	

Assessment 10: Insert a Symbol, Clip Art Image and WordArt in a Sales Workbook
File: EL1-U2-A10-CISales.xlsx

Steps	Tasks	Criteria	Value	Score
1	Organization, Accuracy	Open **CISales.xlsx**, Save As **EL1-U2-A10-CISales.**	3	
2	Editing, Formatting	**Cell A7:** *Overwrite* text to Económico using Symbol.	3	
3	Inserting	*Insert* a new row at the beginning of the worksheet.	3	
4	Merging	**Cells A1 through D1:** Merge cells	3	
5	Formatting	**Row 1**: increase the height to *141.00 points*	3	
6	Typing, Editing	**Cell A1**: Insert text *to Custom Interiors* as WordArt, fitting in the cell.	3	
7	Copying with screen clipping	a. Open Word, Open CISustomers.docx located the EL1U2 folder on storage medium. b. Make a screenshot of EL1-U2-A10-CSSales.xlsx (screen clipping option) of the customer information in the Word Document. Position the screenshot image below the data in the cells.	4	
8	Formatting	c. Insert a custom footer that prints name at left, file name at right.		
9-11	Editing, Finishing	d. Data and screenshot should display on the same page. Print the worksheet. e. EL1-U2-A10-CISales.xlsx. Close word document.	3	
		TOTAL POINTS	**25**	

Assessment 11: Insert and Format a Shape in a Budget Workbook
File: EL1-U2-A11-SEExpenses.xlsx

Steps	Tasks	Criteria	Value	Score
1	Organization, Accuracy	Open **SEExpenses.xlsx**, Save As **EL1-U2-A11-SEExpenses.**	3	
2	Editing, Formatting	Make the following changes to the worksheet as shown in Figure U2.1: f. **A1 through D1**: merge cells g. **A1 through D1**: Add fill to the cells as show in Figure *(Green Accent 6, Lighter 40% fill color)* h. Increase the height of **row 1** to approximate size shown in Figure. i. **Cell A1**: type *SOLAR*, Alt + Enter, type *ENTERPRISES*. (**Text**: *20 point Calibri bold, center and middle aligned, font color to Green, Accent 6, Darker 25%)* j. Insert the sun shape (*Basic Shapes* section) Apply *orange shape fill* (Orange option in *Standard Colors* section); change the shape outline to *Green, Accent 6, Darker 25%.* Copy the shape in the cell and then size and position the shapes as shown in Figure.	10	

Steps	Tasks	Criteria	Value	Score
3	Finishing	Save, print close **EL1-U2-A11-SEExpenses.xlsx**	2	
		TOTAL POINTS:	**15**	

Writing Activities

Activity 1: Prepare a Projected Budget
File: **EL1-U2-Act1-MFBudget.xlsx** and **EL1-U2-Act1-MFMemo.docx**

Steps	Tasks	Criteria	Value	Score
1	Accuracy, Typing, Formatting	Create a departmental budget worksheet (department has a budget of $1,450,000) with the following information that shows the projected yearly budget, the budget items in the department, the percentage of the budget, and the amount for each item. The percentages for the proposed budget items are: Salaries, 45%; Benefits, 12%; Training, 14%; Administrative Costs, 10%; Equipment, 11%; Supplies, 8%.	10	
2	Organization, Finishing	Save as **EL1-U2-Act1-MFBudget**, print, then close.	3	
3	Writing	[OPTIONAL EXERCISE] In Word 2010, write a memo to McCormack Funds Finance Department explaining that proposed annual department budget is attached for their review. Comments and suggestions are to be sent within one week.	4	
4	Organization, Finishing	Save the Word document as **EL1-U2-Act1-MFMemo**, print, then close document.	3	
		TOTAL POINTS	**20**	

Activity 2: Create a Travel Tours Bar Chart
File: EL1-U2-Act2-CTTours.xlsx

Steps	Tasks	Criteria	Value	Score
1	Accuracy, Typing, Formatting	At a blank workbook, prepare a worksheet including the following information: **Scandinavian Tours** **Country** **Tours** **Booked** Norway 52 Sweden 62 Finland 29 Denmark 38	6	
2	Graphing, Formatting	Use the information in the worksheet to create and format a bar chart as a separate sheet.	5	
3	Organization, Finishing	Save as **EL1-U2-Act2-CTTours**, print only the sheet containing the chart, then close workbook.	4	
		TOTAL POINTS	**15**	

Activity 3: Prepare a Ski Vacation Worksheet
File: **EL1-U2-Act3-CTSkiTrips.xlsx**

Steps	Tasks	Criteria	Value	Score
1	Typing, Enhancement, Formatting, Formulas	At a blank workbook, prepare worksheet for Carefree Travels that advertises snow skiing trip. Include the following information in the announcement: • At the beginning of the worksheet, create company logo that includes company name *Carefree Travels* and a clip art image related to travel. • Include heading *Whistler Ski Vacation Package* in the worksheet. • Include the following below the heading: • Round-trip air transportation: $395 • Seven nights hotel accommodations: $1,550 • Four all-day ski passes: $425 • Compact rental car with unlimited mileage: $250 • Total price of the ski package: (calculated) • Include the following somewhere in the worksheet: • Book your vacation today at special discount prices. • Two-for-one discount at many local ski resorts.	12	
2	Organization, Finishing	Save, print, close **EL1-U2-Act3-CTSkiTrips**, print, and then close.	3	
		TOTAL POINTS	15	

Internet Research

Find Information on Excel Books and Present the Data in a Worksheet
File: **EL1-U2-IR-Books.xlsx**

Steps	Tasks	Criteria	Value	Score
1	Research, Accuracy, Typing	Use the Internet to locate two companies that sell new books. At the first new book company site, locate three books on Microsoft Excel. Record title, author, and price for each book. At the second new book company site, locate the same three books and record the prices.	5	
2	Accuracy, Typing, Formatting	Create Excel worksheet that includes the following: Name of each new book company; title and author of the three books; prices for each book from the two sites. Create a hyperlink for each book company to the website on the Internet.	7	
3	Organization, Finishing	Save as **EL1-U2-IR-Books**, print, then close workbook.	3	
		TOTAL POINTS	15	

Job Study

Create a Customized Time Card for a Landscaping Company
File: **EL1-U2-JS-TimeCard.xlsx**

Steps	Tasks	Criteria	Value	Score
1	Accuracy	Locate a time card template using the search words *weekly time sheet portrait*. Download and use to create a customized time card workbook for your company.	3	
2	Editing, Enhancement, Formatting	With template open, insert additional blank rows to increase spacing above the Employee row. Insert a clip art image related to landscaping or gardening, then position and size it attractively in the form. Include a text box with the text *Lawn* and *Landscaping Specialists* inside the box, then format, size, and position the text attractively in the form.	7	
3		Fill in the form for the current week with the following employee information: Employee = Jonathan Holder Manager = (Student name) Employee phone = (225) 555-3092 Employee email = None Regular hours = 8 hours for Monday, Tuesday, Wednesday, Thursday Overtime = 2 hours on Wednesday Sick hours = None Vacation = 8 hours on Friday Rate per hour = $20.00 Overtime pay = $30.00	12	
4	Organization, Finishing	Save as **EL1-U2-JS-TimeCard**, print, then close workbook.	3	
		TOTAL POINTS	**25**	

Benchmark Excel 2013 Level 2, Chapter 1

Skills Check

Assessment 1: Use Conditional and Fraction Formatting
File: **EL2-C1-A1-RSRServRpt.xlsx**

Steps	Tasks	Criteria	Value	Score
1-2	Opening, Saving	Open **RSRServRpt.xlsx**. Save As **EL2-C1-A1-RSRServRpt**.	1	
3	Formatting	Apply the following formatting changes to worksheet: • Format C6:C23 to fractions using type *As quarters (2/4)* • Format rate codes in D6:D22 with the 3 Traffic Lights (Rimmed) icon • Format parts values in F6:F22 to color cell with *Light Red Fill* for cells equal to zero • Format total invoice values in G6:G22 using *Red Data Bar* option in *Gradient Fill* section of Data Bars side menu.	8	
4	Saving, Printing	Save, print, and close **EL2-C1-A1-RSRServRpt.xlsx**.	1	
		TOTAL POINTS	**10**	

Assessment 2: Apply Custom Number Formatting
File: **EL2-C1-A2-RSRServRpt.xlsx**

Steps	Tasks	Criteria	Value	Score
1-2	Opening, Saving	Open **EL2-C1-A1-RSRServRpt.xlsx**. Save As **EL2-C1-A2-RSRServRpt**.	1	
3	Creating, Applying Custom Number Formats	Create and apply the following custom number formats: • Create custom number format that displays *hrs* one space after the values in C6:C23 • Create custom number format that displays *RSR-* in front of each work order number in B6:B22	8	
4	Saving, Closing	Save, print, and close **EL2-C1-A2-RSRServRpt.xlsx**. Print and close document.	1	
		TOTAL POINTS	**10**	

Assessment 3: Use Custom AutoFilter; Filter and Sort by Color
File: **EL2-C1-A3-RSRServRpt.xlsx**

Steps	Tasks	Criteria	Value	Score
1-2	Opening, Saving	Open **EL2-C1-A2-RSRServRpt.xlsx**. Save As **EL2-C1-A3-RSRServRpt**.	1	

3-5	Filtering	Using the Oct worksheet: Select A5:G22 and turn on Filter feature. Filter worksheet as follows: • Use filter arrow button in *Hours Billed* column, display invoices where hours billed is between 1.75 and 3.75 hours. • Filter *Parts* column by color to show only those invoices for which no parts were billed • Using the Nov worksheet: • Clear filter from *Date* column • Filter worksheet by icon associated with rate code 3	10	
6	Defining Custom Sort	Using the Dec worksheet: • Remove the filter arrows from the worksheet. • Make any cell active within invoice list • Open Sort Dialog box • Define three sort levels as follows: ◦ Sort by Rate Code, Sort On Cell Icon, Order Red Traffic Light (On Top) ◦ Sort by Rate Code, Sort On Cell Icon, Order Yellow Traffic Light (On Top) ◦ Sort by Rate Code, Sort On Cell Icon, Order Green Traffic Light (On Top)	3	
7-8	Printing, Saving	Print worksheet. Save and close **EL2-C1-A3-RSRServRpt.xlsx**.	1	
		TOTAL POINTS	**15**	

Assessment 4: Create, Edit, and Delete Formatting Rules

File: **EL2-C1-A4-VIVPay-Oct31.xlsx**

Steps	Tasks	Criteria	Value	Score
1-2	Opening, Saving	Open **VIVPay-Oct31.xlsx**. Save As **EL2-C1-A4-VIVPay-Oct31**.	1	
3	Creating, Applying Formatting Rules	Create and apply two conditional formatting rules for values in Pay Rate column as follows: • Apply Light Blue fill color to values from *7.50 to 8.00* • Apply light green fill color to values greater than 8.00	4	
4	Creating, Applying Formatting Rules	Create a conditional formatting rule for *Gross Pay* column that will format values in Dark Red font color if employee has worked overtime hours.	4	
5	Quick Analysis button	Use the Quick Analysis button to find the top 10% for the *Gross Pay* column	1	
6-7	Editing, Formatting	Edit formatting rule for *Cell Value <7.5* by changing fill color to Light Orange. Use the Quick Analysis button to delete the formatting rule for Overtime Hours	4	
8-9	Printing, Saving	Print revised worksheet. Save then close **EL2-C1-A4-VIVPay-Oct31.xlsx**.	1	
		TOTAL POINTS	**15**	

Visual Benchmark

Format a Billing Summary

File: **EL2-C1-VB-BillingsOct5to9.xlsx**

Steps	Tasks	Criteria	Value	Score
1-2	Opening, Saving	Open **BillingsOct8to12.xlsx**. Save As **EL2-C1-VB-BillingsOct8to12**.	1	
3	Formatting	Format the worksheet to match Figure 1.10 using the following information: • Data in *Billing Code* column formatted to add text *Amicus* #- in front of code number in blue font color of code number • Icon sets are used in *Attorney Code* column and same icon set should be applied in *Attorney Code Table* section of worksheet • Data bars added to values in *Legal Fees* column edited to change bar appearance to *Turquoise, Accent 3* gradient fill • Values below1500.00 in *Total Due* column are conditionally formatted and worksheet sorted by font color used for conditional format	8	
4	Saving, Printing	Save, print, and close **EL2-C1-VB-BillingsOct5to9.xlsx**.	1	
		TOTAL POINTS	**10**	

Case Study

Part 1

File: **EL2-C1-CS-P1-USIncomeStats.xlsx**

Steps	Tasks	Criteria	Value	Score
1	Opening, Saving	Open **USIncomeStats.xlsx**. Save As **EL2-C1-CS-P1-USIncomeStats.xlsx**.	1	
2	Formatting	Format data using color to differentiate income levels. Apply color formatting to: *Average Median Income Range* • Less than 45,000 • Between 45,00 and 55,000 • Great than 55,000 • Use color formats to distinguish from each other.	6	
3	Creating Reference Table	Create reference table starting in E3 that provides a legend to read the colors.	2	
4	Saving, Printing	Save and close **EL2-C1-CS-P1-USIncomeStats.xlsx**.	1	
		TOTAL POINTS	**10**	

Part 2

File: **EL2-C1-CS-P2-USIncomeStats.xlsx**

Steps	Tasks	Criteria	Value	Score
1	Saving	In order to keep original file, **EL2-C1-CS-P1-USIncomeStats.xlsx** intact, save worksheet as **EL2-C1-CS-P2-USIncomeStats**.	1	
2	Sorting	Sort in descending order from highest income level to lowest. • Do not include Entries in row 3 for United States average in sort operation.	4	
3	Filtering	After sorting, filter median incomes to display the top 20 states.	3	
4	Creating List	Add contact telephone list next to Top 20 state data. Create list using telephone numbers provided below in a suitable location: Yolanda (cell) 800 555 3117 Yolanda (office) 800 555 4629 Yolanda (home) 800 555 2169 Yolanda (fax) 800 555 6744 Apply special number format for phone numbers to ensure data is displayed consistently.	6	
5	Saving, Printing	Save and print **EL2-C1-CS-P2-USIncomeStats.xlsx**.	1	
		TOTAL POINTS	**15**	

Part 3

File: **EL2-C1-CS-P3-USIncomeStats.xlsx**

Steps	Tasks	Criteria	Value	Score
1	Applying Conditional Formatting	With **EL2-C1-CS-P2-USIncomeStats.xlsx** still open, apply conditional formatting using either a two-color or three-color scale to the filtered cells in Colum C (exclude the United States median income at top of column).	8	
2	Saving, Printing	Save As **EL2-C1-CS-P3-USIncomeStats.xlsx**. Print worksheet. *If color printer not available, student should write on printout the two- or three-color scale conditional formatting option applied to filtered values in Column C.*	2	
		TOTAL POINTS	**10**	

Part 4

File: **EL2-C1-CS-P4-USIncomeStats.xlsx**

Steps	Tasks	Criteria	Value	Score
1	Gathering Information	Using the Internet, go to URL www.census.gov/ and find page that describes the history of the Census Bureau.	1	
2	Typing Text	In new sheet in same file as median income data, type in column A five to seven interesting facts student learned about the bureau from the website.	6	
3	Formatting	Adjust width of column A. Apply wrap text or shrink to fit formatting to improve the appearance.	2	

Steps	Tasks	Criteria	Value	Score
4	Saving, Printing	Save revised workbook as **EL2-C1-CS-P4-USIncomeStats.xlsx**. Print worksheet and close workbook.	1	
		TOTAL POINTS	**10**	

Benchmark Excel 2013 Level 2, Chapter 2

Skills Check

Assessment 1: Create Range Names and Use the Lookup Function

File: **EL2-C2-A1-RSROctLaborCost.xlsx**

Steps	Tasks	Criteria	Value	Score
1-2	Opening, Saving	Open **RSROctLabor.xlsx**. Save As **EL2-C2-A1-RSROctLabor**.	1	
3	Creating Range Names	Create the following range names: • F7:F22 *LaborCost* • I3:J5 *RateChart*	3	
4-5	Creating VLOOKUP	Change the range name for the range named *Hr* to *Hours*. In E7, create VLOOKUP formula to return correct hourly rate based on technician code in D7. Use range name *RateChart* within formula to reference hourly rate chart. Make sure Excel returns values for exact matches only.	6	
6	Creating or Copying Formulas	Copy VLOOKUP formula in E7 and paste to E8:E22. In F7 create formula to multiply the named range *Hours* by the hourly rate in cell E7. Copy formula in F7 and paste to F8:F22. Create formula in F23 to sum column.	3	
7	Printing	Preview and print worksheet.	1	
8	Saving, Printing	Save and close **EL2-C2-A1-RSROctLabor.xlsx**.	1	
		TOTAL POINTS	**15**	

Assessment 2: Use Conditional Statistical and Math Functions

File: **EL2-C2-A2-RSROctLabor.xlsx**

Steps	Tasks	Criteria	Value	Score
1-2	Opening, Saving	Open **EL2-C2-A1-RSROctLabor.xlsx**. Save As **EL2-C2-A2-RSROctLabor**.	1	
3	Creating COUNTA Formula	In cell I23, create a COUNTA formula to count number of calls made in October using dates in column A as source range.	4	

Steps	Tasks	Criteria	Value	Score
4	Creating COUNTIF Formula	Using the range names *TechCode*, Create COUNTIF formulas in cells as indicated below: I9: Count number of calls made by Technician 1 I10: Count number of calls made by Technician 2 I11: Count number of calls made by Technician 3	4	
5	Creating COUNTIFS Formulas	In I14 create COUNTIFS formula to count number of calls made by Technician 3 where hours logged were greater than 3.	3	
6	Creating SUMIF Formulas	Using the ranges named *TechCode* and *LaborCost*, create SUMIF formulas in cells as indicated below: J9: Add labor cost for calls made by Technician 1 J10: Add labor cost for calls made by Technician 2 J11: Add labor cost for calls made by Technician 3	4	
7	Creating SUMIFS formulas	Using the ranges named *TechCode, LaborCost* and *Hours,* create a SumIFS formula in cell J14 to add the labor cost for calls made by technician 3 in which the hours logged were greater than three.	4	
8	Creating AVERAGEIF Formula	Using the named ranges *TechCode* and *LaborCost*, create AVERAGEIF formulas for the following cells: J18: Average the labor cost for calls made by technician 1 J19: Average the labor cost for calls made by technician 2 J20: Average the labor cost for calls made by technician 3.	4	
9	Formatting	Format J9:J11, J14, and J18:J20 to Comma Style format.	4	
10	Saving, Printing	Save, print, and close **EL2-C2-A2-RSROctLabor.xlsx**.	2	
		TOTAL POINTS	**30**	

Assessment 3: Use Financial Functions PMT and PPMT
File: **EL2C2A3PrecisionWarehouse.xlsx**

Steps	Tasks	Criteria	Value	Score
1-2	Opening, Saving	Open **PrecisionWarehouse.xlsx**. Save As **EL2-C2-A3-PrecisionWarehouse.xlsx**.	1	
3	Creating Formula	Create PMT formula in D8 to calculate monthly loan payment for proposed loan from New Ventures Capital Inc.	3	
4	Creating Formula	Find principal portion to loan payment for first loan payment in D10 and last loan payment in D11 using PPMT formulas.	2	
5	Creating Formula	In D13 create formula to calculate total cost of loan by multiplying monthly loan payment times 12 times the amortization period in years.	2	
6-7	Saving, Printing	Print worksheet. Save and close **EL2-C2-A3-PrecisionWarehouse.xlsx**.	2	
		TOTAL POINTS	**10**	

Assessment 4: Use Logical Functions
File: **EL2-C2-A4-ACPremiumReview.xlsx**

Steps	Tasks	Criteria	Value	Score
1-2	Opening, Saving	Open **ACPremiumReview.xlsx.** Save As **EL2C2A4ACPremiumReview.xlsx**.	1	
3	Creating Range Names	Create the following range names: • B4:B23 *Claims* • C4:C23 *AtFault* • D4:D23 *Rating* • E4:E23 *Deductible*	3	
4	Creating Formula	Create formula in G4 to display *Yes* if number of At Fault Claims is greater than 1 and Current Rating is greater than 2. Both conditions must test true to display *Yes*; otherwise display *No* in cell. *Hint: Use a nested IF and AND formula.*	3	
5	Creating Formula	Create formula in H4 to display *Yes* if either number of claims is greater than 2 or current deductible is less than $1,000.00; otherwise, display *No* in cell. *Hint: Use a nested IF and OR formula.*	3	
6	Formatting, Copying	Center result in G4 and H4. Copy formulas to G5:G23 and H5:H23 respectively. Deselect range after copying.	3	
7	Printing, Saving	Print, save, and close **EL2-C2-A4-ACPremiumReview.xlsx**.	2	
		TOTAL POINTS	**15**	

Assessment 5: Use the HLOOKUP Function
File: **EL2-C2-A5-JTutorProgressRpt.xlsx**

Steps	Tasks	Criteria	Value	Score
1-2	Opening, Saving	Open **JTutorProgressRpt.xlsx**. Save As **EL2-C2-A5-JTutorProgressRpt.xlsx**.	1	
3-4	Creating Range	Review layout of lookup table in ProgressComments sheet. Data is organized in rows with score in row 1 and grade comment in row 2. Select A1:G2 and create range name *GradeTable*.	3	
5-6	Creating Formula	Deselect range and make StudentProgress the active sheet. Create formula in G4 that will look up student's total score in range named *GradeTable* and return appropriate progress comment.	3	
7	Copying	Copy formula in G4 and paste to G5:G12.	2	
8	Printing, Saving	Print, save, and close **EL2-C2-A5-JTutorProgressRpt.xlsx**.	1	
		TOTAL POINTS	**10**	

Visual Benchmark

Use Lookup, Statistical, and Math Functions in a Billing Summary
File: **EL2-C2-VB1-BillHrsOct5to9.xlsx**

Steps	Tasks	Criteria	Value	Score
1-2	Opening, Saving	Open **BillHrsOct5to9.xlsx**. Save As **EL2-C2-VB1-BillHrsOct5to9**.	1	
3	Creating Formulas	Use the following information to create the required formulas. Create range names to use in all of the formulas so that readers can easily interpret the formula. • In column F, create a formula to look up attorney's hourly rate from the table located at the bottom right of the worksheet • In column G, calculate legal fees billed by multiplying billable hours times the hourly rate • In J6:J9 calculate total legal fees billed by attorney • In J13:J16 calculate average hours bill by attorney	8	
4	Saving, Printing	Save, print, and close **EL2-C2-VB1-BillHrsOct5to9.xlsx**.	1	
		TOTAL POINTS	**10**	

Use Lookup and Logical Functions to Calculate Cardiology Costs
File: **EL2-C2-VB2-WPMCCardioCosts.xlsx**

Steps	Tasks	Criteria	Value	Score
1-2	Opening, Saving	Open **WPMCCardioCosts.xlsx**. Save As **EL2-C2-VB2-WPMCCardioCosts**.	1	
3-4	Creating Formulas	Review range names and cells each name references to become familiar with the worksheet. • Review worksheet shown in Figure 2.9 and complete the worksheet to match the one shown by creating formulas using the following information: • In column G, create a formula to look up surgery fee in the table located at bottom of worksheet. Specify in formula to return result for exact matches only. • In column H insert aortic or mitral valve cost if cardiac surgery required a replacement valve; otherwise place a zero in the cell. *The surgery codes for surgery codes for surgeries that include a replacement valve are* ART *and* MRT. • In column I, calculate postoperative hospital cost by multiplying number of days patient was in hospital by postoperative cost per day. • In column J, calculate total cost as sum of surgery fee, valve cost, and postoperative hospital cost. • Calculate total cost for each column in row 22.	18	
5	Formatting, Saving, Printing	Format the numbers as shown in Figure 2.9 Save, print, and close **EL2-C2-VB2-WPMCCardioCosts.xlsx**.	1	
		TOTAL POINTS	**20**	

Case Study

Part 1

File: **EL2-C2-CS-P1-PBMSales.xlsx**

Steps	Tasks	Criteria	Value	Score
1	Opening, Saving	Open **PBMSales.xlsx**. Save As **EL2-C2-CS-P1-PBMSales.xlsx**.	1	
2	Creating Formulas	Create formulas in rows 3 to 16 in columns H and I. Create range names for data to easily understand formulas. Use the following specifications: • A count of number of stores with gross sales greater than $500,000 • A count of number of stores location in Michigan with sales greater than $500,000 • Average sales for Detroit, Michigan stores • Average sales for Michigan stores established prior to 2004 • Total sales for stores established prior to 2010 • Total sales for Michigan stores established prior to 2010	12	
3	Formatting	Student determines layout, labels, and other formats for statistics section.	6	
4	Saving, Printing	Save and print **EL2-C2-CS-P1-PBMSales.xlsx**.	1	
		TOTAL POINTS	**20**	

Part 2

File: **EL2-C2-CS-P2-PizzaByMarioSales.xlsx**

Steps	Tasks	Criteria	Value	Score
1	Saving	Continue working with the **EL2-C2-CS-P1-PBMSales.xlsx** worksheet. Save as **EL2-C2-CS-P2-PBMSales.xlsx**.	1	
2	Creating Formulas	Use the following specifications: • Create range name for royalty rate table. • Create lookup formula to insert correct royalty percentage for each store in column F. • Create formula to calculate dollar amount of royalty payment based on store's sales times percent value in column F.	7	
3	Formatting	Format royalty percent and royalty fee columns appropriately.	5	
4	Saving, Printing	Print worksheet making sure printout fits on one page. Adjust if necessary. Save revised workbook **EL2-C2-CS-P2-PBMSales.xlsx**.	2	
		TOTAL POINTS	**15**	

Part 3

File: **EL2-C2-CS-P3-PBMSales.xlsx**

Steps	Tasks	Criteria	Value	Score
1	Opening, Saving	Continue working with the **EL2-C2-CS-P2-PBMSales.xlsx** worksheet. Save As **EL2-C2-CS-P3-PBMSales.xlsx**.	1	
2	Using Help, Copying	Using the Help feature to learn about MEDIAN and STDEV functions. Copy A2:E29 to Sheet 2 keeping source column widths.	2	
3	Creating Formulas	Using sales data in column E, calculate the following statistics: • Average sales • Maximum store sales • Minimum store sales • Median store sales • Standard deviation of sales data	10	
3	Formatting	Student determines layout, labels, and other formats.	6	
4	Creating Text Box	Create text below statistics. Write explanation in each box explaining what median and standard deviation numbers mean based on what was learned in Help.	4	
5	Saving, Printing	Print worksheet making sure printout fits on one page. Adjust if necessary. Save and close revised workbook **EL2-C2-CS-P3-PBMSales.xlsx**.	2	
		TOTAL POINTS	**25**	

Part 4

File: **EL2-C2-CS-P4-PBMSales.xlsx**

Steps	Tasks	Criteria	Value	Score
1	Researching	Select two states that in close proximity to Michigan, Ohio, Wisconsin, and Iowa. Research statistics on the Internet. Within each state find population and income statistics for two cities.	4	
2	Opening, Saving	Open **EL2-C2-CS-P3-PBMSales.xlsx**. Save as **EL2-C2-CS-P4-PBMSales.xlsx**.	1	
3	Creating Worksheet	Create new worksheet within Pizza By Mario franchise worksheet. Prepare summary of research findings. Include URLs of sites from which data was obtained.	8	
4	Saving, Printing	Save as **EL2-C2-CS-P4-PBMSales.xlsx**. Print worksheet making sure printout fits on one page. Adjust if necessary. Save and close workbook.	2	
		TOTAL POINTS	**15**	

Benchmark Excel 2013 Level 2, Chapter 3

Skills Check

Assessment 1: Create and Format a Table

File: **EL2-C3-A1-VIVClassics.xlsx**

Steps	Tasks	Criteria	Value	Score
1-2	Opening, Saving	Open **VIVClassics.xlsx**. Save As **EL2-C3-A1-VIVClassics**.	1	
3	Creating Table	Select A4:L30 and create table using Table Style Medium 12.	2	
4	Adding Formulas	Add a calculated column to table in column M. Type the label **Total Cost** as column heading. Create formula in first record that multiplies number of copies in column G times cost price in Column L.	6	
5-6	Formatting	Adjust three rows above table to merge and center across columns A through M. Adjust all column widths to AutoFit. Band columns instead of rows. Emphasize last column in table.	4	
7	Insert Row, Adding Functions	Add *Total* row to table. Add Average functions that calculate average number of copies and average cost price of classic video. Format average value in Copies column of Total row to zero decimals. Format M5-M31 to two decimal places.	3	
8	Formatting, Deleting	Delete video *Blue Hawaii* record. Delete row in table for record with Stock No. CV1015.	3	
9	Saving, Printing	Save, print, and close **EL2-C3-A1-VIVClassics.xlsx**.	1	
		TOTAL POINTS	**20**	

Assessment 2: Use Data Tools

File: **EL2-C3-A2-VIVClassics.xlsx**

Steps	Tasks	Criteria	Value	Score
1-2	Opening, Saving	Open **EL2-C3-A1-VIVClassics.xlsx**. Save As **EL2-C3-A2-VIVClassics**.	1	
3	Inserting Column	Insert new blank column to right of column containing director names. Change column headings to *Director FName* and *Director LName* Split Director names into two columns.	2	
4	Editing	Use the Remove Duplicates feature to find and remove any duplicate rows using *Title* as the comparison column.	2	

Steps	Tasks	Criteria	Value	Score
5	Creating Validation Rules	Create the following validation rules: • Create custom format of "CV-"#### applied to the *Stock No.* column that ensures all new entries are 4 characters in length. • Add input message to column to advise user to enter the last four digits of the stock number. • Student determines title and message text. • Use default error alert options. • Create validation rule that restricts entries in copies column to a maximum number of five. • Create a validation rule that restricts entries in the *Copies* column to less than six. • Do not add an input message, and use default Stop error alert. • Create drop-down list for the *Genre* column with entries provided. Do not enter an input message and use default error alert settings.	6	
6	Adding Record	Add the following record to table to test data validation rules. Initially enter incorrect values in *Stock No.*, *Genre*, and *Copies* columns to make sure rule and messages work correctly. *Stock No.* **CV-1026** *Title* **The Philadelphia Story** *Year* **1940** *Genre* **Comedy** *Stock Date* **12/12/2015** *Director FName* **George** *Director LName* **Cukor** *Copies* **3** *VHS* **No** *DVD* **Yes** *Blu-ray* **Yes** *Category* **7-day rental** *Cost Price* **10.15**	3	
7	Saving, Printing	Save, print, and close **EL2-C3-A2-VIVClassics.xlsx.**	1	
		TOTAL POINTS	**15**	

Assessment 3: Subtotal Records
File: **EL2-C3-A3-VIVClassics.xlsx**

Steps	Tasks	Criteria	Value	Score
1-2	Opening, Saving	Open **EL2-C3-A2-VIVClassics.xlsx.** Save As **EL2-C3-A3-VIVClassics.xlsx.**	1	
3-5	Formatting	Remove Total row, and remove emphasis from last column in table. Convert table to normal range. Adjust all column widths to AutoFit.	5	
6	Sorting	Sort the list first by genre, then by director's last name, and then by title of video. Use default sort values and sort order for each level.	3	

Steps	Tasks	Criteria	Value	Score
7	Inserting Subtotals	Add subtotals using the Subtotal button in Outline group of DATA tab to *Total Cost* column to calculate sum and average total costs of videos by genre.	3	
8-9	Displaying Level, Showing Details	Display worksheet at Level 2 of outline. Show details for Comedy, Drama, and Family genres.	2	
10-11	Printing, Saving	Print worksheet. Save and close **EL2-C3-A3-VIVClassics.xlsx**.	1	
		TOTAL POINTS	**15**	

Visual Benchmark

1: Using Table and Data Tools in a Call List
File: **EL2-C3-VB1-WPMCallList.xlsx**

Steps	Tasks	Criteria	Value	Score
1-2	Opening, Saving	Open **WPMCallList.xlsx**. Save As **EL2-C3-VB1-WPMCallList.xlsx**	1	
3	Formatting	Format and apply data tools as required to duplicate worksheet in Figure 3.10 using the following information: • Worksheet has *Table Style Medium 5* applied to table range • Table is sorted by three levels using fields *Designation, Hourly Rate*, and *Hire Date* • Shift cost multiplies hourly rate times 8 hours • Split names into two columns (using Flash Fill) • Include *Total* row and apply appropriate banded options	8	
4	Saving, Printing	Save, print, and close **EL2-C3-VB1-WPMCallList.xlsx**.	1	
		TOTAL POINTS	**10**	

2: Using Subtotals in a Call List
File: **EL2-C3-VB2-WPMCallList.xlsx**

Steps	Tasks	Criteria	Value	Score
1-2	Opening, Saving	Open **EL2-C3-VB1-WPMCallList.xlsx**. Save As **EL2-C3-VB2-WPMCallList.xlsx**.	1	
3-4	Creating Subtotals	Create subtotals and view revised worksheet at appropriate level to display as shown in Figure 3.11.	3	
5	Saving, Printing	Save, print, and close **EL2-C3-VB2-WPMCallList.xlsx**.	1	
		TOTAL POINTS	**5**	

Case Study

Part 1

File: **EL2-C3-CS-P1-NuTrendsMktPlans.xlsx**

Steps	Tasks	Criteria	Value	Score
1	Opening, Saving	Open **NuTrendsMktPlans.xlsx**. Save As **EL2-C3-CS-P1-NuTrendsMktPlans.xlsx**.	1	
2	Sorting	Sort table first by consultant's last name, then by marketing campaign's start date, both in ascending order. Split consultant names into two columns.	6	
3	Formatting	Format using the following specifications: • Improve formatting of dollar values. • Add Total row to sum the columns containing dollar amounts. • Add formatting to titles above table that are suited to colors in table style student selected. • Make other formatting changes to improve appearance of worksheet.	5	
4	Saving, Printing	Save **EL2-C3-CS-P1-NuTrendsMktPlans.xlsx**. Print worksheet in landscape orientation with width scaled to 1 page.	3	
		TOTAL POINTS	**15**	

Part 2

File: **EL2-C3-CS-P2-NuTrendsMktPlans.xlsx**

Steps	Tasks	Criteria	Value	Score
1	Saving	With **EL2-C3 CS-P1-NuTrendsMktPlans.xlsx** open save as **EL2-C3-CS-P2-NuTrendsMktPlans.xlsx**.	1	
2	Creating Formulas	Include the following information: • Total marketing plan budget values managed by each consultant as well as total planned expenditures by month. • Average marketing plan budget managed by each consultant as well as average planned expenditures by month.	6	
3	Saving, Printing	Save **EL2-C3-CS-P2-NuTrendsMktPlans**. Set printout to display only the total and average values for each consultant as well as grand average and grand total. Print and close worksheet.	3	
		TOTAL POINTS	**10**	

Part 3

File: **EL2-C3-CS-P3-NuTrendsMktPlans.xlsx**

Steps	Tasks	Criteria	Value	Score
1	Opening, Saving	Open **NuTrendsMktPlans.xlsx**. Save As **EL2-C3-CS-P3-NuTrendsMktPlans**.	1	
2	Using Help, Inserting	Use the Help feature to learn how to filter a range of cells using Advanced Filter button in Sort & Filter group of DATA tab and how to copy rows that meet filter criteria to another area of worksheet. • Printout request needs to show original data at top of worksheet and few blank rows below. Marketing plan details for Yolanda Robertson's clients with a campaign starting after January 31, 2012. • Using the information, insert three new rows above worksheet and use these rows to create criteria range.	2	
3	Filtering, Copying	Filter list as specified above. Rows that meet criteria should be copied below worksheet starting in cell A21.	5	
4	Inserting Title	Add appropriate title to describe copied data in cell A20.	2	
5	Formatting	Make formatting changes to improve appearance of worksheet.	4	
6	Saving, Printing	Save revised workbook. Print and close **EL2-C3-CS-P3-NuTrendsMktPlans**.	1	
		TOTAL POINTS	**15**	

Part 4

File: **EL2-C3-CS-P4-NuTrendsSalaryAnalysis.xlsx**

Steps	Tasks	Criteria	Value	Score
1	Researching	Use the Internet to find information on current salary ranges for a market researcher in the United States. If possible, find salary information that is regional to student's state for a minimum of three cities. Find a low salary and a high salary for a market research in each city. Find a minimum of three and a maximum of five resources.	4	
2	Creating Worksheet	Create worksheet that summarizes results of research with the following specifications: • Include Web site addresses as hyperlinked cells next to salary range information. • Organize data as a table. • Apply table formatting options so data is attractively presented and easy to read. • Add Total row to table. • Include Average function to find average salary from three cities.	10	
3	Saving, Printing	Save As **EL2-C3-CS-P4-NuTrendsSalaryAnalysis.xlsx**. Print worksheet and close workbook.	1	
		TOTAL POINTS	**15**	

Benchmark Excel 2013 Level 2, Chapter 4

Skills Check

Assessment 1: Summarize Data in Multiple Worksheets Using Range Names
File: **EL2-C4-A1-NADQ1Fees.xlsx**

Steps	Tasks	Criteria	Value	Score
1-2	Opening, Saving	Open **NADQ1Fees.xlsx**. Save As **EL2-C4-A1-NADQ1Fees**.	1	
3	Creating Range Names	Create a range name in F13 of each worksheet to reference the total fees earned by the dentist for the quarter as follows: • Name F13 in the Popovich worksheet *PopovichTotal* • Name F13 in the Vanket worksheet *VanketTotal* • Name F13 in the Jovanovic worksheet *JovanovicTotal*	3	
4	Adding Label	In the FeeSummary worksheet, type the following label in A6: **Quarter 1 fees for Popovich, Vanket, and Jovanovic**.	1	
5	Inserting Formula	In F6, create a Sum formula to add the total fees earned by each dentist using the range names created in Step 3.	2	
6	Formatting	Format F6 to Accounting Number Format style and adjust column width to AutoFit.	2	
7-8	Saving, Printing	Print FeeSummary worksheet. Save and close **EL2-C4-A1-NADQ1Fees.xlsx**.	1	
		TOTAL POINTS	10	

Assessment 2: Summarize Data Using Linked External References
File: **EL2-C4-A2-PFSalesSum.xlsx**

Steps	Tasks	Criteria	Value	Score
1-2	Opening, Saving	Open **PFSalesSum.xlsx**. Save As **EL2-C4-A2-PFSalesSum**.	1	
3-4	Opening, Inserting Titles	Open **PFQ1.xlsx**, **PFQ2.xlsx**, **PFQ3.xlsx**, and **PFQ4.xlsx**. Title all open workbooks.	2	
5-7	Creating Formulas	Starting in cell B5 in the **EL2-C4-A2-PFSalesSum.xlsx** workbook, create formulas to populate cells in column B by linking to appropriate source cell in **PFQ1.xlsx**. *Hint: After creating first formula, edit entry in B5 to use a relative reference to the source cells (instead of absolute) so formula can be copied and pasted in B5 to B6:B9.* Create formulas to link to appropriate source cells for second, third, and fourth quarter sales. Close four quarterly sales workbooks. Click Don't Save when prompted to save changes.	6	
8-10	Saving, Printing	Maximize **EL2-C4-A2-PFSalesSum.xlsx**. In cell B5, break the link to PFQ1.xlsx. Print and close workbook.	1	
		TOTAL POINTS	10	

Assessment 3: Summarize Data Using 3-D References
File: **EL2-C4-A3-JuneEntries.xlsx**

Steps	Tasks	Criteria	Value	Score
1	Opening, Saving	Open **JuneEntries.xlsx**. Save **As EL2-C4-A3-JuneEntries.**	1	
2	Using 3-D References	With AttendanceSummary worksheet active, summarize data in the three park worksheets using 3-D references as follows: • Make B7 the active cell and create a 3-D formula to sum attendance values in the three park worksheets for Day 1. Copy and paste formula to remaining cells in column B to complete summary to Day 16. • Make E7 the active cell and create a 3-D formula to sum attendance values in three park worksheets for Day 17. Copy and paste formula to remaining cells in column E to complete summary to Day 31. • Type label **Total Vehicle and Individual Entrances** in A24. • Create Sum formula in E24 to computer grand total. • Apply comma formatting options to grand total to make total stand out.	18	
3	Printing, Saving	• Print AttendanceSummary worksheet. • Save and close **EL2-C4-A3-JuneEntries.xlsx**.	1	
		TOTAL POINTS	**20**	

Assessment 4: Summarize Data in a PivotTable and PivotChart
File: **EL2-C4-A4-BillingSummary3Q.xlsx**

Steps	Tasks	Criteria	Value	Score
1-2	Opening, Saving	Open **BillSummary3Q.xlsx**. Save As **EL2-C4-A4-BillingSummary3Q.xlsx**.	1	
3	Creating PivotTable Report	Create PivotTable report in a new worksheet as follows: • Display range named *ThirdQ* and insert a PivotTable in a new worksheet • Add the *AttorneyLName* field as columns. • Add the *Area* field as rows • Sum the *Fees Due* field	3	
4-6	Formatting, Printing	• Apply the Pivot Style Medium 2 style to the PivotTable • Apply comma formatting with no decimal places • Change the column widths of B through H to 13 characters, right-align the *Martinex*, *ODonovan*, *Sullivan*, *Williams*, and *Grand Total* labels in Column A. • Name the worksheet *PivotTable* and change the following: • Cell A1, type **Associate Billing Summary**, change the font to 14-point Copperplate Gothic Bold. Merge and center the text across the PivotTable. • Cell A2, type October – December 2015 and change the font to 14-point Copperplate Gothic Bold, merge and center the text across the PivotTable. • Change to landscape orientation, print the PivotTable.	8	

Steps	Tasks	Criteria	Value	Score
7-9	Creating, Filtering PivotChart	Create a PivotChart from PivotTable using the 3-D Stacked column chart type. Move chart to its own sheet named *PivotChart*. Apply Style 7 to the PivotChart and filter the PivotChart by the attorney *Martinez*.	5	
10-11	Printing, Saving	Print the PivotChart. Save and close **EL2-C4-A4-BillingSummary3Q.xlsx**.	3	
		TOTAL POINTS	**20**	

Assessment 5: Filtering a PivotTable Using A Slicer and Timeline
File: **EL2-C4-A5-BillingSummary3Q.xlsx**

Steps	Tasks	Criteria	Value	Score
1-2	Opening, Saving	Open **EL2-C4-A4-BillingSummary3Q.xlsx**. Save As **EL2-C4-A5-BillingSummary3Q.xlsx**.	1	
3-5	Viewing Report, Inserting Slicer Panes	View PivotTable report in PivotTable sheet. Remove the filter to display all of the attorney names and insert a Slicer pane for the *Area* field; move the Slicer pane below the PivotTable.	14	
6	Filtering	Use Slicer pane to filter PivotTable by *Corporate*. Using the Shift key, select Divorce.	2	
7	Filtering	Insert the Timeline pane, filter the PivotTable for Oct to Nov 2015.	2	
9-10	Printing, Saving	Print PivotTable report. Save and close **EL2-C4-A5-BillingSummary3Q.xlsx**.	1	
		TOTAL POINTS	**20**	

Assessment 6: Creating and Customizing Sparklines
File: **EL2-C4-A6-PFSalesSum.xlsx**

Steps	Tasks	Criteria	Value	Score
1-2	Opening, Saving	Open **EL2-C4-A2-PFSalesSum.xlsx**. Save As **EL2-C4-A6-PFSalesSum.xlsx**.	1	
3-7	Creating, Customizing Sparklines	Create and customize using the following specifications: • Select H5-H9 and insert Line Sparklines referencing data range B5:E9. • Show high point and markers on each line. • Change Sparkline color to *Dark Blue*. • Change width of column H to 21 characters. • Type label **Region Sales by Quarter** in H4.	12	
8	Printing, Saving	Change page orientation to landscape and print worksheet. Save and close **EL2-C4-A6-PFSalesSum.xlsx**.	2	
		TOTAL POINTS	**15**	

Visual Benchmark

1: Summarizing Real Estate Sales and Commission Data

File: **EL2-C4-VB-HillsdaleOctSales.xlsx**

Steps	Tasks	Criteria	Value	Score
1-2	Opening, Saving	Open **HROctSales.xlsx**. Save As **EL2-C4-VB-HROctSales**.	1	
3	Creating PivotTable	Create PivotTable report shown in Figure 4.11 in new worksheet named *PivotTable*. Use *Pivot Style Medium 11* and set column widths to 18.	4	
4	Creating PivotChart Report	Create PivotChart report shown in Figure 4.12 in new worksheet named *PivotChart*. Use 3-D Clustered Column chart and Style 11.	4	
5-6	Saving, Printing	Print PivotTable and PivotChart sheets. Save and close **EL2-C4-VB-HROctSales.xlsx**.	1	
		TOTAL POINTS	**10**	

Case Study

Part 1

File: **EL2-C4-CS-P1-PBMRpt.xlsx**

Steps	Tasks	Criteria	Value	Score
1	Opening, Saving	Open **PBMSales&Profits.xlsx**. Save As **EL2-C4-CS-P1-PBMRpt.xlsx**.	1	
2	Creating PivotTable Report	Create PivotTable report using the following specifications: • Include average gross sales and average net income by city by state. • Organize layout of report *(Hint: Add more than one numeric field to Values list box)*. User determines layout. • Remove grand totals at right of report so that grand total row appears only at bottom of PivotTable. *(Hint: Use Grand Totals button in Layout group of PivotTable Tools Design tab)*.	8	
3	Formatting	• Apply formatting options to improve appearance and to be sure report will print on one page.	4	
4	Saving, Printing	Print report in landscape orientation. Rename worksheet containing report *PivotTable*. Save **EL2-C4-CS-P1-PBMRpt.xlsx**.	2	
		TOTAL POINTS	**15**	

Part 2

File: **EL2-C4-CS-P2-PBMRpt.xlsx**

Steps	Tasks	Criteria	Value	Score
1	Opening, Saving	With **EL2-C4-CS-P1-PBMRpt.xlsx** open save as **EL2-C4-CS-P2-PBMRpt.xlsx**.	1	
2	Creating PivotChart	Include the following information to create a PivotChart: • Create PivotChart in new sheet named PivotChart • Graph the average net income data for state of Michigan only • Determine appropriate chart style and elements. • Be sure chart is of professional quality	8	
3	Saving, Printing	Print chart. Save and close **EL2-C4-CS-P2-PBMRpt.xlsx**.	1	
		TOTAL POINTS	10	

Part 3

File: **EL2-C4-CS-P3-PBMRpt.xlsx**

Steps	Tasks	Criteria	Value	Score
1	Opening, Saving	Open **EL2-C4-CS-P1-PBMRpt.xlsx**. Save As **EL2-C4-CS-P3-PBMRpt**.	1	
2	Using Help, Changing Display	Use the Help feature to learn how to modify a numeric field setting to show values as ranked numbers from largest to smallest. Change display of average sales to show the values ranked from largest to smallest using City as the base field. Remove *Net Income* field from PivotTable. Remove grand total row at bottom of PivotTable.	9	
3	Formatting	Make formatting changes to improve appearance of worksheet.	4	
4	Saving, Printing	Print PivotTable. Save and close **EL2-C4-CS-P3-PBMRpt.xlsx**.	1	
		TOTAL POINTS	15	

Part 4

File: **EL2-C4-CS-P4-PizzaFranchiseComparison.xlsx**

Steps	Tasks	Criteria	Value	Score
1	Researching	Use the Internet to research sales and net income information of a pizza franchise with which student is familiar.	4	
2	Creating Worksheet	Create worksheet that summarizes results of research with the following specifications: • Compare total annual sales and net income values of pizza franchise researched with the Pizza By Mario Information in the **EL2-C4-CS-P1-PBMRpt.xlsx**. • Provide URL of website used to obtain the competitive data.	10	

Steps	Tasks	Criteria	Value	Score
3	Creating Chart	Create chart that visually presents comparison data.	4	
4	Saving, Printing	Save As **EL2-C4-CS-P4-PizzaFranchiseComparison.xlsx**. Print comparison data and chart. Close workbook.	2	
		TOTAL POINTS	**20**	

Benchmark Excel 2013 Level 2, Unit 1 Performance Assessment

Assessing Proficiency

Assessment 1: Conditionally Format and Filter a Help Desk Worksheet
File: **EL2-U1-A1-RSRHelpDesk.xlsx**

Steps	Tasks	Criteria	Value	Score
1-2	Opening, Saving	Open **RSRHelpDesk.xlsx**. Save As **EL2-U1-A1-RSRHelpDesk**.	1	
3	Formatting	Apply conditional formatting using the Quick Analysis to values in *Priority* column.	3	
4	Creating Custom Format	Create custom format for values in *Time Spent* column. Format should display leading zeroes, two decimal places, and text *hrs.* at end of entry separate by one space from number.	3	
5	Creating Conditional Formatting Rules	Create two conditional formatting rules for values in T*ime Spent* column as follows: • For all entries where time spent is less than 1 hour, apply bold and Olive Green, Accent 3, Lighter 80% fill color. • For all entries where time spent is more than 2 hours, apply Yellow fill color.	4	
6	Filtering	Filter worksheet by the Yellow fill color applied in *Time Spent* column.	2	
7	Printing	Print filtered worksheet.	1	
8-9	Clearing Filter, Printing, Saving	Clear filter and filter arrow buttons. Print worksheet. Save and close **EL2-U1-A1-RSRHelpDesk.xlsx**.	1	
		TOTAL POINTS	**15**	

Assessment 2: Use Conditional Logic Formulas in a Help Desk Worksheet
File: **EL2-U1-A2-RSRHelpDesk.xlsx**

Steps	Tasks	Criteria	Value	Score
1-2	Opening, Saving	Open **EL2-U1-A1-RSRHelpDeskRpt.xlsx.** Save As **EL2-U1-A2-RSRHelpDesk.xlsx.**	1	
3	Creating Range Names	• Create range names for the following ranges: • Name cells in A4:E6, which will be used in a lookup formula • Name entries in *Operator ID* column • Name values in *Time Spent* column • Name cells in *Status* column • Student determines appropriate names.	2	
4-11	Creating Formulas	• Creating formulas with the following specifications: • Create COUNTA formula in I4 to count number of help desk calls in March using column A as the source range. • Create COUNTIF formulas in I5 and I6 to count number of active calls (I5) and number of closed calls (I6). • Create COUNTIF formulas in K3 through K6 to count calls assigned to Operator ID 1, 2, 3, and 4, respectively. Use range names in formulas. • Create SUMIF formulas in L3 through L6 to calculate total time spent on calls assigned to Operator ID 1, 2, 3, and 4, respectively. Use range names in formulas. Format results to display two decimal places. • Create AVERAGEIF formulas in M3 through M6 to find average time spent on calls assigned to Operator ID 1, 2, 3, and 4, respectively. Use range names in formulas. Format results to display two decimal places. • Create HLOOKUP formula with exact match in G8 to return last name for operator assigned to the call. Use the range name for lookup table in formula. • Create HLOOKUP formula with exact match in H8 to return first name for operator assigned to call. Use range name for lookup table in formula. • Copy HLOOKUP formulas in G8:H8 and paste to remaining rows in list.	16	
12	Saving, Printing	Save, print, and close **EL2-U1-A2-RSRHelpDesk.xlsx.**	1	
		TOTAL POINTS	**20**	

Assessment 3: Use Table and Data Management Features in a Help Desk Worksheet

File: **EL2-U1-A3-RSRHelpDesk.xlsx**

Steps	Tasks	Criteria	Value	Score
1-2	Opening, Saving	Open **EL2-U1-A2-RSRHelpDesk.xlsx**. Save as **EL2-U1-A3-RSRHelpDesk.xlsx**.	1	
3-6	Inserting, Formatting	• Create the file number in column F using the ticket number in column B followed by a dash, the priority in column C, followed by a dash and the Operator ID. • Format A7:J30 as a table with Table Style Medium 20 table style. • Add a calculated column to the table in column K that multiplies the time spent times 15. Use the column heading *Cost* in cell K7. • Apply comma formatting, two decimal places. • Add a Total row to the table, display totals for columns I and K	8	
7	Formatting	Add emphasis to the last column in the table and band the columns instead of the rows.	2	
8	Formatting	Create a drop-down list for the Operator ID column that displays entries 1, 2, 3, and 4.	2	
9	Validation Rule	Create a validation rule in the *Time Spent* column that prevents any value greater than 3 to be entered. Create any appropriate messages for both input and errors.	2	
10	Adding Records	Add two records above the total in row 31: Dates: 03/31/2015 and 03/31/2015 Ticket No's: 14424 and 14425 Priority: 2 and 2 Type of call: Email and Password Operator ID: 3 and 4 File No: 14424-2-3 and 14425-2-4 Time Spent: .75 and .25 Status: Active and Closed	3	
11-16	Filtering, Saving and closing	Filter to display the *Closed* status and print. Filter to display the *Closed* status and type of call of *Password* and print. Clear both filters. Save, print, and close **EL2-U1-A3-RSRHelpDesk.xlsx**.	2	
		TOTAL POINTS	**20**	

Assessment 4: Add Subtotals and Outline a Help Desk Worksheet

File: **EL2-U1-A4-RSRHelpDesk.xlsx**

Steps	Tasks	Criteria	Value	Score
1-2	Opening, Saving	Open **EL2-U1-A3-RSRHelpDesk.xlsx**. Save As **EL2-U1-A4-RSRHelpDesk.xlsx**.	1	
3-4	Editing	Remove Total row from table. Convert table to a normal range.	2	

Steps	Tasks	Criteria	Value	Score
5	Sorting	Sort list first by operator's last name, then by operator's first name, then by call priority, and finally by type of call; all in ascending order.	5	
6	Inserting	Add subtotal to list at each change in operator last name to calculate the total cost of calls by operator.	2	
7-8	Displaying, Printing	Display outlined worksheet at level 2 and print worksheet. Display outlined worksheet at level 3 and print worksheet.	4	
9	Saving	Save and close **EL2-U1-A4-RSRHelpDesk.xlsx**.	1	
		TOTAL POINTS	15	

Assessment 5: Use Financial and Text Functions to Analyze Data for a Project
File: **EL2-U1-A5-ACLoan.xlsx**

Steps	Tasks	Criteria	Value	Score
1-2	Opening, Saving	Open **ACLoan.xlsx**. Save As **EL2-U1-A5-ACLoan**.xlsx.	1	
3	Creating Formulas	Create formulas to analyze cost of loan from NEWFUNDS TRUST and DELTA CAPITAL as follows: • In C10 and E10, calculate monthly loan payment from each lender • In C12 and E12, calculate principal portion of each payment for first loan payment • In C14 and E14, calculate total loan payments that will be made over the life of the loan from each lender	9	
4-5	Using Text Functions	In E20, use text function =*PROPER* to return loan company for loan that represents the lowest total cost to AllClaims Insurance. In E21, use text function =*LOWER* to return loan application number for loan company name displayed in E20.	4	
6	Saving, Printing	Save, print, and close **EL2-U1-A5-ACLoan.xlsx**.	1	
		TOTAL POINTS	15	

Assessment 6: Analyze Sales Using a PivotTable, a PivotChart, and Sparklines
File: **EL2-U1-A6-PrecisPreBulkSales.xlsx**

Steps	Tasks	Criteria	Value	Score
1-2	Opening, Saving	Open **PreBulkSales.xlsx**. Save As **EL2-U1-A6-PreBulkSales.xlsx**.	1	
3	Creating PivotTable	Select A4:I22 and create a PivotTable in a new worksheet named *PivotTable* as follows: • Add *Category* field as report filter field • Add *Distributor* field as row labels • Sum North, South, East, and West sales values. • Name the worksheet PivotTable	6	

Steps	Tasks	Criteria	Value	Score
4-6	Formatting, Printing	Apply formatting options to PivotTable to make data easier to read and interpret. Insert a Slicer for the Model and show the data for *PD-1140, PD-1150, and PD-1155.* Move the Slicer pane under the PivotTable and print the PivotTable and Slicer pane on one sheet.	3	
7-10	Creating PivotChart, Printing	Create PivotChart in separate sheet named *PivotChart* that graphs data from PivotTable in a 3-D Clustered Column chart. Move the legend to the bottom of the chart. Apply the Style 3 format to the chart and print.	6	
11	Creating Sparklines	Make Sheet1 active and create Sparklines in J5:J22 that show North, South, East, and West sales in a line chart. Set width of column J to 18. Customize Sparklines by changing Sparkline color and adding data points. Student determines data points and colors. Type appropriate label in J4 and add additional formatting to improve appearance.	8	
12	Printing, Saving	Save, print, and close **EL2-U1-A6-PreBulkSales.xlsx**.	1	
		TOTAL POINTS	**25**	

Assessment 7: Link to an External Data Source and Calculate Distributor Payments

File: **EL2-U1-A7-PreDistPymnt.xlsx** and **EL2U1A7PreSource.xlsx**

Steps	Tasks	Criteria	Value	Score
1-4	Opening, Saving	Open **PreDistPymnt.xlsx**. Save As **EL2-U1-A7PreDistPymnt.xlsx**. Open **EL2-U1-A6-PreBulkSales.xlsx**. Save As **EL-U1-A7-PreSource.xlsx**.	1	
5-7	Editing, Saving	Make PivotTable worksheet active. Remove any filters, delete the Slicer pane and then edit the PivotTable Fields so that *Sum of Total* is the only numeric field displayed in the table. Save **EL2-U1-A7-PreSource.xlsx**. Arrange display of two workbooks vertically.	4	
8-9	Creating Linked External References	Create linked external references starting in D6 in **EL2-U1-A7-PreDistPymnt.xlsx** to appropriate sources cells in PivotTable in **EL2-U1-A7-PreSource.xlsx** so that distributor payment worksheet displays total sales for each distributor. Close **EL2-U1-A7-PreSource.xlsx**.	4	
10-11	Formatting	Maximize **EL2-U1-A7-PreDistPymnt.xlsx**. Format D6:D8 to comma style with no decimal places defaults.	2	

Steps	Tasks	Criteria	Value	Score
12	Calculating	Using data in illustrated chart, calculate payment owed for distributors in H6:H8. Perform calculation using either one of the following two methods: • Create a nested IF statement; OR • Create a lookup table in worksheet that contains sales ranges and three percentage values. Next, add a column next to each distributor with a lookup formula to return correct percentage and then calculate payment using total sales times percent value.	4	
13	Formatting	Format H6:H8 to Comma Style number format.	2	
14	Creating Formulas, Formatting	Add label *TOTALS* in B10. Create formulas in D10 and H10 to calculate total sales and total payments respectively. Format totals and adjust column widths as necessary.	6	
15	Printing	Print worksheet. Write the GETPIVOTDATA formula for D6 at bottom of printout.	2	
16	Breaking link	Break link to external references. Convert formulas to their existing values.	3	
17	Printing, Saving	Save, print, and close **EL2-U1-A7-PreDistPymnt.xlsx**.	2	
		TOTAL POINTS	**30**	

Writing Activities

Activity 1: Create a Worksheet to Track Video Rental Memberships

File: **EL2-U1-Act01-VIVMemberships.xlsx**

Steps	Tasks	Criteria	Value	Score
1	Creating Worksheet	Worksheet needs to provide in list format the following information: • Date annual membership needs to be renewed • Customer name • Customer telephone number • Membership level • Annual membership fee • Discount on movie rentals • Table U.1 provides the three memberships levels and discounts	6	
2	Adding Formulas	Use lookup table to populate cells containing membership fee and discount level. Create drop-down list for cell containing membership level that restricts the data entered to three membership categories. Use special number format for telephone number column so all telephone numbers include area code and are displayed in consistent format.	9	

Steps	Tasks	Criteria	Value	Score
3	Adding Records	Enter a minimum of five sample records to test worksheet with student settings. Format enough rows with data features to include at least 35 memberships.	4	
5-6	Saving, Printing	Save As **EL2-U1-Act01-VIVMemberships.xlsx**. Print and close worksheet.	1	
		TOTAL POINTS	**20**	

Activity 2: Create a Worksheet to Log Hours Walked in a Company Fitness Contest

File: File: **EL2-U1-Act02-FitProgram.xlsx**

Steps	Tasks	Criteria	Value	Score
1	Creating Worksheet	Worksheet needs to total each department's totals by month and summarize data to show total distance walked for entire company at end of year as follows: • Create separate worksheets for each department: Accounting, Human Resources, Purchasing, and Marketing • Enter miles or kilometers walked by day • Calculate statistics by department to show total distance walked, average distance walked, number of days in month in which employees walked during their lunch hour • When calculating average and number of days, include only those days in which employees logged a distance (do not include days in which employees did not log any distance) • Create summary worksheet that calculates total of all miles or kilometers walked for all four departments	15	
2	Adding Information	Enter at least five days of sample data in each worksheet to test settings.	4	
3	Saving, Printing	Save As **EL2-U1-Act02-FitProgram.xlsx**. Print entire workbook and close workbook.	1	
		TOTAL POINTS	**20**	

Activity 2A: Optional Create a Worksheet to Log Hours Walked in a Company Fitness Contest

File: File: **EL2-U1-Act02-FitMemo.docx**

Steps	Tasks	Criteria	Value	Score
1	Researching, Writing	Use the Internet or other sources to find information on health benefits of walking. Write a memo from Human Resources announcing the contests and provide a summary of information on health benefits of walking.	9	
3	Saving, Printing	Save As **EL2-U1-Act02-FitMemo.docx**. Print memo and close file.	1	
		TOTAL POINTS	**10**	

Internet Research

Create a Worksheet to Compare Online Auction Listing Fees
File: **EL2-U1-Act03-AuctionAnalysis.xlsx**

Steps	Tasks	Criteria	Value	Score
1	Researching	Research at least two Internet auction sites for all selling and payment fees associated with selling online. Find out costs for the following activities involved in an auction sale: • Listing fees (insertion fees) • Option features that can be attached to an ad such as reserve bid fees, picture fees, listing upgrades, etc. • Fees paid when item is sold based on sale value • Fees paid to third party to accept credit card payments (such as PayPal)	4	
2	Creating Worksheet	Create worksheet comparing fees for each auction site researched. Include two sample transactions and calculate total fees that would be paid. Add optional features to listing such as picture and/or reserve bid. Assume in both sample transactions the buyer pays by credit card using a third party service.	10	
3	Formatting	Based on your analysis, decide which auction site is a better choice from a cost perspective. Apply formatting options to make worksheet easy to read and explain your recommendation for the lower cost auction site.	5	
4	Saving, Printing	Save As **EL2-U1-Act03-AuctionAnalysis.xlsx**. Print and close worksheet.	1	
		TOTAL POINTS	**20**	

Benchmark Excel 2013 Level 2, Chapter 5

Skills Check

Assessment 1: Convert Columns to Rows; Add Source Cells to Destination Cells; Filter
File: **EL2-C5-A1-CRC.xlsx**

Steps	Tasks	Criteria	Value	Score
1-2	Opening, Saving	Open **CRC.xlsx**. Save As **EL2-C5-A1-CRC**.	1	
3-4	Editing	Copy and paste A4:F12 below worksheet, converting data arrangement so that columns become rows and rows become columns. Delete rows 4 through 13- the original source data rows from worksheet.	4	
5	Formatting	Adjust merge and centering of title rows across top of worksheet, use AutoFit to adjust column widths, apply bold formatting to B4:I4.	4	

Steps	Tasks	Criteria	Value	Score
6-7	Copying	Copy values in *Shipping* column. Paste values to *Total Cost* values using Add operation so that Total Cost includes shipping fee. Copy *Compact* values and past only validation rule to *Mid-Size* and *SUV* columns.	5	
8	Saving, Printing	Save, print, and close **EL2-C5-A1-CRC.xlsx**.	1	
		TOTAL POINTS	**15**	

Assessment 2: Use Goal Seek

File: **EL2-C5-A2-NationalBdgt.xlsx**

Steps	Tasks	Criteria	Value	Score
1-2	Opening, Saving	Open **NationalBdgt.xlsx**. Save As **EL2-C5-A2-NationalBdgt**.	1	
3-5	Editing	Make D8 the active cell and open Goal Seek dialog box. Find projected increase for Wages and benefits that will make total cost of new budge equal $655,000. Accept the solution Goal Seek calculates.	3	
6	Saving, Printing	Save, print, and close **EL2-C5-A2-NationalBdgt.xlsx**.	1	
		TOTAL POINTS	**5**	

Assessment 3: Use Scenario Manager

File: **EL2-C5-A3-PreCdnTarget.xlsx**

Steps	Tasks	Criteria	Value	Score
1-2	Opening, Saving	Open **PreCdnTarget.xlsx**. Save As **EL2-C5-A3-PreCdnTarget**.	1	
3	Creating Scenarios	Create scenarios to save various percentage data sets for four regions using the following information: • A scenario named *OriginalTarget* that stores current values in K4:K7 • A scenario named *LowSales* with the following values: *East* .20 *West* .32 *Ontario* .48 *Quebec* .37 • A scenario named *HighSales* with the following values: *East* .36 *West* .58 *Ontario* .77 *Quebec* .63	6	
4	Applying Scenario, Printing	Apply *LowSales* scenario and print worksheet.	2	

Steps	Tasks	Criteria	Value	Score
5	Editing	Create a scenario summary displaying cell H18 as the result cell.	2	
6-7	Creating Report, Printing, Saving	Create scenario summary report displaying H18 as the result cell. Print Scenario Summary sheet. Save and close **EL2-C5-A3-PreCdnTarget.xlsx**.	4	
		TOTAL POINTS	**15**	

Assessment 4: Create a Two-Variable Data Table
File: **EL2-C5-A4-NationalHlpDsk.xlsx**

Steps	Tasks	Criteria	Value	Score
1-2	Opening, Saving	Open **NationalHlpDsk.xlsx**. Save As **EL2-C5-A4-NationalHlpDsk**.	1	
3	Creating Two-Variable Data Table	Create a two-variable data table that will calculate the average cost per call in data table for each level of total call minutes logged and at each average cost per minute.	6	
4	Printing, Saving	Save, print, and close **EL2-C5-A4-NationalHlpDsk.xlsx**.	1	
		TOTAL POINTS	**8**	

Assessment 5: Find and Correct Formula Errors
File: **EL2-C5-A5-NationalCapital.xlsx**

Steps	Tasks	Criteria	Value	Score
1-2	Opening, Saving	Open **NationalCapital.xlsx**. Save As **EL2-C5-A5-NationalCapital.xlsx**.	1	
3-6	Correcting Errors	Make D19 the active cell and use Trace Error feature to draw red tracer arrows to find source cell creating the #N/A error. The cost of a Pix firewall is $4,720.00. Enter this data in appropriate cell to correct the *#N/A* error. Remove tracer arrows. Find and correct the logic error in one of the formulas.	8	
7	Printing, Saving	Save, print, and close **EL2-C5-A5-NationalCapital.xlsx**.	1	
		TOTAL POINTS	**10**	

Visual Benchmark

1: Find the Base Hourly Rate for Drum Lessons
File: **EL2-C5-VB1-Lessons.xlsx**

Steps	Tasks	Criteria	Value	Score
1-2	Opening, Saving	Open **Lessons.xlsx**. Save As **EL2-C5-VB1-Lessons.**	1	
3-4	Using Goal Seek	The current hourly rates in B5:B13 are linked to cell named *BaseRate* located in B16. Intermediate-level and advanced-level lessons have $4 and $8 added to hourly base rate. Drum teacher wants to earn $2,645.50 per month from drum lessons instead of current total of $2,292.00. Use Goal Seek to change base hourly rate to required value needed to reach drum teacher's target.	3	
5	Saving, Printing	Save, print, and close **EL2-C5-VB1-Lessons.xlsx**.	1	
		TOTAL POINTS	5	

2: Create Scenarios for Drum Lesson Revenue
File: **EL2-C5-VB2-Lessons.xlsx**

Steps	Tasks	Criteria	Value	Score
1-2	Opening, Saving	Open **Lessons.xlsx**. Save As **EL2-C5-VB2-Lessons.**	1	
3	Creating Scenarios	Examine Scenario Summary report shown in Figure 5.12. Create three scenarios to save the hourly base rates shown: **Low Rate Increase**, **Mid Rate Increase**, and **High Rate Increase**.	6	
4	Generating Report	Generate Scenario Summary report to show monthly revenue for all classes at the three hourly base rates.	3	
5	Formatting	Format report by changing fill color and font color. Add descriptive text in row 7. Student should try to match colors shown in Figure 5.12.	5	
6	Editing	Edit Notes text in B20 so that the sentence correctly references the highlighted color for changing cells.	4	
7-8	Printing, Saving	Print Scenario Summary worksheet. Save and close **EL2-C5-VB2-Lessons.xlsx**.	1	
		TOTAL POINTS	20	

Case Study

Part 1

File: **EL2-C5-CS-P1-PBMStartup.xlsx**

Steps	Tasks	Criteria	Value	Score
1	Opening, Saving	Open **PBMStartup.xlsx**. Save As **EL2-C5-CS-P1-PBMStartup.xlsx**.	1	
2	Applying WhatIf Analysis	Apply what-if analysis to find out the value that is needed for project sales in Year 1 in order to pay back the initial investment in 12 months (instead of 17). Accept proposed solution.	8	
3	Saving, Printing	Print worksheet. Save **EL2-C5-CS-P1-PBMStartup.xlsx**.	1	
		TOTAL POINTS	**10**	

Part 2

File: **EL2-C5-CS-P2-PBMStartup.xlsx**

Steps	Tasks	Criteria	Value	Score
1	Opening, Saving	With **EL2-C5-CS-P1-PBMStartup.xlsx** open, save as **EL2-C5-CS-P2-PBMStartup.xlsx**.	1	
2	Editing	Restore sales for year to the original value of $485,000.	3	
3	Creating Worksheets	Using the information illustrated, set up worksheet to save each model (*Conservative, Optimistic*, and *Aggressive*). Use comma to separate two cell references as the changing cells.	5	
4	Creating Report	Create report that shows the input variables for each model and the impact of each on the number of months to recoup the initial investment.	4	
5	Saving, Printing	Save the revised workbook. Print the summary report.	2	
6	Editing	Switch to worksheet and show model that reduces the number of months to recoup the initial investment to the lowest value.	4	
7	Printing, Saving	Print the worksheet. Save **EL2-C5-CS-P2-PBMStartup.xls**x.	1	
		TOTAL POINTS	**20**	

Part 3
File: **EL2-C5-CS-P3-PBMStartup.xlsx**

Steps	Tasks	Criteria	Value	Score
1	Using Help, Editing	Use the Help feature to find out how to select cells that contain formulas. With **EL2-C5-CS-P2-PBMStartup.xlsx** open and using information learned in Help, select cells within worksheet that contain formulas. Review each formula cell in Formula bar to ensure formula is logically correct. Type the name of the feature used in a blank cell below the worksheet.	4	
2	Printing, Saving	Print and save as **EL2-C5-CS-P3-PBMStartup.xlsx**.	1	
		TOTAL POINTS	5	

Part 4
File: **EL2-C5-CS-P4-PBMStartup.xlsx**

Steps	Tasks	Criteria	Value	Score
1	Researching	Use the Internet to research current lending rates for secured credit lines at a bank.	2	
2	Creating Worksheet	Create worksheet with the following specifications: • Document the current loan rate found on the Internet and the URL of the bank website from which the rate was obtained. • Add two percentage points to lending rate to compensate the owners for the higher risk associated with financing the startup. • Create linked cell in the new worksheet to the Total Estimated Initial Investment in Sheet 1. • Calculate monthly loan payment for a term of five years.	8	
3	Formatting	Add appropriate labels to describe the date. Format worksheet to improve the appearance of the worksheet.	4	
4	Saving, Printing	Save As **EL2-C5-CS-P4-PBMStartup.xlsx**. Print loan worksheet.	1	
		TOTAL POINTS	15	

Benchmark Excel 2013 Level 2, Chapter 6

Skills Check

Assessment 1: Enter and Display Workbook Properties; Insert Comments

Files: **EL2-C6-A1-NationalLicenses.xlsx; EL2-C6-A1-NationalLicenses.docx**

Steps	Tasks	Criteria	Value	Score
1-2	Opening, Saving	Open **NationalLicenses.xlsx**. Save As **EL2-C6-A1-NationalLicenses**.	1	
3-4	Editing Properties	Type following text in appropriate workbook properties: • *Add an Author:* **Wendy Cheung** • *Title:* **MSO 2013 License Chargeback** • *Subject:* **Journal entry by department** • *Category:* **JE supporting document** • *Status:* **Posted** • *Comments:* **Audit worksheet for Office 2013 site license with internal chargebacks** Remove existing author *Paradigm Publishing Inc.*	5	
5-6	Creating Word Document	Display the Document Information Panel. Insert screen image of the worksheet showing Document Information Panel in a new Word document using either Print Screen with Paste, or the Screenshot feature. Student's name typed a few lines below the screen image.	3	
7-8	Saving, Printing	Save the Microsoft Word document as **EL2-C6-A1-NationalLicenses.docx**. Print document and exit Word.	1	
9-11	Inserting Comments	At Microsoft Excel worksheet, close Document Information Panel. Make B8 the active cell and insert a new comment. Type in the comment box: Check this quantity with Marty. The number seems high. Make B14 the active cell and insert a new comment. Type in the comment box: Make a note in the budget file for next year. This quantity will increase by 5.	4	
12-13	Saving, Printing	Print worksheet with comments displayed on sheet. Save and close **EL2-C6-A1-NationalLicenses.xlsx**.	1	
		TOTAL POINTS	**15**	

Assessment 2: Share a Worksheet, Edit a Shared Workbook, and Print a History Sheet

File: **EL2-C6-A2-PreMfgTargets.xlsx**

Steps	Tasks	Criteria	Value	Score
1-2	Opening, Saving	Open **PreMfgTargets.xlsx.** Save As **EL2-C6-A2-PreMfgTargets**.	1	
3-8	Sharing, Editing	Share the workbook. Change user name to *Lorne Moir* and edit the following cells: C11 from 4,352 to *5520* C18 from *15,241* to *15960* Save the workbook. Change user name to Gerri Gonzales and edit the following cells: F4 from *3,845* to *5126* F9 from *7,745* to *9320* Save the workbook.	6	
9-10	Creating, Printing History Sheet	Create History sheet with a record of changes made to the data by all users. Print History sheet.	2	
11-12	Saving, Changing Name	Save and close **EL2-C6-A2-PreMfgTargets.xlsx**. Change user name back to original user name for the computer student used.	1	
		TOTAL POINTS	**10**	

Assessment 3: Remove Shared Access

File: **EL2-C6-A3-PreMfgTargets.xlsx**

Steps	Tasks	Criteria	Value	Score
1-2	Opening, Saving	Open **EL2-C6-A2-PreMfgTargets.xls**x. Save As **EL2-C6-A3-PreMfgTargets**.	0	
3	Removing Shared Access	Remove shared access to workbook.	1	
4	Closing	Close **EL2-C6-A3-PreMfgTargets.xlsx**.	0	
		TOTAL POINTS	**1**	

Assessment 4: Protect an Entire Worksheet and Add a Password to a Workbook

File: **EL2-C6-A1-NationalLicenses.xlsx**

Steps	Tasks	Criteria	Value	Score
1-2	Opening, Saving	Open **EL2-C6-A1-NationalLicenses.xlsx**. Save As **EL2-C6-A4-NationalLicenses.xlsx**.	1	
3-5	Protecting Worksheet	Protect entire worksheet using password *eL2-A4* to unprotect. Add password *eL2-A4* to open workbook. Save and close **EL2-C6-A4-NationalLicenses.xlsx**.	6	

Steps	Tasks	Criteria	Value	Score
6-7	Testing	Open **EL2-C6-A4-NationalLicenses.xlsx** and test password to open workbook. Close **EL2-C6-A4-NationalLicenses.xlsx**.	3	
		TOTAL POINTS	10	

Assessment 5: Unlock Cells and Protect a Worksheet; Protect Workbook Structure
File: **EL2-C6-A5-PreMfgTargets.xlsx**

Steps	Tasks	Criteria	Value	Score
1-2	Opening, Saving	Open **PreMfgTargets.xlsx**. Save As **EL2-C6-A5-PreMfgTargets.xlsx**.	1	
3-6	Protecting Worksheet	Select range C4:F21 and unlock cells. Deselect range and then protect worksheet using password *eL2-A5* to unprotect. Rename Sheet 1 to *2015MfgTargets*. Protect workbook structure to prevent users from inserting, deleting, or renaming sheets using the password *eL2-A5* to unprotect.	8	
7	Saving	Save **EL2-C6-A5-PreMfgTargets.xlsx**.	1	
		TOTAL POINTS	10	

Assessment 6: Track Changes; Accept/Reject Changes; Print a History Sheet
File: **EL2-C6-A6-PreMfgTargets.xlsx**

Steps	Tasks	Criteria	Value	Score
1-2	Opening, Saving	Open **EL2-C6-A5-PreMfgTargets.xlsx**. Save As **EL2-C6-A6-PreMfgTargets**.	1	
3-7	Editing	Unprotect workbook structure so that new sheets can be added, deleted, renamed, or copied. Turn on Track Changes feature. Change user name to *Grant Antone* and edit the following cells: D4 from *3,251* to *3755* D17 from *5,748* to *6176* Save workbook, change user name to *Jean Kocsis*, and edit the following cells: E6 from *6,145* to *5748* E11 from *2,214* to *3417* Save workbook and change user name back to original user name for computer student used.	9	
8	Accepting, Rejecting Changes	• Accept and Reject changes as follows: Accept D4 Reject D17 Reject E6 Accept E11	2	

Steps	Tasks	Criteria	Value	Score
9	Creating History Sheet, Printing	Create and print History sheet of changes made to worksheet.	2	
10-11	Printing, Saving	Print the 2015MfgTargets worksheet. Save and close **EL2-C6-A6-PreMfgTargets.xlsx**.	1	
		TOTAL POINTS	**15**	

Visual Benchmark

Track Changes; Insert Comments

File: **EL2-C6-VB-PawsParadise.xlsx**

Steps	Tasks	Criteria	Value	Score
1-2	Opening, Saving	Open **PawsParadise.xlsx**. Save As EL2-C6-VB-PawsParadise.	1	
3	Making Changes	Make changes as illustrated in Figure 6.17 and Figure 6.18 making sure changes are associated with the owner's name.	6	
4	Creating History Worksheet, Printing	Create and print a History worksheet scaled to fit on one page. *Note: If work is submitted electronically, create a copy of History worksheet in new workbook since* History worksheet is automatically deleted when file is saved.	2	
5-7	Saving, Printing	Print worksheet with changes highlighted and the comments as displayed on the worksheet. Save and close **EL2-C6-VB-PawsParadise.xlsx**. Change user name back to original user name for computer student used.	1	
		TOTAL POINTS	**10**	

Case Study

Part 1

File: **EL2-C6-CS-P1-PBMNewFranchises.xlsx**

Steps	Tasks	Criteria	Value	Score
1	Opening, Saving	Open **PBMNewFranchises.xlsx**. Save As **EL2-C6-CS-P1-PBMNewFranchises**.	1	
2	Inserting Properties	Add appropriate title and subject to workbook's properties. Include comment text explain that the draft workbook was created in consultation with Nicola Carlucci.	3	
3	Protecting Workbook	Protect workbook to prevent accidental data modifications or erasure when workbook is shared with others. City, state, and store numbers should be protected. Month new store is planned to open and names of prospective franchises can be changed. Share the workbook. Password to unprotect worksheet is *eL2-CS1*. Password to open workbook is *eL2-CS1*.	5	

Steps	Tasks	Criteria	Value	Score
4	Saving	Save **EL2-C6-CS-P1-PBMNewFranchises.xlsx**.	1	
		TOTAL POINTS	**10**	

Part 2

File: **EL2-C6-CS-P2-PBMNewFranchises.xlsx**

Steps	Tasks	Criteria	Value	Score
1	Saving	With **EL2-C6-CS-P1-PBMNewFranchises.xlsx** open, save as **EL2-C6-CS-P2-PBMNewFranchises.xlsx.**	1	
2	Editing	Make sure the user name is correct and make the following changes: Store 138 Franchisee is Jae-Dong Han Store 149 Franchisee is Leslie Posno Save workbook.	2	
3	Editing	Make sure the user name is correct and make the following changes: Store 135, Open in February Store 141, Open in December Save workbook. Display worksheet with all changes highlighted.	2	
4	Creating History Sheet, Printing	Create History sheet. Print worksheet with cells highlighted. Print history sheet. Restore worksheet to exclusive use. Close **EL2-C6-CS-P2-PBMNewFranchises.xlsx**. Change user name back to original user name for computer used by student.	5	
		TOTAL POINTS	**10**	

Part 3

File: **EL2-C6-CS-P3-PBMNewFranchises; EL2-C6-CS-P3-PBM-LScriver.xlsx**

Steps	Tasks	Criteria	Value	Score
1	Opening, Unprotecting, Saving	Open **EL2-C6-CS-P3-PBMNewFranchises.xlsx**. Unprotect worksheet and remove password to open workbook. Save as **EL2-C6-CS-P3-PBM-LScriver.xlsx**.	2	
2	Making Changes	Make sure user name is correct so that the comment boxes display Leonard's name: • Store 136: Opening a second store in Chicago is more likely to occur in April • Store 144: Move this opening to June as resources at head office will be stretched in May • Store 152: Try to open this franchise at the same time as store 151 Show all comments within worksheet.	6	

Steps	Tasks	Criteria	Value	Score
3	Printing, Saving	Print worksheet with comments printed as displayed. Save and close **EL2-C6-CS-P3-PBM-LScriver.xlsx**. Change user name back to original name for computer used by student.	2	
		TOTAL POINTS	10	

Part 4

File: **EL2-C6-CS-P4-PBMPasswords.xlsx; EL2-C6-CS-P4-PBPasswords.docx**

Steps	Tasks	Criteria	Value	Score
1	Researching	Use the Internet to research guidelines for creating strong passwords.	2	
2	Creating Word Document	Create a Microsoft Word document that highlights the components of a strong password. Include a table of do's and don'ts for creating strong passwords in a user-friendly easy-to-understand format. Create a minimum of three examples that show a week password improved by a stronger password. Include a suggestion for how to use the phrasing technique to create strong passwords to they are easier to remember.	12	
3	Saving, Printing	Save the Word documents as **EL2-C6-CS-P4-PBMPasswords**. Print and close **EL2-C6-CS-P4-PBMPasswords.docx**.	1	
		TOTAL POINTS	15	

Benchmark Excel 2013 Level 2, Chapter 7

Skills Check

Assessment 1: Create Macros

Files: **MyMacros-StudentName.xlsm**

Steps	Tasks	Criteria	Value	Score
1	Creating Macros	At a new blank workbook, create the following two macros: • Create a macro named *Landscape* that changes page orientation to landscape, sets custom margins at top = 1 inch; bottom, left, and right = 0.5 inch; and centers worksheet horizontally. Assign macro the shortcut key Ctrl + Shift + Q. Enter appropriate description that includes student's name and date macro was created. • Create a macro named *Ion* that applies the theme named *Ion* and turns off the display of gridlines in the active worksheet. Assign macro the shortcut key Ctrl + T. Enter an appropriate description that includes student's name and date macro was created.	9	

Steps	Tasks	Criteria	Value	Score
2-3	Saving	Save workbook as a macro-enabled workbook named **MyMacros-Student Name**. Leave **MyMacros-Student Name.xlsm** workbook open for next assessment.	1	
		TOTAL POINTS	10	

Assessment 2: Run Macros
File: **EL2-C7-A2-NationalCS.xlsx**

Steps	Tasks	Criteria	Value	Score
1-2	Opening, Saving	Open **NationalCS.xlsx**. Save As **EL2-C7-A2-NationalCS**.	1	
3-4	Running Macros	Press Ctrl + T to run the Ion macro. Press Ctrl + Shift + Q to run the Landscape macro.	3	
5-6	Saving, Printing	Save, print, and close **EL2-C7-A2-NationalCS.xlsx**. Close **MyMacros-Student Name.xlsm**.	1	
		TOTAL POINTS	5	

Assessment 3: Create Macros; Save as a Macro-Enabled Workbook
File: **EL2-C7-A3-NationalCS.xlsm**

Steps	Tasks	Criteria	Value	Score
1-3	Opening, Creating Macros	Open **EL2-C7-A2-NationalCS.xlsx**. Create the following two macros within the current workbook: • Create a macro named *FormulaBarOff* that turns off the display of the Formula bar and protects the worksheet. Do not enter a password to unprotect the sheet. Assign the macro to the shortcut key Ctrl + Shift + M. Enter an appropriate description that includes student's name and date macro was created. • Create a macro names *FormulaBarOn* that turns on display of the Formula bar and unprotects the worksheet. Assign the macro to the shortcut key Ctrl + Shift + B. Enter an appropriate description that includes student's name and date macro was created. Test each macro to make sure shortcut key runs the correct commands.	9	
4-5	Saving	Save revised workbook as a macro-enabled workbook and name it **EL2-C7-A3-NationalCS**. Close **EL2-C7-A3-NationalCS.xlsm**.	1	
		TOTAL POINTS	10	

Assessment 4: Print Macros
File: **EL2-C7-A3-NationalCS.xlsm**

Steps	Tasks	Criteria	Value	Score
1-2	Opening	Open **EL2-C7-A3-NationalCS.xlsm** and enable content. Open Macro dialog box and edit the FormulaBarOff macro.	1	
3-5	Printing	At Microsoft Visual Basic Application Window, click *Print*, and then Print + VBAProject dialog box, click OK. Click on File on Menu bar and click *Close and Return to Microsoft Excel.* Close **EL2-C7-A3-NationalCS.xlsm**.	2	
6-10	Printing	Open **MyMacros-StudentName.xlsm** and enable content. Open dialog box Macro dialog box and edit Landscape macro. At Microsoft Visual Basic Application Window, click *Print*, and then Print + VBAProject dialog box, click OK. Click on File on Menu bar and click *Close and Return to Microsoft Excel.* Close **MyMacros-StudentName.xlsm**.	2	
		TOTAL POINTS	5	

Assessment 5: Customize the Excel Environment
File: **EL2-C7-A5-BillingsDec18.xlsx**

Steps	Tasks	Criteria	Value	Score
1-2	Opening, Saving	Open **BillingsDec18.xlsx**. Save As **EL2-C7-A5-BillingsDec18.xlsx**.	1	
3-5	Formatting	Make the following changes to the Display options: • Turn off the horizontal scroll bar • Turn off sheet tabs • Turn off row and column headers • Turn off gridlines Change current them to Wisp. Freeze first four rows in worksheet.	7	
6-9	Creating Screen Image, Saving, Printing	Create screen image of worksheet with the modified display options and paste image into a new Word document. Type student name a few lines below screen image. Save Word document as **EL2-C7-A5-BillingsDec18**. Print **EL2-C7-A5-BillingsDec18.docx** and exit Word. Save and close **EL2-C7-A5-BillingsDec18.xlsx**.	2	
		TOTAL POINTS	10	

Assessment 6: Create Custom Views
File: **EL2-C7-A6-BillingsDec18.xlsx**

Steps	Tasks	Criteria	Value	Score
1-2	Opening, Saving	Open **BillingsDec18.xlsx**. Save As **EL2-C7-A6-BillingsDec18.xlsx**.	1	
3-12	Creating Custom Views	• Select A4:I23 and custom sort in ascending order by *Attorney* and then by client's *Last Name*. • With A4:I23 selected turn on filter arrows. • Deselect range and then filter the Attorney column to show only those rows with the attorney name *Kyle Williams*. • Create custom view names *Williams* to save filter settings. • Clear filter in the *Attorney* column. • Filter list by *Attorney* named *Marty O'Donovan*. • Create a custom view named *O'Donovan* to save filter settings. • Clear filter in *Attorney* column. • Create custom view named *Martinez* and clear filter from *Attorney* column. • Create custom view named Sullivan and clear filter from *Attorney* column.	12	
13-16	Creating Screen Image, Printing	Open Custom Views dialog box. Create screen image of worksheet with dialog box open and past image into a new Word document. Type student name a few lines below screen image. Save Word document as **EL2-C7-A6-BillingsDec18**. Print **EL2-C7-A6-BillingsDec18.docx** and exit Word. Close Custom Views dialog box; save and close **EL2-C7-A6-BillingsDec18.xlsx**.	2	
		TOTAL POINTS	15	

Assessment 7: Create and Use a Template
File: **EL2-C7-A7-Billings.xlsx; Billings-StudentName.xltx**

Steps	Tasks	Criteria	Value	Score
1	Opening	Open **EL2-C7-A5-BillingsDec18.xlsx**. Turn on display of row and column headers.	1	
2-4	Revising Workbook	Make the following changes to workbook: • Select and delete all of the data below the column headings in row 4 • Delete text in A3 • Edit subtitle in A2 to *Associate Weekly Billing Summary*. Save revised workbook as template named **Billings-StudentName**. Close **Billings-StudentName.xltx**.	4	
5-7	Creating Workbook	Start new workbook based on the **Billings-StudentName.xltx** template. Cell A3, type *November 16 to 20, 2015*. Enter two billings shown in Figure 7.12.	8	

Steps	Tasks	Criteria	Value	Score
8-10	Saving, Printing	Save As **EL2-C7-A7-Billings**. Print **EL2-C7-A7-Billings.xlsx**. Copy Billings-StudentName.xltx from [c]\Users\username\MyDocument\Custom Office Templates folder to theEL2C7 folder on storage medium.	2	
		TOTAL POINTS	**15**	

Visual Benchmark

1: Customize the Ribbon

File: **EL2-C7-VB1-MyRibbon.docx**

Steps	Tasks	Criteria	Value	Score
1-2	Creating Custom Tab, Inserting Screen Image	Create custom tab including groups and buttons shown in Figure 7.13. Insert a screen image in a new Word document that shows the ribbon with custom tab displayed in Microsoft Excel.	4	
3-5	Saving, Printing	Save Word document as **EL2-C7-VB1-MyRibbo**n. Print **EL2-C7-VB1-MyRibbon.docx** and exit Word. Restore ribbon in Excel to its original settings.	1	
		TOTAL POINTS	**5**	

2: Create a Custom Template

File: **EL2-C7-VB2-AudennitaSalesInv.xltm; EL2-C7-VB2-AudennitaInvToVanderwyst.xlsx**

Steps	Tasks	Criteria	Value	Score
1-2	Creating Custom Template	Create custom template that could be used to generate a sales invoice similar to Figure 7.14. Match column widths, row heights, and color formatting. Font in A1 is *Footlight MT Light 36-point* and *Garamond* for remaining cells (18-point in A2 and 12-point elsewhere).Substitute an appropriate clip art image if the one shown is not available on the computer being used. Save workbooks as a template and name it **EL2-C7-VB2-AudennitaSalesInv**.	5	
3-6	Completing Invoice, Printing, Saving	Use the template to fill out sale invoice using data shown in Figure 7.14. Save completed invoice as **EL2-C7-VB2-AudennitaInvToVanderwyst**. Print invoice and close **EL2-C7-VB2-AudennitaInvToVanderwyst.xlsx**. Make copy of custom template and save copy to storage medium in the EL2C7 folder. Delete custom template from computer.	5	
		TOTAL POINTS	**10**	

Case Study

Part 1

File: **EL2-C7-CS-P1-NuTrendMacros.xlsm**

Steps	Tasks	Criteria	Value	Score
1	Creating Macros	Delete Sheet 2 and Sheet 3 form workbook. Rename Sheet1 to *MacroDocumentation.* Document macros with macro names, shortcut keys assigned, and descriptions of actions each macro performs. Create a separate macro for each of the following tasks: • Apply theme named *Organic* and show all comments. • Set active column's width to 20. • Apply conditional formatting to highlight top 10 in a selected list. Accept the default formatting options. • Apply Accounting format with zero decimals. • Create a footer that prints student's name centered at bottom of worksheet.	9	
2	Printing, Editing	Print MacroDocumentation worksheet. Open Macro dialog box and edit first macro. Print the macros in the VBAProject. Close Visual Basic for Applications windo2. Save **EL2-C7-CS-P1-NuTrendsMacros.xlsm**.	1	
		TOTAL POINTS	**10**	

Part 2

File: **EL2-C7-CS-P2-PBMNewFranchiseRev.xlsx**

Steps	Tasks	Criteria	Value	Score
1	Opening, Saving	Open **PBMNewFranchiseRev.xlsx**. Save As **EL2-C7-C2-PS-PBMNewFranchiseRev**.	1	
2	Running Macros	Run each macro created in 1 using the following information: • Set all of the column widths to 20 except column C. • Run the number formatting and the conditional formatting with the values in column E selected. • Run the theme and footer macros.	8	
3	Printing, Saving	Print the worksheet making sure comments print as displayed. Save and close **EL2-C7-C2-PS-PBMNewFranchiseRev.xlsx**. Close **EL2-C7-CS-P1-NuTrendsMacros.xlsm**.	1	
		TOTAL POINTS	**10**	

Part 3

File: **EL2-C7-CS-P3-CustomizeQATMemo.docx**

Steps	Tasks	Criteria	Value	Score
1	Using Help	Use Excel Help to learn how to add a button to the Quick Access toolbar directly from the ribbon. Test information learned by adding Orientation button and New Comment button.	1	
2	Creating Memo	Using Microsoft Word, compose a memo that describes steps to add a button to Quick Access toolbar directly from ribbon. Insert screen image of Quick Access toolbar in Excel that display the buttons that were added. Place image below the memo text.	8	
3	Printing, Saving	Save, print, and close Word memo as **EL2-C7-C3-P3-CustomizeQATMemo.docx**. Exit Word. Remove two buttons added to Quick Access toolbar.	1	
		TOTAL POINTS	10	

Part 4

File: **EL2-C7-CS-P4-DocRecovery.docx**

Steps	Tasks	Criteria	Value	Score
1	Researching	Use Help and the Internet to research Document Recovery messages in Excel.	2	
2	Creating Word Document	Create a Microsoft Word document explaining in student's own words the AutoRecover and AutoSave features. Include explanation that Document Recovery task pane appears after Excel has not been properly closed. Provide advice on how to review files in the pane to make sure data has not been lost.	7	
3	Saving, Printing	Save As **EL2-C7-CS-P4-DocRecovery**. Print and close **EL2-C7-CS-P4-DocRecovery.docx**.	1	
		TOTAL POINTS	10	

Benchmark Excel 2013 Level 2, Chapter 8

Skills Check

Assessment 1: Import Data From Access and a Text File
Files: **EL2-C8-A1-HRS.xlsx**

Steps	Tasks	Criteria	Value	Score
1-2	Opening, Saving	Open **HRS.xlsx**. Save As **EL2-C8-A1-HRS.xlsx**.	1	
3	Importing	Make cell A6 of CPIData worksheet the active cell. Import table named CPI from Access database **NuTrendsCensus.accdb**.	2	
4	Editing	Make the following changes to worksheet: • Apply *Table Style Medium 15* to imported cells. • Format values in all columns *except* column A to one decimal place. • Remove the filter arrow buttons and then center column headings. • If necessary, adjust column widths to accommodate data.	4	
5	Printing	Print CPIData worksheet.	1	
6-7	Importing	Make UIRateMI the active worksheet. Make A6 the active cell. Import comma delimited text file named **UIRateMI.csv**.	2	
8	Editing	Make the following changes to data: • Change width of column B to 8.00 (61 pixels). • Change width of columns C to F to 15.00 (110 pixels).	4	
9-10	Printing, Saving	Print the UIRate-MI worksheet. Save **EL2-C8-A1-HRS.xlsx** and close.	1	
		TOTAL POINTS	15	

Assessment 2: Link Data to a Word Document
File: **EL2-C8-A2-HROctSalesbyDateByRep.xlsx** and **EL2-C8-A2-HROctRpt.docx**

Steps	Tasks	Criteria	Value	Score
1-2	Opening, Saving	Open **HROctSalesByDateRep.xlsx**. Save As **EL2-C8-A2-HROctSalesByDateByRep**.	1	
3-5	Linking to Word, Formatting	With SalesByDate the active worksheet, link A3:G27 at the end of the Word document **HROctRpt.docx**. Change margins in Word document to *Narrow* (Top, Bottom, Left, and Right to 0.5 inch). Save As **EL2-C8-A2-HROctRpt.docx**.	5	
6-9	Editing Excel	Switch to Excel. Deselect range. Change value in F4 to *525000.* Change value in F5 to *212000.* Save **EL2-C8-A2-HROctSalesByDateByRep.xlsx**.	2	

Steps	Tasks	Criteria	Value	Score
10-14	Updating Link, Printing, Saving	Switch to Word, *Update Link.* Print Word document. Break link in Word document. Save **EL2-C8-A2-HROctRpt.docx** and exit Word. Save and close **EL2-C8-A2-HROctSalesByDateByRep.xlsx**.	2	
		TOTAL POINTS	**10**	

Assessment 3: Embed Data in a PowerPoint Presentation
File: **EL2-C8-A2-HROctSalesByDateByRep.xlsx** and **CRCarRpt.pptx**

Steps	Tasks	Criteria	Value	Score
1-2	Opening, Saving	Open **HROctSalesByDateByRep.xlsx**. Save As **EL2-C8-A3-HROctSalesByDateByRep**.	9	
3-5	Creating Column Chart	Make SalesByRep the active worksheet. Display worksheet at outline level 2 (only sales agent names, sale prices, and commissions display). Create column chart in separate sheet to graph sales commissions earned by each sales agent. Student determines appropriate chart style, title, and other chart elements.	4	
6-7	Opening, Saving	Open Powerpoint and the file **HROctRpt.pptx**. Save As **EL2-C8-A3-HROctRpt.pptx**.	1	
8	Embedding Chart	Embed chart created in step 5 on Slide 3.	4	
9-11	Printing, Saving	Print presentation as Handouts with three slides per page. Save **EL2-C8-A3-HROctRpt.pptx** and exit PowerPoint. Save and close **EL2-C8-A3-HROctSalesByDateByRep.xlsx**.	2	
		TOTAL POINTS	**20**	

Assessment 4: Export Data as a Text File
File: **EL2-C8-A4-HROctSalesByDateByRep.csv**

Steps	Tasks	Criteria	Value	Score
1-3	Opening, Saving	Open **HROctSalesByDateByRep.xlsx**. With SalesByDate the active worksheet, save as a CSV (Comma delimited) (*.csv) text file named **EL2-C8-A4-HROctSalesByDateByRep**. Close (if prompted do not save changes) **EL2-C8-A4-HROctSalesByDateByRep.csv**.	1	
4-6	Editing	Start Notepad and open **EL2-C8-A4-HROctSalesByDateByRep.csv**. Delete first two lines at beginning of file that contain the title text from the top of the worksheet. (*Hillsdale Realtors* and end with *Commission*) Delete bottom row in file that contains the commas and the total commission value.	3	

Steps	Tasks	Criteria	Value	Score
7-8	Printing, Saving	Print document. Save **EL2-C8-A4-HROctSalesByDateByRep.csv** and exit Notepad.	1	
		TOTAL POINTS	5	

Assessment 5: Prepare a Workbook for Distribution
File: **EL2-C8-A5-HR2015Sales.xlsx**

Steps	Tasks	Criteria	Value	Score
1-2	Opening, Saving	Open **HR2015Sales.xlsx**. Save As **EL2-C8-A5-HR2015Sales.xlsx**	1	
3-9	Reading Information, Changing Settings, Inserting Screen Shot, Printing	Display the Info backstage area, showing all properties. Read the information in the *Author, Title* and *Subject* property text boxes. Open the Properties dialog box (advanced Properties) and read the information in the Statistics and Custom tabs. Turn on the display of all comments and read the comments that appear. Change to Page layout view and check for a header or footer in the workbook. Use the Document Inspection feature to check the workbook for private and hidden information. Remove all items that display with red exclamation marks Click the REVIEW tab, turn off the Show All Comments feature, go to Normal view. Paste a screen image into a new Word document using the Print Screen with Paste or the Screenshot feature. Type name a few lines below the screen image and print. Exit Word without saving.	2	
10-12	Running Compatibility Feature, Marking as Final	Run Compatibility Feature to check for loss of functionality or fidelity in workbook if saved in earlier Excel version. Save Summary report to new sheet. Print Compatibility Report sheet. Mark workbook as final. Close **EL2-C8-A5-HR2015Sales.xlsx**.	2	
		TOTAL POINTS	5	

Assessment 6: Prepare and Distribute a Workbook

File: **EL2-C8-A6-HR2015Sales.xlsx; EL2-C8-A6-HR2015Sales.pdf; EL2C8A6HR2015Sales.mht**

Steps	Tasks	Criteria	Value	Score
1-2	Opening, Saving	Open **HR2015Sales.xlsx**. Save As **EL2-C8-A6-HR2015Sales**.	1	
3-6	Publishing, Saving	Use Document Inspector feature to remove comments and annotations only from worksheet. Publish worksheet as PDF file named **EL2-C8-A6-HR2015Sales.pdf**. Publish worksheet as single file web page named **EL2-C8-A6-HR2015Sales.mht** with a page title *Hillsdale Realtors.* Save and close **EL2-C8-A6-HR2015Sales.xlsx**.	3	
7	Displaying File Extensions, Printing	Display contents of EL2C8 folder and display file extensions. Paste screen image of folder's content into new Word document. Type student's name a few lines below screen image. Print Word document and exit Word without saving.	1	
		TOTAL POINTS	5	

Visual Benchmark

1: Import, Analyze, and Export Population Data

File: **EL2-C8-VB-PBMReport.docx; EL2-C8-VB-PBMPopData.xlsx**

Steps	Tasks	Criteria	Value	Score
1	Importing Table from Access, Formatting	Create the worksheet shown in **Figure 8.8** by importing PopByState table from the Access database **NuTrendsCensusData.accdb**. Worksheet has *Table Style Light 2* style. Add title rows and change title in B4 as shown. Match other formatting characteristics such as column width, row height, number formatting, alignment, and fill color.	6	
2	Renaming, Printing	Rename worksheet ***PopulationTable***. Print worksheet.	1	
3-4	Creating Chart, Saving	Select A4:B19 and create chart as shown in Figure 8.9 in a new sheet named *PopulationChart*. Chart has Style 12 style applied. The Rounded Rectangle in the Inserts Shapes group on the CHART TOOLS FORMAT tab was used to insert the source information. Use Shape Effects in the Shape Styles group to apply the shadow. Save As **EL2-C8-VB-PBMPopData**.	4	

Steps	Tasks	Criteria	Value	Score
5-6	Copying, Pasting, Printing	Open PBMReport.docx. Use Save As to name **EL2-C8-VB-PBMReport**. Change *Student Name* on page 1 to student's name. Copy and paste Excel chart, positioning the chart between last two paragraphs on page 2. Make formatting adjustments to chart as needed. Save, print, and close Word document **EL2-C8-VB-PBMReport.docx**. Close **EL2-C8-VB-PBMPopData.xlsx**.	4	
		TOTAL POINTS	15	

Case Study

Part 1

File: **EL2-C8-CS-P1-PBMResearch.xlsx**

Steps	Tasks	Criteria	Value	Score
1	Creating Worksheets	Start new workbook and set up three worksheets named using the state names *Illinois, Indiana*, and *Kentucky*. In each sheet use New Web Query feature, display the web page http://quickfacts.census.gov/qfd/, and import People Quickfacts for the state. Delete column A. Add appropriate title merged and centered above imported data and apply formatting to improve appearance of column headings.	9	
2	Saving, Printing	Save As **EL2-C8-CS-P1-PBMResearch**. Print all three worksheets.	1	
		TOTAL POINTS	10	

Part 2

File: **EL2-C8-CS-P2-PBMExpansionResearch.docx**

Steps	Tasks	Criteria	Value	Score
1	Opening, Saving	Open **PBMExpansionResearch.docx**. Save As **EL2-C8-CS-P2-PBMExpansionResearch**.	1	
2	Copying, Pasting	Copy and Paste to Word document the following data from Excel worksheet created in Part 1 for each state (do not include data in USA column). Do not embed or link data: • Households • Persons per household • Median household income At bottom of document, create a reference for data from U.S. Census Bureau. Check with instructor for preferred format for reference.	8	

Steps	Tasks	Criteria	Value	Score
3	Saving, Printing	Save, print, and close Word document **EL2-C8-CS-P2-PBMExpansionResearch,docx**. Close **EL-C8-CS-P1-PBMResearch.xlsx**.	1	
		TOTAL POINTS	**10**	

Part 3

File: **EL2-C8-CS-P3-PBMResearch.xlsx**; **EL2C8CSP3DataConnectionsMemo.docx**

Steps	Tasks	Criteria	Value	Score
1	Using Help	Use Excel Help to learn how to manage connections to external data using Workbook Connections dialog box.	1	
2	Opening, Removing Connections	Open **EL2-C8-CS-P1-PBMResearch.xlsx**. Open Workbook Connections dialog box and using information learned in Help, remove all of the connections.	4	
3	Saving	Save revised workbook as **EL2-C8-CS-P3-PBMResearch.xlsx** and close workbook.	1	
4	Composing Memo	Use Word and compose memo that provides brief explanation of why security warning message about data connections appears when a workbook is opened that contains external content. Base memo on information learned in Help. Be sure memo is composed in student's own words. Include explanation that student created a new copy of workbook with the connections removed.	8	
5-6	Saving, Printing	Save Word memo as **EL2-C8-CS-P3-DataConnectionsMemo.docx**. Print and close document.	1	
		TOTAL POINTS	**15**	

Part 4

File: **EL2-C8-CS-P4-WebMemo.docx**

Steps	Tasks	Criteria	Value	Score
1	Researching	Use Excel Help to learn how to use the Internet Fax feature. Search the Internet to research for at least two fax service providers.	2	
2	Creating Word Document	Using Microsoft Word compose a memo that briefly explains how to use the Internet Fax feature in Excel. Student uses own words. Include in memo the URL of two fax service providers visited and add own recommendation for provider.	7	
3	Saving, Printing	Save As **EL2-C8-CS-P4-WebMemo**. Print and close **EL2-C8-CS-P4-WebMemo.docx**.	1	
		TOTAL POINTS	**10**	

Benchmark Excel 2013 Level 2, Unit 2 Performance Assessment

Assessing Proficiency

Assessment 1: Use Goal Seek and Scenario Manager to Calculate Investment Proposals

File: **EL2-U2-A1-HillsInvtPlan.xlsx**

Steps	Tasks	Criteria	Value	Score
1-2	Opening, Saving	Open **HillsInvtPlan.xlsx**. Save As **EL2-U2-A1-HillsInvtPlan**.	1	
3	Using Goal Seek	Use Goal Seek to find monthly contribution amount client must make in order to increase projected value of the plan to $65,000 at end of the term. Accept solution Goal Seek calculates.	4	
4-5	Assigning Range Name, Creating Scenarios	Assign range name *AvgReturn* to E8. Create three scenarios for changing E8 as follows: *Scenario Name* *Interest Rate* Moderate 5.5% Conservative 4.0% Aggressive 12.5%	5	
6	Applying Scenario, Printing	Apply *Aggressive* scenario. Print worksheet.	2	
7-9	Editing, Creating Report, Printing, Saving	Edit *Moderate* scenario's interest rate to 8.0% and apply the scenario. Create and print a Scenario Summary report. Save and close **EL2-U2-A1-HillsInvtPlan.xlsx**.	3	
		TOTAL POINTS	**15**	

Assessment 2: Calculate Investment Outcomes for a Portfolio Using a Two-Variable Data Table

File: **EL2-U2-A2-HillsResearchInvtTbl.xlsx**

Steps	Tasks	Criteria	Value	Score
1-2	Opening, Saving	Open **HillsResearchInvtTbl.xlsx**. Save As **EL2-U2-A2-HillsResearchInvtTbl.xlsx**.	1	
3	Creating Two-Variable Data Table	Create two-variable data table that calculates projected value of investment at end of term for each monthly contribution payment and at each interest rate in the range A11:G20.	6	
4-7	Formatting	Apply Comma Style format to projected values in table and adjust column widths if necessary. Make E8 the active cell and display precedent arrows. Make A11 the active cell and display precedent arrows. Remove the arrows.	2	
8	Saving, Printing	Save, print, and close **EL2-U2-A2-HillsResearchInvtTbl.xlsx**.	1	
		TOTAL POINTS	**10**	

Assessment 3: Solve an Error and Check for Accuracy in Investment Commission Formulas

File: **EL2-U2-A3-HillsModeratePortfolio.xlsx**

Steps	Tasks	Criteria	Value	Score
1-2	Opening, Saving	Open HillsModeratePortfolio.xlsx. Save as **EL2-U2-A3-HillsModeratePortfolio.xlsx**.	1	
3	Solving Error	Solve the #VALUE! Error in E19. Use formula auditing tools to help find source cell containing the invalid entry.	4	
4	Checking Logic Accuracy	Check logic accuracy of formula in E19 by creating proof formulas below worksheet as follows: • In row 21, calculate amount from customer's deposit that would be deposited into each of the six funds based on the percentages in column B. Example: In B21 create formula to multiply customer's deposit in B19 times percentage recommended for investment in DW Bond fund in B5. Create similar formula for remaining funds in C21:G21. • In row 22, multiply amount deposited to each fund by fund's commission rate. Example: in B22, create formula to multiply value in B21 times the commission rate paid by DW Bond fund in B17. Create similar formula for remaining funds in C22:G22. • In B23, create a SUM function to calculate the total of the commissions for the six funds in B22:G22. Add appropriate labels next to the values created in rows 21 to 23.	9	
5	Saving, Printing	Save, print, and close **EL2-U2-A3-HillsModeratePortfolio.xlsx**.	1	
		TOTAL POINTS	**15**	

Assessment 4: Document and Share a Workbook and Manage Changes in an Investment Portfolio Worksheet

File: **EL2-U2-A4-HillsModPortfolio.xlsx**

Steps	Tasks	Criteria	Value	Score
1-2	Opening, Saving	Open **EL2-U2-A3-HillsModPortfolio.xlsx**. Save As **EL2-U2-A4-HillsModPortfolio**.	1	
3	Entering Data	Enter following data into workbook properties: • *Author:* Logan Whitmore • *Title:* Recommended Moderate Portfolio • *Comments:* Proposed moderate fund • *Subject:* Moderate Investment Allocation	2	
4-5	Creating Word Document, Sharing	Paste screen image of Info tab Backstage view showing all properties into a new Word document. Type student name a few blank lines below image, print document, and exit without saving. Click Review tab and share workbook.	2	

Steps	Tasks	Criteria	Value	Score
6-7	Editing, Saving	Change user name to *Carey Winters* and edit the following cells: • B7 to *15%* • B8 to *10%* Save EL2-U2-A4-HillsModPortfolio.xlsx.	2	
8-9	Editing, Saving	Change user name to *Jodi VanKemenade* and edit the following cells: • D17 to *2.32%* • E17 to *2.19%* Save **EL2-U2-A4-HillsModPortfolio.xlsx**.	2	
10	Creating, Printing	Create and print a History sheet.	1	
11-12	Accepting, Rejecting Changes	Change user name back to original name on computer. Accept and reject changes made to ModeratePortfolio worksheet as follows: • Reject B7 • Reject B8 • Accept D17 • Reject E17	4	
13	Saving, Printing	Save, print, and close **EL2-U2-A4-HillsModPortfolio.xlsx**.	1	
		TOTAL POINTS	15	

Assessment 5: Insert Comments and Protect a Confidential Investment Portfolio Workbook

File: **EL2-U2-A5-HillsModPortfolio.xlsx**

Steps	Tasks	Criteria	Value	Score
1-2	Opening, Saving	Open EL2-U2-A4-HillsModPortfolio.xlsx. Save As EL2-U2-A5-HillsModPortfolio.xlsx.	1	
3-10	Formatting	Make the following changes to workbook: • Remove shared access to workbook. • Hide rows 20 to 23. • Make B17 the active cell and insert a comment. Type Commission rate to be renegotiated in 2015 in comment box. • Copy comment in B17 and paste it to D17 and G17. • Edit comment in G17 to change year from 2015 to 2016. • Protect worksheet to only allow editing in cell B19. Assign the password eL2-U2 to unprotect the worksheet. • Encrypt the workbook with the password eL2-U2. • Save and close EL2-U2-A5-HillsModPortfolio.xlsx.	8	

Steps	Tasks	Criteria	Value	Score
11-14	Editing, Printing, Saving	Complete the following: • Test security features added to work by opening EL2-U2-A5-HillsModPortfolio.xlsx using password *eL2-U2* (created in step 9). Try to change one of the values in range B5:B10 and B17:G17. • Make B19 active cell and change value to *10000*. • Display all comments in worksheet and print worksheet with comments *As displayed on sheet* and with worksheet scaled to fit on 1 page. • Save and close **EL2-U2-A5-HillModPortfolio.xlsx**.	6	
		TOTAL POINTS	15	

Assessment 6: Automate and Customize an Investment Portfolio Workbook
File: **EL2-U2-A6-HillsModPortfolio.xlsx**

Steps	Tasks	Criteria	Value	Score
1-2	Opening, Unprotecting Workbook, Deleting Comments	Open **EL2-U2-A5-HillsModPortfolio.xlsx**. Unprotect worksheet. Turn off display of all comments. Delete comments in B17, D17, and G17.	2	
3	Deleting Custom Views	Display Custom Views dialog box. Delete all custom views in dialog box. Add a new custom view named *ModeratePortfolioOriginalView*.	3	
4-5	Creating and Testing Macros	Create two macros stored in active workbook as follows: • A macro named *CustomDisplay* that applies Metropolitan theme and turns off display of gridlines and row and column headers in current workbook. Assign macro the shortcut key Ctrl + Shift + T. Enter appropriate description that includes student name and date macro was created. • A macro named *CustomHeader* that prints text *Private and Confidential*. Assign macro the shortcut key Ctrl + Shift + H. Enter appropriate description that includes student name and date macro was assigned. • Test macros by opening **EL-U2-A1-HillsInvtPlan.xlsx**. Make InvestmentPlanProposal the active worksheet. Run two macros created in the assessment. View worksheet in Print backstage area.. Close the Print backstage area and then close without saving **EL-U2-A1-HillsInvtPlan.xlsx**.	6	
6	Printing Visual Basic Code	Print Visual Basic program code for the two macros and close Microsoft Visual Basic window. Return to Excel.	2	
7	Creating Custom View	Create custom view *ModeratePortfolioTemplateView*.	3	
8-9	Printing, Saving	Save revised workbook as macro-enabled named **EL2-U2-A6-HillsModPortfolio.xlsm**. Remove password to open workbook. Print worksheet.	2	

Steps	Tasks	Criteria	Value	Score
10-11	Creating, Printing Word Document	Paste screen image of worksheet with the Custom Views dialog box in a new Word document. Type student name a few lines below image. Print document and exit Word without saving. Close Custom Views dialog box and then close **EL2-U2-A6-HillsModPortfolio.xlsm**.	2	
		TOTAL POINTS	**20**	

Assessment 7: Create and Use an Investment Planner Template
File: **EL2-U2-A7-HillsInvPlan-StudentName.xltx** and **EL2U2A7HillsInvPlan.xlsx**

Steps	Tasks	Criteria	Value	Score
1-4	Opening, Editing, Saving	Open **EL2-U2-A2-HillsResearchInvtTbl.xlsx**. Make the following changes: • Change label in A3 to *Investment Planner*. • Change font color of A11 to white (cell will appear to be empty). • Clear contents of E5:E7. • Protect worksheet allowing editing to E5:E7 only. Assign password *eL2-U2* to unprotect worksheet. Save revised workbook as template named **HillsInvPlan-StudentName.xltx** and close template.	8	
5-8	Creating, Saving, Printing	Start new workbook based on template **HillsInvPlan-StudentName.xltx**. Enter the following information in appropriate cells: • *Monthly Contribution* *-475* • *Number of years to invest* *5* • *Forecasted annual interest rate* *4.75%* Save As and print workbook named **EL2-U2-A7-HillsInvPlan.xlsx**.	5	
9	Copying, Deleting	Copy template created in this assessment to EL2U2 folder.	2	
		TOTAL POINTS	**15**	

Assessment 8: Export a Chart and Prepare and Distribute an Investment Portfolio Worksheet
File: **EL2-U2-A8-HillsModPortfolio.xlts** and **EL2U2A8HillsPortfolios.pptx**

Steps	Tasks	Criteria	Value	Score
1-3	Opening, Saving	Open **EL2-U2-A6-HillsModPortfolio.xlsm** and enable content if security warning message bar appears. Start PowerPoint and open **HillsPortfolios.pptx**. Save As **EL2-U2-A8-HillsPortfolios**.	2	
4-7	Copying, Printing, Saving	Copy pie chart from Excel to Slide 7 in PowerPoint presentation. Resize chart on slide and edit legend if necessary to make chart consistent with other charts in presentation. Print presentation as *9 Slides Horizontal Handouts*. Save **EL2-U2-A8-HillsPortfolios.pptx** and exit PowerPoint.	4	

Steps	Tasks	Criteria	Value	Score
8-12	Inspecting, Editing	Deselect chart. Inspect document, leaving all items checked at Document Inspector dialog box. Remove all items that display with red exclamation mark and close dialog box. Change file to type to *.xlsx* and name it **EL2-U2-A6-HillsModPortfolio**. Click Yes when prompted that file cannot be save with VBA Project. Click OK at privacy warning message box. Mark workbook as final. Click OK if privacy warning message box reappears.	2	
13-15	Composing and Sending Email, Printing	Send workbook as XPS document to student in email initiated from Excel. Include appropriate message. Open message window from Inbox in email program and print message. Close message window and exit email. Display Info tab Backstage view showing all properties. Paste a screen image into a new Word document. Type student name a few blank lines below image. Print document and exit Word without saving. Close **EL2-U2-A8-HillsModPortfolio.xlsx**.	7	
		TOTAL POINTS	15	

Writing Activities

Activity: Create a Computer Maintenance Template
File: **EL2-U1-Act1-NationalCMForm.xltx**

Steps	Tasks	Criteria	Value	Score
1	Creating Template	In a new workbook, create a template that can be used to complete the maintenance form electronically. The template should information that identifies the workstation by asset ID number, department in which computer is located, name of employee using computer, name of technician that performs maintenance, date maintenance is perform. Include a column next to each task with a drop-down list with options: *Completed, Not Completed, Not Applicable*. Next to this column include a column in which technician can type notes. At bottom of template include text box with message text: **Save using the file naming standard CMStationID##-yourinitials, where ## is the asset ID. Example: CM-StationID56-JW**	10	
2	Protecting, Saving	Protect worksheet, leaving cells unlocked that technician will fill in. Do not include password for unprotecting sheet. Save template as NationalCMForm-StudentName.	3	
3	Creating Workbook	• Start new workbook based on custom template. Fill out form as if student was technician working on computer to test template's organization and layout.	5	

Steps	Tasks	Criteria	Value	Score
4	Saving, Printing	Save As EL2-U2-Act1-NationalCMForm. Print form scaled to fit one page in height and width. Copy NationalCMForm-StudentName.xltx to storage medium and delete template from computer.	2	
		TOTAL POINTS	**20**	

Internet Research

Activity 1: Apply What-If Analysis to a Planned Move
File: **EL2-U2-Act2-MyFirstYearBudget.xlsx**

Steps	Tasks	Criteria	Value	Score
1	Researching, Creating Workbook	After researching create a workbook based on the following: • Research typical rents for apartments in city of student's choice. • Estimate other living costs in the city include: transportation, food, entertainment, clothes, telephone, cable/satellite, cell phone, Internet, etc. • Calculate total living costs for an entire year. • Research annual starting salaries of student's chosen field of study. Estimate the take home pay at approximately 70% of annual salary. • Use take-home pay and total living costs for the year. Calculate if there will be money left over if will have to borrow money to meet expenses. • Use Goal Seek to find take-home pay needed to earn in order to have $2,000 left over at end of year. Accept solution that Goal Seek provides.	14	
2	Creating Scenarios	Create two scenarios in worksheet as follows: Scenario named *LowestValues* in which you adjust each value down to lowest amount you think is reasonable. Scenario named *HighestValues* in which you adjust each value up to highest amount you think is reasonable. Apply each scenario and notice impact on amount left over at end of year.	6	
3	Creating Scenario Summary Report, Printing	Display worksheet in the *HighestValues* scenario and create a scenario summary report. Print worksheet applying print options as necessary to minimize pages required. Print scenario summary report.	4	
4	Saving	Save As **EL2-U2-Act2-MyFirstYearBudget.xlsx**. Close worksheet.	1	
		TOTAL POINTS	**25**	

Activity 2: Research and Compare Smartphones
File: **EL2-U2-Act2-MyFirstYearBudget.xlsx**

Steps	Tasks	Criteria	Value	Score
1	Researching, Creating Workbook	Research the latest smartphone from three different manufacturers. Features needed include conference calling, email, web browsing, text messaging, and modifying PowerPoint presentations, Word documents, and Excel worksheets. Create a workbook that compares the three smartphones. Organize the worksheet so that main features are along the left side of the page by category and each phone's specifications for those features are set in column. At bottom of each column, provide hyperlink to phone's specifications on the Web. Based on student's perception of best value, provide a brief explanation as to why the phone was selected; place in a comment box in the price cell of selected phone.	18	
2	Saving, Publishing, Printing	Save As **EL2-U2-Act3-Smartphones**. Publish worksheet as single file web page accepting default file name. Change page title to *Smartphone Feature and Price Comparison*. Print web page from Internet Explorer window. Close Internet Explorer and close **EL2-U2-Act3-Smartphones.xlsx**.	2	
		TOTAL POINTS	20	

Job Study

Prepare a Wages Budget and Link the Budget to a Word Document
File: **EL2-U2-JS-GardenviewWageBdgt.xlsx** and **EL2-U2-JS-GardenviewOpBdgt.docx**

Steps	Tasks	Criteria	Value	Score
1	Creating Worksheet	Create worksheet to estimate next year's hourly wages expense using the information provided about hourly paid works and average wage costs in Table U2.1.	14	
2	Formatting	Format worksheet to make use of colors, themes, and/or table features to make budget calculations easy to read.	6	
3	Saving, Printing	Save As **EL2-U2-JS-GardenviewWageBdgt**. Print worksheet adjusting print options as necessary to minimize pages required.	2	
4	Creating Chart	On a separate sheet, create a chart to show the total hourly wages budget by worker category. Student determines chart type and chart options to present information.	4	
5	Opening Word Document, Linking Chart	Open Word document **GardenviewOpBdgt**. Edit year on title page to current year. Edit name and date at bottom of title page to include student's name and current date. Link chart created in Excel to end of Word document.	3	
6	Printing, Saving	Save As **EL2-U2-JS-GardenviewOpBdgt.docx**. Print and close document. Deselect chart and close **EL2-U2-JS-GardenviewWageBdgt.xlsx**.	1	
		TOTAL POINTS	**30**	

Benchmark Excel 2013 Level 1, Unit 1
Supplemental Assessments

Supplemental Assessment 1

Instructions

1. A friend has made several visits to the doctor in the past month because of a serious illness and has asked you to calculate what he will owe after the insurance company has paid its part of the bill. The insurance company usually takes about a month to process a claim and your friend is hoping you can help figure the amount right away so he can plan ahead.
2. Create a worksheet to include the following information from the visits to the doctor. Apply accounting formatting to the *Cost of Visit* column.

	A	B	C
1	**Date of Visit**	**Doctor**	**Cost of Visit**
2	8/6/2015	Yong	$113.00
3	8/10/2015	Yong	$145.00
4	8/12/2015	Loman	$120.00
5	8/13/2015	Yong	$110.00
6	8/14/2015	Loman	$140.00
7	8/17/2015	Loman	$175.00
8	8/20/2015	Loman	$135.00
9	8/21/2015	Walker	$215.00
10	8/24/2015	Walker	$235.00
11	8/27/2015	Loman	$120.00
12	8/28/2015	Yong	$105.00

3. Your friend has a co-payment of $25.00 and the insurance will pay 80% of the remaining cost. In column D create a formula that displays how much the insurance company will pay. In column E, create a formula that displays the amount your friend will have to pay.
4. The insurance company is supposed to respond within 30 days of billing. The doctor's office has said that they will bill three days after the visit. In column F, create a formula that calculates the insurance response date.
5. In cell A13, type the word **Total**. In cell C13, insert a formula that calculates the total cost of the visits. Copy this formula to cells D13 and E13.
6. In cell A14, type the word **Average**. In cell C14, input a formula that calculates the average cost of visit.
7. Format the worksheet to make it easy to read and visually attractive. Add a footer that includes your name.
8. Save the file with the name **EL1-U1-SA1-DoctorVisits**. Make sure the worksheet information fits on one page and then print the worksheet.

Note that the following are suggested rubrics. Instructors should feel free to customize the rubrics to suit your grading standards and/or to adjust the point values.

Suggested Scoring Distribution: Above average: student completes 80% or more of task(s); average = student completes 70-79% of task(s); below average = student completes 69% or less of task(s)

Rubric

Supplemental Assessment 1

File: **EL1-U1-SA1-DoctorVisits.xlsx**

Steps	Tasks	Criteria	Value	Score
2	Typing/ Accuracy/ Editing	Create worksheet and enter data; Accounting format applied to Cost of Visit column	5	
3	Editing	Insurance Pays – column D formula =(C2-25)*0.8	3	
3	Editing	Friend Pays – column E formula =25+(C2-25)*.02 **OR** =C2-D2	3	
4	Editing	Insurance Response Date formula – column F =A2+33	3	
5	Feature/Editing	C13 SUM function (copied to D13, E13)	2	
6	Feature	C14 AVERAGE function	2	
7	Feature	Format the spreadsheet	3	
7	Feature	Insert a Footer	2	
8	Finishing	Save and print	2	
		TOTAL POINTS	25	

Date of Visit	Doctor	Cost of Visit	Insurance Pays	Friend Pays	Insurance Response Date
8/6/2015	Yong	$ 113.00	$ 70.40	$ 42.60	9/8/2015
8/10/2015	Yong	$ 145.00	$ 96.00	$ 49.00	9/12/2015
8/12/2015	Loman	$ 120.00	$ 76.00	$ 44.00	9/14/2015
8/13/2015	Yong	$ 110.00	$ 68.00	$ 42.00	9/15/2015
8/14/2015	Loman	$ 140.00	$ 92.00	$ 48.00	9/16/2015
8/17/2015	Loman	$ 175.00	$ 120.00	$ 55.00	9/19/2015
8/20/2015	Loman	$ 135.00	$ 88.00	$ 47.00	9/22/2015
8/21/2015	Walker	$ 215.00	$ 152.00	$ 63.00	9/23/2015
8/24/2015	Walker	$ 235.00	$ 168.00	$ 67.00	9/26/2015
8/27/2015	Loman	$ 120.00	$ 76.00	$ 44.00	9/29/2015
8/28/2015	Yong	$ 105.00	$ 64.00	$ 41.00	9/30/2015
Total		$ 1,613.00	$ 1,070.40	$ 542.60	
Average		$ 146.64			

Student Name

EL1-U1-SA1-DoctorVisits.xlsx

Supplemental Assessment 2

Instructions

1. Use the Save As command and save the worksheet created in Assessment 1 as **EL1-U1-SA2-DoctorVisits**.
2. Sort the worksheet alphabetically by Doctor and then by Cost of Visit.
3. Apply the Dividend theme and the Blue theme colors to the worksheet.
4. Apply a Total cell style to the total amounts in the Cost of Visit, Insurance Pays, and Friend Pays columns. Apply the 20% - Accent 1 cell style to the average amount in the Cost of Visit column.
5. Apply any additional necessary formatting and make sure the worksheet will fit on one page. Save the workbook and print the worksheet.

Rubric

Supplemental Assessment 2

File: **EL1-U1-SA2-DoctorVisits.xlsx**

Steps	Tasks	Criteria	Value	Score
2	Feature	Sort by Doctor and then by Cost of Visit	4	
3	Feature	IF statement =IF(E13>600,"Yes Loan","No Loan"). This statement could also be done IF(E13<=600, "No Loan","Yes Loan")	4	
4	Finishing	Formatting new information. Save and print.	2	
		TOTAL POINTS	**10**	

Date of Visit	Doctor	Cost of Visit	Insurance Pays	Friend Pays	Insurance Response Date
8/12/2015	Loman	$ 120.00	$ 76.00	$ 44.00	9/14/2015
8/27/2015	Loman	$ 120.00	$ 76.00	$ 44.00	9/29/2015
8/20/2015	Loman	$ 135.00	$ 88.00	$ 47.00	9/22/2015
8/14/2015	Loman	$ 140.00	$ 92.00	$ 48.00	9/16/2015
8/17/2015	Loman	$ 175.00	$ 120.00	$ 55.00	9/19/2015
8/21/2015	Walker	$ 215.00	$ 152.00	$ 63.00	9/23/2015
8/24/2015	Walker	$ 235.00	$ 168.00	$ 67.00	9/26/2015
8/28/2015	Yong	$ 105.00	$ 64.00	$ 41.00	9/30/2015
8/13/2015	Yong	$ 110.00	$ 68.00	$ 42.00	9/15/2015
8/6/2015	Yong	$ 113.00	$ 70.40	$ 42.60	9/8/2015
8/10/2015	Yong	$ 145.00	$ 96.00	$ 49.00	9/12/2015
Total		**$ 1,613.00**	**$ 1,070.40**	**$ 542.60**	
Average		$ 146.64			

Student Name

EL1-U1-SA2-DoctorVisits.xlsx

Benchmark Excel 2013 Level 1, Unit 2
Supplemental Assessments

Supplemental Assessment 1

Instructions

1. Create a workbook named **EL1-U2-SA1-StockPortfolio.xlsx** to track your stock portfolio. Create the following on Sheet1:

Utility Companies	Symbol	# Shares	Closing Price 06/26/2015	Total Value 06/26/2015	Closing Price Current Date	Total Value Current Date	Gain/ Loss	% Gain/ Loss
Ameren Corporation	AEE	50	25.32					
Detroit Edison	DTH	144	37.18					
Southern Company	SO	20	33.92					
Dynegy, Inc.	DYN	16	4.85					
Totals								

2. Rename Sheet1 to *Utilities* and change the tab color to *Green*. Change the page orientation to landscape.
3. Use the Internet to find current stock quotes for each of the utilities above; insert them in the *Closing Price Current Date* column.
4. Insert formulas in the first cell in each column listed below; copy the formula to the other three stocks in the column.
   - Total Value 06/26/2015 = # Shares * Closing Price 06/26/2015
   - Total Value Current Date = # Shares * Closing Price Current Date
   - Gain/Loss = Total Value Current Date - Total Value 06/26/2015
5. Insert formulas in the *Totals* row to calculate the totals for columns C, E, G, H
6. Select cell H6 and define it as *UtilityTotalGL.*
7. Insert a formula in cells I2 through I5 as follows:

   % Gain/Loss = Gain/Loss ¸ UtilityTotalGL (the range you just named in Step 6 above)
8. Apply accounting formatting with a dollar sign and two places past the decimal point to cells D2:H2, E6, G6, and H6; comma style with two places past the decimal point to cells D3:H5; and percent style with two places past the decimal point to cells I2:I5.
9. In cell A11, insert a hyperlink using the text *Stock Quotes* to the website used in Step 3.
10. Insert a new row above row 1 and merge and center cells A1:I1. Adjust the height to 81 points. Insert an applicable WordArt title in row 1.
11. Apply borders and shading to enhance the worksheet. Do not use a predefined table style to format the worksheet.

12. Create a copy of the worksheet, insert it after the Utilities sheet, and rename it *Cars*. Change the tab color to *Yellow*. Change the text of the WordArt title appropriately, change the color of the WordArt title, and change the formatting applied in Step 11 to yellow colors.
13. Delete row 5.
14. Update columns A, B, C, and D as necessary to match the following:

Automobile Companies	**Symbol**	**# Shares**	**Closing Price 06/26/2015**
Ford	F	60	11.53
Toyota	TM	25	71.86
Honda	HMC	45	30.38

15. Use the Internet to find current stock quotes for each of the car companies above; insert them in the *Closing Price Current Date* column. Be sure the rest of the columns are updated.
16. Select cell H6 and define it as a range named *CarTotalGL*.
17. Change the formula in cells I3:I5 to be as follows:
    % Gain/Loss = Gain/Loss ¸ CarTotalGL (the range you just named in Step 16 above)
18. Insert a new sheet after the Cars worksheet tab, rename the sheet to *Stock Portfolio*, and then change the tab color to *Blue*.
19. Adjust the height of row 1 to 81 points. Insert an applicable WordArt title in row 1.
20. Create the following starting in cell A2:

Company	**Gain/Loss**	**% Gain/Loss**
Utilities		
Cars		
Total		

21. Insert a formula in cell B3 that links to the Utilities Total Gain/Loss (H7). Insert a formula in cell B4 that links to the Cars Total Gain/Loss (H6).
22. In cell B5, insert a formula to calculate the total for column B.
23. Insert the following formula in cell C3 and copy the formula to cell C4.
    % Gain/Loss = Gain/Loss ¸ Total Gain/Loss
24. Format cells C3:C4 as a percentage with two places after the decimal point.
25. Apply borders and shading to enhance the worksheet. Do not use a predefined table style to format the worksheet.
26. Insert a footer on each worksheet that includes the file name at the left margin, the page number in the center, and your name at the right margin.
27. Save and print the workbook.

Note that the following are suggested rubrics. Instructors should feel free to customize the rubrics to suit your grading standards and/or to adjust the point values.

Rubric

Supplemental Assessment 1

File: **EL1-U2-SA1-StockPortfolio.xlsx**

Steps	Tasks	Criteria	Value	Score
1	Typing/Accuracy	Create Utilities worksheet and enter data Students answers will vary	2	
2,12,18	Feature	Rename and color sheet names for all 3 sheets	3	
3,15	Internet Research	Search Internet and enter data	3	
4,5	Editing	Insert and copy formulas for Total Value 6/26/2015, Gain/Loss, and Totals	4	
6,16	Feature	Name a range or cell UtilityTotalGL, CarTotalGL	2	
7	Editing	Insert formula in Column I	1	
8,24	Format	Apply accounting formatting, comma style, and percent style to designated cells – all should have two places past the decimal point	2	
9	Feature	Insert hyperlink	2	
10,12,19	Feature	WordArt on all 3 sheets	3	
11,12,25	Feature	Format worksheet – not predefined style	4	
13,14	Editing	Update Cars sheet	2	
17	Editing	Update formula in Column I	1	
20	Editing	Enter data for Stock Portfolio sheet	2	
21	Feature	Insert a formula that is linked to the other sheets	2	
22,23	Editing	Insert a formula for % Gain/Loss and copy Insert total formula	2	
26	Feature	Insert a footer on all three sheets as follows: File name on left Page number in center Student name on right	3	
27	Finishing	Save and print Page numbers at bottom of page should be 1, 2, and 3 as it asks them to print as a workbook.	2	
		TOTAL POINTS	**40**	

Utility Stocks

Utility Companies	Symbol	# Shares	Closing Price 06/26/2015	Total Value 06/26/2015	Closing Price Current Date	Total Value Current Date	Gain/Loss	% Gain/Loss
Ameren Corporation	AEE	50	$ 25.32	$ 1,266.00	$ 28.46	$ 1,423.00	$ 157.00	39.88%
Detroit Edison	DTH	144	37.18	5,353.92	38.39	5,528.16	174.24	44.26%
Southern Company	SO	20	33.92	678.40	36.84	736.80	58.40	14.84%
Dynegy, Inc.	DYN	16	4.85	77.60	5.10	81.60	4.00	1.02%
Totals		230		$ 7,375.92		$ 7,769.56	$ 393.64	

Stock Quotes

EL1-U2-SA1-StockPortfolio.xlsx 1 Student Name

EL1-U2-SA1-StockPortfolio.xlsx

Automobile Companies	Symbol	# Shares	Closing Price 06/26/2015	Total Value 06/26/2015	Closing Price Current Date	Total Value Current Date	Gain/Loss	% Gain/Loss
Ford	F	60	$ 11.53	$ 691.80	$ 11.71	$ 702.60	$ 10.80	13.06%
Toyota	TM	25	71.86	1,796.50	68.22	1,705.50	(91.00)	-110.04%
Honda	HMC	45	30.38	1,367.10	34.00	1,530.00	162.90	196.98%
Totals		130		$ 3,855.40		$ 3,938.10	$ 82.70	

Stock Quotes

EL1-U2-SA1-StockPortfolio.xlsx 2 Student Name

EL1-U2-SA1-StockPortfolio.xlsx

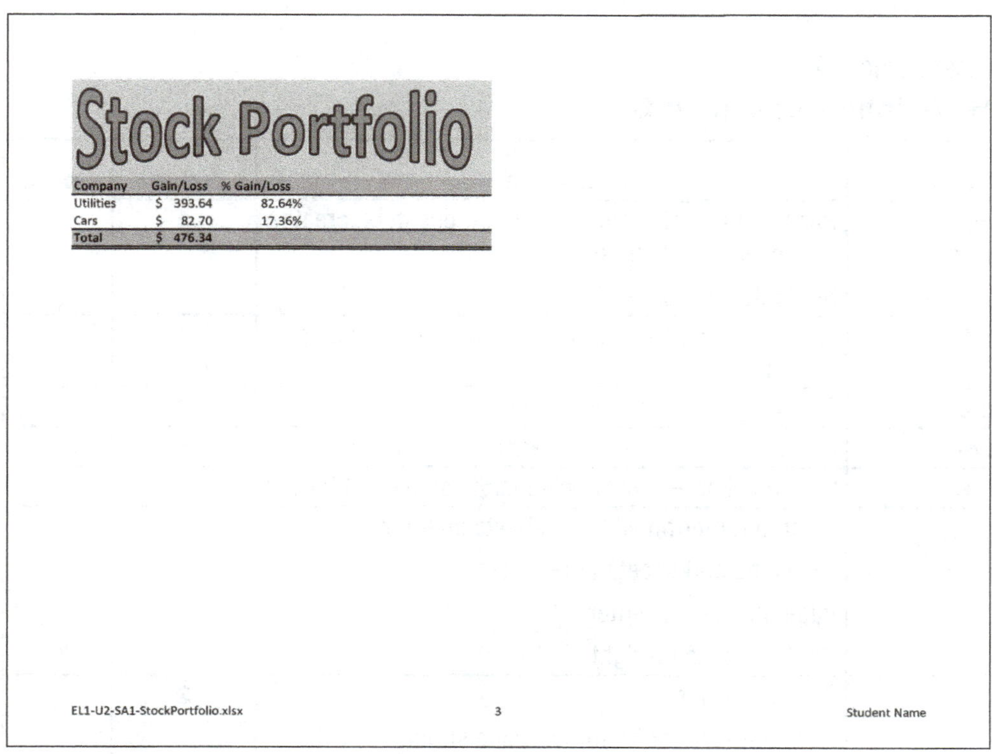

Stock Portfolio

Company	Gain/Loss	% Gain/Loss
Utilities	$ 393.64	82.64%
Cars	$ 82.70	17.36%
Total	$ 476.34	

EL1-U2-SA1-StockPortfolio.xlsx 3 Student Name

EL1-U2-SA1-StockPortfolio.xlsx

Supplemental Assessment 2

Instructions

1. Use a search engine to research roller coaster statistics. Create a worksheet named **EL1-U2-SA2-RollerCoaster.xlsx** that includes the following information for five roller coasters:
   - Name of the coaster
   - Park where it is located
   - State where it is located
   - Length of the ride
   - Top speed
2. Be sure to include an appropriate title and a roller coaster–related clip art image at the top of the worksheet. Format the worksheet with borders and shading.
3. Rename Sheet1 to *Roller Coasters* and change the tab color to *Blue.*
4. Create a bar chart to display the name of the coaster and the length, and a column chart to display the name of the coaster and the top speed. Format both charts to enhance their appearance. Make sure you include an appropriate title. Each chart should appear on its own sheet with an appropriately named tab. On the column chart, draw an arrow to the fastest roller coaster. Input appropriate text in the arrow.
5. Insert a footer on each worksheet that includes the file name and sheet name at the left margin, the page number in the center, and your name at the right margin.
6. Save and print the workbook.

Rubric

Supplemental Assessment 2

File: **EL1-U2-SA2-RollerCoaster.xlsx**

Steps	Tasks	Criteria	Value	Score
1	Internet Research	Research for information on roller coasters, create worksheet and enter data Students answers will vary	4	
2	Format	Format the worksheet including borders, shading, and clip art	4	
3,4	Feature	Rename and color sheet names	2	
4	Feature	Pie chart – create on separate sheet and format	5	
4	Feature	Column chart – create on separate sheet and format	5	
5	Feature	Insert a footer on all three sheets as follows: File name and sheet name on left Page number in center Student name on right	3	
6	Finishing	Save and print Page numbers at bottom of page should be 1, 2, and 3 as it asks them to print entire workbook.	2	
		TOTAL POINTS	**25**	

Roller Coasters of America

Name	Park	State	Length	Top Speed
Wicked Twister	Cedar Point	OH	2700	72
Vertical Velocity	Six Flags Great America	IL	656	70
X-Flight	Six Flags Great America	IL	3000	55
Great Bear	Hersheypark	PA	2800	61
Raptor	Cedar Point	OH	3790	57

EL1-U2-SA2-RollerCoaster.xlsx Roller Coasters 1 Student Name

EL1-U2-SA2-RollerCoaster.xlsx

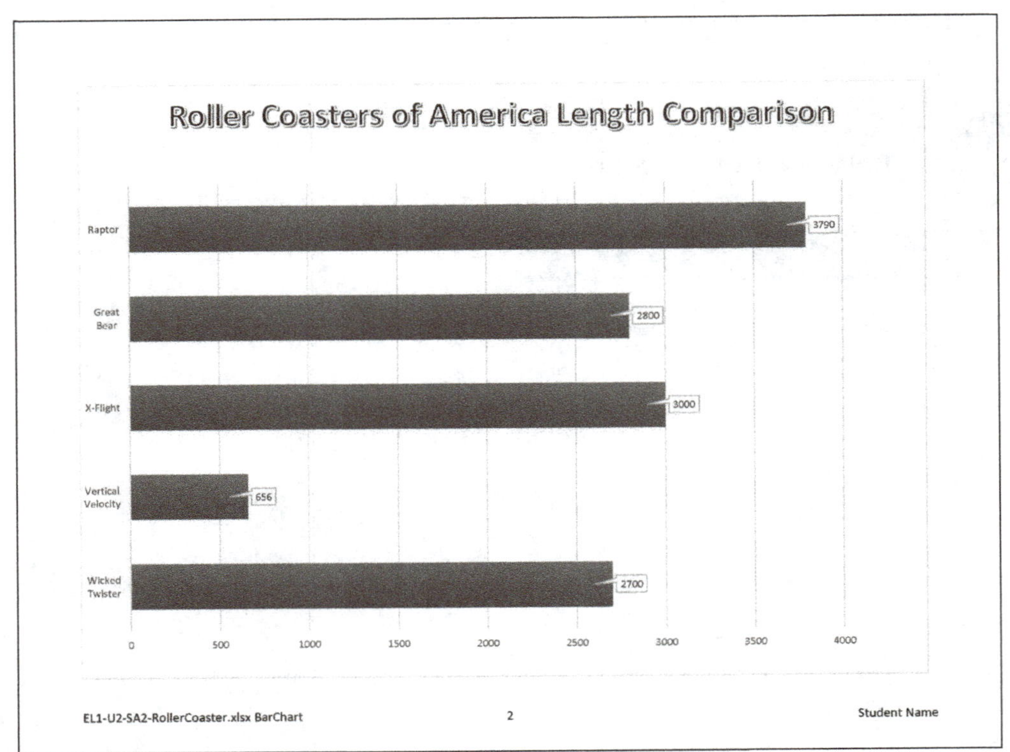

EL1-U2-SA2-RollerCoaster.docx

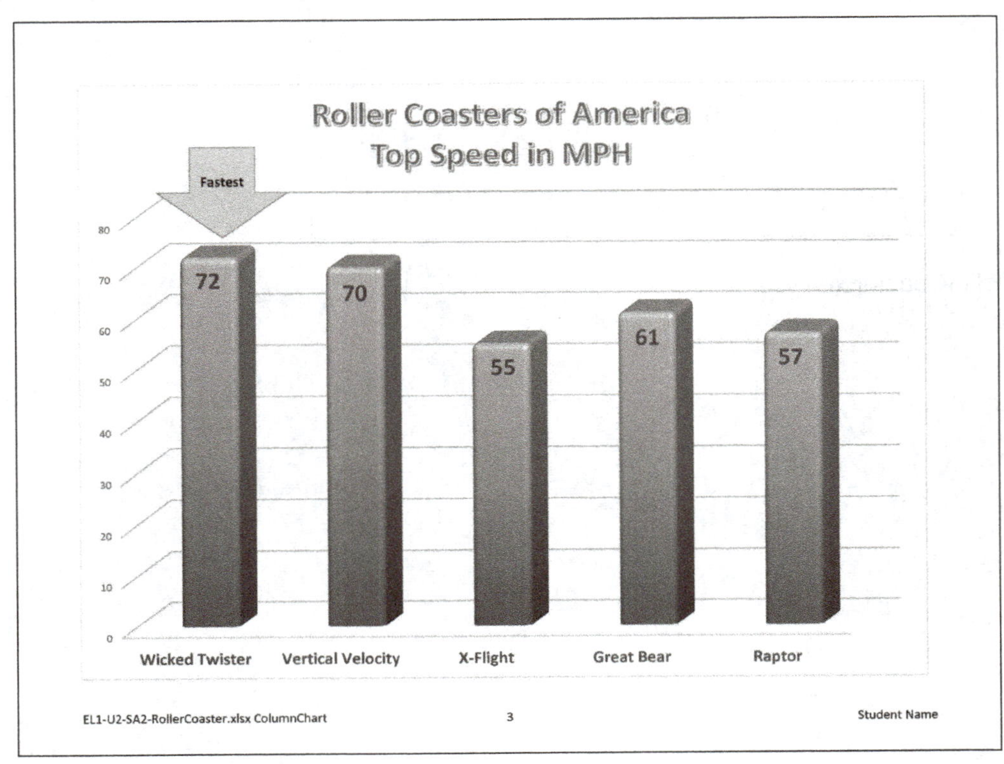

EL1-U2-SA2-RollerCoaster.docx

Benchmark Excel 2013, Level 2, Unit 1
Supplemental Assessments

Supplemental Assessment 1

Instructions

1. Open the data file **EL2-U1-SA1-Gradebook-DataFile.xlsx** that was provided with this project. Save the file with the name **EL2-U2-SA1-Gradebook**.
2. Rename Sheet1 to *CompSci*.
3. Using the Flash Fill or Text to Columns features, split the student names (A4:A12) so that the last name is in column A and the first name is in column B. Insert appropriate column headings in A3 and B3.
4. In column K, calculate the number of missing chapter assignments for each person. An assignment that is missing should have a score of 0.
5. In column L, calculate the overall average grade for each student's chapter assignments and exam. The overall average grade is the average of the contents in columns D through J. In Row 14 for each chapter and exam, create an AVERAGEIF function to calculate the average grade for those students who actually received a grade other than 0. Format both Row 14 and Column L to show one decimal.
6. In column M, calculate the final grade using a nested IF statement using the guidelines below:

A	93-100
B	85-92
C	77-84
D	70-77
F	69 and below

7. Use conditional formatting in the final grade cell using light red fill with dark red text for any student earning an F.
8. Create a named range called *Final* for the range M4:M12. In the *Distribution of Grades* section, use the named range and a function to calculate the number of students who have earned each grade.
9. Add a custom number format to the student number to insert SN- before the number in the cell.
10. Add a header to the worksheet; it should include your name at the left and the sheet name at the right.
11. Add additional formatting to the worksheet as necessary. Do not use a predefined table style to format the worksheet.
12. Save and print the worksheet so that it fits on one page.

Note that the following are suggested rubrics. Instructors should feel free to customize the rubrics to suit your grading standards and/or to adjust the point values.

Rubric

Supplemental Assessment 1

Note: Answers will vary.

File: **EL2-U1-SA1-Gradebook.xlsx**

Steps	Tasks	Criteria	Value	Score*
1	Editing	Open and save the workbook with a different name	1	
2	Editing	Rename Sheet 1 to CompSci	1	
3	Feature	Use the Flash Fill or Text to Columns features to split data in split the student names (A4:A12) so that the last name is in column A and the first name is in column B. Insert appropriate column headings	3	
4	Feature	Column K, number of missing assignments =COUNTIF(D4:I4,0)	3	
5	Feature	Column L, average for chapter assignments and exam =AVERAGE(D4:J4)	2	
	Feature	Row 14, AVERAGEIF to calculate average >0 =AVERAGEIF(D4:D12,">0")	3	
	Editing	Format to Column K and Row 14 to one decimal	1	
6	Feature	Column L, nested IF to calculate grade =IF(L4>=93,"A",IF(L4>=85,"B",IF(L4>=77,"C",IF(L4>=70,"D","F"))))	4	
7	Editing	Conditional formatting Column M, red fill and text for an F grade	2	
8	Feature	Name range M4:M12 Final	2	
	Feature	Distribution of Grades. In the next row, the "A" will vary to "B", etc. =COUNTIF(Final,"A")	5	
9	Feature	B4:B12 format changed to custom "SN-"######	3	
10	Editing	Header to include name at left and sheet name at right	2	
11	Editing	Additional formatting such as bolding, shading, etc.	2	
12	Finishing	Save worksheet and print on one page	2	
		TOTAL POINTS	**36**	

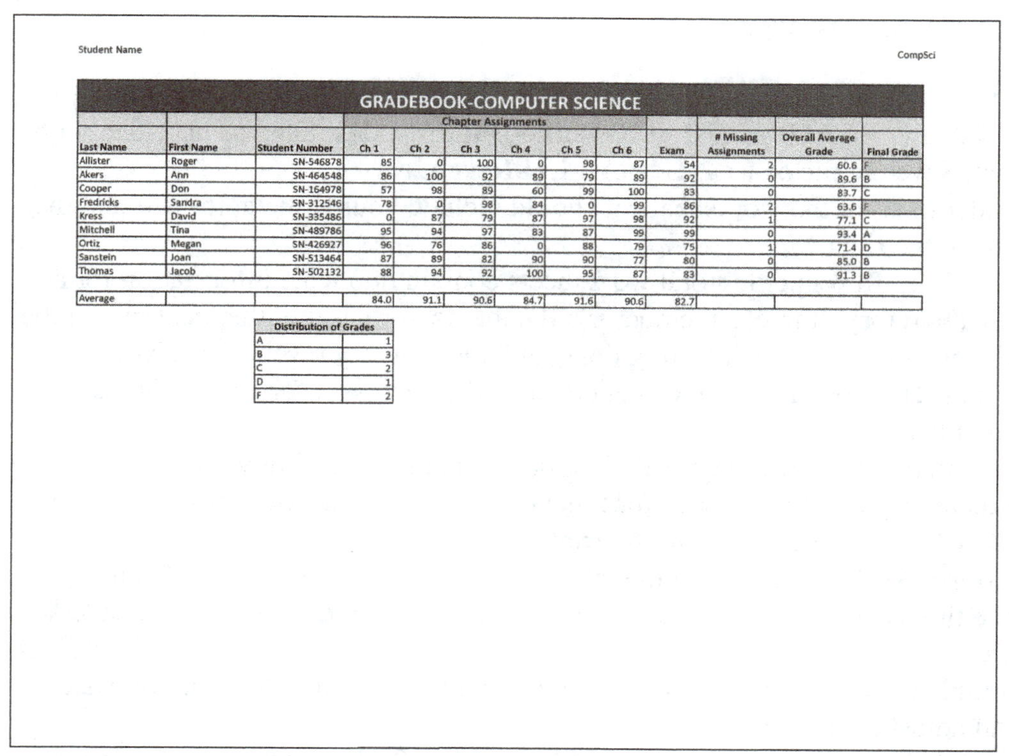

Student Name

CompSci

GRADEBOOK-COMPUTER SCIENCE													
			Chapter Assignments										
Last Name	First Name	Student Number	Ch 1	Ch 2	Ch 3	Ch 4	Ch 5	Ch 6	Exam	# Missing Assignments	Overall Average Grade	Final Grade
Allister	Roger	SN-546878	85	0	100	0	98	87	54	2	60.6	F
Akers	Ann	SN-464548	86	100	92	89	79	89	92	0	89.6	B
Cooper	Don	SN-164978	57	98	89	60	99	100	83	0	83.7	C
Fredricks	Sandra	SN-312546	78	0	98	84	0	99	86	2	63.6	F
Kress	David	SN-335486	0	87	79	87	97	98	92	1	77.1	C
Mitchell	Tina	SN-489786	95	94	97	83	87	99	99	0	93.4	A
Ortiz	Megan	SN-426927	96	76	86	0	88	79	75	1	71.4	D
Sanstein	Joan	SN-513464	87	89	82	90	90	77	80	0	85.0	B
Thomas	Jacob	SN-502132	88	94	92	100	95	87	83	0	91.3	B
Average			84.0	91.1	90.6	84.7	91.6	90.6	82.7			

Distribution of Grades	
A	1
B	3
C	2
D	1
F	2

EL2-U1-SA1-Gradebook-ModelAnswer(Step12).xlsx

Supplemental Assessment 2

Instructions

1. Open the data file **EL2-U1-SA2-LabRevenue-DataFile.xlsx** that was provided with this project. Save the file as **EL2-U2-SA2-LabRevenue**.
2. Add a header to all of the worksheets; it should include your name at the left and the sheet name at the right.
3. The Revenue and Revenue Subtotal worksheets contain duplicate information for a diagnostic laboratory. It tracks the doctor's ID, the doctor's name, the location number where patients go to have their testing done, and the monthly revenue received from each location. The Locations worksheet contains the address information for each location number.
4. Search the Internet to find a diagnostic laboratory that is located in your city. Find five different locations around your city for this laboratory. On the Locations worksheet, fill in the missing address information. Print the worksheet.
5. In the Revenue worksheet, convert the laboratory revenue data to a table. Do not include the title *Laboratory Revenue*. Adjust each column width so that the headers can be read.
6. Add a formula in column P to calculate the yearly revenue. Provide an appropriate header and adjust the column width.
7. Create a validation rule, input message, and error alert for locations in the Revenue worksheet. The location must be 1, 2, 3, 4, or 5.
8. Filter the data to show only Location 1. Print page 1.
9. Make the Revenue Subtotal worksheet active. Calculate subtotals for each month and calculate yearly revenue at each change in name. Adjust column widths where needed and then display the second outline level. Print page 1.
10. Create a copy of the Revenue Subtotal worksheet and rename the copy *PivotTable Data*. On the PivotTable Data worksheet, remove the subtotaling. Create a PivotTable report on a new page to summarize the revenue received by each doctor (*Name*) for January, February, and March. Change the sheet name to *PivotTable*.
11. Add a PivotChart below the PivotTable using a column style. Add an appropriate title to the PivotChart.
12. In Column E of the PivotTable worksheet, create an appropriate Sparkline. Show the high point.
13. Add a header to the worksheet; it should include your name at the left and the sheet name at the right.
14. Adjust the worksheet so that it prints on one page and print the worksheet.
15. Save **EL2-U1-SA2-LabRevenue.xlsx**.

Rubric

Supplemental Assessment 2

File: **EL2-U1-SP2-LabRevenue.xlsx**

Steps	Tasks	Criteria	Value	Score*
1	Editing	Open and save the workbook with a different name	1	
2	Editing	Header to include name at left and sheet name at right	2	
4	Research/ Editing	Search Internet to find diagnostic laboratories Insert locations on Locations worksheet and print	3	
5	Feature	Convert laboratory revenue to a table Adjust column widths so all data can be seen	2	
6	Feature/ Editing	Column P, calculate yearly revenue (include column heading) Format and adjust column width	3	
7	Feature	In Revenue worksheet, create validation rule, input message, and error alert for locations Location must be 1, 2, 3, 4, or 5	3	
8	Feature	Filter data to show only Location 1	3	
	Finishing	Print page 1	1	
9	Feature	In Revenue Subtotal worksheet, calculate subtotals for each month and yearly revenue at each change in name	4	
	Feature	Display the second outline level	2	
	Finishing	Print page 1	1	
10	Editing	Create a copy of Revenue Subtotal and rename it PivotTable Data	1	
	Feature	Create a PivotTable report new page to summarize revenue received by each doctor for January, February, and March	4	
	Editing	Change sheet name to PivotTable	1	
11	Feature	Create PivotChart below PivotTable Column style Title	3	
12	Feature	Column E of PivotTable, add a Sparkline Show the high point	3	
13	Editing	Header to include student name at left and sheet name at right	1	
14	Finishing	Adjust worksheet to print on one page and print	2	
		TOTAL POINTS	**40**	

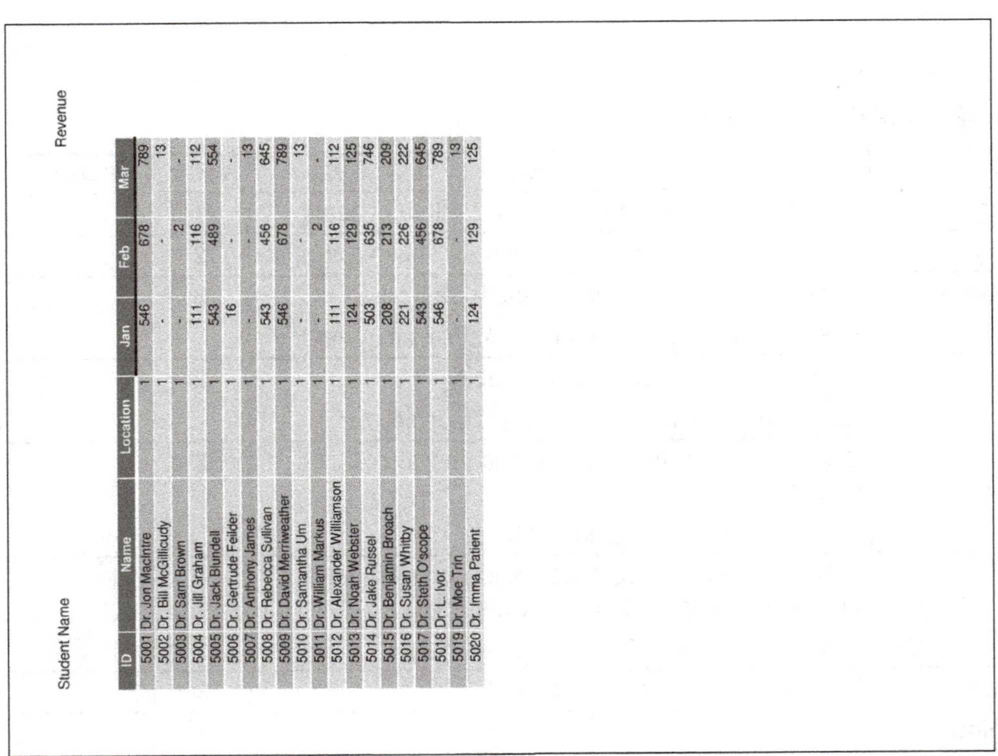

Student Name Revenue

ID	Name	Location	Jan	Feb	Mar
5001	Dr. Jon MacIntre	1	546	678	789
5002	Dr. Bill McGillicudy	1	-	-	13
5003	Dr. Sam Brown	1	-	2	-
5004	Dr. Jill Graham	1	111	116	112
5005	Dr. Jack Blundell	1	543	489	554
5006	Dr. Gertrude Feilder	1	16	-	-
5007	Dr. Anthony James	1	-	-	13
5008	Dr. Rebecca Sullivan	1	543	456	645
5009	Dr. David Merriweather	1	546	678	789
5010	Dr. Samantha Um	1	-	-	13
5011	Dr. William Markus	1	-	2	-
5012	Dr. Alexander Williamson	1	111	116	112
5013	Dr. Noah Webster	1	124	129	125
5014	Dr. Jake Russel	1	503	635	746
5015	Dr. Benjamin Broach	1	208	213	209
5016	Dr. Susan Whitby	1	221	226	222
5017	Dr. Steth O'scope	1	543	456	645
5018	Dr. L. Ivor	1	546	678	789
5019	Dr. Moe Trin	1	-	-	13
5020	Dr. Imma Patient	1	124	129	125

EL2-U1-SA2-LabRevenue-ModelAnswer.xlsx (Step 1 of 3)

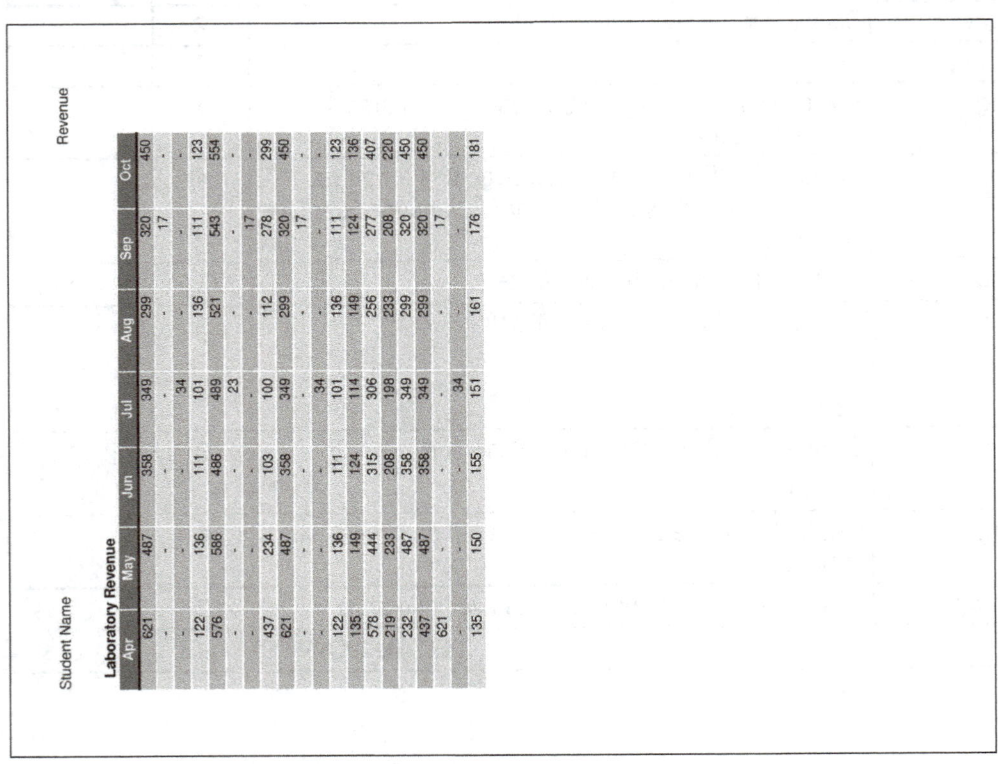

Student Name Revenue

Laboratory Revenue

Apr	May	Jun	Jul	Aug	Sep	Oct
621	487	358	349	299	320	450
-	-	-	-	-	17	-
-	-	-	34	-	-	-
122	136	111	101	136	111	123
576	586	486	489	521	543	554
-	-	-	23	-	-	-
-	-	-	-	-	17	-
437	234	103	100	112	278	299
621	487	358	349	299	320	450
-	-	-	-	-	17	-
-	-	-	34	-	-	-
122	136	111	101	136	111	123
135	149	124	114	149	124	136
578	444	315	306	256	277	407
219	233	208	198	233	208	220
232	487	358	349	299	320	450
437	487	358	349	299	320	450
621	-	-	-	-	17	-
-	-	-	34	-	-	-
135	150	155	151	161	176	181

EL2-U1-SA2-LabRevenue-ModelAnswer.xlsx (Step 2 of 3)

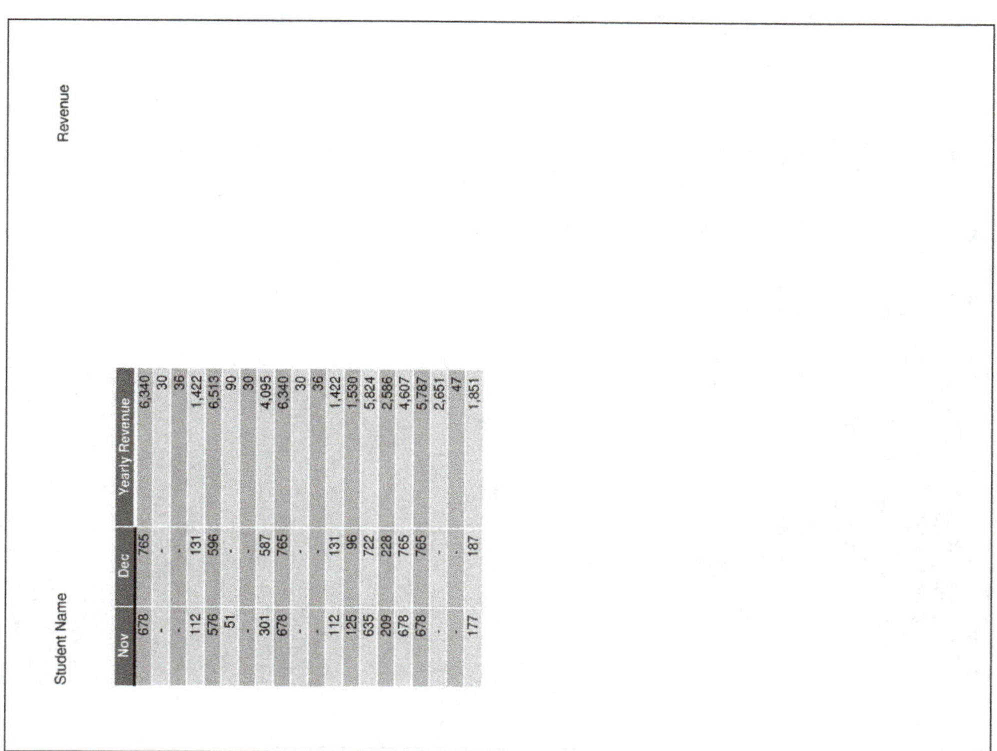

Student Name

Revenue

Nov	Dec	Yearly Revenue
678	765	6,340
-	-	30
-	-	36
112	131	1,422
576	596	6,513
51	-	90
-	-	30
301	587	4,095
678	765	6,340
-	-	30
-	-	36
112	131	1,422
125	96	1,530
635	722	5,824
209	228	2,586
678	765	4,607
678	765	5,787
-	-	2,651
-	-	47
177	187	1,851

EL2-U1-SA2-LabRevenue-ModelAnswer.xlsx (Step 3 of 3)

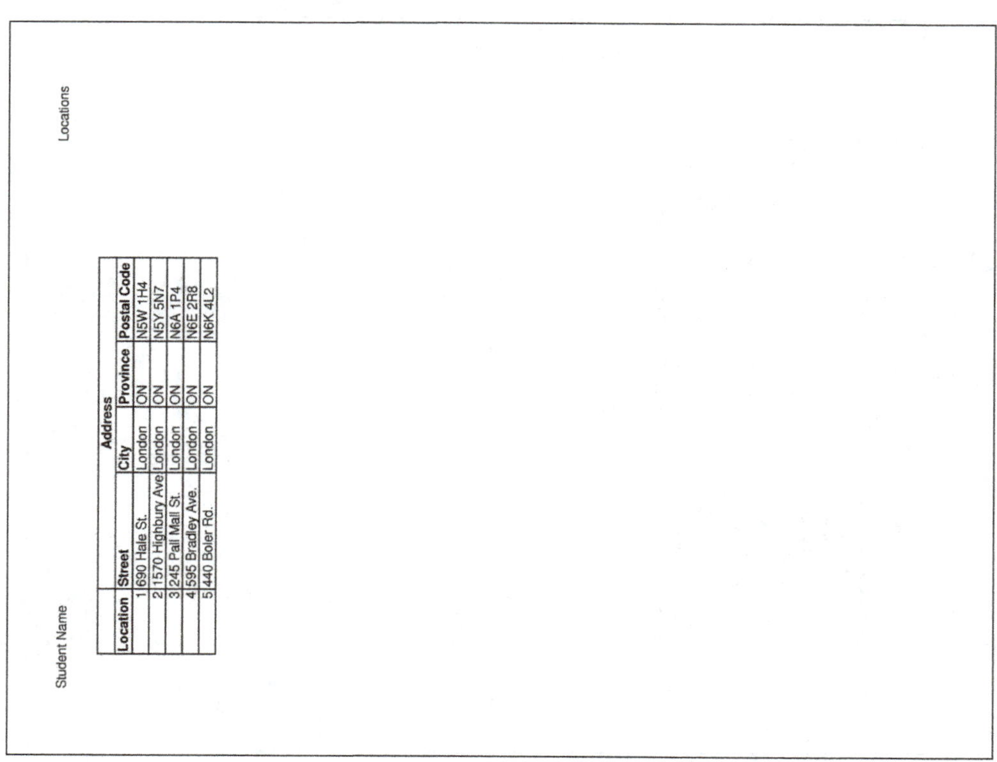

Student Name

Locations

	Address			
Location	Street	City	Province	Postal Code
1	690 Hale St.	London	ON	N5W 1H4
2	1570 Highbury Ave	London	ON	N5Y 5N7
3	245 Pall Mall St.	London	ON	N6A 1P4
4	595 Bradley Ave.	London	ON	N6E 2R8
5	440 Boler Rd.	London	ON	N6K 4L2

EL2-U1-SA2-LabRevenue-ModelAnswer(Step4).xlsx

Student Name Revenue

ID	Name	Location	Jan	Feb	Mar
5001	Dr. Jon MacIntre	1	546	678	789
5002	Dr. Bill McGillicudy	1	-	-	13
5003	Dr. Sam Brown	1	-	2	-
5004	Dr. Jill Graham	1	111	116	112
5005	Dr. Jack Blundell	1	543	489	554
5006	Dr. Gertrude Feilder	1	16	-	-
5007	Dr. Anthony James	1	-	-	13
5008	Dr. Rebecca Sullivan	1	543	456	645
5009	Dr. David Merriweather	1	546	678	789
5010	Dr. Samantha Um	1	-	-	13
5011	Dr. William Markus	1	-	2	-
5012	Dr. Alexander Williamson	1	111	116	112
5013	Dr. Noah Webster	1	124	129	125
5014	Dr. Jake Russel	1	503	635	746
5015	Dr. Benjamin Broach	1	208	213	209
5016	Dr. Susan Whitby	1	221	226	222
5017	Dr. Steth O'scope	1	543	456	645
5018	Dr. L. Ivor	1	546	678	789
5019	Dr. Moe Trin	1	-	-	13
5020	Dr. Imma Patient	1	124	129	125

EL2-U1-SA2-LabRevenue-ModelAnswer(Step8).xlsx

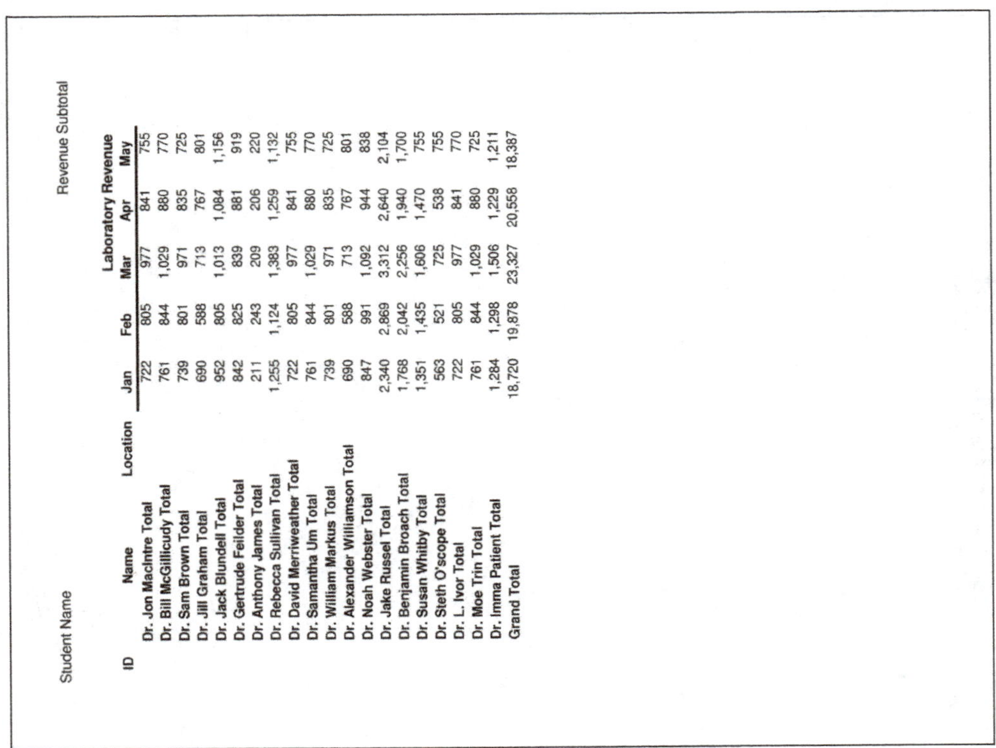

Student Name Revenue Subtotal

ID	Name	Location	Jan	Feb	Mar	Apr	May
					Laboratory Revenue		
	Dr. Jon MacIntre Total		722	805	977	841	755
	Dr. Bill McGillicudy Total		761	844	1,029	880	770
	Dr. Sam Brown Total		739	801	971	835	725
	Dr. Jill Graham Total		690	588	713	767	801
	Dr. Jack Blundell Total		952	805	1,013	1,084	1,156
	Dr. Gertrude Feilder Total		842	825	839	881	919
	Dr. Anthony James Total		211	243	209	206	220
	Dr. Rebecca Sullivan Total		1,255	1,124	1,383	1,259	1,132
	Dr. David Merriweather Total		722	805	977	841	755
	Dr. Samantha Um Total		761	844	1,029	880	770
	Dr. William Markus Total		739	801	971	835	725
	Dr. Alexander Williamson Total		690	588	713	767	801
	Dr. Noah Webster Total		847	991	1,092	944	838
	Dr. Jake Russel Total		2,340	2,869	3,312	2,640	2,104
	Dr. Benjamin Broach Total		1,768	2,042	2,256	1,940	1,700
	Dr. Susan Whitby Total		1,351	1,435	1,606	1,470	755
	Dr. Steth O'scope Total		563	521	725	538	755
	Dr. L. Ivor Total		722	805	977	841	770
	Dr. Moe Trin Total		761	844	1,029	880	725
	Dr. Imma Patient Total		1,284	1,298	1,506	1,229	1,211
	Grand Total		18,720	19,878	23,327	20,558	18,387

EL2-U1-SA2-LabRevenue-ModelAnswer(Step9).xlsx

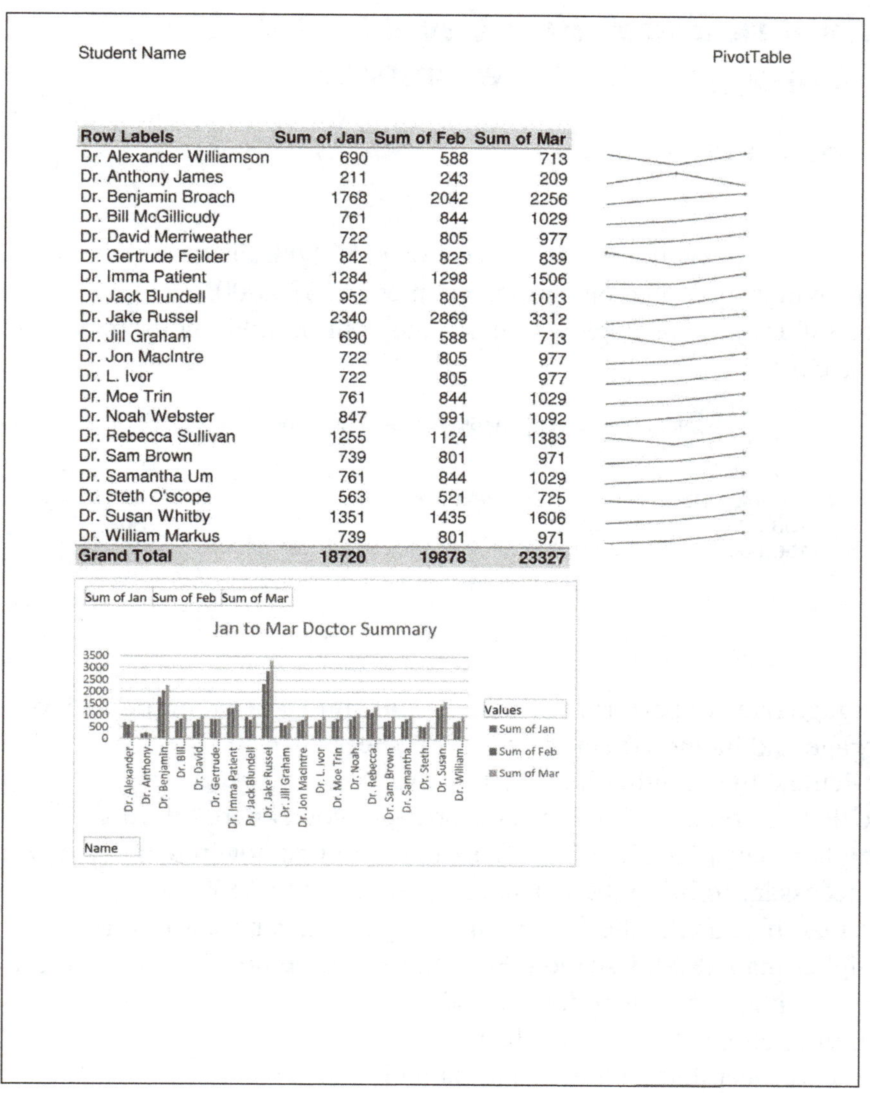

Student Name PivotTable

Row Labels	Sum of Jan	Sum of Feb	Sum of Mar
Dr. Alexander Williamson	690	588	713
Dr. Anthony James	211	243	209
Dr. Benjamin Broach	1768	2042	2256
Dr. Bill McGillicudy	761	844	1029
Dr. David Merriweather	722	805	977
Dr. Gertrude Feilder	842	825	839
Dr. Imma Patient	1284	1298	1506
Dr. Jack Blundell	952	805	1013
Dr. Jake Russel	2340	2869	3312
Dr. Jill Graham	690	588	713
Dr. Jon MacIntre	722	805	977
Dr. L. Ivor	722	805	977
Dr. Moe Trin	761	844	1029
Dr. Noah Webster	847	991	1092
Dr. Rebecca Sullivan	1255	1124	1383
Dr. Sam Brown	739	801	971
Dr. Samantha Um	761	844	1029
Dr. Steth O'scope	563	521	725
Dr. Susan Whitby	1351	1435	1606
Dr. William Markus	739	801	971
Grand Total	**18720**	**19678**	**23327**

EL2-U1-SA2-LabRevenue-ModelAnswer(Step14).xlsx

Benchmark Excel 2013 Level 2, Unit 2
Supplemental Assessments

Supplemental Assessment 1

Instructions

You are considering purchasing a new home with a price of $156,500. From the sale of a previous home and your savings, you plan on a down payment of $30,000.

1. Create a worksheet similar to the one below to calculate your monthly house payment (not including any taxes).

Insert house clip art here	Calculating an Affordable House Payment					
	Selling Price	Down Payment	Interest Rate	Term in Years	Length of Loan in Years	Monthly Payment
	$ 156,500	$ 30,000		10	30	
	$ 156,500	$ 30,000		7	15	

2. Research local mortgage rates to perform the calculations; find a fair rate for a 15-year and a 30-year mortgage and include them in your worksheet.
3. Use a function to calculate the monthly house payment.
4. Assume you decide that, if you take the 30-year mortgage, you cannot afford a monthly payment higher than $550. Use Goal Seek to determine how much of a down payment would be necessary to bring the house payment down to $550.
5. Assume you decide that, if you take the 15-year mortgage, you cannot afford a monthly payment higher than $800. Use Goal Seek to determine how low the interest rate must be to bring the house payment down to $800.
6. Apply formatting of your choice to the worksheet.
7. Add a header to the worksheet that includes your name in the center.
8. Save the worksheet as **EL2-U2-SA1-HousePayment** with the password *L2U2PMT* to open it. Close the worksheet and exit Excel.
9. Open Excel and then open **EL2-U2-SA1-HousePayment.xlsx** using the correct password. Print the worksheet so that it fits on one page. Save and then close **EL2-U2-SA1-HousePayment**.

Note that the following are suggested rubrics. Instructors should feel free to customize the rubrics to suit your grading standards and/or to adjust the point values.

Rubric

Supplemental Assessment 1

Note: Answers will vary.

File name: **EL2-U2-SA1-HousePayment.xlsx**

Steps	Tasks	Criteria	Value	Score*
1	File Management/ Typing	Create worksheet and enter data	5	
	Editing	Insert clip art	2	
2	Research/Typing	Search Internet for 15- and 30-year mortgage interest rates Input rates into worksheet	4	
3	Feature	Calculate monthly house payments using PMT function	3	
4	Feature	Goal Seek, 30-year monthly payment of $550, interest rate stays the same, find down payment	4	
5	Feature	Goal Seek, 15-year monthly payment of $800, find interest rate	4	
6	Editing	Format worksheet	3	
7	Editing/Typing	Header with name in center	2	
8	Feature	Password protect with L2U2PMT as the password	2	
9	Finishing	Open with password; print, save, and then close	1	
		TOTAL POINTS	**30**	

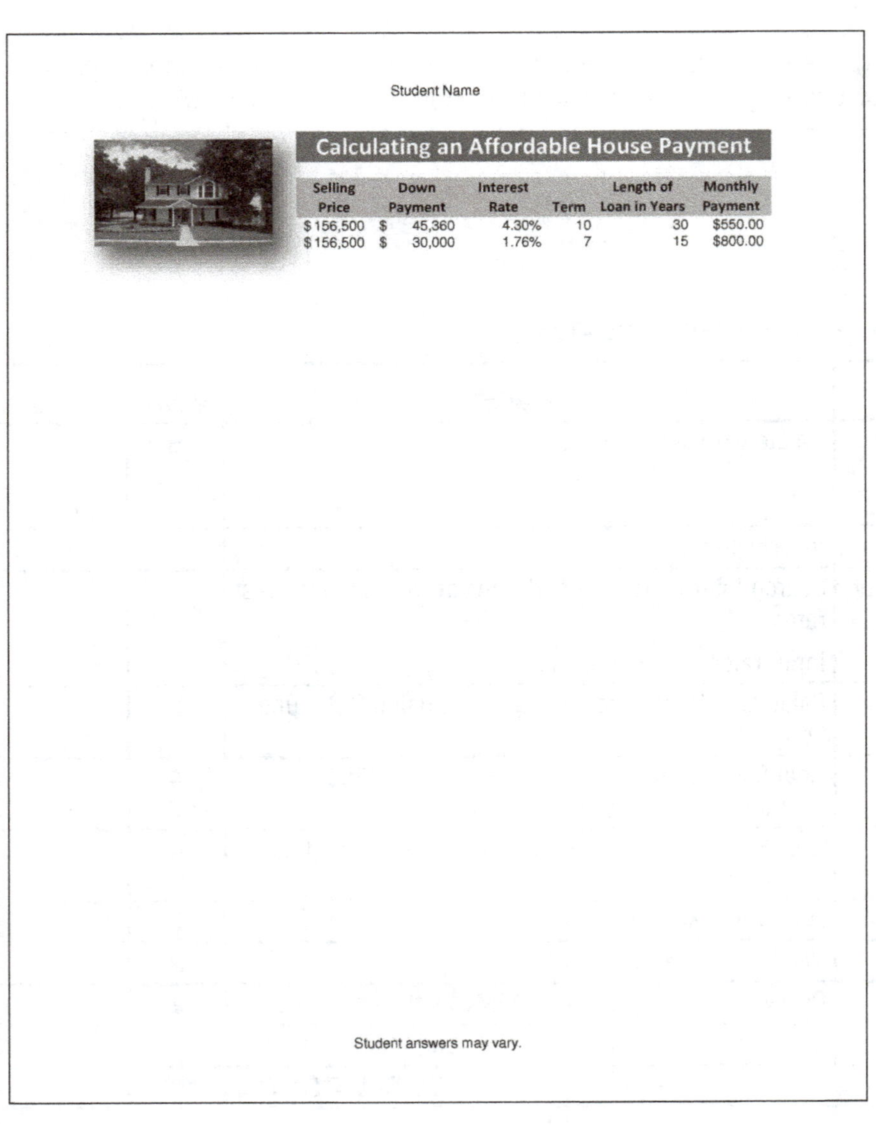
Student Name

Calculating an Affordable House Payment

Selling Price	Down Payment	Interest Rate	Term	Length of Loan in Years	Monthly Payment
$ 156,500	$ 45,360	4.30%	10	30	$550.00
$ 156,500	$ 30,000	1.76%	7	15	$800.00

Student answers may vary.

EL2-U2-SA1-HousePayment-ModelAnswer(Step9).xlsx

Supplemental Assessment 2

Instructions

1. At a new blank worksheet, in cell A1, create a macro and name it *Font*. Use an appropriate description. The macro should change the font to Bookman Old Style 12 points, and autofit the column. Assign the macro to the Ctrl + Shift + L shortcut.
2. Import the **EL2-U2-SA-Mileage-DataFile.txt** file into a worksheet.
3. Merge and center the worksheet title over the worksheet.
4. Run the macro in cells A3, B3, C3, D3. Autofit the columns.
5. Use the Internet to determine the mileage between the home city (St. Louis) and each destination. Enter them in Column C.
6. Save the workbook as a macro-enabled workbook with the name **EL2-U2-SA2-Mileage**. Add a header to the worksheet; it should include your name at the left and the sheet name at the right. Print the worksheet.
7. In Cell E3, insert the heading *Cost*. Apply the Font macro. If the cost per mile is $0.30, calculate the cost for each location (E4:E19). Apply currency formatting with two places past the decimal point.
8. Use the Paste Special function and paste the values (not the formulas) in column E. Autofit the column if necessary. Merge and center the title again.
9. Apply formatting of your choice to the worksheet.
10. Save and print **EL2-U2-SA2-Mileage.xlsm**.
11. Open **EL2-U2-SA2-TravelRoutesMemo-DataFile.docx**. Add your instructor's name and your name as indicated. Update the date to the current date. Save as **EL2-U2-SA2-TravelRoutesMemo**. Embed the data from the Sheet1 worksheet of **EL2-U2-SA2-Mileage.xlsx** at the end of the memo. Remember to go back and enable the macros.
12. Save and print the memo.

Rubric

Supplemental Assessment 2

File names: **EL2-U2-SA2-Mileage.xlsx, EL2-U2-SA2-Travel-Routes-Memo.docx**

Steps	Tasks	Criteria	Value	Score*
1	Feature	Create a macro named Font Add appropriate description Ctrl + Shirt + L = Shortcut font = Bookman Old Style 12 points Autofit the column	5	
2	Feature	Import mileage text file	3	
3	Editing	Merge and center title	1	
4	Feature	Run macro from A3:D3	2	
5	Research/Typing	Determine mileage between St. Louis and each destination. Enter data in Column C.	5	
6	Finishing	Save workbook as macro-enabled Add header with student name at left and sheet name at right Print worksheet	2	
7	Feature/Editing	Column E heading: Cost. Apply macro. Calculate cost at $0.30/mile. Apply currency formatting with two places past the decimal point.	3	
8	Feature	Use Paste Special to paste values instead of formulas in the column.	3	
9	Editing	Format	3	
10	Finishing	Save and print the worksheet.	1	
11	Editing/Feature	Open TravelRoutesMemo Add names Update date Embed worksheet at end of memo Enable the macros	4	
12	Finishing	Save and print the memo	2	
		TOTAL POINTS	**34**	

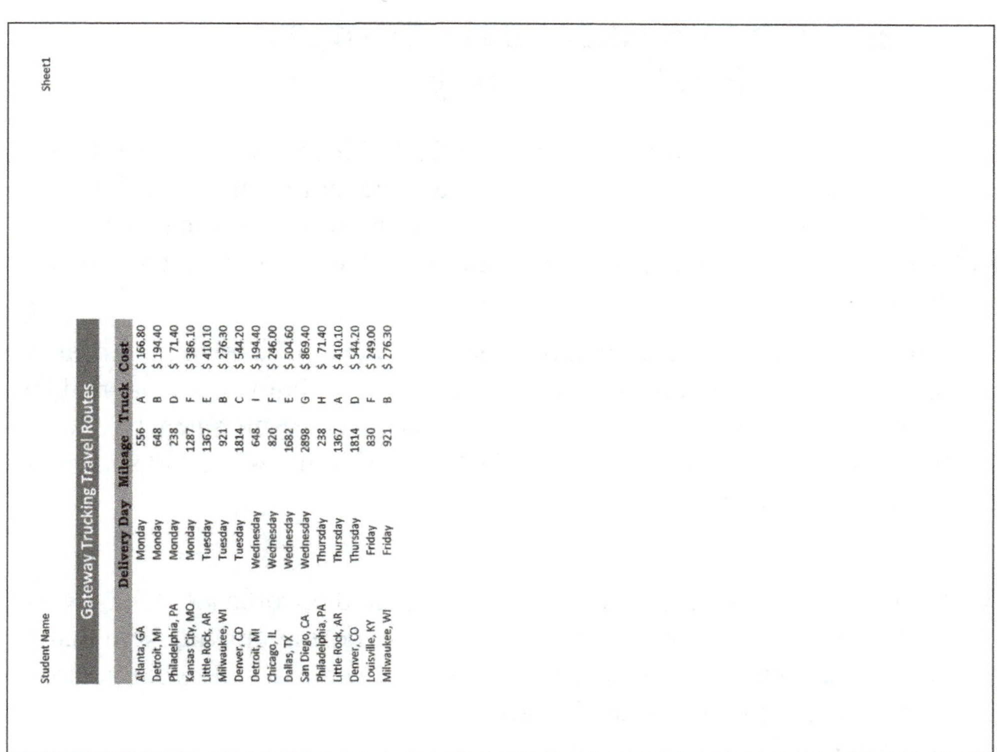

Student Name

Sheet1

Gateway Trucking Travel Routes				
	Delivery Day	Mileage	Truck	Cost
Atlanta, GA	Monday	556	A	$ 166.80
Detroit, MI	Monday	648	B	$ 194.40
Philadelphia, PA	Monday	238	D	$ 71.40
Kansas City, MO	Monday	1287	F	$ 386.10
Little Rock, AR	Tuesday	1367	E	$ 410.10
Milwaukee, WI	Tuesday	921	B	$ 276.30
Denver, CO	Tuesday	1814	C	$ 544.20
Detroit, MI	Wednesday	648	I	$ 194.40
Chicago, IL	Wednesday	820	F	$ 246.00
Dallas, TX	Wednesday	1682	E	$ 504.60
San Diego, CA	Wednesday	2898	G	$ 869.40
Philadelphia, PA	Thursday	238	H	$ 71.40
Little Rock, AR	Thursday	1367	A	$ 410.10
Denver, CO	Thursday	1814	D	$ 544.20
Louisville, KY	Friday	830	F	$ 249.00
Milwaukee, WI	Friday	921	B	$ 276.30

EL2-U2-SA2-Mileage-ModelAnswer(Step10).xlsx

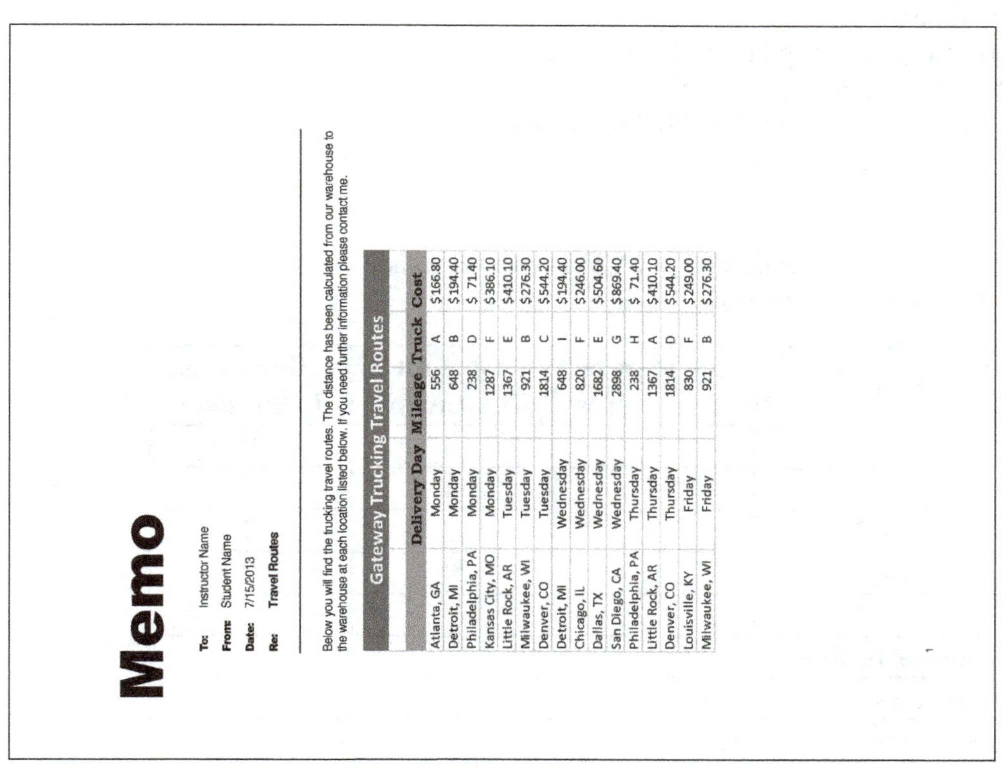

Memo

To: Instructor Name

From: Student Name

Date: 7/15/2013

Re: **Travel Routes**

Below you will find the trucking travel routes. The distance has been calculated from our warehouse to the warehouse at each location listed below. If you need further information please contact me.

Gateway Trucking Travel Routes				
	Delivery Day	Mileage	Truck	Cost
Atlanta, GA	Monday	556	A	$166.80
Detroit, MI	Monday	648	B	$194.40
Philadelphia, PA	Monday	238	D	$ 71.40
Kansas City, MO	Monday	1287	F	$386.10
Little Rock, AR	Tuesday	1367	E	$410.10
Milwaukee, WI	Tuesday	921	B	$276.30
Denver, CO	Tuesday	1814	C	$544.20
Detroit, MI	Wednesday	648	I	$194.40
Chicago, IL	Wednesday	820	F	$246.00
Dallas, TX	Wednesday	1682	E	$504.60
San Diego, CA	Wednesday	2898	G	$869.40
Philadelphia, PA	Thursday	238	H	$ 71.40
Little Rock, AR	Thursday	1367	A	$410.10
Denver, CO	Thursday	1814	D	$544.20
Louisville, KY	Friday	830	F	$249.00
Milwaukee, WI	Friday	921	B	$276.30

EL2-U2-SA2-TravelRoutesMemo-ModelAnswer(Step12).xlsx

Benchmark Excel 2013 Level 1
Final Case Study

Scenario: You are on a temporary work assignment at Body Mechanics & Rehabilitation. BMR provides physiotherapy, massage therapy, and accident rehabilitation. Your expertise in Excel has been requested to assist management in preparing some spreadsheets required for an upcoming meeting. As you work through each activity, additional information will be provided as needed.

This case study will allow you to exercise creativity and polish your Excel skills. In each activity, specific step-by-step instructions may not be provided to simulate a more realistic workplace assignment. Some instructions may appear vague or not comprehensive, but they are purposefully open-ended to allow each student to do original work and showcase individual creativity in problem solving.

Part 1

1. Use an Excel template to create a new sales invoice. Name the worksheet **EL1-FCS-Receipt**. Fill in the worksheet with information of your choosing, making sure that you include at least the following information. In Step 1e, replace with your name. Format to enhance the appearance of the invoice.
   a. Name of company
   b. Clinic's address, phone number, and email
   c. Name and address of the customer
   d. Current date
   e. One 60-minute massage provided by at a price of $74.00
   f. Add 13% sales tax.
   g. Insert the logo called **EL1-FCS-BMRLogo.jpg**.
2. Save and print the worksheet.

Part 2

1. Create a new workbook called **EL1-FCS-Treatment.xlsx**.
2. Place the following information on Sheet1.

Week	30-Minute Treatments	45-Minute Treatments	60-Minute Treatments
Wk 1	3	6	0
Wk 2	5	3	6
Wk 3	8	1	2
Wk 4	2	0	7
Schedule of Fees			
60 minutes	$74		
45 minutes	$60		
30 minutes	$50		

1. Rename the sheet to *Treatments*. Change the color of the tab to *Blue*.
2. Determine the following:
   a. The total number of treatments each week
   b. The total number of 30-, 45-, and 60-minute treatments over four weeks
   c. The average number of 30-, 45-, and 60-minute treatments over four weeks
   d. The weekly income
   e. The monthly income
   f. The total number of minutes worked each week
3. Use an IF statement to determine whether the clinic has met its goal of earning at least $600 per week. If the weekly income is $600 or more, the IF statement should return the value *Target met*; if the weekly income is less than $60, the statement should return the value *Target not met*.

Part 3

1. In row 1, insert the name of the company as WordArt.
2. Insert the logo image **EL1-FCS-BMRLogo.jpg**.
3. Add an appropriate clip art image.
4. Format the spreadsheet to enhance its appearance including shading and borders.

Part 4

1. Create a column chart that shows the total number of treatments on a weekly basis. Place the chart on a new sheet. Name the sheet appropriately and color the tab.
2. Add a title and the company logo (**EL1-FCS-BMRLogo.jpg**). Format the chart to enhance the appearance. Include the total number of treatments on each bar.

Part 5

1. Copy the Treatments worksheet to a new sheet. Rename the sheet *Increase*. Change the color of the tab.
2. Increase the fees by 10%. Show no places past the decimal point. Make sure the weekly and monthly income formulas change.
3. Change the WordArt title to *Tentative 10% Increase*.

Part 6

1. Put your name and the page number as a footer on each worksheet. Ensure that each sheet prints on one page. Print the workbook.
2. Submit all electronic copies of files and folders to your instructor, along with any printouts.

Note that the following are suggested rubrics. Instructors should feel free to customize the rubrics to suit your grading standards and/or to adjust the point values.

Benchmark Excel 2013 Level 1
Final Case Study Rubric

Final Case Study
Files: **EL1-FCS-Receipt.xlsx**
EL1-FCS-Treatment.xlsx

Steps	Tasks	Criteria	Value	Score
		Note: Student's answer may vary.		
Part 1 **1**	Organization/ Accuracy/ Editing	Create a workbook using a sales invoice template.	**3**	
a-g	Editing	Add Name of the company Clinic's address, phone number, and email Name and address of the customer Today's date One 60-minute massage provided by *Student Name* at a price of $74.00 Add 13% sales tax Insert the logo	**5**	
3	Feature	Print the worksheet	**2**	
Part 2 **1,2**	Feature/ Editing	Create workbook and enter information	**5**	
3	Feature	Rename sheet and color tab	**2**	
4	Feature	Determine the following: The total number of treatments each week The total number of 30-, 45-, and 60-minute treatments over 4 weeks The average number of 30-, 45-, and 60-minute treatments over 4 weeks The weekly income The monthly income The total number of minutes worked each week	**10**	
5	Feature	IF statement	**5**	

Steps	Tasks	Criteria	Value	Score
Part 3 **1**	Feature	Name of company as WordArt	**3**	
2	Feature	Insert logo	**2**	
3	Feature	Clip art	**3**	
3	Feature	Format to enhance the worksheet Include shading and borders	**5**	
Part 4 **1**	Feature	Create a pie chart	**5**	
1	Feature	Separate sheet Rename sheet and color tab	**2**	
2	Feature	Add a title and logo Format the chart Add % and week numbers	**4**	
Part 5 **1**	Feature	Copy Treatments sheet and rename it *Increase* Change the color of the tab	**3**	
2	Feature/ Editing	Increase the fees by 10%	**3**	
3	Editing	Change title	**2**	
Part 6 **1**	Feature	Name and page number as footer	**3**	
1	Feature	Print the workbook Make sure each worksheet prints on one page (may display in landscape) Check numbering at bottom of page	**5**	
		TOTAL POINTS	**72**	

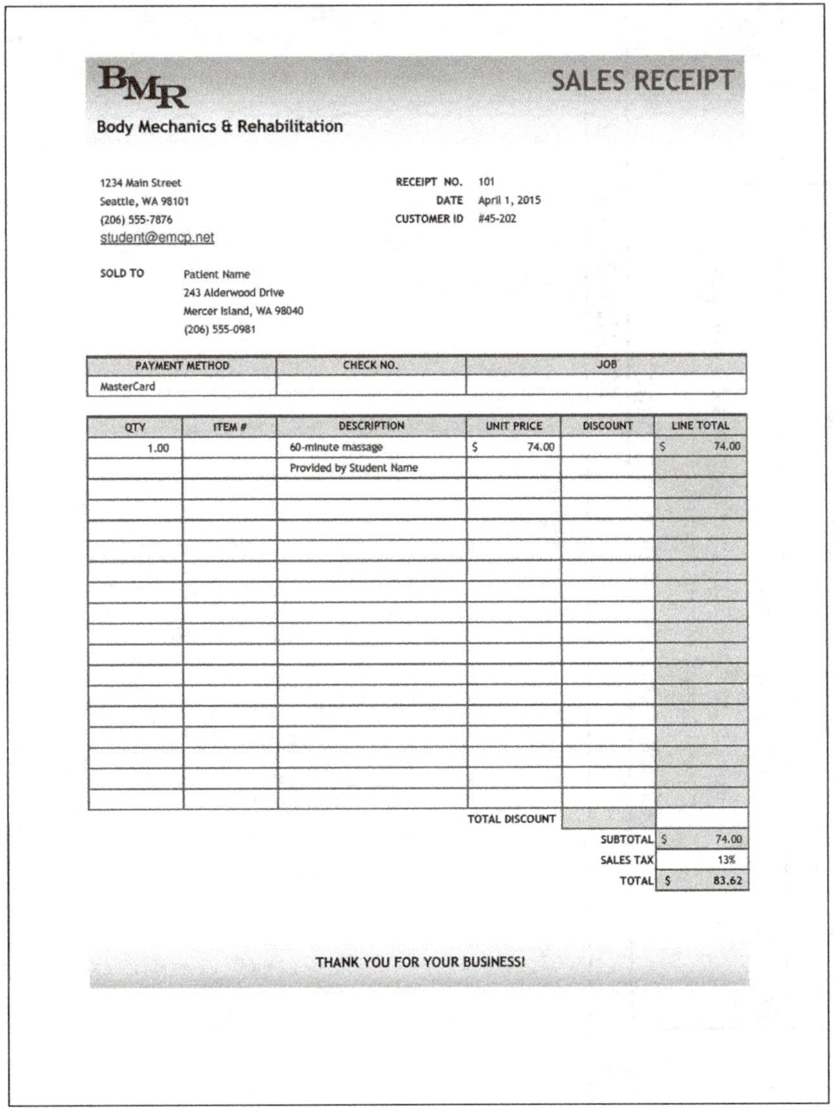

BMR

Body Mechanics & Rehabilitation

SALES RECEIPT

1234 Main Street
Seattle, WA 98101
(206) 555-7876
student@emcp.net

RECEIPT NO. 101
DATE April 1, 2015
CUSTOMER ID #45-202

SOLD TO Patient Name
243 Alderwood Drive
Mercer Island, WA 98040
(206) 555-0981

PAYMENT METHOD	CHECK NO.	JOB
MasterCard		

QTY	ITEM #	DESCRIPTION	UNIT PRICE	DISCOUNT	LINE TOTAL
1.00		60-minute massage	$ 74.00		$ 74.00
		Provided by Student Name			
			TOTAL DISCOUNT		
				SUBTOTAL	$ 74.00
				SALES TAX	13%
				TOTAL	$ 83.62

THANK YOU FOR YOUR BUSINESS!

EL1-FCS-Receipt.xslx

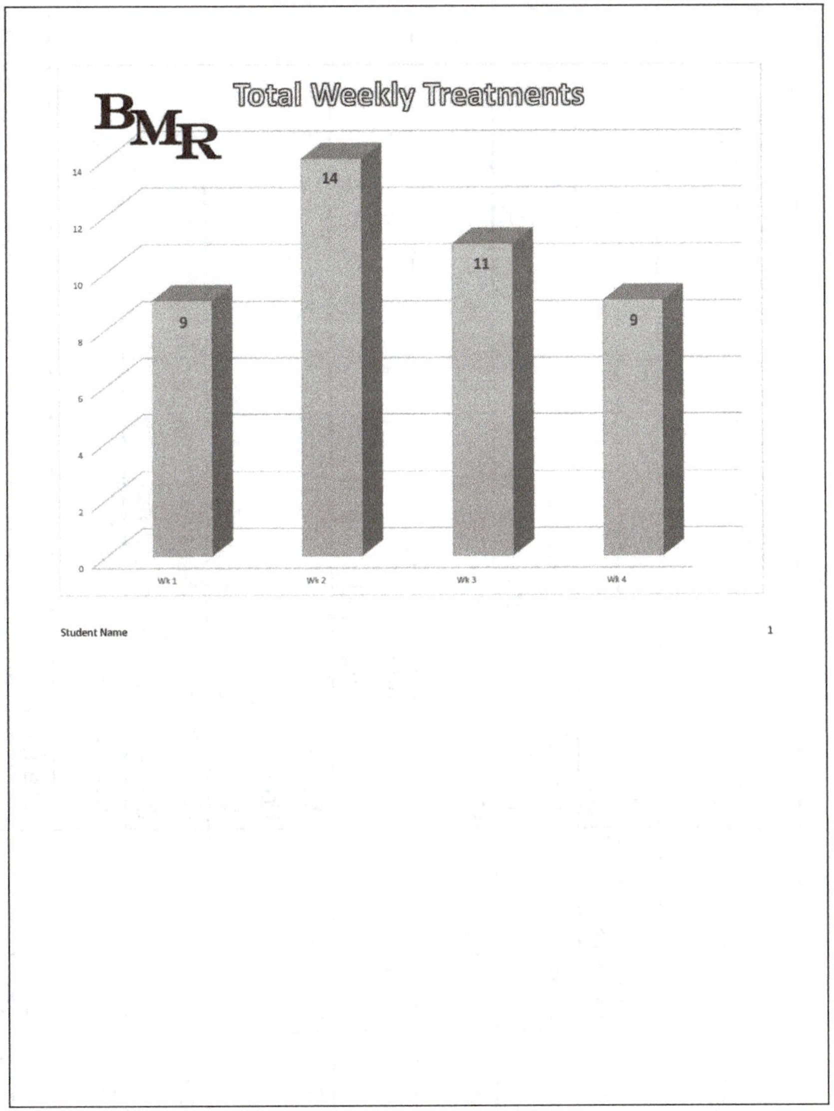

BMR

Student Name 1

EL1-FCS-Treatment.xslx (1 of 3)

BMR Body Mechanics & Rehabilitation

Week	30-Minute Treatments	45-Minute Treatments	60-Minute Treatments	Treatments Per Week	Weekly Income	Minutes Worked	Earning Goal Met?
Wk 1	3	6	0	9	$ 510.00	360	Target not met
Wk 2	5	3	6	14	$ 874.00	645	Target met
Wk 3	8	1	2	11	$ 608.00	405	Target met
Wk 4	2	0	7	9	$ 618.00	480	Target met
Total Number of Treatments	18	10	15				
Average Number of Treatments	4.5	2.5	3.75				
Total Monthly Income					$2,610.00		

Schedule of Fees	
60 minutes	$74
45 minutes	$60
30 minutes	$50

EL1-FCS-Treatment.xslx (2 of 3)

BMR Tentative 10% Increase

Week	30-Minute Treatments	45-Minute Treatments	60-Minute Treatments	Treatments Per Week	Weekly Income	Minutes Worked	Earning Goal Met?
Wk 1	3	6	0	9	$ 561.00	360	Target not met
Wk 2	5	3	6	14	$ 961.40	645	Target met
Wk 3	8	1	2	11	$ 668.80	405	Target met
Wk 4	2	0	7	9	$ 679.80	480	Target met
Total Number of Treatments	18	10	15				
Average Number of Treatments	4.5	2.5	3.75				
Total Monthly Income					$2,871.00		

Schedule of Fees	10% Increase
60 minutes	$81
45 minutes	$66
30 minutes	$55

EL1-FCS-Treatment.xslx (3 of 3)

Benchmark Excel 2013
Level 2 Final Case Study

Scenario: You are on a temporary work assignment at Worldwide Enterprises located in New York. Worldwide Enterprises distributes independent movies to cinemas around the world. Your expertise in Excel has been requested to assist management with various data analysis tasks. As you work through each activity, additional information will be provided as needed.

This case study will allow you to exercise creativity and polish your Excel skills. In each activity, specific step-by-step instructions will not be provided to simulate a more realistic workplace assignment. Some instructions may appear vague or not comprehensive, but they are purposefully open-ended to allow each student to do original work and showcase individual creativity in problem solving.

Activity 1

The manager of Human Resources has downloaded a text file from the company's accounting system. She wants you to create a table. To begin this activity, locate and copy the data file named **EL2-FCS-EmployeeDeptAndSalaryInfo-DataFile.txt**.

a. Import the text file into a new Excel workbook and then adjust column widths as necessary. ***Note: This file is in comma-delimited format.***

b. Use Save As to save the workbook in Excel Workbook and name it **EmployeeInfo-Macros.xlsx**.

c. Rename the worksheet **EmployeeDeptAndSalaryInfo**.

d The human resources manager is concerned about upcoming salary increases. She wants to do some analysis before negotiations begin with each department manager. Using the **EmployeeDeptAndSalaryInfo** worksheet, add statistics to the bottom of the worksheet as follows:

   i) The sum of the salaries for staff in all departments.

   ii) Calculate the total salaries for each department. ***Hint: Use the SUMIF function to calculate the total for each department.***

e. In a separate area adjacent to the statistics created in Step d, create labels similar to the ones shown below.

Projected Salary Costs for 2015:		
Wage Increase	2.5%	
European Distribution		
North American Distribution		
Overseas Distribution		

   Enter formulas to calculate the projected salary costs for each department if a 2.5% wage increase is granted and then calculate the total cost of all salaries at the increased wage. Use a named range for the wage increase.

f. The Human Resources manager is concerned that the wages for the Overseas Distribution department are too high. She wants to know what the wage increase percent would be if she capped the total wages for 2015 for that department at $620,000. Use Goal Seek to find the answer. Do not click OK to change the percent since this salary ceiling affects only one department. Instead, type a note to the manager inside a cell below the projected salary costs in which you state the result that Goal Seek calculated. At this time, the manager is only looking at various wage options; no firm decisions have been made.
g. To further prepare for upcoming wage increase negotiations, the Human Resources manager has asked you to create three versions of projected wage costs for 2015. She wants the three versions stored in scenarios to keep the worksheet uncluttered and avoid confusion. The president has directed the maximum wage increase is 2.5%; however, the company's goal is to settle somewhat lower than this at 1.5%. The manager wants a third scenario calculated that settles the wage increase halfway between the other two rates. Name the three scenarios *Maximum Increase, Goal Increase, and Compromise Increase*, respectively. Save the revised worksheet with the Goal Increase scenario displayed. Create a scenario summary report.
h. Format the worksheet as necessary to produce a professional appearance. Set print options so that the worksheet fits on one page in landscape orientation in an attractive layout. Exclude any cells used for criteria ranges in the print area. Set up a custom header that identifies the printout as *Projected Salary Costs for 2015.* In a custom footer, add your name, the current date, and any other identifying information you routinely use in the course. Save the revised workbook.

Activity 2

The Human Resources manager has asked you to add the following properties to the workbook:

Author	Student Name
Subject	Your course code
Keywords	Employee, Department, Salary
Comments	Any changes must be authorized by the Human Resources Manager

You also need to create macros with shortcut keys that the Human Resources manager can use to perform the sorts shown below on the salary records within the worksheet. Begin each macro with a Go To command that will ensure the active cell is moved to a cell within the list before opening the Sort dialog box. Make sure you put in proper descriptions. Name the macros *SalaryByDept, SalaryByYear, and SalaryByEmpNo,* respectively.

a. Ctrl + Shift + B. Sort all of the salary records first by department in ascending order, then by annual salary in descending order, and then by last name in ascending order.
b. Ctrl + Shift + C. Sort all of the salary records first by year of hire in descending order, then by department in ascending order, and then by last name in ascending order.
c. Ctrl + Shift + D. Sort all of the salary records by employee number in ascending order.

Save the revised workbook as a macro-enabled workbook.

Activity 3

The workbook you have been editing for the Human Resources manager contains confidential salary information. After discussing security issues with her, you have agreed to secure the data using the following methods:

a. Delete the Scenario Summary worksheet. Make active the EmployeeDeptAndSalaryInfo worksheet. Add a comment to the cell containing the wage increase percentage. The comment should inform the reader that three scenarios for wage increases have been stored and then inform the user how to open the Scenarios dialog box.
b. Use the Save As function and save the workbook as **EmployeeInfo-Password**. Assign the following password to open the workbook: *L2FCS*. ***Note: Passwords are case sensitive. Be sure you type the password as shown.***
c. Assign the following password to protect the worksheet: *L2FCS*. Close the **EmployeeInfo-Password.xlsm** workbook.

Activity 4

The Human Resources manager has asked you to research inflation rates on the Internet. Inflation is measured based on the change in the consumer price index (CPI). You need to find the projected inflation rate for 20XX (use the current year). This information will help management with the upcoming salary negotiations.

a. Using **EmployeeInfo-Macros.xlsx** insert a new worksheet into the workbook named and change the tab color to red. Position the new sheet to the right of the EmployeeDeptAndSalaryInfo sheet. Enter the projected inflation rate for 20XX, describe the source of the information, and include a hyperlink to the website from which you obtained the projection. ***Hint: Make sure you locate inflation predictions for the United States. Government agencies often track and forecast economic data such as inflation rates. Consider starting your search from a government source such as the U.S. Department of Commerce Economics and Statistics Administration.***
b. A few rows below the hyperlink, locate a web page that provides historical data on the consumer price index (CPI). Try to find a site that provides 10 years of historical CPI data. The Human Resources manager can use this historical information to compare current inflation with historical rates and the 20XX projected rate. Import the data from the web page into the worksheet using the Web Query feature if the historical data is presented in table format on the web page. If the data is not in a table, use another method to import the data. Above the imported data, include a description of the source from which you obtained the history and the URL of the source.
c. Embed the company's logo (**WorldwideLogo.bmp**) at the top of the InflationProjection worksheet.
d. Below the imported historical CPI data, create and format a chart that plots the CPI. Depending on your data, decide to plot either the monthly CPI for the most recent 12-month history, or, the annual CPI for the previous five years. Add a trendline to the chart to predict the future CPI.

e. Set print options so that the worksheet fits on one page. You determine if the best output is portrait or landscape orientation. Set up a custom header that identifies the printout as *Inflation Research for Salary Negotiations*. In a custom footer, add your name, the current date, and any other identifying information you routinely use in the course. Save the revised workbook.

Submit the electronic copies of the following files to your instructor:

EmployeeInfo-Macros.xlsx
EmployeeInfo-Macros.xlsm
EmployeeInfo-Password.xlsm

Keep a copy of all files completed in this case study until you have received your grade.

Benchmark Excel 2013 Level 2
Final Case Study Rubric

Note: Answers will vary.

Final Case Study

File names: **EmployeeInfo-Macros.xlsx, EmployeeInfo-Macros.xlsm, EmployeeInfo-Password.xlsm**

Step	Tasks	Criteria	Value	Score*
1 a, b	File Management/ Feature	File named properly and data imported correctly.	**3**	
c	Editing	Rename worksheet	**1**	
d	Feature	Totals calculated, grand total and each department's total salaries (SumIF)	**6**	
e	Feature	Projected salaries for 2015 labeled and calculated using a named range for the wage increase	**6**	
f	Feature	Goal Seek results typed below 2015 projections—entry states a 1.4 % increase to cap at $620,000 for the Overseas Distribution department	**3**	
g	Feature	Three scenarios stored, Maximum Increase, Goal Increase, Compromise Increase Wage increase percentage displayed is 1.5% (Goal Increase) Create a scenario summary report	**8**	
h	Feature/ Finishing/Editing	Worksheet formatted Print options set to exclude criteria range Landscape orientation Custom Header, Projected Salary Costs for 2012 Custom Footer, Name, current date	**10**	

2	Editing	Add properties to the workbook Author – Student Name Subject – Your course code Keywords – Employee, Department, Salary Comments – Any changes must be authorized by the Human Resources Manager	**4**	
a, b, c	Feature	Each shortcut key/macro performs the correct sort. Ctrl + Shift + B (SalaryByDept) Ctrl + Shift + C (SalaryByYear) Ctrl + Shift + D (SalaryByEmpNo) Each macro begins with a Go To statement or Ctrl + Home to move the active cell within the database list	**9**	
	File Management	Save the workbook as macro-enabled	**2**	
3a	Editing	Delete Scenario Summary Worksheet Add comment to cell containing wage increase to inform user how to open the Scenarios dialog box	**3**	
b	File Management/ Feature	SaveAs EmployeeInfo-Password Workbook requires password to open the file—L2FCS. Note: Passwords are case sensitive. If this password doesn't work, try the first letter in lower-case format or the @ instead of the 2. Deduct a point if either of these errors occurs	**4**	
c	Feature	Protect the worksheet with L2FCS.	**2**	
4a	Editing	In EmployeeInfo-Macros.xlsx, insert new sheet named InflationProjection and change tab color to red	**2**	
a	Research/Typing	Search Internet for information on inflation rate Enter projected inflation rate Include hyperlink to source web page	**4**	
b	Feature	Historical CPI data imported Include a description of the source data and the URL	**5**	
c	Editing	Company logo at the top of a worksheet	**2**	
d	Feature	Chart created and formatted that plots either one year of monthly CPI or five years of annual CPI	**5**	
	Feature	Trendline added to chart	**2**	
e	Finishing/Typing	Print options set to print on one page either landscape or portrait Custom Header – Inflation Research for Salary Negotiations Custom Footer – Name, current date	**4**	
		TOTAL POINTS	**85**	